INSTRUCTIVE ANECDOTES

ILLUSTRATIVE OF THE

OLD AND NEW TESTAMENTS

Instructive Anecdotes

ILLUSTRATIVE OF THE

Old and New Testaments

BY

John Whitecross

AUTHOR OF

"*Biographies of Pious Men,*" "*Moral and Religious Anecdotes,*"
"*Sabbath Evening Lessons for Families,*" &c., &c.

ELEVENTH EDITION—REVISED

SOLID GROUND CHRISTIAN BOOKS
BIRMINGHAM, ALABAMA USA

Solid Ground Christian Books
PO Box 660132
Vestavia Hills AL 35266
205-443-0311
mike.sgcb@gmail.com
www.solid-ground-books.com

*Instructive Anecdotes Illustrative
of the Old and New Testaments*

by John Whitecross

Taken from the 1878 edition by *Thomas D. Morison*
Glasgow, Scotland – The Eleventh Edition - Revised

First Solid Ground edition in April 2012

Cover design by Borgo Design
Contact them at borgogirl@bellsouth.net

ISBN- 978-159925-279-7

Instructive Anecdotes

ILLUSTRATING THE

Old Testament

OTHER RELATED TITLES

In addition to *Instructive Anecdotes Illustrative of the Old and New Testaments* we have also published the following similar titles:

The Shorter Catechism Illustrated from Christian History and Biography by John Whitecross

This unusual volume follows the doctrinal structure of the classic Puritan catechism, expanding each doctrinal point not with exposition, as is customary, but with many factual stories well selected by the author from a wide range of sources. Thus such subjects as Providence, Prayer and The Ten Commandments are illuminated with telling and sometimes fascinating narratives. First published in 1828, and passing through many editions in the last century, the book has been revised for greater usefulness today.

Anecdotes: Religious, Moral and Entertaining by Charles Buck

Another rare volume alphabetically arranged, and interspersed with a variety of useful observations on subjects from afflictions to young persons. Charles Buck (1771-1815) was a gifted minister of the Gospel best known for his extremely popular Theological Dictionary that is still available today on-line. This volume of anecdotes was once the possession of nearly every clergyman. Spurgeon once told his students that this volume was so well known that it was no longer wise to use it for illustrative purposes. This is no longer the cases, as it has been out of print for more than a century.

Visit us on-line at **solid-ground-books.com**
Call us at **205-443-0311**

PREFACE

TO

OLD TESTAMENT.

THE Compiler of the following Work having, with a very few exceptions, supplied, in a former publication, each chapter of the New Testament with two anecdotes, was naturally led to turn his attention to the Old Testament, with the view of completing his plan. In some of the Books of Moses, the Chronicles, the concluding chapters of Ezekiel, and some other parts of Scripture, considerable difficulty was felt in getting anecdotes to bear on particular passages, and after all, the connection may, in several instances, appear remote. The candid reader will in such cases make allowance. The Compiler has been careful not to admit anecdotes of a light and humorous kind, more calculated to afford amusement than to make any serious impression on the mind. Passages may occur to the recollection of the intelligent reader, to which some of the anecdotes elsewhere applied may be thought more appropriate; their application to these passages, however, would have displaced others from a situation that appeared the most proper. Unless it may have arisen from oversight, none of the anecdotes in the last editions of the other compilations of the author's have been admitted into the present volume. Where the Old Testament is read through in order by children, either in a family or school, an anecdote will be found under each chapter, the reading, or relating of which, may give the exercise an additional interest, and impress some truth of the Word of God more strongly on the mind.

INSTRUCTIVE ANECDOTES
OF THE
OLD TESTAMENT.

BOOK OF GENESIS.

The Creation.

CHAP. i. VER. 16.—God made two great lights; the greater light to rule the day.

THE late Dr Livingston of America, and Louis Bonaparte, Ex-king of Holland, happened once to be fellow-passengers, with many others, on board of one of the North River steam-boats. As the doctor was walking the deck in the morning, and gazing at the refulgence of the rising sun, which appeared to him unusually attractive, he passed near the distinguished stranger, and, stopping for a moment, accosted him thus: "How glorious, Sir, is that object!"—pointing gracefully with his hand to the sun. The Ex-king assenting, he immediately added, "And how much more glorious, Sir, must be its maker, the Sun of Righteousness!" A gentleman, who overheard this short incidental conversation, being acquainted with both personages, now introduced them to each other, and a few more remarks were interchanged. Shortly after, the doctor again turned to the Ex-king, and with that air of polished complaisance, for which he was remarkable, invited him first, and then the rest of the company, to attend a morning prayer. It is scarcely necessary to add, that the invitation was promptly complied with.

The Sabbath.

Chap. ii. ver 3.—And God blessed the seventh day, and sanctified it.

"IT is a little remarkable," says Captain Scoresby, in his voyage to Greenland, "that during the whole of the voyage, no circumstance ever occurred to prevent us engaging in public worship on the Sabbath day. In a few instances, the hour of worship could not be easily kept, but opportunity was always found of having each of the services in succession on a plan adopted at the commencement of the voyage. And it is worthy of observation, that in no instance, when on fishing stations, was our refraining from the ordinary duties of our profession on the Sunday ever supposed, eventually, to have been a loss to us, for we in general found, that if others who were less regardful, or had not the same view of the obligatory nature of the command respecting the Sabbath day, succeeded in their endeavours to promote the success of the voyage, we seldom failed to procure a decided advantage in the succeeding week. Independently, indeed, of the divine blessing on honouring the Sabbath day, I found that the restraint put upon the natural inclinations of the men for pursuing the fishery at all opportunities, acted with some advantage, by proving an extraordinary stimulus to their exertions when they were next sent out after whales. Were it not out of place here, I could relate several instances in which, after our refraining to fish upon the Sabbath, while others were thus successfully employed, our subsequent labours succeeded under circumstances so striking, that there was not, I believe, a man in the ship who did not consider it the effect of the divine blessing."

The Fall.

Chap. iii. ver. 15.—I will put enmity between thee and the woman, and between thy seed and her seed: it shall bruise thy head, and thou shalt bruise his heel.

DURING the Arian controversy, at a general meeting of the ministers of London, at Salters' Hall, Mr Thomas Bradbury had been contending, that those who really believed the doctrine of Christ's divinity, should openly avow it; when, to bring it to the test, he said, "You who are not ashamed to own the deity of our Lord, follow me into the gallery." He had scarcely mounted two or three steps before the opposite party hissed him; when, turning round, he said, "I have been pleading for him who bruised the serpent's head; no wonder the *seed* of the serpent should hiss."

Cain and Abel.

Chap. iv. ver. 8.—It came to pass, when they were in the field, that Cain rose up against Abel his brother, and slew him.

MR. CLARKE, in his Examples, relates the account of two French merchants who were travelling to a fair, and while passing through a wood, one of them murdered the other, and robbed him of his money. After burying him, to prevent discovery, he proceeded on his journey. The dog of the person murdered remained, however, by the grave of his master; and, by his loud and continued howling, attracted the notice of several persons in the neighbourhood, who, by this means, discovered the murder. The fair being ended, they watched the return of the merchants. The murderer no sooner appeared in view, than the dog sprung furiously upon him, who being apprehended, confessed the crime, and was justly executed.

Walking with God.

Chap. v. ver. 22.—Enoch walked with God.

DR. CORNELIUS, of North America, whose death was somewhat sudden, said to the writer of his life, "Tell your own dear people, from me, that they hear for eternity. Last Monday I was in the world, active, but now I am dying; so it may be with any of them. O, if they would but realize the solemn import of the fact, that they hear for eternity, it would rouse them all from slumber, and cause them to attend, without delay, to the things which belong to their eternal peace. Tell Christians to aim at a higher standard of piety, and to live more entirely devoted to Christ and his cause. When one comes to die, he feels that there is an immeasurable disparity between the standard of piety as it now is, and as it ought to be."

The Holy Spirit Striving with Men.

Chap. vi. ver. 3.—And the Lord said, My Spirit shall not always strive with man.

A YOUNG WOMAN, who had lived negligent of the great salvation, not long before she died, burst into tears, and said, "O that I had repented when the Spirit of God was striving with me! but now I am undone." She afterwards exclaimed, "O, how have I been deceived! When I was in health, I delayed repentance from time to time! O that I had my time to live over again! O that I had obeyed the Gospel! but now I must burn in hell for ever. O! I cannot bear it; I cannot bear it!" Not long before she died she said, "Eternity! Eternity! O, to burn throughout eternity!"

Noah and the Ark.

Chap. vii. ver. 9.—There went in two and two unto Noah into the ark, the male and the female, as God had commanded Noah.

THE dominion originally given to man over the inferior animals is still, in a great measure, maintained, notwithstanding his fall, and consequent loss of authority over the brute creation. "Considering the use that is made of the elephant in the East Indies," says Mr Park in his travels, "it may be thought extraordinary that the natives of Africa have not, in any part of this immense continent, acquired the skill of taming this powerful and docile creature, and applying his strength and faculties to the service of man. When I told some of the natives that this was actually done in the countries of the East, my auditors laughed me to scorn; and exclaimed, '*Tobaubo fonnio!*'— (White man's lie.)"

No More Floods.

Chap. viii. ver. 22.—While the earth remaineth, seed-time and harvest, and cold and heat, and summer and winter, and day and night, shall not cease.

A MINISTER going to church one Lord's day morning, when the weather was extremely cold and stormy, was overtaken by one of his neighbours, who, shivering, said to him, "It's very cold, Sir." "Oh," replied the minister, "God is as good as his word still." The other started at his remark, not apprehending his drift, or what he referred to; and asked him what he meant? "Mean," replied he, "why, he promised, about three thousand years ago, and still he makes his word good, that while the earth remaineth, seed-time and harvest, and cold and heat, shall not cease."

Wine Drinking.

Chap. ix. ver. 21.—Noah drank of the wine, and was drunken.

A PERSON in Maryland, who was addicted to drunkenness, hearing a considerable uproar in his kitchen one night, felt the curiosity to step without noise to the door, to know what was the matter; when he found his servants indulging in the most unbounded roars of laughter at a couple of negro boys, who were mimicking himself in his drunken fits!—as how he reeled and staggered—how he looked and nodded—and hiccupped and tumbled. The pictures which these children of nature drew of him, and which had filled the rest with such inexhaustible merriment, struck him with so salutary a disgust, that from that night he became a perfectly sober man, to the great joy of his wife and children.

The Mighty of the Earth.

Chap. x. ver. 8.—Nimrod began to be a mighty one in the earth.

"WHAT right," asks Rollin, "had Alexander over the great number of nations, which did not know even the name of Greece, and had never done him the least injury? The Scythian Ambassador spoke very judiciously, when he addressed him in these words:— 'What have we to do with thee? We never once set our feet in thy country. Are not those who live in woods allowed to be ignorant of thee, and the place from whence thou comest? Thou boastest that the only design of thy marching is to extirpate robbers: thou thyself art the greatest robber in the world.' This is Alexander's exact character, in which there is nothing to be rejected.—A pirate spoke to him," adds the same historian, "to the same effect, and in stronger terms. Alexander asked him, 'What right he had to infest the seas?' 'The same that thou hast,' replied the pirate, with a generous liberty, 'to infest the world; but because I do this in a small ship, I am called a robber; and because thou actest the same part with a great fleet, thou art styled a conqueror.'"

The Tower of Babel.

Chap. xi. ver. 4.—Let us build us a city, and a tower whose top may reach unto heaven.

ACCORDING to Herodotus, the tower of Babel, which was constructed of bricks of bitumen, was a furlong on each side at the base; and Strabo adds, a furlong in height. It consisted of eight towers, built one above another, which, if proportionally high, would make the elevation exactly one mile. The ascent to the top, Rollin informs us, was by stairs winding round it on the outside; that is, there was an easy sloping ascent in the side of the outer wall, which turning by very slow degrees in a spiral line, eight times round the tower, from the bottom to the top, had the same appearance as if there had been eight towers placed upon one another. In these different stories were many large rooms with arched roofs, supported by pillars. Over the whole, on the top of the tower, was an observatory, by the benefit of which the Babylonians became more expert in astronomy than all other nations.

Calling on the Name of the Lord.

Chap. xii. ver. 8.—Abraham pitched his tent, and there he builded an altar unto the Lord, and called on the name of the Lord.

MR. HOWARD, the philanthropist, never neglected the duty of family prayer, even though there was but one, and that one his domestic, to join him in it; always declaring, that where he had a tent, God should have an altar. This was the case, not only in England, but in every part of Europe which they visited together, it being the invariable practice, wherever, and with whomsoever he might be, to tell Thomasson to come to him at a certain hour, at which, well knowing what the direction meant, he would be sure to find him in his room, the doors of which he would order him to fasten; when, let who would come, nobody was admitted till this devotional exercise was over. "Very few," says the humble narrator, "knew the goodness of this man's heart."

Avoiding Strife.

Chap. xiii. ver. 8.—Abraham said unto Lot, Let there be no strife, I pray thee, between me and thee, and between my herdsmen and thy herdsmen; for we be brethren.

MR RICHARDS, missionary in India, on his journey to Meerut, halted under the shade of a tree, in the outskirts of a large village, by the road-side · as he sat there, two of the Zemindars of the neighbourhood came up, and, respectfully saluting him, entreated him to act as an umpire between them, and settle a dispute, in which they had been long involved, about the boundaries of their respective lands. Mr R. declined interfering in the matter; but intimated his readiness to give them information respecting the important concerns of salvation. Having read and explained the Scriptures, they listened with attention and delight. The disputants embraced each other with apparent cordiality, and avowed that they would dispute no more about their lands, but love each other, and strive to seek and serve God.

Humanity.

Chap. xiv. ver. 21.—The King of Sodom said unto Abram, Give me the persons, and take the goods to thyself.

WHEN the Archduke Charles was on his way to Bohemia, to take the command of the army in Germany, as he approached the scene of action, he fell in with a number of wounded, who were abandoned by their companions on the road, for want of horses to draw the carriages in their retreat. The Prince immediately ordered the horses to be unyoked from several pieces of cannon that were retreating, saying, that these brave men were better worth saving than a few pieces of cannon. When General Moreau heard of the benevolent act, he ordered the cannon to be restored, observing, "That he would take no cannon which were abandoned from motives so humane."

Belief and Righteousness.

Chap. xv. ver. 6.—Abraham believed in the Lord; and he counted it to him for righteousness.

MR COOPER, late missionary in the East Indies, had been on one occasion preaching on Justification, at a military station on the Malabar coast; and on giving out the hymn at the end of the service, which was the 109th of the first book of Watts, he paused and remarked, that if any one who did not come to Christ for the bestowment of this righteousness, joined in the singing of this hymn, he was only insulting God. One of the soldiers who was hearing him said, he was as if thunderstruck: "What a wretch must I be," said he, "that I am prohibited from joining in the praises of God!" He went to the barracks under this impression, and found that without an interest in Christ he was a wretch indeed; and now, to all human appearance, he has fled for refuge to that atonement he had formerly neglected.

God Seeing Us.

Chap. xvi. ver. 13.—Thou God seest me.

IN a market-town in Buckinghamshire, several Christians of different denominations united to support and teach a Sabbath school in a neighbouring village. One of the teachers, who was accustomed to address the children and other attendants, on religious subjects, was one Sabbath morning, during winter, very greatly discouraged in the prospect of his duties, and entirely unable to fix on a topic for his usual address. Walking along in this disconsolate state of mind, he found written on the snow, apparently with the stick of some passing traveller, that striking passage of Holy Scripture,—"Thou God seest me." He resolved on making this the foundation of his remarks, and the happy result was the conversion to God of two of his hearers, who became consistent members of a christian church.

Parental Solicitude.

Chap. xvii. ver. 18.—Abraham said unto God, O that Ishmael might live before thee!

IN the house of a good man lived his daughter and her husband, both of them strangers to real religion, and the latter of them immoral. The affectionate exhortations, the holy life, and the prayers of the old man, which were offered every day, in the presence of this son and daughter, as often as he could prevail upon them to come to his bedside, produced no effect upon them. A child, who boarded with them in the cottage, never failed to attend on these occasions: and on the evening of the day in which the old man died, this child said to his daughter, "Mother," for so he usually called her (though no relation), "we shall have no prayer to-night, now grandfather is dead; will not you pray?" "As I can," was the reply. The child, with much simplicity and fervour, urged her request. At length, the poor woman, overcome by her entreaties, and her mind perhaps somewhat softened by the loss she had that day sustained, made her first attempt to call on the name of the Lord. The result was happy; for she has been a praying person ever since, and consistent in her conduct. Her husband soon after became "convinced of sin and righteousness, and of judgment to come;" and is, there is good reason to believe, a truly pious man. This case surely affords a powerful encouragement to parents to persevere in offering up fervent prayer for the conversion of their children, in the hope that their petitions may be heard, though they may not live to witness the answer for them.

The Godly Household.

Chap. xviii. ver. 19.—I know him that he will command his children and his household after him, and they shall keep the way of the Lord, to do justice and judgment.

THE following account is given by Milner in his Church History, of the family order observed by Eleazer, Count of Arian, in the 14th century:—"I cannot," said the Count, "allow blasphemy in my house, nor anything in word or deed, which offends the laws of decorum. Dice and all games of hazard are to be prohibited. Let all persons in my house divert themselves at proper times; but not in a sinful manner. In the morning, reading and prayer must be attended to. Let there be constant peace in my family; otherwise two armies are formed under my roof, and the master is devoured by them both. If any difference arise, let not the sun go down upon your wrath. We must bear with something if we have to live among mankind. Every evening, all the family shall be assembled at a godly conference, in which they shall hear something of God and salvation. Let none be absent on pretence of attending to my affairs. I have no affairs so interesting to me as the salvation of my domestics. I seriously forbid all injustice which may cloak itself under colour of serving me."

Procrastination.

Chap. xix. ver. 14.—Up, get you out of this place; for the Lord will destroy this city. But Lot seemed as one that mocked unto his sons-in-law.

SOME of the unconverted inhabitants of Greenland had heard that the world would be destroyed, and as in that case they would have no where to go to, they expressed a desire to be converted, that they might go with the believers. "But," added they, with that carelessness and procrastination so natural to man, in the things that belong to eternity, "as the destruction will not happen this year, we will come in next season."

Faith Healing.

Chap. xx. ver. 6.—Abraham prayed unto God: and God healed Abimelech.

DR THOMAS BROWN, a physician of considerable celebrity in former days, and author of *Religio Medici*, says, "I never hear of a person dying, though in my mirth, without my prayers and best wishes for the departing spirit. I cannot go to cure the body of my patient, but I forget my profession, and call unto God for his soul."

The Promise of Kindness.

Chap. xxi. ver. 23.—Now, therefore, swear unto me, here, by God, that thou wilt not deal falsely with me, nor with my son, nor with my son's son: but according to the kindness that I have done unto thee, thou shalt do unto me, and to the land wherein thou hast sojourned.

WHEN Mr Bruce was at Shekh Ammer, he entreated the protection of the governor in prosecuting his journey. Speaking of the people who were assembled together, at this time, in the house, he says, "The great people among them came, and after joining hands, repeated a kind of prayer, of about two minutes long, by which they declared themselves and their children accursed, if ever they lifted up their hands against me in the *tell*, or field in the *desert*; or in case that I, or mine, should fly to them for refuge, if they did not protect us at the risk of their lives, their families, and their fortunes; or, as they emphatically expressed it, to the death of the last male child among them."

The Parent's Duty.

Chap. xxii. ver. 10.—Abraham stretched forth his hand, and took the knife to slay his son.

THE following anecdote, and remarks, are found in a note to one of President Davies' sermons. "How astonishing was the rigid justice of Brutus the Elder, who, in spite of all the passions of a father, passed sentence of death upon his own sons, for conspiring against the liberty of their country! While the amiable youths stood trembling and weeping before him, and hoping their fears would be the most powerful defence with a father; while the senate whisper for the moderation of the punishment, and that they might escape with banishment; while his fellow-consul is silent; while the multitude tremble and expect the decision with horror;—the inexorable Brutus rises, in all the stern majesty of justice, and turning to the lictors, who were the executioners, says to them, 'To you, lictors, I deliver them.' In this sentence he persisted, inexorable, notwithstanding the weeping intercession of the multitude, and the cries of the young men, calling upon their father by the most endearing names. The lictors seized them, stripped them naked, bound their hands behind them, beat them with rods, and then struck off their heads; the inexorable Brutus looking on the bloody spectacle with unaltered countenance. Thus the father was lost in the judge; the love of justice overcame all the fondness of the parent; private interest was swallowed up in regard for the public good, and the honour and security of government. This, perhaps, is the most striking resemblance of the justice of Deity that can be found in the history of mankind. But how far short does it fall! How trifling were the sufferings of these youths compared with those of the Son of God! They, too, were criminals,—he was holy and free from sin. How insignificant the law and government for which *they* suffered, to that of the divine! How small the good of the public in the one case to that of the other!"

The Beauty of Courtesy.

Chap. xxiii. ver. 7.—Abraham bowed himself to the people of the land, even to the children of Heth.

SIR WILLIAM COOELS, Governor of Virginia, was conversing one day with a merchant in the street, when he saw a negro pass by who saluted him. Sir William having returned the salutation, the merchant, in surprise, asked him, "How! does your Excellency condescend to bow to a slave?" "To be sure," answered the Governor, "I should be very sorry that a slave should show himself more civil than I."

Prayer in the Fields.

Chap. xxiv. ver. 63.—Isaac went out to meditate (*margin*, to pray) in the field at the even-tide.

A pious young man in the army, not finding a convenient place in the barracks in which he was quartered, went, one night, when dark, into an adjoining field, for the purpose of secret devotion. Two men belonging to the same regiment, in whose breasts enmity had long subsisted against each other, were resolved to end it, as they said, by a battle, being prevented from going, during the day, by the fear of punishment. They were led by Providence to the same part of the field where the young man was engaged in his secret exercises. They were surprised at hearing, as they thought, a voice in the field at that time of night; and much more so, when they drew nearer and heard a man at prayer. They stopped, and gave attention; and, through the divine blessing, the prayer had such an effect on both, as to turn their enmity into love. They instantly took each other by the hand, and cordially confessed that there existed no longer, in their hearts, hatred to each other.

A Good Old Age.

Chap. xxv. ver. 8.—Then Abraham gave up the ghost, and died in a good old age, an old man, and full of years; and was gathered to his people.

THE late Rev. Mr Innes of Gifford, after a life prolonged beyond the days of most men, literally fell asleep; through life a truly peaceful man, his latter end was peculiarly so; without the suffering of disease, or any acute pain, the pins of his tabernacle seem to have been gently loosed. Some days before, one of his parishioners, a farmer, called, and seeing him cheerful, said he was glad to see him so well, and that as mild weather was at hand, he would soon get better, and be visiting them again. He replied, "No, I wish no such flattery; you see here a poor old man on his death-bed, but without alarm I tell you that; hear, and tell all your neighbours, my parishioners, that my comfort now, and hope for eternity, is just the gospel of Christ I have preached to them sixty years, and there is no other." He was wonderfully composed at all times; but a week before his death, one called, and seeing a book of small type before him, asked him if he saw to read without glasses. He said, "O, no; I cannot read even my Bible without glasses; but," strengthening his voice, "I am thankful that I have a Bible that I *have read*, and I can mind some texts that I can see and feel now, as I never did before. O, it is a precious book!"

The Strife Regarding Water.

Chap. xxvi. ver. 20.—The herdmen of Gerar did strive with Isaac's herdmen, saying, The water is ours.

MAJOR ROOKE, in his travels, relates the following circumstance: "One morning when we had been driven, by stress of weather, into a small bay, called Birk Bay, the country around it being inhabited by the Budoos, (Bedoweens,) the noquedah sent his people on shore to get water, for which it is always customary to pay; the Budoos were, as the people thought, rather too exorbitant in their demands, and not choosing to comply with them, returned to make their report to their master: on hearing it, rage immediately seized him, and, determined to have the water on his own terms, or perish in the attempt, he buckled on his armour, and, attended by his myrmidions, carrying their match-locks, guns, and lances, being twenty in number, they rowed to the land. My Arabian servant, who went on shore with the first party, and saw that the Budoos were disposed for fighting, told me that I should certainly see a battle. After a parley of about a quarter of an hour, with which the Budoos amused them till nearly an hundred were assembled, they proceeded to the attack, and routed the sailors, who made a precipitate retreat, the noquedah and two others having fallen in the action, and several having been wounded." Hence, we discover the conformity of the ancient and modern custom of buying the water, and the serious consequences that have ensued from the disputes respecting it.

A Warning.

Chap. xxvii. ver. 45.—Tarry with Laban a few days, until thy brother's fury turn away.

AT the Flintshire assizes, in 1821, T. Dutton was found guilty of wilful murder. At his execution, addressing the spectators, supposed to be about ten thousand, he said, "Young people, all take warning by me; it was *passion* that brought me here."

A Divine Ladder.

Chap. xxviii. ver. 12.—He dreamed, and behold, a ladder set upon the earth, and the top of it reached to heaven.

THE excellent Mr. Hervey did not confine his preaching to *his church alone*, but took every opportunity to preach Christ. On one occasion, he preached from the preceding passage. He considered the ladder as a type of Christ, as the way to the Father. After he had done his duty in the church, as he was coming down the lane leading from it to the parsonage, his hearers, wishing to show their regard to him, generally used to stand on each side of the lane to pay their respects, by bowing and curtseying to him as he passed. As soon as he came to the top of the lane, Mr. Hervey lifted up his hands, and gave a short lecture as he passed, saying, "O, my friends, I beg of God that you may not forget this glorious ladder that Almighty God hath provided for poor sinners!—a ladder that will raise us above our corruption unto the glorious liberty of the sons of God! O, my dear friends and hearers, I beg you will never forget this glorious ladder; but hope you will daily meditate upon it, till you reach the third heaven."

Physical and Mental Beauty.

Chap. xxix. ver. 17.—Leah was tender-eyed; but Rachel was beautiful and well-favoured.

A GENTLEMAN had two children, the one a daughter who was very plain in her person, the other a son, who was very beautiful. One day as they were playing together, they saw their faces in a looking-glass; upon which the boy was so charmed with his beauty, that he extolled it mightily to his sister, who felt these praises as so many reflections on her own features. She accordingly acquainted her father with the affair, and complained of her brother's rudeness to her. Upon this, the old gentleman, instead of being angry, took the children on his knees, and embracing them both with the greatest tenderness, gave them the following advice: "I would have you both look at yourselves in the glass every day; you, my son, that you may be reminded never to dishonour the beauty of your face by the deformity of your actions;—and you, my daughter, that you may take care to hide the defect of beauty in your person, by the superior lustre of a virtuous and amiable conduct."

The Son and the Mother.

Chap. xxx. ver. 14.—Reuben found mandrakes in the field, and brought them unto his mother Leah.

THE three sons of an Eastern lady were invited to furnish her with an expression of their love, before she went a long journey. One brought a marble tablet, with the inscription of her name; another presented her with a rich garland of fragrant flowers; the third entered her presence, and thus accosted her: "Mother, I have neither marble tablet nor fragrant nosegay, but I have a heart: here your name is engraved, here your memory is precious, and this heart, full of affection, will follow you wherever you travel, and remain with you wherever you repose."

Lengthened Service.

Chap. xxxi. ver. 31.—Ye know, that with all my power I have served your father.

Copy of a letter from a master to a young man, on quitting his service after a seven years' apprenticeship.

My dear James,

IN looking forward to the moment of personally parting with thee to-morrow morning, I believe I must forego it. I find it almost as much as I could bear to witness the commencement of the scene this afternoon, though only a spectator. Did I feel less for thee, and towards thee, than I do, I should not have this difficulty; but after passing seven long years under my roof, and thy conduct and conversation, in every respect, being so thoroughly and completely to my satisfaction, and after having been accustomed to regard thee almost as one of my own sons, I do confess that I feel the separation keenly. If thou wilt not think bad of it, I believe we must not meet in the morning, but I hope to get a glimpse of thee when passing on the carriage. And now, my dear friend, in adopting the melancholy word —farewell, how earnestly do I covet that thou mayest emphatically fare well in every sense! and that the great and good Master, whom it is thy desire to serve, may be pleased more and more to guide thee by his counsel, and, in the end, to receive thee into glory.

Most affectionately thine,
GEORGE NAIRN.

Wrestling with God.

Chap. xxxii. ver. 24.—Jacob was left alone; and there wrestled a man with him until the breaking of the day.

IT was the custom of Mr. John Janeway, an eminently pious young minister, to set apart a portion of his time daily for secret retirement and solemn meditation. On one of these occasions a friend of his, unknown to him, observed all that passed. "O! what a spectacle did I see!" says the relator, "surely, a man walking with God, conversing intimately with his Maker, and maintaining a holy familiarity with the great Jehovah. Methought I saw one talking with God. O! what a glorious sight it was! Methinks I see him still; how sweetly did his face shine! O, with what a lovely countenance did he walk up and down, his lips going, his body oft reaching up, as if he would have taken his flight into heaven! His looks, and smiles, and every motion, spake him to be on the very confines of glory. O! had one but known what he was then feeding on! Surely, he had meat to eat which the world knew not of!"

Peace and Brotherly Kindness.

Chap. xxxiii. ver. 4.—Esau ran to meet him, and embraced him, and fell on his neck and kissed him: and they wept.

ON one occasion, when Mr. Nott, a missionary, and his companions, arrived at the island of Tubuai, the whole of the population being engaged in a war, were preparing for battle. The missionary and his friends stepped forward as mediators, saw the leaders of the contending parties, expostulated with them, procured an interview between them, and reconciled their differences. The contending armies threw down their weapons of war, cordially embraced each other, went in company to a new building which was devoted to the service of God, and sat side by side to hear the gospel of peace, which was now published to many of them for the first time

Religious Responsibility.

Chap. xxxiv. ver. 30.—Jacob said to Simeon and Levi, Ye have troubled me, to make me to stink among the inhabitants of the land.

THE Spaniards, by their cruelty to the natives of the island of Cuba, rendered themselves odious, and excited in the minds of the inhabitants the strongest prejudices against their religion. A chief, who had been condemned to be burnt, when brought to the stake was exhorted to embrace Christianity, assured that thereby he would be admitted to heaven. The chief asked if there were any Spaniards in heaven. "Yes," said the priest who attended him, "but they are all good ones." The chief replied, "I cannot bring myself to go to a place where I should meet with but one; therefore, do not speak to me any more of your religion, but let me die."

Faithful Servants.

Chap. xxxv. ver. 8.—Deborah, Rebekah's nurse, died, and she was buried beneath Bethel under an oak.

EXTRACT FROM A MEMOIR OF MRS. C. BERNARD OF SOUTHAMPTON.— "Of her conduct as a mistress, I cannot give a better proof, than that those servants who were worth keeping, staid till they were removed by death or marriage. One of her female servants lived with her, or waited round her person, *forty years;* and the almost unparalleled instance which follows, perhaps reflects as much honour on the man servant as it does on the mistress, or master, (one of her sons.)

It is briefly expressed in the inscription over his grave, which is as follows:

> In Memory of
> Mr Richard Lawrence,
> Who, after living *sixty years* in
> The family of the Bernards above Barr
> Departed this life, 12th Feb. 1795,
> Aged 74 years.
> His humble demeanour,
> His affectionate faithfulness,
> **And** persevering diligence in his station,
> Are best attested by the fact
> Related above.
> His surviving master,
> Mr William Bernard,
> Raises this stone as a memorial
> Of so uncommon an instance of
> PRIVATE EXCELLENCE."

Dukes and Kings.

Chap. xxxvi. ver. 15.—These were dukes of the sons of Esau.

DUKE HAMILTON, a pious young nobleman, during his last illness, was at one time lying on a sofa, conversing with his tutor on some astronomical subject, and about the nature of the fixed stars: "Ah!" said he, "in a very little while I shall know more of this than all of you together." When his death approached, he called his brother to his bed-side, and, addressing him with the greatest affection and seriousness, he concluded by saying:—" And now, Douglas, in a little while you will be a DUKE, but I shall be a KING!"

An Evil Beast.

Chap. xxxvii. ver. 33.—An evil beast hath devoured him; Joseph is, without doubt, rent in pieces.

THE Moravian missionaries, in South Africa, write the following account in their diary:—"July 1, 1830.—George Yager met a very serious accident. Passing through the wood, he encountered a wounded wild buffalo, which immediately attacked him, and gored him in a most terrible manner. George was without arms, and could not defend himself. The buffalo threw him upon his back, and trod upon him, and would have killed him in a short time, had not God heard his cry, and helped him in his great distress. The manner of his deliverance was singular. A large dog, unknown to George, came and attacked the wild beast behind, and while the buffalo defended himself against the dog, George crawled to, and climbed up a tree, where he waited till the buffalo was driven off. Then, first, he discovered how severely he had been wounded; nor was he able to do more than get down and creep into a ditch, where he expected to bleed to death, no human help being at hand. In the night he suffered much from the cold wind. About noon on the second day a boy providentially strayed into that part of the wood, discovered the wounded man, and brought tidings of his situation; upon which, some of our people, with a small cart, conveyed him home. He was, however, so far gone, that we expected he would die under the operation of undressing and washing; but God blessed so effectually the means used, that in a few days hopes could be entertained of his recovery."

Moral Purity.

Chap. xxxviii. ver. 21.—There was no harlot in this place.

THE Rev. Dr Waugh was enlarging one evening, at a public Sabbath School meeting, on the blessings of education ; and, turning to his native country, Scotland, for proof, told his audience the following anecdote :—"At a board-day at the Penitentiary at Millbank, the food of the prisoners was discussed, and it was proposed to give Scotch broth thrice-a-week. Some of the governors were not aware what sort of broth the barley made, and desired to taste some before they sanctioned the measure. One of the officers was accordingly directed to go to the wards and bring a Scotch woman, competent to the culinary task, to perform it in the kitchen. After long delay, the board supposing the broth was preparing all the while, the officer returned, and told their honours *that there was no Scotch woman in the house.*"

In Prison.

Chap. xxxix. ver. 21.—The Lord gave Joseph favour in the sight of the keeper of the prison.

THE respectability of Mr. Bunyan's character, and the propriety of his conduct, while in prison at Bedford, appear to have operated very powerfully on the mind of the jailor, who showed him much kindness, in permitting him to go out and visit his friends occasionally, and once to take a journey to London. It is stated, that some of his persecutors in London, knowing that he was often out of prison, sent an officer to talk with the jailor on the subject ; and, in order to discover the fact, he was to get there in the middle of the night. Bunyan was at home with his family, but so restless that he could not sleep ; he therefore acquainted his wife that, though the jailor had given him liberty to stay till the morning, yet, from his uneasiness, he must immediately return. He did so, and the jailor blamed him for coming in at such an unseasonable hour. Early in the morning the messenger came, and interrogating the jailor, said, " Are all the prisoners safe ?" "Yes." "Is John Bunyan safe ?" "Yes." "Let me see him." He was called, and appeared, and all was well. After the messenger was gone, the jailor, addressing Mr. Bunyan, said, " Well, you may go in and out again just when you think proper, for you know when to return better than I can tell you."

A Dream.

Chap. xl. ver. 7.—Wherefore look ye so sadly to-day ? And they said unto him, We have dreamed a dream, and there is no interpreter of it.

A PIOUS lady, having occasion to go to the country on a visit to some friends, her road lay through a place where a gay acquaintance of hers lived. She called on her ; and, perceiving that she did not look well, and seemed a good deal flurried, she asked the reason. At first she made light of it, but soon afterwards acknowledged that she was a little agitated with a foolish dream she had had the night before, which she related as follows :—" In my sleep, I thought I was in my dining-room, with a large party of friends, when a most frightful figure appeared at the window, and seemed as if he wanted to get in. I asked what it was, and being told that it was Death, I was exceedingly alarmed, and begged they would keep him out ; but in spite of all their efforts, he forced his way in, and pointed his dart at me. I prayed earnestly that he would go away and not hurt me ; on which he said, 'That he would leave me for the present, but in *nine days* he would return and take no denial.' After this, I thought I was carried to a beautiful place, where I saw an immense company of people, who all appeared to be exceedingly happy. I understood it was heaven, and felt greatly disappointed and astonished that I did not find myself happy. I was not able to join in their employments, nor could I understand the cause of their joy. While I was musing on all this, one came to me, whom I supposed to be an angel. I asked him if this was heaven? He answered, 'Yes.' 'How does it happen then,' said I, 'that I am not happy?' 'Because,' he replied, 'it is not your place.' He then asked how I came there? I told him I did not know. On saying this, he conducted me to a door, which opening, I was instantly precipitated towards a most dreadful place, from which issued such doleful groans and piercing shrieks, as awoke me from my sleep." Having given this account of her dream, her visitor spoke to her very seriously, and advised her to consider it as a warning from God to attend to her best interests, and to prepare for death and eternity. Perhaps she would really die at the time when Death said he would return, and how sad would it be if she slighted the admonition, and was found unprepared! This conversation was not relished; and to put an end to it, the poor thoughtless lady rang her bell, and desired the servant to bring her some millinery articles, that had been sent home the day before, to shew them to her friend, who, perceiving her design, very soon left her, and proceeded on her journey. In a fortnight she returned the same way, and as she entered the place where her gay acquaintance resided, she met a splendid funeral, which she was told was her friend's, who had died on the very day mentioned in her dream.

Deserved Esteem.

Chap. xli. ver. 42, 43.—Pharaoh took off his ring from his hand, and put it upon Joseph's hand, and arrayed him in vestures of fine linen, and put a gold chain about his neck: And he bade him to ride in the second chariot which he had.

WHEN the great Duke of Cumberland commanded in Germany, he was particularly pleased with the ability and valour of a sergeant belonging to his own regiment. Having observed the gallantry of this man, and made several inquiries into his private character, his Royal Highness took occasion, after a great exploit which the sergeant had performed, to give him a commission. Some time afterwards he came to the Duke, and entreated his leave to resign the rank he held. Surprised at so extraordinary a request, the Duke demanded the reason, and was told by the applicant that he was now separated from his old companions by his elevation, and not admitted into the company of his brother officers, who considered themselves degraded by his appointment. "Oh! is that the case?" said the Duke, "let the matter rest for a day or two, and I will soon find means of putting an end to your disquietude." The next morning His Royal Highness went on the parade, when he was received by a circle of officers, and while he was engaged in conversation, he perceived his old friend walking, at a distance, by himself. On this the Duke said, "Pray, gentlemen, what has that officer done that he should be drummed out of your councils?" and without waiting for an answer, he went up, took the man by the arm, and thus accompanied, went through all the lines. When the parade was over, Lord

Ligonier respectfully desired His Royal Highness to honour the mess with his presence that day :—" With all my heart," replied the Duke, "provided I bring my friend, here, with me." "I hope so," said his Lordship; and from that day the gentleman's company was rather courted than shunned by the highest officer in the service.

Parental Solicitude.

Chap. xlii. ver. 4.—Benjamin, Joseph's brother, Jacob sent not with his brethren : for he said, Lest peradventure mischief befall him.

MR. SAMUEL FAIRCLOUGH, when at College, became tutor to the Earl of Northampton's son. When his pupil was going on his travels, the Earl made handsome proposals to Mr. Fairclough to accompany him. But consulting his mother on the subject, she, who had lost several sons already, was unwilling to part with him, as Jacob with Benjamin. Upon which, falling on his knees, he said, " Dear mother, though my inclination is strong to travel with such company, since I know your pleasure, I feel, already, far greater satisfaction in denying my own will for yours, than I can in any way find in the journey."

Brotherly Affection.

Chap. xliii. ver. 29.—He lifted up his eyes and saw his brother Benjamin, his mother's son, and said, Is this your younger brother of whom ye spake unto me ?

AS one of the water-bearers at the fountain of the Fauxbourg St Germain, in Paris, was at his usual labours, in 1766, he was taken away by a gentleman in a splendid carriage, who proved to be his own brother, and who, at the age of three years, had been carried to India, where he acquired considerable wealth. On his return to France, he had made inquiry respecting his family ; and hearing that he had only one brother alive, and that he was in the humble condition of a water-bearer, he sought him out, embraced him with great affection, and brought him to his house, where he gave him bills for upwards of a thousand crowns per annum.

The Bondman.

Chap. xliv. ver. 33.—I pray thee, let thy servant abide instead of the lad a bondman to my lord ; and let the lad go up with his brethren.

PAULINUS, a native of Bordeaux, and bishop of Nola, was a man of great benevolence. Under the Vandalic persecution, many Christians were carried slaves out of Italy into Africa, for whose redemption Paulinus expended his whole estate. At last a widow came to him, and entreated him to give her as much as would ransom her son : he told her he had not one penny left; nothing but his own person, which he would freely give to procure her son's ransom. This the woman looked upon as deriding her calamity, and not pitying her case ; but he assured her he was in earnest ; and both took shipping for Africa. On their arrival, Paulinus addressed himself to the prince, begged the release of the widow's son, and offered himself in his room. Paulinus, it is said, then became the prince's slave, who employed him in keeping his garden. His master having discovered who he was, set him at liberty, and gave him leave to ask what he would. He begged the release of all his countrymen then in bondage ; which was granted, and all were joyfully sent home.

Relief to the Dying.

Chap. xlv. ver. 5.—God did send me before you to preserve life.

DURING the 17th century, while the Rev. John Cotton was minister of Boston, intelligence reached that town of the distress of the poor Christians at Sigatea, where a small church existed, the members of which were reduced to great extremity of sufferings by persecution. Mr. Cotton immediately began to collect for them, and sent the sum of £700 for their relief. It is remarkable, that this relief arrived the very day after they had divided their last portion of meal, without any prospect than that of dying a lingering death, and immediately after their pastor, Mr. White, had preached to them from Psalm xxiii. 1. "The Lord is my Shepherd; I shall not want."

The Son and the Father.

Chap. xlvi. ver. 29.—Joseph made ready his chariot, and went up to meet Israel his father, to Goshen, and presented himself unto him; and he fell on his neck, and wept on his neck a good while.

ALI BEY, Sheik Bellet, or chief Bey of Egypt, ordered a person, whom he had occasion to send to Constantinople, to transact some business for him in that city, when there to find out his father, and bring him back with him into Egypt. His agent was successful, and brought him over; and when Daout (or David), which was the name of that Greek priest, who was Ali's father, approached Cairo, the capital of Egypt, where the Sheik resided, Ali went out of the city with a numerous retinue to meet his father, and as soon as he saw him, he fell on his knees and kissed his father's hand. Proceeding afterwards to his palace, Daout's feet having been washed by the domestics, he was led into the Harem, and presented to the Princess Mary (Ali's principal wife) and her child.

Preparing the Tomb.

Chap. xlvii. ver. 30.—I will lie with my fathers, and thou shalt carry me out of Egypt, and bury me in their burying-place.

AT the time when his Majesty George the Third, desirous that himself and family should repose in a less public sepulchre than that of Westminster Abbey, had ordered a royal tomb to be constructed at Windsor, Mr. Wyatt, his architect, waited upon him with a detailed report and plan of the building, and of the manner in which he proposed to arrange its various recesses. The king minutely examined the whole, and when finished, Mr. Wyatt, in thanking his Majesty, said, "he had ventured to occupy so much of his Majesty's time and attention with these details, in order that it might not be necessary to bring so painful a subject again under his notice." To this the good king replied, "Mr. Wyatt, I request that you will bring the subject before me whenever you please. I shall attend with as much pleasure to the building of a tomb to receive me when I am dead, as I would to the decoration of a drawing-room to hold me while living; for, Mr. Wyatt, if it please God that I shall live to be ninety, or an hundred years old, I am willing to stay; but if it please God to take me this night, I am ready to obey the summons."

God appearing to Man.

Chap. xlviii. ver. 3.—Jacob said unto Joseph, God Almighty appeared unto me at Luz, in the Land of Canaan, and blessed me.

THE following remarkable passage was found written by Mr. John Howe with his own hand, in Latin, on a blank leaf of his Bible:—

"Dec. 26, 1689.—After that I had long, seriously, and repeatedly thought within myself, that, besides a full and undoubted assent to the objects of faith, a vivifying savoury taste and relish of them was also necessary, that, with stronger force, and more powerful energy they might penetrate into the most inward centre of my heart, and there, being most deeply fixed and rooted, govern my life; and that there could be no other sure ground whereon to conclude and pass a sound judgment on my good estate God-ward; and after I had, in my course of preaching, been largely insisting on 2 Cor. i. 12, this very morning I awoke out of a most ravishing and delightful dream, that a wonderful and copious stream of celestial rays, from the lofty throne of the Divine Majesty, seemed to dart into my expanded breast.—I have often since, with great complacency, reflected on that very signal pledge of special divine favour, vouchsafed to me on that noted memorable day, and have, with repeated fresh pleasure, tasted the delights thereof."

Waiting on Salvation.

Chap. xlix. ver. 18.—I have waited for thy salvation, O Lord!

AN aged Christian negro, who died a few years ago, was often visited by some pious friends. On one occasion she told them, if it was the will of "Jesus Massa" to call her to-morrow, she should be satisfied to go; if it was His will to spare her some time longer, she should be satisfied to stay. She repeated, that she was waiting for her summons from above; said God spared her a little, and she thanked Him for it. By and by, when He saw His time He would come, and then she would thank Him for that.—The next evening she appeared faint and low, and said she was in pain from head to foot: "Jesus Massa" had sent the pain, and she thanked Him for it. Some day, when He saw good, He would come and take it away. After lingering for some time, still in pain, but prayer and praise ever flowing from her lips, she drew near her end. When in her greatest extremities, she said her Saviour would give her ease when he saw fit, and if he did not give it to her now, he would give it to her yonder, pointing upwards.

Gladness after Sorrow.

Chap. l. ver. 21.—Fear ye not; I will nourish you and your little ones. And he comforted them, and spake kindly unto them.

THE father of that eminent lawyer, Mr Sergeant Glanville, had a good estate, which he intended to settle on his eldest son; but he proving a vicious young man, and there being no hopes of his recovery, he devolved it upon the sergeant, who was his second son, Upon the father's death, his eldest son, finding that what he had considered before as the mere threatenings of an angry old man, were now but too certain, became melancholy; which, by degrees, wrought in him so great a change, that what his father could not prevail in while he lived, was now effected by the severity of his last will. His brother, observing this, invited him, together with many of his friends, to a feast; where, after other dishes had been served up, he ordered one which was covered to be set before his brother, and desired him to uncover it: upon his doing which, the company, no less than himself, were surprised to find it full of writings; and still more when the sergeant told them that he was now doing what he was sure his father would have done, had he lived to see the happy change which now they all saw in his brother; and therefore he freely restored to him the whole estate."

BOOK OF EXODUS.

Fearing God.

Chap. 1. ver. 17.—They feared God, and did not as the King of Egypt commanded them.

WHEN Alexander the Great was rebuilding the temple of Belus, he ordered the Jewish soldiers who were in his army to work as the rest had done; but they could not be prevailed on to give their assistance, excusing themselves by observing, that as idolatry was forbidden by the tenets of their religion, they were not allowed to assist in the building of a temple designed for idolatrous worship; and accordingly not one lent a hand on this occasion. They were punished for disobedience, but all to no purpose; so that, at last, Alexander, admiring the firmness of their resolution, discharged, and sent them home.

Slavery.

Chap. ii. ver. 23.—The children of Israel sighed by reason of bondage.

IT is stated that at least fifty thousand poor creatures are carried away from Africa every year to be made slaves! And their sufferings in the ships, as they cross the sea, as well as on their coming to the place of slavery, are beyond belief. In one instance, a black having been seized and carried off to the coast to be put on board a ship, his mother hastened to offer a sum of money for his freedom. The white man took the money; but—horrid to relate—seized the mother, and two days after, shipped both mother and son for America. The son, indignant at the outrage, stabbed himself, saying, "Thou white man, devourer of blacks, I cannot revenge myself on thee but by depriving thee of my person!" While the rash and forbidden act of this unhappy slave is by no means to be approved, it paints in the blackest colours the treachery, injustice, and cruelty of the wretch that drove him to this awful extremity.

The New Man.

Chap. iii. ver. 11.—Who am I, that I should go unto Pharaoh, and that I should bring the children of Israel out of Egypt?

MR NEWTON, speaking of his situation, after having been settled in London, says, "That one of the most ignorant, the most miserable and the most abandoned of slaves, should be plucked from his forlorn state of exile on the coast of Africa, and at length be appointed minister of the parish of the first magistrate of the first city in the world—that he should then not only testify of such grace, but stand up as a singular instance and monument of it—that he should be enabled to record it in his history, preaching, and writings, to the world at large, is a fact I can contemplate with admiration, but never sufficiently estimate." This reflection, indeed, was so present to his mind on all occasions, and in all places, that he seldom passed a single day anywhere, but he was found referring to the strange event in one way or other.

Hearing by Faith.

Chap. iv. ver. 11.—Who maketh the deaf?

"I HAVE in my congregation," said a venerable minister of the gospel, "a worthy aged woman, who has for many years been so deaf, as not to distinguish the loudest sound, and yet she is always one of the first in the meeting. On asking the reason of her constant attendance, as it was impossible for her to hear my voice, she answered, 'Though I cannot hear you, I come to God's house because I love it, and would be found in his ways; and he gives me many a sweet thought upon the text, when it is pointed out to me; another reason is, because there I am in the best company, in the more immediate presence of God, and amongst his saints, the honourable of the earth: I am not satisfied with serving God in private; it is my duty and privilege to honour him regularly and constantly in public.

Knowing not the Lord.

Chap. v. ver. 1, 2.—Moses and Aaron went in, and told Pharaoh, Thus saith the Lord God of Israel, Let my people go, that they may hold a feast unto me in the wilderness. And Pharaoh said, Who is the Lord, that I should obey his voice to let Israel go? I know not the Lord, neither will I let Israel go.

THE American missionaries having been admitted to an interview with the Emperor of Burmah, presented a petition requesting permission to preach the gospel in his dominions. After the Emperor had perused it, he handed it back without saying a word, and took a tract which was also presented to him. "Our hearts," say the missionaries, "now rose to God for a display of His grace. 'O, have mercy on Burmah! Have mercy on her king!' But, alas! the time was not yet come. He held the tract long enough to read the first two sentences, which assert that there is one eternal God, who is independent of the incidents of mortality; and that, besides Him, there is no God; and then, with an air of indifference, perhaps disdain, he dashed it down to the ground! Moung Zah (one of his ministers) stooped forward, picked it up, and handed it to us. Moung Yo made a slight attempt to save us, by unfolding one of the volumes which composed our present, and displayed its beauty; but His Majesty took no notice. Our fate was decided. After a few moments, Moung Zah interpreted his royal master's will in the following terms:—"In regard to the objects of your petition, his Majesty gives no order; in regard to your sacred books, His Majesty has no use for them; take them away.'"

Depending on God.

Chap. vi. ver. 30.—Moses said before the Lord, Behold I am of uncircumcised lips, and how shall Pharaoh hearken unto me?

"ONE Lord's day," a minister writes in his diary, "my mind was borne down by a sense of my unpreparedness for the work of the day; my fears rose so high, as greatly to affect my body. This fear, as to its nature, was an apprehension of being left to barrenness in the work of the day. Its cause was viewing the greatness of the work, and the weakness of my own abilities, without looking to God. Its cure, I thought, must be a view of the Lord's ability to help me, and a reliance on him for aid. I went to meeting in the depth of fear, but the Lord did not leave me in it after His service began; for both in prayer and preaching I enjoyed unusual liberty. After this my proud heart was too much elated; and the Lord very justly left me to great contractedness in the afternoon."

Sorcerers.

Chap. vii. ver. 11.—Then Pharaoh also called the wise men and the sorcerers; now the magicians of Egypt they also did in like manner with their enchantments.

THE missionaries at Poonah, in the East Indies, speaking of the heathen superstitions, and more particularly describing one that has lately arisen, say—"Narayun Bhas was the son of a labourer, in a small village equidistant from Wall and Satiria. He had been taught, when nine years of age, the art of catching serpents. This wonderful faculty possessed by so young a boy, was given out as proving his origin to be divine. This was soon noised abroad throughout the whole country, and vast numbers flocked from all quarters to see this new divinity. It was given out that he could cleanse lepers, give sight to the blind, &c. As soon as ever we mentioned the miracles of Christ, those of Narayun Bhas were appealed to by the deluders and the deluded. Several lepers were seated by his directions by the side of a rivulet, waiting for a miraculous cure. Things went on in this way for four or five months; at last, some one, to try him, brought a very venomous serpent for him to catch. On this occasion his usual tact was wanting; the serpent bit him, and a few minutes after, the boy died. The eyes of some people seemed to be open to the imposture; others expect that he is immediately to appear again in the family of a Brahmin near this, if he has not already appeared."

The Care of Providence.

Chap. viii. ver. 19.—This is the finger of God.

"I HAVE been thrown from my pony," said a little boy to his father; "but, *by chance*, I am not hurt." "I am glad to hear of your safe escape, my dear child; but you ought to ascribe it to Providence. Chance is blind, and cannot protect us: Providence watches over us all. Look round on nature—on those things most obvious to your senses, the plants, trees, animals, and yourself; lift your eyes to heaven—see the beautiful regularity of the planetary orbs, the return of day and night, and the revolution of seasons; then reflect, can these things be the effect of chance? No; a Supreme Power rules and directs the order of the universe, and holds the chain of events. Learn to acknowledge this great and good Being in everything that befalls you. Look up to His superintending Providence for every blessing you would wish to receive, and every danger you are anxious to avoid, and scorn to be indebted to chance for what you really owe to your Father and your God."

God Performing a Great Work.

Chap. ix. ver. 16.—In very deed for this cause have I raised thee up, for to shew in thee my power; and that my name may be declared throughout all the earth.

"WHEN God is about to perform any great work," says Mr Newton, "he generally permits some great opposition to it. Suppose Pharaoh had acquiesced in the departure of the children of Israel, or that they had met with no difficulties in the way, they would indeed have passed from Egypt to Canaan with ease; but they, as well as the Church in all future ages, would have been great losers. The wonder-working God would not have been seen in those extremities which make his arm so visible. A smooth passage, here, would have made but a poor story."

The Hardening of Pharaoh's Heart.

Chap. x. ver. 20.—The Lord hardened Pharaoh's heart.

IN a conversation with the Vice-Patriarch at the Greek Convent at Cairo, and his secretary, Mr Jowett intimated that it would be desirable that the Greeks in Cairo should possess the Holy Scriptures. "These artisans," observed the secretary, "how can they understand the Scriptures, unless we explain them? How would a common man understand that passage, '*The Lord hardened Pharaoh's heart?*' Would he not be led to think that God was the author of Pharaoh's sin?" "On this show of controversy, I retired," says Mr J., "for a few moments into my own thoughts; and, having paused in that way, which the long pipe with which I was furnished gave an opportunity of doing, I turned to the secretary, and asked how he would explain that passage, which was certainly a difficult one." He replied, "God permitted Pharaoh to remain in his hardened state of nature." "Very well," I said, "the explanation which satisfies you, would most probably satisfy every common reader of the Bible, as it does me."

Praying unto the Lord.

Chap. xi. ver. 7.—But against any of the children of Israel shall not a dog move his tongue, against man or beast; that ye may know how that the Lord doth put a difference between the Egyptians and Israel.

ALTHOUGH it is true, that, in the general course of Divine Providence, "no man knoweth either love or hatred by all that is before them," and that "all things come alike to all," and "there is one event to the righteous and to the wicked," yet there are many instances in which we may "discern between the righteous and the wicked; between him that serveth God, and him that serveth him not," and are called to acknowledge. "Verily there is a reward for the righteous: verily he is a God that judgeth in the earth."—About the time when the gospel was beginning to make its way in Raiatea, one of the South Sea Islands, a canoe, with four men in it, was upset at sea, and the people were thrown into the water. Two of the men having embraced Christianity, immediately cried, "Let us pray to Jehovah; for He can save us."—"Why did you not pray to him sooner?" replied their Pagan comrades; "here we are in the water, and it is useless to pray now." The Christians, however, did cry mightily unto their God, while all four were clinging for life to the broken canoe. In this situation, a shark suddenly rushed towards them, and seized one of the two idolators. His companions held him as fast and as long as they could; but the monster prevailed in the tug between them, and hurried the unfortunate victim into the abyss, marking the track with his blood. After some time the tide bore the surviving three to the reef, when, just as they were cast upon it, a second shark snatched the other idolator with his jaws, and carried off his prey, shrieking in vain for assistance, which the two Christians, themselves struggling with the breakers, could not afford him. This circumstance made a great impression on the minds of their countrymen, and powerfully recommenced to them the "God that heareth prayer."

Early Impressions.

Chap. xii. ver. 26, 27.—When your children shall say unto you, What mean ye by this service? Ye shall say, It is the sacrifice of the Lord's passover.

THE mother of Dr Samuel Johnson was a woman of great good sense and piety; and she was the means of early impressing religious principles on the mind of her son. He used to say, that he distinctly remembered having had the first notice of heaven, "a place

to which good people go," and hell, "a place to which bad people go,"
communicated to him by her, when a little child in bed with her; and
that it might be the better fixed in his memory, she sent him to repeat
it to her man servant. He being out of the way, this was not done;
but there was no occasion for any artificial aid for its preservation·
When the Doctor related this circumstance, he added, "that children
should be always encouraged to tell what they hear that is particularly striking, to some brother, sister, or servant, immediately, before
the impression is erased by the intervention of newer occurrences."

Respect for the Deceased.

Chap. xiii. ver. 19.—Moses took the bones of Joseph with him.

WICKLIFFE, the first English reformer, was seized with palsy,
while engaged in public worship in his church at Lutterworth,
which, in three days, put a period to his life. His body was interred
in the chancel of the church; but the resentment of his enemies did
not terminate with his life. Having first ordered his works to be
burnt, his bones, by a decree of the Council of Constance, were
commanded to be dug up and committed to the flames; which
disgraceful mandate was carried into effect thirteen years afterwards.

Resting on the Lord.

Chap. xiv. ver. 13.—Moses said unto the people, Fear ye not; stand
still, and see the salvation of the Lord.

THE Rev. Mr Monteith, late of Alnwick, on his way from London,
called on the Rev. James Hervey. Being asked by him, What
news in the city? He replied, "Everything is preparing for war;"
upon which Mr Hervey said, with much sweetness and composure,
"Well, God will keep him in perfect peace, whose mind is stayed on
him, because he trusteth in him."

God Controls the Wind.

Chap. xv. ver. 10.—Thou didst blow with thy wind, the sea covered
them.

WHEN the Spaniards, on the defeat of their Invincible Armada,
stung with disappointment, and wishing to detract from the
honour which our brave defenders had acquired, exclaimed, that the
English had little reason to boast, for if the elements had not fought
against them, they would certainly have conquered us; the enlarged
and vivid mind of Queen Elizabeth improved the hint. She commanded a medal to be struck, representing the Armada scattered and
sinking in the back ground; and in the front, the British fleet riding
triumphant, with the preceding passage as a motto round the medal:
"Thou didst blow with thy wind, and the sea covered them." It
becomes us to say in reference to this, as well as many other national
deliverances, "Blessed be the Lord, who hath not given us as a prey
to their teeth."

Preparing for Sunday.

Chap. xvi. ver. 23.—To-morrow is the rest of the holy Sabbath unto
the Lord: bake that which ye will bake to-day, and seethe that ye
will seethe; and that which remaineth over lay up for you, to be kept
until the morning.

"WHILE at tea this evening," says Mr Stewart, missionary at the
Sandwich Islands, "we heard a herald passing through the
district—the manner in which all the general orders of the king and
chiefs are communicated to their vassals—making a proclamation to

the people. On inquiring of the native boys in our yard, we learned that the object of it was to inform the people, that the next day but one would be the Sabbath, and to command them to have all their food prepared on the morrow, and not to break the commandment of God, by working on the 'la tabau'—sacred day. Heralds have very frequently been out on a Saturday evening, to give intelligence of the approach of the Sabbath, and to command its observance; but this is the first time we have heard it notified so seasonably, as to take all excuse from those who disregard it."

Striving with his Maker.

Chap. xvii. ver. 2.—Wherefore do ye tempt the Lord?

A FARMER named Higgins, an inhabitant of Baltonsborough, in Somersetshire, died about the end of 1831. From the time of his marriage in 1793, he became extremely anxious to have a son; but his wife presenting him with three daughters in succession, he became very disconsolate, and even enraged at his repeated disappointment; and vowed, with an oath of imprecation, that should his next child be a daughter, he would never speak to her. Before the birth of his fourth child, he impiously repeated the same solemn vow: the child, however, to his inexpressible joy, proved to be a boy; but the father's satisfaction was of short continuance, for the child, as soon as it began to take notice of surrounding objects, was observed to avoid him, and never could be induced, even for a moment, to remain in his arms. As the boy advanced in years, and the time of articulation arrived, his shyness towards his father became more and more apparent; and it was soon observed, that whilst he conversed freely with his mother and sisters, he never addressed a word to his father, or uttered a syllable in his presence. His shyness was at first thought to be accidental, as his father was much from home; but when the boy had gained the full power of speech, and still observed a constant and marked silence towards him, it became but too evident that Higgins was destined never to hold any conversation with his son. The afflicted parent often entreated him to speak to him and converse with him, but neither entreaties, threats, nor promises, were of the least avail; he even promised him the half of what he possessed, if he would converse, or even speak to him, but it was all to no purpose. The mother also often desired him to oblige his father by talking to him; but his reply was, "No, mother, do you not think I would talk to father if I could? Whenever father approaches me, my voice begins to falter; and before he comes within hearing, the power of speaking entirely fails me." It is remarkable, that the inability of speaking applied to all other males, as well as the father, and continued so for thirty-five years, up to the period of his father's death. Immediately after this occurrence, he began to converse with all around, males as well as females, and he still continues to enjoy the *full* powers of speech. How sinful and dangerous to cherish o express dissatisfaction with the arrangements of the all-wise Providence of God! Woe to him that striveth with his Maker.

Upright Judging.

Chap. xviii. ver. 21, 22.—Thou shalt provide out of the people able men, such as fear God, men of truth, hating covetousness,—and let them judge the people at all seasons.

SIR MATTHEW HALE, in one of his circuits, had a buck sent for his table, by a gentleman who had a trial at the assizes. When

Sir Matthew heard the gentleman's name, he asked, "If he was not the same person that had sent him venison?" And finding he was the same, he told him he could not suffer the trial to go on till he had paid him for his buck. The gentleman observed, that he never sold his vension, and that he did nothing to him which he did not do to every judge who had gone that circuit : the truth of which was confirmed by several gentlemen then present. The Lord Chief Baron, however, would not proceed with the trial till he had paid for the present, upon which the gentleman withdrew the record. At Salisbury, too, the Dean and Chapter having, according to custom, presented him with six sugar loaves in his circuit, he made his servants pay for the sugar before he would try their cause.

Awe Inspiring Impressions.

Chap. xix. ver. 16.—There were thunders and lightnings, and a thick cloud upon the mount, and the voice of the trumpet exceeding loud ; so that all the people that was in the camp trembled.

MR RICHARD MORRIS, pastor of a Baptist Church in England, when a young man, attended, as a spectator, a funeral which he had followed into St Mary's Church, at Stamford. His mind being peculiarly solemnized and softened by the scene, the blast of six trumpets sounded together, to set the evening watch, and reverberated through the dome, striking the whole audience with awe. It was a natural association of ideas, which, at such a moment, called up with peculiar vividness the thought that he must certainly hear the tremendous sound of the trump of God. With this impression fresh upon his mind, Mr Morris retired to his room, and endeavoured to lift up his heart to that God who he knew must be his Judge. His prayer was heard, and although he was at this time, as he confessed, totally unacquainted with the nature of salvation by Jesus Christ, as revealed in the Gospel, as well as with the agency of the Holy Spirit, as necessary to bring the soul to a personal acquaintance with it, yet he was enabled to break off, from this time, his former habits, and to enter, though with very obscure notions, upon a religious life. This trifling occurrence acting with peculiar force upon his imagination, seems to have been the means of permanently arresting his attention, and of giving rise to those workings of conscience which issued in his conversion.

Profane Swearing.

Chap. xx. ver. 7.—Thou shalt not take the name of the Lord thy God in vain : for the Lord will not hold him guiltless that taketh his name in vain.

THE Rev. Ebenezer Erskine, when crossing the Forth from Leith to Kinghorn, had the unhappiness to find himself in the midst of ungodly passengers, who took the most unhallowed liberties with their Creator's name. For a time he was silent, but at last, unable to suppress his concern, and solicitous to curb their blaspheming tongues, he rose from his seat, and taking hold of the mast, uncovered his head, waved his hat, and cried aloud, "O yes! O yes! O yes!" Having thus secured the attention of the astonished passengers and crew, he proceeded, in a solemn and impressive manner, to proclaim that commandment of the moral law which they were flagrantly violating : "Thou shalt not take the name of the Lord thy God in vain : for the Lord will not hold him guiltless that taketh his name in vain." Without adding a single word, he quitted the mast, covered his head, and resumed his seat. The giddy company, however, resolved to harden themselves against the striking reproof. They began first to elbow each other, then to titter, and at last, to be avenged on their kind reprover, they burst into a fit of loud laughter. Their conversation soon became as profane and offensive as before. Among the rest, a lady, laying aside the delicacy of the sex, and regardless alike of the authority of God, and the maxims of politeness, seemed to find a malicious pleasure in giving emphasis to almost every sentence, by intermixing the sacred name, accompanied with smiles of derision and contempt, obviously intended to mortify the venerable man. It pleased God, however, to second the despised warning of his servant, by an alarming admonition of his providence. When they had got to the north of Inchkeith, a tempest suddenly arose; the heavens became black with clouds—the sea raged—the danger was imminent—the pilot, unable to keep hold of the helm, assured them that their fate was inevitable. This unexpected alteration of circumstances produced at least a temporary change on their spirit and appearance. Their sportive gaiety gave place to consternation and despair. The same lady who had acted so insolent a part towards the faithful clergyman, overwhelmed with dismay, now sprang across the boat, and clasped her arms around his neck, exclaiming, "O Sir, if I die here, I will die with you." Through the Divine patience and forbearance, however, they weathered the storm, and reached the harbour in safety.

Loving my Master.

Chap. xxi. ver. 5.—I love my master; I will not go out free.

A GENTLEMAN in Virginia had in his service a negro youth, about fourteen years of age, named Scipio. The gentleman had a son about the same age, to whom Scipio was greatly attached. This youth was taken ill, and was constantly attended by his anxious parents, who relieved each other at proper intervals. One evening, however, being greatly exhausted, they both retired to rest, leaving the patient to the care of a friend who had volunteered her services on the occasion. About two o'clock in the morning, he became very restless, and called for something to drink. The nurse fell asleep, but Scipio had calculated upon such an event, and had concealed himself under the bed. On hearing his young master's voice, he put out his head, saying, "Massa George, wat you want? me come arectly." He arose immediately, but not knowing the contents of three or four bottles which were on the table, he went and called his mistress, to whom he related his adventure. After supplying the wants of her son, she commended the conduct of Scipio, and desired him to go to bed. But the faithful and affectionate youth could not be prevailed on to leave the room, but said, "Poor massa very tired, poor missey very tired, missey go bed; Scipio no tired, Scipio no sit up last night; no go bed now." Soon afterwards the youth recovered, and his father, in reward of Scipio's fidelity, offered him his freedom; but such was his regard for his young master, that he declined the favour, and remained in the family, beloved and respected by all who knew him.

The Righteous Man's Harvest.

Chap. xxii. ver. 4.—If a man shall cause a field or vineyard to be eaten, and shall put in his beast, and shall feed in another man's field; of the best of his own field, and of the best of his own vineyard, shall he make restitution.

IN the last war in Germany, a captain of cavalry was out on a foraging party. On perceiving a cottage in the midst of a solitary valley, he went up and knocked at the door. Out came a Hernouten (better known by the name of United Brethren) with a beard silvered by age. "Father," says the officer, "show me a field where I can set my troopers aforaging." "Presently," replied the Hernouten. The good old man walked before, and conducted them out of the valley. After a quarter of an hour's march, they found a fine field of barley. "There is the very thing we want," said the captain. "Have patience for a few minutes," replied his guide; "you shall be satisfied." They went on, and at the distance of about a quarter of a league farther, they at length reached another field of barley. The troop immediatey dismounted, cut down the grain, trussed it up, and remounted. The officer, upon this, said to his conductor, "Father, you have given yourself and us unnecessary trouble: the first field was much better than this." "Very true, Sir," replied the good old man, "but it was not mine." This stroke goes directly to the heart. I defy an Atheist to produce anything to be compared to this. And surely he who does not feel his heart warmed by such an example of exalted virtue, has not yet acquired the first principles of moral taste.

Resting on the Sabbath Day.

Chap. xxiii. ver. 12.—On the seventh day thou shalt rest; that thine ox and thine ass may rest, and the son of thine handmaid and the stranger may be refreshed.

THE late Sir Edward Wraes, who resided near the city of Bristol, was in the habit of driving his carriage and four, with a corresponding retinue, about the neighbourhood every Sabbath-day. During one of these ungodly excursions, he observed at a distance a group of people listening to a discourse of the late excellent Mr. James Bundy. The baronet ordered his coachman to drive forward to the crowd to see what was going on. He then sat in his open carriage, and listened with attention to Mr. B., who, with his wonted zeal and fidelity, embraced the opportunity of expatiating on the impropriety of misemploying the Lord's day, and of causing our servants and cattle to do the like. The appeal had the desired effect; Sir Edward immediately ordered his servants to return home. Shortly after, calling them into his parlour, he informed them, that for the future he should never take his ride of pleasure on the Lord's day; that they should always have it for their own religious benefit, and which, he hoped, they would zealously improve, by attending some place of public worship. He then sent for Mr. Bundy, and expressed his obligations to him for his faithfulness, and maintained a friendship with him during life.

Obedient unto the Lord.

Chap. xxiv. ver. 7—All that the Lord hath said will we do, and be obedient.

"ABOUT eighteen months ago," says a correspondent in the Christian Herald, "a person called on me, applying for fellowship with our church. His knowledge and conduct, for a considerable time before, had indicated that he was a believer of the Gospel. I asked him what induced him to apply *now*. He told me he had been led to this by his lately having had a dream, of which he gave me the following relation:—Being from home on business, and lodging in an inn in Linton, he, during the night, dreamed that he died; that the coffin was provided for his body, and a number of people were standing round it. He (*i. e.* the disembodied spirit,) with the utmost confidence, addressed them in these words—'You shall now see me ascend into heaven!' He ascended so far, when he felt he could go no farther; but, to his great disappointment, was forced downward to the ground, while a voice addressed him in these words—*You have obeyed but in part.* He awoke in great agitation and distress. He considered his faith and the profession of it, in connection with his notorious neglect of the commands of the Lord Jesus, and could give himself no rest without endeavouring to obey *all* the will of the Lord."

Giving Willingly.

Chap. xxv. ver. 2.—Of every man that giveth it willingly with his heart ye shall take my offering.

TWO ministers collecting for the London Missionary Society in Yorkshire, had twenty guineas brought to them by a man in low circumstances of life. Doubting whether it was consistent with his duty to his family and the world, to contribute such a sum, they hesitated to receive it, when he answered to the following effect:—
"Before I knew the grace of our Lord, I was a poor drunkard; I never could save a shilling; my family were in beggary and rags: but since it has pleased God to renew me by his grace, we have been industrious and frugal; we have not spent many idle shillings, and we have been enabled to put something into the bank, and this I freely offer to the blessed cause of our Lord and Saviour."—This was the second donation from the individual to the same amount.

Loyal to the Scriptures.

Chap. xxvi. ver. 30.—Thou shalt rear up the tabernacle according to the fashion thereof which was shewed thee in the mount.

WHEN Luther, at the diet of Worms, was urged by Eckius, the Pope's legate, to recant, he replied, "I beseech you, give me leave to maintain the peace of my own conscience, which, if I should consent to you, I cannot do. For unless my adversaries can convince me by sound arguments taken out of the Holy Scriptures, I cannot satisfy my conscience. For I can plainly prove, that both Popes and Councils have often erred grievously; and therefore it would be an ungodly thing for me to assent to them, and to depart from the Holy Scriptures, which are plain, and alone cannot err."

The Brazen Altar.

Chap. xxvii. ver. 1, 2.—Thou shalt make an altar of shittim-wood; and thou shalt overlay it with brass.

"THIS brazen altar," says Mr. Henry, "was a type of Christ dying to make atonement for our sins. The wood had been consumed by the fire from heaven, if it had not been secured by the brass; nor could the human nature of Christ have borne the wrath of God, if it had not been supported by a divine power. Christ sanctified himself for his Church, as their altar, John xvii. 19, and by his mediation sanctifies the daily services of his people, who also have *a right to eat of this altar*, Heb. xiii. 10, for they serve at it as spiritual priests. To the horns of this altar poor sinners fly for refuge when justice pursues them, and there they are safe in virtue of the sacrifice there offered!"

Trust in God.

Chap. xxviii. ver. 38.—And it shall be upon Aaron's forehead, that Aaron may bear the iniquity of the holy things, which the Children of Israel shall hallow in all their holy gifts ; and it shall be always upon his forehead, that they may be accepted before the Lord.

"MY confidence is," said the pious Dr Doddridge shortly before his death, "not that I have lived such or such a life, or served God in this or the other manner ; I know of no prayer I ever offered, no service I ever performed, but there has been such a mixture of what was wrong in it, that instead of recommending me to the favour of God, I needed his pardon, through Christ, for the same. Yet I am full of confidence ; and this is my confidence—there is a hope set before me : I have fled, I still fly, for refuge to that hope."

The Priest's Office.

Chap. xxix. ver. 9.—The priest's office shall be theirs.

A PIOUS lady being at one time among a party of gentlemen, by whom the worldly circumstances of ministers became the topic of conversation, remarks were thrown out, of which she could not approve. For a considerable while she said nothing, but at last, opening her mouth with a dignified air, and a decided tone, she put them all to silence with these words, "Well, you may say what you please concerning the situation of ministers, but, let me tell you, that a minister of the *Gospel* holds a more honourable office than a minister of *State*."

Money for Souls.

Chap. xxx. ver. 12.—They shall give every man a ransom for his soul.

AN American missionary states, that during almost seven years that he resided in Malta, he was witness every Monday morning to an affecting and admonitory scene. A man passed through the streets, ringing a bell in one hand, and rattling a box in the other, crying at every corner, "What will you give for the souls ? What will you give for the souls ? The women and children came out of the habitations of poverty, and cast their mites into the box. When it is full, it is carried to a neighbouring convent, to pay the priests for praying the souls of the dead out of purgatory ! Let Protestants be exhorted to "give money for souls" in a far different manner, by assisting Christian missions, and the circulation of the word of God.

Keeping the Sabbath.

Chap. xxxi. ver. 13.—Speak thou also unto the children of Israel, saying, Verily my Sabbaths ye shall keep.

THE Rev. J. S. Smith, in his boyish days, used means to reform his companions from a gross profanation of the Sabbath. Of his zeal in this respect, the following is a pleasing instance. It was a common practice in the neighbourhood where he dwelt, for boys to go out into the fields on the Lord's day to play at foot-ball. Viewing this practice as a great evil, he resolved, if possible, to put a stop to it. To accomplish this purpose, he called several of them together, expostulated with them on the impropriety of their conduct, urged them to renounce it for ever, and advised them to attend some place of worship on the sacred day. This was his first attempt to reform the manners of others, and it succeeded beyond his expectations

Heathen Worship.

Chap. xxxii. ver. 6.—And the people sat down to eat and to drink, and rose up to play.

"THE Chinese," says the Rev. Samuel Dyer, "you know, are very polished idolators. A few evenings since, there was special worship performing in their temple ; and while the worship was proceeding, I was engaged in the temple distributing tracts. A priest saw me, and laughed very contemptuously at me. One poor man entered the temple with a small bundle, and standing at the table in front of the idol, he began to open his bundle, talking with any one near him with the utmost indifference to the service which was going forward ; so little solemnity accompanies their worship. When the bundle was opened, a paper containing sweetmeats, was first presented to the idol ; then the gold paper was prepared for burning ;. and when all was ready the man worshipped ; then tried his fortune ; afterwards burnt his paper money (for the use of the dead), and let off crackers. He then folded up his present of sweetmeats, took them away, and became, I suppose, a spectator of the play, opposite the temple gate. These plays are performed by the Chinese, for their gods to see; and they always bring a concourse of people to the temple."

Seeing God's Face.

Chap. xxxiii. ver. 20.—Thou canst not see my face: for there shall no man see me, and live.

"YOU teach," said the Emperor Trajan to Rabbi Joshua, "that your God is everywhere, and boast that he resides among your nation ; I should like to see him." "God's presence is, indeed, everywhere," replied Joshua, "but he cannot be seen ; no mortal eye can behold his glory." The Emperor insisted. "Well," said Joshua, "suppose we try to look first at one of his ambassadors ?" The Emperor consented. The Rabbi took him into the open air at noonday, and bade him look at the sun in its meridian splendour. "I cannot," said Trajan, "the light dazzles me." "Thou art unable," said Joshua, "to endure the light of one of his creatures, and canst thou expect to behold the resplendent glory of the Creator ? Would not such a light annihilate thee ?"

Resting the Seventh Day.

Chap. xxxiv. ver. 21.—The seventh day thou shalt rest ; in earing-time and in harvest thou shalt rest.

ONE Sabbath, a few children were gathered round the porch of a village church, waiting for the commencement of public worship, when a waggon, with a number of persons in it who were going out on pleasure, stopped, and one of the men called out to the children, "Halloo there, what sort of religion do you have there ?" One of the young lads replied, "A sort of religion that forbids our travelling on the Sabbath."

A Missionary Offering.

Chap. xxxv. ver. 25.—All the women, whose hearts stirred them up in wisdom, spun goat's hair.

A POOR woman, just after a missionary meeting held in the country, called at the lodgings of a minister who had been engaged at the meeting, and told him she had been prevented from attending it, but hoped she was not too late to present a little contribution she wished to make to the Society. The poverty of her appearance induced the minister to say he feared she could not afford to give anything ; but the poor woman assured him, that though she was a widow, and had four children to support by the mangle which she worked, she had contrived to save a little ; and that she should be much grieved if he should refuse to take it. She then untied a bundle she had brought with her, and produced 330 farthings, saying that she had laid by one farthing every day for the year past, excepting those days in which illness had disabled her from working.

Giving Willingly.

Chap. xxxvi. ver. 5.—The people bring much more than enough for the service of the work which the Lord commanded to make.

IT is pleasing to observe the willingness with which many, even of the poorer classes of society contribute to Bible and Missionary Societies. A minister in the country, who had formed a penny-a-week society in his congregation, gives the following account :—"I am happy to inform you that my success has far exceeded my expectations. If our subscriptions continue, the annual amount will be considerable. One hundred subscribers were obtained the first day. The account which the collectors give of their reception among the poor is really affecting ; they found some of them standing at the doors of their humble abodes, with their pence in their hands, and others, whom they had passed by, followed them with their money, saying to the collectors, 'Pray, do not neglect us because we are poor.' A lady in one district called on a poor widow, merely to prevent her feelings from being hurt, and told her that, owing to her poverty she did not expect anything from her. 'O,' replied the poor widow, 'I cannot, poor as I am, refuse giving a penny-a-week towards promoting the cause of that Redeemer who has given me the hope of heaven.' This poor widow has entirely to support five fatherless children ; and yet she, of her penury, thus cast into the missionary treasury. Indeed, from this, and many other pleasing occurrences, it is evident that the poor consider themselves favoured by being thus called upon. The collectors declare that they could not have been better received had they gone to distribute money, instead of receiving it."

Incense and Prayer.

Chap. xxxvii. ver. 25.—He made the incense-altar

THE incense to be burnt daily on the altar, has been justly considered as significant of the intercession of Christ, and the prayers of his people. Hence the Psalmist says, "Let my prayer be set forth before thee as incense."

Of Mr Thomas Hooker, of New England, his biographer says, "He was a man of prayer ; which, indeed, was a ready way to become a man of God. He would say, 'that prayer was the principal part of a minister's work : it was by this that he was to carry on the rest.' Accordingly, he devoted one day a month to prayer, with fasting, before the Lord, besides the public fasts, which often occurred. He would say, 'that such extraordinary favours as the life of religion and the power of godliness, must be preserved by the frequent use of such extraordinary means as prayer, with fasting ; and that if professors grew negligent of these means, iniquity would abound, and the love of many wax cold."

Circulating the Scriptures.

Chap. xxxviii. ver. 8.—He made the laver of brass, and the foot of it brass, of the looking-glasses of the women assembling, which assembled at the door of the tabernacle of the congregation.

"A GENTLEMAN," says Mr Knill, missionary at Petersburg, "resident on the shores of the Caspian, who once cared nothing about Christ or his cause, has, within a few years, become a warm-hearted disciple. Knowing his character, I wrote to him to assist me in the distribution of the Holy Scriptures. To my request he joyfully agreed; but he did not think it sufficient to contribute towards it himself, but he tried to enlist others also in the good work. He mentioned it in particular to a pious lady of his acquaintance, who had just before received a present of a hundred roubles, to purchase a pair of ear-rings. Fired with a hope of promoting the eternal happiness of her fellow-creatures, she determined to sacrifice her ear-rings to the cause of God, and sent the hundred roubles to me. Perhaps this was the first time that ever her attachment to the Saviour had called for a sacrifice; and it must be unspeakably gratifying to her mind, when reviewing the transaction, to feel that she could part with her ornaments for her adorable Redeemer."

Preaching the Gospel.

Chap. xxxix. ver. 30.—Holiness to the Lord.

"IT is plain," says an eminent divine, "from experimental obser- vation of the longest standing, and the greatest compass, that genuine morality is eminently promoted by preaching up the purity of the gospel. The hope that is laid up for us in heaven, whereof we hear by the word of truth, brings forth fruit in us : 'He that has this hope in him, purifies himself, even as God is pure.'—One of the martyrs in Queen Mary's days confessed, that his prejudice against the Protestants was for their insisting so much on faith, and things of a mysterious nature. 'But,' says he 'when among the Papists, I heard nothing but works; I scarce did any. Now, where duties are preached less, I find them practised more.'"

Walking with God.

Gal. 5.—Old Testament.

Chap. xl. ver. 36. 37.—When the cloud was taken up from over the tabernacle, the children of Israel went onward in all their journeys: But if the cloud were not taken up, then they journeyed not till the day that it was taken up.

"NOTHING was more remarkable," says the biographer of Mr Newton, "than his constant habit of regarding the hand of God in every event, however trivial it might appear to others. On every occasion—in the concerns of every hour—in matters public or private, like Enoch, he 'walked with God.' Take a single instance of his state of mind in this respect. In walking to his church he would say, 'The way of man is not in himself,' nor can he conceive what belongs to a single step. When I go to St Mary Woolnoth, it seems the same whether I turn down Lothbury, or go through the Old Jewry; but the going through one street, and not another, may produce an effect of lasting consequence. A man cut down my hammock in sport, but had he cut it down half an hour later, I had not been here, as the exchange of crew was then making. A man made a smoke on the sea-shore, at the same time a ship passed, which was thereby brought to, and afterwards brought me to England."

BOOK OF LEVITICUS.

Giving Cheerfully.

Chap. i. ver. 3.—He shall offer it of his own voluntary will.

WHEN a Missionary Association was first established in Huahine, one of the South Sea Islands, and contributions were solicited, the people were explicitly informed, that they should not be compelled to give any thing; whatever they did, therefore, must be of their own free will. One day a native brought a hog to Hautia, who was the treasurer, and, throwing the animal down at his feet, said, in an angry tone, "Here's a pig for your Society." "Take it back again," replied Hautia camly; "God does not accept *angry pigs.*" He then explained to the man the objects of missionary institutions, and the necessity of those who supported them doing so from right motives, especially enforcing the Scripture words, "The Lord loveth a cheerful giver." The man was obliged to take his hog home again; for though exceedingly chargined to have it rejected—refusal being considered a great affront when a present is offered—Hautia was too conscientious to accept it.

Early Passion for Christ.

Chap. ii. ver. 14.—Thou shalt offer, for the meat-offering of thy first-fruits, green ears of corn dried by the fire.

THE requiring of green ears of corn in the meat-offering, may intimate how acceptable to God early piety is. The following is a pleasing instance:

In the beginning of the last centuary, Mr Hamilton was successively minister of Airth and Stirling. His ministry was distinguished for its warmth and evangelical savor; it was, of course, very acceptable, and much attended. At that time, the dispensation of the Lord's Supper was attended by multitudes from the neighbourhood. On one of these occasions, at Airth, a young person, at a considerable distance, felt a strong desire to attend. This however, was opposed by her elder sister, on account of her tender age and inability to sustain the fatigues of such a journey; but still bent on the execution of her purpose, she so arranged matters on the preceding evening, that her sister could not, even at the earliest hour, go away without awakening her. Finding the determination so strong, her sister no longer opposed it. On the Sabbath morning, she took her young friend to the place of worship. After the celebration of the Lord's Supper, Mr Hamilton addressed the communicants and audience. In the conclusion, he invited sinners, with great fervour and freedom, to the Lord Jesus Christ. The riches of divine grace, in the salvation of perishing sinners, were exhibited in the most alluring and engaging manner. The attention of this young person was excited, and her heart sweetly drawn to the Saviour. This gracious season was remembered and mentioned by her with pleasure to the end of life; and her descendants, to whom her pious example and instructions were rendered useful, still preserve the memory and record of it with a delightful interest. This should encourage parents to bring their children, at an early age, to attend the ordinances of divine grace in public.

BOOK OF LEVITICUS.

Eastern Sheep.

Chap. iii. ver. 9.—The fat thereof, and the whole rump, it shall be take off hard by the backbone.

HERE is a kind of sheep near Aleppo, the tails of which are very broad and large, terminating in a small appendix that turns back upon it. These tails, Dr Russell informs us, are of a substance between fat and marrow, and are not eaten separately, but mixed with the lean meat in many of their dishes, and also often used instead of butter: That a common sheep of this kind, without the head, feet, skin, &c., weighs sixty or seventy English pounds, of which the tail usually weighs fifteen pounds and upwards. This species, he observes, is by much the most numerous.

Evil through Ignorance.

Chap. iv. ver. 2.—If a soul shall sin through ignorance against any of the commandments of the Lord.

A HEBREW merchant had three negroes, very bad characters, who frequently got drunk and robbed him. Observing a sudden change in their conduct, he inquired into the cause. One of the poor fellows replied, "Massa, God Almighty in top!" (above.) He was answered, "Was not God Almighty in top when you got drunk and robbed me?" "Yes, Massa, but *we not know then*." He then asked them how they came to know. They answered, "Massa, we been gone a chapel and preacher tell we so; and now we fraid to get drunk and rob like fore time. God will see, and he will be angry; Him see everything."

Profane Swearing.

Chap. v. ver. 1.—If a soul sin, and hear the voice of swearing, and is a witness, whether he hath seen or known of it; if he do not utter it, then he shall bear his iniquity.

AS the sin referred to in the preceding verse appears to consist in a concealment of the truth, especially when called on oath to declare it, the following anecdote may, in *part* at least, illustrate the passage:—

Captain (afterwards Admiral) Cornwallis, in order to prevent profaneness among the ship's crew, had a book to every mess to insert each offender's name, and appointed forfeits according to the offence. To these rules the captain made himself liable; and, looking over the books one morning when at sea, he found his own name inserted, upon which he sent for the informer, and inquired what he had said, and who was near when he used improper language. Being told that the chaplain was at his elbow, he called for the Reverend gentleman, and asked him if he recollected hearing him say, on the preceding day, "By God." He confessed this, but did not think it came within the meaning of the rules. The captain observed, "It was certainly an irreverent use of the sacred name, and you should have reproved me; you, therefore, shall be punished for neglect, and the informer shall be rewarded with a guinea."

Restoring the Lost Thing.

Chap. vi. ver. 6.—He shall restore—the lost thing which he found.

SOME years ago, a poor shoemaker found, in a street in Liverpool, a bill of exchange for £110. On being informed of its value, with an honest simplicity, he had it cried through the streets by the bellman. Several applications were soon made to him for the bill:

but from the evident eagerness of the applicants, and the large sums offered him as a reward, he suspected that the bill could not be their's. He accordingly took it to a respectable banker's, where it had been drawn, who presently discovered the right owner, and rewarded the shoemaker with five guineas for his honesty. The poor man received it with gratitude, declaring that this sum would do him more good, now that he was assured the bill would go to the true owner, than if he had given it to others and received a larger sum.

Thankfulness.

Chap. vii. ver. 12.—If he offer it for a thanksgiving.

MR. ROMAINE being in company with Mr Hervey, who was unwell, at breakfast time, observed him retire to another part of the room, taking with him a small basin of milk; and overheard him praying over it thus: "Lord, if I obtain no nourishment from this food which thou hast given me, at least let me get thankfulness from it."

Disagreement and Love.

Chap. viii. ver. 9.—He put the mitre upon his head.

IN the reign of King Edward VI., when Mr John Hooper was made bishop, there was much controversy between him and Drs Cranmer and Ridley, about the cap and rochet, &c. When, however, they were all imprisoned in Queen Mary's reign, Dr Ridley wrote to Hooper in the following manner :—"My dear brother, forasmuch as I understand by your works that we thoroughly agree in those things which are the grounds and substantial points of our religion, against which the world so furiously rageth in these days; however, formerly, in certain bye-matters and circumstances of religion, your wisdom and my simplicity have a little jarred, each of us following the abundance of his own sense and judgement; now, I say, be assured, that even with my whole heart (God is my witness) in the bowels of Christ, I love you in the truth, and for the truth's sake, which abideth in us, and shall, by the grace of God, abide for ever."

Repentance.

Chap. ix. ver. 12.—He slew the burnt offering; and Aaron's sons presented unto him the blood, which he sprinkled round about upon the altar.

DES BARREAUX, a foreigner of eminent station, had been a great profligate, and afterwards became a great penitent. He composed a piece of poetry after his conversion, the leading sentiment of which was to the following effect :—"Great God, thy judgments are full of righteousness, thou takest pleasure in the exercise of mercy; but I have sinned to such a height, that justice demands my destruction, and mercy itself seems to solicit my perdition. Disdain my tears, strike the blow, and execute thy judgment. I am willing to submit and adore, even in perishing, the equity of thy procedure. But on what place will the stroke fall that is not covered with the blood of Christ?"

Strong Drink.

Chap. x. ver. 9.—Do not drink wine nor strong drink, thou, nor thy sons with you, when ye go into the tabernacle of the congregation, lest ye die: it shall be a statute for ever throughout your generation.

A GENTLEMAN travelling in Essex, called at the house of a friend, where he met a young minister who was just going to preach in the neighbourhood. The lady of the house offered him a glass of spirits before he entered upon his work, which he accepted. An elderly man, who was present, thus addressed him :—My young friend, let me offer you a word of advice respecting the use of liquors. There was a time when I was as acceptable a preacher you now may be; but by too frequently accepting of the well-designed favours of my friends, I contracted a habit of drinking, so that now I never go to bed sober if I can get liquor. I am, indeed, just as miserable as a creature can be on this side of hell!" About two years after this, the traveller just mentioned had occasion to call again at the same house, and made inquiry concerning the unhappy man, when he was informed that he had been some time dead; and no doubt in consequence of his intemperance. It was stated that, towards the close of his life, he had not drunk to the same excess; but it was only because he could not obtain spirituous liquors.

The Harvest of the Sea.

Chap. xi. ver. 9.—Whatsoever hath fins and scales in the waters, in the seas, and in the rivers, them shall ye eat.

MR. TURNER, in his History of Providence, relates, that when the people of a certain sea-port town (Hastings) in England were in great poverty, and suffered much by scarcity of money and provisions, it pleased God that an unusual and great shoal of herrings came up the river, by which the inhabitants were plentifully supplied for the present; and the week after, a multitude of cod succeeded them, which were supposed to have driven the former into the river before them; by which means the necessities of the poor inhabitants were unexpectedly and remarkably supplied.

An Offering.

Chap. xii. ver. 8.—If she be not able to bring a lamb, then she shall bring two turtles, or two young pigeons.

MR. CHANDLER, in his travels in Asia Minor, informs us, that on their arrival at the town of Guzel-Hissar, they were surprised to see around them innumerable tame turtle-doves, sitting on the branches of trees, on the walls and roofs of houses, cooing unceasingly. Though these creatures migrate in winter, the Jewish worshippers might be supplied with offerings, at any season of the year, from the tame ones they bred up.

Treatment of Lepers.

Chap. xiii. ver. 46.—All the days wherein the plague shall be in him he shall be defiled; he is unclean: he shall dwell alone; without the camp shall his habitation be.

WHILE the law of Moses only required the exclusion of the leper from the camp or town where he formerly resided, the following account of the treatment of one of these unhappy men shows that the dark places of the earth are full of cruelty :—"A Hindoo, of the writer cast," says one of the Baptist Missionaries in India, "who has been in our employment upwards of two years, and of whose veracity I have had proof in many instances, informed me yesterday, that on the 5th or 6th instant, he saw a Hindoo carpenter drowned because he had the leprosy. He was carried from one of the ghauts at Alumgunj in a boat, in the presence of a large assembly of people, and when in deep water put overboard. Two large earthen pots, one filled with sand, the other with barley, were fastened to his shoulders.

The man sunk, but after some time floated on the surface of the water. The people in the boat rowed after him and took him up, *but made sure work of it the second time!"*

Giving according to Means.

Chap. xiv. ver. 22.—Two turtle-doves, or two young pigeons, such as he is able to get.

MR. RICHMOND, during his visit to Iona, frequently preached in the school-house. On one of these occasions, he adverted to the Jewish Missions. The hum of the children was heard, "We will give, we will give!" Some persons present attempted to check their zeal, and keep silence, but all voices were raised in reply, "The bairns will have it, the bairns will have it!" meaning, the children *would* make a collection; and they presented to him the sum of £2, 0s, 9d,—a magnificent offering to him whose grace had touched their hearts and inspired their zeal. Of these poor islanders it might be truly said, "Their deep poverty abounded unto the riches of their liberality."

Eastern Purification.

Chap. xv. ver. 12.—And the vessel of earth that he touched which hath the issue shall be broken: and every vessel of wood shall be rinsed in water.

MR. CLARK was one evening entertained very kindly by a Turk and his family. After leaving the place, the next morning he returned for a book he had left behind, when he found his kind host and all the family employed in breaking and throwing away the earthenware, plates, and dishes, from which his guests had eaten, and purifying the other utensils and articles of furniture, by passing them through fire or water.

The Scape Goat.

Chap. xvi. ver. 22.—And the goat shall bear upon him all their iniquities unto a land not inhabited: and he shall let go the goat in the wilderness.

THE Aswamedha Jug is an ancient rite, in which a horse was brought and sacrificed, with some ceremonies very similar to those prescribed in the Mosaic law. The horse so sacrificed, bears, in place of the sacrificer, his sins with him into the wilderness, into which he is turned adrift, (for, from this particular instance, it seems that the sacrificing-knife was not always employed), and becomes the expiatory victim of those sins. Mr Halhed observes, that this ceremony reminds us of the *scape-goat* of the Israelites; and, indeed, it is not the only one in which a particular coincidence between the Hindoo and Mosaic systems of theology may be traced.

The Doctrine of the Atonement.

Chap. xvii. ver. 11.—It is the blood that maketh an atonement for the soul.

THE first sermon which the late Rev. Robert Hall preached at Cambridge, after he became a settled pastor, was in confirmation of the atonement. Immediately after the service, one of the congregation, who had followed Mr Robinson through all his changes of sentiment until he was hovering over the very undefinable barrier which separates the colder Socinianism from infidelity, went to the vestry, and said, "Mr Hall, this preaching won't do for us; it will only suit a congregation of old women!"—"Do you mean my sermon, Sir, or the *doctrine?*'—"Your *doctrine.*"—"Why is it that the *doctrine* will only do for *old women?*"—Because it may suit the musings of people tottering on the brink of the grave."—"Thank you, Sir," said Mr Hall, "for your concessions. The doctrine will *not suit* people of *any* age if it be not *true;* and if it *be true,* it is equally important at *every* age. So that you will hear it again if you hear me."

A Diabolical Custom.

Chap. xviii. ver 21.—Thou shalt not let any of thy seed pass through the fire to Moloch.

"AN eminent historian," says Dr Doddridge, "speaking of that diabolical custom which so long prevailed amongst the old Carthaginians, of offering their children to a detestable idol, (which was formed in such a manner, that an infant put into its hands, which were stretched out to receive it, would immediately fall into a gulph of fire,) adds a circumstance, which one cannot mention without horror :—That the mothers who, with their own hands, presented the little innocents, thought it an unfortunate omen that the victim should be offered weeping ; and, therefore, used a great many fond artifices to divert it, that, soothed by the kisses and caresses of a parent, it might smile in that dreadful moment in which it was to be given up to the idol. Pardon me, my friends, such is *your* concern for the present ease and prosperity of your children, while their souls are neglected,—a fond solicitude that they may pass smiling into the hands of the destroyer."

Tale-bearing.

Chap. xix. ver. 16.—Thou shalt not go up and down as a talebearer among thy people.

AT a small town in ———shire lives a decent honest woman, who has for more than forty years gained her livelihood by washing in gentlemen's families. She gives the highest satisfaction to all her employers, and has, in several instances, been the whole of that time in the employ of the same families. Indeed, those whom she has once served never wish to part with her. She has one distinguishing excellency, it is this : through all this long course of years, *she has never been known, by either mistress or servant, to repeat in one house what was said or done in another.*

Fortune Telling.

Chap. xx. ver. 27.—A man also, or woman, that hath a familiar spirit, or that is a wizard, shall surely be put to death.

"SOME time since," says one, "I was on a visit in Wiltshire, and a large parcel of tracts had been recently received by the worthy family, which they were sorting for distribution amongst the Sunday school children. Whilst I was looking over the tracts, I cast my eyes upon one that related to fortune-telling ; at that moment the servant entered the parlour, and announced that a woman was at the door, and desired to know if any of the party would have their fortune told. I instantly ran out and accosted the woman, 'So you can tell fortunes !' 'Yes, Sir.' 'And can you tell mine ?' 'Yes.' 'Ah ! I do not wish to have my fortune told, for I am a fortune-teller too.' She looked extremely confused, and faintly replied,—'Indeed, Sir !' 'Yes, and I will tell you your fortune ; it is, that if you continue in your present course of wickedness and deception, neglecting God's salvation, and disregarding the eternal state of your soul, you will be lost for ever and ever ! Let me exhort you to leave off your present sinful course, and pray to God to turn your heart. Are you not ashamed to go about the country and thus impose upon servants and young people ? There,' said I, putting some of the fortune-teller's tracts into her hand, 'go and read these carefully, and sell them instead of the wretched trash you have already, they will procure you a trifle, and be sure to attend to what has been said to you on the subject.' The woman appeared affected with the advice, and, after expressing her thanks, curtseyed, and went away."

Heathen mode of obtaining Salvation.

Chap. xxi. ver. 5.—They shall not make—any cuttings in their flesh.

"A FEW months ago," says Mr George, a missionary in Ceylon, "I witnessed a strange and degrading scene. A fine young man, apparently about twenty-five years of age, being prompted by a chimerical imagination, and the false insinuations of the priests, resolved to render propitious the goddess Ammen, and thereby obtain great advantages. With these hopes, he submitted to a most torturing ceremony, as the goddess to be honoured is supposed to be of a sanguinary temper. She is said to have murdered her own child, and to have drunk its blood. To please this demon, he first discoloured his own body with paints and saffron, so as to look terrible; and having partaken plentifully of narcotics, he proceeded to walk round the temple upon slippers studded with nails, which pierced his bare feet; after which he was supported while he stood on one foot on the point of a pole about six feet high, called calloo. After this, an iron hook, at least five inches long, with two prongs, more than an inch in circumference, was thrust through the skin and muscles of his back and a rope, about forty yards in length, was attached to the ring of the hook. This was held by two men, to prevent the wretched man from destroying himself or others; for if he were to get loose, they said he would run into the fire or water, or commit murder, or whatever the spirit of the goddess, by which he was inspired, might prompt him to do; at least so they believed. In this way, the infatuated man was led round the neighbourhood. The applause of the multitude,— the impulse of his own deluded mind,—the stimulating effect of the narcotics,—and the excruciating pain he endured from the hook, made him quite frantic; so that he would frequently, and with inconceivable agility, bound forwards the length of his rope and attempt to escape, but was prevented by the men who held it. His back was thus lacerated by the prongs of the hook, and the blood occasionally flowing from the wound, and mixing with the paints on his body, made him appear, when in his gesticulations, the most demon-like one could possibly imagine. During the ceremony he was an object of the greatest awe, for the people imagine such a one to be possessed of a supernatural influence, and that all whom he blesses are blessed, and whom he curses are cursed: hence they scrupulously avoid offending him, and to obtain his blessings, are very liberal in their offerings to the Brahmins."

Profaning God's Name.

Chap. xxii. ver. 32.—Neither shall ye profane my holy name.

THE late Dr Gifford, as he was one day showing the British Museum to strangers, was very much vexed by the profane conversation of a young gentleman who was present. The Doctor, taking an ancient copy of the Septuagint, and showing it to him,—"O!" said the gentleman, "I can read this." "Well," said the Doctor, "read that passage," pointing to the third commandment. Here the gentleman was so struck, that he immediately desisted from swearing.

Keeping the Sabbath.

Chap. xxiii. ver. 3.—Ye shall do no work therein : it is the Sabbath of the Lord in all your dwellings.

WHEN Mr Crook and his family arrived on the coast of Otaheite, in the brig Active, they were much surprised that not a single native could be seen all along the shore as the vessel sailed ; nor could they perceive any smoke arising from their dwellings. This excited in the minds of Mr Crook and others, a painful suspicion that the island had been subdued, and all the inhabitants cut off in the wars. In the midst of this agitation of mind, one of the sailors, an Otaheitan, who left Port-Jackson in the Active, observed that the natives were keeping the Sabbath-day : that of late they did no kind of work, nor cooked any victuals, nor went out of their houses except to worship God ; and that the whole of the day was employed in religious worship, or in teaching one another to read. At length the vessel came to anchor in Matavia Bay, and not a native made his appearance till Monday morning, when great numbers repaired to the brig, bringing with them the usual testimonies of hospitality ; thus fully satisfying all on board, that, as before noticed, they had been observing the Sabbath.

Blaspheming the Lord.

Chap. xxiv. ver. 11.—The Israelitish woman's son blasphemed the name of the Lord, and cursed.

ONE evening, as the Rev. William Wilson of Perth was passing along the streets of that town, three soldiers then quartered in it happened to walk behind him, who were indulging in the utterance of most profane and blasphemous language. One of them, on some frivolous account, declared it to be his wish, that God Almighty might damn his soul in hell to all eternity. Mr Wilson immediately turned round, and with a look of dignity and compassion, said, "Poor man, and what if God should say amen, and answer that prayer !" Mr Wilson passed on. The man seemed to stand petrified, and on going home to his quarters, was in such distraction of mind and feeling, that he knew not whither to turn for relief. He was soon afterwards seized with fever, under which he continued to suffer the most awful forebodings of eternal misery. His case was so singular, that many Christians went to visit him, to whom he invariably said he was sure of being beyond the reach of mercy, and that God had sent his angel to tell him so. One of them asked him to describe the appearance of the person who had pronounced this doom on him. He did so, and the visitant at once perceiving that it must have been Mr Wilson, inquired if he would wish again to see him. "Oh," said he, "I would wish above everything to see him, but he will not come near a wretch like me." Mr Wilson was soon brought, and told him of the way of salvation through *Christ crucified*, and encouraged him *to flee for refuge to lay hold upon the hope set before him*. His words being accompanied by Divine power, the poor soldier was enabled to believe in Christ, and thus found peace and comfort to his troubled soul. He soon afterwards recovered, and became a very exemplary Christian ; and, as he felt the army unfavourable to a religious life, Mr W., at his request, used influence, and procured his discharge. He settled in Perth, became a member of the Church, attached himself steadily to Mr Wilson, and was through life a comfort to him, and an ornament to the Christian profession.

Fraternal Love.

Chap. xxv. ver. 35.—And if thy brother be waxen poor, and fallen in decay with thee, then thou shalt relieve him; yea, though he be a stranger, or a sojourner; that he may live with thee.

MR H—, an ingenious artist, being driven out of all employment, and reduced to great distress, had no resource to which to apply except that of an elder brother, who was in good circumstances. To him, therefore, he applied, and begged some little hovel to live in, and some small provision for his support. The brother melted into tears, and said, "You, my dear brother! you live in a hovel! You are a man; you are an honour to the family. I am nothing. You shall take this house and the estate, and I will be your guest, if you please." The brothers lived together without its being distinguishable who was proprietor of the estate, till the death of the elder put the artist in possession of it.

Religion and Courage.

Chap. xxvi. ver. 36.—I will send a faintness into their hearts in the lands of their enemies; and the sound of a shaken leaf shall chase them; and they shall flee, as fleeing from a sword; and they shall fall when none pursueth.

A PASSENGER and a lieutenant were passing the New York Mariners' Church together, when the former observed, "That place will be the ruin of sailors." The lieutenant asked him why. The passenger replied, "By stuffing their heads with religion, and making them unfit for the duties they are called to, especially in fighting the enemy." The lieutenant asked him if he thought that religion made a man less industrious or less brave. The passenger assented to that opinion. The lieutenant, who was about forty-seven years of age, then said, "that he had been the greater part of his life at sea, and had been in many engagements; that he had never seen the religious man shrink from his duty, or be a coward; and that the reason was obvious, for when he goes into an engagement he has but one enemy to engage with, whilst the irreligious man has two: he has to contend with one *within* as well as *without*." The passenger ingenuously acknowledged, that the enemy *within* was certainly the worse of the two, and that the lieutenant had the best of the argument.

Giving the Tithe.

Chap. xxvii. ver. 30.—All the tithe of the land, whether of the seed of the land, or of the fruit of the tree, is the Lord's; it is holy unto the Lord.

JOHN FREDERIC OBERLIN, a minister of the gospel in France, happening to read one day, with more attention than usual, the accounts of the tithes in the Books of Moses, was so struck with some of them, as to resolve from that moment to devote three tithes of all he possessed to the service of God and the poor. The resolution was no sooner made than put into execution, for whatever Oberlin conceived it to be his duty to do, he conscientiously, and without delay, set about it. From that period till the end of his life, even during the most calamitous seasons of the Revolution, he always scrupulously adhered to the plan, and often said that he *abounded in wealth*.

BOOK OF NUMBERS.

True Soldiers.

Chap. i. ver. 3.—All that were able to go forth to war in Israel.

"AT Brussels," says Simpson, in his Visit to Flanders, "and wherever I went in the Netherlands, when the English troops were mentioned, whom they likewise much admired, the natives always returned to the Scotch Highlanders. 'They are good and kind as well as brave. They are the only soldiers who become members of the family, in houses where they are billetted; they even carry about the children, and do the domestic work.' The favourite proverbial form of compliment was, 'Lions in the field, and lambs in the house.' There was a competition among the inhabitants who should have them in their houses; and when they returned wounded, the same house they had left had its doors opened, and the family went out some miles to meet our own Scotchmen. The people had many instances to relate of the generosity of these men; after the battle, many Highlanders, themselves wounded, were seen binding up the wounds of the French, and assisting them with their arm."

Standards.

Chap. ii. ver. 2.—Every man of the children of Israel shall pitch by his standard, with the ensign of their father's house.

PITTS, an eastern traveller, in his account of his return from Mecca, describes those lights by which they travel during the night in the desert, and which are carried on the tops of poles to direct their march. "They are somewhat like iron stoves," says he, "into which they put that dry wood, with which some of the camels are loaded. It is carried in great sacks, which have a hole near the bottom, where the servants take it out as they see the fires need a recruit. Every cotter (or company) has one of these poles belonging to it, some of which have ten, some twelve of these lights on their tops, or more or less; and they are likewise of different figures, as well as numbers; one, perhaps, oval, like a gate, another triangular, or like N, or M, &c. so that every one knows by them his respective cotter. They are carried in the front, and set up at some distance from one another, in the place where the caravan is to pitch, before that comes up. They are also carried by day, not lighted; but yet, by the figure and number of them, the pilgrims are directed to what cotter they belong, as soldiers are, by their colours, where to rendezvous; and without such directions it would be impossible to avoid confusion in such a vast number of people."

On Duty.

Chap. iii. ver. 10.—Aaron and his sons—shall wait on their priest's office.

"IT is most honourable," says Dr. Willet, "for a soldier to die fighting, and for a bishop or pastor to die praying; and, if my merciful God shall vouchsafe to grant me my request, my earnest desire is, that, in writing and commenting upon some part of the Scripture, I may finish my days." This request was granted him, for he was called hence as he was composing a commentary upon Leviticus.

Work in the Lord's Cause.

Chap. iv. ver. 3.—From thirty years old and upwards, even until fifty years old—to do the work in the tabernacle of the congregation.

WHAT indefatigable servant of Christ, the Rev. George Whitefield, preached, in the course of his ministry, which included thirty-four years, eighteen thousand sermons; which was upwards of five hundred in a year. The day preceding his death, he expressed a great desire to enter into his eternal rest; at the same time saying, "Lord, thou knowest I am not weary *of* thy work, though I am often weary *in* it."

Consecrated Water.

Chap. v. ver. 17.—And the priest shall take holy water in an earthen vessel.

SIMILAR to this ordeal, by the water of jealously, is the practice of some of the Africans, among whom Mr. Park travelled. He says, that, "at Baniferile, one of the slatees (slave merchants) returning to his native town, as soon as he had seated himself on a mat by the threshold of his door, a young woman, his intended bride, brought a little water in a calabash, and kneeling down before him, desired him to wash his hands; when he had done this, the girl with a tear of joy sparkling in her eyes, drank the water; this being considered as the greatest proof she could give him of fidelity and attachment."

Strong Drink.

Chap vi. ver. 3.—He shall separate himself from wine and strong drink.

A HEATHEN king, who had been for years confirmed in the sin of drunkenness, by the evil practices of white men on the Sandwich Islands, had been led to forsake the dreadful habit. He said lately to a missionary, "Suppose you put 4000 dollars in one hand, and a glass of rum in the other, you say, you drink this rum, I give you 4000 dollars, I no drink it; you say you kill me, I no drink it."

Speaking with God.

Chap. vii. ver. 89.—When Moses was gone into the tabernacle of the congregation to speak with Him, then he heard the voice of one speaking unto him from off the mercy-seat.

SOME English soldiers, who were quartered on a settlement in Africa, where the climate was hot and unwholesome, attended no place of worship, nor had any clergyman with them. While they were in this situation, a fatal distemper broke out among them, and carried them off daily. A poor negro, who was witness to the case, and probably to their neglect of prayer and other ordinances, made this observation in reference to their conduct—"The English never speak to God Almighty—God Almighty never speaks to them; so the devil comes to fetch them away."

The Service of the Tabernacle.

Chap. viii. ver. 24.—They shall go in to wait upon the service of the tabernacle of the congregation.

THE residence of the late Rev. David Brown, in Calcutta, was at a considerable distance from the Mission Church, where he preached;

BOOK OF NUMBERS.

but no weather ever deterred him from meeting the people at the stated periods of divine service. And when on any occasion, and even in cases of indisposition, he has been urged to postpone the service, he would not consent; for he has observed, "If the hearers once find a minister to be irregular in his attendance on them, they will quickly take courage to become irregular in attending him; but when my congregation sees that no inconvenience whatever makes me neglect them, they will be ashamed to keep away on any frivolous pretext."

Waiting God's Time.

Chap. ix. ver. 18.—At the commandment of the Lord the children of Israel journeyed, and at the commandment of the Lord they pitched: as long as the cloud abode upon the tabernacle they rested in their tents.

THE REV. OLIVER HEYWOOD, having been settled some time at Coley, near Halifax, began to think of entering into the married state. The following are his remarks on this subject:— "After I had continued here a considerable time, I looked out for a suitable help-meet. I was directed to divers, and then stopped in my progress. Many times I had good hopes that I was near a conjugal relation, but was disappointed by some strange means or other. This was no small trouble to me, but was the means of humbling my heart, and sending me more frequently and earnestly to the throne of grace. I was often afraid of missing my way; and as often begged direction, pleading this promise, that God will teach the humble his way, and the meek he will guide in judgment. I desired not to follow my own fancy, but God's counsel. Such observable providences as I noticed about this time, concerning these things, did mightily prevail upon me to wean me from the world, and set my heart on heaven: yea, I have been convinced thereby of the deceit of strong impressions and persuasions that such things would come to pass.— Come, my soul, let me lead thee in a rational way. Stay awhile, and wait God's time, for he is waiting to be gracious to thee, when thou art prepared for the mercy. He will meet thee in his own time and way; and when it comes, it will be the surest and most seasonable blessing that ever thou hadst in thy life. In the meantime, if God cause thee to live more to him, and to have more communion with him, it will be equivalent to the blessing itself." Mr Heywood was at length married on 12th April 1655, to Miss Angier, daughter of a minister in Yorkshire, a lady distinguished for her piety and prudence, her amiable disposition, and personal accomplishments

Journeying Together

Chap. x. ver. 29.—We are journeying unto the place of which the Lord said, I will give it you: come thou with us and we will do thee good; for the Lord hath spoken good concerning Israel.

AFTER Mr Philip Henry, who came to Worthenbury a stranger, had been in the country for some time, his attachment to Miss Matthews, afterwards his wife, became manifest; and it was mutual. Among the other objections urged by her friends against the connection was this—that although Mr Henry was a gentleman, and a scholar and an excellent preacher, he was quite a stranger, and they did not even know where he came from. "True," replied Miss Matthews, "but I know where he is going, and I should like to go with him."

Envy Not.

Chap. xi. ver. 29.—And Moses said unto him, Enviest thou for my sake? Would God that all the Lord's people were prophets, and that the Lord would put his Spirit upon them!

MR. VENN, when removed to the obscurity of Yelling, never appeared to gain acceptance with the rude rustics amongst whom he sojourned; and at length, being incapable of much service, he was assisted by a curate from Wales, who attracted the people surprisingly. "Honest Evans," said he "carries all before him." His family were a little jealous of this unexpected preference; but he rebuked them: "Carry me to hear him," said he, "God honours him, and I will honour him. Have you ever studied the text, brother—'He must increase, but I must decrease?' 'A man can receive nothing except it be given him from heaven.'"

Evil Speaking

Chap. xii. ver. 8.—Wherefore then were ye not afraid to speak against my servant Moses?

THE late Dr Waugh of London, being once present in a company consisting of nearly forty gentlemen, when a young man, who was then a student for the ministry, was entertaining those around him with ungenerous strictures upon a popular preacher in the city, he looked at him for a time with a strong mixture of pity and grief in his countenance. When he had by this manner arrested the attention of the speaker, he mildly but pointedly remarked—"My friend, there is a saying in a good old book, which I would recommend to your reflection: 'The Spirit that dwelleth within us lusteth to envy.'"

The Valley of Eshcol.

Chap. xiii. ver. 23.—And they came unto the brook of Eshcol, and cut down from thence a branch with one cluster of grapes, and they bare it between two upon a staff.

DOUBDAN relates, that, travelling in the country about Bethlehem, he found a most delightful valley, full not only of aromatic herbs and rose-bushes, but planted with vines, which, he supposed, were of the choicest kind; and that it was indeed the valley of Eshcol, whence the spies carried the prodigious branch of grapes to Moses. "It is true," says the writer, "I have seen no such bunches of grapes, not having been here in the time of vintage; but the monks assured me that they still find here some that weigh ten or twelve pounds. As to the wine, I have tasted of it many times, and have always found it the most agreeable of that made in the Holy Land. It is a white wine, which has, however, something of a reddish cast, is somewhat of the muscadel kind, and very delicious to drink, without producing any bad effects."

Murmurings.

Chap. xiv. ver. 27.—I have heard the murmurings of the children of Israel, which they murmur against me.

A PERSON with not very ample means of support was burthened with a large family. A neighbour had just called to tell him of a friend who had got a prize in the lottery, when he was also informed of the birth of his twelfth child. He exclaimed, peevishly, "God sends meat to others, children to me." It so happened that God, at whose government he had so impiously murmured, sent him those riches he longed for. But as he sent him the wished-for wealth, he deprived him of the children he had complained of. He saw them one by one go to the grave before him; and in advanced life, and great affluence, when he endured the stroke of having his last beloved daughter taken from his eyes, he bitterly remembered (it is hoped, with salutary bitterness), his former rebellious murmurings against God.

Sinning Ignorantly.

Chap. xv. ver. 28.—And the priest shall make an atonement for the soul that sinneth ignorantly, when he sinneth by ignorance before the Lord, to make an atonement for him; and it shall be forgiven him.

"DURING part of the time I was in the custom-house employ," says Mr Newton, "I took a certain kind of fee which came into my pocket, which, had I thought it wrong, I would sooner have put my hand into the fire. One day I went into a house, when I saw a book of Mr Wesley's lying on the table, which treated on different kinds of oaths, and showing him how much they were violated. This opened my mind. I mentioned my scruples to the superior, who endeavoured to remove them. He assured me, that the superior, in administering the oath, meant that these prequisites should be taken. This did not satisfy me; I wrote to two clergymen, stating the case, for their council how to act. After hearing their opinions, I took no more fees. My conscience formerly was uninformed, and did not chide me;—nay, on a Saturday evening, when I found I had been successful that week, I thanked the Lord for it."

Dying in Peace.

Chap. xvi. ver. 29.—If these men die the common death of all men, or if they be visited after the visitation of all men, then the Lord hath not sent me.

ABOUT the year 1793, an awful incident occurred at Salem, in the State of New Jersey. There had been a revival of religion, and the pious part of the community had been disturbed with riots and mobs; but, on making application to the civil magistrate, these tumults had been effectually suppressed. The opposers of religion turned their attention to a new method of entertainment; acting in a farcical way at religious meetings, pretending to speak of their experiences, to exhort, &c., in order to amuse one another in a profane theatrical manner. One night, a young actress stood up on one of the benches, pretending to speak of her experience; and, with mock solemnity, cried out, "Glory to God, I have found peace, I am sanctified, I am now fit to die." Scarcely had this unhappy girl uttered these words, before she actually dropped dead upon the floor, and was taken up a lifeless corpse. Struck with this awful visitation, the auditors were instantly seized with inexpressible terror, and every face was covered with consternation and dismay.

The Rod of Aaron.

Chap. xvii. ver. 8.—On the morrow Moses went into the tabernacle of witness; and, behold, the rod of Aaron, for the house of Levi, was budded, and brought forth buds, and bloomed blossoms, and yielded almonds.

THE charitable society for the relief of the widows and children of clergymen, since known by the name of the "Corporation for the Sons of the Clergy," was first commenced in the year 1655. The first sermon was preached at St Paul's, on the 5th of November that year, by the Rev. George Hall, afterwards Bishop of Chester, from the following text:—"The rod of Aaron budded, and bloomed blossoms, and yielded almonds." The preacher enforced the necessity and usefulness of a settled ministry; but his sermon breathed great moderation, considering the rancorous feuds then existing in the Church. These he noticed, "Let these ill-invented terms," said he, "whereby we have been distinguished from each other, be swallowed up in that name which will lead us hand in hand to heaven—the name of Christians. If my stomach, or any of yours, rise against the name of brotherly communion, which may consist with our several principles retained, not differing in substantials, God take down that stomach, and make us see how much we are concerned to keep the unity of the Spirit in the bond of peace. Why should some, in the height of their zeal for the liturgy, suppose there can be no service of God but where that is used? Why should others, again, think their piety concerned and trespassed upon, if I prefer, and think fit to use, a set form? There must be abatements and allowances of each other, a coming down of our punctilios, or we shall never give a good account to God."

Holy Duties.

Chap. xviii. ver. 1.—And the Lord said unto Aaron, thou, and thy sons, and thy father's house with thee, shall bear the iniquity of the sanctuary: and thou and thy sons with thee shall bear the iniquity of your priesthood.

IT was the constant endeavour of the Rev. S. Kilpin to go from the closet to the pulpit. His expression was, "I need to have my heart warmed by the Sun of Righteousness ere I address the hearts of others." He often remarked, "I have preached with self-application to-day, and have been humbled in the dust, or have derived divine light from the subject presented to view, if no one else is benefited." Frequently he exclaimed, after four or five public services on the Sabbath-day, "Never does the blood of Christ appear so valuable as at the close of such a Sabbath. In this fountain I bathe. Lord, pardon the sins of my holy duties."

The Unpurified Man.

Chap. xix. ver. 20.—The man that shall be unclean, and shall not purify himself, that soul shall be cut off from among the congregation, because he hath defiled the sanctuary of the Lord.

A PERSON on a journey, not much acquainted with true religion, after being for some time pensive, exclaimed to his companion, "I never shall forget an expression my friend made on his dying bed some years ago. On being asked what it was, it was said to be this :— 'You must die, as I soon shall; but if your heart be not changed, you cannot enter the kingdom of heaven; and if that be the case, I think we shall never meet again.'"

Trials Known and Unknown.

Chap. xx. ver. 5.—Wherefore have ye made us to come up out of Egypt, to bring us in unto this evil place? It is no place of seed, or of figs, or of vines, or of pomegranates; neither is there any water to drink.

MR CECIL, riding one day with a friend in a very windy day, the dust being very troublesome, his companion wished that they could ride in the fields, where they would be free from dust; and this wish he repeated more than once while on the road. At length they reached the fields, when the flies so teased his friend's horse, that he could scarcely keep his seat on the saddle. On his bitterly complaining, "Ah! Sir," said Mr Cecil, "when you were in the road, the dust was your only trouble, and all your anxiety was to get into the fields; you forgot that the fly was there. Now this is a true picture of human life, and you will find it so in all the changes you make in future. We know the trials of our present situation, but the next will have trials, and perhaps worse, though they may be of a different kind."

Serenity under Discouragement.

Chap. xxi. ver. 4.—The soul of the people was much discouraged because of the way.

A STAGE coach was, a short time since, passing through the interior of Massachusetts, on the way to Boston. It was a warm, summer day, and the coach was filled with passengers, all impatient to arrive at the city at an early hour in the evening. The excessive heat rendered it necessary for the driver to spare his horses more than usual. Most of the passengers were fretting and complaining that he did not urge his horses along faster. But one gentleman sat in the corner of the stage calm and quiet. The irritation, which was destroying the happiness of all the others, seemed not to disturb his feelings in the least. At last the coach broke down as they were ascending a long steep hill, and the passengers were compelled to alight, and travel some distance on foot under the rays of the burning sun. This new interruption caused a general burst of vexatious feelings. All the party, with the exception of the gentleman alluded to, toiled up the hill, irritated and complaining. He walked along, good humoured and happy, and endeavouring by occasional pleasantry of remark to restore good humour to the party. It was known that this gentleman, who was extensively engaged in mercantile concerns, had business which rendered it necessary that he should be in the city at an early hour. The delay was consequently to him a serious inconvenience. Yet, while all the rest of the party were ill-humoured and vexed, he alone was untroubled. At last one asked how it was that he retained his composure under such vexatious circumstances? The gentleman replied, that he could have no control over the circumstances in which he was then placed; that he had commended himself and his business to the protection of the Lord, and that if it were the Lord's will that he should not enter Boston at as early an hour as he desired, it was his duty patiently and pleasantly to submit. With these feelings he was patient and submissive, and cheerful. The day, which to the rest of the party was rendered disagreeable by vexation and complaint, was by him passed in gratitude and enjoyment. And when, late in the evening, he arrived in the city with a serene mind, he was prepared to engage in his duties.

The Word of the Lord.

Chap. xxii. ver. 18.—Balaam said, If Balak would give me his house full of silver and gold, I cannot go beyond the word of the Lord my God, to do less or more.

"FOUR individuals," says a clergyman in Ireland, "have, within a few months, come over to us, having publicly renounced the errors of the Church of Rome. One of these persons, an individual of some little importance amongst them, has been most bitterly persecuted; but, though offered £50 by a near relation, through the medium of her former priest, she refused the bribe, saying, 'Take back the price of sin: Judas betrayed his Master for thirty pieces of silver; I will not deny Christ for fifty pieces of gold.'"

The Death of the Righteous.

Chap. xxiii. ver. 10.—Let me die the death of the righteous, and let my last end be like his.

MR AILMER, rector of Much Hadham, Herts, died in 1625, closing his own eyelids, and with these words in his mouth:—"Let my people know that their pastor died undaunted, and not afraid of death! I bless my God I have no fear, no doubt, no reluctance, but a sure confidence in the sin-overcoming merits of Jesus Christ."

The Star of Jacob.

Chap. xxiv. ver. 17.—There shall come a star out of Jacob.

MR RENWICK, the last of the Scottish martyrs, speaking of his sufferings for conscience' sake, says, "Enemies think themselves satisfied that we are put to wander in mosses, and upon mountains; but even amidst the storms of these last two nights, I cannot express what sweet times I have had, when I had no covering but the dark curtains of night. Yea, in the silent watch, my mind was led out to admire the deep and inexpressible ocean of joy, wherein the whole family of heaven swim. Each *star* led me to wonder what He must be, who is the Star of Jacob, of whom all stars borrow their shining."

Zeal for God.

Chap. xxv. ver. 13.—Phinehas was zealous for his God.

MR ANDREW MELVILLE, professor of divinity at St Andrews, in the reign of James VI., was a very bold and zealous man for the cause of God and truth. When some of his more moderate brethren blamed him for being too hot and fiery, he was wont to reply, "If you see my fire go downwards, set your foot upon it and put it out; but if it go upward, let it return to its own place."

If the Lord Wills.

Chap. xxvi. ver. 9.—They strove against the Lord.

A MINISTER praying for a child apparently dying, said, "If it be thy will, spare——" The wretched and distracted mother, interrupting him, cried, "It *must* be his will; I will have no *ifs*." The child, to the surprise of many, recovered, but lived to break his mother's heart, and was publicly executed at the age of twenty-two.

Guiding the Congregation.

Chap. xxvii. ver. 16, 17.—Let the Lord, the God of the spirits of all flesh, set a man over the congregation—that the congregation of the Lord be not as sheep which have no shepherd.

THE following reflections, occasioned by the death of two ministers residing in the same neighbourhood, who died within two days of each other, have been extracted from an excellent little volume, entitled, "Sacred Aphorisms," by Mr Thomas Pauling—" Two famous lights in one week, are put, not under a bushel, but under a gravestone. God is now calling in his labourers, then who shall gather in his harvest? He is putting out the lights, and who shall guide them to Immanuel's land! God's gardens take a great deal of dressing; and when dressers are taken away, what danger are vineyards in of becoming like the field of the slothful? The loss of a guide in the way to heaven is not a small loss. God pulls out stakes in Zion's hedge, but few are put in to make up the gap. But while we obey the precept, 'Pray ye therefore the Lord of the harvest, that he will send forth labourers into his harvest,' Lord, fulfil thy promise, 'I will give you pastors according to my heart, which shall feed you with knowledge and understanding.'"

The Holy Day.

Chap. xxviii. ver. 25.—On the seventh day ye shall have an holy convocation; ye shall do no servile work.

A PROFESSIONAL gentleman in Berkshire, whom God has made the instrument of very considerable good in the country, was first led seriously to embrace the gospel, from a person's refusing to transact some urgent business with him on the Lord's day.

Violating the Sabbath.

Chap. xxix. ver. 35.—Ye shall do no servile work therein.

WHEN his Majesty George III. was repairing his palace at Kew one of the workmen, who was a pious character, was particularly noticed by the King, and he often held conversations with him of some length upon serious subjects. On Monday morning, his Majesty went as usual to watch the progress of the work, and not seeing this man in his customary place, inquired the reason of his absence. The King was informed that, not having been able to complete a particular job on the Saturday night, they had returned to finish it on the following morning. This man alone had refused to comply, because he considered it a violation of the Christian Sabbath; and, in consequence of what was called his obstinacy, he had been dismissed from his employment. "Call him back immediately," exclaimed the good King; "the man who refused doing his ordinary work on the Lord's day, is the man for me. Let him be sent for." The man was accordingly replaced, and the king ever after showed him particular favour.

The Vow to God.

Chap. xxx. ver. 2.—If a man vow a vow unto the Lord, or swear an oath to bind his soul with a bond; he shall not break his word, he shall do according to all that proceedeth out of his mouth.

THE stage was crowded with passengers as it passed from New York to Boston. It was late in the evening when one of the passengers, a sea captain, endeavoured to excite the attention of the drowsy company, by giving a relation of his own circumstances. He had been at sea in a fine ship; in a dreadful storm his ship had been wrecked, his money and property all destroyed, and every soul on board had been lost, except himself, who had saved his life by being on a plank, at the mercy of the waves, for several days together. The company were interested in this narrative; they pitied the poor unfortunate captain, who was returning home to his family entirely destitute; but they wondered that a man relating such a tale, and telling of an escape almost miraculous, should confirm almost every sentence with an oath. Nothing, however, was said to him. In the morning, when the stage stopped, Mr Bathgate, one of the passengers, invited the captain to walk on before with him, designing to step into the stage when it should come up. The proposal was agreed to, and they walked on alone. Mr B. said, "Did I understand you last night—the stage made much noise—did you say that you had lost your ship?" "Yes." "That you saved your life on a plank?" "Yes." "Let me ask you one more question;—when on that plank, did you not vow to your God, that if he would spare your life, *you would devote that life to his service?*" "None of your business," said the captain angrily. The stage by this time came up, and they entered it. Towards evening, as the stage was entering Providence, the captain informed the company that he should not sup with them, as he was so unfortunate as not to have any money. Mr B. took from his pocket, and offered him a handsome bill. "No," said the captain, "I am poor, yet I am no beggar." "But," replied Mr B., "I do not give it to you as to a beggar, but as to an unfortunate brother. You must learn that I profess to be a *Christian*, and I am taught by my religion to do good unto all men. The gospel prescribes no limits to benevolence; it teaches us to do good to all." The company applauded, and pressed the captain to take the money. He silently put it into his pocket, without even thanking the donor; though his countenance betrayed uneasiness. The company supped together, and the captain bid each adieu, after having asked Mr B. when he left town. He was informed, on the morrow at sunrise. They then parted. The captain went home with a heavy heart, while Mr B. retired to rest. He was surprised, the next morning at day-light, to hear some one rap at the door. He opened it, and beheld the captain standing before him in tears. The captain pressing his hand, said, "Sir, I have not slept a wink since I saw you; I abused you yesterday; I am now come to ask your pardon. I *did*, while on that plank, vow to God, that I would live differently from what I ever had done; and, by God's help, from this time forward, I am determined to do so." The captain could not proceed; they pressed each other's hands, and parted, probably to meet no more in this world.

An Oblation for the Lord.

Chap. xxxi. ver. 50.—We have brought an oblation for the Lord, what every man hath gotten, of jewels, of gold, chains, and bracelets, rings, ear-rings, and tablets.

A MINISTER, preaching for a Missionary Society, remarked, in the course of the sermon, that "if the ladies who came out of Egypt could give their golden trinkets to Aaron, to make a calf for the support of idolatry, surely Christian ladies would not deem it a great sacrifice to give up some of their trinkets, for the noble and benevolent cause of diffusing among the heathen the unsearchable riches of Christ." The next morning a box was sent, by an unknown lady, containing an amber necklace, a pair of gold ear-rings, and a diamond ring, as a present to the Missionary Society.

Sin Cannot be Hidden.

Chap. xxxii. ver. 23.—Be sure your sin will find you out.

"I WAS once applied to," says the late Mr English of Wooburn, in his diary, "by a stranger, in a place where I was labouring for a few Sabbaths only, for a sight of a letter which I had received calumniating his character. I looked at the man and pitied him, and coolly replied, 'It would be a breach of the common principles of society to show confidential letters written to us for the purpose of our doing people good.' He retorted in an angry tone, 'I demand a sight of it, Sir, as an act of justice due to an injured man.' I replied, 'How did you know that I had received a letter concerning you?'

'Know,' said he, 'it was impossible not to know it, your language and manner were so pointed, that it was impossible I should be deceived!' I rejoined. 'Do not be too positive : you have been deceived before now, I suppose ; you may be so again.' 'It is not possible,' said he, 'you described the sin of which I am accused in the clearest language, and looking me in the face, and pointing towards me, you said, sinner, be sure your sin will find you out : I therefore expect from you, Sir, as a gentleman and a Christian minister, that you will give me a sight of the letter, that I may know its contents and repel its charge.' I observed, 'I do not know your name ; to my knowledge I never saw you before ; and as you have not told me in what part of the sermon it was I was so pointed, if I show you any letter I may show you the wrong one ; I shall, therefore, certainly not exhibit any of my letters to you, nor satisfy you whether I have received any one about you, till you describe the case alluded to.' He hesitated, but afterwards described the sin of which he was accused. When he had finished, looking him full in his eyes, assuming a solemn attitude, and using a grave and serious tone of voice, I said,—' Can you look me full in the face, as you must your Judge at the great day of God, and declare that you are innocent of this sin laid to your charge ?' He trembled, turned pale, and his voice faltered ; guilt and anger struggling in his breast, like the fire in the bowels of Mount Etna, and, summoning up his remaining courage, he said,—'I am not bound to make any man my confessor ; and, if I were guilty, no man has a right to hold me up to public observation, as you have done.' I assumed a benignity of countenance, and softened my tone, saying,—' Do you believe the passage I cited—*Be sure your sin will find you out*—is the word of God?' He said,—'It may be.' 'Surely it is,' said I; 'he that made the ear, shall he not hear ? he that made the eye, shall he not see ? Can he have any difficulty in bringing your sin to light ?—Now I will tell you honestly, I never received any letter or information about you whatever, but I am persuaded your sin has found you out; the preaching of the word is one method by which God makes men's sins find them out. Let me entreat you seriously to consider your state and character ; who can tell, God may have intended this sermon for your good ; he may mean to have mercy on you ; this may be the means of saving your neck from the gallows, and your soul from hell ; but let me remind you, you are not there yet, there still is hope.' He held down his head, clenched his hands one into the other, and bursting into tears, said,—' I never met with anything like this—I am certainly obliged to you for your friendship—I am guilty ; and hope this conversation will be of essential advantage to me !'"

Journeyings in the East.

Chap. xxxiii. ver. 1.—These are the journeys of the children of Israel.

PITTS, an eastern traveller, in describing his return from Mecca, says,—"The first day we set out from Mecca it was without any order at all ; but the next day every one laboured to get forward ; and in order to it, there was many times much quarrelling and fighting. But after every one had taken his place in the caravan, they orderly and peaceably kept the same place till they came to Grand Cairo. They travel four camels abreast, which are all tied one after the other, like as in teams. The whole body is called a caravan, which is divided into several cotters, or companies, each of which has its name, and consists, it may be, of several thousand camels ; and they

move, one cotter after another, like distinct troops. In the head of
each cotter is some great gentleman, or officer, who is carried in a
thing like a horse-litter. In the head of every cotter there goes
likewise a sumpter camel, which carries his treasure. This camel
has two bells, about the bigness of our market bells, hanging one on
each side, the sound of which may be heard a great way off. Some
others of the camels have round bells about their necks, some about
their legs, like those which our carriers put about their fore-horses'
necks; which, together with the servants, (who belong to the camels,
and travel on foot,) singing all night, make a pleasant noise; and
the journey passes away delightfully. They say the music makes
the camels brisk and lively. Thus they travel in good order every
day, till they come to Grand Cairo; and were it not for this order,
you may guess what confusion would be among such a vast multitude.
They have lights by night (which is the chief time for travelling,
because of the exceeding heat of the sun by day,) which are carried
on the tops of high poles to direct the hagies, or pilgrims, in their
march."

The Salt Sea.

Chap. xxxiv. ver. 12.—The goings out of it shall be at the salt sea.

A LATE traveller, to whose unpublished journal Dr Russell repeatedly refers in his Description of Palestine, remarks that the
Lake of Sodom, when he visited it, was sunk or hollow, and that the
banks had been recently under water, being still very miry and
difficult to pass. The shores were covered with dry wood, some of it
good timber, which they say is brought by the Jordon from the
country of the Druses. "The water is pungently salt, like oxymuriate
of soda. It is incredibly buoyant. Geddes bathed in it, and when
he lay still on his back or face, he floated with one-fourth at least of
his whole body above the water. He described the sensation as extraordinary, and more like lying on a feather-bed than floating
on water. On the other hand, he found the greatest resistance
in attempting to move through it; it smarted his eyes excessively. I put a piece of stick in, it required a good deal of pressure
to make it sink, and when let go, it bounded out again like
a blown bladder. The water is clear and of a yellowish tinge, which
might be from the colour of the stones at bottom, or from the hazy
atmosphere. There were green shrubs down to the water's edge in
one place, and nothing to give an idea of anything blasting in the
neighbourhood of the sea; the desert character of the soil extending
far beyond the possibility of being affected by its influence."

The Price of Blood.

Chap. xxxv. ver. 31.—Moreover, ye shall take no satisfaction for
the life of a murderer, which is guilty of death, but he shall be surely
put to death.

IN a letter from Lord Seaforth, Governor of Barbadoes, to Lord
Hobart, dated March 18, 1802, his Lordship says, "You will
observe in the last day's proceedings of the Assembly, that the majesty
of the House had taken considerable offence at a message of mine, recommending an act to be passed to make the murder of a slave felony.
At present, the fine for the crime is only £15. A committee of the
whole house was hereupon appointed to prepare an answer to the
Governor's message, which should be 'moderate and respectful, but
calculated to repel insult, evinces that the house understands its

interests, and asserts its rights.' 'Whoso sheddeth man's blood, by man shall his blood be shed,' saith the law of God, in Gen. ix. 6.— 'Whoso sheddeth the blood of a negro,' saith the law of Barbadoes, 'shall pay £15; —and the *humane* legislators resent the proposal of rendering murder felony : they understand their *interest* and their rights too well to conform to the law of God !"

Suitable Marriage.

Chap. xxxvi. ver. 6.—Let them marry to whom they think best; only to the family of the tribe of their fathers shall they marry.

MR PHILIP HENRY used to give two advices, both to his children and others, in reference to marriages. One was, "Keep within the bounds of profession." The other was, "Look at suitableness in age, quality, education, temper," &c. He used to observe, from Gen. ii. 18, "I will make him a help-meet for him;" that where there is not meetness, there will not be much help. He commonly said to his children, with reference to their choice in marriage, "Please God, and please yourselves, and you shall never displease me;" and greatly blamed those parents who conclude matches for their children without their consent. He sometimes mentioned the saying of a pious gentlewoman, who had many daughters—"The care of most people is how to get good husbands for their daughters; but my care is to fit my daughters to be good wives, and then let God provide for them."

BOOK OF DEUTERONOMY.

Conscientious Judgment.

Chap. i. ver. 17.—Ye shall not repect persons in judgment—ye shall not be afraid of the face of man, for the judgment is God's.

DURING Colonel Gardiner's residence at Bankton, the Commander of the King's forces, with several colonels and gentlemen of rank, one day dined with him. When the company assembled, he addressed them with a great deal of respect, and yet with a very frank and determined air, and told them that he had the honour in that district to be a Justice of the Peace, and, consequently, that he was sworn to put the laws in execution, and, among the rest, those against swearing; that he could not execute upon others with any confidence, or approve himself as a man of impartiality and integrity to his own heart, if he suffered them to be broken in his presence by persons of any rank whatever; and that, therefore, he entreated all the gentlemen who then honoured him with their company, that they would please be on their guard; and that if any oath or curse should escape them, he hoped they would consider his legal animadversion upon it as a regard to the duties of his office, and dictates of his conscience, and not as any want of deference to them. The commanding officer immediately supported him in this declaration, as entirely becoming the station in which he was, assuring him he would be ready to pay the penalty if he inadvertently transgressed; and when Colonel Gardiner on any occasion stepped out of the room, he himself undertook to be the guardian of the law in his absence; and, as one of the inferior officers offended during this time, he informed the Colonel, so that the fine was exacted and given to the poor, with the approbation of the company.

Trusting God's Promise.

Chap. ii. ver. 7.—These forty years the Lord thy God hath been with thee; thou hast lacked nothing.

A PIOUS minister in England relates, in a letter to a friend, that, being at one time in great want of money, and knowing not to whom he should apply for aid, he betook himself to prayer, committing his case to the Lord, and seeking direction from him. In a day or two after, a servant called, telling him, that a gentleman wished him to dine with him at Norfolk. The gentleman had come from Bath, after his marriage, to see the minister, as he had been formerly acquainted with him. He presented the minister with ten pounds, as a marriage present, which relieved him from his embarrassments, filled him with gratitude to God for so seasonable a supply of his wants.

The River Jordan.

Chap. iii. ver. 17.—Jordan, and the coast thereof, from Chinnereth even unto the sea of the plain, even unto the salt sea.

MR. CHATEAUBRIAND, describing the present state of the valley through which flows the Jordan, says, "Here and there stunted shrubs with difficulty vegetate upon this inanimate tract; their leaves are covered with salt, which has nourished them, and their bark has a smoky smell and taste. Instead of villages you perceive the ruins of a few towers. Through the middle of this valley flows a discoloured river, which reluctantly creeps towards the pestilential lake by which it is engulphed. Its course amidst the sands can be distinguished only by the willows and the reeds that border it; and the Arab lies in ambush among these reeds to attack the traveller, and to plunder the pilgrim.—Such is the scene famous for the benedictions and curses of Heaven. This river is the Jordan; this lake is the Dead Sea; it appears brilliant, but the guilty cities entombed in its bosom seem to have poisoned its waters. Its solitary abysses cannot afford nourishment to any living creature; never did vessel cut its waves; its shores are without birds, without trees, without verdure; and its waters excessively bitter, and so heavy, that the most impetuous winds can scarcely ruffle their surface."

Keeping God's Statutes.

Chap. iv. ver. 6.—Keep therefore, and do them; for this is your wisdom and your understanding in the sight of the nations, which shall hear all these statutes, and say, Surely this great nation is a wise and understanding people.

"ABOUT twenty years ago," says one, "passing the house where Thomas Paine boarded, the low window was open, and seeing him sitting close by, I stepped in. Seven or eight of his friends were present, whose doubts and his own he was labouring to remove, by a long talk about the story of Joshua commanding the sun and moon to stand still; and concluded by denouncing the Bible as the worst of books, and that it had occasioned more mischief and bloodshed than any book ever printed, and was believed only by fools and knaves. Here he paused; and while he was replenishing his tumbler with his favourite brandy and water, a person asked Mr. Paine if he ever was in Scotland? The answer was, 'Yes.' 'So have I,' continued the speaker; 'and the Scotch are the greatest bigots about the Bible I ever met;—it is their school-book, their houses and churches are furnished with Bibles, and if they travel but a few miles from home their Bible is always their companion ; yet, in no other country where I have travelled, have I seen the people so comfortable and happy. Their poor are not in such abject poverty as I have seen in other countries. By their bigoted custom of going to church on Sundays, they save the wages which they earn through the week, which, in other countries that I have visited, are generally spent by mechanics, and other young men, in taverns and frolics, on Sundays ; and of all the foreigners who land on our shores, none are so much sought after for servants, and to fill places where trust is reposed, as the Scotch. You rarely find them in taverns, the watch-house, alms-house, bride-well, or prison. Now, if the Bible is so bad a book, those who use it most would be the worst of people ; but the reverse is the case.' This was a sort of argument Paine was not prepared to answer, and an historical fact which could not be denied ;—so, without saying a word, he lifted a candle from the table and walked upstairs. His disciples slipped out one by one, and left the speaker and myself to enjoy the scene."

Paternal Respect.

Chap. v. ver. 16—Honour thy father and thy mother, as the Lord thy God hath commanded thee.

A BOY about ten years of age having lost his father, and his mother being ill at an hospital, was sent to the work-house at Shrewsbury. He was set to work, that he might earn, as soon as possible, his own livelihood. He behaved well, and was diligent at his work. Very soon he had a little money given to him as a reward ; and he was told that he might do with it what he pleased. As soon as he had received it, he asked leave of his master to go and see his mother. He took the money with him, and gave it to her. It was not much, but it was all that he had to give ; and the disposition with which it was given was more comforting to his mother than the value of the gift.

Teaching the Children.

Chap. vi. ver. 7.—Thou shalt teach them diligently unto thy children, and shalt talk of them when thou sittest in thine house, and when thou walkest by the way, and when thou liest down, and when thou risest up.

OF the late excellent Mrs. Berry of Warminster, it is said, that her Sabbath evenings were employed in reading the Scriptures, and holding familiar dialogues with her three children. After hearing them repeat a short prayer, and one of Watts' little hymns for children, she seated them each on a separate chair, while with maternal simplicity and endearments, she heard and answered *their* questions, and proposed *her own*. Dismissing the two youngest to rest, the eldest (being now six years old) was retained up a little longer. With him it was her constant Sabbath-evening custom to kneel and pray. At these periods she forgot herself in endeavouring to interest her boy. She would begin with prayer for his father, who, at that moment, was preaching to his people ; then she would pray for her children one by one. After mentioning their names, she either implored forgiveness for them, or expressed her gratitude that "the Great God had made them such good children." Taking this boy one day into the parlour where she usually performed these exercises, his father asked him, if his dear mother did not sometimes kneel with him and pray? With eyes instantly filled with tears, the little disciple artlessly replied, "Yes, father, mother used to kneel at that *chair*, and hold my hand, and pray for father that he might do good, and for me, and Henry, and for little Mary, and for all of us."

Increasing little by little.

Chap. vii. ver. 22.—The Lord thy God shall put out those nations before thee by little and little: thou mayest not consume them at once, lest the beasts of the field increase upon thee.

IT is here supposed, that if Judea should be thinly peopled, the wild beasts would so multiply there as to render it dangerous to the inhabitants. Haynes, when describing his arrival at Cana of Galilee, says, "The approaching Cana, at the close of the day, as we did, is at once terrifying and dangerous. The surrounding country swarms with wild beasts, such as tigers, leopards, jackals, &c., whose cries and howling, I doubt not, as it did me, would strike the boldest traveller, who had not been frequently in a like situation, with the deepest sense of horror." The same traveller, giving an account of his visit to Mount Tabor, on the top of which he found many ruins, remarks, "I amused myself a considerable time in walking about the area, and creeping into several holes and subterraneous caverns among the ruins. My guide perceiving me thus employed, told me I must be more cautious how I ventured into those places, for that he could assure me those holes and caverns were frequently resorted to by tigers in the day-time, to shelter them from the sun; and therefore I might pay dear for gratifying my curiosity."

A Plague of Scorpions.

Chap. viii. ver. 15.—Wherein were fiery serpents and scorpions.

AN Emperor of Persia, who designed to go on a journey into Media, durst not proceed on account of the vast quantity of scorpions that were lying about the road. He sent a great number of stout fellows to destroy those terrible creatures, promising a superior reward to him who killed most. Till this execution was over, he durst not venture his dignified person abroad.

Heathen Images.

Chap. ix. ver. 12.—They have made them a molten image.

A BOY who came to school in India, and was instructed in the doctrines and precepts in religion, was one day ordered by his parents to worship an image they had lately bought. The boy knew, however, that it was sinful, and refused to do so. He patiently endured a great deal of ill treatment; but his parents, seeing, at length, that he was dutiful in all other respects, did not any longer require him to worship their image.

Kindness to Strangers.

Chap. x. ver. 19.—Love ye therefore strangers; for ye were strangers in the land of Egypt.

HAYNES informs us, that having arrived at Nazareth, the end of December, about five in the evening, upon entering the town, he and his party saw two women filling their pitchers with water at a fountain he had described, and about twelve others waiting for the same purpose, whom they desired to pour some into a trough which stood by, that their horses might drink. They had no sooner made the request than the women complied, and filled the trough, and the others waited with the greatest patience. Upon the travellers returning their thanks, one of the women, with great modesty, replied,

"We consider kindness and hospitality to strangers as an essential part of our duty."

Instruction in the Scriptures.

Chap. xi. ver. 19.—Ye shall teach them your children, speaking of them when thou sittest in thine house.

IN Iceland, a custom prevails among the people, of spending their long evenings in a manner which must powerfully tend to promote their religious improvement. The whole family assembles at dusk, and around the lamp, every one except the reader having some kind of work to perform. The reader is frequently interrupted, either by the head, or some of the most intelligent members of the family, who make remarks on various parts of the story, and propose questions with a view to exercise the ingenuity of the children and servants. In this form of exercise the Bible is preferred to every other book. At the conclusion of the labour a prayer is offered, and the exercise is concluded with a psalm. Their morning devotions are conducted in a similar manner at the lamp. What great opportunity for religious instruction of youth!

The Second Commandment.

Chap. xii. ver. 32.—What thing soever I command you, observe to do it; thou shalt not add thereto, nor diminish from it.

AS the second commandment so expressly forbids the use of images in the worship of God, the Roman Catholics omit it in their catechisms and books of devotion, and divide the tenth into two. The Rev. Mr. Temple, one of the American missionaries at Malta, relates the following fact:—"My teacher, a native of Italy, came into my room one morning, and took up a tract then lying on the table, and immediately cast his eyes upon the Ten Commandments, which I had inserted at the end. As soon as he had read the *second* commandment, he confessed much astonishment, and asked whether this was part of the decalogue. I immediately showed him this commandment in Archbishop Martini's Italian translation of the Latin Vulgate. He could not suppress his feelings or surprise on reading this in the Italian Bible, and in a version, too, authorised by the Pope. 'I have lived,' said he, 'fifty years, have been publicly educated in Italy: have had the command of a regiment of men, and fought in many compaigns; but, till this hour, I never knew that such a commandment as this is written in the pages of the Bible.'"

Idol Worship.

Chap. xiii. ver. 17.—There shall cleave nought of the cursed thing to thine hand.

ON one occasion, when the converted natives of Huahine, in the South Sea, and the idolatrous party, were about to engage in battle, two leaders of the Christian party made an offer of peace. They said, "You must soon fall into our hands, or we must soon fall into yours; but, if you will lay down your arms *now*, we will be friends with you." The other party answered. "We will have peace; we will not fight for those false gods any more; we will submit to the true God!" Peace was concluded; a fire was lighted, and the image of Tani, their god, was thrown into the flames, and burnt to ashes before the eyes of both parties. His house was immediately consumed, and his marae, or temple, destroyed. A leader among the converts being congratulated on having been the instrument of accomplishing so great a deliverance of his nation from the thraldom of Satan, he replied, with much emotion, "All my forefathers worshipped Tani: where are they now? It is my mercy to live in better days."

Chewing the Cud.

Chap. xiv. ver. 6.—*Every beast that parteth the hoof, and cheweth the cud, among the beasts, that ye shall eat.*

CHEWING the cud has often been referred to as emblematical of meditation, or the digesting of our spiritual food. Mr. Philip Henry notes in his diary the saying of a pious hearer of his own, as what much affected him:—"I find it easier," said the good man, "to go six miles to hear a sermon, than to spend one quarter of an hour in meditating and praying over it in secret, as I should, when I come home."

Master's Servant.

Chap. xv. ver. 18.—*It shall not seem hard unto thee when thou sendest him away from thee.*

SOME years ago, a respectable gentleman, residing a few miles from New York, actuated by truly Christian feelings, gave a negro and his wife, formerly his slaves, their liberty. This important instrument of writing being prepared and executed in the presence of several ladies and gentlemen, was delivered to the slave; who, after a solemn pause, in broken accents, though in language which conveyed the genuine sentiments of his heart, addressed his benefactors in substance as follows:—"Master and mistress, I thank you for your goodness to me this day. I am a poor African, therefore make allowance for my want of words to express my joy at this great deliverance. As Peter said to the lame man when he healed him, so say I unto you—'Silver and gold have I none, but such as I have I give unto thee.' May the blessing of the Lord be your reward—may he relieve your souls from the bondage of sin and death, as you this day have relieved me from the bonds of slavery—may the blessing of God rest on the heads of your children, and upon your children's children." It was enough:—every heart at the moment felt that keen sensibility which the unexpected address of the free black excited. All was silence—unaffected tears flowed from every eye. The benefit of the same praiseworthy action was experienced by the wife of this happy African. By the piety of his conduct, during a course of years, he has given evidence that he enjoys that liberty wherewith Christ makes his people free.

That which is Just.

Chap. xvi. ver. 20.—*That which is altogether just shalt thou follow.*

MR. ELLIS relates, that two principal chiefs walking by the sea-side came to a place where a fisherman had been sharpening his hooks, but had forgotten his file, which, in the estimation of the natives, is an article of considerable value. As the fisherman had retired from the place, and was totally unknown to the chiefs, they picked up the file, and went on their way. They had not proceeded far before one of them, reflecting on the circumstance, said to the other, "This is not our file; and is not our taking it theft!" "Perhaps it is," replied the other, "yet as the real owner is unknown, I do not know who has a better right to it than ourselves." "I am satisfied," rejoined his companion, "that it is not ours, and therefore think we had better give it away." To this the other consented, and the file was given to the first man they met, accompanied with its little history, and a strict injunction, that inquiry should be made after the proprietor, to whom it should be given if he could be discovered; if not, it was to become his own property.

Worshipping the Sun.

Chap. xvii. ver. 3.—Hath worshipped—either the sun or moon, or any of the host of heaven, which I have not commanded.

THE gospel having spread into Persia, the Pagan priests, who worshipped the sun, persuaded the Emperor Sapor to persecute the Christians in all parts of his empire. Many eminent persons in the Church and State fell martyrs: even thousands were put to death for not worshipping the sun. Usthazares, tutor to the Persian princes, was a Christian. Sapor sent for him, and asked him, "Why he mourned?" He answered, "O King, this grieves me, that I am this day alive, who should rather have died long since, and that I see this sun, which, against my heart and mind, for your pleasure, dissemblingly I appear to worship, but I will never be so mad again, as, instead of the Maker of all things, to worship the things which he hath made." When he was carried away to be beheaded, he desired the King, that for all the faithful services he had done to his father and to him, he would now cause to be proclaimed openly, that Usthazares was beheaded, not for any treachery or crime committed against the King or realm, but only because he was a Christian, and would not, at the King's pleasure, deny his God. This request was granted, and many were established in Christianity at his death, and many had been staggered by his apostacy.

Secret Arts.

Chap. xviii. ver. 10, 11, 12.—There shall not be found among you—a charmer, or a consulter with familiar spirits, or a wizard, or a necromancer. For all that do these things are an abomination unto the Lord.

A WOMAN who lived in the county of Sussex, a few years since, having the ague, and hearing of a man who could charm it away, went to him; he gave her what he called a charm, which was a paper sewed up in a bag, which she was to wear round her neck, and never to open it, for if she did, he told her the complaint would return again. The disease was removed; she continued to wear the bag till the end of four years, when she was stirred up to a concern about her soul, and was taught by the Spirit to see and to feel the exceeding sinfulness of sin. She then, for the first time, began to fear whether this charm was not the work of Satan. For many days she prayed to the Lord to teach her what she ought to do respecting it, and at last she saw it to be her duty to take it off; and opening it, found it thus written on the paper—*Torment her not till she is in hell.* The disease never returned.

Bearing False Witness.

Chap. xix. ver. 16.—If a false witness rise up against any man, to testify against him that which is wrong, &c.

A GENTLEMAN who had suffered much loss in his affairs by the malice of a person who lived in his vicinity, taught a parrot to pronounce, in a clear articulate voice, the Ninth Commandment, "Thou shalt not bear false witness against thy neighbour." He kept the bird hanging in a cage opposite the informer's house, who, whenever he appeared, heard himself saluted with—"Thou shalt not bear false witness against thy neighbour." This exhortation being kept constantly ringing in his ears, became at last so annoying to him, and amusing to everybody else, that, to hide his disgrace, he was forced to remove to a distant part of the town.

Tree Felling.

Chap. xx. ver. 20.—The trees which thou knowest that they be not trees for meat, thou shalt destroy and cut them down.

FORMERLY when the natives of Eimeo felled trees on the mountains, after lopping the branches, they paused, offered a prayer to one of their gods for a safe passage, and then launched the trunk down the side of the slope; standing in silence, holding their breath, and with their eyes following its course till it reached the valley. Once when Mr. Henry, missionary there, was assisting some of his people to procure timber for building the brig Hawes, having descended from the mountain to refresh himself at a brook which ran at the foot of it, he sat down on the bank, and was about to drink, but refrained in the instant, and removed about two yards off, where access to the water seemed more convenient. While drinking there, a tree, which had been felled above, came thundering down with such velocity and force, as scarcely to have been perceived by him before it had plunged with the fore end deep into the earth at the very spot from which he had just risen. He could not regard his escape as otherwise than strikingly providential.

Children of Disobedience.

Chap. xxi. ver. 20.—This our son is stubborn and rebellious, he will not obey our voice.

"I WELL remember," says a writer on Christian education, "being much impressed by a sermon about twenty years ago, when I was a young father, in which the preacher said, were he to select one word as the most important in education, it should be the word *obey*. My experience since has fully convinced me of the justice of the remark. Without filial obedience everything must go wrong. Is not a disobedient child guilty of a manifest breach of the Fifth Commandment? And is not a parent, who suffers this disobedience to continue, an habitual partaker in his child's offence against that commandment? By the disobedience of our first parents, sin came into the world; and through the obedience of the second Adam, are the gates of heaven opened to true believers. The wicked are emphatically styled *the children of disobedience*: and it is clearly the object of the divine plan of salvation to conquer the rebellious spirit of man, and to bring him into a state of humility and submission. Parental authority is one powerful instrument for effecting the change. It is intended to bend the stubborn will, and, by habituating a child to subjection to earthly parents, to prepare him for Christian obedience to his heavenly Father. In proportion as filial obedience is calculated to smooth the way for true religion, filial disobedience must produce the opposite effect. The parent who habitually gives way to it, has appalling reason to apprehend that he is educating his child, not for heaven but for hell.

Brotherly Help.

Chap. xxii. ver. 4.—Thou shalt not see thy brother's ox or ass fall down by the way, and hide thyself from them; thou shalt surely help him to lift them up again.

MR. GEORGE HERBERT, the poet, when walking to Salisbury, saw a poor man, with a poorer horse, fallen under his load. Mr. Herbert perceiving this, put off his canonical coat, and helped the poor man to unload, and after to load his horse. The poor man blessed him for it, and he blessed the poor man, and he gave him money to refresh both himself and his horse; and told him, "If he loved himself, he should be merciful to his beast." At his coming to his musical friends at Salisbury, they began to wonder that Mr. George Herbert, who used to be so clean, came in such a condition; but he told them the occasion; and when one of the company told him, "He had disparaged himself by so dirty an employment," his answer was, "That the thought of what he had done would prove music to him at midnight; and the omission of it would have upbraided and made discord in his conscience, whensoever he should pass by the place."

Care for Strangers.

Chap. xxiii. ver. 24.—When thou comest into thy neighbour's vineyard, then thou mayest eat of grapes thy fill at thine own pleasure.

ABOUT twenty years ago, a land-owner of Patudupee, about fourteen miles from Calcutta, planted an orchard by a public road, placed a person to keep it, and dedicated it to the use of travellers of all descriptions, who are permitted to enter it, and take as much fruit as they can eat.

The Kind-Hearted.

Chap. xxiv. ver. 19.—It shall be for the stranger, for the fatherless, and for the widow; that the Lord thy God may bless thee in all the work of thine hands.

IT is said of Sir Matthew Hale, that he frequently invited his poor neighbours to dinner, and made them sit at table with himself. If any of them were sick, so that they could not come, he sent provisions to them, warm from his own table. He did not confine his bounties to the poor of his own parish, but diffused supplies to the neighbouring parishes, as occasion required. He always treated the old, the needy, and the sick, with the tenderness and familiarity that became one who considered they were of the same nature with himself, and were reduced to no other necessities than such as he himself might be brought to.

The Just Measure.

Chap. xxv. ver. 15.—A perfect and just measure shalt thou have.

A linen merchant in Colerain, offered Dr. Adam Clarke a situation in his warehouse, which he accepted with the consent of his parents. Mr. Baker knew that his clerk and overseer was a religious man, but he was not sensible of the depth of the principle which actuated him. Some differences arose at times about the way of conducting the business, which were settled very amicably. But the time of the great Dublin market approached, and Mr. Baker was busy preparing for it. The master and servant were together in the folding-room, when one of the pieces was found short of the required number of yards. "Come," said Mr. Baker. "it is but a trifle. We shall soon stretch it, and make out the yard. Come, Adam, take one end, and pull against me." Adam had neither ears nor heart to this proposal, and absolutely refused to touch what he thought an unclean thing. The usages of the trade were strongly and variously enforced, but in vain. The young man resolved rather to suffer than to sin. Mr. Baker was therefore obliged to call one of his men less scrupulous, and Adam retired quietly to his desk. Soon after, Mr. Baker, in the kindest manner, stated to him, that it was very clear he was not fit for worldly business, (why not? if any were unfit, it must be the merchant himself,)and wished him to look out for some employment more congenial to his own mind; adding, that he might depend on his friendship in any line of life into which he might enter.

Going to the Lord.

Chap. xxvi. ver. 13.—I have brought away the hallowed things out of mine house, and also have given them unto the Levite.

"SIR," said a poor labouring man to a minister in a letter, "when you preached the missionary sermon last year, I was grieved that I had it not in my power to give what I wished. I thought and thought, and consulted my wife whether there was anything which we could spare without stinting the poor children; but it seemed that we lived as near as possible in every respect, and had nothing but what was absolutely necessary. At last it came into my mind, 'Is that fourpence which goes every week for an ounce of tobacco absolutely necessary?' I had been used to it so long, that I scarcely thought it possible to do without it, however I resolved to try; so, instead of spending the fourpence, I dropped it into a box. The first week I felt it sorely, but the second week it was easier; and in the course of a few weeks it was little or no sacrifice at all; at least I can say, that the pleasure far outweighed the sacrifice. When my children found what I was doing, they wished to contribute also; and if ever they got a penny or halfpenny given them for their own pleasure it was sure to find its way into the box instead of the cake-shop. On opening the box, I have the pleasure to find that our collected pence amounted to one pound, which I now inclose, and pray, that the Lord may give his blessing with it."

Unconfessed Homicide.

Chap. xxvii. ver. 24.—Cursed be he that smiteth his neighbour secretly.

SOME years ago, a man of the name of Cooper died in Gloucestershire. He had long endured great horror of mind; and, about an hour previous to his death, he mentioned the cause of it, which was, that, about forty years before, he had assisted another man, of the name of Horton, (who died two years antecedent to Cooper's death), in murdering one Mr Rice, a surveyor of the roads, whose body they threw into a well, where it was soon after the fact found; but the murderers were not known till now.—How many dreadful secrets will be revealed at the great day, when the Judge of all shall make inquisition for blood.

Bodily Fear Day and Night.

Chap. xxviii. ver. 46.—Thy life shall hang in doubt before thee; and thou shalt fear day and night, and shalt have none assurance of thy life.

A GENTLEMEN, who was for some years British Consul at Tripoli, mentioned some circumstances, which set, in a striking light, the state of fear and degradation in which the Jews there live. If the Bey has a fear or jealously of any man, he sends some one to put a pistol to his head and shoot him. If it happen to be a Christian, remonstrance is made by the consul of his nation. The Bey is quite ready to give satisfaction; he sends some one to shoot the first agent of his cruelty; and then, with an air of great regret, asks the Consul if he is satisfied; if not, he is ready to give him satisfaction still farther. But if the object of his wrath be a Jew, none would think of demanding satisfaction for HIS death. This people feel the curse in full, that among the nations where they are scattered, they should *find no ease, and have none assurance of their life.* They are known by their being campelled to wear a particular dress, which they sometimes change IN THEIR HOUSES, on occasion of their merry-makings; but even in these they are not free, the Moors exercising the privilege of free ingress at any time. When a vessel comes into port, the merchant (a Mahometan) compels every Jew whom he meets by the way, to come and help in unlading, carrying, &c.; nor do they dare to resist.

Worshipping Anything.

Chap. xxix. ver. 17.—Ye have seen their abominations, and their idols, wood and stone.

IN Baitenzorg, a village in the island of Java, there is a street nearly a mile long, inhabited solely by Chinese. Messrs. Tyerman and Bennet, the deputation from the London Missionary Society, called at several of their houses, and found in each an idol of some kind. "That which most surprised us," say they, "was a French engraving of the Emperor Napoleon Bonaparte, in a gilt frame, before which incense was burning; and the old man, to whom the picture belonged, in our presence paid it divine honours, bowing himself in various antic attitudes, and offering a prayer for blessings on himself and family. When we asked him why he worshipped that as a god which came from Europe, and not from his own country, he frankly replied, 'Oh, we worship anything!' In this street are two temples, one a decent building under repair, the other an open shed, on a little mound, consisting of a slight square roof, supported by four pillars. In this sanctuary are several mis-shapen stones, planted on their ends, to which prayers are daily made by beings (in that respect) as stupid as themselves. A cocoa-nut shell was placed in the midst of these blocks, containing some small offerings. We visited two other edifices of similiar construction, and consecrated to gods of the same material as these,—namely, rude upright stones, which, it seems, the rude Malays worship with no less devotion than the shrewd Chinese."

Obedience to God.

Chap. xxx. ver. 8. 9.—Thou shalt return, and obey the voice of the Lord, and do all his commandments: and the Lord thy God will make thee plenteous in every work of thine hand.

THE late Admiral Colpoys, who rose, by industry, to the highest rank and honour in the profession, used to be fond of stating, that on first leaving an humble lodging to join his ship as a midshipman, his landlady presented him with a Bible, and a guinea, saying, —"God bless and prosper you, my lad; as long as you live, never suffer yourself to be laughed out of your money and your prayers." This advice the young sailor sedulously followed through life to his great advantage.

Strong in Faith.

Chap. xxxi. ver. 6.—Be strong, and of good courage, fear **not, nor** be afraid of them; for the Lord thy God, he it is that doth go with thee; he will not fail thee, nor forsake thee.

SOME of the Indian chiefs having become the open enemies of the Gospel, Mr. Elliot, sometimes called the Apostle of the American Indians, when in the wilderness, without the company of any other Englishman, was, at various times, treated in a threatening and barbarous manner by some of those men; yet his Almighty Protector inspired him with such resolution, that he said—"I am about the work of the Great God, and my God is with me; so that I fear neither you, nor all the Sachims (or chiefs) in the country. I will go on, and do you touch me if you dare." They heard him and shrunk away.

Gratitude to the Lord.

Chap. xxxii. ver. 11. Do ye thus requite the Lord, O foolish people and unwise? is not he thy father that hath bought thee? hath he not made thee, and established thee?

A Clergyman in Germany, who had exercised the ministerial office for twelve years, while destitute of faith in, and love to the Redeemer, one day, after baptizing the child of a wealthy citizen, one of the members of his congregation, was invited with some other guests to a collation at this person's house. Directly opposite to him, on the wall, hung a picture of Christ on the cross, with two lines written under it:—

"I did this for thee;
What hast thou done for me?"

The picture caught his attention; as he read the lines they seemed to pierce him, and he was involuntarily seized with a feeling he never experienced before. Tears rushed into his eyes; he said little to the company, and took his leave as soon as he could. On the way home these lines constantly sounded in his ears—divine grace prevented all philosophical doubts and explanations from entering his soul—he could do nothing but give himself up entirely to the overpowering feeling; even during the night, in his dreams, the question stood always before his mind, "What hast thou done for me?" He died in about three months after this remarkable and happy change in his temper and views, triumphing in the Saviour, and expressing his admiration of his redeeming love.

Treasures in the Sand.

Chap. xxxiii. ver. 19.—They shall suck of the abundance of the seas, and of the treasures hid in the sand.

AMONG the hardships experienced by the first settlers in North America, they were sometimes greatly distressed for food, which led the women and the children to the sea side to look for a ship which they expected with provision, but no ship appeared for many weeks; they saw in the sand, however, vast quantities of shell-fish, since called *clams*, a species of mussel. Hunger impelled them to taste, and at length they fed wholly upon them, and were as cheerful and well as they had been before in England, enjoying the best provision. It is added, that a good man, after they had all dined one day on *clams*, without bread, returned thanks to God for causing them to "suck of the abundance of the seas, and of treasures hid in the sand." This text, which they had never before observed particularly, was ever after endeared to them.

Dying in Hope and Peace.

Chap. xxxiv. ver. 5.—Moses, the servant of the Lord, died there, in the land of Moab, according to the word of the Lord.

MRS COOPER, wife of Mr Cooper, late missionary in India, having gone to the Nilgherry hills for the benefit of her health, after her arrival, appeared to be considerably relieved; but the pleasing hope to which this gave rise was ultimately disappointed. She died July 4, 1831, in the hope of a glorious and blessed immortality. "I feel I am fast going," she said, "and that in a little while all will be over. But, oh! do not look so overwhelmed. When you look on my clay-cold cheek, think not of the grave and corruption; but think of me as a redeemed saint in glory, and that will support you." "Such," says Mr Cooper, "were her words to me a few nights before her peaceful departure from this world to glory; and I have endeavoured to act upon them, and calmly to commit her precious remains to the grave, in the assurance that her spirit rests with God, and her body, as a part of the Redeemer's purchase, will be raised in glory, when he comes to be glorified in his saints, and admired in all them that believe.'

BOOK OF JOSHUA.

All good Laws found in the Bible.

Chap. i. ver. 7.—Observe to do according to all the laws which Moses my servant commanded thee: turn not from it to the right hand or to the left, that thou mayest prosper whithersoever thou goest.

MR KAY, missionary in South Africa, was at one time addressing about a hundred and fifty of the natives. Having only his English pocket Testament with him, from which he usually translated into the vernacular tongue of the people, he asked whether any of them was able to read; desiring, at the same time, to know whether they were in possession of a Dutch translation of the Scriptures; on which a New Testament in that language was instantly produced. When he opened it, a small pamphlet fell out, which proved to be a copy of an ordinance issued by the late lieutenant-governor, in July, 1828, for the improvement of the condition of the Hottentots, and other free persons of colour; and for consolidating and amending the laws affecting those persons, agreeably to the recommendations of his Majesty's commissioners of inquiry. This document was carefully inserted between the pages of the sacred volume, "Because," said they, "God's word forms the basis on which all good laws are grounded."

Pursuing.

Chap. ii. ver. 7.—The men pursued after them the way to Jordon unto the fords.

MR RUGGLES, one of the American missionaries in the South Sea Islands, related the following anecdote respecting his father, who was a minister of the gospel:—One day, while he was preaching, a party of Indians came suddenly upon the congregation, scattered them, and carried him away into the forest. At night he was left under the charge of two women, while the men went to rest; but his female keepers, as well as the faithful dogs, falling asleep also, he took the opportunity to make his escape. He had not fled far before he heard the alarm-cry, and the crashing of the bushes behind warned him that the enemy were already in close pursuit of him. In his distress he crept, with little hope of safety, into a hollow tree, at whose feet there happened to be an opening through which he could squeeze his body, and stand upright within. The Indians soon rushed by in full chase, without stopping to search his retreat, and what is more extraordinary, their dogs had previously smelled about the root of the tree, and ran forward without barking, as they had discovered nothing.

Early Rising.

Chap. iii. ver. 1.—Joshua rose early in the morning.

FREDERICK II. King of Prussia, used to rise early; and he gave strict orders to his attendants never to suffer him to sleep longer than four o'clock in the morning, and to pay no attention to his unwillingness to rise. One morning, at the appointed time, the page whose turn it was to attend him, and who had been long in his service, came to his bed and awoke him. "Let me sleep but a little longer," said the monarch; "I am still much fatigued." "Your majesty has given positive orders I should wake you so early," replied the page. "But another quarter of an hour more." "Not one minute," said the page; "it has struck four; I am ordered to insist upon your majesty's rising." "Well," said the king, "you are a brave lad; had you let me sleep on, you would have fared ill for your neglect."

Remembrances.

Chap. iv. ver. 21, 22.—When your children shall ask their fathers in time to come, saying, What mean these things ?—Then ye shall let your children know, saying, Israel came over Jordon on dry land.

THE Secretary of the American Education Society, visiting Dr Payson, shortly before his death, asked for a message which he might carry from him to beneficiaries, when he received the following impromptu :—"What if God should place in your hand a diamond, and tell you to inscribe on it a sentence which should be read at the last day, and shown there as an index of your own thoughts and feelings, what care, what caution would you exercise in the selection ! Now this is what God has done. He has placed before you immortal minds, more imperishable than the diamond, on which you are about to inscribe every day and every hour, by your instructions, by your spirit, or by your example, something which will remain and be exhibited for or against you at the judgment-day."

Two Methods.

Chap. v. ver. 13.—Art thou for us, or for our adversaries ?

A PLAIN, honest Christian, on being called, by a profligate worldling, "a Methodist," replied, "Sir, whether you are aware of it or not, you are equally a Methodist with myself." "How? how?" rejoined the scoffer, with many oaths. "Pray, be calm," said the other, "there are but two methods, the method of salvation, and the method of damnation; in one of these you certainly are; in which, I leave with you to decide." The scoffer was silenced.

Purity.

Chap. vi. ver. 18.—In any wise keep yourself from the accursed thing.

ANSELM, Archbishop of Canterbury, who died in the beginning of the twelfth century, said, "If I should see the shame of sin on the one hand, and the pain of hell on the other, and must, of necessity, choose one, I would rather be thrust into hell without sin, than go into heaven with sin."

The Hardest Commandment.

Chap. vii. ver. 21.—When I saw among the spoils a goodly Babylonish garment, and two hundred shekels of silver, and a wedge of gold of fifty shekels weight, then I coveted them, and took them.

"AS I stood one day by Mr Jeffreys," says Mrs Jeffreys in her Journal, "catechising the children, I asked them which of the commandments was most difficult to observe? One after a long pause, mentioned one, and another a different precept; till, at last, a boy, about twelve years old, said, 'The last is the hardest.' Mr Jeffrey said, 'Why is it so, my boy?' He replied, 'Because, for one who is poor, to see another possessing a great deal of money, a great deal of clothes, and much cattle and rice, without wishing for some of them, is very hard; I think no person can keep this commandment.'"

Presenting the Scriptures to the People.

Chap. viii. ver. 35.—There was not a word of all that Moses commanded which Joshua read not before all the congregation of Israel, with the women, and the little ones, and the strangers that were conversant among them.

QUEEN ELIZABETH, on the morning of her coronation, agreeably to the custom of releasing prisoners at the inauguration of a prince, went to the chapel; and in the great chamber, one of her courtiers, who was well known to her, presented her with a petition, and before a number of courtiers, besought her,—"That now this good time there might be four or five principal prisoners more released; they were the four evangelists and the apostle Paul, who had been long shut up in an unknown tongue, as it were in prison, so as they could not converse with the common people." The queen answered very gravely, "That it was best first to inquire of them whether they would be released or no."

Keeping the Oath.

Chap. ix. ver. 19.—The princes said unto the congregation, We have sworn unto them by the Lord God of Israel: now therefore we may not touch them.

JOHN, King of France, left in England two of his sons as hostages for the payment of his ransom. One of them, the Duke of Anjou, tired of his confinement in the Tower of London, escaped to France. His father, more generous, proposed instantly to take his place; and when the principal officers of his court remonstrated against his taking that honourable but dangerous measure, he told them, "Why, I myself was permitted to come out of the same prison in which my son was, in consequence of the treaty of Bretagne, which he has violated by his flight. I hold myself not a free man, at present. I fly to my prison. I am engaged to do it by my word; and if honour were banished from all the world, it should have an asylum in the breast of kings." The magnanimous monarch accordingly proceeded to

England, and became the second time a prisoner in the Tower of London, where he died in 1384.

Hailstones in the East.

Chap. x. ver. 11.—The Lord cast down great stones from heaven upon them unto Azekah, and they died: they were more which died with hailstones than they which the children of Israel slew with the sword.

ALBERTUS AQUENSIS relates, that when Baldwin I. in the time of the Crusades was with his army in the mountains of Arabia, beyond the Dead Sea, they had to encounter with the greatest dangers, from a horrible hail, terrible ice, unheard-of rain and snow, which were such, that thirty of the foot died of cold.—"Something of this kind, I presume," adds Harmer, "the Canaanites suffered in their flight from Joshua, in a mountainous part of Judea. But it must have been much more destructive to people that were fleeing before their enemies, than to those Albertus mentions; as they doubtless had thrown away their clothes in part for the sake of expedition, dared not stop for shelter, and were running along in a mountainous place among precipices.

Faith for the Battle.

Chap. xi. ver. 6. The Lord said unto Joshua, be not afraid because of them; for to-morrow, about this time, I will deliver them up all slain before Israel.

DURING the awful moments of preparation for the battle of Camperdown, Admiral Duncan called all his officers upon deck, and in their presence prostrated himself in prayer before the God of Hosts, committing himself and them, with the cause they maintained, to his sovereign protection, his family to his care, his soul and body to the disposal of his providence. Rising then from his knees, he gave command to make an attack, and achieved one of the most splendid victories in the annals of England.

The Giants.

Chap. xii. ver. 4.—Og was of the remnant of the giants.

FERDINAND MAGELLAN, when wintering with his crew in St. Stephen's Bay, on the coast of Patagonia, South America, is said, one day, to have seen approaching a man of great stature, dancing and singing, and putting dust upon his head, as they supposed, in token of peace. This overture for friendship was, by Magellan's command, quickly answered by the rest of his men; and the giant approaching, testified every mark of astonishment and surprise. His face was broad, his colour brown, and painted over with a variety of tints; each cheek had the resemblance of a heart drawn upon it; his hair was approaching to whiteness; he was clothed in skins, and armed with a bow. Being treated with kindness, and dismissed with some trifling presents, he soon returned with many more of the same stature; two of whom the mariners decoyed on board. Nothing could be more gentle than they were in the beginning; they considered the fetters that were preparing for them as ornaments, and played with them like children with their toys; but when they found for what purpose they were intended, they instantly exerted their amazing strength, and broke them in pieces with a very easy effort.

Aged and Humble Minded.

Chap. xiii. ver. 1.—Thou art old and stricken in years, and there remains yet much land to be possessed.

WHEN Mr. John Elliot, from advanced age and infirmities, was laid aside from his former employments, he sometimes said, with an air peculiar to himself, "I wonder for what the Lord Jesus lets me live. He knows that I now can do nothing for him."—Speaking of his labours among the American Indians, he expressed himself thus :—"There is a cloud, a dark cloud, on the work of the gospel among the poor Indians. The Lord revive and prosper that work, and grant that it may live when I am dead. It is a work which I have been doing much about. But what have I said? I recall that word. My doings! Alas! they have been poor, and small, and I will be the man that shall throw the first stone at them." He died in 1690, aged eighty-six.

Singleness of Purpose.

Chap. xiv. ver. 8.—I wholly follow the Lord my God.

MR. CHARLES, an eminently pious minister at Bala, having previously spoken of "the single eye" which we should possess in all our concerns and proceedings, thus writes respecting a party who were going to emigrate from North Wales to America :—" I hope that those you hinted at as intending to emigrate to America possess this single eye. It will be of more use to them in steering their course across the Atlantic than the polar star; and without it they had better eat barley-bread or oaten cakes on the barren rocks in Wales."

Oriental Respect.

Chap. xv. ver. 18.—Achsah lighted off her ass; and Caleb said unto her, What wouldst thou?

"THE *alighting* of those that ride," says Harmer, "is considered in the East as an expression of *deep respect*; so Dr. Pococke tells us, that they are wont to descend from their asses in Egypt, when they came near some tombs there, and that Christians and Jews are obliged to submit to this.—So Hasselquist tells Linneus, in one of his letters to him, that Christians were obliged to alight from their asses in Egypt, when they met with commanders of the soldiers there. This he complains of as a bitter indignity; but they that received the compliment, without doubt, required it as a most pleasing piece of respect."

National Bravery.

Chap. xvi. ver. 10.—They drave not out the Canaanites that dwelt in Gezer.

WHEN the Romans, under Agricola, first carried their arms into the northern parts of Britain, they found it possessed by the Caledonians, a fierce and warlike people. Notwithstanding every exertion, the Romans were never able to conquer these Caledonians; they only retained, for a short time, small portions of their territories, which they occasionally invaded. The most northern boundary of the Roman Empire in Scotland was a wall which the Emperor Severus erected between the Firths of Forth and Clyde; but this boundary the bravery of the Caledonians did not permit them long to preserve. At a subsequent period, Adrian, Emperor of the Romans, in order to preserve his conquests, erected a second wall between

Newcastle and Carlisle, which became the boundary of his empire; and the country between these two walls was possessed alternately by the Romans and Caledonians.

A Great People.

Chap. xvii. ver. 14.—I am a great people, forasmuch as the Lord has blessed me hitherto.

FROM the rapidity with which the population of the United States of America has hitherto increased, and is diffusing itself over the wide and fertile continent of which it is in possession, the most magnificent anticipations are formed by the Americans themselves of the future greatness of their nation. "Let us assume," say they, "what appears highly probable, that the people of the United States will ultimately spread themselves over the whole North American continent west of the Mississippi, between the parallels 30° and 49°, as far as the Pacific Ocean. This will be found to add 1,800,000 square miles to the territory east of the Mississippi, and, putting both together, the area of the United States, thus enlarged, will be 2,700,000 square miles. A surface of such extent, if peopled to the density of Massachusetts, would contain two hundred millions; or if peopled to the density of Great Britain and Ireland, four hundred and thirty millions. If the population of the United States continue to multiply in the same proportion as hitherto, it is demonstrable that the two hundred millions, necessary to people this vast territory, will be produced within a century."

Indolence.

Chap. xviii. ver. 3.—How long are ye slack to go to possess the land?

"IN an affair of the highest consequence," says Mr. Hervey, in one of his letters, "how negligent is the community; I mean, in the long expected reformation of the liturgy, in which, excellent as it is on the whole, there are some passages so justly exceptionable, that every bishop in the kingdom will tell you he wishes to have them expunged; and yet, I know not for what political or timid reasons, it continues just as it did. Had our first reformers been thus *indolent*, we still had been Papists."

The City of Tyre.

Chap. xix. ver. 29.—The strong city Tyre.

THE destruction of old Tyre, which was situated on the continent of Phenicia, by Nebuchadnezzar, King of Babylon—the dispersion of the inhabitants, and their flight by sea into other regions—the subsequent restoration of its commerce and wealth in that part of the city, or New Tyre, which was built on an island half a mile distant from the shore—the siege and destruction of this latter by Alexander the Great—the casting of the stones, and timber, and dust—the ruins of the old or continental city, into the water;—yea, the scraping of her dust from off her, which were done by that conqueror, in forming a mound from the shore to the island in carrying on the siege of the new city—the smiting of the power in this latter in the sea by her capture, and the annihilation of her commerce—the burning of the city—the slaughter of many of her inhabitants—and the selling of others into captivity, form the most prominent historical facts relative to Tyre, and are each the fulfilment of a prophecy. The destruction of the first city by Nebuchadnezzar and the Chaldeans took place in the year 573 before Christ ; the insular city began to flourish 70 years after, and its siege and capture took place 330 years before the birth of the Saviour.

Slaying Unawares.

Chap. xx. ver. 3.—The slayer that killeth any person unawares, and unwittingly, may flee thither.

WHILE William II., surnamed Rufus, was hunting in the New Forest, Hampshire, he was shot by an arrow that Sir Walter Tyrrel discharged at a deer, which, glancing from a tree, struck the King to the heart. He dropped dead instantly ; while the innocent author of his death, terrified at the accident, put spurs to his horse, hastened to the sea-shore, embarked for France, and joined the Crusade that was then setting out for Jerusalem.

The Promises of the Bible.

Chap. xxi. ver. 45.—There failed not ought of any good thing which the Lord had spoken unto the house of Israel : all came to pass.

MR. CECIL, during a severe illness, said to a person who spoke of it, "It is all Christ. I keep death in view. If God does not please to raise me up, he intends me better. 'I know whom I have believed.' How little do we think of improving the time while we have opportunity ! I find every thing but religion only vanity.—To recollect a promise of the Bible : *this* is substance ! Nothing will do but the Bible. If I read authors, and hear different opinions, I cannot say *this* is truth ! I cannot grasp it as substance ; but the Bible gives me something to *hold*. I have learned more within these curtains than from all the books I ever read."

Equitable Division.

Chap. xxii. ver. 8.—Return with much riches unto your tents, and with very much cattle, with silver and with gold, and with brass, and with iron, and with very much raiment : divide the spoil of your enemies with your brethren.

IN September 1801, W. T. M., Esq., departed this life ; and, dying without a will, his large property, which was chiefly landed estate, devolved to his eldest son. By this circumstance, the eight younger children were unprovided for ; but this gentleman, with a generosity seldom equalled, but which does honour to Christianity, immediately made over to his younger brother and sisters three considerable estates (it is said of the value of ten thousand pounds), which were about two-thirds of the whole property. This munificence is the more extraordinary, as he had a young and increasing family of his own. On a friend's remonstrating with him on his conduct, his answer was, " I have enough ; and am determined that all my brothers and sisters shall be satisfied."

Improper Matrimonial Connections.

Chap. xxiii. ver. 12, 13.—If ye make marriages with them—they shall be snares and traps unto you, and scourges in your sides, and thorns in your eyes.

THE Rev. S. Kilpin of Exeter had been preaching on the subject of marriage, and pointing out the evil of improper connections. A gentleman called on him next day to thank him for the discourse, adding, that his state of mind when he entered Exeter was most distressing, as he was on the very point of complying with a dreadful temptation, which would have embittered his future life. He had been a disciple of Christ, and was anxious to consecrate his life to the service of his adorable Master, and had sought a helpmate to strengthen his hands in serving God. A lady, whom he deemed pious, had accepted his addresses; but, when every customary arrangement was made, she had dishonourably discarded him. His mind was so exceedingly wounded and disgusted, that he had determined to choose a wife who made no profession of religion, and had fixed on another object for his addresses, with every prospect of success, although he had not as yet mentioned his intention to her. He added, "But the providence of God led me, an entire stranger, to this city, to your meeting-house. You may suppose that your subject arrested my attention. You appeared to be acquainted with every feeling of my soul. I saw my danger, and perceived the temptation, and the certain ruin of my peace, if the dreadful snare had not been broken. You, Sir, under God, have been my deliverer. By the next Sabbath I should have been bound in honour to an enemy of that Saviour whom I adore; for although she is moral, and externally correct, yet she knows not the Saviour but by name. I could not leave the city in peace until I had sought to make this communication."

Thinking of Succeeding Generations.

Chap. xxiv. ver. 13—Of the vineyards and olive-yards which ye planted not do ye eat.

A very poor and aged man, busied in planting and grafting an apple-tree, was rudely interrupted by this interrogation:—"Why do you plant trees, who cannot hope to eat the fruit of them?" He raised himself up, and, leaning upon his spade, replied, "Some one planted trees before I was born, and I have eaten the fruit; I now plant for others, that the memorial of my gratitude may exist when I am dead and gone."

BOOK OF JUDGES.

Long Deferred Punishment.

Chap. i. ver. 7.—Adoni-Bezek said, Threescore and ten kings, having their thumbs and their great toes cut off, gathered their meat under my table: as I have done, so God hath requited me.

THE history of a respected citizen of the town of Acton is remarkable, on account of his seven sons, who, though not otherwise deformed, were quite dumb. The father was constantly sorrowing over his sons, and could not comprehend why God visited him so dreadfully, more than other fathers. One day he accompanied them to a neighbouring farm, and where an old Swiss sold refreshments. The afflicted father looked with much feeling at his sons, who sat blooming and healthy round the table. The tears started in his eyes, and exclaimed, "O God! why have I deserved this?" The old Swiss, who had overheard him, drew him on one side, and said, with honesty, "I see you are downcast at the affliction of your sons; but I do not wonder at it. Do you not remember (I knew you from your youth) when a boy, how you laid snares for the birds, and when caught tore heir tongues out of their mouths, and then with malignant joy let them fly away? How often have I not warned you! Oh, the birds under the heavens, who could not praise God with their tongues, have accused you, and you shall never hear the sweet name of father from the lips of your children."

Undesirable Society.

Chap. ii. ver. 2.—Ye shall make no league with the inhabitants of this land.

ON one occasion, the late Mr. Hall of Bristol having mentioned, in terms of panegyric, Dr. Priestley, who was eminent in scientific attainments, but deeply imbued with Socinian principles, a gentleman who held Dr. P.'s theological opinions, tapping him on the shoulder, said, "Ah, Sir, we shall have you among us soon, I see." Mr. Hall started, and, offended by the tone in which this was uttered, hastily replied, "*Me* amongst *you*, Sir! *me* amongst *you!* Why, if that were the case, I should deserve to be tied to the tail of the great red dragon, and whipped round the nethermost regions to all eternity!"

Undue Fatness.

Chap. iii. ver. 17.—Eglon was a very fat man.

MR. STEWART, in his account of the Sandwich Islands, says, "The nobles of the land are so strongly marked by their external appearance, as at all tim e to be easily distinguishable from the common people. They seem, indeed, in size and stature, to be almost a distinct race. They are all large in their frame, and often excessively corpulent; while the common people are scarcely of the ordinary height of Europeans, and of a thin rather than full habit. Keopuolani, the mother of Kiho-Kiho, and Taumuarii, King of Tauai, are the only chiefs arrived at years of maturity I have yet seen, who are not heavy, corpulent persons. The governess of Tauai, the sister of Taumuarii, is said to be remarkably so; Namokana, one of the queens of Tamehameha is exceedingly corpulent; her sisters Kaahumanu and Kalakua, nearly the same; and her brother Kuakini, governor of Humaii, though little more than twenty-five years old, is so remarkably stout, as to be unequal to any exertion, and scarcely able to walk without difficulty. This immense bulk of person is supposed to arise from the care taken of them from their earliest infancy; and from the abundance and nutritious quality of their food, especially that of poe, a kind of paste made from the taro, an esculent root, a principal article of diet. They live on the abundant resources of the land and the sea; and, free from all toil and oppression, their only care is, '*to eat, and to drink, and to be merry.*'"

Truthfulness.

"Chap. iv. ver. 20.—Sisera said unto her, Stand in the door of the tent; and it shall be, when any man doth come and enquire of thee and say, Is there any man here? that thou shalt say, No.

BISHOP ATTERBURY was once addressed by some of his right reverend coadjutors to the following effect:—"My Lord, why will you not suffer your servants to deny you, when you do not care to see company? It is not a lie for them to say, your lordship is not at home, for it deceives no one; everybody knowing it means only your lordship is busy." He replied, "My Lords, if it is, which I doubt, consistent with sincerity, yet I am sure it is not consistent with that sincerity which becomes a Christian bishop."

The Pen and the Sword.

Chap. v. ver. 14.—Out of Zebulun came they that handle and pen of the writer.

ONE night, in the year 1745, when the rebels were expected to make an attack on the town of Stirling, the Rev. Ebenezer Erskine, minister there, presented himself in the guard-room, fully accoutred in the military garb of the times. Two literary gentlemen of the place happened to be on guard the same night; and surprised to see the venerable clergyman in this attire, recommended to him to go home to his prayers, as more suitable to his vocation. "I am determined," was his reply, "to take the hazard of the night along with you; for the present crisis requires the *arms* as well as the *prayers* of all good subjects." He remained with them, accordingly, all that night; but no formal attack was then made.

Heathen Altars.

Chap. vi. ver. 31.—If he be a god, let him plead for himself, because one has cast down his altar.

A CHIEF in Tahiti, one of the South Sea Islands, informed Messrs Tyreman and Bennet, that when Pomare, the king, abjured heathenism, he ordered the chief to take an axe and chop his gods to pieces. Though exceedingly terrified with the anticipation of the consequences, should they resist and retaliate, as the priests threatened, he nevertheless determined to put their divinity to the proof, and with a trembling hand began the work, when, no evil following, he completed it with all his might. After the last decisive battle, Pomare commanded his people to go to the great marae, or temple, at Taiarabu, and fetch out Oro (the god of war,) and commit him, together with all the rabble of blocks that occupied his chamber of imagery, to the flames. This was a perilous enterprise; a few bold spirits, however, were found to attempt it. These marched to the marae, but, instead of entering, fired into the house where the idols were kept, saying, "Now, ye gods, if ye be gods, and have any power, come forth and avenge the insults which we offer you." The multitude who had assembled to witness the sacrilege stood amazed—not less at the impotence of the deities, than the rashness of the assailants. The house was afterwards pulled down, when the wooden inhabitants were shot through and through, and then burnt to ashes.

Dreams.

Chap. vii. ver. 13.—When Gideon was come, behold, there was a man that told a dream unto his fellow, and said, Behold, I dreamed a dream, and, lo, a cake of barley bread tumbled into the host of Midian, and came unto a tent, and smote it that it fell, and overturned it, that the tent lay along.

A PERSON in Southampton, who was a stone-mason, and who had purchased an old building for the materials, previous to his pulling it down, came to Mr Watts (father of the celebrated Dr Watts) under some uneasiness, in consequence of having dreamed that a large stone in the centre of an arch fell upon him and killed him. On asking Mr Watts his opinion in the case, he answered him to this effect:—" I am not for paying any great regard to dreams, nor yet for utterly slighting them. If there is such a stone in the building as you saw in your dream; (which he told him there really was,) my advice to you is, that you take great care, in taking down the building, to keep far enough off from it." The mason resolved that he would; but having forgot his dream, he went too near this stone, and it actually fell upon him, and crushed him to death.

Pacifying Anger.

Chap. viii. ver. 2, 3.—Gideon said unto them, What have I done now in comparison of you? &c. Then their anger was abated toward him when he had said that.

THE late Lord Bottetourt, in passing through Gloucester, soon after the cider-tax, in which he had taken a part that was not very popular in that country, observed himself burning in effigy in one of the streets of that city. He stopped his coach, and giving a purse of guineas to the mob that surrounded the fire, said, "Pray, gentlemen, if you will burn me, at least do me the favour to burn me like a gentleman. Do not let me linger; I see that you have not faggots enough." This good-humoured and ready speech appeased the fury of the people immediately, and they gave him three cheers, and permitted him to proceed quietly on his journey.

Wine and the Scriptures.

Chap. ix. ver. 13.—The vine said unto them, Should I leave my wine, which cheereth God and man, and go to be promoted over the trees?

THE witty Earl of Rochester being once in company with King Charles II., his Queen, chaplain, and some ministers of state, after they had been discoursing on public business, the king, of a sudden, exclaimed, "Let our thoughts be unbended from the cares of State, and give us a generous glass of wine, that cheereth, as the Scripture saith, both God and man." The Queen, hearing this, said, she thought there could be no such text in Scripture, and the idea was little less than blasphemy. The king replied that he was not prepared to turn to chapter and verse, but he was sure he had met with it in his Scripture reading. The chaplain being appealed to, was of the same opinion with the Queen. Rochester, suspecting the King to be right, slipt out of the room to inquire if any of the servants were conversant with the Bible. They mentioned David, the Scotch cook, who always carried a Bible about with him; and being called David recollected the text, and where to find it. Rochester ordered him to be in waiting, and returned to the King. The company still conversing on the same subject, Rochester proposed calling in David, who, he said, was acquainted with the Scriptures. David appeared, and being asked the question, produced his Bible, and read the text. The King smiled, the Queen asked pardon, and the chaplain blushed. The chaplain declining, David was applied to for an exposition of the text. "How much wine cheereth man," David remarked, "your Lordship knows; and that it cheereth God, I beg leave to say, that, under the Old Testament dispensation, there were meat-offerings and drink-offerings, the latter consisting of wine, which was typical of the blood of the Mediator; that, by a metaphor, was said to cheer God, as he was well pleased in the way of salvation he had appointed; whereby his justice was satisfied, his law fulfilled, his mercy reigned, his grace triumphed, all the divine perfections harmonized, the sinner was saved and God in Christ glorified."

Burning Idols.

Chap. x. ver. 16.—They put away the strange gods from among them.

ONE of the deacons in the church at Eimeo, is also a chief and a judge of the island; and both, in his official and private character, is venerated by his people, and regarded by the missionaries, who bear testimony, that by his uniform christian demeanour, he has hitherto adorned that gospel, which he was the first in Eimeo, publicly to confess, by throwing his idols into the flames. This he did in the presence of his countrymen, who stood shuddering at his hardihood, and expecting that the evil spirits, to whom the senseless stocks were dedicated, would strike him dead on the spot for the profanation. He remained unharmed, however, and it was not long before other chiefs followed his example, and the people joining in with them, the temples, the altars, the images of Satan were universally overthrown, and, in various instances, the churches of the true God have been erected on the very sites of the demolished temples of heathenism.

An Oath unto God.

Chap. xi. ver. 35.—I have opened my mouth unto the Lord, and I cannot go back.

HIS Majesty George III., while the Catholic question was under consideration, being very much pressed by one of his ministers to assent to the total removal of the restrictions under which the Catholics lay, with great firmness replied, "My Lord, if it will be for the good of the country, I will lay my head upon the block; but I cannot forswear myself, by going contrary to the oath I took at my coronation."

Inconsiderate Reproach.

Chap. xii. ver. 4.—The men of Gilead smote Ephraim, because they said, Ye Gileadites are fugitives.

A Negro who was servant to an officer on board a seventy-four gun ship, was observed to be often alone, and was asked why he shut himself up so much. He said the boys of the ship mocked him because he was a negro, and he was afraid he should be tempted to be in a passion with them.

No Moderation.

Chap. xiii. ver. 4.—Drink not wine nor strong drink.

A Gentleman, of the most amaible disposition, had contracted confirmed habits of intemperance. His friends persuaded him to come under a written engagement, that he would not drink, except *moderately*, in his own house, or the house of a friend. In a few days he was brought home in a state of bestial intoxication. His apology to a gentleman, a short time after, was, that had the engagement allowed no intoxicating liquor whatever, he was safe; "but if," said he, "I take the half-full of a thimble, I have no power over myself at all." He has practised entire abstinence since, and is strong and well.

Humility.

Chap. xiv. ver. 6.—He rent the lion as he would have rent a kid, and he had nothing in his hand: but he told not his father nor his mother what he had done.

"ON a visit to London," says the Rev. J. Campbell, in a letter to a minister, "I was expressing a great desire to see the late Mr. Charles of Bala, with whom I had corresponded for three years concerning a remarkable revival which had taken place under his ministry. Mr C. happening to be in town at the same time, your father kindly took me to Lady Ann Erskine's, where he resided. We spent there two happy hours. Your father requested Mr C. to favour us with a brief outline of the circumstances which led to the remarkable revival at Bala and its surrounding region, its progress, &c. He did so for upwards of an hour. On our leaving him, your father said, 'Did you not observe the wonderful humility of Mr C. in the narrative he gave? never having once mentioned *himself*, though he was the chief actor and instrument in the whole matter.'"

Dwelling among the Rocks.

Chap. xv. ver. 8.—He went down and dwelt in the top of the rock Etam.

WHEN the Grand Seignior ordered the Bashaw of Damascus to make the Emir Faccardine a prisoner, the latter shut himself up in the hollow of a great rock, with a small number of his officers, where the Bashaw besieged him some months, and was on the point of blowing up the rock, when the Emir surrendered on conditions, 1634. "A lively comment, I have always thought this," adds Harmer in his 'Observation,' "on Samson's retiring, after various exploits against the Philistines, to the top of the rock Etam; and on his surrendering himself afterwards into the hands of the men of Judah, sent by the Philistines, to take him."

Cruel Sport.

Chap. xvi. ver. 27.—All the lords of the Philistines were there: and there were upon the roof about three thousand men and women, that beheld while Samson made sport.

IMPROPER and cruel amusements are often attended with danger; and the end of such mirth is heaviness.—Some years ago, at the termination of a fair, annually held at Rochdale, in Lancashire, it was determined to bait a bull, for the gratification of a great number of persons, whose tastes are as savage as their amusements are cruel, and accordingly, the poor beast was tied to a stake at the edge of the river, near the bridge. The radius of the cord was about six yards, and the animal in making the circle was frequently three feet deep in water. The crowd collected to witness this sight was great, and the number of people on and near the bridge made it difficult to pass: the sides of the river were also thronged with spectators of every age and sex, and many were seen near the bull up to their middle in water, jumping with ecstasy at the sport. At every revolution the animal made to disengage himself from the dogs, people were seen tumbling over each other in mud and water up to the knees, and the shouts of joy occasionally expressed could only have been equalled by the yell of savages. This sport continued for about three hours, when a considerable portion of the parapet wall leading to the bridge gave way, from the extreme pressure of the crowd, and five persons were killed on the spot. Other four persons died shortly afterwards of the wounds they received, making nine in the whole who lost their lives, besides a considerable number who were severely wounded. The stones being large, they fell with overwhelming weight; and from the pressure of the crowd near the wall, numbers of the spectators were precipitated along with the stones on the people below. One woman had her thighs broken, and a young man had his arm completely cut from his body, besides others who were severely bruised. May not this calamity be regarded as a token of God's displeasure against such wanton cruelty?

Restoration of Money.

Chap. xvii. ver 4.—He restored the money unto his mother.

SOME time ago, a gentleman residing in the vicinity of York received an anonymous letter, appointing a meeting in the oat-market, when, as the letter stated, something would be communicated for his advantage. The gentleman kept the appointment, and was accosted by a respectable looking man, who proposed that they should go to an inn together. The gentleman consented; and having entered a private room, they both sat down at a table, when the stranger presented his new friend with £60, which he said was his property. The gentleman refused to take it without an explanation; but the stranger then presented him with £60 more, and said that was also due besides, as interest of the money (simple and compound) during the time he held his property. He afterwards gave the following explanation to the gentleman:—"More than twenty years ago, you had an uncle, whose property you now possess; his age and infirmities rendered it expedient for him to have a housekeeper to manage his affairs. My sister was that housekeeper. Some time after his death she found £60 folded up in one of her trunks, which she believed to have belonged to him at the time of his death. She sent for me, gave it into my hands, and requested that I would restore it to you as the lawful heir of her master's property. This I promised to do; but being embarrassed in my circumstances at the time, I made use of it for my own purposes. Years have passed away, and I have prospered in business, till I am now able to make the proper restitution. I do it to the utmost, and with pleasure; and I do assure you, that this transaction has taken a very heavy weight from my distressed mind." Various circumstances then occurred to the gentleman's mind, which left no doubt of the stranger's story.

Industry and Vice.

Chap. xviii. ver. 7.—The people dwelt careless—and there was no magistrate in the land, that might put them to shame in anything.

THE good effect of magistracy, and of a system of labour in prison, will appear by the following anecdote:—"I have heard," says the celebrated Howard, "that a countryman of ours, who was a prisoner in the Rasp House at Amsterdam several years, was permitted to work at his own trade, shoemaking, and by being constantly kept employed, was quite cured of his vices that were the cause of his confinement. My informant added, that the prisoner received at his release a surplus of his earnings, which enabled him to set up his trade in London, where he lived in credit; and at dinner commonly drank, 'Health to his worthy masters at the Rasp House at Amsterdam.'"

Generous Hospitality.

Chap. xix. ver. 20, 21.—The old man said, Peace be with thee; howsoever, let all thy wants lie upon me; only lodge not in the street. So he brought him into his house, and gave provender unto the asses: and they washed their feet, and did eat and drink.

THE lamented Mungo Park, when suffering under the pangs of hunger, rode up to the Dooty's house, in a Foulah village, but was denied admittance; nor could he even obtain a handful of corn either for himself or his horse. "Turning," says he, "from this inhospitable door, I rode slowly out of the town; and perceiving some low Scotland huts without the walls, I directed my steps towards them, knowing that in Africa, as well as in Europe, hospitality does not always prefer the highest dwellings. At the door of one of these huts an old motherly-looking woman sat spinning cotton. I made signs to her that I was hungry, and enquired if she had any victuals with her in the hut. She immediately laid down her distaff, and desired me, in Arabic, to come in. When I had seated myself on the floor, she set before me a dish of kouskous that had been left the preceding night, of which I made a tolerable meal; and in return for this kindness, I gave her one of my pocket handkerchiefs, begging, at the same time, a little corn for my horse, which she readily brought me. Overcome with joy at so unexpected a deliverance, I lifted up my eyes to heaven; and whilst my heart swelled with gratitude, I returned thanks to that gracious and bountiful Being, whose power had supported me under so many dangers, and had now spread for me a table in the wilderness."

Gathering to Prayer.

Chap. xx. ver. 1.—All the children of Israel went out, and the congregation was gathered together as one man, from Dan even to Beer-sheba, with the land of Gilead, unto the Lord in Mizpeh.

FARMER has the following quotation from Pocock's Travels, which he seems to consider as the remains of ancient Eastern usages, and illustrative of the preceding passage: "Near Cairo, beyond the mosque of Sheikh Duise, and the neighbourhood of a burial-place of the sons of some Pashas, on a hill, is a solid building of stone, about three feet wide, built with ten steps, being at the top about three feet square, on which the Sheikh mounts to pray on any extraordinary occasion, when all the people go out, as at the beginning of a war: and here in Egypt, when the Nile does not rise as they expect it should; and such a place they have without all the towns throughout Turkey.

Kings made by Men.

Chap. xxi. ver. 25.—In those days there was no king in Israel; every man did that which was right in his own eyes.

SELDON, in his book entitled, "Table Talk," in the article "King," says, "A King is a thing which men have made for their own sakes, for quietness sake, just as in a family one man is appointed to buy the meat. If every man buy what the other liked not, or what the other bought before, there would be confusion. But that charge being committed to one, he, according to his discretion, pleases all. If they have not what they would have one day, they shall have it the next, or something as good."

BOOK OF RUTH.

Loyalty to Affection.

Chap. i. ver. 16, 17.—Ruth said, Entreat me not to leave thee, or to return from following after thee: for whither thou goest, I will go; and where thou lodgest, I will lodge.—The Lord do so to me, and more also, if ought but death part thee and me.

M. DELLEGLAIE being ordered from a dungeon at Lyons to the Conciergerie, departed thither. His daughter, who had not quitted him, asked to be admitted into the same vehicle, but was refused. The heart, however, knows no obstacles: though she was of a very delicate constitution, she performed the journey on foot. She followed for more than a hundred leagues the carriage in which her father was drawn, and only left it to go into some town and prepare his food; and in the evening, to procure some covering to facilitate his repose in the different dungeons which received him. She ceased not for a moment to accompany him, and watch over his wants, till the Conciergerie separated them. Accustomed to brave jailors, she did not despair of disarming oppressors. During three months, she every morning implored the most influential members of the Committee of Public Safety, and finished by overcoming their refusals. She reconducted her father to Lyons, happy at having rescued him; but she was not permitted to enjoy her work here below. Overcome by the excess of fatigue she had undergone, she was taken ill on the road and died.

The Lord Recompenses.

Chap. ii. ver. 11, 12.—It hath fully been shewed me all that thou hast done unto thy mother-in-law—The Lord recompense thy work, and a full reward be given thee of the Lord God of Israel, under whose wings thou art come to trust.

A FEMALE servant, who was past the prime of life, in an inferior station, but much respected for her piety and integrity, had saved a little money from her wages, which, as her health was evidently on the decline, would probably soon be required for her own relief. Hearing that her aged parents were, by unavoidable calamity, reduced to extreme indigence, and having reason to fear they were strangers to the comforts of religion, she obtained leave to visit them; shared with them the little she had, and used her utmost endeavours to make them acquainted with the consolations and supports of the gospel, apparently not without success. Being reminded by an acquaintance that, in all probability, she would soon stand in need of what she had saved, she replied, "that she could not think it her duty to see her aged parents pining in want while she had more than was needful for her present use, and that she trusted God would find her some friend, if he saw good to disable her for service." Having continued to assist her parents till their death, she was soon after deprived of health, so as to become incapable of labour. God, in a wonderful manner, however, raised her up friends where she had least expected them. For years she was comfortably supported, and circumstances were at length so ordered, that her maintenance to the end of her life was almost as much ensured as anything can be in this uncertain world.

The Model Man.

Chap. iii. ver. 18.—The man shall not be in rest until he have finished the thing this day.

"I KNOW nothing of that man's creed," said a person of a religious tradesman with whom he dealt, "because I never asked him what he believed; but a more honourable, punctual, generous tradesman, I never met with in my life. I would as soon take *his word* for a thousand pounds, as I would another man's *bond* for a shilling. Whatever he promises he performs, and to the time also."

Care for the Aged.

Chap. iv. ver. 15.—He shall be unto thee a restorer of thy life, and a nourisher of thine old age.

A WIDOW, who had been left with an only son, when she became aged, was much distressed at the thought of being under the necessity of going to the poor-house, or of living on alms. Her son was now eighteen years of age; he was healthy and strong; and he assured her, that while he was able to work for her, she should be obliged to nobody. He therefore took a little cottage for her on the edge of the forest; carried her to it; and got into the service of a farmer in the neighbourhood as a day-labourer. His mother lived nine years after this; during which time he maintained her with great cheerfulness and kindness; nor had she ever assistance from any other person. He denied himself every little indulgence which young men of that age often take, that he might maintain his mother.

FIRST BOOK OF SAMUEL.

Praying for the Children.

Chap. i. ver. 27, 28.—For this child I prayed; and the Lord hath given me my petition which I asked of him: Therefore also I have lent him to the Lord; as long as he liveth he shall be lent to the Lord. And he worshipped the Lord there.

IN the vicinity of Philadelphia, there was a pious mother, who had the happiness of seeing her children, in very early life, brought to the knowledge of the truth; walking in the fear of the Lord, and ornaments in the Christian church. A clergyman, who was travelling, heard this circumstance respecting this mother, and wished very much to see her, thinking that there might be something peculiar in her mode of giving instruction, which rendered it so effectual. He accordingly visited her, and inquired respecting the manner in which she discharged the duties of a mother in educating her children. The woman replied, that she did not know that she had been more faithful than any christian mother would be, in the religious instruction of her children. After a little conversation, she said, "While my children were infants on my lap, as I washed them, I raised my heart to God, that he would wash them in that blood which cleanseth from all sin: as I clothed them in the morning, I asked my heavenly Father to clothe them with the robe of Christ's righteousness: as I provided them food, I prayed God would feed their souls with the bread of heaven, and give them to drink of the water of life. When I have prepared them for the house of God, I have pleaded that their bodies might be fit temples for the Holy Ghost to dwell in. When they left me for the week-day school, I followed their infant footsteps with a prayer, that their path through life might be like that of the just, which shineth more and more unto the perfect day. And as I committed them to the rest of the night, the silent breathing of my soul has been, that their heavenly Father would take them to his embrace, and fold them in his paternal arms."

The Church and the Children.

Chap. ii. ver. 18.—Samuel ministered before the Lord, being a child; girded with a linen ephod.

THE Rev. John Brown was born in 1722, in the county of Perth, in Scotland. In a narrative of his experience, he remarks, "I reflect on it as a great mercy, that I was born in a family which took care of my Christian instruction, and in which I had the privilege of God's worship, morning and evening. About the eighth year of my age, I happened, in a crowd, to push into the church at Abernethy, on a Sacrament Sabbath. Before I was excluded I heard a minister speak much in commendation of Christ; this, in a sweet and delightful manner captivated my young affections, and has since made me think that children should never be kept out of church on such occasions."

Unrestrained Children.

Chap. iii. ver. 13.—His sons made themselves vile, and he restrained them not.

A GENTLEMAN once observed an Indian standing at a window, looking into a field where several children were at play. The gentleman asked the interpreter what was the conversation. He answered, "The Indian was lamenting the sad estate of those orphan children." The interpreter inquired of him why he thought them orphans? The Indian with great earnestness replied, "Is not this the day on which you told me the white people worship the Great Spirit? If so, surely these children, if they had parents, or any persons to take care of them, would not be suffered to be out there playing and making such a noise! No! no! they have lost their fathers and mothers, and have no one to take care of them!"

Fearing God.

Chap. iv. ver. 7.—The Philistines were afraid; for they said, God is come into the camp. And they said, Woe unto us.

THE father of three orphan children, lately taken under the care of the Southampton Committee for the improvement of the Gipsies, had lived an athiest, but such he could not die. He had often declared there was no God; but before his death, he called one of his sons to him, and said,—"I have always said there was no God, but now I know there is; I see him now." He attempted to pray, but knew not how! And many other gipsies have been so afraid of God, that they dreaded to be alone.

A Heathen god.

Chap. v. ver. 4.—The head of Dagon, and both the palms of his hands, were cut off upon the threshold: only the stump of Dagon was left to him.

A MISSIONARY in the East Indies passed a place which had fallen into decay, although it had been the dwelling-place of a god, where, during the last dry season a buffalo had been sacrificed for obtaining rain. The missionary inquired after the god, of which nothing remained, and was answered by the people that, "*the white ants had eaten him.*"

Providence.

Chap. vi. ver. 9.—It was a chance that happened to us.

A CARELESS sailor, on going to sea, remarked to his religious brother:—" Tom, you talk a great deal about religion and Providence, and if I should be wrecked, and a ship was to heave in sight and take me off, I suppose you would call it a merciful Providence. It's all very well, but I believe no such thing—these things happen, like other things, by mere chance, and you call it Providence, that's all!" He went upon his voyage, and the case he had put hypothetically was soon literally true; he was wrecked, and remained upon the wreck three days, when a ship appeared, and, seeing their signal of distress, came to their relief. He returned, and in relating it, said to his brother, " O Tom, when that ship hove in sight, my words to you came in a moment into my mind—it was like a bolt of thunder: I have never got rid of it; and now I think it no more than an act of common gratitude to give myself up to Him who pitied and saved me."

Especial Prayer.

Chap. vii. ver. 5.—I will pray for you unto the Lord.

AN eminent minister in the north of Scotland, remarkable for his fervour, was once praying, in the public assembly, for various classes of sinners. Among others he prayed for *profane sinners*, that notwithstanding all the enormity of their offences, God would pardon them through the Lord Jesus Christ. A profane swearer, who was present, felt deeply interested, and lived to manifest a thorough conversion to God, and by the Divine blessing, the effect and answer of the prayer which had been offered for *that class of sinners* to which he belonged.

Hard Rulers.

Chap. viii. ver. 17.—He will take the tenth of your sheep; and ye shall be his servants.

A POOR man in one of the Sandwich Islands, by some means obtained the possession of a pig, when too small to make a meal for his family. He secreted it at a distance from his house, and fed it till it had grown to a size sufficient to afford the desired repast. It was then killed, and put into the oven, with the same precaution of secrecy: but when almost prepared for appetites, whetted by long anticipation to an exquisite keenness, a caterer of the royal household unhappily came near, and, attracted to the spot by the savoury fumes of the baking pile, deliberately took a seat till the animal was cooked, and then bore off the promised banquet without ceremony or apology.

Bringing Presents.

Chap. ix. ver. 7.—If we go, what shall we bring the man?—There is not a present to bring to the man of God, what have we?

"THIS day," says Maundrell, "we all dined at Consul Hasting's house; and after dinner went to wait upon Ostan, the bassa of Tripoli, having first sent our present, as the manner is among the Turks, to procure a propitious reception. It is counted uncivil to visit in this country without an offering in hand. All great men expect it as a kind of tribute due to their character and authority; and look upon themselves as affronted, and indeed defrauded, when this compliment is omitted. Even in familiar visits amongst inferior people, you shall seldom have them come without bringing a flower, or an orange, or some other such token of their respect to the person visited; the Turks in this point keeping up the ancient Oriental customs hinted, 1 Sam. ix. 7. "If we go, (says Saul) what shall we bring the man of God? there is not a present," &c. which words are questionless to be understood in conformity to this Eastern custom, as relating to a token of respect, and not a price of divination."

Father and Son.

Chap. x. ver. 2.—Lo, thy father—sorroweth for you, saying, What shall I do for my son?

IN the Rothesay Castle, which was lately wrecked, a father with his child was near the helm, grasping his hand, till the waves, rolling over the quarter-deck, and taking with them several persons who were standing near them, it was no longer safe to remain there. The father took his child in his hand, and ran towards the shrouds, but the boy could not mount with him. He cried out, therefore,— "Father! father! do not leave me." But finding that his son could not climb with him, and that his own life was in danger, he withdrew his hand. When the morning came, the father was conveyed on shore with some other passengers who were preserved, and as he was landing he said within himself, "How can I see my wife, without having our son with me?" When, however, the child's earthly parent let go his hand, his heavenly Father did not leave him. He was washed off the deck, but happily clung to a part of the wreck on which some others of the passengers were floating. With them he was almost miraculously preserved. When he was landing, not knowing of his father's safety, he said, "It is of no use to take me on shore, now I have lost my father." He was, however, carried much exhausted to the same house where his father had been sent, and actually placed in the same bed, unknown to either, till they were clasped in each other's arms.

Unseemly Anger.

Chap. xi. ver. 6.—The Spirit of God came upon Saul when he heard those tidings, and his anger was kindled greatly.

WHEN Bonaparte retreated from before Acre, the tyrant Djezzar Pasha, to avenge himself on the Franks, inflicted a severe punishment on the Jewish and Christian inhabitants of Saphet. It is said that he had resolved to massacre all the believers in Moses and Jesus Christ who might be found in any part of his dominions, and had actually sent orders to Nazareth and Jerusalem to accomplish his barbarous designs. But Sir Sidney Smith, on being apprised of his intention, conveyed to him the assurance, that if a single Christian head should fall, he would bombard Acre, and set it on fire. The interposition of the British admiral is still remembered with heartfelt gratitude by all the inhabitants, who looked upon him as their deliverer. "His word," says Burkhardt, "I have often heard both Turks and Christians exclaim, was like God's Word—it never failed."

Unceasing Prayer.

Chap. xii. ver. 23.—God forbid that I should sin against the Lord in ceasing to pray for you.

ONE Lord's day morning, Mr Whitefield, with his usual fervour, exhorted his hearers to give up the use of the means for the spiritual good of their relations and friends *only with their lives;* remarking that he had a brother, for whose spiritual welfare he had used every means. He had warned him and prayed for him; and, apparently, to no purpose, till a few weeks ago, when his brother to his astonishment and joy, came to his house, and with many tears declared, that he had come up from the country, to testify to him the great change that divine grace had wrought upon his heart; and to acknowledge with gratitude his obligation to the man whom God had made the instrument of it. Mr Whitefield added, that he had that morning received a letter, which informed him, that on his brother's return to Gloucestershire, where he resided, he dropped down dead as he was getting out of the stage-coach, but that he had previously given the most unequivocal evidence of his being a new man in Christ Jesus.—" Therefore," said Mr W., " let us pray always for ourselves and for those who are dear to us, and never faint.'

Disobeying God's Commands.

Chap. xiii. ver. 13.—Samuel said to Saul, Thou hast done foolishly; thou hast not kept the commandment of the Lord thy God, which he commanded thee.

WILLIAM IX., Duke of Aquitaine and Earl of Poitiers, was a violent and dissolute prince, and often indulged himself in improper behaviour at the expense of religion. Though he had contracted a very suitable marriage, and one with which he was satisfied for some time, he parted from his wife without reason, to marry another who pleased him better. The bishop of Poitiers, where he resided, was a holy prelate, named Peter. He could not brook so great a scandal, and having employed all other means in vain, he thought it his duty to excommunicate the Duke. As he began to pronounce the anathema, William furiously advanced, sword in hand, saying, " Thou art dead, if thou proceedest." The bishop, as if afraid, required a few moments to consider what was most expedient. The duke granted it, and the bishop courageously finished the rest of the formula of excommunication. After which, extending his neck— " Now strike," said he, " I am quite ready." The astonishment which this intrepid conduct produced in the duke disarmed his fury, and saying, ironically, " I don't like you well enough to send you to heaven," he contented himself with banishing him.

Wars and Rumours of Wars.

Chap. xiv. ver. 47.—Saul fought against all his enemies on every side, against Moab, and against the children of Ammon, and against Edom, and against the kings of Zobah, and against the Philistines: and whithersoever he turned himself, he vexed him.

BONAPARTE, referring to the seige of Acre, says, "I see that this paltry town has cost me many men, and occupies much time; but things have gone too far not to risk a last effort. If we succeed, it is to be hoped we shall find in that place the treasures of the pasha, and arms for three hundred thousand men. I will raise and arm the whole of Syria, which is already greatly exasperated by the cruelty of Djezzar, for whose fall you have seen the people supplicate Heaven at every assault. I advanced upon Damascus and Aleppo; I recruit my army by marching into every country where discontent prevails; I announce to the people the abolition of slavery, and of the tyrannical government of the pashas; I arrive at Constantinople with armed masses; I overturn the dominion of the Mussulman. I found in the East a new and mighty empire, which shall fix my position with posterity; and perhaps I return to Paris by Adrianople or Vienna, having annihilated the house of Austria."

Living by the Sword and Dying by the Sword.

Chap. xv. ver. 33.—As thy sword hath made women childless, so shall thy mother be childless among women.

PERSECUTORS, and others who have unjustly shed the blood of their fellow-creatures, have often, in the righteous Providence of God, met with a violent death or been visited by signal judgments. —Nero was driven from his throne, and perceiving his life in danger, became his own executioner; Domitian was killed by his own servants; Hadrian died of a distressing disease, which was accompanied with great mental agony; Severus never prospered in his affairs after he persecuted the church, and was killed by the treachery of his son; Maximinus reigned but three years, and died a violent death; Decius was drowned in a marsh, and his body never found; Valerian was taken prisoner by the Persians, and after enduring the horrors of captivity for several years, was flayed alive; Dioclesian was compelled to resign his empire, and became insane; Maximianus Herculeus was deprived of his government and strangled; Maximianus Galerius was suddenly and awfully removed by death; and Severus committed suicide.

The Power of Music.

Chap. xvi. ver. 23.—When the evil spirit from God was upon Saul, David took a harp, and played with his hand: so Saul was refreshed, and was well, and the evil spirit departed from him.

SULTAN AMURATH, having laid seige to Bagdad, and taken it, ordered 30,000 Persians to be put to death, though they had submitted and laid down their arms. Amongst these unfortunate victims was a musician. He besought the officer who had the command to see the Sultan's orders executed, to spare him but for a moment, and permit him to speak to the emperor. The officer indulged him, and, being brought before the Sultan, he was suffered to give a specimen of his art. He took up a kind of psaltery, which resembles a lyre, and has six strings on each side, and accompanied it with his voice. He sung the taking of Bagdad, and the triumph of Amurath. The pathetic tones and exulting sounds of the instrument, together with the alternative plaintiveness and boldness of his strains, melted even Amurath; he suffered him to proceed, till overpowered with the harmony, tears of pity gushed forth, and he revoked his cruel orders. In consideration of the musician's abilities, he not only ordered those of the prisoners who remained alive to be spared, but gave them their liberty.

The Lion.

Chap. xvii. ver. 37.—The Lord delivered me out of the paw of the lion.

MR CAMPBELL relates a singular escape of a Bushman child from being devoured by a lion. The child was only four years of age, and was sleeping beside its parents in a half-open hut. About midnight the child awoke, and sat by a dull fire. The father happening to awake about the same time, looked at his child, and while looking, a lion came to the opposite side of the fire. The child, ignorant of his danger, was not afraid, but spoke to it, and sportingly threw live cinders at it, on which the lion snarled, and approaching nearer, when the child seized a burning stick, and playfully thrust it into its mouth, when the lion scampered off as fast as he could run. The father witnessed all this, but was afraid to interfere, lest himself, as well as his child, should have been torn to pieces by the ferocious animal.

God-like Men.

Chap. xviii. ver. 12.—Saul was afraid of David, because the Lord was with him.

"IT has often struck me as a singular inconsistency," says a writer in the London Evangelical Magazine, " on the part of those who are in the habit of profaning the name and attributes of the Most High, that although they are in no degree impressed by the idea of the omnipresence of God, (who hears and takes cognizance of every oath which they utter,) they are often awed into silence by the presence of a fellow mortal, if they know him to be a pious man. The late Mr Marr was a striking proof of the correctness of this remark. He was a man of extensive property and influence, and a most inveterate swearer. In the company of his inferiors, superiors, or equals, it was all the same. Oath after oath rolled from his tongue. And yet there was one man in whose presence Mr M. was never known to swear. And who was he? A man of high rank and political power? Not at all. He was one of Mr M.'s own tenants. But he was a pious man; a fearless defender of the honour of his Divine Master; and of him Mr M. could not help standing in awe."

Escape from Death.

Chap. xix. ver. 10.—Saul sought to slay David even to the wall with the javelin; but he slipt away out of Saul's presence, and he smote the javelin into the wall: and David fled, and escaped that night.

MR JOHN KNOX was accustomed to sit at the head of the table in his own house, with his back to the window; yet on a certain night, such was the impression on his mind, that he would neither sit in his own chair, nor allow any other person to sit in it, but sat on another chair with his back to the table. That very night, a bullet was shot in at the window, purposely to kill him, but the conspirators missed him; the bullet grazed the chair in which he used to sit, lighted on the candlestick, and made a hole in the foot of it; which it is said is yet to be seen.—The Earl of Morton, who attended Mr Knox's funeral, when the corpse was put into the ground, said, "Here lies the body of him, who, in his lifetime, never feared the face of man, and though oftened threatened with dag and dagger, hath ended his days in peace and honour."

Deliverance from Danger.

Chap. xx. ver. 3.—There is but a step between me and death.

WHEN we consider the frailty, shortness, and uncertainty of human life, these words of David will appear applicable to mankind in general; there are particular cases, however, in which they apply with peculiar propriety. The following is a remarkable instance:—

A short time ago, a respectable old gentleman in Perth, before he was aware, had placed himself in the way of an enraged bull, which was ranging through the streets, preceded by a large crowd of people who were flying from it in all directions. The gentleman, finding himself suddenly by the side of the bull, placed himself as quickly as possible against a wall, in the hope that it might pass without giving him any molestation. The enraged animal, however, made an instantaneous and furious onset, but happily for the life of the intended victim, it was possessed of enormously large horns, which, instead of coming in contact with his body, actually inclosed him, and struck the wall with tremendous force, one horn on each side of the terrified gentleman. The bull, hurt by the reaction, ran quickly off, without inflicting injury. Deliverance from a danger so imminent calls for the liveliest gratitude to the God of providence.

The Word of the Lord.

Chap. xxi. ver. 2.—The king hath commanded me a business, and he hath said unto me, Let no man know anything of the business whereabout I send thee.

FROM the circumstances in which we know David was placed, the account given of himself to Ahimelech, must appear untrue, and contrary to the Scripture rule of speaking the truth every man to his neighbour.—At a meeting of an Auxiliary Bible Society in London, Mr. Dudley related that a friend of his, who had subscribed a guinea a year to one of the Southwark Societies, and whose servants had also become members of it, intimated to him that he could no longer give his support to such societies. On being asked the reason, he replied, "That they had ruined his servants : he had had one of the best women-servants in the world ; but, on a late occasion, when he wished to be denied to a person who called, and bid her say he was not at home, she told him she could not say so." "Why so ?" said he. "I have read my Bible," she replied, "and cannot tell a lie."—Mr. Dudley, however, on conversing with his friend, who was a man of sense, convinced him that he was wrong in supposing that the Bible had ruined his servant. It was far more probable that she who was taught to tell lies *for* him, would soon learn to tell lies *to* him. His friend, instead of withdrawing his subscription, immediately doubled it.

Hateful Commands.

Chap. xxii. ver. 17.—The king said unto the footmen that stood about him, Turn, and slay the priests of the Lord ; but the servants of the king would not put forth their hand to fall upon the priests of the Lord.

WHEN the infamous Catherine of Medicis had persuaded Charles IX. of France to massacre all the Protestants in the kingdom, that detestable prince sent orders to the governors of the different provinces to put all the Hugonots to death in their respective districts. —"Sire," answered one Catholic governor, who will ever be dear to humanity, "I have too much respect for your Majesty not to persuade myself that the order I have received must be forged ; but if, which God forbid, it should be really your Majesty's order, I have too much respect for your Majesty to obey it."

Providential Care.

Chap. xxiii. ver. 26, 27.—Saul and his men compassed David and his men round about to take them.—But there came a messenger unto Saul, saying, Haste thee, and come ; for the Philistines have invaded the land.

MR. ALEXANDER PEDEN, a Scotch Covenanter, with some others, had been, at one time, pursued both by horse and foot, for a considerable way. At last, getting some little height between them and persecutors, he stood still, and said, "Let us pray here, for

if the Lord hear not our prayer and save us, we are all dead men."
He then prayed, saying, "O Lord, this is the hour and the power of
thine enemies, they may not be idle. But hast thou no other work
for them than to send them after us? Send them after them to whom
thou wilt give strength to flee, for our strength is gone. Twine them
about the hill, O Lord, and cast the lap of thy cloak over puir auld
Saunders, and thir puir things, and save us this ae time, and we will
keep it in remembrance, and tell to the commendation of thy guid-
ness, thy pity and compassion, what thou didst for us at sic a time."
And in this he was heard, for a cloud of mist immediately intervened
between them and their persecutors; and in the meantime orders
came to go in quest of James Renwick, and a great company with
him.

Bless thine Enemy.

Chap. xxiv. ver. 19.—If a man find his enemy, will he let him go
well away?

TASSO being told that he had a fair opportunity of taking advantage of a very bitter enemy:—"I wish not to plunder him,"
said he, "but there are things I wish to take from him; not his honour, his wealth, or his life, but his ill-will."

Unfitting Joy.

Chap. xxv. ver. 36, 37.—Nabal held a feast in his house, like the
feast of a king: and Nabal's heart was merry within him, for he was
very drunken:—But—when the wine was gone out of Nabal, his
heart died within him, and he became as a stone.

A MR. LAMONT, from his earliest years, looked with anxious
desire to the period of his possessing the living of G——, to
which he was the nearest heir. Some years ago the incumbent died.
When intelligence was brought Mr. Lamont, he collected all his
friends, and treated them with a sumptuous feast for three days.
He drank so large a quantity of wine upon this occasion, that he became deranged, was inhibited, and put in confinement, and his elder
son took possession of his living.

Be Merciful.

Chap. xxvi. ver. 8.—Then said Abishai to David, God hath delivered
thine enemy into thine hand this day; now therefore let me smite
him, I pray thee, with the spear even to the earth at once, and I will
not smite him the second time.

ARCADIUS, an Argive, was incessantly railing at Philip of Macedon.
Venturing once into the dominions of Philip, the courtiers reminded their prince, that he had now an opportunity to punish
Arcadius for his past insolences, and to put it out of his power to
repeat them. The king, however, instead of seizing the hostile
stranger, and putting him to death, dismissed him, and loaded with
courtesies and kindnesses. Some time after Arcadius's departure
from Macedon, word was brought that the king's old enemy was become one of his warmest friends, and did nothing but diffuse his
praises wherever he went. On hearing this, Philip turned to his
courtiers, and asked, with a smile—"Am not I a better physician
than you?"

Among Strangers.

Chap. xxvii. ver. 7.—David dwelt in the country of the Philistines.

THE celebrated philanthropist, Howard, who spent the best part of his life in travelling over all the countries of Europe—" to plunge into the infection of hospitals—to survey the mansions of sorrow and pain—to remember the forgotten, and to visit the forsaken, under all climes,"—was not unhappy amidst his toils. In a letter from Riga, during his last journey, he says, "I hope I have sources of enjoyment that depend not on the particular spot I inhabit ; a rightly cultivated mind, under the power of religion and the exercise of beneficent dispositions, affords a ground of satisfaction little affected by *heres* and *theres*."

The Evil Spirit.

Chap. xxvii. ver. 8.—Saul said, I pray thee, divine unto me by the familiar spirit, and bring me him up whom I shall name unto thee.

AN honest tradesman came one day to the late John Frederic Oberlin, pastor of Waldbach, in France, informing him that a ghost, habited in the dress of an ancient knight, frequently presented itself before him, and awakened hopes of a treasure buried in his cellar. He had often, he said, followed, but had always been so much alarmed by a fearful noise, and a dog which he fancied he saw, that the effort had proved fruitless, and he returned as he went. The affair so entirely absorbed his mind, that he could no longer apply to his trade with his former industry, and had, in consequence, lost nearly all his custom. He, therefore, urgently begged Oberlin would go to his house, and conjure the ghost, for the purpose of either putting him in possession of the treasure, or of discontinuing its visits. Oberlin replied, that he did not trouble himself with the conjuration of ghosts, and endeavoured to waken the notion of an apparition in the man's mind, exhorting him to seek for worldly wealth by application to his business, prayer, and industry. Observing, however, that his efforts were unavailing, he promised to comply with the man's request. On arriving, at midnight, at the tradesman's house, he found him in company with his wife and several female relations, who still affirmed that they had seen the apparition. They were seated in a circle in the middle of the apartment. Suddenly the whole company turned pale, and the man exclaimed, "Do you see, Sir, the count is standing opposite to you?" "I see nothing." "Now, Sir," exclaimed another terrefied voice, "he is advancing towards you." "I still do not see him." "Now, he is standing just behind your chair." "And yet I cannot see him ; but, as you say he is so near me, I will speak to him." And then, rising from his seat, and turning towards the corner where they had said he stood, Oberlin continued,—" Sir count, they tell me you are standing before me, although I cannot see you, but this shall not prevent me from informing you, that it is scandalous conduct on your part, by the fruitless promise of a hidden treasure, to lead an honest man, who has hitherto faithfully followed his calling, into ruin—to induce him to neglect his business—and to bring misery upon his wife and children, by rendering him improvident and idle. Begone, and delude them no longer with such vain hopes." Upon this the people assured him that the ghost vanished at once. Oberlin went home, and the poor man taking the hint which in his address to the count he had intended to convey, applied to business with his former alacrity, and never again complained of his nocturnal visitor.

Eastern Fountains.

Chap. xxix. ver. 1.—The Israelites pitched by a fountain which is in Jezreel.

WILLIAM ARCHBISHOP of Tyre, informs us that the christian kings of Jerusalem used to assemble their forces at a fountain between Nazareth and Sepphoris, which was greatly celebrated on that account. This being considered as the centre of their kingdom, they could from thence march more conveniently to any place where their presence was required. He mentions also another fountain near a town called Little Gerinum, which, he says, was the ancient Jezreel. Near this, Saladin pitched his camp, for the benefit of its waters, while Baldwin king of Jerusalem had, as usual, assembled his army at the first-mentioned place.

Reviving the Fainting.

Chap. xxx. ver. 11, 12.—They found an Egyptian in the field, and brought him to David, and gave him bread, and he did eat; and they made him drink water; and when he had eaten, his spirit came again to him; for he had eaten no bread, nor drunk any water, three days and three nights.

ALEXANDER, the late Emperor of Russia, in one of his journeys, came to a spot where they had just dragged out of the water a peasant, who appeared to be lifeless. He instantly alighted, had the man laid on the side of the bank, and immediately proceeded to strip him, and to rub his temples, wrists, &c. Dr. Wyllie, his majesty's physician, attempted to bleed the patient, but in vain; and after three hours' fruitless attempts to recover him, the doctor declared it was useless to proceed any farther. The emperor entreated Dr. Wyllie to persevere, and make another attempt to bleed him. The doctor, though he had not the slightest hope of success, proceeded to obey the injunctions of his majesty, who, with some of his attendants, made a last effort at rubbing. At length the emperor had the inexpressible satisfaction of seeing the blood make its appearance, while the poor peasant uttered a feeble groan. His majesty, in a transport of joy, exclaimed that this was the brightest day of his life, while tears stole involuntarily down his cheek. Their exertions were now redoubled; the emperor tore his handkerchief, and bound the arm of the patient, nor did he leave him till he was quite recovered. He then had him conveyed to a place where proper care could be taken of him, ordered him a considerable present, and afterwards provided for him and his family.

A Sinful Death.

Chap. xxxi. ver. 4.—Saul said unto his armour-bearer, Draw thy sword, and thrust me through therewith.

THE father of a family in the province of Silesia, in Germany, having determined to put an end to his life, loaded his gun, and placing the muzzle to his mouth, called one of his children, only eight years of age, and desired him to pull the trigger. The poor child, ignorant of the consequences of his obedience, did as he was desired, and thus became innocently the destroyer of his father.

SECOND BOOK OF SAMUEL.

Treachery Punished.

Chap. i. ver. 15.—David called one of the young men, and said, Go near and fall upon him. And he smote him that he died.

PAPIRIUS CARBO, the Roman consul, being impeached as an accomplice in the assassination of the second Africanus, one of his servants, whom he had affronted, stole the box in which his master kept all his papers, and carried it to Licinius Crassus, who was employed to make good the indictment. Crassus was at enmity with Papirius, and these papers would have furnished him with ample matter to gratify it; but the generous Roman had such an abhorrence of the treachery, that he sent back the slave in chains, and the box unopened, saying, that he had rather let an enemy and a criminal escape unpunished, than destroy him by base and dishonourable means.

Unavailing Expostulation.

Chap. ii. ver. 22, 23.—Abner said again to Asahel, Turn thee aside from following me: wherever should I smite thee to the ground?—Howbeit he refused to turn aside: wherefore Abner, with the hinder end of the spear, smote him under the fifth rib, that the spear came out behind him; and he fell down dead there, and died in the same place.

WHEN Colonel Blackadder was a very young man, an unhappy affair took place between him and a brother officer, Captain Saville, which was said to have originated in some trifling verbal dispute while over their wine in a company after dinner. Captain Saville, it appears, had taken offence at some expression dropt by his friend in conversation, as if intended to call in question his veracity. Meeting with him sometime afterwards, he reminded him of the alleged insult, and insisted upon having immediate satisfaction. His friend, astonished and unconscious of giving offence, asserted his innocence, as he could recollect of nothing he had said that could have the least tendency to asperse or injure his character. In vain, however, did he attempt to justify himself, and to show him that the words he had used were on a trifling occasion, and not capable of the construction he put upon them. In vain, did he assure him, that if he had given him just provocation, he was ready to make any proper apology, or any concession or reparation he had a right to demand. In a paroxysm of rage, and incapable of listening to reason, Captain Saville drew his sword, and rushed on Lieutenant Blackadder, who, for some time, kept retreating and expostulating, willing to terminate the dispute in some more amicable way. At length, finding all his remonstrances ineffectual, and perceiving his own life in danger, he saw himself obliged, in self-defence, to close with his antagonist. An unfortunate thrust soon laid the captain at his feet. The consequences of this rash misadventure might have proved fatal to himself, but happily the whole contest was seen from the ramparts of the town, by several soldiers, who bore witness to the necessity under which he was laid to defend his life. The matter was speedily adjusted; and after a regimental trial, the lieutenant was honourably acquitted. The event, however, was too solemn, and made too deep an impression

Eastern Mourning.

Chap. iii. ver. 31.—David said to Joab, and to all the people that were with him, Rend your clothes, and gird you with sackcloth, and mourn before Abner. And king David himself followed the bier.

A MERCHANT of the town of Ghinnah, in Upper Egypt, was murdered while on a journey from Ghinnah to Cosire. Irwin gives an account of the mourning which took place while he stopped in the town:—"The tragedy," he says, "which was lately acted near Cosire, gave birth to a mournful procession of females, which passed through the different streets of Ghinnah this morning, and uttered dismal cries for the death of Mahomet, (the merchant who was murdered.) In the centre was a female of his family, who carried a naked sword in her hand, to intimate the weapon by which the deceased fell. At sundry places the procession stopped, and danced around the sword, to the music of timbrels and tabors. They paused a long time before us, (Irwin and his companions had been on ill terms with the merchant,) and some of the women made threatening signs to one of our servants; which agrees with the caution we received to keep within doors. It would be dangerous enough to face this frantic company, whose constant clamour and extravagant gestures gave them all the appearance of the female Bacchanals of Thrace recorded of old."

Unexpected Results.

Chap. iv. ver. 10.—When one told me, saying, Behold, Saul is dead, (thinking to have brought good tidings,) I took hold of him, and slew him in Ziklag, who thought that I would have given him a reward for his tidings.

A CERTAIN Roman, in the days of Paganism, called Titus Manlius, was extremely ill-treated by his father, for no other reason than a defect in his speech. A tribune of the people brought an accusation against the father before the people, who hated him for his imperious conduct, and were determined to punish him with severity. The young man came one morning very early from his father's country farm, where he was forced to live in the style of a slave, and finding out the house of the tribune who had impeached his father, compelled him to swear that he would immediately drop the prosecution. Oaths being at that time held inviolable in Rome, the tribune declared before the people that he withdrew his charge against old Manlius, because his son Titus had obliged him to promise upon oath that he would carry it no farther. The people, charmed with the filial piety of Titus to an unnatural father, not only forgave the old man, but next year advanced his generous son to the supreme honours of the state.

Praying for Protection.

Chap. v. ver. 22, 23.—The Philistines came up yet again, and spread themselves in the valley of Rephaim. And David inquired of the Lord.

"IN the number of providential interpositions in answer to prayer," says Le Clerc, "may be placed what happened on the coast of Holland in the year 1672. The Dutch expected an attack from their enemies by sea, and public prayers were offered for their deliverance. It came to pass, that when their enemies waited only for the tide, in order to land, the tide was retarded, contrary to its usual course, for twelve hours; so that their enemies were obliged to defer the attempt to another opportunity, which they never found, because a storm arose afterwards, and drove them from the coast.

Household Benediction.

Chap. vi. ver. 20.—Then David returned to bless his household.

SIR THOMAS ABNEY kept up regular prayer in his family, during all the time he was Lord Mayor of London; and in the evening of the day he entered on his office, he, without any notice, withdrew from the public assembly at Guildhall after supper, went to his house, there performed private worship, and then returned to the company.

Building in Hope.

Chap. vii. ver. 12, 13.—When thy days be fulfilled, and thou shalt sleep with thy fathers, I will set up thy seed after thee.—He shall build an house for my name.

WHEN the late Rev. J. Brewer of Birmingham laid the foundation of a large meeting-house for worship, having been in declining health some time before, he said, on that occasion—"You are going to build a chapel here for the exercise of my ministry, and with the hope and intention that I should labour in it; and yet most probably, when you meet again for the purpose of opening it, you may have to walk over my sleeping dust." This solemn and affecting premonition was soon realized, and his disconsolate people had to perform a painful duty in following the remains of their beloved pastor into this unfinished edifice.

God and the Bible.

Chap. viii. ver. 6.—And the Lord preserved David whithersoever he went.

SAMUEL PROCTOR, a class-leader in the Methodist Society, was formerly a grenadier in the first regiment of foot guards, and took part in the struggle on the plains of Waterloo. He always carried a small Bible in one pocket, and a hymn book in the other. In the evening of June 16th, his regiment was ordered to dislodge the French from a wood, of which they had taken possession, and from which they annoyed the allied army. While thus engaged, he was thrown a distance of four or five yards, by a force on his thigh, for which he could not account at the time; but when he came to examine his Bible, he saw, with lively gratitude to the Preserver of his life, what it was that had thus driven him. A musket ball had struck him where his Bible rested, and penetrated nearly half through the volume. All who saw the ball said it would undoubtedly have killed him, had it not been for the Bible, which served as a shield. The Bible is kept as a sacred deposit, and laid up in his house, like the sword of Goliath in the tabernacle.

The King's Table.

Chap. ix. ver. 10.—Thou shalt bring in the fruits, that thy master's son may have food to eat; but Mephibosheth thy master's son shall eat bread always at my table.

"THE eating at courts," says Harmer, "is of two kinds; the one public and solemn, the other private: might not the intention of these passages, that speak of a right to eat at a royal table, be to point out a right to a seat there when the repast was public and solemn? Understanding things," he adds, "after this manner, removes embarrassments from what is said concerning Mephibosheth. Though he was to eat at all public times at the king's table, yet he would want the produce of his lands for food at other times. It was very proper also for David to mention to Ziba the circumstances of his being to eat at all public times as one of his own sons, at the royal table, that Ziba might understand it would be requisite for him to bring the produce of the lands to Jerusalem ; and that in such quantities, too, as to support Mephibosheth in a manner answerable to the dignity of one that attended at public times at court. 'Thou shalt bring in the fruits that thy master's son may have food to eat : *and* (for that, I apprehend, is the particle our translators should have made use of, not *but*) Mephibosheth, thy master's son, shall eat always at my table.'

The Lesson of the Beard.

Chap. x. ver. 5.—Tarry at Jericho until your beards be grown.

A VERY young clergyman, who had just left college, presented a petition to the King of Prussia, requesting that his Majesty would appoint him inspector in a certain place where a vacancy had just happened. As it was an office of much consequence, the King was offended at the presumption and importunity of so young a man, and instead of any answer to the petition, he wrote underneath, "2 Book of Samuel, Chap. x. ver. 5," and returned it. The young clergyman was eager to examine the quotation, but, to his great disappointment, found the words "Tarry at Jericho until your beards be grown."

Noble Abstinence.

Chap. xi. ver. 11.—Uriah said unto David, The ark, and Israel, and Judah, abide in tents ; and my lord Joab, and the servants of my lord, are encamped in the open fields : shall I then go unto my house, to eat and to drink ?

A VETERAN officer on the French service, being reduced without a pension, and with a young family, worked hard to support them by daily labour, in an obscure part of the country. He had one son, however, in the military school at Paris, where he had every comfort and conveniency of life that could be wished ; yet the generous youth refused to take anything but bread and water. When asked the reason, he replied, "His father's family had nothing else, and he could not think of living luxuriously, while they were starving." This coming to the ears of the Duke de Choiseul, he rewarded the son, and settled a pension on his father.

Invocation for the Child.

Chap. xii. ver. 16.—David besought God for the Child ; and David fasted, and went in, and lay all night upon the earth.

"MY mother," says Legh Richmond, "had six children ; three of whom died in infancy. A very affecting circumstance accompanied the death of one of them, and was a severe trial to her maternal feelings. Her then youngest child, a sweet little boy, only just two years old, through the carelessness of his nurse, fell from a bed-room window upon the pavement beneath. I was at that time six years of age, and happened to be walking upon the very spot when the distressing event occurred. I was, therefore, the first to take him up. I delivered into our agonized mother's arms the poor little sufferer. The head was fractured, and he survived the fall only about thirty hours. I still preserve a very lively and distinct remembrance of the struggle between the natural feelings of a mother, and the spiritual resignation of the Christian. She passed the sad interval of suspense in almost continual prayer, and found God a present help in time of trouble. Frequently during that day did she retire with me ; and as I knelt beside her, she uttered the feelings and desires of her heart to God. I remember her saying, 'If I cease praying for five minutes, I am ready to sink under this unlooked-for distress ; but, when I pray, God comforts and upholds me : his will, not mine, be done.' Once she said, 'Help me to pray, my child : Christ suffers little children to come to him, and forbids them not ;—say something.' 'What shall I say, mamma ? Shall I fetch a book ?' 'Not now,' she replied ; 'speak from your heart, and ask God that we may be reconciled to his will, and bear this trial with patience.'"

Drink and Death.

Chap. xiii. ver. 28.—Mark ye now when Ammon's heart is merry with wine, and when I say unto you, Smite Ammon ; then kill him.

"AT our village feast or wake," says one, "there is much drunkenness and rioting. Sunday has been the chief day of gaiety in former years. On the Sunday evening last year, seeing the public-house yard full of drinkers, a person went in amongst them with tracts, and offered them at the tables. The first tract offered was, 'Are you prepared to die ?' The man who took it, read the title aloud and said, 'No, Sir, I am not.' He was asked, 'Is this the place to prepare to die ?' He said, 'No, Sir, I think not.' He then took up his hat, and said, 'I will be off immediately,'—carried the tract away in his hand, and left the village to go home. In half an hour the public-house yard was clear."

Water at Burial.

Chap. xiv. ver. 14.—We must needs die, and are as water spilt on the ground, which cannot be gathered up again.

THE Rev. Mr Jowett, when describing the funeral services of the Greeks, says, "The corpse was now carried out into the church-yard. A slab lifted up, discovered that the whole church-yard is hollow under ground. The body was put into a meaner wooden coffin, and lowered into the grave. I did not observe that they sprinkled earth upon it as we do ; but, instead of this, a priest concluded the ceremony by pouring a glass of water on the head of the corpse. I did not learn what this meant ; but it brought to my mind that touching passage in 2 Samuel xiv. 14. 'For we must needs die, and are as water spilt on the ground, which cannot be gathered up again.'"

Resignation.

Chap. xv. ver. 26.—If he thus say, I have no delight in thee ; behold here am I, let him do to me as seemeth good unto him.

MR HEY, an eminent surgeon, early in the year 1778, received a stroke upon his thigh, which threatened the complete suspension of his professional labours. The remedies applied under his own direction, and those of his medical friends, proved altogether unserviceable ; and it appeared in the highest degree probable to himself and them, that he would never regain the power of walking. He was the father of a large family, and was soon to be the parent of the eleventh child. He was in full business, and had the most reasonable prospect of distinction and emolument, as creditable to himself as advantageous to his family. Mr Hey felt this afflictive dispensation of Divine Providence as every considerate man in similiar circumstances would feel it—he was deeply affected by it; but his language and conduct were constantly expressive of the most humble submission, and meek acquiescence in the Divine will. To an intimate friend who was lamenting the apparent consequences of a disorder which extinguished all his prospects of future usefulness, he replied, "If it be the will of God that I should be confined to my sofa, and he command me to pick straws during the remainder of my life, I hope I should feel no repugnance to his good pleasure."

An Unnatural Son.

Chap. xvi. ver. 11.—Behold, my son, which came forth of my bowels, seeketh my life.

A PIOUS father, alive to the importance of his trust, neglected nothing, in order to give a good education to his son. Good examples, pious instructions, and sound advice, were all employed to this purpose; but a bad temper and criminal propensities obtained the ascendancy in the soul, and drove the reckless youth to multiplied irregularities, which rung the heart of his parent, and caused the most pungent sorrow. This unnatural son, listening to the suggestions of a wicked heart, formed the horrible project of assassinating his father, that he might at once become possessed of his property, and, of course, that he might be able to indulge, to a greater extent, in licentiousness. The unhappy father received the painful intelligence, through a medium which left no doubt on his mind concerning the fact. Stung with grief, and resolving to make a last effort to touch a heart so lost to itself, the father said one day to his son, " My son, would you take a walk with me ? Your company will give me pleasure." The son consented to the proposal, perhaps with the view of executing his barbarous intention. The father conducted him insensibly to a solitary place, in the deepest recesses of an extensive forest. Then stopping suddenly, he addressed his son in the following terms :—" My son, I have been told, and have no doubt of the fact, that you have formed the desperate resolution of murdering me. Notwithstanding the many just grounds of complaint which I have against you, still you are my son, and I love you still, and wish to give you a last token of my tenderness. I have led you into this forest, and to this solitary place, where none are to witness our conduct, and where none can have the smallest knowledge of your crime." Thus, drawing a dagger, which had been concealed, "There, my son," said he, "there is a dagger ;—take your will of me—execute the cruel design which you have formed against my life—put me to death according to your resolution—I shall, at least, in dying here, save you from falling into the hands of human justice ;—this shall be the last evidence of my tender attachment to you ; in my extreme grief, this shall be some consolation to me, that I shall save your life, whilst you deprive me of mine." The son, struck and astonished, could not refrain from crying ; he burst into a flood of tears—threw himself at his father's feet—implored the forgiveness of his foul offence —protested before God, that he would change his conduct to the best and most benevolent of fathers. He kept his word,—renouncing his ruinous irregularities, and causing consolation and joy, somewhat proportioned to the grief and sorrows of soul which he had given to his father.

Unavailing Regret.

Chap. xvii. ver. 23.—When Ahithophel saw that his counsel was not followed, he saddled his ass, and arose, and gat him home to his house to his city, and put his household in order, and hanged himself.

AN avowed infidel, whose language and conduct had been most profane, and who had boldly argued for man's right to kill himself when he found it expedient, swallowed a quantity of opium which put an end to his life. Among his papers was found one, on which was written, "I have this moment swallowed a vial of tincture of opium, consequently my life will be but short. Whether there will be a heaven or a hell, I leave parsons to divine." The part of the manuscript which followed was blotted, and concluded thus : "My hand trembles, my eyes grow dim, I can see to write no more ; but he that would be happy should be religious."

The Disobedient Son.

Chap. xviii. ver. 9.—Absalom's head caught hold of the oak, and he was taken up between the heaven and the earth ; and the mule that was under him went away.

UNNATURAL and disobedient children are often, in the righteous retributions of Providence, punished for their wickedness. Mr Clark mentions the case of Adolf, son of Arnold, Duke of Guelders, who, dissatisfied that his father should live so long, came upon him one night as he was going to bed, took him prisoner, obliged him to go on foot in a cold season, barelegged as he was, and then shut him a close prisoner in a dark dungeon for six months. Such disobedience and cruelty did not, however, go long unpunished ; for shortly after, the son was apprehended, kept for a long time in prison, and after his release, was slain in a battle with the French.

Kingly Greatness.

Chap. xix. ver. 21, 22.—Abishai said, Shall not Shimei be put to death for this, because he cursed the Lord's anointed ?—And David said—Shall there any man be put to death this day in Israel ? for do not I know that I am this day King over Israel ?

LOUIS XII. of France had been Duke of Orleans before his elevation to the crown. During that time, a French nobleman had offered him several unjust and gross indignities. After his accession to the throne, some courtiers hinted to him, that it was now in his power to avenge the affronts he had formerly received. His Majesty's answer is truly worthy of being remembered—"God forbid, that the King of France should remember the quarrels of the Duke of Orleans."

Noble and Peaceful.

Chap. xx. ver. 19.—I am one of them that are peaceable and faithful in Israel.

THE excellent conduct of Mr Swartz, missionary in India, was such as to secure the confidence of all ranks of people. In the time of war, when the fort of Tanjore was in a distressed situation, a powerful enemy at hand, and not provision enough even for the garrison, and when, to add to this distress, the neighbouring inhabitants, who, by ill-treatment, had lost all confidence in the Europeans, and the Rajah had in vain entreated the help of the people, the only hope left was in Mr Swartz. "We have all lost our credit," said the Rajah to an English gentleman ; "let us try whether the inhabitants will trust Mr Swartz." Accordingly, he was desired to make an agreement with them. There was no time to be lost. The Seapoys fell as dead people, being emaciated with hunger. The streets were lined with dead bodies every morning. He sent, therefore, letters in every direction, promising to pay, with his own hands, for every bullock that might be taken from the enemy In a day or two he got above a thousand bullocks. He sent catechists and other Christians into the country, at the risk of their lives, who returned in a short time, and brought into the fort a great quantity of corn. Thus the fort was saved ; and when all was over, he paid all the people, made them a small present, and sent them away.

Regard for the Dead.

Chap. xxi. ver. 10.—Rizpah—suffered neither the birds of the air to rest on them by day, nor the beasts of the field by night.

TIMOLEON, the Corinthian, being in a battle with the Argives, and seeing his brother fall dead with the wounds he had received, he instantly leaped over his dead body, and with his shield protected it from insult and plunder ; and though sorely wounded in this generous enterprise, he would not, by any means, retreat to a place of safety, till he had seen the corpse carried off the field by his friends.

Worshipping among the Heathen.

Chap. xxii. ver. 50.—I will give thanks unto thee, O Lord, among the heathen, and I will sing praises unto thy name.

"THE Sabbath here," says Mr. Stewart, referring to the Sandwich Islands, "is a most interesting day to the Christian and Missionary. The number of decently dressed heathens who flock to the humble temple of the only true God—the attention and seriousness with which many of them listen to the words of eternal life proclaimed in their own language, by the ambassadors of Jesus Christ—the praises of Jehovah chanted in this untutored tongue, necessarily produce a lively and joyful impression on the pious mind. Of this I saw a pleasing instance only two Sabbaths since. An officer from one of the ships in port—a serious young man—spent the interval between the English and native services with me at the Mission-House. As the congregation began to assemble, he accompanied me to the door of the chapel, intending to take leave when the exercises should begin, as he was unacquainted with the language, and had been already longer from his ship than he designed ; but after standing a few minutes, and seeing hundreds of natives assembling quietly and seriously from various directions, he suddenly exclaimed, while tears glistened in his eye, "*No !—this is too much—I cannot go till I worship with these heathen !*"

A Covenant with God.

Chap. xxiii. ver. 5.—Although my house be not so with God, yet he hath made with me an everlasting covenant, ordered in all things, and sure : for this is all my salvation, and all my desire, although he make it not to grow.

"I HAVE been for these two months past and more," writes the Rev. Mr. Charles, a little before his death, "in a state of great bodily debility, supposed by the doctors to be the effects of over-exertion of body and mind. I had frequent pains, and was confined to the house ; and I was frequently on the bed I was not fit for anything that required exertion either of body or mind, and was recommended to indulge myself in rest and cessation from all work, as the most likely way to restore my strength. Through mercy I am now much better.

free from pain, though still languid. I have found great support from the last words of David,—the everlasting covenant, 'well-ordered in all things and sure,' containing *all my salvation.* Though I was feeble, I found strong ground to stand upon, and I rejoiced in it. When heart and flesh fail, here is strength for my heart, and a portion —all my salvation, for ever. I cannot now pen on this paper what I saw in it; but I saw *enough*, and that for ever. God remembered me and showed me the best things he had,—a salvation in a covenant made by himself. This salvation in a covenant is well arranged, well ordered; everything is provided for—the glory of God, his law, and government; and everything which pertains to the safety and eternal felicity of those in his covenant. It is all sure; the covenant itself, and all its privileges, are all sure. May God the Holy Ghost keep our minds in constant and clear views of this covenant; and we shall be enabled to rejoice in tribulation, and in hope of the glory of God."

Receiving Payment.

Chap. xxiv. ver. 24.—The king said unto Araunah, Nay; but I will surely buy it of thee at a price.

WHEN Mr. Campbell went upon his first mission to Africa, the Bible Society sent along with him a number of Bibles to be distributed to a Highland regiment stationed at the Cape of Good Hope. Arrived there, the regiment was drawn out in order to receive the Bibles. The box which contained them, and Mr. C., were placed in the centre; and on his presenting the first Bible to one of the men he took out of his pocket *four shillings and sixpence* for the Bible, saying, "I enlisted to serve my King and my country, and I have been well and regularly paid, and will not accept of a Bible as a present, when I can pay for it." His example was instantly followed by all the regiment.

FIRST BOOK OF KINGS.

The Spoiled Son.

Chap. i. ver. 6.—His father had not displeased him at any time in saying, Why hast thou done so?

A YOUNG man, as he was going to the place of execution, desired to whisper something into his mother's ear; but when he came, instead of whispering, he bit off her ear, telling her, that it was because she did not chastise him for his faults when a boy he was brought to such an unhappy end.

Under Divine Guidance.

Chap. ii. ver. 1, 2, 3.—David—charged Solomon his son, saying, I go the way of all the earth: be thou strong, therefore, and shew thyself a man; and keep the charge of the Lord thy God, to walk in his ways, —that thou mayest prosper in all that thou doest, and whithersoever thou turnest thyself.

THE following is said to have been a part of Alfred the Great's dying advice to his son Edward:—"My son, I feel that my hour is coming: My countenance is wan: My days are almost done: We now must part. I shall go to another world, and thou shalt be left alone in all my wealth. I pray thee (for thou art dear, my child) strive to be a father and a lord to thy people ; be thou the children's father, and the widow's friend ; comfort thou the poor, and shelter the weak ; and with all thy might, right that which is wrong ; and, son, govern thyself by law ; then shall the Lord love thee, and God, above all things, shall be thy reward ; call upon him to ADVISE thee in all thy need and so he shall HELP thee better to do that which thou wouldest."

The Stranger Child.

Chap. iii. ver. 20.—She arose at midnight, and took my son from beside me, while thine handmaid slept, and laid it in her bosom, and laid her dead child in my bosom.

SOME time ago, a lady, apparently labouring under considerable fatigue, called at a cottage in the neighbourhood of Turnham-Green, in the vicinity of London, and applied for refreshment, for which she tendered a bank note. The inhabitant, a female, left the house for the purpose of procuring change, and on her return, with great surprise, found the stranger gone. On hearing, as she believed the cry of her infant, she hastened to its cradle ; but to her utter dismay, discovered her own had been taken away, and another of a tawny colour placed in its stead. Cash to the amount of £100 was fastened to its breast. It is said the poor woman, influenced by the pecuniary gift, has become reconciled to the event, and treats the child with maternal fondness.

Trees in the East.

Chap. iv. ver. 25.—Judah and Israel dwelt safely, every man under his vine and under his fig-tree.

PLANTATIONS of trees about houses are found very useful in hot countries, to give them an agreeable coolness. The ancient Israelites seem to have made use of the same means, and probably planted fruit-trees, rather than other kinds, to produce that effect. "It is their manner, in many places," says Sir Thomas Row's chaplain, speaking of the country of the Great Mogul, "to plant about, and amongst their buildings, trees which grow high and broad ; the shadow keeps their houses by far more cool ; this I observed in a special manner, when we were ready to enter Amadavar ; for it appeared to us as if we had been entering a wood rather than a city."

Wood Floats.

Chap. v. ver. 9.—My servants shall bring them down from Lebanon unto the sea ; and I will convey them by sea in floats unto the place that thou shalt appoint me. and will cause them to be discharged there, and thou shalt receive them : and thou shalt accomplish my desire, in giving food for my household.

THE rafts, or timber floats, on the Rhine, consist of the fellings of almost every German forest, which, by streams, or short land carriage, can be brought to the Rhine. The rafts, when compacted, are said to be of the following dimensions :—The length is from 700 to 1000 feet ; the breadth from 50 to 90 feet ; the depth when manned by the whole crew, is usually seven feet above the surface of the water. Five hundred labourers of different classes are employed, maintained, and lodged during the voyage ; and a little street of deal huts is built upon it for their reception. The captain's apartments are distinguished from the others by being better built. The provisions for the voyage, on board such a float, are fifteen or twenty thousand pounds of fresh meat, forty or fifty thousand pounds of bread, ten or fifteen thousand pounds of cheese, with proportioned quantities of other articles. When the float is in readiness for moving, and each individual is at his post, the pilot, who stands on high, near the rudder, takes off his hat, and calls out, "Let us all pray." In an instant, there is the happy spectacle of all these numbers on their knees, imploring a blessing on their undertaking. The anchors, which were fastened on the shore, are now brought on board, the pilot gives a signal, and the rowers put the whole float in motion, while the crews of the several boats, attending on the float, ply round it to facilitate the departure. Dort, in Holland, is the destination of these floats, the sale of one of which occupies several months, and frequently produces thirty thousand pounds, or more.

Work Completed.

Chap. vi. ver. 38.—The house was finished throughout all the parts thereof.

MR. CHARLES had a strong and ardent desire to procure a correct and indefective edition of the Bible for his Welsh countrymen; therefore his toil and labour were very great, though without any remuneration from man. While engaged in this work, he acknowledged that he had a strong wish to live until it was completed; "and then," said he, "I shall willingly lay down my head and die." He lived to see it completed; and he expressed himself very thankful to the Lord for having graciously spared him to witness the work finished; and the last words ever written by him, as it is supposed, were these, with reference to this work—"It is now finished."

Upright Judgment.

Chap. vii. ver. 7.—He made a porch for the throne, where he might judge, even the porch of judgment

SIR MATTHEW HALE, when Chief Baron of the Exchequer, was very exact and impartial in his administration of justice. He would never receive any private addresses or recommendations from the greatest persons in any matter in which justice was concerned. A noble duke once went to his chamber, and told him, "That, having a suit in law to be tried before him, he was then to acquaint him with it, that he might the better understand it when it should come to be heard in Court." Upon which Sir Matthew interrupted him, and said, "He did not deal fairly, to come to his chamber about such affairs, for he never received any information of causes but in open Court, where both parties were to be heard alike;" and would not allow him to proceed. His grace went away, not a little dissatisfied, and complained of it to the king as a rudeness that was not to be endured. But his Majesty bade him content himself that he was no worse used, saying, "He verily believed he would have used himself no better, if he had gone to solicit him in any of his own causes."

The King before the Lord.

Chap. viii. ver. 22.—Solomon stood before the altar of the Lord, in the presence of all the congregation of Israel, and spread forth his hands towards heaven.

MR. CHAMBERLAIN, an American missionary, giving an account of the opening of a new meeting-house in the Sandwich Islands, says, "Probably not fewer than 4000 persons were present, including most of the great personages of the nation. We were exceedingly gratified with the appearance of the King on this occasion and also of his sister, the Princess Harieta Keopuolani. An elegant sofa, covered with damask of a deep crimson colour, had been placed for them in the front of the pulpit. The King in his rich Windsor uniform sat at one end, and his sister in a superb dress at the other Before the religious services commenced, the King arose from his seat, stepped to a platform in front of the pulpit, directly behind the sofa, called the attention of the congregation, and, addressing himself to the chiefs, teachers, and people generally, said, that this house, which he had built, he now publicly gave to God, the maker of heaven and earth, to be appropriated to his worship; and declared his wish, that his subjects should worship and serve God, obey his laws, and learn his word. The religious exercises were appropriate; and when these were closed, the princess arose from her seat, and, taking her stand upon the platform, called the attention of the chiefs and people anew to what her brother had said, and exhorted them to remember and obey. She said God was the King above, to whom they should give their hearts, and render constant homage. At the closing exercise of the occasion, the King stood up, and saying, "E pule kakou" (let us pray), addressed the throne of grace. In this act of worship, using the plural number, he gave the house anew to God, acknowledged him as his sovereign, yielded his kingdom to him, confessed his sinfulness, prayed for help, for teaching—supplicated his mercy as a sinner, a great sinner, needing mercy, pardon and cleansing—prayed to be preserved from temptation, and delivered from evil. He prayed for the different classes of his subjects; for the chiefs, teachers, learners, and common people; for the missionaries and foreign residents; and concluded, in a very appropriate manner, by ascribing unto God the kingdom, and the power, and the glory, to the world everlasting."

Establishing the Throne.

Chap. ix. ver. 4, 5.—If thou wilt keep my statutes and my judgments—then I will establish the throne of thy kingdom upon Israel for ever.

WHEN his Majesty George III. came to the crown, his speech from the throne was worthy of the sovereign of a free people:— "The civil and religious rights of my loving subjects," said the monarch, "are equally dear to me with the most valuable prerogatives of my crown: and as the surest foundation of the whole, and the best means to draw down the divine favour upon my reign, it is my fixed purpose to countenance and encourage the practice of true religion and virtue." In consonance with this declaration, his Majesty soon after issued a proclamation against vice, among the high and the low; and his public regard to the rights of conscience, as well as the whole tenor of his private conduct, were a practical comment on his speech during the whole of his life.

An Awful End.

Chap. x. ver. 7.—The half was not told me.

A MINISTER once preached from the preceding words, in a country village in Lincolnshire. They were considered in an accommodated view, as appropriate to the felicity of the righteous, and also as awfully aplicable to the case of the ungodly, throughout the endless ages of eternity. When speaking on the latter head, a man exceedingly intoxicated rushed into the room, and sat down, who, nevertheless, behaved with decorum during the service. After worship was concluded, it was found that he had thus intruded himself in consequence of a wager. Some one offered to lay him a tankard of ale that he durst not enter in. "Yes," added he, with an oath; "and if *hell-door* was open, I would go in." In a few days, Death, the king of terrors, arrested his awful progress, cut the brittle thread of life, and consigned him over to the retributions of eternity.

Deserved Approbation.

Chap. xi. ver. 28.—Jeroboam was a mighty man of valour: and Solomon seeing the young man that he was industrious, he made him ruler over all the charge of the house of Joseph.

A PERSON whose talents had raised him to a high station, went to return his thanks to the minister by whom he had been elevated. The minister remarked, "You have no thanks to return to me; I had but the public good in view, and you would not have had my approbation, if I had found anybody more deserving of it than yourself."

The Effect of Kindness.

Chap. xii. ver. 7.—If thou wilt be a servant unto this people this day, and will serve them, and answer them, and speak good words to them, then they will be thy servants for ever

SOME courtiers observed to the Emperor Sigismond, that, instead of destroying his conquered foes, he admitted them to favour. "Do I not," replied the monarch, "effectually destroy my enemies, when I make them my friends?"

Mourning.

Chap. xiii. ver. 30.—They mourned over him, saying, Alas, my brother!

MR. FOUNTAIN, a missionary in the East Indies, says, "One morning I heard a noise, and found a number of women and girls assembled to lament over the grave of a lad, who had been killed by a wild buffalo ten days before. The mother sat on earth at one end of the grave, leaning upon it, and exclaiming, 'O, my child! O, my child!' At the other end of the grave sat another female, expressing her grief in a similar manner."

The Kind of Priest Required.

Chap. xiv. ver. 13.—In him there is found some good thing toward the Lord God of Israel in the house of Jeroboam.

A LITTLE boy, who was educated in one of the London Hibernian Schools, in the county of Roscommon, was seized by sickness, and confined to his bed. In a few days his dissolution seemed to be near. The parents of the boy, being Roman Catholics, sent immediately for the priest, to have the rites of their Church administered, which in their estimation was the only preparation for heaven. On the arrival of the priest, the boy seemed much confused, and astonished why he came. "Your visit," said the boy, "was altogether unnecessary: I have no need of your help or assistance: I have a great High Priest on the right hand of the Majesty in the heavens, able to save to the uttermost all that come unto God by Him: He lives for evermore, to make intercession; and it is such a priest as I require." The priest, perceiving it to be in vain to reason at such a time, and knowing the boy to have been made acquainted with the Bible, went off. The child requested his parents to send for his schoolmaster, who stated that he never witnessed such a scene—it was altogether unexpected. The boy was always silent; though he was attentive to the instructions given at school, he never once hinted a change in his sentiments. In the course of conversation, he was asked, was he afraid to die? "No," replied the boy, "my Redeemer is Lord of the dead and living; I love him for his love to me, and soon I hope to be with him, to see his glory."

God and Means.

Chap. xv. ver. 23.—In the time of his old age Asa was diseased in his feet.

"ASA was sick but of his feet," says Bishop Hall, "far from his heart; yet, because he sought to the physicians, and not to God, he escaped not. Hezekiah was sick to die; yet, because he trusted to God, and not to physicians, he was restored. Means, without God, cannot help; God, without means, can, and often doth. I will use good means, not rest in them."

Killing his Father.

Chap. xvi. ver. 10.—Zimri went in and smote him, and killed him—and reigned in his stead.—*See* 2 Kings ix. 31.

THE cruel Al Montaser, having assassinated his father, was afterwards haunted by remorse. As he was one day admiring a beautiful painting of a man on horseback, with a diadem encircling his head, and a Persian inscription, of which he inquired the meaning, he was told that it signified—" I am Shiunyeh, the son of Kosru, who murdered my father, and possessed the crown only six months!"— He turned pale, as if struck by a sentence of death. Frightful dreams interrupted his slumbers, and he died at the early age of twenty-five.

God Providing.

Chap. xvii. ver. 6.—The ravens brought him bread and flesh in the morning, and bread and flesh in the evening; and he drunk of the brook.

WHILST the cruel persecution, carried on by the Emperor Maximilian was raging, the ancestors of the celebrated Basil, along with a few servants, fled for safety to a certain cave in the side of a mountain. There they remained above seven years, exposed to the inclemency of the weather, and subsisted upon bread alone. But their God who fed the Israelites in the desert with manna and quails, directed unprovided and unexpected caterers to visit them—namely, a number of fat stags, which approached to the place of their retreat, though no person was pursuing them. Of these they killed what was necessary for their present wants, and conveyed the rest, which made no opposition, but went willingly, to a place of confinement, to be reserved for future use. "So true," adds the pious Witsius, "is that observation of the Psalmist, 'The young lions do lack and hunger, but they that seek the Lord shall not want any good thing.'"

The Chosen of the Lord.

Chap. xviii. ver. 4.—It was so, when Jezebel cut off the prophets of the Lord, that Obadiah took an hundred prophets, and hid them by fifty in a cave, and fed them with bread and water.

MR. DAVID ANDERSON, once minister of Walton-upon-Thames, fearing the return of Popery, went, with his wife and five small children, to reside at Middleburgh, in Zealand. Some time after, he was reduced to the greatest distress, but was restrained by modesty from making his case known. One morning, however, after he had been at prayer with his family, when they were all in tears together, because his children asked for bread for breakfast, and he had none to give them, the bell rang, and Mrs. Anderson found a person at the door, who gave her a paper containing forty pieces of gold, which, he said, a gentleman had sent her. Soon after a countryman brought a horse loaded with provisions; but neither of the messengers would say from whom they were sent. Afterwards, money was regularly conveyed to Mr. Anderson to pay his rent, and ten pounds sterling every quarter; yet, to the day of his death, he never discovered who was his benefactor. But Mr. John Quick, pastor of the English church at Middleburgh, in 1681, was told by a gentleman then in the magistracy, that he carried the money to Mr. Anderson, being then apprentice to a pious merchant of the place; who observing a grave English minister apparently in want and dejected, privately inquired into his circumstances; and, with all possible secrecy, made him those remittances, saying, "God forbid that any of Christ's ambassadors should be strangers and in distress, and we neglect to assist them."

A Word in Season.

Chap. xix. ver. 9.—What dost thou here, Elijah?

A HAND-BILL, with the title, "WHAT DOEST THOU HERE, ELIJAH?" came into the hands of a German reformed clergyman in Maryland, who was so much pleased with it, that he determined to translate it into German for the benefit of a part of his congregation. He had only commenced translating it, when he was called out, and Mr. Elijah —— coming in during his absence, was so much struck with the title, that he took it up and carried it away with him. The clergyman came in, and learning from his wife that he had taken it, went in pursuit of him, being desirous to finish the translation. As he passed a certain house, he saw him, through an open window, engaged with some ungodly associates in a game of chance. The clergyman, thrusting his hand into the window, struck Elijah gently on the shoulder, saying, "What doest thou here, Elijah?" It proved a word in season, and was the means of calling him from the devious paths of sin and folly into the narrow way that leads to life.

Wise Submission

Chap. xx. ver. 31.—His servants said unto him, Behold, now, we have heard that the kings of the house of Israel are merciful kings: let us, I pray thee, put sackloth on our loins, and ropes upon our heads, and go out to the king of Israel; peradventure he will save thy life.

THE Tusculani, a people of Italy, having offended the Romans, Camillus, at the head of a considerable army, marched to subdue them. Conscious of inability to make successful resistance, they declined all thoughts of opposition, set open their gates, and every man applied himself to his proper business, resolving to submit, where they knew it was in vain to contend. Camillus, on entering their city, was struck with the singularity of their conduct, and thus addressed them:—"You only of all people have found out the true method of abating the Roman fury, and your submission has proved your best defence. Upon these terms, we can no more find in our hearts to injure you, than, upon other terms, you could have found power to oppose us." The chief magistrate replied, "We have so sincerely repented of our former folly, that in confidence of that satisfaction to a generous enemy, we are not afraid to acknowledge our fault." The mercy of God in Christ is a powerful encouragement to sinners to return to him. The goodness of God leadeth to repentance.

Envy.

Chap. xxi. ver. 2.—Ahab spake unto Naboth, saying, Give me thy vineyard, that I may have it for a garden of herbs, because it is near unto my house ; and I will give thee for it a better vineyard than it ; or, if it seem good to thee, I will give thee the worth of it in money.

NEAR Potsdam, in the reign of Frederick the Great, was a mill which interfered with a view from the windows of Sans Souci. Annoyed by this eye-sore to his favourite residence, the king sent to inquire the price for which it would be sold by the owner. "For no price," was the reply of the sturdy Prussian ; and in a moment of anger, Frederick gave orders that the mill should be pulled down. "The King may do this," said the miller quietly folding his arms, "but there are laws in Prussia ;" and forthwith he commenced proceedings against the monarch, the result of which was, that the court sentenced Frederick to rebuild the mill, and to pay besides a large sum of money as compensation for the injury which he had done. The King was mortified, but had the magnanimity to say, addressing himself to his courtiers, "I am glad to find that just laws and upright judges exist in my kingdom."—About five or six years ago, the present head of the honest miller's family, who had in due course of time succeeded to the hereditary possession of his little estate, finding himself, after a long struggle with losses occasioned by that war which brought ruin into many a house besides his own, involved in pecuniary difficulties that had become insurmountable, wrote to the present King of Prussia, reminding him of the refusal experienced by Frederick the Great at the hands of his ancestor, and stating that, if his majesty now entertained a similar desire to obtain possession of the property, it would be very agreeable to him, in his present embarrassed circumstances, to sell the mill. The King immediately wrote, with his own hand, the following reply :—

"My dear neighbour—I cannot allow you to sell the mill ; it must remain in your possession as long as one member of your family exists ; for it belongs to the history of Prussia. I lament, however, to hear that you are in circumstances of embarrassment ; and I therefore send you 6000 dollars (about £1000 sterling,) to arrange your affairs, in the hope that this sum will be sufficient for the purpose.

Consider me always your affectionate neighbour,
"FREDERICK WILLIAM."

The Fallen King.

Chap. xxii. ver. 34.—A certain man drew a bow at a venture, and smote the king of Israel between the joints of the harness.

SPEED, in his History of Britain, informs us that Richard I. was besieging a castle with his army, when the besieged offered to surrender if he would grant them quarter. He, however, refused their request, and threatened to hang every one of them. Upon this, a certain soldier on the ramparts charged his bow with a square arrow, and, praying that God would vouchsafe to direct the shot, and deliver the innocent from oppression, he discharged the shaft upon the ranks of the besiegers. The arrow struck the king himself, inflicting a wound of which he soon afterwards died, and the objects of his vengeance were thus delivered.

SECOND BOOK OF KINGS.

Divine Punishment.

Chap. i. ver. 14.—Behold, there came down fire from heaven, and burnt up the two captains of the former fifties with their fifties: therefore let my life be precious in thy sight.

IN 1682, some soldiers came to break up a meeting where Mr. Browning, who had been ejected from Desborough, in Northamptonshire, was, and to apprehend him. The constable of the place, who was present, admonished them to be well-advised in what they did—"For," said he, "when Sir —— was alive, he eagerly prosecuted these meetings, and engaged eight soldiers of the country troop to assist him, whereof myself was one. Sir —— himself is dead; six of the soldiers are dead; some of them were hanged, some of them broke their necks; and I myself fell off my horse, and broke my collar-bone, in the act of persecuting them. This has given me such a warning, that, for my part, I am resolved never to meddle with them more."

Religious Exercises.

Chap. ii. ver. 15.—The sons of the prophets came to meet Elisha.

IN the reign of Queen Elizabeth, there were public theological exercises, called *prophesyings*, which appear to have been beneficial to both ministers and people. Lord Bacon gives the following account of them:—"The ministers within a district did meet upon a week-day, in some principal town, where there was some grave ancient minister, who was president, and an auditory admitted of gentlemen, or other persons of leisure. Then every minister, successively, beginning with the youngest, did handle one and the same part of scripture, spending severally some quarter of an hour, or better, and in the whole some two hours; and so the exercise being begun and concluded with prayer, and the president giving a text for the next meeting, the assembly was dissolved; and this was, as I take it, a fortnight's exercise, which, in my opinion, was the best way to frame and train up preachers to handle the word of God, as it ought to be handled, that hath been practised. For we see orators have their declamations, lawyers have their moods, logicians their sophisms, and every practice of science hath an exercise of erudition and initiation, before men come to the life; only preaching, which is the worthiest, and wherein it is most dangerous to do amiss, wanteth an introduction and is ventured and rushed upon at the first."

Heathen Sacrifice.

Chap. iii. ver. 27.—The king of Moab took his eldest son, that should have reigned in his stead, and offered him for a burnt-offering upon the wall.

MR. BUCHANAN, giving an account of the procession of the idol Juggernaut, says, "After the tower had proceeded some way, a pilgrim announced that he was ready to offer himself a sacrifice to the idol. He laid himself down in the road before the tower, as it was moving along, lying on his face, with his arms stretched forwards. The multitude passed round him, leaving the space clear, and he was crushed to death by the wheels of the tower. A shout of joy was raised to the god. He is said to *smile* when the libation of blood is made. The people throw cowries, or small money, on the body of the victim, in approbation of the deed. He was left to view a considerable time ; and was then carried to a place a little way out of the town, called by the English Golgotha, where the dead bodies are usually cast forth, and where dogs and vultures are ever seen. There I have just been reviewing his remains." Dr. B. adds,—"I beheld another distressing scene at the Place of Skulls,—a poor woman lying dead, or nearly dead ; and her two children by her, looking at the dogs and vultures which were near. The people passed by without noticing the children. I asked them where was their home. They said, 'They had no home, but where their mother was.' Oh, there is no pity at Juggernaut !—no mercy, no tenderness of heart in Molech's kingdom."

Humble Minded.

Chap. iv. 13.—Wouldst thou be spoken for to the king, or to the captain of the host? And she answered, I dwell among mine own people.

JOE MARTIN, an Indian chief now residing in New Brunswick, was interrogated a short time ago, by a professional gentleman who holds an important office under government, whether he would accept the commission of a captain among the Indians, which, he observed, it was in his power to procure for him ; to which the Indian made the following reply :—" Now Joe Martin love God, pray to God ; now Joe Martin humble ; certain not good to make Indian proud ; when Indian proud, him forget God : for this reason Joe Martin never must be captain !" He accordingly declined it.

Gifts Refused.

Chap. v. ver. 16.—As the Lord liveth, before whom I stand, I will receive none. And he urged him to take it ; but he refused.

WHEN great presents were sent to Epaminondas, the celebrated Theban general, he used to observe,—" If the thing you desire be good, I will do it without any bribe, even because it is good : if it be not honest, I will not do it for all the goods in the world." He was so great a contemner of riches, that, when he died, he left not enough to discharge the expenses of his funeral.

Feeding the Adversary.

Chap. vi. ver. 22.—Set bread and water before them, that they may eat and drink, and go to their master.

AFTER the dispersion of the Spanish Armada in 1588, Joan Lomes de Medina, who had been general of twenty hulks, was, with about two hundred and sixty men, driven in a vessel to Anstruther in Scotland, after suffering great hunger and cold for six or seven days. Notwithstanding the object for which this fleet had been sent, and the oppressive conduct of the Spaniards to the Scottish merchants who traded with them, these men were most humanely treated. Mr. James Melvil, the minister, told the Spanish officer first sent on shore, that they would find nothing among them but Christianity and works of mercy. The laird of Anstruther, and a great number of the neighbouring gentlemen, entertained the officers ; and the inhabitants gave the soldiers and mariners kail, pottage, and fish ;—the minister having addressed his flock, as Elisha did the King of Israel in Samaria, "Give them bread and water."

Physical and Spiritual Life.

Chap. vii. ver. 4.—If we sit still here, we die. Now therefore come, and let us fall unto the host of the Syrians : if they save us alive, we shall live ; and if they kill us, we shall but die.

"IT is just a year this day," says Mrs Judson, "since I entertained a hope in Christ. About this time in the evening, when reflecting on the words of the lepers, 'If we enter into the city, then the famine is in the city, and we shall die there ; and if we sit still here, we die also ; and felt that if I returned to the world, I should surely perish ; if I staid where I then was, I should perish ; and I could but perish, if I threw myself on the mercy of Christ. Then came light, and relief, and comfort, such as I never knew before."

Tampering with Principle.

Chap. viii. ver. 13.—Hazael said, But what! is thy servant a dog, that he should do this great thing?

ONE of the early Christians, on being asked by a friend to accompany him to the amphitheatre, to witness the gladiatorial combats with wild beasts, expressed his utmost abhorrence of the sport, and refused to witness a scene, condemned alike by humanity and Christianity. Overcome at length by the continued and pressing solicitations of his friend, whom he did not wish to disoblige, he consented to go ; but determined that he would close his eyes as soon as he had taken his seat, and keep them closed during the whole time that he was in the amphitheatre. At some particular display of strength and skill by one of the combatants, a loud shout of applause was raised by the spectators, when the Christian almost involuntarily opened his eyes ; being once open, he found it difficult to close them again ; he became interested in the fate of the gladiator, who was then engaged with a lion. He returned home, professing to dislike, as his principles required him to do, these cruel games ; but still his imagination ever and anon reverted to the scenes he had unintentionally witnessed. He was again solicited by his friend, who perceived the conquest that had been made, to see the sport. He found less difficulty now than before in consenting. He went, sat with his eyes open, and enjoyed the spectacle. Again and again he took his seat with the pagan crowd ; till at length he became a constant attendant at the amphitheatre, abandoned his Christian principles, relapsed to idolatry, died a heathen, and left a fatal proof of the deceitfulness of sin.

Deferred Retribution.

Chap. ix. ver. 31.—Had Zimri peace, who slew his master?

MR. FORDYCE, in his Dialogues on Education, relates the following striking incident, which he says occurred in a neighbouring state. A jeweller, a man of good character and considerable wealth, having occasion to leave home on business at some distance, took with him a servant. He had with him some of his best jewels, and a large sum of money. This was known to the servant, who, urged by cupidity, murdered his master on the road, rifled him of his jewels and money, and suspending a large stone round his neck, threw him into the nearest canal. With the booty he had thus gained, the servant set off to a distant part of the country, where he had reason to believe that neither he nor his master was known. There he began to trade, at first in a very humble way, that his obscurity might screen him from observation; and in the course of many years he seemed to rise, by the natural progress of business, into wealth and consideration, so that his good fortune appeared at once the effect and reward of industry and virtue. Of these he counterfeited the appearance so well, that he grew into great credit, married into a good family, and was admitted into a share of the government of the town. He rose from one post to another, till at length he was chosen chief magistrate. In this office he maintained a fair character, and continued to fill it with no small applause, both as governor and judge; until one day, as he presided on the bench with some of his brethren, a criminal was brought before him, who was accused of murdering his master. The evidence came out fully: the jury brought in their verdict that the prisoner was guilty, and the whole assembly waited the sentence of the court with suspense. The president appeared to be in unusual disorder and agitation of mind; his colour changed often; at length he rose from his seat, and descending from the bench, placed himself close to the unfortunate man at the bar, to the no small astonishment of all present. "You see before you," said he, addressing himself to those who had sat on the bench with him, "a striking instance of the just award of heaven, which this day, after thirty years' concealment, presents to you a greater criminal than the man just now found guilty." He then made a full confession of his guilt, and of all its aggravations: —"Nor can I feel," continued he, "any relief from the agonies of an awakened conscience, but by requiring that justice be forthwith done against me in the most public and solemn manner." We may easily suppose the amazement of all the assembly, and especially of his fellow judges. However, they proceeded, upon his confession, to pass sentence upon him, and he died with all the symptoms of a penitent mind.

Obtrusive Godliness.

Chap. x. ver. 16.—Jehu said, Come with me, and see my zeal for the Lord.

MR JOHN FOX, the author of the "Book of Martyrs," was once met by a woman who showed him a book she was carrying, and said, "See you not that I am going to a sermon?" The good man replied, "If you will be ruled by me, go home, for you will do little good to-day at church." "When, then," asked she, "would you counsel me to go?" His reply was—"When you tell no one beforehand."

God and the King.

Chap. xi. ver. 12.—He brought forth the king's son, and put the crown upon him, and gave him the testimony: and they made him king and anointed him; and they clapped their hands, and said, God save the king.

AT the coronation of his Majesty George III., after the anointing was over in the abbey, and the crown put upon his head with great shouting, the two archbishops came to hand him down from the throne to receive the sacrament. His Majesty told them he would not go to the Lord's Supper, and partake of that ordinance, with the crown upon his head; for he looked upon himself, when appearing before the King of kings, in no other character than in that of a humble Christian. The bishops replied, that although there was no precedent for this, it should be complied with. Immediately he put off his crown, and laid it aside; he then desired that the same should be done with respect to the queen. It was answered, that her crown was so pinned on her head, that it could not be easily taken off; to which the king replied, "Well, let it be reckoned a part of her dress, and in no other light." "When I saw and heard this," says the narrator, "it warmed my heart towards him; and I could not help thinking, that there would be something good found about him towards the Lord God of Israel."

Personal Influence.

Chap. xii. ver. 2.—Jehoash did that which was right in the sight of the Lord all his days, wherein Jehoiada the priest instructed him.

THE late Dr. Finlay, president of Princetown College, had once in his congregation, a man over whom intemperate drinking had got the dominion. But when the pastor discovered the fact, he applied himself most anxiously to the reformation of the wanderer. His commanding eloquence in the pulpit was seconded by most earnest and impressive appeals in private. Everything was united in Dr. Finlay, to shew the utmost effect of talent and piety—the power of his personal presence—his watchful care and tender solicitude—and, when he preached on the end of the drunkard, the thunder of his eloquence, the effect was irresistible, and the parishioner abstained from liquor many years. At length Dr. Finlay fell sick, and the unhappy man, in his turn, showed a corresponding anxiety for his minister's health. He often sent to inquire how the president was; and as the accounts became more unfavourable, his anxiety became distressing. At length the answer came, that Dr. Finlay was dead: "Then," said he, "I am a lost man." He returned to his house, resumed his cups, and soon drank himself to death.

The Death of the Godly.

Chap. xiii. ver. 14.—Elisha was fallen sick of his sickness whereof he died: and Joash the king of Israel came down unto him, and wept over his face, and said, O my father, my father! the chariot of Israel, and the horsemen thereof!

THE Rev. John Gibb of Cleish, in Fifeshire, at one time travelled during a storm to the extremity of his parish, to comfort a godly man in his dying moments. The cottage being solitary, and owing to the inclemency of the weather, no other person venturing that evening to visit the family, he watched with them all night, performing with alacrity every kind office in his power; and when he returned home next day, remarked that it was no small honour to sit up a winter's night with an heir of glory, or, (in his own homely but expressive language,) with *a piece of heaven's plenishin'*.

Vanity of Worldly Glory.

Chap. xiv. ver. 10.—Thou hast indeed smitten Edom, and thine heart hath lifted thee up; glory of this, and tarry at home; for why shouldest thou meddle to thy hurt, that thou shouldest fall, even thou, and Judah with thee?

WHEN Pyrrhus, King of Epirus, was making great preparations for his intended expedition into Italy, Cineas, the philosopher, took a favourable opportunity of addressing him thus:—" The Romans, Sir, are reported to be a warlike and victorious people; but if God permit us to overcome them, what use shall we make of the victory?"—"Thou askest," said Pyrrhus, "a thing that is self-evident. The Romans once conquered, no city will resist us; we shall then be masters of all Italy." Cineas added—"And having subdued Italy, what shall we do next?" Pyrrhus, not yet aware of his intentions, replied,—"Sicily next stretches out her arms to receive us." "That is very probable," said Cineas, "but will the possession of Sicily put an end to the war?" "God grant us success in that," answered Pyrrhus, "and we shall make these only the forerunners of greater things; for then Lybia and Carthage will soon be ours; and these things being completed, none of our enemies can offer any farther resistance." "Very true," added Cineas, "for then we may easily regain Macedon, and make an absolute conquest of Greece; and when all these are in our possession, what shall we do then?"— Pyrrhus, smiling, answered, "Why then, my dear friend, we will live at our ease, drink all day long, and amuse ourselves with cheerful conversation." "Well, Sir," said Cineas, "and why may we not do all this *now*, and without the labour and hazard of enterprise so laborious and uncertain?" Pyrrhus, however, unwilling to take the advice of the philosopher, ardently engaged in these ambitious pursuits, and at last perished in them.

Cruel Slaughter.

Chap. xv. ver 16.—Menahem smote Tiphsah, and all that were therein, and the coasts thereof from Tirzah: because they opened not to him, therefore he smote it.

"IT was in the spring of 1799," says Dr. Russell, "that the French general (Bonaparte) who had been informed of certain preparations against him in the pashalic of Acre, resolved to cross the desert which divides Egypt from Palestine at the head of ten thousand chosen men. El Arish soon fell into his hands, the garrison of which were permitted to retire, on condition that they should not serve again during the war. Gaza likewise yielded, without much opposition, to the overwhelming force by which it was attacked. Jaffa set the first example of a vigorous resistance; the slaughter was tremendous; and Bonaparte, to intimidate the towns from showing a similar spirit, gave it up to plunder, and the other excesses of an enraged soldiery. A more melancholy scene followed—the massacre of nearly four thousand prisoners who had lain down their arms. Napoleon alleged, that these were the very individuals who had given their parole at El Arish, and had violated their faith by appearing against him in the fortress which had just fallen. On this pretext he commanded them all to be put to death, and thereby brought a stain upon his reputation which no casuistry on the part of his admirers, and no consideration of expediency, military or political, will ever succeed in removing."

Princes and Priests.

Chap. xvi. ver. 11.—Urijah the priest built an altar according to all that King Ahaz had sent from Damascus.

"I WAS sorry to see," says Mr. Hervey in a letter to Mr. Ryland, "from a paragraph in a late newspaper, that, by the command of the prince, the tragedy of Douglas was reacted at the theatre-royal. Ah! this one source, one copious source, of our miseries! If *princes will encourage* such corrupting sources of entertainment, there never will be wanting *ministers of the gospel to write for them*, and magistrates to attend them. O that the Prince of the kings of the earth would give our rulers, and all that are in authority, to discern the things that are excellent!"

Taught to fear God.

Chap. xvii ver. 28.—One of the priests came and dwelt in Bethel, and taught them how they should fear the Lord.

WHEN the Rev. Mr Charles, of Bala in Wales, met a poor man or woman on the road, he used to stop his horse, and make the inquiry—"Can you read the Bible?" He was so much in the habit of doing this, that he became everywhere known from this practice. "The gentleman who kindly asked the poor people about the Bible and their souls," was Mr. Charles. Meeting one day with an old man, on one of the mountains, he said to him,—"You are an old man, and very near another world." "Yes," said he, "and I hope I am going to heaven." "Do you know the road there,—do you know the word of God?" "Pray, are you Mr. Charles?" said the old man. He suspected who he was from his questions. He was frequently thus accosted when asking the poor people he met with about their eternal concerns. "Pray, are you Mr. Charles?" was often the inquiry. When he had time, he scarcely ever passed by a poor man on the road, without talking to him about his soul, and his knowledge of the Bible. When he found any ignorant of the Word of God, and not able to read it, he represented to them, in a kind and simple manner, the duty and necessity of becoming acquainted with it, and feelingly and compassionately set before them the awful state of those who leave the world without knowing the word of God, and the way of saving the soul. He sometimes succeeded in persuading them to learn to read; and the good he thus did was no doubt very great.

Presents in the East.

Chap. xviii. ver. 31.—Thus saith the king of Assyria, Make an agreement with me by a present.

AMONG eastern nations it has always been usual to bring presents when people visit one another; they never appear before a prince or great man without having something to offer. Modern travellers tell us that, even when poor people visit, they bring a flower, or fruit, or some such trifle. One person mentions a present of fifty radishes; and when Bruce, the Abyssinian traveller, had agreed, at the request of a chief, to take a poor sick Arab with him for a great distance, the poor man presented him with a dirty cloth containing about ten dates. Mr. Bruce remarks, that he mentions this to show how important and necessary presents are considered in the east; whether they be dates or diamonds, a man thinks it necessary to offer something.

Profane Swearing

Chap. xix. ver. 22.—Whom hast thou reproached and blasphemed? and against whom hast thou exalted thy voice, and lifted up thine eyes on high? even against the Holy One of Israel.

MR. HARRIS, the minister of Hanwell, during the civil wars, frequently had military officers quartered at his house. A party of them, being unmindful of the reverence due to the holy name of God, indulged themselves in swearing. The doctor noticed this, and on the following Sabbath preached from these words:— "Above all things, my brethren, swear not." This so enraged the soldiers, who judged the sermon was intended for them, that they swore they would shoot him if he preached on the subject again. He was not, however, to be intimidated; and on the following Sabbath, he not only preached from the same text, but inveighed in still stronger terms against the vice of swearing. As he was preaching, a soldier levelled his carbine at him; but he went on to the conclusion of his sermon, without the slightest fear or hesitation.

The Spiritual House

Chap. xx. ver. 1.—Set thine house in order; for thou shalt die, and not live.

A WOMAN in Suffolk was taken ill, with but small hopes of recovery. She had heard or read something about *setting her house in order*, and thinking it referred only to earthly things, said to those about her, she blessed God she had arranged all her matters, and got everything to her liking, except putting a few more feathers into one of her beds. If her attention was directed to worldly affairs only, while the concerns of her soul were overlooked, there is reason to fear she was ill prepared for dying.

Evil Enchantments.

Chap. xxi. ver. 6.—He observed times, and used enchantments, and dealt with familiar spirits and wizards.

IN a book entitled, "A guide to grand jurymen, in cases of witchcraft," written by Mr. Bernard more than two hundred years ago, is the following relation:—"Mr. Edmunds of Cambridge was one that, for a time, professed to help men to goods or money stolen; and was once by the heads of the university questioned for witchcraft, as he confessed to me, when he had better learned Christ, and had given over his practice that way. He told me two things, (besides many other, in a whole afternoon's discourse at Castle Kiningham, in Essex,) never to be forgotten:—1st, That by his art he could find out him that stole from another, but not himself. 2d, That the ground of this art was not so certain but that he might mistake; and so peradventure accuse an honest man instead of the offender, and therefore gave it over; albeit, he said he might have made two hundred pounds per annum of his skill."

The Book of God.

Chap. xxii. ver. 10. Shaphan the scribe showed the king, saying, Hilkiah the priest hath delivered me a book: and Shaphan read it before the king.

"I RESIDE," says a Scripture reader in Ireland, "with a very friendly family, in a large and well-inhabited village, where all are Roman Catholics, except two families professedly Protestant. The whole of this population never heard of the Bible, and are, consequently, very dark and ignorant. On the Sabbath, I read a considerable portion of it to the family in the morning, and in the afternoon. They were greatly surprised to see so small a book contain such wonderful things, and inquired how I obtained it, and what country it came from? I informed them it was the Book of God; that it was written by the holy Prophets of the Lord, many hundred years ago; and that it contained an account of the nativity, life, and death of the Son of God, &c. They were all perfectly astonished, and after I had read a few chapters in the beginning of Matthew, the man of the house ran out in haste to two of his next door neighbours, and brought them in to see and hear "the Book of God," (for by this name my little Bible is now known.) These individuals also expressed their surprise, and, after hearing me read of the birth, miracles, and death of our Saviour they went out and brought their wives to hear the same glorious news."

Leaving the Dead Alone.

Chap. xxiii. ver. 18.—Let him alone: let no man move his bones. So they let his bones alone, with the bones of the prophet that came out of Samaria.

WHILE the troops of Charles V. were quartered at Wirtenberg, in 1547, a year after Luther's death, a soldier gave the reformer's effigy, in the church of the castle, two stabs with his dagger; and the Spaniards earnestly desired that his tomb might be pulled down, and his bones dug up and burnt; but the emperor observed,—"I have nothing farther to do with Luther; he has henceforth another Judge, whose jurisdiction it is not lawful for me to usurp. Know that I make no war with the dead, but with the living, who still make war with me." He would not, therefore, permit his tomb to be demolished; and forbade any attempt of that nature, upon pain of death.

Bloody Cruelty.

Chap. xxiv. ver. 4.—He filled Jerusalem with innocent blood, which the Lord would not pardon.

CHARLES IX. of France was a cruel and persecuting monarch, (witness the massacre at Paris in 1572,) and died in a very wretched state. He expired, bathed in his own blood, which burst from his veins, and in his last moments he exclaimed,—"What blood! —what murders!—I know not where I am!—how will all this end? —what shall I do?—I am lost for ever!—I know it!"

Kindness versus Pride.

Chap. xxv. ver. 27, 28.—Evil-merodach, king of Babylon, in the year that he began to reign, did lift up the head of Jehoiachin, king of Judah, out of prison: and he spake kindly to him.

MR HOWARD, the philanthropist, was once honoured with a visit from the governor of Upper Austria, accompanied by his countess. The governor asked him what was the state of the prisons in the province of Upper Austria.—"The worst," he replied, "in all Germany, particularly in the condition of the female prisoners; and I recommend your countess to visit them personally, as the best means of rectifying the abuses in their management." "I!" said the countess, haughtily, "I go to prisons!" and instantly both descended the stair-case so rapidly, as to alarm him lest some accident should befal them. But notwithstanding the precipitancy of their retreat, he called after her in a loud voice, "Madam, remember that you are a woman yourself, and must soon, like the most miserable female in the dungeon, inhabit a small space of that earth from which you equally originated."

FIRST BOOK OF CHRONICLES.

Kings and their Ways.

Chap. i. ver. 50.—When Baal-hanan was dead, Hadad reigned in his stead.

ROBERT, the eldest son of William the Conquerer, was a prince who inherited all the bravery of his family and nation, but was rather bold than prudent, rather enterprising than politic. Earnest after fame, and even impatient that his father should stand in the way, he aspired to that independence to which his temper, as well as some circumstances in his situation, conspired to invite him. He had formerly, it seems, been promised by his father the government of Maine, a province of France, which had submitted to William, and was also declared successor to the dukedom of Normandy. However, when he came to demand an execution of these engagements, he received an absolute denial ; (of the king's breach of promise we do not approve), the monarch shrewdly observed, that *it was not his custom to throw off his clothes till he went to bed.*

Giving in Marriage.

Chap. ii. ver. 35.—Sheshan gave his daughter to Jarha his servant to wife.

HARMER remarks, that the people of the East frequently marry their slaves to their daughters, when they have no male issue, and those daughters are what we call great fortunes : That Hassan, who was Kiaia of the Asaphs of Cairo, that is to say, the colonel of four or five thousand men who go under that name, was the slave of a predecessor in that office, the famous Kamel, and married his daughter : for Kamel, according to the custom of the country, gave him one of his daughters in marriage, and left him, at his death, one part of the great riches he had amassed in the course of a long and prosperous life. "What Sheshan then did," adds Harmer, "was, perhaps, not so extraordinary as we may have imagined, but perfectly conformable to old Eastern customs, if not to the arrangements of Moses ; at least it is, we see, just the same with what is now practised."

Scripture Biography.

Chap. iii. ver. 5.—These were born unto David ; Shimea, and Shobab, and Nathan, and Solomon.

A YORKSHIRE priest, in an alehouse which he used to frequent, spoke very disrespectfully of Archbishop Cranmer, saying, that he had no more learning than a goose. Lord Cromwell, being informed of this, committed the priest to Fleet prison. When he had been there for a few weeks, he sent a relation of his to the archbishop to beg his pardon, and to sue for a discharge. Cranmer immediately sent for him, and, after a gentle reproof, asked the priest whether he knew him ? The priest replied, "No." He asked him why he should then make so free with his character. The priest excused himself by stating that he was in drink ; but this Cranmer said was a double fault. He told the priest, that if he were inclined to try his abilities as a scholar, he should have liberty to oppose him in any science he pleased. The priest humbly asked his pardon, and confessed himself to be very ignorant, and to understand nothing but his mother tongue. "No doubt, then," said Cranmer, "you are well versed in the English Bible, and can answer any questions out of that; pray tell me who was David's father?" The priest, after some hesitation, told him he could not recollect his name. "Tell me, then," said Cranmer, "who was Solomon's father?" The poor priest replied, that he had no skill in *genealogies*, and could not tell. The archbishop then, advising him to frequent *alehouses* less, and his *study* more, and admonishing him not to accuse others for want of learning, till he was master of some himself, set him at liberty, and sent him home to his cure.

Evil Doing.

Chap. iv. ver. 10.—Jabez called on the God of Israel, saying, O that thou wouldest keep me from evil, that it may not grieve me! And God granted his request.

A MAN who was executed for the crime of murder, said in his last moments,—"Oh, if I had gone to prayer that morning when I committed the sin for which I am now to die, O Lord God, I believe thou wouldest have kept back my hands from that sin."

God in the Battle.

Chap. v. ver. 20.—They were helped against them, and the Hagarites were delivered into their hand, and all that were with them: for they cried to God in the battle, and he was entreated of them; because they put their trust in him.

"THIS day is one of the greatest Ebenezers in my life," says Colonel Blackadder in his Diary, after the battle of Malplaquet. "We have fought a battle, and, by the mercy and goodness of God, have obtained a great and glorious victory. We attacked the enemy in their camp, a strong camp, and strongly entrenched by two days' working. The battle began about seven in the morning, and continued till about three in the afternoon. It was the most deliberate, solemn, and well-ordered battle that ever I saw; a noble and fine disposition, and as finely executed. Every one was at his post; and I never saw troops engage with more cheerfulness, boldness, and resolution. For my own part, I was nobly and richly supplied, as I have always been on such occasions, with liberal supplies of grace and strength as the occasions of the day called for. I never had a more pleasant day in my life. My mind was stayed, trusting in God; I was kept in perfect peace. All went well with me; and not being in a hurry and hot action, I had time for plying the throne of grace. God gave me faith and communion with himself, sometimes prayer and sometimes praise, as the various turns of Providence gave occasion; sometimes for the public, sometimes for myself. The next morning I went to view the field of battle, to get a preaching from the dead, which might have been very edifying; for in all my life I have not seen the dead lie so thick as they were in some places. The potsherds of the earth are dashed together: and God makes the nations a scourge to each other, to work his holy ends, and to sweep off sinners from the earth. It is a wonder to me the British escaped so cheap, who are the most heaven-daring sinners in the whole army; but God's judgments are a great deep. I bless thee, O Lord, who bringest me back in peace, while the carcases of others are left a prey in the fields to the beasts and birds."

The Service of Song.

Chap. vi. ver. 31.—*These are they whom David set over the service of song in the house of the Lord.*

"DR. WATT," says Mr. Montgomery, "may almost be called the inventor of hymns in our language; for he so far departed from all precedent, that few of his compositions resemble those of his forerunners.—Every Sabbath, in every region of the earth where his native tongue is spoken, thousands and tens of thousands of voices are sending the sacrifices of prayer and praise to God, in the strains which he prepared for them a century ago; yea, every day 'he being dead yet speaketh' by the lips of posterity, in these sacred lays, some of which may not cease to be sung by the ransomed on their journey to Zion, so long as the language of Britain endures— a language now spreading through all lands whither commerce, civilization, or the gospel, are carried by merchants, colonists, or missionaries."

Mourning Many Days.

Chap. vii. ver. 22.—*Ephraim their father mourned many days, and his brethren came to comfort him.*

THE eldest son of the Rev. Legh Richmond, having, contrary to his father's wishes, preferred a sea-faring life, he went on board the Arniston, a merchant vessel, for Ceylon, which he reached in 1815. More than a twelvemonth after, Mr. Richmond received the painful account that the vessel had been wrecked, and that all on board had perished, with the exception of six persons, whose names were specified, but that of his son was not among the number. The whole family went into mourning; and the father sorrowed for his lost child with a sorrow unmitigated by the communication of any cheering circumstance as to the state of his mind, and his fitness for so sudden a change. Three months afterwards, a letter was delivered to Mr. Richmond, in the hand-writing of the very son whom he mourned as dead, announcing that he was alive—that circumstances had prevented his setting sail in the Arniston, of whose fate he seemed to be unconscious; and communicating details of his present engagements and future prospects! The transition of feeling to which the receipt of this letter gave rise produced an effect almost as overwhelming as that which the report of his death had occasioned. The family mourning was laid aside, and Mr. Richmond trusted he might recognize, in the signal interposition of Divine Providence, a ground for hope that his child's present deliverance was a pledge of that spiritual recovery, which was now alone wanting to fill up the measure of his gratitude and praise.

Many Sons.

Chap. viii. ver. 40.—*The sons of Ulam were mighty men of valour— and had many sons.*

THE Rev. Moses Browne, an excellent minister, was thus addressed by a friend :—" You have a very large family, Sir; you have just as many children as the patriarch Jacob had." "True," answered the good old divine, "and I have also Jacob's God to provide for them."

Cups of Union.

Chap. ix. ver. 28.—*Certain of them had the charge of the ministering vessels, that they should bring them in and out by tale.*

MR. JOHN BARNSTON, in the reign of Charles I., was the judge of a certain consistory court, when a churchwarden was sued for a chalice which had been stolen out of his house. "Well," said the doctor, "I am sorry the cup of union should be the cause of difference among you. I doubt not but either the thief will, out of remorse, restore it, or some other, as good, will be sent to you." Accordingly, the doctor, by his secret charity, provided another.

Unrighteous Inquisitiveness.

Chap. x. ver. 13. Saul died for his transgression, and also for asking counsel of one that had a familiar spirit, to inquire of it.

LORD BYRON, when a boy, was warned by a fortune-teller, that he should die in the 37th year of his age. That idea haunted him, and in his last illness, he mentioned it as precluding all hope of his recovery. It repressed, his physician says, that energy of spirit so necessary for nature in struggling with disease. He talked of two days of the week as his unlucky days, on which nothing would tempt him to commence any matter of importance; and mentioned as an excuse for indulging such fancies, that his friend Shelly, the poet, had a familiar who had warned him that he should perish by drowning, and such was the fate of that highly gifted but misguided man.

Slaying Wild Animals.

Chap. xi. ver. 22.—Benaiah went down and slew a lion in a pit in a snowy day.

IN the beginning of May, 1815, the British army in India, from the hot winds and bad weather, became so sickly, that the troops were ordered into quarters. "On the 6th of May," says the brave officer who is the subject of this anecdote, "we passed through a forest, and encamped on its skirts, near a small village, the head man of which entreated us to destroy a large tiger, which had killed seven of his men; was in the daily habit of stealing his cattle; and had that morning wounded his son. Another officer and myself agreed to attempt the destruction of this monster. We immediately ordered seven elephants, and went in quest of the animal, which we found sleeping under a bush. The noise of the elephants awoke him, when he made a furious charge upon us, and my elephant received him with her shoulder; the other six turned about and ran off, notwithstanding the exertions of their riders, and left me in the above situation. I had seen many tigers, and had been at the killing of them, but never so large a one as this. The elephant shook him off; I then fired two balls, and the tiger fell; but, again recovering himself, he made a spring at me. I escaped him, and he seized the elephant by her hind leg, then receiving a kick from her, and another ball from me, he let go his hold, and he fell a second time. Thinking he was by this time disabled, I very unfortunately dismounted, intending to put an end to his existence with my pistols, when the monster, who was only crouching to take another spring, made it that moment, and caught me in his mouth; but it pleased God to give strength and presence of mind; I immediately fired into his body, and finding that had little effect, used all my force; happily disengaged my arm; and then directing my pistol to his heart, I at length succeeded in destroying him, after receiving twenty-five severe wounds."

Good and Loyal.

Chap. xii. ver. 39.—They were with David three days, eating and drinking: for their brethren had prepared for them.

AT the restoration of Charles II., the Rev. Roger Turner preached a sermon, which concluded with the following excellent admonitions :—" Do not drown your reason, to prove your loyalty—pray for the King's health, but drink only for your own. Go now and ring your bells; but beware in the meantime, that you hold not fast Solomon's cords of sin, or the prophet's cart-ropes of iniquity, and thereby pull down judgment upon your heads. You may kindle bonfires in the streets, but beware that you kindle not the fire of God's displeasure against you by your sins. In a word, for God's sake, for your King's sake, for your own soul's sake, be *good*, that you may be *loyal!"*

Of the Lord.

Chap. xiii. ver. 2.—David said unto all the congregation of Israel, If it seem good unto you, and that it be of the Lord our God, &c.

SHORTLY after the defeat of La Hogue, James II. being in conversation with the superior of a convent of nuns, the lady took occasion to express her sorrow, that it had not pleased God to hear the prayers so many persons had offered up for his success in that expedition. The king making no reply, the abbess began to repeat what she had said, when the king interrupted her—" Madame, I heard very well what you said : and the reason why I made no answer was, that I was unwilling to contradict you, and be obliged to let you see I am not of your opinion ; we seem to think, that what you asked was better than what it pleased God to do; whereas, I think what he orders is best; and that, indeed, nothing is well done but what is done by him."

Fame.

Chap. xiv. ver. 17.—The fame of David went out into all lands.

BOERHAAVE, who died in 1738, in his 70th year, was the most celebrated physician of his age. His private virtues, extenisve knowledge, and distinguished reputation, have been rarely equalled, and never surpassed. His celebrity as a public teacher in the University of Leyden drew together crowds of pupils from all the surrounding countries. A person in China wrote a letter to him, addressed in the following general manner :—" To the illustrious Boerhaave, Europe ;" which, notwithstanding, was as readily brought to him, as if his residence had been particularly specified.

The King of Kings.

Chap. xv. ver. 29.—Michal—saw King David dancing and playing ; and she despised him in her heart.

THE Duke of Norfolk, seeing Sir Thomas More, when he was Lord Chancellor, sitting in the choir in his parish church, singing the service, said, "Fie, fie, my lord! the Lord Chancellor of England a parish priest, and a paltry singing man? You dishonour the King !" —"No, my lord," replied Sir Thomas, "it is no shame for the King if his servant serve his Sovereign and Saviour, who is the King of kings."

Household Devotion.

Chap. xvi. ver. 43.—David returned to bless his house.

BARON AUGUSTE DE STAEL, grandson of Monsieur Neckar, Minister of Finance in France, was an experimental farmer at Coppet, on the borders of Switzerland, and a truly pious man. He visited England in quest of the means of improving his race of horses; and one morning, at an early hour, he called upon Mr. Gate, who was to assist him with his advice in the purchase of some horses to take to Coppet. When introduced, he entered directly into conversation upon the immediate object of his visit, and which was a very interesting one, for both of them were warmly attached to the pursuits of agriculture. His friend, however, appeared to the baron to be somewhat embarrassed, and at length begged to be excused for a little while, only a short half hour; which he invited the baron to pass till his return, in looking over some engravings which he placed before him. The native politeness of the baron felt the great delicacy of having thus put his friend to inconvenience, and he expressed his sorrow that he had thereby rendered it necessary for him to apologise. His friend replied, "You must know then that this is just the time for our morning family prayers. My family and my servants are all now assembled, and they wait only for me. You will be good enough, therefore, to pardon my request to leave you; so soon as this duty, which we never omit, shall be concluded, I will return immediately to you." The baron at once said, "I have also a favour to beg of you: shall I be acting indiscreetly if I ask permission to join your family, and so unite with them in this pious duty?" His friend granted with pleasure what the baron had asked with so much manifest desire, and he became witness of the serious and edifying manner in which the assembled family listened to the reading of the Scriptures, and to the prayers offered by his friend the head of the family. "How valuable for me were those delicious moments," said the baron, "which I passed in the bosom of that happy family, where, when I entered, I had no other expectation than to receive some advice upon the purchase of horses!"

Unlooked for Honour.

Chap. xvii. ver. 16.—Who am I—that thou hast brought me hitherto?

THE works of the late Rev. John Newton were introduced to the notice of King George III. by the Earl of Dartmouth; and the high estimation in which his Majesty held them was communicated by the same nobleman to Mr. N., when the worthy minister observed, "Who would have thought that I should ever preach to majesty!"

Judgment and Justice.

Chap. xviii. ver. 14.—David—executed justice and judgment among all his people.

LORD CHIEF JUSTICE HOLT was one of the ablest and most upright judges that ever presided in a court of justice. Such was the integrity and firmness of his mind, that he could never be brought to swerve in the least from what he esteemed law and justice. He was remarkably strenuous in nobly asserting, and as rigorously supporting, the liberties of the subject, to which he paid the greatest regard; and would not even suffer a reflection, tending to depreciate them, to pass uncensured, or without a severe reprimand. He lost his place, as Recorder of London, for refusing to expound the law suitably to the King's designs. He asserted the law with such intrepidity, that he incurred, by turns, the indignation of both Houses of Parliament.

Behaving Valiantly.

Chap. xix. ver. 13.—Be of good courage, and let us behave ourselves valiantly for our people, and for the cities of our God.

AN officer of distinction and tried valour refused to accept a challenge sent by a young officer, but returned the following answer:—" I fear not your sword, but the sword of my God's anger. I dare venture my life in a good cause, but cannot hazard my soul in a bad one. I will charge up to the cannon's mouth for the good of my country, but I want courage to storm hell!"

A Giant.

Chap. xx. ver. 6.—At Gath, there was a man of great stature.

MAXIMINUS, the Roman Emperor, was a man of gigantic stature, being reported to have been upwards of eight feet high, and of proportionable size and strength. He is said to have eaten forty pounds of flesh, and to have drunk six gallons of wine, each day. He was of a savage and cruel disposition, and a persecutor of the Christians.

Contributing.

Chap xxi. ver. 24.—I will not take that which is thine for the Lord, nor offer burnt offerings without cost.

A LITTLE girl at Lyons, in France, asked her mother to give her a small sum of money to subscribe to the Bible Society of that city. The mother, who was always anxious that her child should consider the ground of her actions, explained to her that she would not really herself be a subscriber unless it was with her own money; and suggested to her that she might earn a trifle, if she liked to do some sewing beyond her usual work. The little girl gladly undertook this, and thus became a monthly subscriber *with her own money.*

Spending for God.

Chap. xxii. ver. 14.—Behold, in my trouble I have prepared for the house of the Lord an hundred thousand talents of gold, &c.

LADY HUNTINGDON, with an income of only £1200 a-year, did much for the cause of religion. She maintained the college she had erected, at her sole expense; she erected chapels in most parts of the kingdom; and she supported ministers who were sent to preach in various parts of the world.—A minister of the gospel, and a person from the country, once called on her ladyship. When they came out, the countryman turned his eyes towards the house, and, after a short pause, exclaimed, "What a lesson! Can a person of her noble birth, nursed in the lap of grandeur, live in such a house, so meanly furnished,—and shall I, a tradesman, be surrounded with luxury and elegance? From this moment I shall hate my house, my furniture, and myself, for spending so little for God, and so much in folly"

Melody in the Heart.

Chap. xxiii. ver. 30.—To stand every morning to thank and praise the Lord.

ONE of the Moravian brethren, going very early one morning to let out their sheep, heard uncommonly sweet singing in a tent, and drawing near, found it was the head of the family performing his morning devotions with his people. Beckoning to the others to come, "We stood still," say the brethren in their diary, "and listened to this sweet melody with hearts exceedingly moved, and with eyes filled with tears, and thought these people were, no longer than two years ago, savage heathens, and now they sing to the Lamb that was slain, so charmingly that it strikes the inmost soul."

Casting Lots.

Chap. xxiv ver. 31.—These likewise cast lots.

JOSEPHUS, the Jewish historian, on one occasion, had taken refuge in a cave, with forty desperate persons, who determined to perish rather than to yield to their enemies, and who proposed to kill him first, as the most honourable man in the company. When he could not divert them from their frantic resolution of dying, he had no other refuge than to engage them to draw lots who should be killed, the one after the other; and, at last, only he and another remained, whom he persuaded to surrender to the Romans.

Equal before God.

Chap. xxv ver. 8.—As well the small as the great, the teacher as the scholar.

LEWIS the IX., King of France, was found instructing a poor kitchen-boy; and being asked why he did so, replied, "The meanest person hath a soul as precious as my own, and bought with the same blood of Christ."

Dedication to the Lord's Cause.

Chap. xxvi. ver. 27.—Out of the spoils won in battles did they dedicate to maintain the house of the Lord.

MR. HOPPER, one of the assistant missionaries to the Choctaw Nation, in North America, relates in his journal the following affecting instance of benevolence while at Steubenville:—"What most of all affected our hearts was, that a poor African, who, it is believed, is a devout servant of God, came forward, and gave a coat, obtained by making brooms after performing his task in the field. Mr. M'Curdy informed us, that both that man and his wife are praying souls. They are slaves. O! is it not truly animating, is it not enough to touch the tenderest sensibilities of the soul, to see an Ethiopian in such circumstances, thus moved at hearing the Macedonian cry, and thus extending the hand of charity. Should every professed disciple of Christ make such sacrifices as did this poor African, at no distant period would the precious gospel be preached to all nations."

Kings' Counsellors.

Chap. xxvii. ver. 33, 34.—Ahithophel was the king's counsellor—and the general of the king's army was Joab.

MR. WATHEN, the celebrated oculist, in one of his interviews with King George III., observed to his Majesty, "I have often thought of the words of Solomon, 'When the righteous are in authority, the people rejoice;' and if your Majesty could always appoint servants of that character, the voice of rejoicing would be heard throughout the empire."—"Wathen," replied the King, "these are the men I have sought; but when I have required their services, I have often been disappointed; for I find men distinguished by habits of piety prefer retirement; and that, generally speaking, the men of the world must transact the world's business."

A Father's Advice.

Chap. xxviii. ver. 9.—Thou, Solomon my son, know thou the God of thy father, and serve him with a perfect heart, and with a willing mind.

THE REV. A. DUNCAN, in his Will, says, "I earnestly beseech my children, as they would have God's blessing and mine, that they set God before their eyes, walk in his ways, living peaceably in his fear, in all humility and meekness; holding their course to heaven, and comforting themselves with the glorious and fair-to-look-on heritage, which Christ hath consigned to them, and to all that love him. Now, farewell, sinful world, and all that is in thee! Farewell, dear wife, blessed partner of all my weals and woes! Farewell, dear children, now no longer mine, for I have in faith turned you all over to the unerring care of Him that gave you to me, in hopes of meeting you in my prepared habitation above! Farewell, Sabbaths, pulpit, and pulpit-work; my delight, my joy, my soul's comfort! Farewell, church, and all spiritual friends, till I meet you at home in glory!"

Willing to Give.

Chap. xxix. ver. 5.—Who then is willing to consecrate his service this day unto the Lord?

A MINISTER of the gospel, conversing with Lady Huntingdon about the wants of a family that appeared to be in distress, her ladyship observed, "I can do for them but very little. I am obliged to be a spectator of miseries which I pity but cannot relieve; for when I gave myself up to the Lord, I likewise devoted to him all my fortune, with this reserve, that I would take with a sparing hand what might be necessary for my food and raiment, and for the support of my children, should they live to be reduced. I was led to this from a consideration that there were many benevolent persons, who had no religion, who would feel for the temporal miseries of others, and help them; but few, even among professors, who had a proper concern for the awful condition of ignorant and perishing souls. What, therefore, I can save for a while out of my own necessaries I will give them; but more I dare not take without being guilty of sacrilege."

SECOND BOOK OF CHRONICLES.

Asking God.

Chap. i. ver. 7.—In that night did God appear unto Solomon, and said unto him, Ask what I shall give thee.

AS a little boy was paring an apple which had been given to him after dinner, the following question was put to him by a lady: "Supposing God were to tell you he would give you whatever you chose to ask him for, what would you ask him to give you?"—"Do you mean to eat?" inquired the little boy. "No," replied the lady; "I mean of all things you can think of that you like, what would you ask him for?" The child laid down his apple, and seemed for a few seconds to be lost in thought; then looking up at the lady, he answered, "I would ask God to give me a new heart."

Humble Mindedness.

Chap. ii. ver. 6.—Who am I then that I should build him an house?

"FROM low circumstances," says the late Mr. Brown of Haddington, "God hath, by his mere grace, exalted the orphan to the highest station in the church; and I hope hath given me some success, not only in preaching and in writing, but also in training up many for the ministry. He chose me to be his servant, and took me from the sheep-fold, from following the ewes great with young; he brought me to feed Jacob his people, and Israel his inheritance. Lord, what am I, and what is my father's house, that thou hast brought me hitherto!"

Temporal and Spiritual Houses.

Chap. iii. ver. 1.—Solomon began to build the house of the Lord.

CRISTNO, a converted Hindoo, made the following observation in a conversation he had with some others:—"The Hindoos," said he, "when they have built a new house, consider it unclean and untenantable till they have performed an offering, and then they take up their abode in it. So God, he does not dwell in earthly temples, however magnificent; his residence is in the heart. But how shall he dwell with man? The sacrifice of Christ must be offered: then the house, the heart, in which this sacrifice is received, becomes the habitation of God through the Spirit."

Various Sorts of Temples.

Chap. iv. ver. 22.—The snuffers, and the basons, and the spoons, and the censers, of pure gold.

ETHELWOLD, Bishop of Winchester, in the time of King Edgar, sold the gold and silver vessels belonging to the church, to relieve the poor people during a famine, saying, "There was no reason that the senseless temples of God should abound in riches, while his living temples were perishing with hunger."

Rejoicing.

Chap. v. ver 13.—They lifted up their voice with the trumpets, and cymbals, and instruments of music, and praised the Lord, saying, For he is good; for his mercy endureth for ever.

"PLUTARCH tells us," says Flavel, "that when Titus Flaminius had freed the poor Grecians from the bondage with which they had been long ground by their oppressors, and the herald was to proclaim in their audience the articles of peace he had concluded for them, they so pressed upon them, (not half of them being able to hear,) that he was in great danger to have lost his life in the press: at last, reading them a second time, when they came to understand distinctly how their case stood, they shouted for joy, crying, 'A Saviour! A Saviour!' that they made the very heavens ring again with their acclamations, and the very birds fell down astonished. And all that night the poor Grecians, with instruments of music and songs of praise, danced and sung about his tent, extolling him as a god that had delivered them. But surely you have more reason to be exalting the Author of your salvation, who, at a dearer rate, had freed you from a more dreadful bondage. O ye that have escaped the eternal wrath of God, by the humiliation of the Son of God, extol your great Redeemer, and for ever celebrate his praises."

God Hearing Prayer.

Chap. vi. ver. 29, 30.—What prayer, or what supplication soever shall be made of any man, or of all thy people Israel, when every one shall know his own sore, and his own grief, and shall spread forth his hands in this house:—then hear thou from heaven thy dwelling-place.

SECOND BOOK OF CHRONICLES.

THE Rev. Mr. Nicholson, a pious minister in England, was, at a former period of his life, excessively attached to dancing and card-playing; and breaking off these, he suffered a great conflict. He made many vows and offered many prayers against them; but was still overcome by the power of temptation;—yet an old puritanic saying which he met with in a magazine, forcibly impressed his mind; "That praying will make a man leave off sinning; or sinning will make him leave off praying." "Well, then," said Mr. N., "I will pray against my sins as long as I have breath to do it." The Lord heard him, and delivered him from the temptation of which he complained.

Plagues and Pestilence.

Chap. vii. ver. 13.—If I send pestilence among my people.

A DREADFUL plague raged at Moscow, in the year 1771. The physicians were, therefore, called together, to give their opinion as to the nature of the disease. All, except one, agreed that it was the plague. Measures were taken to prevent its becoming general; and most of the principal families quitted the city. But the winter proving extremely severe and few new cases occurring, all fear of the plague ceased, the city was again filled with inhabitants. On the 11th of March, the physicians were again assembled, the disease having appeared in a factory where 3000 persons were employed in making clothes At the end of July, the number of deaths in the city, which does not in general exceed fifteen in a day, amounted to two hundred; in the middle of August to four hundred; at the end of August to six hundred; and by the middle of September to more than a thousand in a day! The plague was considered as a mark of the divine vengeance for having neglected the worship of God. The deaths continued to the proportion of twelve hundred a-day, till the 10th of October, when, in the mercy of God, they began to diminish, and by the close of the year the plague ceased in Moscow, and in the whole Russian empire. Seventy thousand persons are said to have been cut off by this awful visitation; nearly one-half of the whole population."

Ships and Sailors.

Chap. viii. ver. 18.—Huram sent him ships, and servants that had knowledge of the sea.

WHEN the late Rev. Charles Buck was once preaching in Silver Street chapel, a sailor passing along, seeing a gateway which seemed to lead to a place of worship, thought within himself, "I am shortly going to sea, I shall perhaps never have another opportunity; I will go in." During the sermon, something so deeply impressed his mind, that he determined to inquire the name of the preacher, which he never forgot. He went to sea, and all his impressions wore away; but after his return he was taken ill, and was visited by some pious gentlemen, who found him very ignorant. He acknowledged his neglect of divine things, but said there was a religion which he liked, and that was what he once heard a Mr. Buck preach in Silver Street chapel. They continued their visits, and at length witnessed his happy death. One of his last expressions was, "I now take my cable, and fix it on my anchor, Jesus, and go through the storm." But what makes this circumstance more interesting, is, that the landlord of the house where this sailor was lodging was himself brought to a state of repentance, by listening at the door to hear what was going on between this man and his pious visitors.

Living Wisely.

Chap. ix. ver. 7.—Happy are these thy servants, which stand continually before thee, and hear thy wisdom.

THE advantage of serving in a pious family, and receiving the benefit of religious instruction, will appear from the last mentioned of the two following cases, which is rendered more apparent from the contrast presented in the first:—

Esther and Mary Jones were orphans, who, as soon as they were old enough to go to service, were received into opulent families. Esther's mistress was a lover of pleasure, rather than a lover of God. She ran the round of folly and amusement through the week, and on the Sabbath received company at home. Her servants had no time to attend to their souls, and they soon ceased to remember that they were immortal. Poor Esther learned of her mistress to love dress, and to play at cards; she frequented the theatres whenever it was in her power; and proceeding from step to step in vice, she was hurried in her thoughtless career into an untimely grave. Her sister, meanwhile, had been placed by Providence among the excellent of the earth. Morning and evening the household was assembled for prayer. A portion of each was devoted to the study of the Bible; and on Sabbath evenings the master and mistress imparted religious instruction to their domestics, and inquired how former instructions prospered. Mary soon became a Christian, and, by a holy life, manifested her love to her God and Saviour. She, too, died young, but her latter end was peace; and to the last she blessed God for having appointed her lot in a pious family.

Grievous Burdens.

Chap. x. ver. 4.—Ease thou somewhat the grievous servitude of thy father, and his heavy yoke that he put upon us, and we will serve thee.

IN answer to a petition of the Lord Mayor and Aldermen of the City of London, to George I. in 1718, his Majesty said, "I shall be glad, not only for your sakes, but my own, if any defects, which may touch the rights of my good subjects, are discovered in my time, since that will furnish me with the means of giving you and all my people an indisputable proof of my tenderness of their privileges.

Improper Priests.

Chap. xi. ver. 15.—He ordained him priests for the high places (2 Kings xii. 13.—He made priests of the lowest of the people.)

WHEN Bishop Andrews first became bishop of Winton, a distant relation, a blacksmith, applied to him to be ordained, and provided with a benefice. "No," said his lordship, "you shall have the best *forge* in the country: but every man in his own order and station."

National Sins.

Chap. xii. ver. 2. Shishak king of Egypt came up against Jerusalem, because they had transgressed against the Lord.

A NOBLE English captain, who, when Calais was lost, (which was the last footing the British had in France) being jeered by a Frenchman, and asked, "Now, Englishman, when will you come back to France?" replied, "O Sir, mock not, when the sins of France are greater than the sins of England, the Englishmen will come again to France."

Heathen Infatuation.

Chap. xiii. ver. 9.—A priest of them that are no gods.

WHEN the altars were overthrown, and the idols burnt, in Huahine, a South Sea island, the image of Oro, their principal god, was also demanded by the regenerators of their country, that execution might be done upon it. An old priest, in attendance on the god, seeing his craft in danger, hid the god—a shapeless log of timber—in a cave among the rocks. Hautia, the person engaged in destroying these remains of idolatry, was not, however, to be trifled with, nor could such a nuisance as the pestilent stock, to which human beings had been sacrificed, be permitted to exist any longer on the face of the earth, lest the plague of idolatry should again break out among its reclaimed followers. He insisted upon its being brought forth, and committed to the flames, in presence of the people, who had but a day before trembled and fallen down before it, This was done; but still the priest himself held to the superstition of his fathers, though he had seen their god consumed to ashes by mortal men with impunity; and he ceased not to spurn at the religion of the strangers, till one Sabbath morning, when, in contempt of the day, he went out to work in his garden; on returning to his house, he became blind in a moment. This awful dispensation appears to have been blessed to him, and while blindness fell on his outward, light fell on his inward vision; and his conduct since has been conformable to his profession.

Calling for God's Assistance.

Chap. xiv. ver. 11, 12.—Help us, O Lord our God; for we rest on thee, and in thy name we go against this multitude. O Lord, thou art our God; let not man prevail against thee.—So the Lord smote the Ethiopians before Asa, and before Judah; and the Ethiopians fled.

A REMARKABLE instance of attention to the blessing of the Divine Being was exhibited in the conduct of the valiant and pious Admiral Duncan, previous to his celebrated action at Camperdown. During the awful moments of preparation, he called all his officers upon deck, and in their presence prostrated himself in prayer before the God of Hosts, committing himself and them, with the cause they maintained, to his sovereign protection, his family to his care, his soul and body to the disposal of his providence. Rising then from his knees, he gave command to make the attack, and achieved one of the greatest victories in the annals of England.

Troublous Times.

Chap. xv. ver. 5.—In those times there was no peace to him that went out, nor to him that came in.

OF the pious and excellent Mr. Shaw, a friend writes—"I have known him spend part of many days, and nights too, in religious exercises, when the times were so dangerous, that it would hazard an imprisonment to be worshipping God with five or six people likeminded with himself. I have sometimes been in his company for a whole night together, when we have been obliged to steal to the place in the dark, and stop in the voice by cloathing and fast closing the windows, till the first day-break down a chimney has given us notice to be gone."

Unrighteous Anger.

Chap. xvi. ver. 10.—Asa was wroth with the seer, and put him in the prison-house, for he was in a rage with him because of this thing.

MR. RUMSEY, a pious physician, speaking of his sinful infirmities, observed, "I have to lament the irritability of my temper in my old age." He had been fond of repeating a conversation which he had in the early part of his life with a pious friend. He observed to this person, that he thought if he arrived at old age, he should be subject to fewer temptations than at an earlier period; but his more experienced friend told him, that "the devil had a bait for every age," and Mr. Rumsey was at length fully convinced of the truth and value of the remark.

Teaching the Scriptures.

Chap. xvii. ver. 9.—They taught in Judah, and had the book of the law of the Lord with them, and went about throughout all the cities of Judah, and taught the people.

THE Rev. S. Blair, and the Rev. William Tennant, were sent by the synod on a mission to Virginia. They stopped one evening at a tavern for the night, where they found a number of persons, with whom they supped in a common room. After supper, cards were introduced, when one of the gentlemen politely asked them if they would not take a cut with them, not knowing that they were clergymen. Mr. T. pleasantly answered, "With all my heart, gentlemen, if you can convince us that thereby we can serve our master's cause, or contribute anything towards the success of our mission." This drew some smart reply from the gentlemen; when Mr. T. with solemnity added, "We are ministers of the gospel of Jesus Christ; we profess ourselves his servants; we are sent on his business, which is to persuade mankind to repent of their sins, to turn from them, and to accept of that happiness and salvation which are offered in the gospel." This very unexpected reply, delivered in a tender, though solemn manner, and with great apparent sincerity, so engaged the attention of the gentlemen, that the cards were laid aside, and an opportunity was afforded for explaining, in a social conversation, during the rest of the evening, some of the leading doctrines of the gospel, to the satisfaction and apparent edification of the hearers.

Imprisoned Wrongfully.

Chap. xviii. ver. 26, 27.—Put this fellow in the prison, and feed him with bread of affliction, and with water of affliction until I return in peace. And Micaiah said, If thou certainly return in peace, then hath not the Lord spoken by me.

IN October, 1663, Mr. Steel, and Mr. Philip Henry, two non-conformist ministers, together with some of their friends, were apprehended, and brought prisoners to Hanmer, under pretence of some plot said to be on foot against the government; and there they were kept under confinement some days; on which Mr. Henry writes:—"It is sweet being in any condition with a clear conscience. 'The sting of death is sin,' and so of imprisonment also. It is the first time I was ever a prisoner, but perhaps may not be the last. We felt no hardship, but we know not what we may." Being soon after dismissed, Mr. Henry returned to his tabernacle with thanksgivings to God, and a hearty prayer for his enemies, that God would forgive them. The very next day after they were released, Sir Evans Lloyd, governor of Chester, at whose instigation they were brought into that trouble, died, as was reported, of a drunken surfeit.

Judging for God.

Chap. xix. ver. 9.—Jehoshaphat said to the judges, Take heed what ye do: for ye judge not for man, but for the Lord, who is with you in the judgment.

PEPER the Great frequently surprised the magistrates by his unexpected presence in the cities of the empire. Having arrived without previous notice at Olonez, he went first to the regency, and inquired of the governor how many suits were depending in the court of chancery? "None, sire," replied the governor. "How happens that?" "I endeavour to prevent law-suits, and conciliate the parties; I act in such a manner that no traces of difference remain on the archives; if I am wrong, your indulgence will excuse me." "I wish," replied the Czar, "that all governors would act on your principles. Go on, God and your sovereign are equally satisfied."

Song and Victory.

Chap. xx. ver. 22.—When they began to sing and to praise, the Lord set ambushments against the children of Ammon, Moab, and mount Seir, which were come against Judah: and they were smitten.

WE have often heard of prayer doing wonders: but instances also are not wanting, of praise being accompanied with signal events. The ancient Britons, in the year 420, obtained a victory over an army of the Picts and Saxons, near Mold, in Flintshire. The Britons unarmed, having Germanus and Lupus at their head, when the Picts and Saxons came to the attack, the two commanders, Gideonlike, ordered their army to shout *Alleluia* three times over, at the sound of which, the enemy, being suddenly struck with terror, ran away in the greatest confusion, and left the Britons masters of the field. A stone monument, to perpetuate the remembrance of this *Halleluiah* victory, is said to remain to this day in a field near Mold.

Cruel Fratricide.

Chap. xxi. ver. 4.—When Jehoram was risen up to the kingdom of his father, he strengthened himself, and slew all his brethren with the sword.

UPON the death of Selimus the Second, which happened in the year 1582, Amurah the Third succeeded in the Turkish empire; at his entrance upon which he caused his five brothers, Mustapha, Solymon, Abdalla, Osman, and Sinager, without pity or commiseration, to be strangled in his presence, and gave orders that they should be burned with his dead father; an ordinary thing with Mahometan princes, who, to secure to themselves the empire without rivalship, hesitate not to pollute their hands with the blood of their nearest relations. It is said of this Amurah, when he saw the fatal bow-string put about the neck of his younger brother, that he was seen to weep, but it seems they were crocodile tears, for he held firmly to his bloody purpose.

Evil Conduct.

Chap. xxii. ver. 4.—Ahaziah did evil in the sight of the Lord, like the house of Ahab: for they were his counsellors, after the death of his father, to his destruction.

TAYLOR, the well-known infidel, was boasting one day, that the greater part of the youth in Great Britain had embraced his sentiments. "O," said a gentleman present, "I have till now been unable to account for the increase of juvenile delinquency, but your assertion puts the matter beyond doubt." Taylor, as may easily be imagined, was quite confounded, and unable to reply.

Advice to Royalty.

Chap. xxiii. ver. 11.—They brought out the king's son, and put upon him the crown, and gave him the testimony, and made him king.

ROBERT BARCLAY, the defender of the Quakers, dedicated his Apology to Charles II., and addressed his Majesty in the following words:—"There is no king in the world who so experimentally testifies of God's providence and goodness; neither is there any who rules so many free people, so many true Christians; which thing renders thy government more honourable, thyself more considerable, than the accession of many nations filled with slavish and superstitious souls. Thou hast tasted of prosperity and adversity, knowest what it is to be banished thy native country, to be overruled as well as to rule and sit upon the throne—and being oppressed, thou hast reason to know how hateful the oppressor is both to God and man. If, after all those warnings and advertisements, thou doest not turn to the Lord with all thy heart, but forget him who remembereth thee in thy distress, and give up thyself to follow lust and vanity, surely great will be thy condemnation."

Being Stoned.

Chap. xxiv. ver. 21.—They conspired against Zechariah, and stoned him with stones.

MR. WHITEFIELD, preaching one Sabbath afternoon, in Oxmantour-Green, a place frequented by the Ormond and Liberty boys, as they call them, narrowly escaped with his life. Being war time, he took occasion to exhort his hearers not only to fear God, but to honour the king; and prayed for success to the king of Prussia. In the time of sermon and prayer, a few stones were thrown at him, which did no hurt. But when he was done, and thought of returning home the way he came, to his great surprise access was denied; and he was obliged to go nearly half a mile from one end of the Green to the other, through hundreds of papists, &c., who, finding him unattended, threw volleys of stones upon him from all quarters, and made him reel backwards and forwards, till he was almost breathless and all over with blood. At last, with great difficulty, he staggered to the door of a minister's house, which was kindly opened to him. For a while he continued speechless, and panting for breath; but his weeping friends having given him some cordials, and washed his wounds, a coach was procured, in which, amidst the oaths, imprecations, and threatening of the popish rabble, he got safe home, and joined in a hymn of thanksgiving with his friends. In a letter, written just after this event, he says,—"I received many blows and wounds; one was particularly large, and near my temples. I thought of Stephen, and was in hopes, like him, to go off in this bloody triumph, to the immediate presence of my Master."

Deaf to Good Advice.

Chap. xxv. ver 16.—I know that God hath determined to destroy thee, because thou hast done this, and hast not hearkened unto my counsel.

A MAN at New Orleans set out on a Sabbath morning to cross a river, on some worldly business. As he could find no boat, but one which was fastened to a tree by a lock, he attempted to get that. Some persons who were present requested him to desist from his purpose. But he replied, that he would either go to the other side of the river, or to hell. He therefore broke the lock, and entered the boat. But he had not gone far, when it upset. The spectators were so impressed that it was a judgment from God, that they stood amazed, till it was too late to afford him any help, and he was launched into a boundless eternity, in the midst of his impiety.

Cities of the Philistines.

Chap. xxvi. ver. 6.—Uzziah went forth and warred against the Philistines, and broke down the wall of Gath, and the wall of Jabneh, and the wall of Ashdod, and built cities about Ashdod, and among the Philistines.

"IN the time of the Crusades," says Harmer, "when the ancient city of the Philistines, called Askelon, had frequently made inroads into the territories of the kingdom of Jerusalem, the Christians built two strong castles, not far from Askelon; and finding the usefulness of these structures, King Fulk, in the spring of the year of our Lord 1138, attended by the patriarch of Jerusalem and his other prelates, proceeded to build another castle, called Blanche Guarda, which he garrisoned with such soldiers as he could depend upon, furnishing them with arms and provisions. These, watching the people of Askelon, often defeated their attempts; and sometimes they did not content themselves with being on the defensive, but attacked them, and did them great mischief, gaining the advantage. This occasioned those who claimed a right to the adjoining country, encouraged by the neighbourhood of such a strong place, to build many villages, in which many families dwelt, concerned in tilling the ground, and raising provisions for other parts of their territories. Upon this the people of Askelon, finding themselves encompassed round by a number of inexpugnable fortresses, began to grow very uneasy at their situation, and to apply to Egypt for help by repeated messages."

Doing Right.

Chap. xxvii. ver. 2.—Jotham did that which was right in the sight of the Lord.

JULIUS DRUSUS, a Roman tribune, had a house that in many places lay exposed to the view of the neighbourhood. A person came and offered, that for five talents he would so alter it, that it should not be liable to that inconvenience. "I will give thee ten talents," said Drusus, "if thou canst make my house conspicuous in every room of it, that so all the city may behold in what manner I lead my life." It would be well for us to recollect, that we are all thus continually exposed to the eye of God.

"Awake, asleep, at home, abroad,
We are surrounded still with God."

Kindness to the Defeated.

Chap. xxviii. ver. 15.—The men rose up and took the captives, and with the spoil clothed all that were naked among them, and arrayed them, and shod them and gave them to eat and to drink, and anointed them, and carried all the feeble of them upon asses, and brought them to Jericho, the city of palm trees, to their brethren.

THE REV. WILLIAM GORDON, minister of Alvey in Kincardineshire, was one of the most ardent of the Scottish royalists of 1745. During all the troubles, previous to the decisive conflict of Culloden, he delivered from the pulpit animating exhortations to his flock, to hold themselves in readiness to shed the last drop of their blood in defending the throne, which formed the sole barrier between their religious privileges and sweeping destruction. Yet when the rebels were scattered, wounded, outlawed, and pursued by the arm of justice, this benevolent pastor was the bold advocate and agent of mercy, professing, that as gratitude for a signal deliverance from ecclesiastical despotism, and as Christians forgiving their enemies, every loyal subject should obliterate all remembrance of the injuries they suffered from the opposite party, and relieve their wants and distresses. When the hostile armies were known to have moved northward, Mr. Gordon ordered a large quantity of malt to be brewed into ale, and huge piles of oat cakes to be prepared, telling his wife that he was sure many unfortunate men must pass that way, and all ought to have meat and drink, with dressings for their wounds, whatever might be the side they had espoused. After the battle of Culloden, great numbers of officers and men received refreshments from Mrs. Gordon; and every part of the house, except one room, was filled with the wounded.

Be not Negligent.

Chap. xxix. ver. 11.—My sons, be not now negligent; for the Lord hath chosen you to stand before him, to serve him, and that ye should minister unto him.

THE REV. T. CHARLES of North Wales, at a time when unemployed in the ordinary work of his ministry, and hesitating what steps he should take in a change contemplated by him, had the following striking dream:—The day of judgment, with all its awful accompaniments, appeared to him. He saw millions assembled before the Judge; and what attracted his notice particularly, was the trial of the idle and slothful servant, as recorded in Matth. xxv. He imagined these dreadful sounds uttered from the judgment seat,—"Take him, and bind him hand and foot, and cast him into outer darkness; there shall be weeping and gnashing of teeth." He thought this a representation of his own case; it seemed to say to him, as Nathan said to David, "Thou art the man." When he awoke, he felt greatly alarmed. The dream distressed him exceedingly. The fear of being like the idle and unprofitable servant greatly harassed his mind. Having such a dream when he was doing nothing, he could not but be much affected by it. It bore every appearance of being sent as a warning to him; and, by his subsequent activity, he appears to have improved it to the best of purposes.

Unseemly Laughter.

Chap. xxx. ver. 10.—They laughed them to scorn, and mocked them

SECOND BOOK OF CHRONICLES.

SOME time ago, a man was tried at Cambridge, for a robbery committed on an aged gentlewoman in her own house. The judge was Baron Smith, a man of an amiable character for religion. He asked the gentlewoman, if the prisoner at the bar was the person who robbed her?—"Truly, my Lord," said she. "I cannot positively say it was he, for it was duskish when I was robbed, so dark that I could hardly discern the features of his face." "Where were you when he robbed you?" "I was in a closet that joins to my bedchamber, and he had got into my house while my servant had gone out on an errand." "What day of the week was it?" "It was the Lord's day evening, my lord." "How had you been employed when he robbed you?" "My lord, I am a Protestant dissenter ; I had been at the meeting that day, and had retired into my closet in the evening for prayer and meditation on what I had been hearing through the day." She had no sooner uttered these words, than the court, which was crowded with some hundreds of students, rang with a peal of loud laughter. The judge looked round the court as one astonished, and with a decent solemnity laid his hands upon the bench, as if he was going to rise, and with no small emotion of spirit, spoke to the following effect:—"Good God! where am I? Am I in the place of one of the universities of this kingdom, where, it is to be supposed, that young gentlemen are educated in the principles of religion, as well as in all useful learning? and for such to laugh in so indecent a manner, on hearing an aged Christian tell that she retired into her closet on a Lord's day evening, for prayer and meditation! Blush and be ashamed all of you, if you are capable of it, as well you may ; and if any of your tutors are here, let them blush also to see in how irreligious a manner their pupils and students behave." And then turning to the lady, he said, "Don't be discouraged, Madam, by this piece of rude and unmannerly, as well as irreligious usage ; you have no reason to be ashamed of what you have on this occasion, and in this public manner, said ; on the contrary, you may glory in it. It adds dignity to your character, and shame belongs to them who would expose it to ridicule."

Giving.

Chap. xxxi. ver. 5.—The tithe of all things brought they in abundantly.

AT the conclusion of a meeting of a religious society connected with Surrey Chapel, a gentleman on the platform arose and said "I hope every one will *give a little.*" Upon which the venerable Rowland Hill got up, and exclaimed in a voice and manner truly characteristic, "I hope every one will *give a deal.*"

Mockery Requited.

Chap. xxxii. ver. 16.—His servants spake yet more against the Lord God, and against his servant Hezekiah.

THERE was in a populous Swiss village a pious and excellent clergyman, who preached and lived with such holy zeal and exemplary piety, that many were converted under his ministry. But there lived in the same place a wicked and abandoned character, who not only slighted all the means of grace, but turned the most serious matters into ridicule, and made a laughing-stock of the preacher's expressions. One morning, he came very early to the public house, and began to intoxicate himself with liquor, profaning the name and word of God, and ridiculing the term of conversion. "Now," says he,

"I myself will become a convert," turning himself from one side to the other, and dancing about in the room with a variety of foolish gestures. He quickly left the room, fell down the stairs, broke his neck, and expired, exhibiting an awful monument of God's most righteous vengeance, which sometimes even in this life overtakes those that profane his holy name.

Strange Gods and Bad Books.

Chap. xxxiii. ver. 15.—He took away the strange gods, and the idol out of the house of the Lord, and all the altars that he had built in the mount of the house of the Lord, and in Jerusalem, and cast them out of the city.

SOME years before the revolution in France, a lady, who was a bookseller in Paris, attracted by the reputation of Father Beauregard, an eloquent preacher, went to the church of Notre-Dame to hear him. His discourse was particularly levelled against irreligious books; and the lady had cause enough to reproach herself on that account, having been in the habit of selling many publications which were contrary to religion and good manners. Interest had blinded her as it does many others in the same line of business; but penetrated by the sermon, she was convinced that impious and licentious books poison the mind; and she was compelled to acknowledge that those who print, or sell, or contribute to circulate them in any way whatever, are so many public poisoners, whom God will, one day, call to account for the evils they occasion. Impressed with these sentiments, she went to the preacher, and, with tears in her eyes said to him, "You have rendered me a great service, by giving me to see how culpable I have been in selling many impious books; and I entreat you to finish the good work you have begun, by taking the trouble to come to my warehouse to examine all the books which are in it, and to put aside all those which may be injurious to morals or religion. Whatever it costs me, I am determined to make the sacrifice: I had rather be deprived of a part of my property, than consent to lose my soul." Accordingly Father Beauregard paid her a visit next day to examine her books. When he had separated the good from the bad, she took the latter, and, in his presence, cast them, one after another, into a great fire she had taken care to provide. The price of the works thus consumed amounted, it is said, to about 6000 livres. She made the sacrifice without regret; and, from that time, endeavoured to sell no books but what might tend to counteract the evil done by others. While most will admire this example, few, it is to be feared, will follow it.

Reverence for Godly Matters.

Chap. xxxiv. ver. 27.—Thine heart was tender, and thou didst humble thyself before God.

A LADY who had been in company with the late Mr. Hall of Bristol, and who had been speaking of the Supreme Being with great familiarity, but in religious phraseology, having retired, he said, "I wish I knew how to cure that good lady of her bad habit. I have tried, but as yet in vain. It is a great mistake to affect this kind of familiarity with the King of kings, and speak of him as though he were a next-door neighbour, from the pretence of love. Mr. Boyle's well-known habit was infinitely to be commended. And one of our old divines, I forget which, well remarks, that, 'Nothing but ignorance can be guilty of this boldness; and there is no divinity but in a humble fear, no philosophy but shows itself in silent admiration!'"

Sincere Mourning.

Chap. xxxv. ver. 24.—All Judah and Jerusalem mourned for Josiah.

THE Rev. James Hervey was buried under the middle of the communion-table in the chancel of Weston-Favel, on Friday the 28th of December 1758, in the presence of a numerous congregation, full of regret for the loss of so excellent a pastor. A person who was present says, "Mr. Maddock (Mr. Hervey's curate) was in tears; some were wringing their hands, others sobbing; many were silently weeping, but all seemed inwardly and sincerely grieved, as their looks sufficiently testified; bearing a visible witness of his worth and their sorrow."

Mocking God's Messengers.

Chap. xxxvi. ver. 16.—They mocked the messengers of God, and despised his words, and misused his prophets.

"I HAVE generally," says one of the Baptist missionaries in India, "been three or four hours every day in actual contact with people. Frequently I go and return in good spirits, but sometimes I am low enough. Good spirits are commonly necessary in dealing with my poor people, for there is generally a great deal among them that is very provoking. I frequently tell them that it is a regard for their welfare that leads me to do as I do; and the declaration is received with a sneer. On two or three occasions, a number of little children have been officiously seated before me, as an intimation that I say nothing worthy the attention of men. The people often call after me as I go about: One cries, 'Juggernaut! Juggernaut!' another perhaps says with a contemptuous smile, 'Won't you give me a book?' Soon after, perhaps a third says, 'Sahib! I will worship Jesus Christ!' and a fourth exclaims, 'Victory to Juggernaut the Ruler!" Among these infatuated people, I fear that the utmost propriety in spirit and demeanour would be no protection from very frequent insults. In spite of the most affectionate addresses of which I am capable, and in the midst of them, the people in malicious derision, shout, 'Juggernaut! Juggernaut!' and seem determined, as it were, with one heart and voice, to support their idols, and resist Jesus Christ. I hope he will, ere long, act for himself; and then floods of pious sorrow will stream from the haughtiest eyes, and the grace now scorned will be sought with successful earnestness."

BOOK OF EZRA.

Free-will Offerings.

Chap. i. ver. 4.—The free-will offering for the house of God.

"IT has been frequently wished by Christians," says the late Dr. Payson of America, "that there were some rule laid down in the Bible, fixing the proportion of their property which they ought to contribute to religious uses. This is as if a child should go to his father and say, 'Father, how many times in the day must I come to you with some testimonial of my love? How often will it be necessary to show my affection for you?' The father would at once reply, 'Just as often as your feelings prompt you, my child, and no oftener.' Just so Christ says to his people: 'Look at me, and see what I have done and suffered for you, and then give me just what you think I deserve. I do not wish any thing forced.'"

Giving Freely.

Chap. ii. ver. 68.—Some of the chief of the fathers, when they came to the house of the Lord which is at Jerusalem, offered freely for the house of God, to set it up in its place.

"It HAPPENED," says Dr. Franklin, "to attend one of Mr Whitefield's sermons, in the course of which I perceived he intended to finish with a collection, and I silently resolved he should get nothing from me. I had in my pocket a handful of copper money, three or four silver dollars, and five pistoles of gold. As he proceeded I began to soften, and conclude to give the copper. Another stroke of his oratory made me ashamed of that, and determined me to give the silver; and he finished so admirably, that I emptied my pockets into the collector's dish, gold and all."

Fear and Persecution.

Chap. iii. ver. 3.—Fear was upon them because of the people of those countries.

THE Hussites, driven out of their country by persecution, sought an asylum in the mountains, the thickest forests, and the clefts and recesses of rocks, far removed from the society of other men. They kindled their fires only in the night, lest their places of retreat should be discovered by the smoke. And during the winter, when snow lay on the ground, they used the precaution, when going out, to walk one after the other, the last person dragging a bush after him to erase the marks of their feet. It may easily be conceived to what hardships the Brethren must have been exposed during this period. Yet all the privations and sufferings they endured were amply compensated to them by the rewards of a good conscience, and the divine consolations they derived from the perusal of the Scriptures, and from spiritual conversation. In these exercises they often spent whole nights.

Charged with Sedition.

Chap. iv. ver. 15.—This city is a rebellious city, and hurtful unto kings and provinces, and they have moved sedition within the same.

IT was a frequent charge brought against the non-conformist ministers, that they were a factious and turbulent people; that their meetings were for the sowing of sedition and discontent, and such like. The clergyman of Whitewell Chapel, where Mr. Philip Henry used to attend, was sometimes an accuser of those good men. Referring to an occasion of this kind, Mr. Henry writes :—"Mr. Green at chapel to-day seemed to say something without reflection; 'Mark them that cause divisions, serving their own belly.' Lord," adds the good man, "I can only appeal to thee, and say, if I seek myself in what I do, or my own things, and not the good of souls, and the advancement of thy glory; if I do it in any respect to divide, then fill my face with shame, and let my enemies have power over me. But if otherwise, Lord, take my part, and plead my cause, and clear my integrity, for thy mercy's sake."

Ingenuous good Work.

Chap. v. ver. 5.—The eye of their God was upon the elders of the Jews, that they could not cause them to cease.

DURING the revolution in France, the Ban de la Roche, (a mountainous canton in the north-east of that kingdom,) alone seemed to be an asylum of peace in the midst of war and carnage. Though every kind of worship was interdicted throughout France, and almost all the clergy of Alsace, men of learning, talents, and property, were imprisoned—John Frederick Oberlin, pastor of Walbach, was allowed to continue his work of benevolence and instruction unmolested. His house became the retreat of many individuals of different religious persuasions, and of distinguished rank, who fled thither, under the influence of terror, from Strasbourg and its environs, and who always received the most open-hearted and cordial reception, though it endangered his own situation. "I once," says a gentleman, who was then residing at Walbach, "saw a chief actor of the revolution in Oberlin's house, and in that atmosphere he seemed to have lost his sanguinary disposition, and to have exchanged the fierceness of the tiger for the gentleness of the lamb."

Hinder not Sincere Conviction.

Chap. vi. ver. 7.—Let the work of this house of God alone ; let the governor of the Jews, and the elders of the Jews, build this house of God in his place.

DURING the reign of George III., a bill was brought into the House of Commons, by Mr. Michael Angelo Taylor, which would have materially abridged the rights of Dissenters ; and it actually had gone through two readings without opposition, when it was stopped in its progress by the liberal interference of the king himself. His Majesty sent for Mr. Wyndham, who was then in administration, and said to him, "You may pass that bill through both houses as fast as you please, but I will never sign it ;" adding these emphatic words, "There shall be no persecution in my reign." The bill was withdrawn, and no more was heard of it.

Godly Judges.

Chap. vii. ver. 25.—Set magistrates and judges, which may judge all the people that are beyond the river, all such as know the laws of thy God ; and teach ye them that know them not.

"IN the year 1772," says one, "I spent the summer in London, and being upon a visit to a family at Ware, in Hertfordshire, we one day went to Hertford, it being the summer assizes. Lord Chief Baron Smith presided on the bench, whom I had heard much of, as being a godly and spiritual man, as well as an upright and judicious judge. The first morning he sat at Nisi Prius, and I thought him very sensible and knowing, or, what the lawyers call learned, in his profession : but the next morning he had to try three criminals ; I forget the offences, but they were all capital, and the prisoners were tried separately, and found guilty. The venerable judge, in passing the sentence of the law upon them, was very solemn. He stated to them separately, the aggravation of the particular crime of each, and the necessity that the laws of the country, and the security of the people, should be maintained by the punishment of the offenders, 'which punishment,' he added, 'I am now to pronounce upon you , this it is painful for me to do, but it is a duty imposed on me by my office to pronounce, That you be taken from hence to the place from whence you came,' &c. His subsequent address affected the audience, however it might the criminals :—' Prisoners, so we see that the law worketh wrath against transgressors, and the divine law on us and all mankind as sinners, who have come short of the glory of God. But God, who is rich in mercy, hath provided a glorious salvation, in which you and I may find abundent relief. He sent his own Son to seek and save the lost, and to give himself a sacrifice for sin, that whosoever believeth in him should not perish, but have everlasting life. The blood of Jesus Christ, the Son of God, cleanseth from all sin. I am a sinner like you ; but pleading that blood, I found mercy ; and therefore recommend that blood to you. Go ye and do likewise."

Humbled before God.

Chap. viii. ver. 21.—I proclaimed a fast there, at the river of Ahava, that we might afflict ourselves before our God, to seek of him a right way for us, and for our little ones, and for all our substance.

THE Rev. William Tennant was once passing through a town in the State of New Jersey, in America, in which he was a stranger, and had never preached ; and stopping at a friend's house to dine, was informed, that it was a day of fasting and prayer in the congregation, on account of a very severe drought, which threatened the most dangerous consequences to the fruits of the earth. His friend had just returned from church, and the intermission was but half-an-hour. Mr. Tennant was requested to preach, and with great difficulty consented, as he wished to proceed on his journey. At church, the people were surprised to see a preacher, wholly unknown to them, ascend the pulpit. His whole appearance, being in a travelling dress, covered with dust, wearing an old-fashioned large wig, discoloured like his clothes, and a long meagre visage, engaged their attention, and excited their curiosity. On his rising up, instead of beginning to pray, as was the usual practice, he looked around the congregation with a piercing eye, and after a minute's profound silence, addressed them with great solemnity in the following words :—"My beloved brethren, I am told you have come here to-day to fast and pray : a very good work indeed, provided you have come with a sincere desire to glorify God thereby. But if your design is merely to comply with a customary practice, or with the wish of your church officers, you are guilty of the greatest folly imaginable, as you had much better have staid at home, and earned your three shillings and sixpence. But if your minds are indeed impressed with the solemnity of the occasion, and you are really desirous of humbling yourselves before Almighty God, your heavenly Father, come, join with me, and let us pray." This had an effect so extraordinary on the congregation, that the utmost seriousness was universally manifested. The prayer and the sermon added greatly to the impressions already made, and many had reason to bless God for this unexpected visit, and to reckon this day one of the happiest in their lives.

Treatment of Jews.

Chap. ix. ver. 7.—For our iniquities have we been delivered into the hand of the kings of the lands, to the sword, captivity, and to spoil, and to confusion of face, as it is this day.

THE Rev. W. B. Lewis, in a letter of February 1824, says, "Those Jews in Jerusalem who endeavour to obtain a livelihood by the work of their hands, are frequently forced to give up their time, and

BOOK OF NEHEMIAH.

to work for the ungrateful Turk without payment. Sometimes a mere trifle is thrown to the Jew; but, in either case, if he attempts to reason with the Turk, he is threatened with the bastinado, and I know not what.—Rabbi Solomon P. is an engraver of seals. In the open street he was accosted by a Turk, who produced a large stone, and told him to cut out a seal. Solomon replied it was not in his power, for he only knew how to engrave, not to cut and prepare the stone. The Turk thereupon laid hold of him by his beard, drew his sword, kicked him, and cut and struck him unmercifully. The poor man cried, but there was no one to assist him. Turks in the street passed by unconcerned; and the wounded Jew sought redress in vain from the officers of justice."

Hoping On.

Chap. x. ver. 2.—Yet now there is hope in Israel concerning this thing.

AN old gentleman once said, "I cannot but lament my folly and madness, in not obeying the voice of conscience in my youth. By this time I might have been an old man in Christ; but I am not born yet. Unhappy me! but, by the grace of God, I will not give it up yet. There are promises which I can sometimes lay hold of. God helping me, I will go on to seek his face, and practise what I know."

BOOK OF NEHEMIAH.

Mourning and Fasting.

Chap. i. ver. 4.—I sat down and wept, and mourned certain days and fasted, and prayed before the God of heaven.

IN a sea-port town in New England lived a pious mother who had six daughters. At the age of sixty, she had been for many years the subject of disease, which confined her to her house, and almost to her room. To a Christian friend she remarked, "I have not for these many years known what it is to go to the house of God, in company with his people, and to take sweet counsel with them. But I have another source of grief greater than this; one that weighs down my spirits day and night, while disease and pain bear my body towards the grave. I have six daughters; two are married and live near me, and four are with me; but not one of them is pious. I am alone. I have no one for a Christian companion. O that even one of them were pious, that I might walk alone no longer!" Such was her language. She was evidently a woman with a sorrowful spirit, beseeching the Lord with much entreaty. Soon after this, a revival of religion commenced in the neighbourhood, of which her four single daughters were among the first subjects. A fifth was soon added to the number; but the other, the eldest, was unmoved. "Mother," said one of the converts, "let us all unite in observing a day of fasting and prayer for our unawakened sister." The day was observed. Of this the subject of their prayers had no knowledge; but on the same day, while engaged in her domestic concerns at home, her mind was solemnly arrested, and she was soon after added to the Christian sisterhood. The praying mother lived a few years to enjoy their Christian society; and they were followers of her who was first removed to inherit the promises.

Despised and Contemned.

Chap. ii. ver. 19.—They laughed us to scorn, and despised us.

THE Moravian missionaries in Greenland endured much mockery and opposition from the rude inhabitants, when communicating to them the knowledge of divine truth. When the missionaries told them they meant to instruct them about the will of God, they were met by the taunt, "Fine fellows, indeed, to be our teachers! We know very well you yourselves are ignorant, and must be taught by others!" If they tarried more than one night with them, they used all their endeavours to entice them to participate in their wanton and dissolute sports; and when they failed in this, they mocked and mimicked their reading, singing, and praying, practising every kind of droll antic; or they accompanied their devotions by drumming or howling hideously. Nor did the poverty of the brethren escape their keenest ridicule, or most cutting sarcasms. They even pelted them with stones, climbed upon their shoulders, destroyed their goods, and maliciously tried to spoil their boat, or drive it out to sea.

Speaking and Acting.

Chap. iii. ver. 1.—The high priest rose up, with his brethren the priests, and they builded.

TWO architects were once candidates for the building of a certain temple at Athens. The first harangued the crowd very learnedly upon the different orders of architecture, and showed them in what manner the temple should be built. The other, who got up after him, only observed—"That what his brother had spoken he could do;" and thus he at once gained the cause. Such is the difference between the *speculative* and *practical* Christian.

Boastful Contempt.

Chap. iv. ver. 3, 4.—Tobiah the Ammonite was by him; and he said, Even that which they build, if a fox go up, he shall even break down their stone-wall. Hear, O our God; for we are despised: and turn their reproach upon their own head.

VOLTAIRE boasted, that with one hand he would overturn the edifice of Christianity, which required the hands of twelve apostles to build; but at the present time, the very press which he employed at Ferney for printing his blasphemous works, is actually used at Genoa for printing the Holy Scriptures; so that the very engine he set to work, to destroy the Bible, is now engaged in circulating its sacred truths.

Unselfish Conduct.

Chap. v. ver. 15.—The former governors, that had been before me, were chargeable unto the people, and had taken of them bread and wine, besides forty shekels of silver—but so did not I, because of the fear of God.

THE late Rev. Robert Hall of Bristol was much grieved with the want of economy in managing the finances of some of our public institutions. "When you consider, Sir," said he, "the sources from which these monies are derived, and the objects to which they are intended to be appropriated, there ought to be no improvident expenditure of any kind. I know a Mr. —— who is employed in travelling and collecting for the Bible Society; he puts up at the principal inn in the place where he happens to visit, and rather than exert himself to rise early and travel in the stage coach, I have heard that he takes a post-chaise at the expense of the society. These things ought not to be countenanced. I invariably endeavour to travel on such occasions, Sir, outside of the coach, and when, from indisposition, I am compelled to hire a post-chaise, I pay the extra expense out of my own pocket."

The Post of Duty.

Chap. vi. ver. 11.—Should such a man as I flee? and who is there, that, being as I am, would go into the temple to save his life? I will not go in.

WHEN the Danes laid siege to Canterbury, the principal inhabitants persuaded Alphage, the archbishop, to retreat. "God forbid," said he, "that I should tarnish my character by such conduct, and be afraid to go to heaven because a violent death may be across the passage.—God be thanked, I do not know that I have given the enemy any just occasion to use me ill. 'Tis true I have converted several of them to Christianity; but if this be a fault, I shall be happy in suffering for it. What! have I disobliged them by ransoming some of my countrymen, and by supporting those in their captivity whom I was not able to redeem? If you think the Danes are enraged against me for reproving them for their immorality and injustice, I cannot help that, for unless I give a wicked man warning, his blood will be required at my hands. I think it unbecoming my station to desert my countrymen in time of danger, and make provision for myself. What, can I be less than an hierling, if, when I see the wolf ready to devour my sheep, I presently run away, and leave them to shift for themselves? It is, therefore, my resolution to stand the shock, and submit to the order of Providence." The town was soon after taken, and the inhabitants plundered and murdered. Alphage could not bear to see the poor inhabitants suffer in that manner, and went and begged the Danes to spare the people, and turn their rage against him. They slew about 7000 of the people, and put the bishop in a dungeon for several months. They proposed to him to redeem his liberty with the sum of £3000, but Alphage could not satisfy the demand. He was put to death at Greenwich in 1012.

The Gates of the City.

Chap. vii. ver. 3.—I said unto them, Let not the gates of Jerusalem be opened until the sun be hot; and while they stand by, let them shut the doors and bar them.

DOUBDAN, an eastern traveller, returning from the river Jordan to Jerusalem, in 1652, tells us, "That when he and his companion arrived in the valley of Jehoshaphat, they were much surprised to find that the gates of the city were shut, which obliged them to lodge on the ground at the door of the sepulchre of the blessed virgin, to wait for the return of day, along with more than a thousand other people, who were obliged to continue there the rest of the night, as well as they. At length, about four o'clock, seeing everybody making for the city, they also set forwards, with the design of entering by St. Stephen's gate, but they found it shut, and above two thousand people, who were there in waiting, without knowing the cause of all this. At first they thought it might be too early, and that it was not customary to open so soon; but an hour after, a report was spread that the inhabitants had shut their gates, because the peasants of the country about had formed a design of pillaging the city in the absence

Eager for Scripture Teaching.

Chap. viii. ver. 3.—The ears of all the people were attentive unto the book of the law.

MR. WADDEL, who went lately to the West Indies as a missionary, thus writes in his journal:—After service was over, and I had gone into the room beside that in which I preached, the people, by a messenger, begged I would return. Having done so, they all rose up, and several in different parts of the room, in name of the rest, begged I would not go away, but reside among them, and preach to them the good word. I assured them it would make me quite happy to do so; but that——. Here they all interrupted me, crying out almost with one voice, 'O stay and make us hear the gospel; tell us the good word and we will all hear it.' I said that I was glad to see them wishing to hear the good word of God, and I hoped that they would soon get the blessing they wanted, of a minister to live among them;—if not me, yet someone else. 'Thank you, massa; God bless you, massa,' they cried out, and then begged I would myself stop among them. I said, 'If it were the will of God, it would afford me great pleasure to do so.' 'O, it is the will of God,' said they all immediately. I had often heard of the Macedonian cry, Come over and help us,' but here I witnessed it."

The Book of Books.

Chap. ix. ver. 13.—Thou gavest them right judgments and true laws, good statutes and commandments.

"FOR my part," says Mr. Hervey, "I propose to addict myself with more incessant assiduity to this delightful and divine study of the book of God. Away, my Homer, I have no need of being entertained by you, since Job and the prophets furnish me with images much more magnificent, and lessons infinitely more important. Away, my Horace; nor shall I suffer any loss by your absence, while the sweet singer of Israel tunes his lyre, and inspirits me with the noblest strains of devotion; and even my prime favourite, my Virgil, may withdraw, since in Isaiah I enjoy all his correctness of judgment, and all his beautiful propriety of diction."

Buying and Selling on the Sabbath.

Chap. x. ver. 31,—If the people of the land bring ware, or any victuals, on the Sabboth-day to sell—we would not buy it of them on the Sabbath.

SOON after the Rev. Mr. Galland came to Holmfirth, in the West Riding of Yorkshire, he was grieved at the profane custom of buying and selling on the Lord's-day, and set about reforming the abuse, not without some degree of success. He went through the village, and obtained a promise from every individual concerned, to discontinue the practice if all the rest would. After succeeding thus far, he called them all together, and procured a joint agreement, that in future they would not buy or sell on the Sabbath.

Great Men.

Chap. xi. ver. 14.—Zabdiel the son of one of the great men.

MR. SAMUEL HARDY, a non-conformist minister, had a peculiar freedom in addressing persons of high rank, without anything of rusticity. When Lord Brook lay on his death-bed, he went to him, and spoke to this effect :—" My Lord, you of the nobility are the most unhappy men in the world : nobody dares to come near to you to tell you of your faults, or to put you in the right way to heaven." Hereby he prepared the way for dealing closely with his Lordship, without giving him any offence.

Rejoicing in the Faith.

Chap. xii. ver. 43.—That day they offered great sacrifices, and rejoiced ; for God had made them rejoice with great joy.

"ON a Sabbath evening," says the Rev. Mr Stewart in his 'Visit to the South Seas,' " while walking the main deck, I perceived an open-hearted young fellow, with whom I had formed some acquaintance, leaning against a gun ; and going up to him, said, 'Well, J——, how has the day gone with you ?' 'One of the happiest I ever knew, Sir,' was his reply ; 'and I have heard many of the crew say the same. I never expected such a Sabbath at sea ; earth can scarce know a better.' Adding, on further conversation, ' when I had been on board the Guerrier several weeks, before you, Sir, joined us, without any public worship, I began to fear I had made a bad choice in coming to this ship ; but I was mistaken ; this will be a happy voyage to me ; and I believe the time will yet come, when the ship herself will be called *the happy Guerrier !*' His face beamed with pleasure as he spoke, and I rejoiced to meet one so warm-hearted and seemingly pious."

Profaning the Sabbath.

Chap. xiii. ver. 17.—I contended with the nobles of Judah, and said unto them, What evil thing is this that ye do, and profane the Sabbath-day ?

THE late venerable Bishop Porteous, when on the brink of the grave, felt that he could not depart in peace till he had expressed his disapprobation of the profanation of the Lord's day so prevalent in his diocese. "I had, for some time past," he says, "observed in several of the papers, an account of a meeting, chiefly of military gentlemen, at an hotel of the west end of the town, which was regularly announced, as held every other Sunday during the winter season. This appeared to me, and to every friend of religion, a needless and wanton profanation of the Christian Sabbath, which, by the laws both of God and man, was set apart for very different purposes ; and the bishops and clergy were severally censured for permitting such a glaring abuse of that sacred day to pass without notice or reproof. I determined that it should not, and therefore thought it best to go at once to the fountain-head, to the person of the highest and principal influence in the meeting, the Prince of Wales. [He was then, it is said, wrapped in flannel, and carried to Carlton-House.] I then requested the honour of an audience, and a personal conference with him on this subject. He very graciously granted it, and I had a conversation with him of more than half an hour. He entered immediately into my views, and confessed that he saw no reason for holding the meeting on Sundays, more than any other day of the week ; and he voluntarily proposed that the day should be changed from Sunday to Saturday for which he said that he would give immediate orders."

BOOK OF ESTHER.

Personal Conviction.

Chap. i. ver. 8.—The drinking was according to the law; none did compel: for so the king had appointed to all officers of his house, that they should do according to every man's pleasure.

"THE evening of this day," (Feb. 25, 1785,) says the Rev. David Brown in his journal, "was remarkable for a debate, in which my sentiments respecting song-singing, drinking to excess, &c., were brought to the test. After my glass of claret, I declined taking more; when the captain *forcibly* urged me, and would have taken my glass and filled it; but, with a determined air, I told him, he might attempt as easily to shake Gibraltar as to *shake me* from my purpose. It was replied, 'Then you must sing.' I told them, I considered it as inconsistent with my character, and I could not oblige them by a violation of my judgment. The captain observed, that we ought to accommodate ourselves to the spirit of the company we sit down with, and that it was only good breeding, and harmless to do so. I replied that I was a great advocate for liberty; that I gave large scope to others to follow their own judgments; and that I valued myself on this prerogative of man. I had opinions I could not part with to oblige any company whatsoever; that man must be dastardly and unprincipled, who would, to please others, act contrary to his judgment, and thus give up the most precious right of human nature. That respecting the innocency of table-singing, I would not hesitate to affirm that some songs were really criminal, and by no rules of morality in the world to be justified: and that to me all seemed improper and inconsistent. I added, that it was contrary to good sense, as well as good breeding, and all the laws of freedom, to press a person after such a declaration; and that I did not doubt but the present company, every one of them, would have as contemptible an opinion of me as I deserved, should I comply and give up my opinion; and concluded by answering to the captain's argument, saying, that I did not believe it would give him any satisfaction to hurt my feelings, but that I should disoblige him by granting what they had asked. To this the captain made a short and proper answer, that I should never more be pressed to anything disagreeable, or contrary to my judgment, as long as I was in his ship."

Anger Appeased.

Chap. ii. ver. 1—The wrath of King Ahasuerus was appeased.

MR. P——, a solicitor in London, had a shrewd little boy of about six years old. The child was playing one day when his father came into the room in a violent passion, a thing unusual with him. The child was amazed to see his father so agitated; he dropped his playthings, looked at his father for a moment, and walked up to him and caught his hand, and said, with an earnest look, "Why, father, you are in a passion, are you not?" This rebuke instantly dispelled his father's passion, and for years afterwards the effect of it remained, and checked any improper heat.

Personal Honour.

Chap. iii. ver. 2—All the king's servants that were in the king's gate, bowed, and reverenced Haman.

AN English country clergyman was bragging in a large company of the success he had in reforming his parishioners, on whom his labours, he said, had produced a wonderful change for the better. Being asked in what respect, he replied, that when he came first among them, they were a set of unmannerly clowns, who paid him no more deference than they did to one another; did not so much as pull off their hats when they spoke to him, but bawled out as roughly and familiarly as though he were their equal; whereas now, they never presumed to address him but cap in hand, and in a submissive voice made him their best bow when they were at ten yards' distance, and styled him your reverence at every word. A Quaker, who had heard the whole patiently, made answer, " And so, friend, the upshot of this reformation, of which thou hast so much carnal glory, is, that thou has taught thy people to worship thyself."

Eastern Raiment.

Chap. iv. ver. 4.—The queen sent raiment to clothe Mordecai, and to take away his sackcloth; but he received it not.

AN ambassador in the East informs us, that he was invited, with his companions, to dine with an eastern monarch. The interpreter told them that it was the custom that they should wear, over their own garments, the best of those which the king had sent them. At first they hesitated, and did not like to have their own robes hidden; but being told that it was expected from all ambassadors, and that the King would be much displeased if they came into his presence without his robes, they complied.

Individual Vanity.

Chap. v. ver. 11.—Haman told them of the glory of his riches, and the multitude of his children, and all the things wherein the king had promoted him.

A LADY whom the Hon. and Rev. W. B. Cadogan was one day visiting, having made many inquiries and remarks relating to his birth, family, and connections, " My dear madam," said Mr. C., "I wonder you can spend so much time upon so poor a subject! I called to converse with you upon the things of eternity!"

Sleeplessness Blessed.

Chap. vi. ver. 1.—On that night could not the king sleep; and he commanded to bring the book of records of the Chronicles; and they were read before the king.

A FEW years ago, a good man at Gravesend had retired to rest late on the Saturday night, having first secured the doors and windows of his house and shop. Weary, however, as he was with the labours of the week, he found it impossible to sleep; and having tossed about his bed for an hour or two without rest, he resolved to rise and spend an hour in the perusal of the Bible, as preparatory to the engagements of the Sabbath. He went downstairs with the Bible under his arm, and advancing towards one of the outer doors, he found several men who had broken into his house, and who, but for this singular interruption, would probably, in a very short period, have deprived him of the whole of his property.—Unbroken sleep, in the general, is a blessing, but sometimes the want of sleep is a mercy. The King of Persia was thus led to the knowledge of the facts that in the end prevented the massacre of all the Jews in his empire, which had been decreed to take place.

Evil Motives.

Chap. vii. ver. 4.—We are sold, I and my people, to be destroyed, to be slain, and to perish.

DON PEDRO, one of the Spanish captains taken by Sir Francis Drake, being examined before the Lords of the Privy Council, respecting their design of invading England, replied, "To subdue the nation, and root it out."—"And what meant you," said the Lords, "to do with the Catholics?"—"To send them, good men," said he, "directly to heaven, and you heretics to hell."—"For what end were your whips of cord and wire?"—"To whip you heretics to death." "What would you have done with the young children?"—"They above seven years old should have gone the way their fathers went; the rest should have lived in perpetual bondage, branded in the forehead with the letter L. for Lutheran."

Gladness in Believing.

Chap. viii. ver. 16.—The Jews had light, and gladness, and joy.

CAMBO, a negro in one of the Southern states of America, being desired to give some account of his conversion, proceeded as follows:—"While in my own country, (Guinea) me had no knowledge of the being of a God; me thought me should die like the beasts. After me was brought to America, and sold as a slave, as me and another servant of the name of Bess were working in the field, me began to sing one of my country songs, 'It is time to go home;' when Bess say to me, 'Cambo, why you sing so for?' Me say, 'Me no sick, me no sorry; why me no sing?' Bess say, 'You better pray to your blessed Lord and Massah, to have mercy on your soul.' Me look round, me look up, me see no one to pray to; but the words sound in my ears, 'Better pray to your Lord and Massah!' By and by me feel bad—sun shine sorry—birds sing sorry—land look sorry, but Cambo sorrier than them all. Then me cry out, 'Mercy, mercy, Lord! on poor Cambo!'—By and by, water come in my eyes, and glad come in my heart. Then sun look gay—woods look gay—birds sing gay—land look gay, but poor Cambo gladder than them all. Me love my Massah some; me want to love him more."

Peace.

Chap. ix. ver. 30.—Mordecai sent the letters unto all the Jews—with words of peace and truth.

A HISTORIAN who lived at the period of the Norman Conquest, in mentioning some kings of England before Alfred, with short appropriate epithets, names him with the simple but expressive addition of "The truth-teller."—A good man observed that *peace* was so desirable an object, that he would sacrifice everything but *truth* to obtain it.

The Good of the People.

Chap. x. ver. 3.—Mordecai was accepted of the multitude of his brethren, seeking the wealth of his people, and speaking peace to all his seed.

MR. HOWARD, the philanthropist, with the view of promoting the health and comfort of his tenants, pulled down all the cottages on his estate, and rebuilt them in such a situation, and on such a plan, as to preserve them from the damp of the soil. To each of these neat and simple habitations he allotted a piece of garden ground, sufficient to supply the family of its occupier with potatoes and other vegetables.

He always let the cottages thus so materially improved at the original rent of twenty to thirty shillings a-year; so that there was scarcely a poor person in the village who was not anxious to have the privilege, which however was not so promiscuously or thoughtlessly conferred, but uniformly reserved for the industrious, the sober, and the deserving; and these were required, as a condition of their enjoying it, to attend regularly some place of worship, and to abstain from public-houses, and from pernicious amusements. To secure their compliance with these rules, he made them tenants at will. The natural consequence of these excellent regulations, was a tenantry distinguished by their happiness, order, neatness, and morality; possessing and enjoying a great portion of temporal comfort, and carefully taught the grounds on which to build their hopes for eternity,—namely, on Christ and him crucified.

BOOK OF JOB.

No Repining.

Chap. i. ver. 21, 22.—The Lord gave, and the Lord hath taken away; blessed be the name of the Lord.—In all this Job sinned not, nor charged God foolishly.

A PIOUS lady, who had lost a very promising child, was one day sitting with her little daughter of about three years of age by her side, and conversing with her respecting the death of her little brother. She told her that God had taken him to heaven, and as she spoke she wept. The little girl, after a few moments of pensive thought, asked her mother, "Was it *proper* for God to take H—— to heaven?" To which she replied in the affirmative. "Well, then," said she, "if it was proper for God to take him away, what do you cry for, mamma?"

Receiving from God.

Chap. ii. ver. 10.—What! shall we receive good at the hand of God, and shall we not receive evil?

THE Oriental philosopher, Lokman, while a slave, being presented by his master with a bitter melon, immediately ate it all. "How was it possible," said the master, "for you to eat so nauseous a fruit?" Lokman replied, "I have received so many favours from you, that it is no wonder I should once in my life eat a bitter melon from your hand." The generous answer of the slave struck his master to such a degree, that he immediately gave him his liberty. With such sentiments of *gratitude, submission,* and *ready* obedience, should men receive sorrows and afflictions from the hand of God.

The Grave.

Chap. iii. ver. 19.—The small and great are there.

AFTER Saladin the Great had subdued Egypt, passed the Euphrates and conquered cities without number—after he had retaken Jerusalem, and performed extraordinary exploits in those wars which superstition had stirred up for the recovery of the Holy Land, he finished his life in the performance of an action, which ought to be transmitted to the latest posterity. A moment before he uttered his last sigh, he called the herald, who had carried his banners before him in all his battles ; he commanded him to fasten to the top of a lance the shroud in which the dying prince was soon to be buried. "Go," said he, "carry the lance, unfurl the banner ; and, while you lift up this standard, proclaim—'This, this is all that remains of all the glory of Saladin the Great, the conqueror and King of the empire.'"

The Lion.

Chap. iv. ver. 10.—The roaring of the lion, and the voice of the fierce lion.

RUBENS, a celebrated artist, when painting a lion from the only living specimen he ever had in his power to study, expressed a desire to see him in the act of roaring. Anxious to please him, the keeper plucked a whisker of the royal beast, and with such success, that he daily repeated the experiment. Rubens, however, perceived such deadly wrath in the countenance of the animal, that he begged the man to desist : the hint was at first regarded, but too soon neglected. The consequence was dreadful ; the enraged lion struck down the keeper, and lay upon him the whole day : in the evening he was shot by a body of guards ; but in the agonies of death the keeper was torn to pieces.

Physically Chastened.

Chap. v. ver. 17.—Behold, happy is the man whom God correcteth ; therefore despise not thou the chastening of the Almighty.

DR. WATTS, from his early infancy to his dying day, scarcely ever knew what health was ; but however surprising it may appear, he looked on the affliction as the greatest blessing of his life. The reason he assigned for it was, that being naturally of a warm temper, and an ambitious disposition, these visitations of Divine Providence weaned his affections from the world, and brought every passion into subjection to Christ. This he often mentioned to his dear friend, Sir Thomas Abney, in whose house he lived many years.

Inhabitants of the Water.

Chap. vi. ver. 15.—My brethren have dealt deceitfully as a brook, and as the stream of brooks they pass away.

"TO-DAY," says Mr. Whitefield in the journal of his first voyage to Georgia, "Colonel C. came to dine with us ; and in the midst of our meal, we were entertained with a most agreeable sight. It was a shark, about the length of a man, which followed our ship, attended with five smaller fishes, called *pilot-fish*, much like our mackerel, but larger. These, I am told, always keep the shark company ; and, what is most surprising, though the shark is so ravenous a creature, yet let it be ever so hungry, it will not touch one of them. Nor are they less faithful to him ; for, as I am informed, if the shark is hooked, very often these little creatures will cleave close to his fins, and are often taken up with him.—Go to the pilot-fish, thou that forsakest a friend in adversity, consider his ways, and be ashamed."

Life a Burden.

Chap. vii. ver. 16.—I would not live alway.

DR. DWIGHT'S mother lived to be more than a hundred years of age. When she was a hundred and two, some people visited her on a certain day, and while they were with her, the bell was heard to toll for a funeral. The old lady burst into tears, and said, "When

will the bell toll for me ? It seems that the bell will never toll for me.
I am afraid that I shall never die."

"How gladly my spirit would part
From all that around me I see!
There is but one lingering wish in my heart ;—
'Tis away from the earth and its sorrows to be.
Oh! when will the bell toll for me ?"

Industry.

Chap. viii. ver. 7.—Though thy beginning was small, yet thy latter end should greatly increase.

LATELY died, aged 68, Richard Holt, Esq., banker, and father of the Corporation of Grantham. In this gentleman there is a strong proof of the effect of industry and persevering application to business. In early life he commenced with a small capital as a grocer and tallow-chandler on the premises where he died : he was but rarely seen except behind his counter, or in his counting-house, where he continued with unabated diligence till within a week of his death, leaving, it is generally believed, property to the amount of upwards of £100,000.

Sudden Death.

Chap. ix ver. 23.—If the scourge slay suddenly, he will laugh at the trial of the innocent.

AT a meeting of ministers in Leicestershire, about seventy years ago, among other subjects, one of them proposed the above passage for discussion. Deep seriousness pervaded the conversation, while each minister gave his thoughts upon the text. When it came to the turn of a Mr. Christian to speak, he dwelt upon the subject with an unusual degree of feeling. He considered it as referring to the *sudden death* of the righteous ; and was expatiating very largely on the desireableness of such an event, and the happy surprise with which it would be attended ; when, behold, amidst a flood of rapturous tears, he took his flight, while the words were still faultering on his tongue! The brethren did not at first perceive that he was dead ; but thought the strength of his feelings had forbid his utterance. At their next social meeting, Mr. Woodman preached on the occasion from 2 Kings ii. 11. "And it came to pass, as they still went on and talked, that, behold, there appeared a chariot of fire, and horses of fire, and parted them both asunder ; and Elijah went up by a whirlwind into heaven."

Growth in Religion.

Chap x. ver. 15.—If I be righteous, yet will I not lift up my head.

SOME time after Mr. Newton had published his Omicron's Letters, and described the three stages of growth in religion—from the *blade*, the *ear*, and the *full corn in the ear*—distinguishing them by the letters A, B, and C, a conceited young minister wrote to Mr. N., telling him that he read his own character accurately drawn in that of C. ; Mr. N. wrote in reply, that in drawing the character of C, or full maturity, he had forgotten to add, till now, one prominent feature of C's character, namely—that C *never knew his own face.*

Bereavement.

Chap. xi. ver. 10.—If he cut off—or gather together, then who can harden him ?

TO a lady who was bitterly lamenting the death of an infant child, Bishop Heber related the following beautiful apologue, as one with which he had himself been affected.—A shepherd was mourning over the death of his favourite child, and in the passionate and rebellious feeling of his heart, was bitterly complaining, that what he loved most tenderly, and was in itself most lovely, had been taken from him. Suddenly, a stranger of grave and venerable appearance stood before him, and beckoned him forth into the field. It was night, and not a word was spoken till they arrived at the fold, when the stranger thus addressed him : " When you select one of these lambs from the flock, you choose the best and most beautiful among them ; why should you murmur, because I, the good Shepherd of the sheep, have selected from those which you have nourished for me, the one which was most fitted for my eternal fold ? " The mysterious stranger was seen no more, and the father's heart was comforted.

Evil Prosperity.

Chap. xii. ver. 6.—The tabernacles of robbers prosper, and they that provoke God are secure ; into whose hand God bringeth abundantly.

DR. ARBUTHNOT, after commenting on the great riches and unparalleled iniquities of the infamous Charties, concludes ; " O, indignant reader ! think not his life useless to mankind. Providence connived at his execrable designs, to give to after ages a conspicuous proof and example of how small estimation is exorbitant wealth in the sight of God, by his bestowing it on the most unworthy of mortals !"

Trust in God.

Chap. xiii. ver. 15.—Though he slay me, yet will I trust in him."

THE late Rev. John Butterworth, a minister of England, speaking of his religious experiences, says, " One day as I was reading in a book called the 'Marrow of Modern Divinity,' a sentence from Luther was quoted, which was this, 'I would run into the arms of Christ, if he stood with a drawn sword in his hand.' This thought came bolting into my mind—' so will I too ;'—and those words of Job occurred —'Though he slay me, yet will I trust in him.' My burden dropped off ; my soul was filled with joy and peace through believing in Christ ; a *venturesome believing*, as Mr. Belcher calls it, was the means of setting me at liberty ; nor have I ever been in such perplexity, respecting my interest in Christ, since that time ; though I have had various trials in other respects."

Where is He ?

Chap. xiv. ver. 10.—Man dieth and wasteth away ; yea, man giveth up the ghost, and where is he ?

ONE Lord's day, the Rev. Mr Button, of London, preached at Hurlington from the above text. After a variety of pertinent remarks on the morality of man, and the state of the soul after death, Mr. B. suggested that it was possible some one or other in the congregation might be removed by death that day ; and that being the case, it became each one to put the question to himself—"Where am I likely to be ? In heaven or in hell ?"—Returning to the afternoon service, Mr B. was met at the meeting-house door by one of the members of the church, who said, " An affecting providence, Sir, has just taken place ! The congregation is assembled, and a man in the gallery is now fallen down, apparently dead : he is carried into the vestry." A medical gentleman was immediately sent for, who said that the person had died of an apoplectic fit. The awakening providence produced a deep solemnity in the congregation. "Be ye also ready; for at such an hour as ye think not, the Son of Man cometh."

Pray without Ceasing.

Chap. xv. ver. 4.—Yea, thou castest off fear, and restrainest prayer before God.

AN aged person, who had been many years a well-esteemed member of the church, at length became a drunkard, and was excommunicated, and died in awful circumstances. Some of his dying words were these—"I often prayed unto God for a mercy, which he still denied me. At length I grew angry at God; whereupon I grew slack in my acquaintance with the Lord: ever since which he hath dreadfully forsaken me; and I know that now he hath no mercy for me."

The Shadow of Death.

Chap. xvi. ver. 16.—On my eyelids is the shadow of death.

MR. GEORGE MOIR, an eminently pious man, after having been worn out by a long and painful illness, was told by his wife, that the change of his countenance indicated the speedy approach of death. "Does it!" he replied; "bring me a glass." On looking at himself in the glass, he was struck with the appearance of a corpse which he saw in his countenance: but giving the glass back, he said, with calm satisfaction, "Ah! death has set his mark on my body, but Christ has set his mark upon my soul."

Mockers Reproved.

Chap. xvii. ver. 2.—Are there not mockers with me?

WHEN the late Rev. John Brown of Whitburn was going to London by sea, in 1814, some fellow passengers of the baser sort, knowing or guessing his profession, were resolved to play off their profane wit upon him; with this design they wrote him a note, saying, that as they presumed he was one that was acquainted with, and could apply the "balm of Gilead," they were anxious he would prescribe for a young woman who was under great distress of mind. Having read the note, and perceiving at once the spirit of it, he went down to the cabin from which it had been brought to him, and holding it open in his hand, said, "Gentlemen, it is of little importance what insults you offer me personally, but I cannot, and will not, bear to see Him, whose I am, and whom I serve, insulted. Mock not, lest your bands be made strong." The effect of his appearance and address were such, that during the rest of the passage he was treated with the utmost respect.

Counted as Beasts.

Chap. xviii. ver. 3.—Wherefore are we counted as beasts, and reputed vile in your sight?

"THE present number in the girl's school," says Mrs. Mault in a letter from the East Indies, "is fifty-eight; and some of them are interesting children. About one-third of these girls are slaves; and as the children of slaves here are always the property of the mother's master, we have formed the resolution, that each girl, by her own industry, shall purchase her freedom before she leaves the school.—It will give you some idea in what light slaves are viewed by the higher castes, who are their masters, when I mention one circumstance. A girl in the school had become big enough to work in her master's field : he therefore came to make his claim to her. I asked him if it would not be well for her to learn to read ? and whether he should not allow her to do so ? He replied, " It may be well for you to instruct her, as you will get a better place in heaven thereby ; but it is enough for me if my bullocks and slaves do the work required in the fields ? " Here you see man, who is immortal, classed with the brutes which perisheth. And this is not a solitary instance ; for the lower classes in society here are not allowed to enjoy even the same privileges as cows, and some other of the brute creation ! "

My Redeemer Liveth.

Chap. xix. ver. 25.—I know that my Redeemer liveth, and that he shall stand at the latter day upon the earth.

" I HAVE seen," says Mr. Hervey, " Dr. Glyn's poem, entitled, ' The Day of Judgment.' It is not without elegance and pathos ; but its chief deficiency is, that it neglects to ascribe proper honour to *Christ.* He is, indeed, slightly hinted at in one chosen line ; but he should have been made the most distinguishing figure throughout the whole piece. All judgment is committed to him. It is *Christ* who will come in the clouds of heaven ; we must all appear before the judgment-seat of *Christ.* This, to the believer, is a most delightful consideration—*My Redeemer is my Judge !* He who died for me, passes the final sentence. Look ! how great is his majesty and glory ! so great is my atonement and propitiation."

Wealth and Contentment.

Chap. xx. ver. 22.—In the fulness of his sufficiency he shall be in straits.

" I KNEW a man," says one, " that had wealth and riches, and several houses, all beautiful, and ready furnished, and who would often trouble himself and his family by removing from one house to another. Being asked by a friend why he removed so often, he replied, it was to find content in some one of them, ' Content,' said his friend, ' ever dwells in a meek and quiet soul.' "

Frivolity.

Chap. xxi. ver 12, 13.—They take the timbrel and harp, and rejoice at the sound of the organ.—They spend their days in wealth, and in a moment go down to the grave.

MR. and Mrs. Geddes, who lived in the state of New York, had risen from poverty and obscurity to wealth and distinction. Their prosperity appears, however, to have been unsanctified, and they were led to indulge in those amusements which tend to banish serious reflection and to bring the whole soul under the debasing influence of this world. One evening, memorable in the annals of amusements in the place where they lived, Mrs. Geddes was present. All was hilarity and mirth around her ; but from some cause, Mrs. Geddes had not her accustomed flow of spirits. She had been slightly indisposed, but was now apparently well. She did not, however, fully participate in the general mirth that surrounded her. A gentleman present, who was an intimate acquaintance, attempted to rally her : " Why, Mrs. Geddes, you seem rather sober ; are you becoming serious, or are you growing old ? " " I am not very serious." replied Mrs. Geddes, " and not so old but that I can dance, and if you doubt it, I will dance with you." The offer was joyfully accepted. " Give place, ladies," said the gentleman, as he led her into the forming circle, "Mrs. Geddes is going to join with us." New joy animated all countenances ; the music gave forth its thrilling strains. "On with the dance !" seemed the impulse of every heart. The dance went on ; Mrs. Geddes moved a few steps, and sunk down a lifeless corpse !

Have Compassion.

Chap. xxii. ver. 7.—Thou hast not given water to the weary to drink and thou hast witholden bread from the hungry.

AN Indian, who had not met with his usual success in hunting, wandered down to a plantation, among the back settlements of Virginia, and seeing a planter at his door, asked him for a morsel of bread, for he was very hungry. The planter bid him "Begone, for he would give him none." "Will you give me then a cup of your beer ?" said the Indian. "No ; you shall have none here," replied the planter. "But I am very faint," said the savage ; "will you give me only a draught of cold water ?" "Get you gone, you Indian dog, you shall have nothing here," said the planter. It happened some time after, that the planter went on a shooting party up into the woods, where, intent upon his game, he missed his company, and lost his way, and night coming on, he wandered through the forest, till he espied an Indian wigwam. He approached the savage's habitation, and asked him to show him the way to a plantation, on that side of the country. "It is too late for you to go there this evening, Sir," said the Indian, "but if you will accept of my homely fare, you are welcome." He then offered him some venison, and such other refreshments as his store afforded, and having laid some bear-skins for his bed, he desired that he would repose himself for the night, and he would awake him early in the morning, and conduct him on his way. Accordingly, in the morning they set off, and the Indian led him out of the forest, and put him on the road he was to go. But just as they were taking leave, he stepped before the planter, and turning round, stared full in his face, and bid him say, "whether he recollected his features." The planter was now struck with horror, when he beheld in his kind protector, the Indian whom he had so harshly treated. He confessed that he knew him, and was full of excuses for his brutal behaviour ; to which the Indian replied, "When you see a poor Indian fainting for a cup of cold water, don't say again, 'Get you gone, you Indian dog !'" The Indian then wished him well on his journey, and left him. It is not difficult to say which of these had the best claim to the name of Christian.

The Word of God.

Chap. xxiii. ver. 12.—I have esteemed the words of his mouth more than my necessary food.

"BEING in company," says one, "with a young officer in the East India Company's service, lately arrived, he mentioned that one of the seamen died on their passage home, and when that happens, it is a custom among shipmates to sell all their clothes by auction, and this was done to the person alluded to. In his chest was a Bible, which was put up by itself at sixpence ; it presently got up to twelve shillings, and the captain desired the auctioneer to knock it down, as it was too much for it, he said. And my informant added, he had no doubt but it would have been sold for a guinea, if they had been let alone. He also said, that a Bible was considered a valuable acquisition by many of the seamen on board that ship ; and that frequently, at leisure hours, one person read the Scriptures to many of his shipmates, who were all attention to hear."

Human Murder.

Chap. xxiv. ver. 14.—The murderer, rising with the light, killeth the poor and needy, and in the night is as a thief.

SOMETIMES murders, secretly committed, have been brought to light in a very remarkable manner. The following is an instance taken from an American newspaper : "In the village of Manchester, Vermont, several years since, R. Colvin, a man of respectable connections and character, suddenly and mysteriously disappeared; all search and inquiry proved futile and in vain, until within a few weeks, a person dreamed that he had appeared to him, and informed him that he had been murdered by two persons whom he named, and that he had been buried in such a place, a few rods distant from a sapling, bearing a particular mark, which he minutely described. The same dream occurred three times successively before he awoke, and each time the deceased seemed very solicitous for him to follow. Upon awaking, his feelings were wrought up to such a degree, and he was so impressed with a belief of the fact, that he determined to collect some friends, and follow the directions laid down in the dream. He did so, and discovered, to his great surprise, not only a tree marked precisely as described, but also the appearance of a grave ; and upon digging, found a human skeleton ! After this discovery, Stephen and Jesse Brown, the persons implicated in the dream, were apprehended, and put in confinement, and, after a few days, confessed the deed. They were tried, convicted, and sentenced to be executed on the 18th of January last." (1820.)

Justification.

Chap. xxv. ver. 4.—How then can man be justified with God ?

ABOUT the year 1100, amidst the almost universal darkness of popery, there was a form of consolation to the dying, said to be written by Anselm, archbishop of Canterbury ; and in the year 1475, printed in Germany. It was in the following words :—"Go to, then, as long as thou art in life,—put all thy confidence in the death of Christ alone,—confide in nothing else,—commit thyself wholly to it,—mix thyself wholly with it,—roll thyself wholly on it ; and if the Lord God will judge thee, say, 'Lord, I put the death of our Lord Jesus Christ between me and thy judgment, otherwise, I contend not with thee :'—and if he say, 'Thou art a sinner,' reply, 'Put the death of our Lord Jesus Christ between me and my sins :'—and if he say, 'Thou hast deserved damnation,' let thine answer be, 'Lord, I spread the death of our Lord Jesus Christ between me and my demerits ; I offer his merits for the merits I should have had and have not.' If he still insist that he is angry at thee, reply again, 'Lord, I put the death of the Lord Jesus Christ between me and thine anger.''

Understanding God Fully.

Chap. xxvi. ver. 14.—The thunder of his power who can understand ?

"WERE I fully able to describe God," says Epictetus, 'I should be God myself, or God must cease to be what he is."

Terrors at Sea.

Chap. xxvii. ver. 20.—Terrors take hold on him as waters.

VOLNEY, a French infidel, was on board a vessel during a violent storm at sea, when the ship was in imminent danger of being lost; he threw himself on the deck, crying in agony, "Oh, my God! my God!" "There is a God, then, Monsieur Volney?" said one of the passengers to him. "O yes," exclaimed the terrified infidel, "there is, there is! Lord save me." The ship, however, got safely into port. Volney was extremely disconcerted when his confession was publicly related; but excused it by saying, he was so frightened by the storm that he did not know what he said, and immediately returned to his atheistical sentiments.

Living Wisely.

Chap. xxvii. ver. 28.—Unto man he said, Behold the fear of the Lord, that is wisdom; and to depart from evil is understanding.

MR HERVEY, in a letter to a friend, gives the following account of his views and feelings, when brought to the gates of death by a severe illness:—"Were I," says he, "to enjoy Hezekiah's grant, and have fifteen years added to my life, I would be much more frequent in my applications to a throne of grace. We sustain a mighty loss by reading so much and praying so little. Were I to renew my studies, I would take my leave of these accomplished trifles—the historians, the orators, the poets of antiquity—and devote my attention to the Scriptures of truth. I would sit with much greater assiduity at my Divine Master's feet, and desire to know nothing but Jesus Christ and him crucified. This wisdom, whose fruits are peace in life, consolation in death, and everlasting salvation after death—this I would trace, this I would seek, this I would explore, through the spacious and delightful fields of the Old and New Testament."

Ready to Perish.

Chap. xxix. ver. 13.—The blessing of him that was ready to perish came upon me.

A GENTLEMAN from the country, passing through the streets of the metropolis, saw a poor man who had formerly been employed by him as a labourer, and his circumstances were those of extreme poverty and distress. He had come up to London to seek employment, but, failing to obtain it, was reduced to a state of extreme destitution. The gentleman gave him a shilling, and passed on, scarcely recollecting the circumstance, till it was recalled to his mind by the man himself, whom, about twelve months afterwards, he met again, and whose decent clothing and cheerful looks indicated a favourable change in his circumstances. "Sir," said the poor fellow, "I am bound to bless you and pray for you as long as I live; that shilling you gave me has been the making of me: bad enough I wanted it for food; but I was resolved first to turn it round: so I went up and down one of the principal streets, and collected as many hare-skins as it would purchase; these I disposed of, and contented myself with such food as the profits would afford, still reserving the shilling as my stock in trade. By degrees I saved a little more, and to you, Sir, I am indebted for the foundation of it all. But for your timely aid, I might have perished. May a blessing attend you as long as you live."

Grief for the Poor.

Chap. xxx. ver. 25.—Did I not weep for him that was in trouble? was not my soul grieved for the poor?

ONE Sabbath evening, as Mr. Cruden, the author of the Concordance to the Bible, was returning from a place of worship, he accidentally fell in with a man whose appearance betrayed anxious sorrow, fixed melancholy, and deep despair. This was too interesting an object to the sympathising mind of Mr. Cruden, to be carelessly neglected, and making up to the man, he tenderly accosted him, and in course of conversation learned that the extreme poverty of his family, together with some other causes, had driven him to the desperate resolution of committing suicide. With the most affectionate tenderness, Mr. C. expostulated with the man on the wickedness of his intention, counselled him against the perpetration of the deed, administered such friendly consolations, and accompanied the whole with present pecuniary assistance, and promises of future support, that the poor man was prevented from his horrid purpose, and returned home to his family in the most cheerful state of mind.

Justice to the Widow.

Chap. xxxi. ver. 16.—If I have withheld the poor from their desire, or have caused the eyes of the widow to fail.

WHEN Sir Thomas More was Lord Chancellor, he decreed a gentleman to pay a sum of money to a poor widow, whom he had wronged; to whom the gentleman said, "Then I hope your lordship will grant me a long day to pay it." "I will grant your motion," said the Chancellor, "Monday next is St Barnabas' day, which is the longest day in the year; pay it to the widow that day, or I will commit you to the Fleet."

Speaking Back.

Chap. xxxii. ver. 14.—Job hath not directed his words against me; neither will I answer him with your speeches.

MR. NEWTON of London was a very candid and friendly critic, and was often applied to by young authors for his opinions and remarks, which he would give very candidly, and sometimes under the name of Nibblings. On one of these occasions, a practical essay was put into his hand which he approved; but a letter was appended, addressed to an obscure and contemptible writer, who had said very unwarrantable and absurd things on the subject, and whom therefore the writer attacked with little ceremony. The following is a specimen of some of Mr. Newton's nibblings: "Were the affair mine, I would take no notice of Mr. Black, but, if I did, it should be with the hope, at least with the desire, of doing good, even to him. This would make me avoid every harsh epithet. He is not likely to be benefited by calling him a fool. The Evangelists simply relate what is said and done, and use no bitterness nor severity, even when speaking of Herod, Pilate, or Judas. I wish their manner was more adopted in controversy."

The Dream.

Chap. xxxiii. ver. 15, 16.—In a dream, in a vision of the night, when deep sleep falleth upon men, in slumberings upon the bed; then he openeth the ears of men, and sealeth their instruction.

"A POOR man," says the late Rev. Thomas Scott, "most dangerously ill, of whose religious state I entertained some hopes, seemed to me in the agonies of death. I sat by his bed for a considerable time, expecting to see him expire; but at length he awoke as from sleep, and noticed me. I said, 'You are extremly ill.' He replied, 'Yes; but I shall not die this time.' I asked the ground of this extraordinary confidence, saying, that I was persuaded he would not recover. To this he answered, 'I have just dreamed that you, with a very venerable-looking person, came to me; he asked you what you thought of me: *What kind of tree is it? Is there any fruit?* You said, *No, but there are blossoms. Well, then,* he said, *I will spare it a little longer.*' All reliance upon such a dream I should, in other circumstances, have scouted as enthusiasm and presumption; but it so exactly met my ideas as to the man's state of mind, which, however, I had never communicated to him, and the event, much beyond all expectation, so answered his confidence, by his recovery, that I could not but think there was something peculiar. On his recovery, this man for a time went on very well; but afterwards he gave up all attention to religion, and became very wicked; and, when I reminded him of what has been related, he treated the whole with indifference, not to say with profane contempt. But I have since learned, from very good authority, that, after I left that part of the country, (the neighbourhood of Olney,) he was again brought under deep conviction of sin; recollected and dolefully bemoaned his conduct towards me, and with respect to his dream, and became a decidedly religious character."

Away from God.

Chap. xxxiv. ver. 29.—When he hideth his face, who then can behold him? whether it be done against a nation, or against a man only.

THE late Rev. Ebenezer White, a pious minister in Chester, was subject to frequent depression of spirits. In a letter to his mother, some time before his death, he says,—"In addition to my bodily evils, I am the subject of great darkness and stupidity of mind. I can hardly think on divine things, or indeed any thing, for my mind is as feeble as my body. I have, however, sense enough left to hear some awful voices in this rod. God seems to say, 'Who sent you into my vineyard?—What hast thou to do to declare my statutes?—Give an account of thy stewardship!—Cast out the unprofitable servant!—Let another take his office!'—I have many other dismal impressions; and my confidence is far too weak to efface them. My only hope is the broad ground of the gospel declaration, as that, 'Christ came to save sinners—His blood cleanseth from all sin—He is able to save,' &c. And sometimes, but very rarely, I have a humble hope that God intends to save me, though it be as by fire."

God blesseth Man.

Chap. xxxv. ver. 11.—Who teacheth us more than the beasts of the earth, and maketh us wiser than the fowls of heaven?"

LUTHER tells us of two cardinals, who, as they were riding to the council of Constance, saw a shepherd in the field weeping. One of them being affected with it, rode up to him to comfort him, and coming near to him, desired to know the reason of his weeping. The shepherd was unwilling to tell him at first, but at last he told him, saying, "I looking upon this toad, considered that I never praised God as I ought, for making me such an excellent creature as a man, comely and reasonable. I have not blessed him that made me not such a deformed toad as this." The cardinal hearing this, and considering that God had done far greater things for him than for this poor shepherd, fell senseless from his mule; his servants lifting him up, and bringing him to the city, he recovered his senses, and cried out, "O, St. Austin! how truly didst thou say, the unlearned rise and take heaven by force, and we, with all our learning, wallow in flesh and blood!"

God is Mighty.

Chap. xxxvi. ver. 5.—Behold, God is mighty, and despiseth not any.

THE late Rev. Thomas Charles of Bala, North Wales, in a letter to a friend, remarks:—" You say that you are *without all sense and feeling in religion.* I might ask you as the Lord did Jonah,—' Doest thou well to complain?' Is there not abundantly more cause to be thankful? Think of the Lord's goodness, love, and mercy; and this will effectually give you both sense and feeling. I often find myself in the frame of mind you describe. But when so, if I can but take (and I have been often able) even an obscure view of the Lord's goodness to me, so unfeeling a creature, then my heart begins to melt, and I recover in some degree my spiritual senses. It was so with me a few days ago, when the words of Elihu affected me exceedingly:— ' Behold, God is mighty, and despiseth not any.' I did not know, previously, what to do with myself, feeling myself totally devoid of every thing good. But these words—' despiseth not any '—so much affected me that I could not but go to the Lord, notwithstanding my coldness and insensibility; and I repeated the words as my apology for coming. ' Thou despiseth not any, therefore I will and must come to thee. He did not frown upon me for my boldness, but filled me with good things. Think as bad as you please of yourself; but be sure to think well of God."

The Snow.

Chap. xxxvii. ver. 6.—He saith to the snow, Be thou on the earth.

IN a work, called *Voyages aux Alpes*, which has recently been published in Paris, a curious account is given of an avalanche which occurred in Switzerland many years ago. During the absence of a Swiss farmer, his cottage and stable were, by the fall of the avalanche, enclosed in snow; his wife and daughter were at the time in the stable. Six weeks afterwards, the snow having melted a little, an opening was effected, and the two females were found alive, having been supported by the milk of the cow during that long period. The space left free from the snow was sufficient for air, and there was a good winter's stock of provisions for the cow near the stable.

The Waters Frozen.

Chap. xxxviii. ver. 30.—The waters are hid as with a stone, and the face of the deep is frozen.

A MISSIONARY who had brought over a native from India, was surprised one day by her saying to him, "O, Sir, what wicked men these sailors are! What do you think they have been telling me! They have been telling me that in England, sometimes the water gets so hard that men can stand upon it; but do you think I believe them; *no*, I don't!" The missionary replied, "But it is so, my dear, and now you believe it, don't you?" "Yes," said she, "I believe it, because *you* say so: but *how* can it be?"

The Eagle.

Chap. xxxix. ver. 28, 29.—She dwelleth and abideth on the rock.— From thence she seeketh the prey.

SIR ROBERT SIBBALD relates, that a woman in the Orkney Islands, having left her child, of about one year old, in a field, while she went to some distance, an eagle passing by took up the infant by its clothes, and carried it to her nest on a neighbouring rock; which being observed by some fishermen, they instantly pursued the eagle, attacked her nest, and brought back the child unhurt.

Speaking to God.

Chap. xl. ver. 4, 5.—Behold, I am vile; what shall I answer thee? I will lay mine hand upon my mouth.—Once have I spoken, but I will not answer; yea, twice, but I will proceed no farther.

"IT has been often observed," says Dr. Owen, in his 'Doctrine of Justification,' "that the school-men themselves, in their meditations and devotional writings, speak a language quite different from that which they use in their disputes and controversies; and I had rather learn what men really think on this head from their prayers than from their writings. Nor do I remember that I ever heard any good man, in his prayers, use any expressions about justification, wherein anything of self-righteousness was introduced. Nor have I observed that any public liturgies, (the Mass-Book excepted,) guide men in their prayers before God, to plead anything for their acceptance with him, or as the means or condition thereof,—but grace, mercy the righteousness and blood of Christ alone."

A Strange Incident.

Chap. xli. ver. 25.—When he raiseth up himself, the mighty are afraid.

"I HAVE to report," says a Protestant clergyman in the county of Donegal, in Ireland, "a most awful and unparelleled event, which took place in Inverbay, on Saturday last. Five men in a yawl were in pursuit of a shoal of sprats, for bait, with hand-loops, when a whale in pursuit of the shoal, with open jaws, came in immediate contact with the yawl. Feeling the yawl, the monster closed his jaws and crushed it to pieces, with the exception of the two ends, in one of which was a young lad, in the act of putting out his loop; he was the only one out of the five that escaped. One man was found crushed, and fastened to a piece of the floating wreck. This sad accident took place within seventy yards of the deep shelving shore of Ballysigad; a hundred boats were at the time fishing about a mile distant. A bunch of hair from the gills of the whale, fastened in a shiver of the wreck, confirmed the idea that the boat was destroyed in the way described, which those on shore, and those in the boats, agree in attesting."

The Power of Prayer.

Chap. xlii. ver. 10.—And the Lord turned the captivity of Job, when he prayed to his friends.

"I WAS lately informed," says a missionary, "by a pious and able minister, in Somersetshire, that on the evening when the first permanent impressions were made on his mind, his pious mother was detained at home. But she spent the time devoted to public worship in secret prayer, for the salvation of her son; and so fervent did she become in these intercessions, that, like our Lord in Gethsemane, she fell on her face, and remained in fervent supplications till the service had nearly closed. Her son, brought under the deepest impressions by the sermon of his father, went into a field after the service, and there prayed most fervently for himself. When he came home the mother looked at her son with a manifest concern, anxious to discover whether her prayers had been heard, and whether her son had commenced the all-important inquiry, 'What shall I do to be saved?' In a few days the son acknowledged himself to be the subject of impressions of which none need be ashamed; impressions which lay the foundation of all excellence of character here, and of all blessedness hereafter."

BOOK OF PSALMS.

The Bitter Life.

Psalm i. ver. 1.—Blessed is the man that walketh not in the counsel of the ungodly, nor standeth in the way of sinners, nor sitteth in the seat of the scornful.

"I HAVE considered it as a great favour of God," says Dr. Hopkins of America, "that I was born and educated in a religious family, and among a people, in a country town, where a regard to religion and morality was common and prevalent; and the education of children and youth was generally practised in such a degree, that young people were generally orderly in their behaviour, and abstained from those open vices, which were then too common in sea-ports and populous places. I do not recollect that I ever heard a profane word from the children and youth with whom I was conversant, while I lived with my parents, which was till I was in my fifteenth year."

Divine Punishment.

Ps. iii. ver. 9.—Thou shalt break them with a rod of iron; thou shalt dash them in pieces like a potter's vessel.

FELIX, Earl of Wurtemburg, one of the captains of the Emperor Charles V., being at supper at Augsburg, in company with many who were threatening the sorest punishments on the persons of the pious Christians of that day, swore, before them all, that before he died he would ride up to his spurs in the blood of the Lutherans. That same night he was choked, probably by the bursting of a blood-vessel, which filled his throat, and at once removed him from the world.

God as a Shield.

Ps. ii. ver. 3.—Thou, O Lord, art a shield for me

LUTHER, when making his way into the presence of Cardinal Cajetan, who had summoned him to answer for his heretical opinions at Augsburg, was asked by one of the cardinal's minions, where he should find a shelter, if his patron, the Elector of Saxony, should desert him? "Under the shield of heaven!" was the reply. The silenced minion turned round, and went his way.

Evening Blessing.

Ps. iv. ver. 8.—I will both lay me down in peace, and sleep, for thou, Lord, only makest me dwell in safety.

A GENTLEMAN states, that many years ago he was present at the opening of a dissenting place of worship, in the town of Beaconsfield, in England. After hearing the late Mr. Cook of Maidenhead, and spending the day very agreeably, he took up his lodgings at the principal inn. When he entered the house, he found the late Rev. Matthew Wilks in the travellers' room. Before supper, Mr. Wilks rang the bell, and inquired at the master of the house if he had a Bible? He replied that he had. Mr. Wilks said, with much kindness of manner, "It is always my practice to return thanks to God for the mercies of the day, and to entreat his protection at night; and if you, and your wife, and servants, will come in, I shall be glad," The master of the house made no objection, and his wife and servants, and other persons present, came in. Mr. W. read the Scriptures, and engaged in prayer, in which he manifested much spirituality and fervour.

Morning Prayers.

Ps. v. ver. 3.—My voice shalt thou hear in the morning, O Lord; in the morning will I direct my prayer unto thee, and will look up.

"IN the days of our fathers," says Bishop Burnet, "when a person came early to the door of his neighbour, and desired to speak with the master of the house, it was as common a thing for the servants to tell him with freedom,—'My master is at prayer,' as it is now to say, 'My master is not up.'"

Praying in Faith.

Ps. vi. ver. 9.—The Lord hath heard my supplication; the Lord will receive my prayer.

A MINISTER of the gospel, in the north of England, had a dissolute son, who was an officer. The father had long sought the eternal welfare of his wicked child, but apparently in vain. On one occasion a remark was made to the father on the hopelessness of his son's condition. He replied by expressing his confidence, that so many prayers would not be lost. At length the father died. The son was still a profligate. Some time after his father's decease, the son was riding the horse on which his father had been accustomed to travel to preach the gospel, when a thought to the following effect darted into his mind:—"Poor creature, you used to carry a saint, and now you carry a devil." The issue was, he embraced religion, and his father's prayers were answered.

Forgive thine Enemy.

Ps. vii. ver. 4.—I have delivered him that without cause is mine enemy.

WHEN Bruce the traveller was in Abyssinia, one of the governors, according to the custom of the country, sent him twelve horses, saddled and bridled, desiring him to fix on one for his own use. The groom urged Bruce to mount one of them, assuring him it was a most excellent animal, and very quiet and safe to ride. It proved that the horse was extremely vicious, of which the man was well aware, and apparently had selected him with a malicious intention. The traveller, however, was well skilled in horsemanship; and, after a severe contest, he successfully curbed the unruly animal, completely exhausted him, and descended unhurt. The governor expressed the greatest surprise and concern at the transaction, and most solemnly protested his entire innocence of any design in it, adding, that the groom was already in irons, and before many hours passed would be put to death. "Sir," said the traveller, "as this man has attempted my life, according to the laws of the country, it is I that should name his punishment." "It is very true," replied the governor; "take him, and cut him in a thousand pieces, if you please, and give his body to the kites." "Are you really sincere in what you say?" asked Bruce, "and will you have no after excuses?" He swore solemnly that he would not. "Then," said Bruce, "I am a Christian; the way my religion teaches me to punish my enemies, is, by doing good for evil, and therefore, I keep you to the oath you have sworn. I desire you to set this man at liberty, and put him in the place he held before; for he has not been undutiful to you." Every one present seemed pleased with these sentiments; one of the attendants could not contain himself, but, turning to the governor, said, "Did not I tell you what my brother thought about this man? He was just the same all through Tigre." The governor, in a low voice, very justly replied, "A man that behaves as he does, may go through any country."

Reminded of Duty by a Child.

Ps. viii. ver. 8.—Out of the mouth of babes and sucklings hast thou ordained strength.

R., a little boy not more than four years old, having been accustomed from a very early age to bow at the throne of grace, while his parents engaged in domestic worship, feels so lively an interest in that holy duty, that whenever he is absent from the service, he weeps, and discovers much concern. He has been attached to the exercise from his infancy. One morning, when he was but fifteen months old, his father, having some particular business pressing upon his attention, was preparing hastily to leave the house, without discharging his duty as the priest of his household. As soon as the child perceived this, he ran to a chair, and knelt down. His father still proceeding to go out, he rose up, ran after him, and took hold of his coat to conduct him from the door to the usual place at which he knelt while engaged in social worship. This affecting deportment of the infant brought the father to tears, and compelled him to stay and perform the duty devolving upon him.

Knowing and Trusting God.

Ps. ix. ver. 10.—They that know thy name will put their trust in thee: for thou, Lord, hast not forsaken them that seek thee.

DURING Mr. Legh Richmond's last illness, a friend was speaking to him of the immense value and importance of their religious principles, when he raised himself upright in his chair, and with great solemnity of manner, said,—"Brother, we are only half awake—we are none of us more than half awake!—The enemy, as our poor people would say, has been very busy with me. I have been in great darkness— a strange thought has passed through my mind—it is all delusion.—Brother, brother, strong evidences, nothing but strong evidences will do at such an hour as this. I have looked here and looked there for them—all have failed me—and so I rest myself on the sovereign, free, and full grace of God, in the covenant by Christ Jesus; and there brother, (looking at his friend with a smile of tranquillity quite indescribable,) *there* I have found peace."

The Thoughts of the Wicked.

Ps. x. ver. 4.—God is not in all his thoughts.

A CHILD, instructed in a Sabbath school, on being asked by his teacher if he could mention a place where God was *not*, made the following beautiful and unexpected reply,—"Not in the thoughts of the wicked."

God sees All.

Ps. xi. ver. 4.—His eyes behold, his eyelids try the children of men.

A MAN who was in the habit of going into a neighbour's corn-field to steal the ears, one day took his son with him, a boy of eight years of age. The father told him to hold the bag, while he looked if any one was near to see him. After standing on the fence, and peeping through all the corn rows, he returned and took the bag from the child, and began his guilty work. "Father," said the boy, "you forgot to look somewhere else." The man dropt the bag in a fright, and said, "Which way, child?" supposing he had seen some one. "You forgot to look up to the sky, to see if God was noticing you." The father felt this reproof of the child so much, that he left the corn, returned home, and never again ventured to steal; remembering the truth his child had taught him, that the eye of God always beholds us.

Flattery.

Ps. xii. ver. 2.—With flattering lips, and with a double heart, do they speak.

WHEN a flattering priest told the emperor Constantine, that his godliness and virtues justly deserved to have in this life the empire of the world, and in the future life, to reign with the Son of God; the emperor cried,—"Fie—fie for shame! let me hear no more such unseemly speeches, but rather suppliantly pray to my Almighty Maker, that in this life, and in the life to come, I may be reckoned worthy to be his servant."

Spiritual Sight.

Ps. xiii. ver. 3.—Lighten my eyes, lest I sleep the sleep of death.

A LITTLE daughter of Charles I. died when only four years old. When on her death-bed, she was desired by one of her servants to pray. She said she could not say her long prayer, meaning the, "Our Father;" but that she would try to say her short one. "Lighten my darkness, O Lord God, and let me not sleep the sleep of death." As she said this, she laid her little head on the pillow, and expired.

Self-Righteousness.

Ps. xiv. ver. 3.—They are all gone aside, they are altogether become filthy; there is none that doeth good, no, not one.

AN influential country gentleman, and patron of a church, who, in his way, showed great kindness to a clergyman, was hearing the minister preach on a subsequent Sabbath. When the patron had reached home immediately after attending church, he said, "Here is gratitude for you; here I and my family have shown this man the greatest kindness, and the return he makes when he gets into the pulpit, is to tell us that we are great sinners unless we repent. He preaches that our good works go for nothing before God. This sermon will do very well for a penitentiary, a Newgate; but before a genteel and respectable audience, to tell them that they are sinners, is the most extraordinary conduct that they ever met with."

Evil Speaking.

Ps. xv. ver. 3.—He that backbiteth not with his tongue, nor doeth evil to his neighbour, nor taketh up a reproach against his neighbour.

"NO man," observes one of the friends of the late Dr. Waugh, "was more careful to defend the character of his brethren in anything defensible. On one occasion a minister, then a young man, having animadverted, in a company where Dr. W. was present, on the talents of another minister, in a manner which he thought might leave an unfavourable impression on the minds of persons present, he observed, 'I have known Mr. —— many years, and I never knew him speak disrespectfully of a brother in my life.'"

Saintly Companionship.

Ps. xvi ver. 3.—To the saints that are in the earth, and to the excellent, in whom is all my delight.

"ON Saturday, about ten o'clock," says the Rev. T. Charles of North Wales, in a letter, "I set out from Bristol. Just as I came to the outside of the gate of the city, I met a dear friend, and one whom Jesus loves. I was exceedingly glad to see him. I never expected to see him this side of eternity. He had been in a dangerous decline for this half-year; but now, through mercy, he is wonderfully recovered. He has nothing to depend on but providence; and the Lord put it into the heart of a rich merchant in the city to support and provide for him amply during the whole of his illness; so that, though possessing nothing, he had everything to enjoy. He turned his horse back, with the intention of accompanying me a mile or two. We talked; and our horses carried us one mile after another, till we had ridden fifteen miles; and both ourselves and our horses wanted some refreshment. His conversation was exceedingly savoury, and truly profitable; suited to one who had been, in his own apprehension and that of others, on the borders of heaven. I cannot look on our meeting, but as a particular appointment and blessing from providence. We stayed two hours together at the inn, and parted at last with much regret. You would have smiled to see our eyes fixed on each other, till distance obstructed our sight. Communion of saints is a blessing indeed. I would not, for anything, have it expunged from our creed."

Beholding God's Face.

Ps. xvii. ver. 15.—As for me, I will behold thy face in righteousness. I shall be satisfied, when I awake, with thy likeness.

A YOUNG man who died some years ago, when feeling the approach of death, is said to have uttered these rapturous expressions—"I find now it is no delusion! My hopes are well founded! Eye hath not seen, nor ear heard, neither hath it entered into the heart of man to conceive the glory I shall shortly partake of! Read your Bible! I shall read mine no more!—no more need it! Can this be dying? This body seems no longer to belong to the soul! It appears only as a curtain that covers it; and soon I shall drop this curtain, and be set at liberty! I rejoice to feel these bones give way, as it tells me, I shall shortly be with my God in glory!"

By the Power of God.

Ps. xviii. ver. 29.—By thee I have run through a troop, and by my God have I leaped over a wall.

DURING the rebellion of 1745, Colonel Gardiner accompanied the Rev. Ebenezer Erskine of Stirling to a meeting of the gentlemen of the town; and when endeavouring to inspire the company with the same ardour of patriotic heroism which glowed in his own bosom, he proceeded to state the deficiencies of the enemy's force in arms, in numbers, and in military talents; and affirmed that, were he at the head of a certain regiment which he once had the honour to command, he would not be afraid to encounter their whole army. Mr. Erskine standing by him, and marking his expressions, tapped him gently on the shoulder, and thus whispered in his ear, "Colonel, say, *under God.*" That great man, whose piety was equal to his courage, replied, smiling, "O yes, Mr. Erskine, I mean that, and having God for our general, we must be conquerors."

Better than Gold.

Ps. xix. ver. 10.—More to be desired are they than gold, yea, than much fine gold.

ABOUT the beginning of January 1818, four workmen, belonging to the Custom-House in Paris, who had often occasion to work for Mr. Week, a member of the Society of Friends, went to receive their new-year's gift. On seeing them, he informed them that he had provided for them fifteen francs, (twelve shillings and sixpence,) or, if they preferred it, which he would strongly recommend, a Bible. "Fifteen francs," said he, "are of little consequence, you will soon have spent them; but the word of God will remain with you, and you will always find in it consolation and advice." The eldest of the four said, "As for me, I should very much like the word of God, but it would be useless to me, as I cannot read; and if it makes no difference——" "Oh," said Mr. Week, "if you prefer the money, here it is." The next two also, on some account or other, preferred the francs, and Mr. Week then addressed the youngest, advising him to choose the Bible. "Since you say it is such an excellent book, I would rather," said the young man, "have it, and will read a chapter every day to my mother." "Let me hear how you can read it," said Mr. Week, and gave him one of the four Bibles, On opening it, he found a piece of gold worth forty francs. "You see," said Mr. Week, "the word of God already favours thee. Go home to thy mother." He was unable to express his gratitude. We may judge how the others looked, when they found each of the Bibles contained forty francs.

Trusting in God.

Ps. xx. ver. 7.—Some trust in chariots, and some in horses; but we will remember the name of the Lord our God.

HIS MAJESTY GEORGE III. was one day looking at the plate which had been recently brought from Hanover, and observing one of the articles with the arms of the Electro-rate engraved upon it, he said to the domestic who attended him, "This belonged to King George II.; I know it by the Latin inscription," which he read, adding, "In English it is, *I trust in my sword.* This," said he, "I always disliked; for had I nothing to trust in but my sword, I well know what would be the result; therefore, when I came to the crown, I altered it. My motto is—'I trust in the truth of the Christian religion.'" He then, with his usual condescension, said, "Which of the two inscriptions do you like best?" The attendant replied, "Your Majesty's is infinitely preferable to the other." He said, "I have ever thought so, and ever shall think so: for therein is my trust and confidence." He continued, "Think you, is it possible for any one to be happy and comfortable within himself, who has not that trust and confidence? I know there are those who affect to be at ease while living in a state of infidelity; but it is all *affectation;* it is only the *semblance of happiness*—THE THING ITSELF IS IMPOSSIBLE."

Evil Intentions.

Ps. xxi. ver. 11.—They imagined a mischievous device, which they were not able to perform.

A SAVAGE in the South Sea Islands, one day meeting two children wandering alone among the mountains, stopped them, and told the poor creatures he should kill, roast, and eat them. The boys said, "Do it, do it; and don't pretend that you will, and then you won't." He assured them that they should find he was not frightening them with a false pretence, for he would do as he said. Accordingly he kindled a fire, and was going—as the children, who durst not attempt to run away, said afterwards—to kill, disembowel, and bake them, in the manner that hogs are slaughtered and cooked. Meanwhile some girls coming suddenly in sight, and shrieking with alarm, the wretch fled into the woods. He was, however, soon hunted out, taken, and brought to justice. On his trial he did not deny his cannibal purpose; wherefore, on the testimony of the two lads, he was convicted and condemned to be hanged within a fortnight. The sentence was executed, and he confessed its justice.

The Meek.

Ps. xxii. ver. 26.—The meek shall eat and be satisfied.

THE Rev. Ebenezer Erskine having gone to assist the Rev. Mr. Grier of the College Church, Edinburgh, in administering the Lord's Supper, he lodged in the same house with Janet Paterson, a pious woman, whom he highly esteemed, (being kindly entertained, very probably under her own roof.) Finding him somewhat depressed in spirit on Sabbath morning, she reminded him of the promise—"The meek shall eat and be satisfied,"—adding, that these words had frequently been made sweet to her soul, on his account. Mr. Grier preached on that text,—"My flesh is meat indeed, and my blood is drink indeed;" and the first words he read to be sung after sermon, were the same that Janet Paterson had suggested for his encouragement in the morning. This, he says, melted his heart, and called forth ardent wishes that the promise might be accomplished to his soul.

Anointing the Head.

Ps. xxiii. ver. 5.—Thou anointest my head with oil; my cup runneth over.

"I CONFESS," says Captain Wilson, "that, since my return from India, I have been forcibly struck with several things, which prove the Scriptures to be an eastern book. For instance, the language of one of the Psalms, where David says, 'Thou anointest my head with oil, my cup runneth over,' most likely alludes to a custom which continues to this day. I once had this ceremony performed on myself, in the house of a rich Indian, in the presence of a large company. The gentleman of the house poured upon my hands and arms, a delightfully odoriferous perfume, put a golden cup into my hand, and poured wine into it till it ran over, assuring me, at the same time, that it was a great pleasure to him to receive me, and I should find a rich supply in his house. I think the inspired poet expressed his sense of the Divine goodness by this allusion."

Seeking God.

Ps. xxiv. ver. 6.—This is the generation of them that seek him.

OF the Rev. Mr. Blackerby it is said—" He was much in prayer :— much in closer prayer—much in walking prayer—much in conjugal prayer, for he prayed daily with his wife alone—much in family prayer, daily with his own family—and almost daily with some other family. He used to ride about from family to family, and only alight and pray with them, and give them some heavenly exhortation, and then went away to some other family. Also, he was very much in fasting and prayer."

Seeing Rightly.

Ps. xxv. ver. 15.—Mine eyes are ever toward the Lord.

RIGHT USE OF THE EYES.—An old author says, "We ought not to look for that in the law, which can only be found in the gospel —not to look for that in ourselves, which can only be found in Christ —not to look for that in the creature which can only be found in the Creator—not to look for that on earth, which can only be found in heaven."

The House of God.

Ps. xxvi. ver. 8.—Lord, I have loved the habitation of thy house, and the place where thine honour dwelleth.

MR. W. SPARSHALT, many years an officer in his Majesty's navy, was so remarkable for his attachment to the house and ordinances of God, that he was never known to absent himself from his own place of worship except once, during his whole religious career; and though at times he was so afflicted with deafness that he could not hear a word, he nevertheless continued to fill his place in the sanctuary. He said that he felt it his duty thus to honour divine institutions, and that he felt an advantage in it. In this case he was accustomed to read and meditate on the hymns sung, and the Scriptures which were read : in the time of prayer he prayed for himself, and during the sermon he would get a friend to show the text, and would employ his mind in reflection on it. In this way it is probable that he derived more benefit from the means of grace than many who are not thus afflicted.

Depending on God.

Ps. xxvii. ver. 10.—When my father and my mother forsake me, then the Lord will take me up.

THE following circumstance occurred some years ago at Warrington, and is related by a gentleman of respectability :—"About three weeks ago, two little boys decently clothed, the eldest appearing about thirteen, and the youngest eleven, called at the lodging-house for vagrants in this town, for a night's lodging ; the keeper of the house very properly took them to the vagrants' office to be examined, and if fit objects, relieved. The account they gave of themselves was extremely affecting. It appeared, that but a few weeks had elapsed since these poor little wanderers had resided with their parents in London. The typhus fever in one day carried off both father and mother, leaving them orphans in a wide world, without a home and without friends. After the death of their parents, having an uncle in Liverpool, they resolved to throw themselves upon his protection. Tired, therefore, and faint, they arrived in this town on their way. Two bundles contained their little all ; in the younger boy's was found a neatly covered and carefully preserved Bible. The keeper of the lodging-house, addressing the little boy, said—'You

178 ANECDOTES OF THE OLD TESTAMENT.

have neither money nor meat; will you sell me this Bible? I will give you five shillings for it.' 'No,' replied he, the tears rolling down his cheeks, 'I will starve first.' 'Why do you love the Bible so much?' He answered, 'No book has stood my friend so much as my Bible.' 'Why, what has your Bible done for you?' He answered, 'When I was a little boy, about seven years of age, I became a Sunday scholar in London. Through the kind attention of my master, I soon learned ro read my Bible; this Bible, young as I was, showed me that I was a sinner; it also pointed me to a Saviour, and I thank God that I found mercy at the hands of Christ, and I am not ashamed to confess him before the world. The Bible has been my support all the way from London; hungry and weary, often have I sat down by the wayside to read my Bible, and found refreshment from it.' He was then asked, 'What will you do when you get to Liverpool, should your uncle refuse to take you in?' He replied, 'My Bible tells me, *When my father and my mother forsake me, then the Lord will take me up.*'"

Evil Society.

Ps. xxviii. ver.—Draw me not away with the wicked, and with the workers of iniquity.

A GENTLEMAN, at breakfast with Mr. Newton, told the company of two seamen, under sentence of death for the mutiny at Bantry-bay, having been brought to the knowledge of Jesus. The sentence being remitted, they were sent to the hulks at Woolwich. This gentleman providentially met with a letter from one of them to his father, in which he complained most pathetically of the dreadful company with which he was surrounded. The letter, altogether, was a most Christian one, and very well expressed. The writer was afraid of relapsing into his former profligacy, if he continued amongst horrid company in the hulks. Upon hearing this relation, Mr. Newton remarked, "They would be in a more dangerous situation, were they placed amongst a set of smooth reasoners in the higher circles of life:—at present they are kept on watch; in the other case they would be off their guard, and more likely to receive damage."

Lightning and Thunder.

Ps. xxix. ver. 7.—The voice of the Lord breaketh the cedars.

SOME time ago, about thirty persons were engaged in haymaking in Yorkshire. At a time when the rain was pouring down in torrents, the lightning awfully vivid, and the thunder rolling with tremendous crashes over their heads, they were all hastening, with one accord, to the offered shelter of a beautiful large oak tree; but by the persuasions of their master's brother, who happened to be with them, and who had heard of accidents frequently occurring from the attraction which trees afforded to the lightning, they were induced to forego their first intention, and to take shelter under some of the hay. Scarcely had they reached the hay, when they saw that tree, under which they had been so eager to shelter themselves, struck with the lightning, the large trunk split from the top to the bottom, and all the leaves blasted and withered. How grateful should these men have been for so merciful a preservation from danger so imminent!

Ultimate Happiness.

Ps. xxx. ver. 5.—Weeping may endure for a night, but joy cometh in the morning.

THE Rev. James Hog of Carnock, an eminent minister, was long under deep mental distress. When he had lived in Holland for a considerable time, it pleased God unexpectedly to impart a great measure of light to his mind. "O how sweet," says he, "the light was to me, who had been shut up in a dark dungeon! for sometimes I could do nothing but cry, 'Send out by the light and thy truth.' After I had thus cried, not without some experience of a gracious answer, and expectation of more, I quickly found my soul brought out of prison, and breathing in a free and heavenly air; altogether astonished at the amazing mercy and grace of God."

The Evil Doer.

Ps. xxxi. ver. 23.—The Lord preserveth the faithful, and plentifully rewardeth the proud doer.

WHEN the Rev. Mr. Galland was minister at Ilkiston, in Nottinghamshire, an ungodly man threatened his life, because he supposed his preaching had contributed to the fanaticism of his son's wife,—a crime that could not be forgiven. He vowed no less vengeance than death, and sought an opportunity to execute it; but the Lord, who defends his people, took care of his servant, and shielded his head in the hour of danger. Having heard that there was a prayer-meeting at his son's house, on the Sabbath morning, he repaired thither with the instrument of death; having been hardened to his purpose by drinking all the preceding night. His companions in wickedness, however, endeavoured to dissuade him from his design and to wrest the knife from his hand, with which he meant to perform the murderous deed. He repaired to the place, breathing threatening and slaughter: but he was disappointed of his victim; his information respecting the meeting was incorrect. Divine judgment overtook him, however,—for on his return he fell into a ditch, and was found dead.

God's Guidance.

Ps. xxxii. ver. 7.—Thou art my hiding-place: thou shalt preserve me from trouble; thou shalt compass me about with songs of deliverance.

COWPER the poet, who was subject to mental derangement, once resolved to throw himself into the Thames.—For this purpose, he got into the hackney coach, and desired the man to drive him to Blackfriars Bridge. The man drove all over London, but could not find the place; this was unaccountable, as the driver was well acquainted with London. "O!" said Cowper, "you have driven me quite far enough, drive me home again." He went into his room, and composed the beautiful hymn :—

"God moves in a mysterious way,
His wonders to perform;" &c.

The Human Heart.

Ps. xxxiii. ver. 15.—He fashioneth their hearts alike.

WHEN Mr. Occam, the Indian preacher, was in England, he visited Mr. Newton of London, and they compared experiences. "Mr. Occam," says Mr. Newton, "in describing to me the state of his heart, when he was a blind idolater, gave me, in general, a striking picture of what my own was in the early part of my life; and his subsequent views correspond with mine, as face answers to face in a glass."

The Lord Provides.

Ps. xxxiv. ver. 9.—O fear the Lord, ye his saints; for there is no want to them that fear him.

A POOR widow, left with three small children, who lived in the adjoining parish to St Mary's Leicester, and to whom Mr. Robinson's preaching had been useful, and who was in the constant practice of going to his Tuesday evening lecture, was one of these evenings sitting spinning at her wheel, engaged in deep meditation, her soul longing for the courts of the Lord. While thus engaged, the sound of St Mary's bells caught the ear of one of her children, who were playing in her little apartment. The child instantly ran to his mother, exclaiming, "Mother, don't you go to church?" The poor woman heavily sighed, and said, "No, my dear, if I don't stop at home and spin this wool, you will have no supper." By this time the other two children had come to her wheel; and having heard what had been said, the youngest eagerly exclaimed, "O, man, go *turch;* God send us supper." Struck by this remark of her child, she set aside her wheel, and went to the church. Having got wet in returning home, she sat by her little fire, drying her clothes, when a neighbour entered the room, and said, "Betty I owe you twopence, and I am come to pay you." Betty answered, "Why, neighbour, I don't know you owe me ought." "Yes, but I do; I borrowed twopence of you *a year and a half* since, and it is just come into my mind." She then paid her the twopence, and bid her good-night. The poor widow was filled with surprise and gratitude, and immediately sent one of her children to buy a cake, and thus satisfied the wants of nature.

The Christian Spirit.

Ps. xxxv. ver. 13, 14.—But as for me, when they were sick, my clothing was sackcloth: I humbled my soul with fasting; and my prayer returned into mine own bosom.—I behaved myself as though he had been my friend or my brother.

THE late Mr. Brown of Haddington manifested a singular readiness to forgive his enemies. Notwithstanding the abuse he received from some ministers, when a student, it was remarked that he was never heard to speak evil of them, nor so much as to mention the affair. A dissenting clergyman, who had used him rudely, being reduced to poverty, he sent him money, and in a way which concealed the benefactor. After the clergyman's decease, he offered to take one of his destitute orphans, and bring him up with his own children. To certain writers who reviled him from the press, he meekly replied, "But now that the fact is committed, instead of intending to resent the injury these reverend brethren have done me, I reckon myself, on account thereof, so much the more effectually obliged, by the Christian law, to contribute my utmost endeavours towards the advancement of their welfare, spiritual or temporal, and am resolved, through grace, to discharge these obligations, as Providence gives me opportunity for the same. Let them do to, or with me, what they will, may their portion be redemption through the blood of Jesus, even the forgiveness of sins according to the riches of his grace; and call me what they please, may the Lord call them, 'The holy people, the redeemed of the Lord; sought out, a city not forsaken.'"

Spiritual Bread.

Ps. xxxvi. ver. 8.—They shall be abundantly satisfied with the fatness of thy house : and thou shalt make them drink of the rivers of thy pleasures.

A LITTLE girl said to a gentleman who was never known to enter the house of God—"Sir, why don't you go to church ; for I am sure, such as you are, you need food as well as myself ?" The gentleman answered her, "Pray, who feeds you, and what kind of food is it that you receive at church ?" She replied, "Sir, it is God who feeds me there, and his word is the food I am supplied with ; and I assure you, that though my mother, being very poor, is sometimes scarcely able to give me food to eat, yet, fed as I am every Sunday with the bread of life, I never know what the pains of hunger are." The gentleman, astonished at what he heard from the little girl, resolved from that time to attend the service of the sanctuary ; and he has adhered to his determination, and now feels and confesses the great pleasure and profit that arises from a constant attendance on the means of grace.

Trust in God.

Ps. xxxvii. ver. 8.—Trust in the Lord, and do good : so shalt thou dwell in the land, and verily thou shalt be fed.

A GOOD man, overwhelmed with trouble, and unable to extricate himself, or procure a friend in the hour of necessity, came to the resolution, as a last resource, of leaving his native country. There remained one Lord's day more previous to his departure, and from an apprehension that it would be the last he should ever spend in his own land, it impressed him with more than usual solemnity. When at the house of God, the text which the minister selected for the subject of his discourse was the preceding—"Trust in the Lord, and do good ; so shalt thou dwell in the land, and verily thou shalt be fed." On hearing these words, he found his attention particularly arrested ; nor did he feel himself less interested in the sermon, every sentence of which appeared peculiarly applicable to his circumstances, and led him to conclude the whole to be the voice of Providence. Impressed with this conviction, he changed his purpose, and resolved to struggle against the torrent of adversity, and await the pleasure of his God concerning him. The appointed time to favour him soon arrived. The Lord quickly turned his captivity like that of Job, and caused his latter end to be more blessed than his beginning.

Intended Murder.

Ps. xxxviii. ver. 12.—They also that seek after my life lay snares for me.

WHILE Mr. George Wishart was preaching at Dundee, Cardinal Beaton employed a popish priest to assassinate him. One day after the sermon was ended, and the people had departed, the priest stood waiting at the bottom of the stairs, with a dagger in his hand, under his gown. But Mr. Wishart, having a sharp piercing eye, and seeing the priest as he came, said to him, "My friend, what would you have ?" And immediately seizing the dagger, took it from him. The priest, being terrified, fell down upon his knees, confessed his intention, and craved pardon. A noise being hereupon raised, the people said, "Deliver the traitor to us, or we will take him by force ;" and they burst in at the gate. But Wishart, taking the priest in his arms, said—"Whosoever hurts him shall hurt me, for he hath done me no mischief, but much good, by teaching me more heedfulness for the time to come." And thus he appeased them, and saved the priest's life.

Telling the Truth.

Ps. xxxix. ver. 1.—I said, I will take heed to my ways, that I sin not with my tongue.

DR. JOHNSON, giving advice to an intimate friend, said,—"Above all, accustom your children constantly to tell the truth, without varying in any circumstance." A lady present emphatically exclaimed, "Nay, this is too much; for a little variation in narrative must happen a thousand times a day, if one is most perpetually watching." "Well, Madam," replied the doctor, "and you ought to be perpetually watching. It is more from carelessness about truth, than from intentional lying, that there is so much falsehood in the world."

Preaching.

Ps. xl. ver. 9.—I have preached righteousness in the great congregation; lo, I have not refrained my lips.

DR. PAYSON'S "ruling passion was strong in death." His love for preaching was as invincible as that of the miser for gold, who dies grasping his treasure. He directed a label to be attached to his breast, with the words, "Remember the words which I spake unto you, while I was yet present with you"; that they might be read by all who came to look at his corpse, and by which he, being dead, still spake. The same words, at the request of his people, were engraven on the plate of the coffin, and read by thousands on the day of his interment.

Evil Speaking.

Ps. xli. ver. 5.—Mine enemies speak evil of me.

MR. PHILIP HENRY used to remind those who spoke evil of people behind their backs of that law.—"Thou shalt not curse the deaf." Those that are absent are deaf, they cannot right themselves, and therefore say no ill of them. A friend of his, inquiring of him concerning a matter which tended to reflect upon some people; he began to give him an account of the story, but immediately broke off, and checked himself with these words,—"But our rule is, *to speak evil of no man,*" and would proceed no farther in the story. The week before he died, a person requested the loan of a particular book from him. "Truly," said he, "I would lend it to you, but that it rakes in the faults of some, which should rather be covered with a mantle of love."

Where is God.

Ps. xlii. ver. 3.—Where is thy God?

DURING the American war, a British officer, walking out at sunrising, observed at some distance an old man, whom he supposed taking aim at some game. When come up to him, the officer took him by the arm, and said, "What are you about?" The old man made no reply, but waved his hand expressive of his desire for him to stand at a distance. This not satisfying the inquirer, he repeated the question, when the native again waved his hand. At length, somewhat astonished, the officer said, "You old fool, what are you about?" To which he answered, "I am worshipping the GREAT SPIRIT." The question was then asked, "Where is he to be found?" To which the old man replied, "Soldier! *where is he not?*" and with such energy of expression as made the officer confess he should never forget it to his dying day.

Heavenly Light.

Ps. xliii. ver. 3.—O send out thy light and thy truth.

IT is recorded of one of the Reformers, that when he had acquitted himself in a public disputation with great credit to his Master's cause, a friend begged to see the notes which he had been observed to write, supposing that he had taken down the arguments of his opponents, and sketched the substance of his own reply. Greatly was he surprised to find that his notes consisted simply of these ejaculatory petitions, "More light Lord—more light, more light!"

Trust in God.

Ps. xliv. ver. 6, 7.—For I will not trust in my bow, neither will my sword save me.—But thou hast saved us from our enemies, and hast put them to shame that hated us.

DURING the revolutionary war of America, General Washington's army was reduced at one time to great straits, and the inhabitants of the part of the country where his army was encamped, were much alarmed at the prospect of its destruction. One of them, who left his home with an anxious heart, one day, as he was passing the edge of a wood near the camp, heard the sound of a voice. He stopped to listen, and looking between the trunks of the large trees, he saw General Washington engaged in prayer. He passed quietly on, that he might not disturb him, and on returning home, told his family, that he was cheered with a confident hope of the success of the Americans, for their leader did not trust to his own strength, but sought aid from the Hearer of prayer, who promised in his word—"Call unto me, and I will answer, and show thee great and mighty things which thou knowest not."

Fine Clothes.

Ps. xlv. ver. 13.—The king's daughter is all glorious within: her clothing is of wrought gold.

ONE day a poor pious woman called upon two elegant young ladies, who received her with christian affection, regardless of her poverty, and sat down in the drawing room to converse with her upon religious subjects. While thus employed, their brother, a gay youth, came in, and appeared astonished to see his sisters thus situated and employed. One of them instantly started up, saying,—"Brother, don't be surprised; this is a King's daughter, though she has not yet got on her fine clothes."

God with us.

Ps. xlvi. ver. 11.—The Lord of hosts is with us; the God of Jacob is our refuge.

THE late Rev. John Wesley, after a long life of great labour and usefulness, concluded his course in peace and holy triumph. A short time before his departure, a person coming into the room, he strove to speak to him, but could not. Finding they could not understand him, he paused a little, and with all the remaining strength he had, cried out,—*The best of all is, God is with us;*" and then lifting up his dying arm in token of victory, and raising his feeble voice with a holy triumph, not to be expressed, he again repeated the heart-reviving words—" *The best of all is, God is with us.*"

Song Praise.

Ps. xlvii. ver. 6.—Sing praises to God, sing praises: sing praises unto our King, sing praises.

"AMONG others of our edifying compositions," says Mr. Hervey in a letter to Dr. Watts, "I have reason to thank you for your Sacred Songs, which I have introduced into the service of my Church; so that in the solemnities of the Sabbath, and in a lecture on the week-day, your muse lights up the incense of our praise, and furnishes our devotions with harmony.

God a Refuge.

Ps. xlviii. ver. 3, 4, 5.—God is known in her palaces for a refuge.—For, lo, the kings were assembled, they passed by together.—They saw it, and so they marvelled; they were troubled, and hasted away.

DURING the Rebellion in Ireland in 1793, the rebels had long meditated an attack on the Moravian settlement at Grace-Hill, Wexford county. At length they put their threat in execution, and a large body of them marched to the town. When they arrived there, they saw no one in the streets nor in the houses. The brethren had long expected this attack, but true to their christian profession, they would not have recourse to arms for their defence, but assembled in their chapel, and in solemn prayer besought Him in whom they trusted, to be their shield in the hour of danger. The ruffian band, hitherto breathing nothing but destruction and slaughter, were struck with astonishment at this novel sight. Where they expected an armed hand, they saw it clasped in prayer—where they expected weapon to weapon, and the body armed for the fight, they saw the bended knee and humble head before the altar of the Prince of Peace. They heard the prayer for protection—they heard the intended victims asking mercy for their murderers—they heard the song of praise, and the hymn of confidence, in the "sure promise of the Lord." They beheld in silence this little band of Christians—they felt unable to raise their hand against them—and, after lingering in the streets, which they filled for a night and a day, with one consent they turned and marched away from the place, without having injured an individual, or purloined a single loaf of bread. In consequence of this signal mark of protection from heaven, the inhabitants of the neighbouring villages brought their goods, and asked for shelter in Grace-Hill, which they called the City of Refuge.

Fearing Sin.

Ps. xlix. ver. 3.—Wherefore should I fear in the days of evil, when the iniquity of my heels shall compass me about?

A FRIEND, surprised at the serenity and cheerfulness which the Rev. Ebenezer Erskine possessed in the immediate view of death and eternity, put the question,—" Sir, are you not afraid of your sins?" "Indeed no," was his answer; "ever since I knew Christ, I have never thought highly of my frames and duties, nor am I *slavishly* afraid of my sins.'

Evil Speaking.

Ps. l. ver. 20.—Thou sittest and speakest against thy brother.

THE late Rev. S. Pearce of Birmingham was a man of an excellent spirit. It was a rule with him to discourage all evil speaking;

nor would he approve of just censure, unless some good and necessary end was to be answered by it. Two of his distant friends being at his house together, one of them, during the temporary absence of the other, suggested something to his disadvantage. He put a stop to the conversation, by observing—"He is here :—take him aside, and tell him of it by himself: you may do him good."

Repentance.

Ps. li. ver. 3.—I acknowledge my transgressions; and my sin is ever before me.

SIR JOHN BRENTON, royal navy, brought home from the Cape of Good Hope a clever little Hottentot boy, and in a letter to Dr. Philip, states that a change had taken place in the character of the boy; in proof of which he adds,—"A clergyman asked him which character in the Old Testament he would rather have been, if it were left to his choice. The boy replied, 'David's.' 'Why David's rather than Solomon's, whose reign was so glorious?' 'Why? We have evidence of David's repentance,' said the lad, 'but I don't find any thing in the Bible that enables me to draw the same satisfactory conclusion concerning the repentance of Solomon.'"

Punishment from God.

Ps. lii. ver. 5.—God shall likewise destroy thee for ever; he shall take thee away, and pluck thee out of thy dwelling-place, and root thee out of the land of the living.

MR. ROWE, a non-conformist minister, who had been ejected from Litchet, was informed against for preaching in a cottage among his old parishioners. He escaped into another county; but many of the hearers were apprehended and carried before a justice, who hearing that Mr. Rowe's text had been, "Mortify your members which are upon the earth," profanely burlesqued the words, and uttered many indecencies. Not long after, he was seized with a mortal disease, which was of such a nature, that on his death-bed he declared it was a just judgment on him for his profaneness in this instance. The informer himself soon afterwards had the use of one side taken from him, and died in that state: and a peace officer, who had assisted him in disturbing the meeting, was within a few weeks killed by his own cart, directly opposite to the house where the meeting was held.

The Fool's Saying.

Ps. liii. ver. 1.—The fool hath said in his heart, There is no God.

THE three young men who were executed in Edinburgh, in 1812, immediately after committing the robberies for which they suffered, had gone to Glasgow; and one evening they heard the family with whom they lodged employed in the worship of God. This struck their minds exceedingly, and suggested the question,—Whether there is a God and a world to come? After some discussion they came to this conclusion,—"That there is no God, and no world to come!"—a conclusion, as they themselves acknowledged, to which they came on this sole ground—and how much of the infidelity that abounds in the world rests on no better?—that *they wished it to be so.*

The Reward of Evil Doers.

Ps. liv. ver. 5.—He shall reward evil unto mine enemies.

IN the reign of Henry VII., Dr. Whittington, a bishop's chancellor, having condemned a pious woman to the flames at Chipping, Sodbury, went to that town to witness the courageous manner in which she set her seal to the truth of the gospel. On his return from that affecting scene, a furious bull passed through the crowd, none of whom suffered from him, gored the chancellor, and suddenly inflicted death in a most awful manner.

Prayer to God.

Ps. lv. ver. 17.—Evening, and morning, and at noon will I pray, and cry aloud: and he shall hear my voice.

"A SHORT time since," says a lady, "I was one evening with a friend, after having dismissed my children for the night, when a servant came in and whispered to me that my eldest boy, about six years of age, was crying very much, and said he must speak to me. As it was very unusual for me to hear such an account of him, I was much concerned and hastened to his bedroom, when I found him in the greatest distress and agitation. On inquiring the cause, he said, 'O, mamma, nurse has put me to bed without hearing me say my prayers, and I dare not go to sleep without asking God to watch over me while I sleep.' As he had been some time in bed, and was quite feverish from agitation, I feared his taking cold, and desired him to kneel on the bed. He gave me a most expressive look, and replied, 'No, mamma, I must kneel on the floor; God will not listen to me if I say my prayers in bed.' Such views had he of the spiritual nature of prayer, and of the reverence due to the Great Creator.

Divine Protection.

Ps. lvi. ver. 9.—When I cry unto thee, then shall mine enemies turn back.

THE REV. THOMAS BRADBURY, having one evening called his servants to family worship, which he regularly observed, they came up stairs without recollecting to shut the area door, next the street. Some fellows seeking to commit robbery, happened to observe the door open, and one of them getting over the palisadoes, entered the house. Creeping up stairs, he heard the old gentleman praying, that God would preserve his house from *thieves*. The man was so struck as to be unable to persist in his wicked design. He therefore returned and told the circumstance to his companions, who abused him for his timidity. But the man himself was so affected, that soon after he related the event to Mr. B., and became an attendant on his ministry.

Refuge in God.

Ps. lvii. ver. 1.—In the shadow of thy wings will I make my refuge, until these calamities be overpast.

AT one time, when a pious minister of the gospel was passing over a hill, a lark, pursued by a hawk, took refuge in his bosom; he kindly lodged the little refugee, till, having reached a considerable distance from its persecutor, he gave it liberty to soar and sing in safety. The circumstance suggested to his mind a train of happy thoughts, which he brought forward in a discourse from Psalm xxxiv. 22.—" The Lord redeemeth the soul of his servants; and none of them that trust in him shall be desolate."

Will not Hearken.

Ps. lviii. ver. 4, 5.—They are like the deaf adder that stoppeth her ear; which will not hearken to the voice of charmers, charming never so wisely.

The preceding passage has been often referred to, as expressing the unwillingness of sinners to receive divine truth, and to comply with the call of the gospel. The following anecdote exhibits an instance of this kind :—

THE late Mr. Friend, with some other missionaries, on one occasion met a number of heathen, including several Brahmins, and during the interview they were plainly and coarsely told, that they were gross deceivers, who were about to ensare the people. "Anxious that we should not leave this band of idolaters," adds Mr. Friend, "without reading to them some portion of truth, I proposed that a tract should be read. No sooner, however, was that proposed, than an old man rose and said, 'Nay, excuse me, I must make my salaam : this may do for a bazaar, but it will not do here; we are not to be taken in your net; you will not make converts of us.' Probably superstition as well as fear prompted this conduct, for the natives declare that there is a spell in our books. True, the gospel is the power of God unto salvation to every one that believeth : but, alas for those who refuse to hear its message ! These poor creatures were sad examples of those whom the god of this world hath blinded, lest the light of the glorious gospel of Christ, who is the image of God, should shine unto them."

Sins of the Mouth.

Ps. lix. ver. 12.—For the sin of their mouth, and the words of their lips, let them even be taken in their pride ; and for cursing and lying which they speak.

SOME years ago, a person of considerable property and eminence in the city of N——, who lived in habits of impiety and profaneness, was seized by an indisposition, which induced him to call a medical gentleman ; but being disappointed for a time, by his absence from home, he fell into a violent agitation, which was vented in horrid imprecations. As soon as the medical gentleman arrived, he was saluted with volleys of oaths. The violence of his agitation broke a blood-vessel ; so that oaths and blood continued to flow from his mouth till he could speak no longer ; and in this situation he expired. The physician was much affected by the awful dispensation.—Bishop Hall observes that "suddenness of death certainly argues anger, when it finds us in an act of sin. God strikes some, that he may warn all."

Dependence on God.

Ps. lx. ver. 11, 12.—Give us help from trouble ; for vain is the help of man.—Through God we shall do valiantly ; for he it is that shall tread down our enemies.

HENRY IV. of France uttered the following prayer just before a battle, in which he obtained a complete victory :—"O Lord of Hosts ! who canst see through the thickest veil, and closest disguise ; who viewest the bottom of my heart, and the deepest designs of my enemies ; who hast in thine hands, as well as before thine eyes, all the events which concern human life ; if thou knowest that my reign will promote thy glory, and the safety of thy people ; if thou knowest that I have no other ambition in my soul, but to advance the honour of thy holy name, and the good of this state; favour, O great God ! the justice of my arms, and reduce all the rebels to acknowledge him, whom thy sacred decrees, and the order of a lawful succession, have made their sovereign ; but if thy good providence has ordered it otherwise, and thou seest that I should prove one of those kings whom thou givest in thine anger, take from me, O merciful God, my life and my crown; make me this day a sacrifice to thy will; let my death end the calamities of France, and let my blood be the last that is spilt in this quarrel."

The Scripture Rock.

Ps. lxi. ver. 2.—Lead me to the Rock that is higher than I.

A FEW days before the death of a pious little girl, her father had been preaching from the above passage. Upon rejoining his afflicted father, the text was mentioned, and an outline of the sermon given, with which she appeared powerfully arrested. Upon the remark being made, that Christ is constantly spoken of both in the Old and New Testament as a Rock, especially in the Psalms, and how delightful it was to the believer, that when placed upon this Rock, the storms of life or of death could not remove him, for there he was safe, she seemed to derive much strength and comfort from what had been brought to her notice; and in all the subsequent readings of the Psalms, whenever the Rock was spoken of, she stopped her mother, saying, "Here, mamma, is the Rock again."

Gold in the Heart.

Ps. lxii. ver. 10.—If riches increase, set not your heart upon them.

SOME years before the death of the Rev. Andrew Fuller, a friend had taken him to the bank, when one of the clerks, to whom he had occasion to speak, showed him some ingots of gold. Mr. Fuller seemed to tarry as he balanced one of them in his hand, while his companion was in haste to be gone. Thoughtfully eyeing the gold, he said, as he laid it down, "How much better is it to have this in the *hand* than in the *heart!*"

The Sanctuary.

Ps. lxiii. ver. 2.—To see thy power and thy glory, as I have seen thee in the sanctuary.

THE Rev. Ebenezer Erskine, on the first Sabbath after his settlement at Stirling, allowed the congregation to continue singing considerably longer than usual, before he rose to offer up the first prayer. Some of his elders, who had observed the circumstance, and apprehended that it was the consequence of indisposition, when they saw him next day, made kind inquiries respecting his health. He told them, that his delaying so long to stand up was owing to no bodily complaint: "but the days of grace he had enjoyed at Portmoak (where he was formerly minister) came afresh to his remembrance, with these words, 'I am the God of Bethel;' and his mind was so overpowered, that he scarcely knew how to rise."

The Wicked.

Ps. lxiv. ver. 7, 8.—God shall shoot at them with an arrow; suddenly shall they be wounded.—So they shall make their own tongue to fall upon themselves: all that see them shall flee away.

THE striking fact, detailed in the following lines of poetry, took place in the spring of 1812, at a public-house in Rochester, in the county of Kent:—

> Now to my tale and ditty
> I beg you'll lend an ear;
> Two sailors in a city
> Began to curse and swear.

The one was a brawler, a slave to his sin,
On mischief was bent, and in haste to begin :
In a tempest of wrath he swore he would fight,
Take vengeance on *Robert*, and kill him outright.
Alas ! how this wretch was transported with rage,
He deserv'd to be iron'd and put in a cage.
The old man, the landlord, himself interfer'd,
He raised his voice, and his arms he uprear'd :
" Suppose, wicked rascal, God *you* should strike dead,
And send you to hell with his curse on your head !"
The sailor replied, with an oath most severe,
" God *cannot* do that—give the tankard of beer ;
If he can—to the regions of hell I will sink,
Before this good liquor of your's I shall drink !"
    The tankard he seized, with an oath most profane,
But he instantly *fell*, as one that was slain !
He spoke not a word, nor a sigh did he heave,
The judge would not grant him one moment's reprieve ;
The terror created, each mind petrified,
To think that a *man* his great Maker defied !
They gaz'd on his corpse—ah ! the spirit was fled,
The stroke was severe—now the sinner was dead.

Unexpected answer to Prayer.

Ps. lxv. ver. 5.—By terrible things in righteousness wilt thou answer us, O God of our salvation.

THE Rev. Dr. Lathrop of America, illustrating in a sermon the sentiment, that "God often answers prayer in a way we do not expect," introduced the following facts :—" A poor African negro was led, while in his own country, by the consideration of the works of nature, to a conviction of the existence and benevolence of a Supreme Being. Impressed with this fact, he used daily to pray to this Great Being, that by some means or other he might more distinctly know him. About this time he was taken, with many others, and sold for a slave. For a while he hesitated as to the view he had taken of God, and thought that if there did indeed exist a just and good Being, as he had supposed, he would not allow fraud and iniquity to prevail against innocence and integrity. But after a while this poor slave was introduced into a pious family in New England, where he was instructed in Christianity and enabled to rejoice in God as his friend. He was now persuaded of the fact, that adverse providences are often the means of answering our prayers, and conducting us to the greatest happiness.

Thankfulness.

Ps. lxvi. ver. 16.—Come and hear, all ye that fear God, and I will declare what he hath done for my soul.

"WHILE I was in Edinburgh last," says the Rev. Ebenezer Erskine in his diary, March 13, 1711, "on the Wednesday after the sacrament, Jean Rauvit came to see me in my chamber ; and she and I entered on spiritual discourse. She told me that she had been made to have a very savoury remembrance of me several times, about this occasion of the sacrament, both before and after it. She told me what expressions of the Lord's love she has had, and what nearness she had been admitted to, at this sacrament. O what wonders of free grace and love has the Lord displayed towards her ! She is a person of more nearness to God than any that I know.

How much of his image is discernable in her! What gravity and solidity! Something of Christ in almost every word she speaks, and a sweet savour of heaven."

Glorious Days.

Ps. lxvii. ver. 5, 6.—Let the people praise thee, O God; let all the people praise thee.—Then shall the earth yield her increase; and God, even our own God, shall bless us.

IT is said that Bishop Porteous, four days previous to his death, inquired of one of his friends, how the Bible Society was succeeding in some great town, in which it had been proposed; and on being informed that all denominations had embraced it with ardour, and that the church had taken the lead, a momentary glow of satisfaction flushed his pallid cheeks, he raised himself on his chair, as if youth had been revived, and exclaimed, "Then you will see glorious days!"

New Claim on God.

Ps. lxviii. ver. 5—A Father of the fatherless, and a judge of the widows, is God in his holy habitation.

WHEN the Rev. William Wilson of Perth was on his death-bed, his son Gilbert, who was eleven years of age, hearing of his distress, hurried home from Abernethy, where he was attending school. But his father was gone when he arrived at Perth. As he approached the house, he observed some persons who had been waiting on his deceased parent, withdrawing; and from their appearance, could easily perceive what had taken place. He rushed into the room, where he found his mother, and the rest of the children, in tears. "Mother," said the interesting youth, grasping her hand, "we have a new claim on God to-day. You, my dear mother, have a claim on him for a husband, and my sisters, brother, and myself, have a claim on him for a father."

Much Zeal.

Ps. lxix. ver. 9.—The zeal of thine house hath eaten me up.

AN Indian having heard from a white man some strictures on zeal, replied, "I don't know about having *too much zeal*, but I think it is better the pot should boil over, than not boil at all."

Trouble and Prayer.

Ps. lxx. ver. 5.—I am poor and needy; make haste unto me, O God; thou art my help and my deliverer; O Lord, make no tarrying.

WHEM Melancthon was entreated by his friends to lay aside the natural anxiety and timidity of his temper, he replied, "If I had no anxieties, I should lose a powerful incentive to prayer; but when the cares of life impel to devotion, the best means of consolation, a religious mind cannot do without them. Thus, trouble compels me to prayer, and prayer drives away trouble."

Old Age.

Ps. lxxi. ver. 18.—Now also, when I am old and gray-headed, O God, forsake me not.

MARTIN BUCER was visited in his last sickness by several learned men, and among others, by Mr. John Bradford, who, on taking leave of him to go to preach, told him he would remember him in his prayers; on which Bucer, with tears in his eyes, said, "Cast me not off, O Lord, now in my old age, when my strength faileth me." Soon after, he said, "He hath afflicted me sore; but he will never, never cast me off." Being desired to arm himself with faith, and a steadfast hope in God's mercies against the temptations of Satan, he said, "I am wholly Christ's, and the devil has nothing to do with me; and God forbid that I should not now have experience of the sweet consolation in Christ."

The Earth filled with God's glory,

Ps. lxxii. ver. 18, 19.—Blessed be the Lord God, the God of Israel, who alone doeth wondrous things—and let the whole earth be filled with his glory.

AT a last public meeting, Dr. Penny related the following anecdote of a lady of distinction, of deep piety and zeal for the cause of God, in whom "the ruling passion" was remarkably strong in death. She was just sinking into the arms of death, when he thought he would repeat aloud the account of the success in the South Sea Islands. The dying saint had for some time ceased to speak or to move; she was not, however, insensible; for, on hearing the intelligence, she was somewhat roused, and distinctly articulated, "Now blessed be the Lord God of Israel, who only doeth wondrous things; and let the whole earth be filled with his glory!" Scarcely had she ceased to utter these words, when she commenced singing the Song of Moses and the Lamb in heaven.

Humbling Oneself.

Ps lxxiii. ver. 22.—So foolish was I, and ignorant; I was as a beast before thee.

THE late Rev. John Brown being asked, when on his death-bed, if he remembered on his preaching on this text, "So foolish was I, and ignorant; I was as a beast before thee," he replied, "Yes I remember it very well; and I remember, too, that when I described the beast, I drew the picture from my own heart. But O, amazing consideration! 'Nevertheless I am continually with thee; thou hast holden me by my right hand.'"

Habitations of Cruelty.

Ps. lxxiv. ver. 20.—Have respect unto the covenant; for the dark places of the earth are full of the habitations of cruelty.

WHEN Messrs. Tyerman and Bennett visited Matavai, one of the South Sea Islands, Mr. Nott, one of the missionaries there, assured them, that *three-fourths* of the children were wont to be murdered as soon as they were born, by one or other of the unnatural parents, or by some person employed for that purpose—wretches being found who might be called infant-assassins by trade. He mentioned having met a woman, soon after the abolition of the diabolical practice, to whom he said, "How many children have you? "This one in my arms," was her answer. "And how many did you kill?" She replied, "*Eight!*" Another woman, to whom the same questions were put, confessed that she had destroyed *seventeen!* Nor were these solitary cases. Sin was so effectually doing its own work in these dark places of the earth, that, full as they were of the habitations of cruelty and wickedness, war, profligacy, and murder, were literally exterminating a people unworthy to live; and soon would the cities have been wasted without inhabitants, the houses without a man, and the land being utterly desolate. But the gospel stepped in, and the plague was stayed. Now the mothers nurse their infants with the tenderest affection.

The Wicked.

Ps. lxxv. ver. 4.—I said unto the fools, Deal not foolishly; and to the wicked, Lift not up the horn.

A MINISTER of the gospel having made several attempts to reform a profligate, was at length repulsed with, "It is all in vain, doctor, you cannot get me to change my religion." "I do not want that," replied the good man; I wish religion to change you!"

God to be Feared.

Ps. lxxvi. ver. 7.—Thou, even thou, art to be feared, and who may stand in thy sight when once thou art angry?

WHEN Rabbi Jochanan Ben Zachai was sick, his disciples came to visit him; and when he saw them, he began to weep. They said to him, "Rabbi, the light of Israel, the right hand pillar, the strong hammer, wherefore dost thou weep?" He answered, "If they were carrying me before a king of flesh and blood, who is here to-day, and to-morrow in the grave, who, if he were angry with me, his anger would not last for ever; if he put me in prison, his prison would not be everlasting; if he condemned me to death, that death would not be eternal; whom I could soothe with words, or bribe with riches; yet even in such circumstances I should weep. But now I am going before the King of kings, the holy and blessed God, who liveth and endureth, who, if he be angry with me, his anger will last for ever; if he put me in prison, his bondage will be everlasting; if he condemn me to death, that death will be eternal; whom I cannot soothe with words, nor bribe with riches; when farther, there are before me two ways, the one to hell, and the other to paradise, and I know not into which they are carrying me, shall I not weep?"

Despondency.

Ps. lxxvii. ver. 2.—My soul refused to be comforted.

MR. BAXTER, giving an account of Mr. James Nalton, a holy minister, but subject to occasional depression of spirits, says, "Less than a year before his death, he fell into a grievous fit of melancholy, in which he was so confident of his gracelessness, that he usually cried out, 'O, not one spark of grace, not one good desire or thought! I can no more pray than a post. If an angel from heaven would tell me that I have true grace, I would not believe him.' And yet at that time did he pray very well; and I could demonstrate his sincerity so much to him in his desires and life, that he had not a word to say against it, but yet was harping still on the same string, and would hardly be persuaded that he was melancholy. It pleased God to recover him from his fit, and shortly after he confessed that what I said was true, that his despair was all the effect of melancholy, and rejoiced much in God's deliverance."

Instructing the Children.

Ps. lxxviii. ver. 4.—We will not hide them from their children, shewing to the generation to come the praises of the Lord.

"IT has been my manner for a long time," says Mr. Boston in his Memoirs, "besides the catechising of the parish every year, to have days of catechising for those of the *younger sort*, and they met in the kirk once a-fortnight, sometimes once a-week, sometimes in my house. I learnt it from Mr. Charles Gordon, a grave learned man, minister of Ashkirk. By this course I got several young people of both sexes trained up to a good measure of knowledge; some of them to this day are solid and knowing Christians; and the whole youth of the parish, who were disposed, and had access to wait on, came together, and as occasion required: sometimes these meetings were closed with a warm exhortation to practical religion."

Irreligious Mockery.

Ps. lxxix. ver. 10.—Wherefore should the heathen say, Where is their God?

MR. THOMAS WORTS was ejected, in 1662, from the church of Burningham, Norfolk, and was afterwards pastor of a congregation at Guestwick, in the same county. He was brought from Burningham into Norwich, with a sort of brutal triumph, his legs being chained under the horse's belly. As he was conducted to the castle, a woman looking out of a chamber-window, near the gate through which he was brought in, called out in contempt and derision, "Worts, where's now your God?" The good confessor in bonds desired her to turn to Micah vii. 10. She did so, and was so struck with the passage, that she was a kind friend to him in his long confinement.

The Cedars of Lebanon.

Ps. lxxx. ver. 10.—The boughs thereof were like the goodly cedars.

MAUNDRELL, in giving a description of the cedars of Lebanon, says, "I measured one of the largest, and found it twelve yards six inches in girth, and yet sound, and thirty-seven yards in the spread of its boughs. At about five or six yards from the ground it was divided into five limbs, each of which was equal to a great tree."

Persistent Disobedience.

Ps. lxxxi. ver. 11, 12.—My people would not hearken to my voice; and Israel would none of me. So I gave them up unto their own hearts' lust; and they walked in their counsels.

A GENTLEMAN called his sons around his dying bed, and gave them the following relation:—"When I was a youth, the Spirit strove with me, and seemed to say, 'Seek religion *now;*' but Satan suggested the necessity of waiting till I grew up, because it was incompatible with youthful amusement; so I resolved I would wait till I grew up to be a man. I did so, and was then reminded of my promise to seek religion; but Satan again advised me to wait till middle age, for business and a young family demanded all my attention. Yes, I said, I will do so; I will wait till middle age. I did so; my serious impressions left me for some years. They were again renewed, conscience reminded me of my promises; the Spirit said, 'Seek religion now; but then I had less time than ever; Satan advised my waiting till I was old; then my children would be settled in business, and I should have *nothing* else to do; I could then give an undivided attention to it. I listened to his suggestion, and the Spirit ceased to strive with me. I have lived to be old, but *now* I have no desire as formerly to attend to the concerns of my soul; my heart is hardened. I have *resisted* and *quenched* the Spirit, now there is no hope; already I feel a hell within, the beginning of an eternal misery. I feel the gnawings of that worm that never dies. Take warning from my miserable end; seek religion now; let nothing tempt you to put off this important concern." Then in the greatest agonies he expired. It is dreadful to trifle with the Spirit of God!

Defending the Poor.

Ps. lxxxii. ver. 3, 4.—Defend the poor and fatherless: do justice to the afflicted and needy.—Deliver the poor and needy: rid them out of the hand of the wicked.

WHERE lived in the city of Zurich a person who, though an unworthy character, was a member of its Senate. During the time he was Prefect over a district of the Canton, he had committed innumerable acts of the grossest injustice,—yea, such flagrant crimes, that all the country people reproached and cursed him; but no one dared to prosecute him, as he was related to several members of the Zurich Government, and son-in-law to the chief magistrate of the city. Mr. Lavater, the celebrated physiognomist, having often heard of the atrocities of the Prefect, committed against even helpless widows and orphans, and having duly examined into them, felt an irresistible desire to plead the cause of the poor and oppressed. He was aware that his supporting this cause would expose him to the frowns of the great and the mighty, and occasion much anxiety to his friends; but conceiving it to be his duty, he determined to proceed. Having prepared himself by earnest prayer, and consulted an intimate friend, he addressed a letter to the Prefect, in which he strongly reproached him for his detestable actions, and plainly signified his intention to bring him to public justice, should he not restore his spoils within two months. The time having elapsed, and no restoration having been made, Mr. Lavater proceeded to print a solemn indictment against him, which he caused to be delivered to every member of the Zurich Government. At first he concealed his name; but when called upon, he came forward in the most open manner, nobly avowed and fully proved the points of his indictment before the whole Senate, had the satisfaction to see the wicked Prefect (who, conscious of his guilt, had saved himself by flight) solemnly condemned by law, his unjust property confiscated, and restoration made to oppressed poverty and innocence.

Conscious Stricken.

Ps. lxxxiii. ver. 15.—Persecute them with thy tempest, and make them afraid with thy storm.

WHEN the celebrated Mr. Blair, of the seventeenth century, was deposed by Bishop Bramble of Derry, in Ireland, he cited the bishop to appear before the tribunal of Christ, to answer for that wicked action. "I appeal," said the bishop, "from the justice of God to his mercy."—"Your appeal," replied Mr. Blair, "is likely to be rejected; because, in prohibiting us the exercise of our ministry, you act against the light of your own conscience." The bishop was shortly after smitten with sickness, and when Dr. Maxwell, his physician, inquired at him what was his particular complaint, after a long silence, he replied, "It is my conscience!"—"I have," rejoined the doctor, "no cure for that." This confession the friends of the bishop endeavoured to suppress; but the Countess of Andes, who had it from the doctor's mouth, and who was worthy of credit, used to say, "No man shall bear witness of it to the glory of God, who smote him for persecuting Christ's faithful servants."

In the Sanctuary.

Ps. lxxxiv. ver. 10.—A day in thy courts is better than a thousand : I had rather be a door-keeper in the house of my God, than to dwell in the tents of wickedness.

A MAN who lived in a house by himself, had always been in the practice of going to public worship, but some years previous, for a considerable time, he had found so little comfort in hearing the gospel, that more than once he had debated with himself if it would not be as well to remain at home on the Lord's day. One Saturday night he made up his mind that he would not attend sermon next day, and went to rest with this resolution on his mind. What was his surprise, when he awoke from his sleep, to find that the Sabbath was nearly gone. "When I awoke," said he, "*it was the evening of the Sabbath.* I was struck with the reproof. I had basely resolved that I should not worship God in his house on his own day, and he did not allow me to awake to spend it in any other manner. The reproof was of use to me ; since that time I have never trifled with my duty of seeking God in his sanctuary, and I hope I have done it often since that time with much comfort."

The Peace of God.

Ps. lxxxv. ver. 8.—He will speak peace unto his people, and to his saints ; but let them not turn again to folly.

AN eminent servant of Christ, being suddenly introduced into a large and respectable assembly, was requested to deliver an extemporary address on "The Peace of God." To this request he replied, in terms of the deepest humiliation, that it was impossible for him, at present, to speak on that subject, as he had unhappily deprived himself of that invaluable blessing by his unfaithfulness to God. He then sat down, silently humbling himself before the Lord. This frank confession became the means, it is said, of the conversion of one of the company.

Answering Prayer.

Ps. lxxxvi. ver. 7.—In the day of my trouble I will call upon thee : for thou wilt answer me.

IT is well known that many of the good men who were driven from this country to America, by persecution, in the seventeenth century, had to endure great privations. In the month of June, 1623, their hopes of a harvest were nearly blasted by drought, which withered up their corn, and made the grass look like hay. All expected to perish with hunger. In their distress they set apart a day for humiliation and prayer, and continued their worship for eight or nine hours. God heard their prayers, and answered them in a way which excited universal admiration. Although the morning of that day was clear, and the weather very hot and dry during the whole forenoon, yet before night it began to rain, and gentle showers continued to fall for many days, so that the ground became thoroughly soaked, and the drooping corn revived.

The City of God.

Ps. lxxxvii. ver. 3.—Glorious things are spoken of thee, O city of God.

FULGENTIUS, being at Rome, and observing the glory of the Roman nobility, the triumphant pomp of King Theodoric, and the universal splendour and gaiety of that city, was so far from being impressed in favour of what he saw, that, raising up his thoughts to heavenly joys, he said to some of his friends that accompanied him, "How beautiful must the celestial Jerusalem be, since terrestrial Rome is so glittering! If such honour be given to lovers of vanity, what glory shall be imparted to the saints, who are lovers and followers of truth!"

Mental Trouble and Death.

Ps. lxxxviii. ver. 3.—My soul is full of troubles, and my life draweth nigh unto the grave.

MR JOHNSON gives the following account of one of the school girls, about fifteen years of age, at Regent's Town, Sierra Leone :—"She always complained of the depravity of her heart. I was called up this morning about one o'clock, by the woman who attends the sick in the Female Hospital. I found this poor girl in great distress of mind. She cried aloud, 'Massa, what shall I do? what shall I do? I am going to die now, and my sins be too much. I thief—I lie—I curse—I do bad too much—I bad past all people, and now me must die!—What shall I do?' I spoke to her on the ability and willingness of Jesus to save her. She said that she had prayed to Jesus to pardon her sins, but did not know whether he had heard her prayers. After I had spoken to her for some time, she became calm, and appeared to be in earnest prayer. I saw her again after family prayer. She appeared quite composed, and spoke a few words with great difficulty, to express her peace of mind. I visited her once more; and, on asking her how she did, she said with great difficulty, 'I pray;' and soon afterwards departed."

Death.

Ps. lxxxix. ver. 48.—What man is he that liveth, and shall not see death? shall he deliver his soul from the hand of the grave?

MR PHILIP HENRY, at the monthly lectures at his house, preached upon the four last things, death, judgment, heaven, and hell, in many particulars, but commonly with a new text for every sermon. When he had, in many sermons, finished the first of the four, a person who used to hear him sometimes, inquiring of his progress in his subjects, asked him if he had done with death, meaning that subject concerning death; to which he pleasantly replied—"No, I have not done with him yet. I must have another turn with him, and he will give me a fall; but I hope to have the victory at last."

Our Years.

Ps xc. ver. 9.—We spend our years as a tale that is told.

A MINISTER in Scotland, preaching a sermon to his congregation on the last Sabbath of the year 1793, on contrasting the shortness of life with eternity, and having mentioned the preceding passage of Scripture, fell back, and immediately expired.

The Plague.

Ps. xci. ver. 3.—Surely he shall deliver thee from the noisome pestilence.

LORD CRAVEN lived in London when that sad calamity, the plague, raged. His house was in that part of the town since called Craven Buildings. On the plague growing epidemic, his Lordship, to avoid the danger, resolved to go to his seat in the country.

His coach and six were accordingly at the door, his baggage put up, and all things in readiness for the journey. As he was walking through his hall, with his hat on, his cane under his arm, and putting on his gloves, in order to step into his carriage, he overheard his negro, who served him as postillion, saying to another servant, "I suppose, by my Lord's quitting London to avoid the plague, that his God lives in the country, and not in town." The poor negro said this in the simplicity of his heart, as really believing a plurality of Gods. The speech, however, struck Lord Craven very sensibly, and made him pause. "My God," thought he, "lives everywhere, and can preserve me in town as well as in the country. I will even stay where I am. The ignorance of that negro has just now preached to me a very useful sermon. Lord, pardon this unbelief, and that distrust of thy providence, which made me think of running from thy hand." He immediately ordered his horses to be taken off from the coach, and the baggage to be taken in. He continued at London, was remarkably useful among his sick neighbours, and never caught the infection.

Family Worship.

Ps. xcii. ver. 1, 2.—It is a good thing to give thanks unto the Lord, and to sing praises unto thy name, O most High:—To shew forth thy loving-kindness in the morning, and thy faithfulness every night.

"ABOUT twelve years ago," writes one, in a letter to a minister, "I had occasion to pass a toll-bar in the west of Fife, and happened to enter into conversation with the toll-keeper, whom I found a very intelligent, and apparently a truly pious old man. In the course of our conversation, the great decline even in the outward forms of religion was mentioned; and as a striking proof of this, the toll-keeper remarked—'When I was a young man, about fifty years ago, I left Aberdeen, and came to work as a journeyman flax-dresser in a respectable town in the county of Fife; and for the two first weeks or so after I arrived, curiosity led me out every morning at the breakfast hour to see the town, and at this time every door was shut, and the inmates engaged at family worship, except two doors which I never observed to be shut; but these families perhaps might have some reasonable excuse for not being employed like their neighbours. The two doors I remember most distinctly at this day, and could point them out. And before I left the town, about a year ago, it was nearly as rare to see a shut door for the purpose of family worship, as it was at the former period to see an open one!'" What matter of deep regret, when so becoming and important an exercise is abandoned!

God's Testimonies.

Ps. xciii. ver. 5.—Thy testimonies are very sure: holiness becometh thine house, O Lord, for ever.

THE late Rev. Claudius Buchanan, shortly after he had visited the principal parts of Europe, was met on the streets of London by an old Highlander of Scotland, who was an intimate acquaintance of his father. In order to have a little conversation, they went into a public-house, and took some refreshment.—Young Claudius gave his countryman a very animated description of his tour, and of the wonders he had seen upon the Continent. The old man listened with attention to his narrative, and then eagerly inquired whether his religious principles had not been materially injured by mixing among such a variety of characters and religions. "Do you know what an infidel is?" said Buchanan. "Yes," was the reply. "Then," said he, "I am an infidel; and have seen the absurdity of all those nostrums my good old father used to teach me in the north; and can *you*," added he, "seriously believe that the Bible is a revelation from the Supreme Being?"—"I do."—"And pray tell me what may be your reasons?"—"Claude," said the good old Highlander, "I know nothing about what learned men call the *external* evidences of revelation, but I will tell you why I believe it to be from God. I have a most depraved and sinful nature, and, do what I will, I find I cannot make myself holy. My friends cannot do it for me, nor do I think all the angels in heaven could. One thing alone does it,—the reading and believing what I read in that blessed book—that does it. Now, as I know that God must be holy, and a lover of holiness, and as I believe that book is the only thing in creation that produces and promotes holiness, I conclude that it is from God, and that he is the author of it."

Sudden Death.

Ps. xciv. ver. 23.—He shall cut them off in their own wickedness.

THE following is an extract of a letter from a minister in a small sea-port town in Scotland:—"I have just now heard of a dreadful scene. One ———, for many years master of a coasting vessel, an inhabitant of this place, had, in his younger days, made a distinguished profession of religion; and, among the small but respectable body to which he belonged, he was deemed an eminent Christian. Many years ago this man became a Deist—nay, an avowed Athiest, and made the Being of Deity and a future state the subjects of his ridicule and profane mockery. For horrid swearing and lewdness he had perhaps few equals in Scotland. Last night, in a public-house, when in a rage of swearing, he dropt into eternity in a moment, by the rupture of a blood-vessel. How awful, to be hurried into the tribunal of God, in the very act of blasphemy!"

To-day.

Ps. xcv. ver. 7, 8.—To-day, if ye will hear his voice,—Harden not your heart.

RABBI ELIEZER said, "Turn to God *one* day before your death." His disciples said, "How can a man know the day of his death?" He answered them, "Therefore you should turn to God TO-DAY. Perhaps you may die *to-morrow;* thus, every day will be employed in returning."

God's Rule.

Ps. xcvi. ver. 10.—Say among the heathen that the Lord reigneth: the world also shall be established, that it shall not be moved: he shall judge the people righteously.

AT a public festival at Raiatea, a South Sea island, some of the chiefs and others addressed the company, in brief and spirited appeals to their memory, of the abominations of past times, and to their gratitude for the glorious and blessed changes which the Gospel of Christ had wrought among them. They compared their present manner of feasting, their improved dress, their purer enjoyments, their more courteous behaviour, the cleanliness of their persons, and the delicacy of their language in conversation, with their former gluttony, nakedness, riot, brutality, filthy customs, and obscene talk. One of the speakers observed, "At such a feast as this, a few years ago none but kings, or great chiefs, or strong men, could have got anything good to eat; the poor, and the feeble, and the lame, would have been trampled under foot, and many of them killed in the quarrels and battles that followed the gormandizing and drunkenness." "This," said another, "is the reign of Jehovah—that was the reign of Satan. Our kings might kill us for their pleasure, and offer our carcases to the Evil Spirit; our priests and our rulers delighted in shedding our blood. Now, behold, our persons are safe, our property is our own, and we have no need to fly to the mountains to hide ourselves, as we used to do, when a sacrifice was wanted for Oro, and durst not come back to our homes till we heard that a victim had been slain and carried to the marae."

The Earth Rejoicing.

Ps. xcvii. ver. 1.—The Lord reigneth; let the earth rejoice; let the multitude of isles be glad thereof.

DURING a certain juncture at the beginning of the present century, when a French invasion was generally dreaded, Mrs. Scott, a pious gentlewoman, happened to be in company with a number of ladies, who began, with a sorrowful countenance, to express themselves in a tone of most distressing apprehension regarding the consequences of that deprecated event; but after listening for a little to their melancholy language, she proceeded to reprove their immoderate solicitude and timidity, saying, "Come, my ladies, lay aside your unbelieving fears, remember that *the Lord reigns.*"

The Coming of the Lord.

Ps. xcviii. ver 8, 9.—Let the floods clap their hands: let the hills be joyful together before the Lord: for he cometh to judge the earth: with righteousness shall he judge the world, and the people with equity.

"THERE is an account come," says Ebenezer Erskine in his diary, "of the arrival of King George, and a great rejoicing for it in Edinburgh. I see the fires and illuminations of that city reflected on the skies. O how will the heavens reflect and shine with illuminations, when the King of kings, and Lord of lords, shall erect his tribunal in the clouds, and come in his own glory, and his Father's glory, and in the glory of the holy angels! O what a heartsome day that will be! When Christ, who is our life, shall appear, then shall we appear with him in glory. We shall then lift up our heads with joy, because it shall be a time of refreshing from the presence of the Lord."

Receiving God's Name.

Ps. xcix. ver. 3.—Let them praise thy great and terrible name; for it is holy.

A CERTAIN American planter had a favourite domestic negro, who always stood opposite to him when waiting at the table. His master being a profane character, often took the name of God in vain, when the negro immediately made a low and solemn bow. On being asked why he did so, he replied, that he never heard that *great name* mentioned, but it filled his whole soul with reverence and awe. Thus, without offence, he cured his master of a criminal and pernicious custom.

Thanksgiving.

Ps. c. ver. 14.—Enter into his gates with thanksgiving; and into his courts with praise: be thankful unto him, and bless his name.

"THERE is a tradition," says Dr. Franklin, "that in the planting of New England, the first settlers met with many difficulties and hardships, as is generally the case when a civilized people attempt establishing themselves in a wilderness country. Being men of piety, they sought relief from heaven by laying their wants and distresses before the Lord on frequent set days of fasting and prayer. Constant meditation and discourse on their difficulties kept their minds gloomy and discontented; and like the children of Israel, they were disposed to return to Egypt, which persecution had induced them to abandon. At length, when it was proposed in one of their assemblies to proclaim a fast, a farmer of plain sense rose and remarked, that the inconveniences they suffered, and concerning which they had so often wearied Heaven with their complaints, were not so great as might have been expected, and were diminishing every day as the colony strengthened; that the earth began to reward their toil, and to furnish liberally for their subsistence; that the seas and rivers were full of fish, the air sweet, the climate healthy; and above all, that they were in the full enjoyment of their civil and religious liberty: he therefore thought, that reflecting and conversing on these subjects would be more comfortable, as tending more to make them contented with their situation; and that it would be more becoming the gratitude they owed the Divine Being, if, instead of a Fast, they should appoint a Thanksgiving. His advice was taken, and from that day to this, they have, in every year, observed circumstances of public felicity, sufficient to furnish cause for a Thanksgiving-day; which is therefore constantly ordered, and religiously observed."

The Pious Poor.

Ps. ci. ver. 6.—Mine eyes shall be upon the faithful of the land that they may dwell with me.

A TRULY pious man, of rank and influence in society was in the habit of entertaining and admitting to a degree of intimacy persons of very humble circumstances in life, if they only gave evidence of true religion. A friend of his, who was accustomed to measure everything according to the standard of this world, rallied him on the subject of his associates, intimating his surprise that he should admit to his hospitality and friendship persons of so obscure an origin, and of so little estimation among men. He replied, in a tone of unaffected humility, that as he could scarcely hope to enjoy so elevated a rank as they in the future world, he knew not why he should despise them in the present. The reproof came home to the feelings of the proud man, and he was silent; conscience whispering, meanwhile, how dim were his prospects of rising in the future world to an equality with the pious poor if his Christian friend was in danger of falling below them.

Man's Days.

Ps. cii. ver. 11.—My days are like a shadow that declineth; and I am withered like grass.

THE following inscription, in the choir of St Saviour's Church, Southwark, is on a tablet at the base of a monument of Richard Humble, Gentleman, who was an Alderman of London in the reign of James I.:—

"Like to the damask rose you see,
Or like the blossom on the tree,
Or like the dainty flower of May,
Or like the morning of the day,
Or like the sun, or like the shade,
Or like the gourd which Jonas had :
E'en so is man, whose thread is spun,
Drawn out, and cut, and so is done !
The rose withers, the blossom blasteth,
The flower fades, the morning hasteth,
The sun sets, the shadow flies,
The gourd consumes, the man he dies !"

Trusting versus Seeing.

Ps. ciii. ver. 3.—Who satisfieth thy mouth with good things.

MR. NEWTON, once speaking in reference to the preceding passage, said, "Bring a man to see the best covered table in the world, looking at it might gratify his eyes, but would never satisfy his mouth. We must taste before we can see that God is good."

The Darkness.

Ps. civ. ver. 20, 21.—Thou makest darkness, and it is night, wherein all the beasts of the forest do creep forth. The young lions roar after their prey.

SIR JOHN GAYER, a wealthy citizen of London, and a merchant of the first eminence, in the reigns of King James and Charles 1., was at one time travelling with a caravan of merchants across the deserts of Arabia, when, by some strange mistake, he separated from his companions, and night overtook him before he became sensible of his danger He in vain endeavoured to gain the caravan ; and he was brought into all the horrors of darkness, in the midst of a dreary desert. No place of refuge was near, and he seemed the destined prey of the savage animals which he heard roaring for food a short distance from him. In this awful situation, he resigned himself, like a true Christian, to the disposal of his God. Falling on his knees, he prayed fervently, and promised, that if heaven would rescue him from impending danger, the whole produce of his merchandize should be given as an offering in benefaction to his native country. At this moment a lion of tremendous size was approaching him. Death appeared inevitable ; but whether it was owing to the prayers of the pious knight, or to the generous nature of the noble animal, the fact was, that the lion, after prowling round him, bristling his shaggy hair, and eyeing him, apparently with fierce intent, suddenly stopped short, turned round and walked quietly away, without offering him the slightest injury. The knight continued in the same suppliant posture till the morning dawned, when he pursued his journey, and happily came up with his friends, who had considered him as lost. The remainder of his voyage was prosperous ; he disposed of his freight to advantage, and reached England with increased wealth. In fulfilment of his engagement, he distributed to different charities considerable sums, but particularly to the poor of his own parish ; and among other donations, he bequeathed two hundred pounds to the church of St Catharine Cree, to be laid out in the purchase of an estate, the profits of which were also to be applied to the poor, on condition that a sermon should be occasionally preached in that church, to commemorate his deliverance from the jaws of the lion.

Holiness a Defence.

Ps. cv. ver. 15.—Touch not mine anointed, and do my prophets no harm.

THE Rev. James Garie, with some other ministers, attempted, in 1790, amidst much opposition, to disseminate the gospel in some of the darkest parts of Ireland. One evening a man entered his room with a pistol, threatening to take away his life. Mr. Garie, holding up a small Bible, advanced towards him, and with a smiling countenance, looked him full in the face. Struck with his mild and innocent appearance, the man immediately retired from him, and his life was preserved.

Submission.

Ps. cvi. ver. 15.—He gave them their request; but sent leanness unto their soul.

A LADY in the south of England, had a little boy who was very ill. On being told there was no hope of his recovery, she became almost frantic, and opened her mouth, not in prayer to God for her own submission and her child's salvation, but in positive declaration that her child should not be taken from her. "O God, thou shalt not take my child—he shall not die," was her prayer. The prayer was answered. The child did not die. He recovered; and his mother lived to see him taken to the gallows!

Faith in God.

Ps. cvii. ver. 24.—These see the works of the Lord, and his wonders in the deep.

IN the early part of the career of the Rev. John Wesley, influenced by a desire to do good, he undertook a voyage to Georgia. During a storm on the voyage he was very much alarmed by the fear of death, and being a severe judge of himself, he concluded that he was unfit to die. He observed the lively faith of the Moravians, which, in the midst of danger, kept their minds in a state of tranquillity and ease, to which he and the English on board were strangers. While they were singing at the commencement of their service, the sea broke over them, split the mainsail in pieces, covered the ship, and poured in between the decks, as if the great deep had already swallowed them up. The English screamed terribly—the Moravians calmly sung on. Mr. Wesley asked one of them afterwards, if he were not afraid?" He answered, "I thank God, no." "But, were not your women and children afraid?" He replied, mildly, "No: our women and children are not afraid to die." These things struck him forcibly, and strengthened his desire to know more of these excellent people.

God's Mercy.

Ps. cviii. ver. 4.—Thy mercy is great above the heavens.

TO a person under distress of mind, Mr. Hervey says in a letter, "Don't select such a terrifying text for your meditation, as in your letter you tell me you have done. It is as improper as if you should eat the coldest melon, or use the most slight covering, when shivering with an ague. Choose, the morning after you receive this letter, (by way of antidote to the texts of your own selecting) the following for your meditation:—'His mercy is great above the heavens.' 'His mercy endureth for ever.' Put together these two expressions, and see whether they don't amount to more than either your imprudencies or your distress. You have, to be sure, done amiss in the matter of —God forbid I should justify your conduct! but let it not be said, let it not be surmised, it is beyond the reach of God's immeasurable goodness to pardon, or of Christ's immense merits to expiate the sin. None can tell, none can think, what mercy there is with the Lord. There is a wide difference between humiliation and despair; draw near to Christ with a humble boldness."

Ingratitude.

Ps. cix. ver. 4.—For my love they are my adversaries: but I give myself unto prayer.

MR. BURKITT, in his diary, relates his having met at one time with a very unjust and unexpected accusation from a person whom he had faithfully served, and sought to oblige. "The consciousness of my own innocence," he adds, "supported me, and I hope God will do me good by all. Some persons had never had a particular share in my prayers but for the injuries they have done me."

Willing Service.

Ps. cx. ver. 3.—Thy people shall be willing in the day of thy power

A DEIST, whose infidelity was shaken by the conversation of his little daughter, who attended a Sabbath school, was induced to attend the preaching of the gospel. The Holy Spirit accompanied it with his blessing. On the following November 5th, he convened his family together, and having made a bon-fire of his infidel books, they all joined in singing that hymn,—"Come, let us join our cheerful songs," &c.

Trusting in Providence.

Ps. cxi. ver. 5.—He hath given meat unto them that fear him: he will ever be mindful of his covenant.

MR. MERCER, a pious and zealous curate in Yorkshire, was in circumstances of pecuniary distress; but at the same time, he had frequent experience of the Lord's goodness to his family in their straits. Once, when in great want of the necessaries of life, a five-guinea note was sent them by the carrier; but from whom, they never could learn. On another occasion, their stock, both of coals and money, was exhausted. Having no prospect of a supply, they retired to rest that evening—"Cast down, but not in despair." In the morning, after praying with his wife, Mr. Mercer took a walk out on the highway, still continuing the devout exercise of prayer, when he was met by the post. Without being able to assign a reason why, he felt an impression which led him to ask, " Have you a letter for me ?" To which the person replied in the affirmative. Upon receiving the letter, he immediately opened it, and found it to be an anonymous epistle, with five pounds enclosed. Soon after this, a friend brought a cow for their service; and towards evening, another friend sent them a cart-load of coals. Thus, without making known their case to any one, except the Lord God of Elijah, they received in one day a seasonable supply of money, milk, and coals.

The Poor.

Ps. cxii. ver. 9.—He hath dispersed: he hath given to the poor; his righteousness endureth for ever; his horn shall be exalted with honour.

TIBERIUS II. was so liberal to the poor, that his wife blamed him for it. Speaking to him once of his wasting his treasure by this means, he told her, "He should never want money so long as, in obedience to Christ's command, he supplied the necessities of the poor." Shortly after this, he found a great treasure under a marble table which had been taken up; and news was also brought him of the death of a very rich man, who had left his whole estate to him.

Elevating the Humble.

Ps. cxiii. ver. 7, 8.—He raiseth up the poor out of the dust, and lifteth the needy out of the dung-hill; that he may set him with princes, even with the princes of his people.

MR. BROWN of Haddington, during his last illness, having one day come in from his ride, was scarcely set down, when he began expressing his admiration of the love of God : "O! the sovereignty of grace! How strange that I, a poor cottager's son, should have a chaise to ride in; and what is far more wonderful, I think God hath often given me rides in the chariot of the new covenant; in the former case, he hath raised me from the dunghill, and set me with great men; but in the latter, he hath exalted the man, sinful as a devil, and made him to sit with the prince of the kings of the earth. O, astonishing! astonishing! astonishing!"

The Jordan.

Ps. cxiv. ver 3.—Jordan was driven back.

CHATEAUBRIAND, describing the emotions he felt on his approach to this celebrated river, says, "I had surveyed the great rivers of America with that pleasure which solitude and nature impart; I had visited the Tiber with enthusiasm, and sought with the same interest the Eurotas and the Cephisus; but I cannot express what I felt at the sight of the Jordan. Not only did this river remind me of a renowned antiquity, and one of the most celebrated names that the most exquisite poetry ever confided to the memory of man; but its shores likewise presented to my view the theatre of the miracles of my religion. Judea is the only country in the world that revives in the traveller the memory of human affairs and of celestial things, and which, by this combination, produces in the soul a feeling and ideas which no other religion is capable of exciting.

Heathen Idols.

Ps. cxv. ver. 5.—They have mouths, but they speak not; eyes have they, but they see not, &c.

MR THOMAS, missionary in India, was one day travelling alone through the country, when he saw a great many people waiting near a temple of their false gods. He went up to them, and as soon as the doors were opened, he walked into the temple. Seeing an idol raised above the people, he walked boldly up to it, held up his hand, and asked for silence. He then put his fingers on its eyes, and said, 'It has eyes, but it cannot see! It has ears, but it cannot hear! It has a nose, but it cannot smell! It has hands, but it cannot handle! It has a mouth, but it cannot speak! Neither is there any breath in it!" Instead of doing injury to him for affronting their gods and themselves, they were all surprised; and an old Brahmin was so convinced of his folly by what Mr Thomas said, that he also cried out, "It has feet, but it cannot run away!" The people raised a shout, and being ashamed of their stupidity, they left the temple, and went to their homes.

God's Servants.

Ps. cxvi. ver. 16.—O Lord, truly I am thy servant; I am thy servant, and the son of thine handmaid.

"BESIDES the common mercy of being born in a Christian land," says General Burn, "God was pleased to bestow on me another, which is not common to all his children; that of being born of godly parents, and surrounded on all sides by truly pious relations. Infant reason no sooner dawned, than they began to use every possible means to give that reason a right bias towards its proper object; and they daily approached a throne of grace with fervent prayer for their helpless child, before he knew how to pray for himself. When a rude unthinking boy at school, I have sometimes stood at my pious grandmother's closet door, and how many heart-affecting groans and ardent supplications have I heard poured forth for me, for which I then never imagined there was the smallest occasion! Yet, if the prayers of the righteous avail much, (and surely I can confirm the truth of this scripture,) how greatly am I indebted to God, who blessed me with such parents!"

Merciful Kindness.

Ps. cxvii. ver. 2.—His merciful kindness is great towards us.

ONE day a female friend called on the late Rev. William Evans, a pious minister in England, and asked him how he felt himself. "I am weakness itself," he replied; "but I am on the *Rock*. I do not experience those transports which some have expressed in the view of death; but my dependence is on the *mercy* of God in Christ. Here my religion *began*, and here it must *end*."

Trust.

Ps. cxviii. ver. 8.—It is better to trust in the Lord, than to put confidence in man.

"CHRISTIANS might avoid much trouble and inconvenience," says Dr. Payson, "if they would only believe what they profess—that God is able to make them happy without anything else. They imagine, if such a dear friend were to die, or such and such blessings to be removed, they should be miserable; whereas God can make them a thousand times happier without them. To mention my own case—God has been depriving me of one blessing after another; but as every one was removed, he has come in, and filled up its place; and now when I am a cripple, and not able to move, I am happier than ever I was in my life before, or ever expected to be; and if I had believed this twenty years ago, I might have been spared much anxiety."

The Lesson of Affliction.

Ps. cxix. ver. 71.—It is good for me that I have been afflicted.

A YOUNG man, who had been long confined with a diseased limb, and was near his dissolution, was attended by a friend, who requested that the wound might be uncovered. When this was done, "There," said the young man, "there it is, and a precious treasure it has been to me; it saved me from the folly and vanity of youth; it made me cleave to God as my only portion, and to eternal glory as my only hope; and I think it has now brought me very near to my Father's house."

The Bible a Delight.

Ps. cxix. ver. 92.—Unless thy law had been my delight, I should then have perished in mine affliction.

A PERSON who subscribed to the Bible Society of Nismes, in France, gave the following account of himself to one of the office-bearers of the Society:—" Under the late emperor (Bonaparte) I was attached to the army ; and being taken prisoner and carried to England, I was confined in one of the prison-ships. There, huddled together one above the other, and deprived of everything that could tend to soften the miseries of life, I abandoned myself to dark despair, and resolved to make away with myself. In this state of mind, an English clergyman visited us, and addressed us to the following effect:—'My heart bleeds for your losses and privations, nor is it in my power to remedy them ; but I can offer consolation for your immortal souls ; and this consolation is contained in the word of God. Read this book, my friends ; for I am willing to present every one with a copy of the Bible, who is desirous to possess it.'—The tone of kindness with which he spoke, and the candour of this pious man, made such an impression upon me, that I burst into tears. I gratefully accepted a Bible ; and in it I found abundant consolation, amidst all my miseries and distresses. From that moment the Bible has become a book precious to my soul ; out of it I have gathered motives for resignation and courage to bear up in adversity ; and I feel happy in the idea that it may prove to others what it has been to me."

Sorrow for the Ungodly.

Ps. cxix. ver. 136.—Rivers of waters run down mine eyes, because they keep not thy law.

A DEAF and dumb boy, thirteen years of age, educated in the Institution at Edinburgh, after an absence of four years, went home to see his mother. When he entered her house, in company with his benefactor, she was sitting in a state of intoxication which greatly affected him. He took his pencil, and thus attempted to show her the evil and danger of such conduct, and gave her much good advice. After retiring with his friend, at whose house he went to lodge, his countenance became very sorrowful, and the tears trickled down his cheeks. His friend asked him the occasion of all this, when he wrote, that he was thinking, if he got to heaven, how sorry he should be not to find his mother there.

The Peace-maker.

Ps. cxx. ver. 7.—I am for peace.

THE late John Dickinson, Esq., of Birmingham, was often called by way of distinction, "The Peace-maker ;" and such was his anxiety to keep the bonds of peace from being broken—such was his solicitude to heal the breach when made, that he would stoop to any act but that of meanness—make any sacrifice but that of principle—and endure any mode of treatment, not excepting even insult and reproach. From the high estimate in which his character was held, he was often called upon to act as umpire in cases of arbitration, and it was but rarely, if ever, that the equity of his decisions were impeached. On one occasion, two men were disputing in a public-house about the result of an arbitration, when a third said, "Had John Dickinson anything to do with it ?"—"Yes," was the reply. "Then

The Lord a Protector.

Ps. cxxi. ver. 5.—The Lord is thy keeper.

IN the year 1752, Dr. Gill had a memorable escape from death in his own study. One of his friends had mentioned to him a remark of Dr. Halley, the celebrated astronomer, that close study preserves a man's life, by keeping him out of harm's way; but one day, after he had just left his room to go to preach, a stack of chimneys was blown down, forced its way through the roof of the house, and broke his writing table, in the very spot where a few minutes before he had been sitting. The doctor very properly remarked afterwards to his friend, "A man may come to danger and harm in the closet as well as in the highway, if he be not protected by the special care of Divine Providence."

Public Worship.

Ps. cxxii. ver. 1.—I was glad when they said unto me, Let us go into the house of the Lord.

MR JOEL BARLOW of Hartford, in New England, (author of the Advice to Privileged Orders,) meeting the Rev. Mr Strong, of the same place, one day, asked him why he did not publish the set of sermons he had so long promised the world? "There is one subject," replied Mr. Strong, "I cannot get master of." "What is that?" said Mr Barlow. "To reconcile the profession of the Christian religion," said Mr. S., "with non-attendance on public worship."

The Proud.

Ps. cxxiii. ver. 4.—The contempt of the proud.

DEMETRIUS, one of Alexander's successors, was so proud and disdainful, as not to allow those who transacted business with him liberty of speech; or else he treated them with so much rudeness, as obliged them to quit his presence in disgust. He suffered the Athenian ambassadors to wait two whole years before he gave them audience; and by the haughtiness of his behaviour at last provoked his subjects to revolt from his authority, and expel him from his throne.

Depending on God.

Ps. cxxiv. ver. 8.—Our help is in the name of the Lord, who made heaven and earth.

"I WELL remember," says an eminent minister in North Wales, "that when the spirit of God first convinced me of my sin, guilt, and danger, and of the many difficulties and enemies I must encounter, if ever I intended setting out for heaven, I was often to the last degree frightened; the prospect of those many strong temptations and vain allurements to which my youthful years would unavoidably expose me, greatly discouraged me. And I often used to tell an aged soldier of Christ, the first and only Christian friend I had any acquaintance with for several years, that I wished *I* had borne the burden and heat of the day like *him*. His usual reply was—'That so long as I feared, and was *humbly dependent upon God*, I should *never fall*, but certainly prevail.' I have found it so. O, blessed be the lord, that I can now raise up my Ebenezer, and say, 'Hitherto hath the Lord upheld me.'"

God Shields His People.

Ps. cxxv. ver. 2.—As the mountains are round about Jerusalem, so the Lord is round about his people from henceforth, even for ever.

A CHIEF in Eimeo (a South-Sea island), having embraced the gospel, became an object of hatred and abhorrence to the idolaters. A party of these conspired to kill him, when he and a few other pious persons were assembled together in the evening for prayer. The ruffians came secretly upon them, armed with muskets, and, levelling their pieces, were about to destroy the whole group at a volley. Their deliverance was singularly providential: the marked victims within knew nothing of the lurking assassins without; yet were the latter restrained from executing their diabolical purpose by an influence, which, as they afterwards declared, they could not understand. Seized with sudden horror at the deed on which they had been so desperately bent, they threw down the murderous engines, and, rushing into the room, confessed their guilt. The Christians received them with so much kindness, and so freely forgave them—thus heaping coals of fire upon their head—that they were utterly overcome, and went away, promising never to molest them again; and they kept their word.

Great Things Done.

Ps. cxxvi. ver. 3.—The Lord hath done great things for us, whereof we are glad.

WHEN the deputation from the London Missionary Society, in 1821, visited Eimeo, five of the deacons of the Church there came to express their joy at their arrival. The deputation most heartily returned their congratulations, by declaring their wonder and delight at beholding what great things the Lord had done for them. One of these, who was spokesman for his brethren, said, among other strong observations, "We are brands plucked out of the burning. Satan was destroying, and casting us, one after another, into the flames of hell; but Jehovah came and snatched us out of his hands, and threw water upon the fire that was consuming us—so we were saved!"

Building the House.

Ps. cxxvii. ver. 1.—Except the Lord build the house, they labour in vain that build it.

IT is the custom in the valleys of the canton of Berne, when the father of a family builds a house, and the walls are raised to their full height, to request the minister of the parish to pray to God inside. The workmen meet together, and unite in thanking the Lord for his care hitherto, and entreat a continuance of it through the more dangerous part that remains. A blessing terminates this pious ceremony, the pastor retires, the workmen return to their labours, and the noise of hammers begins to be heard again.

Grandchildren.

Ps. cxxviii. ver. 6.—Thou shalt see thy children's children.

THE REV. HENRY ERSKINE'S father's family was uncommonly large, consisting of thirty-three children; and so great was the number of grandchildren, with whom this venerable patriarch, for some time prior to his death, was surrounded, that, according to tradition, he could not recollect them by face, and when he happened to see them, frequently proposed the friendly question,—" Who are you, my little man?"

The Ungodly Punished.

Ps. cxxix. ver. 5.—Let them all be confounded that hate Zion.

THE disease of which Herod the Great died, and the misery which he suffered under it, plainly showed that the hand of God was then in a signal manner upon him; for not long after the murders at Bethlehem, his distemper, as Josephus informs us, daily increased in an unheard-of manner. He had a lingering and wasting fever, and grievous ulcers in his entrails and bowels; a violent colic, and insatiable appetite; a venomous swelling in his feet; convulsions in his nerves; a perpetual asthma, and offensive breath: rottenness in his joints and other members; accompanied with prodigious itchings, crawling worms, and intolerable smell: so that he was a perfect hospital of incurable distempers.

Forgiveness.

Ps. cxxx. ver. 4.—There is forgiveness with thee, that thou mayest be feared.

ONE MR. DAVIES, a young man, being under religious impressions, opened his mind to Dr. Owen. In the course of conversation, Dr. Owen said, "Young man, pray, in what manner do you think to go to God?" Mr. Davies replied, "through the Mediator, Sir." "That is easily said," observed Dr. Owen; "but I assure you, it is another thing to go to God through the Mediator, than many who make use of the expression are aware of. I myself preached some years, while I had but very little, if any, acquaintance with access to God through Christ, until the Lord was pleased to visit me with a sore affliction, by which I was brought to the brink of the grave, and under which my mind was filled with horror: but God was graciously pleased to relieve my soul by a powerful application of Ps. cxxx. 4. 'But there is forgiveness with thee, that thou mayest be feared.' From this text I received special light, peace, and comfort, in drawing near to God through the Mediator; and on this text I preached immediately after my recovery:"—Perhaps to this exercise of mind we owe his excellent exposition of this Psalm.

Humble Minded.

Ps. cxxxi. ver. 1.—Lord, my heart is not haughty, nor mine eyes lofty.

IF good men cannot always use this language of David, it is their prevailing desire that they should be able to do so, and if at any time they have been exalted above measure, like Hezekiah, they will humble themselves for the pride of their hearts. "I was this day tempted with pride," says the Rev. Ebenezer Erskine in his diary, "and a vain elation of mind, on the composure of a sermon which pleased me, and which I was composing for Edinburgh Sacrament, on the 20th of this month (8th March, 1715). It is a wonder that the Lord—he who beholds the proud afar off—does not blast me in some visible way, on this account. I prayed to the Lord to deliver me from pride of gifts. O it is a hateful sin. O Lord, keep me from it, and help me to be humble, to be like Christ; and to preach Christ, and not to preach myself."

Righteousness and Joy.

Ps. cxxxii. ver. 9.—Let thy priests be clothed with righteousness; and let thy saints shout for joy.

"I HOPE," says Dr. Doddridge, "my younger brethren in the ministry will pardon me, if I entreat their particular attention to this admonition—Not to give the main part of their time to the *curiosities* of learning, and only a few fragments of it to their great work, the *cure of souls;* lest they see cause in their last moments to adopt the words of dying Grotius, perhaps with much more propriety than he could use them—'I have lost a life in busy trifling.'"

Dwelling in Unity.

Ps. cxxxiii. ver. 1.—Behold, how good and how pleasant it is for brethren to dwell together in unity!

A LITTLE boy seeing two nestling birds pecking at each other, inquired of his elder brother what they were doing. "They are quarrelling," was the answer. "No," replied the child, "that cannot be, they are *brothers.*"

Maker of Heaven and Earth.

Ps. cxxxiv. ver. 3.—The Lord—made heaven and earth.

ALPHONSUS X., King of Leon and Castile, was one of the most learned men of his age. He acquired a profound knowledge of astronomy, philosophy, and history, and composed books on the motions of the heavens, and the history of Spain, that are highly commended. But no one can be mentioned as a more striking proof that the wisdom of the world is foolishness with God. So vain, presumptuous, and impious, was this philosophical king, that one of his sayings was—"If I had been of God's Privy Council when he made the world, I would have advised him better."

Heathen Idols.

Ps. cxxxv. ver. 15.—The idols of the heathen are silver and gold, the work of men's hands.

A NATIVE gentleman of India, in relating his history to one of the missionaries, says—"My father was officiating priest of a heathen temple, and was considered, in those days, a superior English scholar; and by teaching the English language to wealthy natives, realized a very large fortune. At a very early period, when a mere boy, I was employed by my father to light the lamps in the pagoda, and attend to the various things connected with the idols. I hardly remember the time when my mind was not exercised on the folly of idolatry. These things I thought were made by the hand of man, can move only by man, and whether treated well or ill, are unconscious of either. Why all this cleaning, anointing, illuminating? &c. One evening, these considerations so powerfully wrought on my youthful mind, that instead of placing the idols according to custom, I threw them from their pedestals, and left them with their faces in the dust. My father, on witnessing what I had done, chastised me so severely, as to leave me almost dead. I reasoned with him, that if they could not get up out of the dust, they were not able to do what I could; and that instead of being worshipped as gods, they deserved to lie in the dust, where I had thrown them. He was implacable, and vowed to disinherit me, and as the first step to it, sent me away from his house. He relented on his death-bed, and left me all his wealth."

The Mercy of the Lord.

Ps. cxxxvi. ver. 1.—O give thanks unto the Lord; for he is good: for his mercy endureth for ever.

"THIS day, August 8, 1722," writes Ebenezer Erskine in his diary, "I could not think there was the least spark of grace or good in me, or about me; and I was thinking that I should never see the Lord any more. But O the trophies and triumphs of free grace; for this night in family prayer the Lord did begin to loose my bonds, and both heart and tongue were loosed together, to my surprise; and it was ordered in providence, that, *in my ordinary in secret* this night, I did sing Psalm cxxxvi., where twenty-six times it is repeated, 'His grace and mercy never faileth;' and O, the repetition of this word at every other line was sweet. I began to hope that I shall sing it as a new song through eternity, that 'His grace never faileth, his mercy endureth for ever.' And I think that none in heaven will have more occasion to raise their hallelujahs of praise to free grace than I have."

Forget not the Lord.

Ps. cxxxvii. ver. 5, 6.—If I forget thee, O Jerusalem, let my right hand forget her cunning.—If I do not remember thee, let my tongue cleave to the roof of my mouth; if I prefer not Jerusalem above my chief joy.

WHEN Bishop Beveridge was on his death-bed, he did not know any of his friends or connections. A minister with whom he had been well acquainted, visited him. When conducted into his room, he said, "Bishop Beveridge, do you know me?" "Who are you?" said the bishop. Being told who the minister was, he said that he did not know him. Another friend came, who had been equally well known, and accosted him in a similar manner; to whom he made a similar reply. His *wife* then came to his bed-side, and asked him if he knew *her* "Who are you?" said he. Being told she was his wife, he said he did not know her. "Well," said one, "Bishop Beveridge, do you know the Lord Jesus Christ?"—"JESUS CHRIST!" said he, reviving, as if the name had upon him the influence of a charm, "O, yes! I had known him these forty years. Precious Saviour! He is my only hope?"

Blessed in the midst of Trouble.

Ps. cxxxviii. ver. 7.—Though I walk in the midst of trouble, thou wilt revive me.

MR. PATRICK MACWARTH, who lived in the west of Scotland, whose heart the Lord, in a remarkable way, opened, was, after his conversion, in such a frame, so affected with the discoveries of the love of God, and of the blessedness of the life to come, that for some months together he seldom slept, being so taken up in wondering at the kindness of his Redeemer. His life was distinguished for tenderness of walk, and near communion with God. One day, after the death of his son, who was suddenly taken away, he retired alone for several hours, and afterwards appeared so remarkably cheerful, that inquiry was made why he looked so cheerful in a time of such affliction. He replied "He had got that in his retirement with the Lord, which, to have it afterwards renewed, he would gladly lose a son every day"

Profane Swearing.

Ps. cxxxix. ver. 20.—Thine enemies take thy name in vain.

MR. WHITE, a substantial tradesman of London, had been imprisoned and fined for non-conformity. In the course of his examination, the Lord Chief Justice, not being pleased with an answer given, profanely swore by the holy name of God. This did not pass unnoticed by the good puritan, who reproved his lordship in the following delicate and modest manner :—" I would speak a word, which I am sure will offend, *and yet I must speak it.* I heard the name of God taken in vain; if I had done it, it had been a greater offence than that which I stand here for."

In Battle.

Ps. cxl. ver. 7.—Thou hast covered my head in the day of battle.

"A SHORT time since," says one, "I had an opportunity of seeing a young man who mingled in the sad scene at Waterloo. It was the first time he had seen such a sight; and at the approach of so vast a number of men and horses, armed with their instruments of death, he was naturally filled with consternation and fear. Calling to recollection what his pious father had often told him, to seek the protection of God, who is a present help in the hour of danger, he retired to a private place, and implored the protection of the Almighty. A very wicked lieutenant, who was in the regiment, the 7th—, overheard him, and laughing, said, 'There is no danger of you being killed to-day,' and treated the duty of prayer in a very light manner. They went both to the field, where, in a short time, they were called to engage; and the second volley from the enemy separated the lieutenant's head from his body." How much better to have imitated the conduct of the young man, in committing himself to God's protection, who could either have preserved him unhurt, or prepared him by his grace for sudden death!

Kind Reproof.

Ps. cxli. ver. 5.—Let the righteous smite me, it shall be a kindness; and let him reprove me, it shall be an excellent oil, which shall not break my head.

IT is related in the "Life of Mrs. Savage," an excellent sister of the Rev. Matthew Henry, that when some respectable pious gentlemen were one Sabbath evening assembled together, they unhappily engaged in conversation unsuitable to the day. Betty Parsons, a good old woman, overhearing them, said, "Sirs, you are making work for repentance." This short and seasonable rebuke restrained them, and turned their conversation into a better channel.

Spiritual Darkness.

Ps. cxlii. ver. 7.—Bring my soul out of prison, that I may praise thy name.

AS the advancement of the Divine glory should be the chief end of all our actions, so it will be found the most powerful plea in prayer.—A man once complained to his minister, that he had prayed for a whole year that he might enjoy the comforts of religion, but found no answer to his prayers. His minister replied, "Go home now and pray, 'Father, glorify thyself.'"

Dependence on God.

Ps. cxliii. ver. 9.—Deliver me, O Lord, from mine enemies; I flee unto thee to hide me.

GUSTAVUS ADOLPHUS, King of Sweden, when in his camp before Werben, had been alone, at one time, in the cabinet of his pavilion some hours together, and none of his attendants at these seasons durst interrupt him. At length, however, a favourite of his having some important matter to tell him, came softly to the door, and, looking in, beheld the king very devoutly on his knees at prayer. Fearing to molest him in that exercise, he was about to withdraw his head, when the king espied him, and, bidding him come in, said, "Thou wonderest to see me in this posture, since I have so many thousands of subjects to pray for me ; but I tell thee, that no man has more need to pray for himself than he, who, being to render an account of his actions to none but God, is, for that reason, more closely assaulted by the devil than all other men besides."

Our Sons.

Ps. cxliv. ver. 12.—That our sons may be as plants grown up in their youth.

A CAMPANIAN lady, who was very rich, and fond of pomp and show, in a visit to Cornelia, a Roman lady, having displayed her diamonds, pearls, and richest jewels, earnestly desired Cornelia to let her see her jewels also. This amiable lady diverted the conversation to another subject, till the return of her sons from the public schools. When they entered their mother's apartments, she said to her visitor, pointing to them, "These are my jewels, and the only ornaments I admire ; and such ornaments, which are the strength and support of society, add a brighter lustre to the fair than all the jewels of the east."

Father and Son.

Ps. cxlv. ver. 4.—One generation shall praise thy works to another, and shall declare thy mighty acts.

THE mother of a Sabbath School boy, about thirteen years of age, who had just lost her husband, overwhelmed with grief, exclaimed, " O, how shall we miss your father at morning and evening prayer ! " —" Yes, mother," said the boy, " we *shall* miss him ; but, *for all that,* we must not forget nor *omit* it, and if you will permit me, I will try." The excellent boy continued to officiate as leader in the devotional exercises of the family.

The Poor.

Ps. cxlvi. ver. 7.—Which giveth food to the hungry.

"BEING detained," says General Burn, " on board the Cormorant at Cowes, in the Isle of Wight, for nearly a month, by strong westerly winds, I grew weary, and being anxious to know something about the Royal George, I set off early one fine morning in the passage-boat for Portsmouth, purposely to inquire at the Admiral's office if she was soon expected in port. I fully intended to have returned to Cowes by the first boat, as I had just money enough left for that purpose ; but to my great sorrow, about noon it began to blow a most violent gale, so that none of the boats would venture out for several days. Never was I placed in a more distressing situation. A perfect stranger in Portsmouth, with only a few pence in my pocket, I continued walking round and round the ramparts nearly the whole of the day, till I was so completely worn out with fatigue and hunger, that the violence of the wind almost drove me off my legs. Night was approaching ; finding it impossible to continue in this state much longer, and being well nigh distracted, I began to devise schemes where I should rest, and I should satisfy craving appetite. At last I fixed on the following expedient :—Having a pair of silver buckles on my shoes, the gift of an affectionate sister, I determined, though grieved at the deed, to take them to some Jew in the town, and exchange them for metal ones, in hope that the overplus would procure me a lodging, and purchase some food. Just as I was stepping off the rampart to put my plan into execution, I was accosted in a very friendly manner by an old acquaintance, who shook me by the hand, and asked me if I had dined. When I answered in the negative, he replied, 'Then come along with me; we are just in time.' By this friend I was plentifully supplied for a few days, till the weather permitted me to return to my ship at Cowes. Thus the same compassionate God who feeds the ravens when they cry, was at no loss to find means to supply the wants of an ungrateful mortal, who did not then seek him by prayer, nor acknowledge the benefit so seasonably bestowed; but having been since several times at Portsmouth, I have walked round the ramparts with a glad heart, in the recollection of this mercy, praising the Lord under a feeling sense of his goodness."

Snow and Storm.

Ps. cxlvii. ver. 16.—He giveth snow like wool.

MR CLARK, a pious minister, during a fall of snow, once walked from Frome to Bristol, a distance of twenty-four miles, to preach; after which, he wrote the following lines to a friend:—

"On Friday last, as well you know,
 I went away in flakes of snow:
 I took the road the horses trod,
 And travell'd on to serve my God;
 And though I had not horse's strength,
 Yet safely reached the end at length.
 May I so safely reach the shore
 Where storms and tempests are no more!
 What though we meet with on the road
 Some little things that incommode,
 The end will more than overpay
 For all the troubles of the way!"

Praising God.

Ps. cxlviii. ver. 13.—Let them praise the name of the Lord; for his name alone is excellent.

"I REMEMBER," says Mr Hervey, "a very ingenious gentleman once showed me a composition in manuscript, which he intended for the press, and asked my opinion; it was moral, it was delicate, it was highly finished; but I ventured to tell him there was one thing awanting, the name and merits of the divinely excellent Jesus, without which I feared the God of heaven would not accompany it with his grace, and without which I was sure the enemy of souls would laugh it to scorn. The gentleman seemed to be struck with surprise. 'The *name of Jesus!*' he replied; 'this single circumstance would frustrate all my expectations, would infallibly obstruct the sale, and make readers of refinement throw it aside with disdain.' I can never think," adds Mr Hervey, "the spread of our performances will be obstructed by pleasing him who has all hearts and events in his sovereign hand." He further adds, on publishing Theron and Aspasia—"I am willing to put the matter to a trial, and myself to practise the advice I gave. So far from secreting the amiable and majestic name of JESUS, and the adorable TRINITY, that I have printed them in grand and conspicuous capitals; that all the world may see I look upon it as my highest honour to acknowledge, to venerate, to magnify my God and Saviour ; and if he has no power over the hearts of men, or nothing to do with the events of the world—if acceptance and success are none of his gifts, have no dependence on his smile, then I am content, perfectly content, to be without them."

Singing Aloud.

Ps. cxlix. ver. 5.—Let the saints be joyful in glory : let them sing aloud upon their beds.

A PIOUS little boy who attended a Sabbath School, a few hours before his death broke out into singing, and sung so loud, as to cause his mother to inquire what he was doing. "I am singing my sister's favourite hymn, mother." "But why, my dear, so loud ?"— "Why !" said he, with peculiar emphasis, "because I am so happy." Just before his death, with uplifted hands, he exclaimed, " Father ! Father! take me, Father !" His parent went to lift him up, when, with a smile, he said, "I did not call you, father ; but I was calling to my heavenly Father to take me ; I shall soon be with him ;" and then expired.

Praising the Lord.

Ps. cl. ver. 6.—Let every thing that hath breath praise the Lord. Praise ye the Lord.

MR JOHN JANEWAY, on his death-bed, said, "Come, help me with praises, all is too little : come, help me, O ye glorious and mighty angels, who are so well skilled in this heavenly work of praise. Praise him, all ye creatures upon the earth ; let every thing that hath being help me to praise him. Hallelujah, hallelujah, hallelujah ! Praise is now my work, and I shall be engaged in that sweet employment for ever."

BOOK OF PROVERBS.

In Safety.

Chap. i. ver. 33.—Whoso hearkeneth unto me shall dwell safely, and shall be quiet from fear of evil.

AN old man, a priest in one of the South Sea Islands, who had lived in affluence under the idolatrous system, having been converted to Christianity, became comparatively poor. Being asked, afterwards, whether he did not repent of having embraced a religion which had cost him so much, he calmly replied, "O, no !—while I was an idolater and a priest, I could never lie down to sleep in peace. I was always in fear of being robbed or murdered before morning. Often have I awoke in the night, trembling with horror ; and then I have sprung up and run among the bushes to hide myself, lest any one should come to kill me. Now I go to rest without suspicion ; I sleep soundly, and never run into the bush for safety, because I know no danger. I might lie on my mat till it rotted beneath me, before any one would hurt me, by night or by day. I am happy ; and therefore I do not repent of what I have done."

Knowledge.

Chap. ii. ver. 4.—If thou seekest for her as silver, and searchest for her as for hid treasure.

VERY near Colombo is a school built in a beautiful and romantic situation, on the high bank of a noble river, across which a bridge of boats had recently been thrown for the convenience of the public. A number of fine little boys residing on the side of the river, opposite the school, were exceedingly anxious to enjoy the benefits of the instruction which it afforded, but were utterly unable, from their poverty, to *pay the toll* for passing this bridge four times every day, to and from school. In removing this serious difficulty, the little fellows showed at once their eagerness to obtain instruction, and their native ingenuity. Wearing only a light cloth around them, according to the custom of the country, they were accustomed to assemble on the bank in the morning, and the larger boys binding up the books of the smaller ones, which they had home with them to learn their tasks, to tie them on the back of their heads, *and swim over*, the little ones following them. And this inconvenience they constantly encountered rather than be absent from school.

Better than Silver and Gold.

Chap. iii. ver. 14.—The merchandise of it is better than the merchandise of silver, and the gain thereof than fine gold.

MR. JOHN ELLIOT was once on a visit to a merchant, and finding him in his counting-house, where he saw books of business on the table, and all his books of devotion on the shelf, he said to him, "Sir, here is earth on the table, and heaven on the shelf. Pray, don't think so much of the table as altogether to forget the shelf."

Keeping the Heart.

Chap. iv. ver. 23.—Keep thy heart with all diligence : for out of it are the issues of life.

THE REV. JOHN FLAVEL being in London in 1672, his old bookseller, Mr. Boulter, gave him the following relation :—"That some time before, a young gentleman came into his shop, to inquire for some play-books. He told him he had none, but showed him Mr. Flavel's small treatise of Keeping the Heart, entreated him to read it, and assured him it would do him more good than any play-book. The gentleman read the title, and glancing upon several pages here and there, broke out into profane expressions. Mr. Boulter begged him to buy and read it, and told him he had no reason to censure it so severely. At last he bought it, but told him he would not read it. 'What will you do with it then?' said the bookseller. 'I will tear and burn it.' 'Then,' said Mr. B., 'you shall not have it.' Upon this the gentleman promised to read it, and Mr. B. told him, if he disliked it upon reading, he would return him his money. About a month after this, the gentleman came to the shop again, and with a serious countenance thus addressed Mr. B. : 'Sir, I most heartily thank you for putting this book into my hands. I bless God that moved you to do it,—it hath saved my soul : blessed be God that ever I came into your shop." He then bought a hundred of the books, and told him he would give them to the poor who could not buy them.

Regardless of Instruction.

Chap. v. ver. 11.—How have I hated instruction, and my heart despised reproof!

"DURING my residence in India," says one, "I frequently visited a British soldier, who was under sentence of death, for having, when half intoxicated, wantonly shot a black man. In some of my visits to the jail, a number of other prisoners came and sat down with this man, to listen to a word of exhortation. In one instance I spoke to them particularly on the desireableness of studying the Bible!—'Have any of you a Bible?' I inquired;—they answered, 'No.' 'Have any of you ever possessed a Bible?'—a pause ensued. At last the murderer broke silence, and amidst sobs and tears confessed that he once had a Bible: 'But O,' said he, 'I sold it for drink. It was the companion of my youth. I brought it with me from my native land, and have since sold it for drink; *O if I had listened to my Bible, I should not have been here!*'"

The Mothers' Influence.

Chap. vi. ver. 20.—Forsake not the law of thy mother.

"WHEN I was a little child," said a good man, "my mother used to bid me kneel beside her, and place her hand upon my head while she prayed. Before I was old enough to know her worth, she died, and I was left much to my own guidance. Like others, I was inclined to evil passions, but often felt myself checked, and, as it were, drawn back by the soft hand on my head. When I was a young man, I travelled in foreign lands, and was exposed to many temptations: but when I would have yielded, that same hand was upon my head, and I was saved. I seemed to feel its pressure as in the days of my happy infancy, and sometimes there came with it a voice in my heart,—a voice that must be obeyed,—'O, do not this wickedness, my son, nor sin against thy God.'"

The Evil Way.

Chap. vii. ver. 27.—Her house is the way to hell, going down to the chambers of death.

A YOUNG man, on reaching the door of a theatre, overheard one of the doorkeepers calling out, "This is the way to the *pit*." Having had some instruction in the word of God in early life, he interpreted what the man said, that the employments of the theatre led to hell. The thought haunted him, made him cease frequenting such amusements; he became attentive to the concerns of his soul, and was afterwards a preacher of the gospel.

The Bible and Good Government.

Chap. viii. ver. 15.—By me kings reign, and princes decree justice.

THE Bible is the foundation of all good government, as it instructs rulers and subjects in their respective duties. A French lady once said to Lord Chesterfield, that she thought the Parliament of England consisted of five or six hundred of the best informed and most sensible men in the kingdom. "True, Madam, they are generally supposed to be so." "What, then, my lord, can be the reason that they tolerate so great an absurdity as the Christian religion?" "I suppose, Madam," replied his lordship, "it is because they have not been able to substitute anything better in its stead; when they can, I do not doubt but in their wisdom they will readily adopt it."

The Clamorous Woman.

Chap. ix. ver. 13.—A foolish woman is clamorous.

A SHORT time since, a mechanic at Winford, near Middlewick, being ill, and unable to attend his work as usual, his wife reproached him bitterly; and in the course of the altercation that ensued, worked herself into a furious passion, venting the most horrible and blasphemous imprecations on the poor man. In the midst of her frenzy, she suddenly lost the use of her sight and speech, became almost completely paralyzed, and died in a few hours afterwards.

Wanton Sport.

Chap. x. ver. 23.—It is as sport to a fool to do mischief.

SOME years ago, at a place near Penzance, some men and boys, accompanied by two young women, having fastened a bullock's horn to the tail of a dog, turned the affrighted animal loose, and followed with brutal exultation. The dog, pursued by its savage tormentors, ran down a lane, when meeting a cart, drawn by two horses, laden with coals, the horses took fright; the driver, who was sitting on the shafts of the cart, was thrown off, and the wheels passing over his head, he was killed on the spot. The persons who had occasioned this melancholy accident immediately suspended their chase of the dog, and the young women, on coming up, found that the lad just killed was their *brother*. We shall not attempt to describe their feelings. The deceased was about seventeen years of age.

The Benevolent.

Chap. xi. ver. 24.—There is that scattereth, and yet increaseth.

"WHEN I consider my earthly-mindedness," says the late Mr. Brown of Haddington, "I admire the almighty grace of God, in so disposing my heart, that it has been my care rather to manage frugally what God provided for me, than greedily to grasp at more. I have looked upon it also as a gracious over-ruling of my mind that though I have often grudged paying a penny or two for a trifle, the Lord hath enabled me cheerfully to bestow as many pounds for pious purposes; and, owing to a kind Providence, my wealth, instead of being diminished, by this means is much increased. From experience, I can testify, that liberality to the Lord is one of the most effectual means of making one rich :—'There is that scattereth, and yet increaseth; and there is that witholdeth more than is meet, and it tendeth to poverty.'"

Kindness to Animals.

Chap. xii. ver. 12.—A righteous man regardeth the life of his beast.

THE REV. JONATHAN SCOTT never neglected his horse at home or abroad; nor would he, either from inattention or false delicacy, confide, without inspection, in the care of any man. He has been known, at the house of a friend, when he has thought his beast in any way neglected, to strip and thoroughly clean him with his own hands—administering at once to the comfort of his horse, and reproof to the servant of his friend—and even in his prayers he was accustomed, especially in his journeys, to pray for the strength and support of his animal, as addressing a God whose care and providence extended to all his creatures.

Duty and Punishment.

Chap. xiii. ver. 24.—He that spareth his rod hateth his son: but he that loveth him chasteneth him betimes

"A CHILD," says Mr. Abbott of Ameria, "a short time since was taken ill with that dangerous disorder, the croup. It was a child most ardently beloved, and ordinarily very obedient. But in this state of uneasiness and pain, he refused to take the medicine which it was needful without delay to administer. The father finding him resolute, immediately punished his sick and suffering son under these circumstances, and fearing that his son might soon die, it must have been a most severe trial to the father; but the consequence was, that the child was taught that sickness was no excuse for disobedience; and while his sickness continued, he promptly took whatever medicine was prescribed, and was patient and submissive. Soon the child was well. Does any one say that this was cruel? It was one of the noblest acts of kindness which could have been performed. If the father had shrunk from duty here, it is by no means improbable that the life of the child would have been the forfeit."

Unnatural Laughter.

Chap. xiv. ver. 13.—Even in laughter the heart is sorrowful; and the end of that mirth is heaviness.

A FRENCH physician was once consulted by a person who was subject to most gloomy fits of melancholy. He advised his patient to mix in scenes of gaity, and particularly to frequent the Italian theatre; and added, "If Carline does not expel your gloomy complaint, your case must be desperate indeed." The reply of the patient is worthy the attention of all those who frequent such places in search of happiness, as it shows the unfitness and insufficiency of these amusements. "Alas! Sir, *I am Carline;* and while I divert all Paris with mirth, and make them almost die with laughter, I myself am dying with melancholy and chagrin."

Devotion and Poverty.

Chap. xv. ver. 16.—Better is little with the fear of the Lord, than great treasure and trouble therewith.

A MISSIONARY in India says, "I rode to Nallamaram and saw some people of the congregation there, together with the catechist. The clothes of one of the women were rather dirty, and I asked her about it. 'Sir,' said she, 'I am a poor woman, and have only this single dress.' 'Well, have you always been so poor?' 'No, I had some money and jewels, but a year ago, the Maravers (thieves) came and robbed me of all. They told me,' she said, '*If you will return to heathenism, we shall restore to you everything.* 'Well, why did you not follow their advice? Now you are a poor Christian.' 'O, Sir, she replied, 'I would rather be a *poor Christian* than a *rich heathen.* Now I can say respecting my stolen property, "The Lord gave it, and the Lord h..th taken it again."

The Humble Spirit.

Chap. xvi. ver. 19—Better it is to be of an humble spirit with the lowly, than to divide the spoil with the proud.

A FRENCH writer remarks, that "the modest deportment of those who are truly wise, when contrasted with the assuming air of the young and ignorant, may be compared to the different appearance of wheat, which, while its ear is empty, holds up its head proudly, but as soon as it is filled with grain, bends modestly down, and withdraws from observation."

True Friendship.

Chap. xvii. ver. 17.—A friend loveth at all times; and a brother is born for adversity.

WHEN SOCRATES was building a house for himself at Athens, being asked by one who observed the littleness of the design, why a man so eminent should not have an abode more suitable to his dignity? He replied, that he should think himself sufficiently accommodated if he should see the narrow habitation filled with real friends. Such was the opinion of this great master of human nature, concerning the unfrequency of such a union of minds as might deserve the name of friendship; that among the multitudes whom vanity, or curiosity, civility, or veneration brought around him, he did not expect that very spacious apartments would be necessary to contain all who should regard him with sincere kindness, or adhere to him with steady fidelity.

Speaking Sincerely.

Chap. xviii. ver. 4.—The words of a man's mouth are as deep waters, and the well-spring of wisdom as a flowing brook.

"FOR my part," says Mr. Hervey, "when Christ and his righteousness are the subject of conference, I know not how to complain of poverty. I feel no weariness; but could rather delight to talk of them without ceasing.—Would not you expect to hear of engagements and victories from a soldier? Would any be surprised to find a merchant discoursing of foreign affairs, or canvassing the state of trade? Why, then, should not the agents for the court of heaven treat of heavenly things? Why should not their whole conversation savour of their calling? Why should they be one thing when they bend the knee or speak from the pulpit, and quite a different one when they converse in the parlour?"

The Heathen Poor.

Chap. xix. ver. 7.—All the brethren of the poor do hate him; how much more do his friends go far from him; he pursueth them with words, yet they are wanting to him.

IN giving an account of the state of the Sandwich Islands, the missionaries state that the helpless and dependant, whether from age or sickness, are often cast from the habitations of their relatives and friends, to languish and to die—unattended and unpitied. An instance recently came to their knowledge, in which a poor wretch thus perished within sight of their dwelling, and having lain uncovered for days and nights in the open air, most of the time pleading in vain to his family, still within the hearing of his voice, for a drink of water. And when he was dead, his body, instead of being buried, was merely drawn so far into the bushes, as to prevent the offence that would have arisen from the corpse, and left a prey to the dogs who prowl through the district in the night.

Good for Evil.

Chap. xx. ver. 22.—Say not thou, I will recompense evil.

A GENTLEMAN once sent his servant to John Bruen, Esq., of Stapleton, in the county of Chester, forbidding him ever to set a foot upon his ground; to whom he sent this truly Christian reply:—
"If it please your master to walk upon my grounds, he shall be very welcome; but if he will please to come to my house he shall be still more welcome." By this meek reply, the gentleman was softened into kindness, and became his friend ever after.

The Robber.

Chap. xvi. ver. 7.—The robbery of the wicked shall destroy them.

BISHOP HALL relates the case of an old plain man in the country, into whose solitary dwelling some thieves broke. Taking advantage of the absence of his family, aud finding him sitting alone by his fireside, they fell violently upon him; when one of them, presenting his dagger to the old man's breast, swore that he would presently kill him if he did not instantly deliver to them the money which they knew he had lately received. The old man, looking boldly into the face of the villain, replied, with an undaunted courage—"Nay, if I were killed by thee, I have lived long enough; but I tell thee, son, unless thou mend thy manners, thou wilt never live to see half my days.

Personal Knowledge.

Chap. xxii. ver. 19.—That thy trust may be in the Lord, I have made known to thee this day, even to thee.

A GENTLEMAN being one day much struck with the scriptural knowledge of an old lady, with whom he was conversing, asked her how she had attained such an extensive acquaintance with the word of God? To this question she made the following reply:—"Sir, much is lost by not considering the word of God as addressed to us as individuals. For these thirty years, I have read the word of God, carefully attended to every part of it, as if I had been the only person in the world to whom it was addressed; and, if I know anything above my neighbours, under the blessing of God, I owe it entirely to this practice."

Giving the Heart.

Chap. xxiii. ver. 26.—My son, give me thine heart.

A HINDOO, after spending some years in seclusion, and in endeavouring to obtain the mastery of his passions, came to a mission station, where he thus accosted the missionary:—"I have a flower, a precious flower, to present as an offering; but as yet I have found none worthy to receive it." Hearing of the love of Christ, he said, "I will offer my flower to Christ, for he is worthy to receive it." This flower was his heart. Jesus accepted it, and after a short time, transplanted it to bloom in the bowers of Eden.

Evil Thoughts.

Chap. xxiv. ver. 9.—The thought of foolishness is sin.

A JEW of Morocco, who read Hebrew with Mr Jowett, once told him that "God is so merciful that he will not punish our evil thoughts, unless they break out into act; then, and not till then, they become sin. Our good thoughts, on the contrary, even if we should not find opportunity to put them in practice, will be counted as good deeds, as much as if they had been performed." "I urged," says Mr J., "all that I could against such a pernicious maxim. He made one exception—'The thought of idolatry is sin; but to INTEND to commit murder, adultery, drunkenness, &c., is no sin, unless the act is committed.'"

Thine Enemy

Chap. xxv. ver. 21, 22.—If thine enemy be hungry, give him bread to eat; and if he be thirsty, give him water to drink:—For thou shalt heap coals of fire upon his head, and the Lord shall reward thee.

DURING the persecuting times in England, two persons from Bedford went early one morning to the house of a pious man, who rented a farm in the parish of Keysoe, with the intention of apprehending and imprisoning him in Bedford jail for non-conformity. The good man knew their intention, and desired his wife to prepare breakfast, at the same time kindly inviting his visitors to partake with them. In asking a blessing or in returning thanks for the food, he pronounced emphatically these words—"If thine enemy hunger, feed him; if he thirst, give him drink,"—by which means the hearts of his persecutors were so far softened that they went away without taking him into custody.

Flattery.

Chap. xxvi. ver. 28.—A flattering mouth worketh ruin.

A CLERGYMAN in New England, eminent both for talents and humility, was one day accosted by a parishioner, who highly commended some of his performances, of which the clergyman himself had a very low opinion. After patiently hearing him a few minutes, the clergyman replied, "My friend, all that you say gives me no better opinion of myself than I had before, but gives me a much worse opinion of you."

Friends.

Chap. xxvii. ver. 10.—Thine own friend, and thy father's friend, forsake not.

THE late excellent Mr Cathcart of Drum was in the practice of keeping a diary, which, however, included one particular department, seldom to be found in like cases. Mr Cathcart describes his plan and object in the following words:—"A memorial of acts of kindness, that as memory is liable to fail, and as the kindness and friendship of former times may be forgotten, the remembrance of friendly offices done to the writer or his family, or to his particular friends, might be preserved, in order that he may himself repay the debt in grateful acknowledgments while he lived, and that his family after him might know to whom their father owed obligations, and might feel every debt of gratitude due by him as an obligation on themselves."

Robbing a Father.

Chap. xxviii. ver. 24.—Whoso robbeth his father or his mother, and saith, It is no transgression; the same is the companion of a destroyer.

ABOUT the end of the year 1774, the following unnatural robbery was committed. A tradesman and his wife had occasion to go out of town, and on their return home, horrible to relate, they were stopped by two of their own sons. The father expostulated with them for some time, as did also their mother, without effect. One of them drove a pistol against his mother's eye, and it was feared she would lose the sight of it. The father died shortly after of a broken heart, and apprehensions were entertained that the mother would not long survive.

The Just and the Unjust.

Chap. xxix. ver. 27.—An unjust man is an abomination to the just; and he that is upright in the way is abomination to the wicked.

THE late Rev. Jonathan Scott, who had been for some time an officer in the army, and an irreligious man, says in a letter to a friend, "I find that before I left the regiment, in order to go to Shrewsbury, I began to be a suspected person. Attending the ministry of such a notorious person as dear Romaine, and associating with some Christian people, were sufficient to cause suspicions that I was turned this, and turned that. Upon my rejoining the regiment, I found that it was no longer bare suspicion. Now they are convinced

I am turned an arrant Methodist: and in this their persuasion is a very lucky one for me; for now they begin to think my company not worth being over-solicitous about; and I am sure you will readily believe that a very little of theirs is enough to satisfy me; or, more properly speaking, to dissatisfy me, so as to be tired of it, since their whole conversation consists in idle, vain nonsense, larded with horrid oaths and filthy obscenity; this is the more shocking to me, as I must sometimes be present at it, and have it not in my power to remedy it."

Mocking a Father.

Chap. xxx. ver. 17.—The eye that mocketh at his father, and despiseth to obey his mother, the ravens of the valley shall pick it out, and the young eagles shall eat it.

MR ADAM CLARKE, when a boy, having one day disobeyed his mother, she took the Bible, and read and commented on the preceding passage in a very serious manner.—The poor culprit was cut to the heart, believing the words had been sent immediately from heaven. He went out into the field with a troubled spirit, and was musing on this awful denunciation of Divine displeasure, when the hoarse croak of a raven sounded in his conscience an alarm more terrible than the cry of fire at midnight! He looked up, and soon perceived this most ominous bird, and actually supposing it to be the raven of which the text spoke coming to pick out his eyes, he clapped his hands on them, and with the utmost speed ran home, to escape the impending danger.

Drunkenness.

Chap. xxxi. ver. 5.—Lest they drink, and forget the law, and pervert the judgment of any of the afflicted.

PHILIP, King of Macedon, having drunk too much wine, determined a cause unjustly, to the hurt of a poor widow, who, when she heard his decree, boldly cried out, "I appeal to Philip *sober*." The king, struck with this strange appeal, began to recover his senses, heard the cause anew, and finding his mistake, ordered her to be paid, out of his own purse, double the sum she was to have lost.

BOOK OF ECCLESIASTES.

Vanity of Life.

Chap. i. ver. 14.—I have seen all the works that are done under the sun; and, behold, all is vanity and vexation of spirit.

MR LOCKE, about two months before his death, drew up a letter to a certain gentleman, and left this direction on it, "To be delivered to him after my decease." In it are these remarkable words: —"This life is a scene of vanity that soon passes away, and affords no solid satisfaction, but in the consciousness of doing well, and in the hopes of another life. This is what I can say upon experience, and what you will find to be true, when you come to make up the account."

Days of Vanity.

Chap. ii. ver. 2.—I said of laughter, It is mad: and of mirth, What doeth it?

THE Rev. Jonathan Scott, meeting at one place with some ladies, who came to speak to him after preaching, one of them said, "Do you remember, Sir, dancing with us at such a time and place?" He replied, "O yes, Madam, I remember it very well; and am much ashamed of those days of my vanity; but, Madam, you and I are many years older now, and so much nearer death and eternity." He then proceeded to speak of the great things of God.

Doing Good.

Chap. iii. ver. 12.—I know that there is no good in them, but for a man to rejoice, and to do good in his life.

WHEN Colonel Gardiner was raised from being Major, he observed that it was as to his personal concern much the same to him, whether he had remained in his former station or been elevated to this, but that if God should by this means honour him as an instrument of *doing more good* than he could otherwise have done, he should rejoice in it.

Envy.

Chap. iv. ver. 4.—I considered every right work, that for this a man is envied of his neighbour.

"DIONYSIUS the tyrant," says Plutarch, "out of envy, punished Philoxenius, the musician, because he could sing; and Plato the philosopher, because he could dispute better than himself."

Good Resolves.

Chap. v. ver. 5.—Better is it that thou shouldest not vow, than that thou shouldest vow and not pay.

"MONDAY evening," writes Mrs. Judson, "the daughters of —— sent to invite me and my sisters to spend the evening with them, and make a family visit. I hesitated a little, but considering that it was to be a family party merely, I thought I could go without breaking my resolutions. Accordingly I went, and found that two or three other families of young ladies had been invited. Dancing was soon introduced—my religious plans were forgotten—I joined with the rest—was one of the gayest of the gay—and thought no more of the new life I had begun. On my return home, I found an invitation from Mrs. See in waiting, and accepted it at once. My conscience let me pass quietly through the amusements of that evening also; but when I retired to my chamber, on my return, it accused me of breaking my most solemn resolution. I thought I should never dare to make others, for I clearly saw that I was unable to keep them."

Good out of Evil.

Chap. vi. ver. 12.—Who knoweth what is good for man in this life.

A MINISTER of Bristol, preaching on the preceding text, introduced the following anecdote into his discourse, related to him by his father, who knew the circumstance to be true. A gentleman in an extensive line of business in a distant part of the country, left his house with an intention of going to Bristol fair; but when he proceeded about half way on his journey he was seized with a violent fit of illness, which detained him several days at the place; and as the fair was by this time nearly over, he was induced to return home. Some years after, the same gentleman happening to be on business at some place where the assizes for the country were held, was present at the execution of a criminal who was then about to suffer. Whilst he was mixed with the crowd, the criminal intimated a wish to speak with him, and signified that he had something to communicate to him. The gentleman approached, and was addressed to the following effect:—"Do you recollect having intended such a time to go to Bristol fair?" "Yes," replied the gentleman, "perfectly well." "It is well you did not," said the criminal, "for it was the intention of myself and several others, who knew that you had a considerable sum of money about you, to way-lay and rob, and, if I mistake not, murder you, to escape detection."

House of Mourning.

Chap. vii. ver. 2.—It is better to go to the house of mourning, than to go to the house of feasting: for that is the end of all men; and the living will lay it to his heart.

WHEN the late Rev. W. Moorhouse, of Huddersfield, was one day during his last illness talking of the heavenly state, which he expected soon to enter, one of his friends said to him, "You think too much about another world; think and talk a little of this life." He replied, "Oh, but I am going there! and, whether I talk about it or not, I must go, for I am fast hastening to an unseen world; the outward man is fast decaying, and it will soon be 'dust to dust.'" With his eyes very devoutly raised, and exhibiting an animated countenance, he then exclaimed—

> "There is a house not made with hands,
> Eternal and on high;
> And here my waiting spirit stands,
> Till God shall bid it fly."

Influence of Wisdom.

Chap. viii. ver. 1.—Who is as the wise man?—a man's wisdom maketh his face to shine, and the boldness of his face shall be changed.

MR. PHILIP HENRY used to remark, "that it is strange to see sometimes what an awe arises upon the spirits of wicked men, from the very company and presence of one eminent in holiness; they dare not do then, as they dare and do at other times. One having dined with Mr. John Dod, said afterwards, that he did not think it could have been possible to have forborne swearing so long."

Wisely Merry.

Chap. ix. ver. 7.—Eat thy bread with joy, and drink thy wine with a merry heart; for God now accepteth thy works.

THE Rev. Samuel Whiting, a learned and useful minister in New England, being at one time on a journey, some persons in an adjoining room of the inn were excessively noisy and clamorous in their mirth. Mr. Whiting, as he passed by their door, looked in upon them, and with a sweet majesty only dropped these words:—"Friends, if you are sure that your sins are pardoned, you may be wisely merry." These words not only stilled their noise for the present, but also had a great effect afterwards on some of the company.

Eating Wisely.

Chap. x. ver. 17.—Thy princes eat in due season, for strength, and not for drunkenness.

A MAN of temperate habits was once dining at the house of a free drinker. No sooner was the cloth removed from the dinner table than wine and spirits were produced, and he was asked to take a glass of spirits and water, "No, thank you," said he, "I am not ill." "Take a glass of wine, then," said his hospitable host, "or a glass of ale." "No, thank you," said he, "I am not thirsty." These answers called forth a loud burst of laughter.—Soon after this, the temperate man took a piece of bread from the side-board, and handed it to his host, who refused it, saying that he was not hungry. At this the temperate man laughed in his turn. "Surely," said he, "I have as much reason to laugh at you for not eating when you are not hungry, as you have to laugh at me for declining medcine when not ill, and drink when I am not thirsty."

The Judgment.

Chap. xi. ver. 9.—Know thou, that for all these things God will bring thee into judgment.

A PERSON in a stage coach, who had indulged in a strain of speech which betrayed licentiousness and infidelity, seemed hurt that no one either agreed or disputed with him. "Well," he exclaimed, as a funeral procession slowly passed the coach, "there is the last job of all." "No!" replied a person directly opposite to him "No! *for* AFTER *death is the judgment.*" The speaker was silenced.

The Days of Youth.

Chap. xii. ver. 4.—Remember now thy Creator in the days of thy youth.

AN old man, one day taking a child on his knee, entreating him to seek God *now*—to pray to him—and to love him : when the child, looking up at him, asked, "But why do not *you* seek God?" The old man, deeply affected, answered, "I would, child ; but my heart is *hard*—my heart is *hard.*"

SONG OF SOLOMON.

Love and the World.

Chap. i. ver. 4.—We will remember thy love more than wine : the upright love thee.

IN a letter from the Rev. Dr. Judson, missionary at Burmah, addressed to American females, the following anecdote is related ;—"A Karem woman offered herself for baptism. After the usual examination, I inquired *whether she could give up her ornaments for Christ.* It was an unexpected blow. I explained the spirit of the gospel. I appealed to her own consciousness of vanity. I read to her the apostle's prohibition (1 Tim. 11. 9.) She looked again and again at her handsome necklace, and then, with an air of modest decision, that would adorn, beyond all ornaments, any of my sisters whom I have the honour of addressing, she took it off, saying, '*I love Christ more than this.*'"

The Shadow of the Almighty.

Chap. ii. ver. 2.—I sat down under his shadow with great delight.

THE Rev. Isaac Toms, of Hadleigh, in England, remarked to one of his daughters, on her return from a long visit to her friends,— "I have heard of Dryden's contentment, when sitting under the statue of Shakspeare; and that Buffon, the celebrated natural historian, felt himself happy at the feet of Sir Isaac Newton; but," said he, pointing to a picture which hung over his desk, "here you find me under the shadow of good Richard Baxter. Yet, my dear," added the venerable saint, "the most desirable situation in which we can be placed, is to be *under the shadow of the Almighty;* under the protection of the great Redeemer."

The Crown.

Chap. iii. ver. 11.—Behold king Solomon with the crown.

THE following is an extract from a letter written by Mr Strachan, one of the heralds at the coronation of his majesty, George III.— "After the king was crowned, and invested with all his royal dignity, all the peers were allowed the privilege of putting on their crowns,— they looked like a company of kings, as in some sense they were. But immediately they came, one by one, and laid down their crowns at their sovereign's feet, in testimony of their having no power or authority but what they derived from him; and having each kissed his sceptre, he allowed each of them to kiss himself; upon which their crowns were restored to them, and they were all allowed to reign as subordinate kings. This could not miss bringing to mind what is recorded in the Revelation, of the whole redeemed company, who are said to be kings and priests unto God, and who are to reign with Jesus Christ for ever and ever; their casting down their crowns, and saying, 'Thou art worthy to receive power and majesty.' I thought with myself, were I so happy as to make one of that innumerable company, redeemed from among men, I should not envy all the nobles in England what they are now enjoying."

A Well of Life.

Chap. iv. ver. 11.—Thy lips, O my spouse, drop as the honey-comb; honey and milk are under thy tongue.

MR HERVEY, in a letter, says—"I have lately seen that most excellent minister of the ever-blessed Jesus, Mr Jones. I dined, supped, and spent the evening with him at Northampton, in company with Dr Doddridge, and two pious ingenious clergymen of the Church of England, both of them known to the learned world by their valuable writings; and surely I never spent a more delightful evening, or saw one that seemed to make nearer approaches to the felicity of heaven. A gentleman of great worth and rank in the town invited us to his house, and gave us an elegant treat; but how mean was his provision, how coarse his delicacies, compared with the fruit of my friend's lips!—they dropped as the honey-comb, and were a well of life."

Catholicity.

Chap. v. ver. 1.—Eat, O friends; drink, yea, drink abundantly, O beloved.

WHILE the American army, under the command of General Washington, lay encamped in the environs of Marristown, N. J., the Lord's Supper was to be administered in the Presbyterian church of that village. In a morning of the previous week, the general visited the house of the Rev. Dr Jones, then pastor of that church, and thus accosted him:—"Doctor, I understand that the Lord's Supper is to be celebrated with you next Sabbath; I would learn if it accords with the canons of your church to admit communicants of another denomination?" The Doctor rejoined, "Most certainly; ours is not the Presbyterian table, General, but the Lord's table; and we hence give the Lord's invitation to all his followers, of whatever name." The General replied, "I am glad to hear it—that is as it ought to be; but as I was not quite sure of the fact, I thought I would ascertain it from yourself, as I purpose to be with you on that occasion. Though a member of the church of England, I have not exclusive partialities." The Doctor re-assured him of a cordial welcome, and the General was found seated with the communicants next Sabbath.

The Moon.

Chap. vi. ver. 10.—Fair as the moon.

THE Rev. Ebenezer Erskine has the following entry in his diary, of September 23, 1713:—"I was this day at Kirkness and Ballingry, with my wife; and upon the way home, towards the twilight, a little after sun-set, the moon appeared in the east, about the full; and it pleased the Lord to give me some views of his power and glory in that creature. It appeared to me to be a vast body, bright and glorious, hanging pendular upon nothing, supported only by the power of the eternal God. I wondered how there could be an atheist in the world, that looked on this glorious creature, wherein there appeared so much of the wisdom and power of the Creator."

Early Rising.

Chap. vii. ver. 12.—Let us get up early to the vineyards.

MORIER, when he travelled in Persia, observed the people sleeping on the house-tops; he noticed that the women were generally up first, and stirring about with activity at an early hour.—Lord Mansfield, a celebrated judge in England, used to ask any aged person who came before him as a witness, about his manner and habits of life; and he said that among the many hundreds he had spoken to, he always found that they were early risers, however they might differ in other respects.

Love.

Chap. viii. ver. 7.—If a man would give all the substance of his house for love, it would utterly be contemned.

A BOY, not five years of age, hearing his parent read the parable of the Wedding Garment, and remark on the concluding sentence—"For many are called, but few are chosen,"—that it may be understood of such as profess to believe in Christ, but are not approved by him; asked *why* they were not approved? He was referred to the parable, which showed that there was something greatly wanting in them. "But what," said he, "is it, that is wanting, that Jesus should approve them? *It is love to Jesus Christ?*"

BOOK OF ISAIAH.

The Forgiveness of Sins.

Chap. i. ver. 18.—Though your sins be as scarlet, they shall be white as snow; though they be red like crimson, they shall be as wool.

A SAILOR on watch, was one evening walking backwards and forwards on deck, when a sudden squall of wind caused the vessel to give a heavy lurch. The sailor was driven against one of the stauncheons, and somewhat injured. He gave vent to his anger by a dreadful oath—cursing the wind, the ship, the sea, and (awful to mention) the Being who made them. Scarcely had this horrid oath escaped his lips, when it appeared to roll back upon his mind with such awful force, that, for a moment or two, he thought he saw the sea parting, and the vessel going down. During the whole of that night, the dreadful oath haunted his mind like a spectre, and its consequences appeared to bring his certain damnation. For several days he was in the deepest distress of mind, till, happening to turn over some things in his chest, he found a leaf in the Bible wrapped about one of the articles in it, containing nearly the whole of the first chapter of Isaiah. The reading of the above passage, in particular, deeply impressed his mind, and, together with his subsequent attendance on the means of grace, was the means of relieving him from his distress, and he was enabled to believe that the Lord had forgiven his great sin.

No more War.

Chap. ii. ver. 4.—They shall beat their swords into plow-shares, and their spears into pruning-hooks · nation shall not lift up sword against nation, neither shall they learn war any more.

THE Rev. Mr Orsmond, missionary in Eimeo, says—"A few weeks ago, I overheard some chiefs conversing among themselves; the following are a few of the expressions which I caught.—'But for our teachers, our grass on the hill, our fences and houses, would have been fire ashes long ago—(meaning that there would have been wars, in which their houses would have been burned, had not Christianity been established.) But for the gospel, we should now have been on the mountains, squeezing moss for a drop of water; eating raw roots, and smothering the cries of our children by filling their mouths with grass, dirt, or cloth. Under the reign of the Messiah, we stretch out our feet at ease; eat our food, keep our pig by the house, and see children, wife, and all, at table in the same house. We do not know our ancestors, our kings and our parents; and we were all blind, till the birds flew across the great expanse with good seeds in their mouths, and planted them among us. We now gather the fruit, and have continual harvest. It was God who put into the hearts of those strangers to come to us. We have nothing to give them. They are a people who seek our good; but we are a people of thorny hands, of pointed tongues, and we have no thoughts. If God were to take our teachers from us, we should soon be savage again. They are the great roots to the tree on the high hill; the wind strikes it, twists it, but cannot level it to the ground, for its roots are strong. Our hearts delighted in war, but our teachers love peace, and, we now have peace.'"

Pride in Dress.

Chap. iii. ver. 22, 23.—The changeable suits of apparel, and the mantles, and the wimples, and the crisping-pins.—The glasses, and the fine linen, and the hoods, and the vails.

THE Rev. John Harrion, a dissenting minister at Denton in Norfolk, had two daughters who were much too fond of dress, which was a great grief to him. He had often reproved them in vain; and preaching one Sabbath day on the sin of pride, he took occasion to notice, among other things, pride in *dress*. After speaking some considerable time on this subject, he suddenly stopped short, and said, with much feeling and expression, "But you will say, *Look at home.* My good friends, I do look at home, till my heart aches."

Purification.

Chap. iv. ver. 4.—When the Lord shall have washed away the filth of the daughters of Zion, and shall have purged the blood of Jerusalem from the midst thereof, by the spirit of judgment, and by the spirit of burning.

"I REMEMBER," says Mr Whitefield, "some years ago, when I was at Shields, I went into a glass-house ; and, standing very attentive, I saw several masses of burning glass of various forms. The workman took a piece of glass, and put into one furnace, then he put it into a second, and then into a third. I said to him, 'Why do you put it through so many fires ?' He answered, 'O, Sir, the first was not hot enough, nor the second, therefore we put it into a third, and that will make it transparent.'" This furnished Mr Whitefield with a useful hint, that we must be tried and exercised with many fires, until our dross be purged away, and we are made fit for the owner's use.

Strong Drink.

Chap. v. ver. 22.—Woe unto them that are mighty to drink wine, and men of strength to mingle strong drink.

TWO young men, lately drinking together in a public-house, in a village near Huntingdon, fell into a conversation as to who could drink most without being intoxicated. One of them said to the other, "I will call for a half-crown's worth of gin : if you finish the liquor I will pay for it—if not, you shall." The other agreed to the proposal, and drank till he fell from the chair, when he was carried home, and soon after died. How awful to meet death in such a state!

Telling the People.

Chap. vi. ver. 9.—He said, Go and tell this people, Hear ye, indeed, but understand not ; and see ye, indeed, but perceive not.

"ON the morning before I was licensed," says the late Rev. John Brown, "that text was much impressed on my spirit, 'He said, Go and tell this people, Hear ye indeed, but understand not ; and see ye indeed, but perceive not,' &c. Since I was ordained at Haddington, I know not how often it hath been heavy to my heart to think how much this scripture hath been fulfilled in my ministry. Frequently I have had an anxious desire to be removed by death, from being a plague to my poor congregation. Often, however, I have checked myself, and have considered this wish as my folly, and begged of the Lord, that if it were not for his glory to remove me by death, he would make me successful in my work."

Flies in the East.

Chap. vii. ver. 18.—The Lord shall hiss for the fly that is in the uttermost part of the rivers of Egypt.

VINISAUF, speaking of the army under Richard I., a little before he left the Holy Land, and describing them as marching on the plain not far from the sea-coast, says, "The army stopping a while there, rejoicing in the hope of speedily setting out for Jerusalem, were assailed by a most minute kind of fly, flying about like sparks, which they called *cincinellac.* With these the whole neighbouring region round about was filled. These most wretchedly infested the pilgrims, piercing with great smartness the hands, necks, throats, foreheads, and faces, and every part that was uncovered, a most violent burning tumour following the punctures made by them, so that all that they stung looked like lepers." He adds, "that they could hardly guard themselves from this most troublesome vexation, by covering their heads and necks with veils."

In Trouble.

Chap. viii. ver. 21.—They shall fret themselves, and curse their king and their God, and look upward.

GENERAL BURN, in describing the effects of a violent storm that assailed the vessel in which he was returning to England, off the coast of Whitehaven, says, "As beings imagining they had but a few moments to live, all strove with dying eagerness to reach the quarter-deck, but we had scarcely raised ourselves upright when the ship struck a second time, more violently than before, and again threw us all prostrate. The scene was enough to make the heart of the stoutest sinner tremble. I very well remember the agony of one of my poor messmates. This man had acquired considerable property in Jamaica, and during the voyage, like the rich man in the parable, was frequently devising plans of future happiness. At this awful moment, he exclaimed bitterly against the treatment of heaven, that had made him spend so many toilsome years in a scorching and unhealthy climate to procure a little wealth; and when with pain and trouble he had heaped it together, had tantalized him with a sight of the happy shore, where he expected peaceably to enjoy it; but now with one cruel sudden stroke had defeated all his hopes. The cutting reflections and bitter complaints which came from this man's mouth expressed such black despair, that he appeared more like a fiend of the bottomless pit, than a sinner yet in the land of hope."

Do not Seek the Lord.

Chap. ix. ver. 13.—The people turneth not unto him that smiteth them, neither do they seek the Lord of hosts.

A CHRISTIAN friend, visiting a good man under great distress and afflicting dispensations, which he bore with such patient and composed resignation, as to make his friend wonder and admire it—inquired how he was enabled so to comfort himself? The good man said, "The distress I am under is indeed severe; but I find it lightens the stroke very much, *to creep near to him who handles the rod;*" adding, "But where else, save in the religion of Christ, could such a sufferer find such a support!"

Boasting.

Chap. x. ver. 15.—Shall the axe boast itself against him that heweth therewith; or shall the saw magnify itself against him that shaketh it?

WHEN Bonaparte was about to invade Russia, a person who had endeavoured to dissuade him from his purpose, finding he could not prevail, quoted to him the proverb, "Man *proposes*, but God *disposes;*" to which he indignantly replied, "I *dispose* as well as propose." A Christian lady, on hearing the impious boast, remarked, "I set that down as the turning point of Bonaparte's fortunes. God will not suffer a creature with impunity thus to usurp his prerogative."

It happened to Bonaparte just as the lady predicted. His invasion of Russia was the commencement of his fall.

Knowing God.

Chap. xi. ver. 9.—They shall not hurt or destroy in all my holy mountain : for the earth shall be full of the knowledge of the Lord, as the waters cover the sea.

IN the eleventh century, the effect of the gospel in Denmark was such as to prove at once its divine origin, and its benign tendency. Adam of Bremen, an historian, thus expresses it :—" Look at that very ferocious nation of the Danes ; for a long time they have been accustomed, in the praises of God, to resound Alleluia ! Look at that piratical people ; they are now content with the fruits of their own country. Look at that horrid region, formerly altogether inaccessible on account of idolatry ; now they eagerly admit the preacher of the word."—To refer to a more recent instance : the inhabitants of the South Sea are now professedly Christian, and improvement in their circumstances keeps pace with that of their morals. Theft is almost unknown among them. Family prayer is set up in every house, and private prayer is almost universally attended to. The people look up to the missionaries as their oracle in all their troubles of body and mind, civil and religious. They were once the cruel slaves of Satan, destroying themselves and their infant offspring. Now, women are restored to their proper rank in society, a new generation of young ones is springing up, beloved by their parents ; and the face of things is wonderfully altered, so that we are constrained to say, "This is the Lord's doing, and it is marvellous in our eyes."

Ultimate Praise to God.

Chap. xii. ver. 1.—In that day thou shalt say, O Lord, I will praise thee : though thou wast angry with me, thine anger is turned away, and thou comfortedst me.

THE late Rev. Thomas Scott, during his last illness, sometimes wanted that comfort which he usually enjoyed ; and though *hope* as to his final salvation generally predominated, yet he would say, " Even one fear, *where infinity is at stake*, is sufficient to countervail all its consoling effects." Having received the Sacrament, at the conclusion of the service, he adopted the language of Simeon, " Lord, now lettest thou thy servant depart in peace, for my eyes have seen thy salvation." Through the remainder of the day, and during the night, he continued in a very happy state of mind. To one who came in the evening, he said, "It was beneficial to me : I received Christ last night : I bless God for it." He then repeated, in the most emphatic manner, the whole twelfth chapter of Isaiah. The next morning he said, " This is heaven begun. I have done with darkness *for ever—for ever.* Satan is vanquished. Nothing now remains but salvation with eternal glory—*eternal glory.*"

Babylon.

Chap. xiii. ver. 20, 21.—It shall never be inhabited, neither shall it be dwelt in from generation to generation ;—but wild beasts of the desert shall lie there ; and their houses shall be full of doleful creatures.

WHEN Babylon was first deserted of its inhabitants, the Persian kings turned it into a park for hunting, and kept their wild beasts there. When the Persian empire declined, the beasts broke loose, so that, when Alexander the Great marched eastward, he found

Babylon a perfect desert. He intended to restore Euphrates to its ancient channel, but the design not having been completed, the river overflowed its banks, and the greater part of that once celebrated city became a lake or pool of water. Theodorus, who lived about four hundred years after Christ, tells us that Babylon was the receptacle of snakes, serpents, and all sorts of noxious animals, so that it was dangerous to visit it. Benjamin of Toledo, a Jew, who visited it in 1112, informs us that few remains of it were left, nor were there any inhabitants within many miles of it. Rawolffe, a German, who travelled to the east in 1572, found it very difficult to discover the place on which it stood, nor could the neighbouring inhabitants give him proper directions. Mr Hanway, a later traveller, with every assistance that could be procured, spent several days in endeavouring to ascertain its situation, but in vain, so completely has it been swept with the besom of destruction from the face of the earth.

The Prisoner.

Chap. xiv. ver. 17.—That opened not the house of his prisoners?

MR WILLIAM JENKYN, one of the ejected ministers in England, being imprisoned in Newgate, presented a petition to King Charles II. for a release, which was backed by an assurance from his physicians that his life was in danger from his close imprisonment; but no other answer could be obtained than this, "Jenkyn shall be a prisoner as long as he lives."—A nobleman having some time after heard of his death, said to the king, "May it please your Majesty, Jenkyn has got his liberty." Upon which he asked, with eagerness, "Aye! who gave it him?" The nobleman replied, "A greater than your Majesty—the King of kings;" with which the king seemed greatly struck, and remained silent.

Eastern Mourning.

Chap. xv. ver. 4.—Hesbon shall cry, and Elealeh; their voice shall be heard even unto Jahaz.

SIR JOHN CHARDIN, giving an account of the Eastern lamentations, says, "Their sentiments of joy, or of grief, are properly transports; and their transports are ungoverned, excessive, and truly outrageous. When any one returns from a long journey, or dies, his family burst into cries, that may be heard twenty doors off; and this is renewed at different times, and continues many days, according to the vigour of the passion. Especially are these cries long in the case of death, and frightful; for the mourning is right-down despair, and an image of hell. I was lodged, in the year 1676, at Ispahan, near the Royal Square; the mistress of the next house to mine died at that time. The moment she expired, all the family, to the number of twenty-five or thirty people, set up such a furious cry, that I was quite startled, and was above two hours before I could recover myself."

Suffering for Conscience Sake.

Chap. xvi. ver. 4.—Let mine outcasts dwell with thee, Moab.

MR PHILIP HENRY, one of the non-conformist ministers, when silenced from preaching, by the act of uniformity, took comfort himself, and administered comfort to others from the preceding passage. "God's people," he observed, "may be an outcast people, cast out of men's love, their synagogues, their country; but God will own his people when men cast them out; they are *outcasts*, but they are *his*, and some way or other he will provide a *dwelling* for them."— Shortly before his death, the same pious man observed that, though many of the ejected ministers were brought very low, had many children, were greatly harassed by persecution, and their friends generally poor and unable to support them; yet, in all his acquaintance, he never knew, nor could remember to have heard of, any nonconformist minister in prison for debt.

Trust in God,

Chap. xvii. ver. 7.—At that day shall a man look to his Maker, and his eyes shall have respect to the Holy One of Israel.

THE Rev. Mr Charles had at one time the prospect of obtaining a situation in North Wales, which he much wished; but, as in a former instance, he eventually failed. The place appears to have been lost through the remissness of a friend, who was commissioned to treat for the situation. "If I had not, at *that moment*," says Mr C., "seen the hand of God in it, I should have been very angry indeed with Mr Smith. Every thing is under the control of the all-wise God. To see and believe this will make us perfectly easy and resigned, even in the greatest disappointments. How true it is, 'that he that believeth in Him shall not be *moved*.' And what a blessed thing it is to obtain a firmness and stability which nothing can shake; no, not even the wreck of nature."

Eastern Boats.

Chap. xviii. ver. 2.—That sendeth ambassadors by the sea, even in vessels of bulrushes upon the waters.

"WE went up the river Euphrates," says an eastern traveller, "this afternoon. Our boat was of a peculiar make. In shape it was like a large round basket: the sides were of willow, covered over with bitumen, a sort of pitch; the bottom was made with reeds; it had two men with paddles, one of whom paddled towards him, and the other pushed from him. This sort of boat is common on the Euphrates, and may be of the same kind as the vessels of bulrushes upon the waters spoken of by Isaiah."

A Saviour.

Chap. xix. ver. 20.—The Lord shall send them a Saviour, and a great one, and he shall deliver them.

THE Rev. Mr Grimshawe stated, at a recent meeting of the Religious Tract Society, that a few years ago he met with Mr Colemeister, who had laboured among the Esquimaux for thirty-four years, and had first translated the four Gospels into the Esquimaux language. Among a variety of interesting questions Mr Grimshawe put to him, he thought that he would question him upon a point of some curiosity and difficulty, respecting his translation. Knowing how imperfect barbarous languages are, and how inadequate to express any abstract idea, Mr G. requested him to say how he translated the word *Saviour* in the Gospel. Mr Colemeister said, "Your question is remarkable, and perhaps the answer may be so too. It is true the Esquimaux have no word to represent the Saviour, and I could never find out that they had any direct notion of such a friend. But I said to them, 'Does it not happen sometimes when you are out fishing that a storm arises, and some of you are lost, and some saved?' They said, 'O yes, very often.'—'But it also happens that you are in the water, and owe your safety to some brother or friend who stretches out his hand to help you?'—'Very frequently.'—'Then what do you call that friend?" They gave me in answer a word of their language, and I immediately wrote it against the term Saviour in Holy Writ, and ever after it was intelligible to them."

The Misery of Prisoners.

Chap. xx. ver. 4.—The King of Assyria shall lead away the Egyptians prisoners, and the Ethiopians captives, young and old, naked and barefoot.

ABOUT a mile from the new town of St. Nicholas, in Russia, Mr. Howard, the philanthropist, inspected four rooms for six recruits and prisoners of war. The number crowded into these rooms was upwards of three hundred, many of whom were extremely ill, and supplied with provisions of the worst quality. Going back to the town, accompanied by the physician and several officers, he found fifty objects of such extreme wretchedness, as, in the whole course of his extensive visits to the abodes of misery and vice, he had never before seen together. Most of them were recruits, in the prime of life, many of whom were dying upon a bed of hard, coarse reeds, without linen or coverlids, or any thing to protect them but a few remnants of their old clothes; their persons indescribably filthy, and their shirts in rags. After viewing other scenes of misery, he makes the following reflection:—"Let but a contemplative mind reflect a moment upon the condition of these poor destitute wretches, forced from their homes and all their dearest connections, and compare them with those one has seen, cheerful, clean, and happy, at a wedding or village festival;—let them be viewed quitting their birth-place, with all their little wardrobe, and their pockets stored with rubles, the gifts of their relations, who never expect to see them more; now joining their corps in a long march of one or two thousand wersts; their money gone to the officer who conducts them and defrauds them of the government allowance; arriving fatigued and half-naked in a distant dreary country, and exposed immediately to military hardships, with harassed bodies, and dejected spirits; and who can wonder that so many droop and die in a short time without any apparent illness? The devastations I have seen made by war among so many innocent people, and this in a country where there are such immense tracts of land unoccupied, are shocking to human nature."

Earthly Glory.

Chap. xxi. ver. 16.—Within a year according to the years of an hireling, and all the glory of Kedar shall fail.

"I REMEMBER," observes one, "having heard a sensible person say he could never covet the office of chief magistrate of London, because that honour continued only one year. Might not the idea be justly extended to all the honours and enjoyments of this life? None of them are permanent."

Untimely Levity.

Chap. xxii. ver. 12, 13.—In that day did the Lord God of hosts call to weeping, and to mourning, and to baldness, and to girding with sackcloth:—And behold joy and gladness, slaying oxen and killing sheep, eating flesh and drinking wine: let us eat and drink, for tomorrow we shall die.

IN the midst of the distresses with which France was harrassed in the reign of Charles VII., and whilst the English were in pos-

session of Paris, Charles amused himself and his mistresses with balls
and entertainments. The brave La Here, coming to Charles one day
to talk to him on some business of importance, whilst the luxurious
Prince was occupied in arranging one of his parties of pleasure, was
interrupted by the Monarch, who asked him what he thought of his
arrangement. "I think, Sire," said he, "it is impossible for any one
to lose his kingdom more pleasantly than your Majesty."

For a Good Cause.

Chap. xxiii. ver. 18.—Her merchandise and her hire shall be holiness to the Lord.

MR. FISK, in giving an account of his missionary labours in Egypt,
says, "I have also become acquainted with the masters of several
English merchant vessels, one of whom I learn has prayers daily with
his men, and reads a sermon to them regularly on the Sabbath. Another has given me an interesting account of the 'Floating Ark, for
the support of which he is a subscriber, and in which he attends
worship when at London. This vessel, he says, was originally a sixty-four gun ship, was purchased by a company of merchants in London,
and application was then made to them by the Port of London
Society, to obtain it as a place of worship for seamen. The merchants
replied, 'If you want it for *that* purpose, we make a donation of it; if
for any *other* object, we charge you £3000.'"

In Tribulation.

Chap. xxiv. ver. 15.—Glorify ye the Lord in the fires.

ANN MEIGLO, a poor distressed woman in the parish of Portmoak,
when visited by Mr. Ebenezer Erskine, said to him, "O, Sir, I am
just lying here, a poor useless creature."—"Think you," said he. "I
think, Sir, what is true, if I were away to heaven, I would be of some
use to glorify God without sin."—"Indeed, Annie," said Mr. Erskine,
"I think you are glorifying God by your resignation and submission
to his will, and that in the face of many difficulties, and under many
distresses. In heaven the saints have no burdens to groan under;
your praises, burdened as you are, are more wonderful to me, and, I
trust, acceptable to God."

Victorious over Death.

Chap. xxv. ver. 8.—He will swallow up death in victory.

MR. LIVINGSTONE, speaking of Josias Welsh, says, "On the
Sabbath afternoon before his death, which was on Monday
following, I heard of his sickness, and came to him about eleven
o'clock at night, and Mr. Blair about two hours thereafter. He had
many gracious discoveries, as also some wrestling and exercise of mind.
One time he cried out, 'O for hypocrisy!' on which Mr. Blair said,
'See how Satan is nibbling at his heels before he enter into glory.' A
very little before he died, being at prayer by his bedside and the
word 'victory' coming out of my mouth, he took hold of my hand,
and desiring me to forbear a little, and clapping his hands, cried
out, 'Victory, victory, victory, for evermore!' He then desired me to
go on, and in a little expired. His death happened on the 23d of June,
1634."

The Resurrection.

Chap. xxvi. ver. 19.—Thy dead men shall live, together with my
dead body shall they arise.

A MAN in Scotland, who had some years before buried his wife, and several of his children, one day stood leaning over a low wall, intently gazing on the spot in the churchyard, where he had deposited their dear remains. A person observing his thoughtful attitude, asked him what occupied his mind? "I am looking," he said, "at the dust that lies there, and wondering at the indissoluble union betwixt it and the Lord Jesus Christ, who is in glory."

Making Peace with God.

Chap. xxvii. ver. 5.—Let him take hold of my strength, that he may make peace with me; and he shall make peace with me.

"I THINK," says one, "I can convey the meaning of this passage, so that every one may understand it, by what took place in my own family within these few days. One of my little children had committed a fault, for which I thought it my duty to chastise him. I called him to me, explained to him the evil of what he had done, and told him how grieved I was that I must punish him for it. He heard me in silence, and then rushed into my arms, and burst into tears. I could sooner have cut off my arm than have then struck him for his fault: he had taken hold of my strength, also he had made peace with me."

Teaching the Children.

Chap. xxviii. ver. 9.—Whom shall he teach knowledge? and whom shall he make to understand doctrine? them that are weaned from the milk, and drawn from the breasts.

A VENERABLE old minister, in New Hampshire, lodging at the house of a pious friend, observed the mother teaching some short prayers and hymns to her children. "Madam," said he, "your instructions may be of far more importance than you are aware:·my mother taught me a little hymn when a child, and it is of use to me to this day. I never close my eyes to rest, without first saying—

'Now I lay me down to sleep,
I pray thee, Lord, my soul to keep:
If I should die before I wake,
I pray thee, Lord, my soul to take.'"

Likened to a Thirsty Man.

Chap. xxix. ver. 8.—As when a thirsty man dreameth, and behold, he drinketh; but he awaketh, and, behold, he is faint, and his soul hath appetite.

MR. PARK, speaking of the great want of water in Africa, says, "I frequently passed the night in the situation of Tantalus. No sooner had I shut my eyes, than fancy would convey me to the streams and rivers of my native land; there, as I wandered along the verdant bank, I surveyed the clear stream with transport, and hastened to swallow the delightful draught; but, alas! disappointments awakened me, and I found myself a lonely captive perishing of thirst, amidst the wilds of Africa."

Saying Smooth Things.

Chap. xxx. ver. 10.—Prophesy not unto us right things; speak unto us smooth things, prophesy deceits.

A DISSENTING minister, preaching very practically, was found fault with by his people, who gave him to understand that they must part with him, if he did not alter the strain of his preaching

The minister, having a family, shrunk for a time, but it preyed upon his health, which his wife observing, plainly told him that he distrusted God out of fear of man, and was unfaithful; and begged of him to preach according to his conscience, and leave the event to God. Accordingly he did so, and was expelled. But just at that time, a larger meeting, with a better salary, and a more lively people, being vacant, he was invited thither, and settled among them; lived in plenty, and preached with acceptance and usefulness, till removed by death.

The Lion.

Chap. xxxi. ver. 4.—The lion and the young lion roaring on his prey, when a multitude of shepherds is called forth against him, he will not be afraid of their voice, nor abase himself for the noise of them.

AN instance of the courage of the lion is related in the account of one who had broken into a walled enclosure for cattle. The people of the farm, with the intention of destroying him on his return, stretched a rope across the entrance, to which several guns were fastened in a direction to discharge their contents into his body, so soon as he should push against the cord with his breast. But the lion approached the rope, and struck it away with his foot; and without showing any alarm, in consequence of the reports of the guns, he went fearlessly on, and devoured the prey he had before left untouched.

Clothed with Righteousness.

Chap. xxxii. ver. 2.—A man shall be as an hiding-place from the wind, and a covert from the tempest; as rivers of water in a dry place; as the shadow of a great rock in a weary land.

A PIOUS minister, some years ago, being called upon to preach a sermon for the benefit of a Sabbath School in Northamptonshire, was led to enlarge in his discourse on the necessity of being clothed with the Redeemer's righteousness, as the only means of security from the wrath to come. While speaking, a violent storm of thunder and lightning came on, accompanied with rain and hail. The lightning struck a tree in the churchyard, shivered it to pieces, and drove a part of it through one of the windows. The congregation, alarmed, began to fly for safety in all directions. The minister entreated them to remain in the house of God: reminding them, that if they were protected from their sins by the righteousness of Christ, let storms, lightnings, or even death come, they were perfectly safe. In pursuing his discourse, his attention was attracted to one of the Sabbath school girls, who was standing near the pulpit, and who appeared to be peculiarly impressed by the sermon. Calling at her parent's house next day, the mother told him that her daughter had met with a disappointment, as she expected to go to the fair that day; but a circumstance had occurred that would prevent her. "What, my dear," said the minister, "are you fond of going to fairs?" The child immediately replied, "O no, Sir; I don't want to go to the fair; I now only want to be clothed in that robe of righteousness which you were speaking of yesterday, that I may see Jesus Christ." The minister entered into conversation with her, and found her mind so deeply impressed, that he had good reason to believe that a saving change was wrought on her soul. He left her, intending to repeat his visit next day, but received information of her death; having been found dead in the garden.

Bribery.

Chap. xxxiii. ver. 15.—That shaketh his hands from holding of bribes.

THE borough of Hull, in the reign of Charles II., chose Andrew Marvell, a young gentleman of little or no fortune, and maintained him in London for the service of the public. His understanding, integrity, and spirit, were dreadful to the then infamous administration. Persuaded he would be theirs, if properly asked, they sent his old school-fellow, the lord treasurer Danby, to renew acquaintance with him in his garret. At parting, the lord treasurer slipped into his hand £1000, and then went to his chariot. Marvell, looking at the paper, called after the Treasurer, "My Lord, I request another moment." They went up again to the garret, and the servant boy was called, "I ask, child, what had I for dinner yesterday?" "Don't you remember, Sir, you had the little shoulder of mutton that you ordered me to bring from a woman in the market." "Very right, child. What have I for dinner to-day?" "Don't you know, Sir, that you bid me lay by the blade-bone to broil?" "It is so; very right, child, go away." My Lord, do you hear that? Andrew Marvell's dinner is provided; there is your piece of paper, I want it not; I know the sort of kindness you intended; I live here to serve my constituents, the ministry may seek men for their purpose; I am not one."

The Raven.

Chap. xxxiv. ver. 11.—The raven shall dwell in it.

IN the centre of a grove near Shelbourne, there stood an oak, which, though on the whole shapely and tall, jutted out to a great excrescence near the middle of the stem. On this tree a pair of ravens had made their nest for so many years, that it was called the "Raven-tree." Many attempts had been made to reach the nest; but when the climbers arrived at the swelling, it jutted out so in their way, and was so far beyond their grasp, that the boldest were defeated. Thus the birds continued to build unmolested, till the fatal day on which the tree was to be levelled. This was in the month of February when these birds usually sit. The saw was applied to the trunk. The wedges were inserted into the opening, the woods echoed with the heavy sound of the axe and the mallet, and the tree nodded to its fall; but still the dam persisted in sitting. At last, when it gave way, the bird was flung from the nest, and though her parental affection deserved a better fate, was whipped down by the twigs, which brought her dead to the ground.

In Heaven.

Chap. xxxv. ver. 10.—They shall obtain joy and gladness, and sorrow and sighing shall flee away.

DURING the last illness of the Rev. John Wilson of Dundee, he was visited by Mr Ralph Erskine; and while conversing together on the happiness of the better country, where the saints are perfect in knowledge and in love, a pious lady present, who was warmly attached to the national church, addressed Mr Erskine in these words, "Aye, Sir, there will be no Secession in heaven." "O, Madam," he instantly replied, "you are under a mistake; for in heaven there will be a complete secession from all sin and sorrow." "With pleasure," said Mr Wilson, "do I adopt that view of Secession."

A King's Power.

Chap. xxxvi. ver. 13.—Rabshaketh stood and cried with a loud voice in the Jews' language, and said, Hear ye the words of the great king, the king of Assyria.

IN the reign of king James II., Mr Baxter was committed prisoner to the King's Bench, by the warrant of Lord Chief Justice Jefferies, for some alleged seditious passages in his Pharaphrase on the New Testament. When brought to his trial, being very much indisposed, he moved, by his counsel, for further time ; but the judge cried out in a passion : " I will not give him a minute's time to save his life : we have had to deal with other sorts of persons, but now we have a saint to deal with. I know how to deal with saints as well as sinners. Yonder stands Oates in the pillory, and he says he suffers for truth, and so says Baxter ; but if Baxter did but stand on the other side of the pillory with him, I would say, two of the greatest rogues and rascals in the kingdom stood there ! " Mr Baxter, beginning to speak for himself, Jefferies said to him, "Richard, Richard, dost thou think we will hear thee poison the court? Richard, thou art an old fellow, an old knave : thou hast written books enow to fill a cart, every one as full of sedition, I may say treason, as an egg is full of meat. Hadst thou been whipt out of thy writing trade forty years ago, it had been happy. I know thou hast a mighty party ; and I see a great many of the brotherhood in corners, to see what will become of their mighty Don, and a Doctor of the party—meaning Dr. Bates—at your elbow ; but by the grace of God Almighty, I'll crush them all." After farther mockery and insult from this blustering judge, Mr Baxter was condemned to pay a heavy fine, and to remain in prison till it was paid. He continued in prison two years, when, from a change of measures, he was set at liberty.

Heathen Gods.

Chap. xxxvii. ver. 19.—And have cast their gods into the fire ; for they were no gods, but the works of men's hands, wood and stone ; therefore they have destroyed them.

IN a letter written by a French Jesuit, about a hundred years ago, it is stated, that at a place several leagues westward of Madras, some masons, who had embraced Christianity, were employed by a Brahmin to repair the embankment of a reservoir of water. It is customary among the Hindoos to place in such situations a number of small idols made of stone. These the workmen designedly buried in the earth which they threw up to strengthen the embankment. The Brahmin coming to inspect their progress, said, "I see nothing of our gods, what have you done with them !" "What is it you mean, Sir ?" replied the overseer ; "I saw a heap of *stones*, which I thought would be of use to strengthen the embankment ; but as for *gods* I saw nothing of the kind." "Those were the things you ought to have taken care of," said the Brahmin ; " did you not know they were our gods?" " Those things," answered the overseer, "I understand as well as anybody : it is my business to do so ; and, take my word for it, Sir, they were nothing but stones ; if they were gods, as you say they are, they could easily get up again into their old places."

Renewed Life.

Chap. xxxviii. ver. 5.—I have heard thy prayer, I have seen thy tears : behold I will add unto thy days fifteen years.

IN the autumn of 1799, the late Rev. T. Charles of Bala met with an afflicting dispensation. While travelling over Mount Migneint, in Carnarvonshire, on a freezing night, one of his thumbs became frost bitten. It was so severely affected, that he was taken very ill, and his life was in danger. To prevent mortification, it was deemed necessary to have it amputated. This affliction was very trying both to his family and to his people. When he was considered to be in a dangerous state, a special prayer-meeting was called by the members of the chapel at Bala. Fervent supplications were offered up in his behalf. Several prayed on the occasion; and one person in particular was much noticed at the time, for the very urgent and importunate manner with which he prayed. Alluding to the fifteen years added to Hezekiah's life, he, with unusual fervency, entreated the Almighty to spare Mr C.'s life at least fifteen years. He several times repeated the following words, with such melting importunity, as greatly affected all present:—"Fifteen years more, O Lord; we beseech thee to add fifteen years more to the life of thy servant. And wilt thou not, O our God, give fifteen years more for the sake of thy church and thy cause?" Mr C. heard of this prayer, and it made a deep impression on his mind. He afterwards frequently mentioned it as a reason why he should make the best use of his time, saying, that his fifteen years would soon be completed. The last time that he visited South Wales, and was asked when he should come again, his answer was, at least to some, that his fifteen years were nearly up, and that he should probably never visit them again. He mentioned this to several of his friends the last year of his life, and especially to his wife. It is remarkable, his death occurred just at the termination of the fifteen years. What is not less remarkable, it was during this time that he performed the most important acts of his life. It was during this time that he wrote the most valuable of his works; established Sabbath Schools; was one means of originating the Bible Society; and was instrumental in doing great good both to Scotland and Ireland.

Happy Days.

Chap. xxxix. ver. 8.—There shall be peace and truth in my days.

"I WELL remember," says Dr. Gibbons, "that discoursing with the late Sir Conyers Jocelyn, about Mr Baxter and Dr. Watts, he pleasantly but very truly observed, nearly in these words, that 'The latter went to heaven on a bed of down, in comparison with the former.' Such was the distinguishing privilege with which this holy man was favoured, not only to his own great comfort, but to the great benefit of the church and the world, who might, had his feeble frame been hunted down by persecution, or locked up in a damp suffocating prison, have been deprived, in a great measure, of his numerous and useful writings."

God a Spirit.

Chap. xl. ver. 18.—To whom then will ye liken God? or what likeness will ye compare unto him?

ONE day, when Mr Richards, missionary in India, was conversing with the natives, a Fakeer came up, and put into his hand a small stone about the size of a sixpence, with the impression of two human likenesses sculptured on the surface; he also proffered a few grains of rice, and said, "This is Mahadeo?" Mr Richards said, "Do you know the meaning of Mahadeo!" The Fakeer replied, "No."

Mr R. proceeded, "Mahadeo means the Great God—He who is God of gods, and besides whom there can be no other. Now, this Great God is a Spirit; no one can see a spirit, who is intangible. Whence, then, this visible impression on a senseless, hard, immoveable stone? To whom will ye liken God or what likeness will ye compare unto Him? God is the high and lofty One that inhabiteth eternity, whose name is Holy. He hath said, 'I am Jehovah; there is no God besides me.'" The poor Fakeer was serious, respectful, attentive; continually exclaiming, "Your words are true."

God with Us.

Chap. xli. ver. 10.—Fear thou not; for I am with thee.

ONE Sabbath, lately, Mr Winder, at Edgeworth-moor, near Bolton, was preaching from the preceding text. He commented on the fear of death, which solemn subject had been suggested by the awfulness of the thunder storm which then hung over the place. The preacher was supposing the possibility that in this storm some one or more present might be struck dead. The words had just escaped his lips, when the lightning broke upon the house, shattering or removing some of the materials of the building, and producing great consternation and disorder in the assembly. No serious injury, however, was done, and after some degree of composure was attained, the congregation sung, "Praise God from whom all blessings flow," and prayed, as it may be supposed, with much devotional fervour.

At Sea with God.

Chap. xlii. ver. 10.—Sing unto the Lord a new song, and his praise from the end of the earth, ye that go down to the sea, and all that is therein.

A VERY young sailor observed to a gentleman that he should never forget the thrill of joy that he felt during his last voyage. One night, or rather early in the morning, a fine starlight morning, as they were running down the trades, with the sea smooth as oil, more than two thousand miles from land, and at that time, as he thought, equally far from any vessel upon the vast Atlantic, he started from his monotonous pacing fore and aft upon the deck, by a sound like a burst of voices; he at first conceived it to be the dying echoes of a fired cannon, probably some vessel in distress. Again he heard it in loud and distinct sounds, and found, at length, it was the harmony of voices, singing, as he judged from the tune, one of the hymns used at the Bethel prayer-meetings. The voices evidently were at a great distance, but, borne over the wide space of the water, reached in soft and pleasing music, and caused him to feel a joyful recollection of the song heard by the shepherds, whilst watching their flocks by night in the fields of Bethlehem. When the morning opened upon them, an English ship was observed to the westward. "Sir," said he, "I can give you no idea of my gladness in anticipating that the day was coming, and now opened upon us like the morning, when every ship should be navigated by men fearing God, and working righteousness."

Why Man was Created.

Chap. xliii. ver. 7.—I have created him for my glory.

MR JOHN THOMSON, a pious merchant in Musselburgh, and father-in-law of the Rev. John Brown of Haddington, used to relate, that in his eleventh year, when he was walking one Sabbath morning to public worship in the church at Abbotshall, he was arrested by the importance of the first question in the Shorter Catechism, "What is the chief end of man?" This led him into a train of inquiry, which was the means, in the hand of the Spirit of God, of making him acquainted with the present fallen and guilty state of man, and of the only method of recovery, through the mercy of God, by the righteousness of Christ.

The Heathen.

Chap. xliv. ver. 9.—They that make a graven image are all of them vanity; and their delectable things shall not profit.

ONE day, a missionary among the Gentoos took with him a little boy from the school, to a shady place, where many people were passing, and set him to read aloud. When some began to listen, he conversed with the boy about what he was reading. The subject was —the absurdity of idolatry; and a Brahmin in the crowd said, "My little fellow, why do you speak so lightly of the gods of your fathers?" The boy replied in a loud voice, "Speak lightly of them! Why, they have eyes, and see not; they have mouths, and speak not; they have ears, and hear not; they are vanity and a lie; and why not speak lightly of them?" The Brahmin walked away confounded.

The Ends of the Earth.

Chap. xlv. ver. 22.—Look unto me, and be ye saved, all the ends of the earth; for I am God, and there is none else.

WHEN the Rev. Andrew Fuller first visited Scotland, a notoriously wicked and abandoned woman, seeing a number of persons thronging the doors of a chapel, felt her curiosity awakened, and being informed that an Englishman was to preach, she mingled with the crowd and entered the place. Mr Fuller took the preceding passage for his text, "What, then," she exclaimed in her heart, "surely there is hope even for me! Wretch as I am, I am not beyond the ends o the earth." She listened with eager delight while the good man proclaimed the free salvation of the gospel. Hope sprung up in her heart, a hope which purified as well as comforted; and the grace of God taught her to "deny ungodliness and worldly lusts, and to live soberly, righteously, and godly in the present world."

God and Old Age.

Chap. xlvi. ver. 4.—Even to your old age, I am he.

A FRIEND conversing with the late Mr Brown of Haddington, about a sermon which Mr B. had preached on these words, "Even to your old age, I am he," he observed that he remembered discoursing on this text; and then added, with a sort of cheerfulness, "I must say, that I never yet found God to break his word in this; no, notwithstanding all the provocations which I have given him."

No Throne.

Chap. xlvii. ver. 1.—Come down, and sit in the dust, O virgin daughter of Babylon; and sit on the ground: there is no throne, O daughter of the Chaldeans.

A MEDAL was struck by Vespasian on the subjugation of the Jews. on the reverse is seen a palm-tree, and a woman sitting on the *ground* at the foot of it, with her head leaning on her arm, weeping; and at her feet different pieces of armour, with this legend, "Judea capta," (taken.) Thus was exactly fulfilled the saying of the same prophet, "And she, being desolate, shall sit upon the ground."

In Affliction.

Chap. xlviii. ver. 10.—I have chosen thee in the furnace of affliction.

A YOUNG man, who lived on Rowley Common, Kent, and had been a very profligate character, while working as a mason, fell from a scaffolding twenty feet high, and was seriously injured. Both his legs were broken, and several of his ribs, and his spine was injured. He lay long on the bed of affliction, when he was visited by a clergyman. He felt deep convictions of sin, but was ignorant of the way of salvation: this was explained to him; he received with eagerness the news of pardon through the atonement of Christ, and was enabled to commit his soul into the Redeemer's hands. His nurse said, "When I went to him first, he was such an impatient, wicked-tempered man, that it was impossible to live with him; but a gentleman came to read the Bible to him for some days, and after that he became like a child, so that it grieved my heart to leave him." On his sick-bed he learned to read and write, and his efforts were blessed to the conversion of his sister. He died in peace.

The King's Protection.

Chap. xlix. ver. 23.—And kings shall be thy nursing fathers.

MR LEIFCHILD was one of a deputation from the three denominations of dissenting ministers in London, who waited on his late majesty, George IV. with an address on his accession to the throne, and were most graciously received. The address alluded to the happiness and protection they enjoyed under the fostering care and parental sway of his beloved and revered father, and expressed an humble but earnest hope, that he would imitate his example, and follow his steps. After his majesty had read the written answer, and before they took leave, one of the deputation said, they feared they had occasioned his majesty too much trouble: when the king said, "You give me no trouble, my friends; I derive the most heartfelt satisfaction and pleasure from your excellent address. It will be the endeavour of my life to imitate the example of my beloved father; and be assured, while I sway the sceptre of these realms, there shall not be the smallest bar to the freest religious toleration."

Eastern Punishment.

Chap. l. ver. 6.—I gave my back to the smiters, and my cheeks to them that plucked off the hair: I hid not my face from shame and spitting.

MR HANWAY, in his Travels, has recorded a scene very much resembling that alluded to by the prophet:—"A prisoner was brought, who had two large logs of wood fitted to the small of his leg, and rivetted together; there was also a heavy triangular collar of wood about his neck. The general asked me if that man had taken my goods. I told him I did not remember to have seen him before. He was questioned some time, and at length ordered to be beaten with sticks, which was performed by two soldiers with such severity, as if they meant to kill him. The soldiers were then ordered to spit in his face, an indignity of great antiquity in the East. This, and the cutting of beards, which I shall have occasion to mention, brought to my mind the sufferings recorded in the prophetical history of our Saviour, Isaiah l. 6."

The Reproach of Man.

Chap. li. ver. 7.—Fear ye not the reproach of men, neither be ye afraid of their revilings.

A POOR man, who had heard the preaching of the gospel, and to whom it had been greatly blessed, was the subject of much profane jesting and ridicule among his fellow-workmen and neighbours. On being asked if these daily persecutions did not sometimes make him ready to give up his profession of attachment to divine truth, he replied, "No! I recollect that our good minister once said in his sermon, that if we were so foolish as to permit such people to laugh us out of our religion, till at last we dropped into hell, they could not laugh us out again."

A Pure Life.

Chap. lii. ver. 11.—Touch no unclean thing; go ye out of the midst of her; be ye clean, that bear the vessels of the Lord.

A LITTLE girl, between four and five years of age, on her return from hearing a preacher whom she much loved, said to her mother, "Mother, I can tell you a little of Mr Henry's sermon : he said, 'Touch not the unclean thing.'" Her mother, with a view to try if she understood the meaning of these words, replied, "Then, if Mr Henry said so, I hope you will take care not to touch things that are dirty, in future." The little girl smiled, and answered, "O, mother, I know very well what he meant." "What did he mean?" said her mother. "He meant *sin*, to be sure," said the child; "and it is all the same as if Mr Henry had said, 'You must not tell lies, nor do what your mother forbids you to do, nor play on Sunday, nor be cross, nor do any such things as these, mother.'"

The Great Atoner.

Chap. liii. ver. 5.—He was wounded for our transgressions, he was bruised for our iniquities.

THE late Rev. William Shrubsole of Sheerness, one holiday, casually took up a folio volume, written by Isaac Ambrose. He opened it, and began to read that part of it which treats of "Looking to Jesus," as carrying on the work of man's salvation in his death. He was much affected at the relation of the sufferings of Christ, and sensibly interested at the inquiry which the author makes,—Who were the persons that brought the Divine Sufferer into so much distress? "I was convinced," he said, "that I was deeply concerned in that horrid transaction; and from this time I date the Lord first penetrated my dark mind with the dawn of heavenly light and salvation."

Restored in the Faith.

Chap. liv. ver. 7, 8.—For a small moment have I forsaken thee; but with great mercies will I gather thee.

MR. WHITE, on the power of godliness, says, "A precious holy man told me of a woman that was six years in desertion; and, by God's providence, hearing Mr. Rollock preach, she of a sudden fell down, overwhelmed with joy, crying out, 'O, he is come, whom my soul loveth!' and so was carried home for dead: and for divers days after, she was filled with exceeding joy, and had such pious and singularly ravishing expressions, so fluently coming from her, that many came to hear the rare manifestations of God's grace in her; and amongst the rest that went to hear, there was one that could write short-hand, who yet a great while stood so amazed at her expressions, that he could not write; at last, recovering himself, he wrote a whole sheet of paper; which this minister read, and told me, that of all the expressions that ever he read in the book of martyrs, or elsewhere, he never read any so high as the lowest of them."

The Present Time.

Chap. lv. ver. 6.—Seek ye the Lord while he may be found, call ye upon him while he is near.

A YOUNG man, on whom sentence of death was passed, said, two days before his execution, "I am afraid that nothing but the fear of death and hell makes me seek the Saviour now, and that I cannot expect to find him. The words, 'Seek ye the Lord *while* he may be found,' trouble my mind very much, that they show me that there is a time when he may *not* be found."

The Lord's Day.

Chap. lvi. ver. 2.—Blessed is the man—that keepeth the Sabbath from polluting it.

A GENTLEMAN, who had been using the boat of Thomas Mann, a pious waterman on the Thames, asked him if he did not make seven days in a week? "No, Sir," replied Thomas; "I hope I know better than to do that. That would be taking what does not belong to me. The Lord's day is not mine; and therefore I never work on that day."

Reviving the Heart.

Chap. lvii. ver. 15.—I dwell in the high and holy place, with him also that is of a contrite and humble spirit, to revive the spirit of the humble, and to revive the heart of the contrite ones.

AT one time, when Ebenezer and Ralph Erskine both preached on the Monday after the celebration of the Lord's Supper at Glasgow, the former delivered an excellent discourse, with his accustomed animation and dignity, while the latter fell considerably short of his usual fluency and fervour. Shortly after the close of the worship, when the two brothers had an opportunity of conversing privately together, Ebenezer gently intimated to Ralph, that it appeared to him, the sermon he had preached that day was not so substantial and interesting as usual; on which Ralph made a reply to this effect: "True, brother! but if my poor sermon humble me, perhaps I shall reap greater advantage from it, than you from your great sermon."

Strong Words.

Chap. lviii. ver. 1.—Cry aloud, spare not; lift up thy voice like a trumpet, and shew my people their transgression, and the house of Jacob their sins.

THE energy of the Rev. Rowland Hill's manner at times, and the power of his voice, were almost overwhelming. Once, at Wotton, he was completely carried away by the impetuous rush of his feelings, and, raising himself to his full stature, he exclaimed, "Because I am in earnest, men call me enthusiast; but I am not; mine are the words of truth and soberness. When I first came into this part of the country, I was walking on yonder hill; I saw a gravel pit fall in and bury three human beings alive. I lifted up my voice for help so loud, that I was heard in the town below, at a distance of a mile; help came, and rescued two of the poor sufferers. No one called me an *enthusiast* then ; and when I see eternal destruction ready to fall upon poor sinners, and about to entomb them irrecoverably in an eternal mass of woe, and call aloud to them to escape, shall I be called an enthusiast now ? No, sinner, I am not an enthusiast in so doing ; I call on thee *aloud* to fly for refuge to the hope set before thee in the gospel of Jesus Christ."

The Word of God.

Chap. lix. ver. 21.—My words which I have put in thy mouth, shall not depart out of my mouth, nor out of the mouth of thy seed, nor out of the mouth of thy seed's seed.

MR. PHILIP HENRY, in a sermon preached in 1659, mentioned it as the practice of a worthy gentleman, that, in renewing his leases, instead of making it a condition that his tenants should keep a hawk or a dog for him, he obliged them that they should keep a Bible in their houses for themselves, and should bring up their children to learn to read, and be catechized. "This," said the gentleman, "will be no charge to you, and it may oblige them to that which otherwise they would neglect."

The Everlasting Light.

Chap. lx. ver. 20.—Thy sun shall no more go down ; neither shall thy moon withdraw itself : for the Lord shall be thine everlasting light, and the days of thy mourning shall be ended.

THE narrator of the loss of the Kent remarks, "Some of the soldiers near me having remarked that the sun was setting, I looked round, and never can I forget the feelings with which I regarded his declining rays. I had previously felt deeply impressed with the conviction that the ocean was to be my bed that night ; and had, I imagined, sufficiently realized to my mind both the last struggles and the consequences of death. But as I continued solemnly watching the departing beams of the sun, the thought that it was really the very last I should ever behold, gradually expanded into reflections, the most tremendous in their import. It was not, I am persuaded, either the retrospect of a most unprofitable life, or the direct fear of death, or of judgment, that occupied my mind at the period I allude to ; but a broad, illimitable view of eternity itself. I know not whether the thought would have hurried me, had I not speedily seized, as with the grasp of death, on some of those sweet promises of the gospel, which give to an immortal existence its only charms ; and that naturally enough led back my thoughts, by means of the brilliant object before me, to the contemplation of that 'blessed city, which hath no need of sun, neither of the moon, to shine in it ; for the glory of God doth lighten it, and the Lamb is the light thereof.'"

Good Tidings.

Chap. lxi. ver. 1.—The Lord hath anointed me to preach good tidings unto the meek : he hath sent me to bind up the broken-hearted.

DURING a time of great awakening in America, through the instrumentality of Mr. Whitefield, Mr. Rowland, a truly pious and eloquent man, being invited to preach in the Baptist church of Philadelphia, proclaimed the terrors of the divine law with such energy to those whose souls were already sinking under them, that not a few fainted away. His error, however, was publicly corrected by the Rev. Gilbert Tennent, who, standing at the foot of the pulpit, and seeing the effect produced on the assembly, interrupted and arrested the preacher by this address :—"Brother Rowland, is there no balm in Gilead ?—is there no physician there ?" Mr. Rowland, on this, immediately changed the tenor of his address, and sought direct to the Saviour those who were overwhelmed with a sense of their guilt."

The Silent Watchmen.

Chap. lxii. ver. 6.—I have set watchmen upon thy walls, O Jerusalem, which shall never hold their peace day nor night : ye that make mention of the Lord, keep not silence.

"THESE people," says one, "are in the road to ruin, who say to their ministers, as the Jews did of old to their prophets—'Prophecy not;' or what amounts to the same thing, 'speak unto us smooth things, prophesy deceits.' I well remember having read in an ancient author the following remarkable and appropriate account:—'News came to a certain town, once and again, that the enemy was approaching; but he did not then approach. Hereupon in anger the inhabitants enacted a law, that no man, on pain of death, should bring again such rumours, as the news of an enemy. Not long after, the enemy came indeed; besieged, assaulted, and sacked the town, of the ruins of which nothing remained, but this proverbial epitaph—*Here once stood a town that was destroyed by silence.*'"

Our Father.

Chap. lxiii. ver. 16.—Doubtless thou art our Father.

"I HAVE been told of a good man," says Mr M. Henry, "among whose experiences, which he kept a record of, after his death, this, among other things, was found, that such a time in secret prayer, his heart, at the beginning of the duty, was much enlarged in giving to God those titles which are awful and tremendous, in calling him the great, the mighty, and the terrible God; but going on thus, he checked himself with this thought, 'And why not my Father ?'"

The Potter and the Clay.

Chap. lxiv. ver. 8.—We are the clay, and thou art our potter.

DURING the siege of Barcelona by the Spaniards and English in the war of the succession, in 1705, an affecting incident occurred, which is thus related by Captain Carleton in his memoirs. "I remember I saw an old officer, having his only son with him, a fine man about twenty years of age, going into the tent to dine. Whilst they were at dinner, a shot from the Bastion of St. Antonio took off the head of his son. The father immediately rose up, first looking down upon his headless child, and then lifting up his eyes to heaven, whilst the tears ran down his cheeks, only said, *Thy will be done.*" Such a conception of God's will is entirely erroneous. The incident, however, shows the father's idea of the matter.

Unexpected Meetings.

Chap. lxv. ver. 25.—I am found of them that sought me not.

MR. WHITEFIELD relates, in one of his sermons, the conversion of a Mr. Crane, who was afterwards appointed steward of the Orphan-House in Georgia. Being determined to spend an evening at the play-house, he went first to Drury-Lane, but the house being quite full, he resolved to go to Covent-Garden; having got thither, he found that house full also, so that he could not gain admittance. He was determined, however, to get entertainment some way or other; and therefore set off to hear Mr. Whitefield. It pleased God to apply

Sunday Observance.

Chap. lxvi. ver. 23.—From one Sabbath to another, shall all flesh come to worship before me, saith the Lord.

MR THOMAS HAWKES, a respectable and pious tradesman in London, when about to go to church one Lord's day, was sent for, to attend on a person of high rank, about some worldly affairs. Mr H. expressed his surprise to the groom, and asked him if he knew what day it was, and intimated that the message must certainly refer to the next day. The groom assured him that was not the case; but that his master must see him immediately. He then desired the groom to present his duty to the distinguished personage, and inform him that he always made a point of attending the worship of God on that day; but that he would wait on the illustrious individual next morning; which accordingly he did, and was received with wonted civility.

BOOK OF JEREMIAH.

Brave in the Lord.

Chap. i. ver. 8.—Be not afraid of their faces; for I am with thee to deliver thee, saith the Lord.

MR MAURICE, one of the non-conformist ministers in Shropshire, experienced many remarkable deliverances in the providence of God, when in danger of being apprehended by his enemies after his ejection. At one time, a constable found him preaching and commanded him to desist; but Mr. Maurice, with great courage, charged him in the name of the Great God, whose message he was then delivering, to forbear molesting him, as he would answer it at the great day. The constable, awed by his solemn manner, sat down trembling, heard him patiently to the end of his discourse, and then quietly left him.

Punishment of Conscience.

Chap. ii. ver. 26.—The thief is ashamed when he is found.

ROBERT AGNEW, foreman to a respectable nurseryman at some distance from town, who had lived with his employers ten years, and had a good character, one Saturday night, after applying for his wages, claimed pay for a young man up to that day, whom he had discharged some days before. His master said, looking him steadily in the face, "Robert, do you want to cheat me, by asking wages for a man that you discharged yourself eight days ago?" He had no sooner said this, than the miserable conscience-stricken man's blood forsook his face, as if he had been stabbed to the heart. When his master saw him so much affected, he told him that he might still labour as he had done, but that after such a manifestly dishonest attempt, his character, and the confidence in it, were gone for ever. On Monday, Robert made his appearance, but was utterly an altered man. The agitation of his mind had reduced his body to the feebleness of an infant's. He took his spade and tried to use it, but in vain; and it was with difficulty that he reached home. He went to bed immediately; medical aid was procured, but to no purpose, and the poor fellow sunk under the sense of his degradation, and expired on Wednesday forenoon! His neighbours who attended him, say, that a short time before he died, he declared, that the agony consequent on the loss of his character as an honest man, which he had for so many years maintained, was the sole cause of his death.

Pastors' Teaching.

Chap. iii. ver. 15.—I will give you pastors according to mine heart, which shall feed you with knowledge and understanding.

THE late Rev. Robert Hall of Bristol was once asked what he thought of a sermon which had been delivered by a proverbially fine preacher, and which had seemed to excite a great sensation among the congregation:—"Very fine, Sir," he replied, "but a man cannot feed upon flowers."

Weak Head and Bad Heart.

Chap. iv. ver. 22.—They are sottish children, and they have none understanding: they are wise to do evil, but to do good, they have no knowledge.

A GAY young fellow, who piqued himself on the character of a libertine, was expatiating upon the qualifications necessary to form a perfect and accomplished debauchee; when, having finished his tirade, he turned to one of the company present, who seemed to receive this sally very gravely, and whom, therefore, he wished to insult, and asked his opinion. Not at all disconcerted at his insolence, the gentleman replied very dryly, "It appears to me, Sir, that you have omitted two of the most important and essential qualifications." "Indeed! and pray what may they be?" "An excessively weak head, and a thoroughly bad heart." The rake was silent, and soon afterwards left the company.

The Ruler of the Waves.

Chap. v. ver. 22.—The Lord, which has placed the sand for the bound of the sea by a perpetual decree, that it cannot pass it: and though the waves thereof toss themselves, yet can they not prevail; though they roar, yet can they not pass over it.

THOMAS MANN, a pious waterman on the Thames, being once employed to row a party of pleasure, one of the number, a young lady, proposed singing "Rule Britannia," when Mann remarked, that he had heard Mr Newton say, "GOD rules the waves, not Britannia."

Bad Company.

Chap. vi. ver. 10.—The word of the Lord is unto them a reproach: they have no delight in it.

THE Rev. John Eliot, styled The Apostle of the Indians, was once asked by a pious woman, who was vexed with a wicked husband, and bad company frequently infesting her house on his account, what she should do? "Take," said he, "the Holy Bible into your hand when bad company comes in, and that will soon drive them out of the house."

Religious Villany.

Chap. vii. ver. 9, 10.—Will ye steal, murder, and commit adultery, and swear falsely—And come and stand before me in this house, which is called by my name?

BOOK OF JEREMIAH.

TWO Greeks, notorious for their piracies and other crimes, were lately tried and condemned, and three days after executed. In the course of the trial, it appeared that the beef and anchovies, on board one of the English vessels which they pirated, were left untouched, and the circumstances under which they were left appeared to the court so peculiar, that the culprits were asked the cause of it. They promptly answered, that *it was at the time of the great fast when their church eat neither meat nor fish!* They appeared to be most hardened and abandoned wretches, enemies alike to their own and every other nation, and yet rigidly maintaining their *religious* character; and while they were robbing, plundering, and murdering, and stealing the women and children of their countrymen, and selling them to the Turks, and committing other atrocious deeds, they would have us understand that they were not so wicked as to taste meat or fish, when prohibited by the canons of their church!

Rejecting God's Word.

Chap. viii. ver. 9.—They have rejected the word of the Lord; and what wisdom is in them?

A GENTLEMAN was arguing with a deist on the absurdity of rejecting Christianity without examination. He owned that he never knew a person examine the subject, who did not afterwards embrace it; but excused himself from examining, under the plea that to do so was analogous to drinking brandy, which always produced intoxication. "Is it not honourable to Christianity," says the gentleman, "to have enemies, who must give up the exercise of their reason before they reject it?"

Personal Conceit.

Chap. ix. ver. 23.—Let not the wise man glory in his wisdom.

IN 1201, Simon Tournay, after he had excelled all his contemporaries at Oxford in learning, and became so eminent at Paris as to be made the chief doctor of the Sorbonne, grew so proud, that while he regarded Aristotle as superior to Moses and Christ, he considered him as but equal to himself! He became such an idiot at length, as not to know one letter in a book, or one thing he had ever done.

God's Care of His Own.

Chap. x. ver. 25.—Pour out thy fury upon the heathen that know thee not, and upon the families that call not on thy name.

A CREDIBLE historian informs us, that about one hundred and fifty years ago, there was an earthquake in Switzerland, by which part of a mountain was thrown down, which fell upon a village that stood under it, and crushed every house and inhabitant to atoms, except the corner of one cottage, where the master of the house with his family were together praying unto God.

Two Lives.

Chap. xi. ver. 19.—Let us cut him off from the land of the living.

"YOU take a life from me that I cannot keep," said one of the martyrs to his persecutors, "and bestow a life upon me that I cannot lose; which is as if you should rob me of counters, and furnish me with gold."

The Death Bed.

Chap. xii. ver. 5.—How wilt thou do in the swelling of Jordan?

ANECDOTES OF THE OLD TESTAMENT.

THE Rev. Richard Hooker, just before his death, said, "I have lived to see that this world is made up of perturbations; and I have been long preparing to leave it, and gathering comfort for the dreadful hour of making my account with God, which I now apprehend to be near; and though I have, by his grace, loved him in my youth, and feared him in my age, and laboured to have a conscience void of offence to him, and to all men; yet if thou, Lord, shouldst be extreme to mark what I have done amiss, who can abide it? And, therefore, where I have failed, Lord, show mercy to me; for I plead not my righteousness, but the forgiveness of my unrighteousness, for his merits, who died to purchase a pardon for penitent sinners."

Prayer for the Unrepented.

Chap. xiii. ver. 17.—But if ye will not hear it, my soul shall weep in secret places for your pride.

A GAY, dissipated young man, went one day to his pious mother, and said, "Mother, let me have my best clothes, I am going to a ball to-night." She expostulated with him, and urged him not to go, by every argument in her power. He answered, "Mother, let me have my clothes, I will go, and it is useless to say anything about it." She brought his clothes; he put them on, and was going out. She stopped him, and said, "My child, do not go." He said he would; she then said to him, "My son, while you are dancing with your gay companions in the ball-room, I shall be out in that wilderness praying to the Lord to convert your soul." He went; the ball commenced; but instead of the usual gaiety, an unaccountable gloom pervaded the whole assembly. One said, "We never had such a dull meeting in our lives;" another, "I wish we had not come, we have no life, we cannot get along;" a third, "I cannot think what is the matter." The young man instantly burst into tears, and said, "I know what is the matter; my poor old mother is now praying in yonder wilderness for her ungodly son." He took his hat, and said, "I will never be found in such a place as this again," and left the company. To be short, the Lord converted his soul. He became a member of the church—was soon after taken ill—and died happy.

The Giver of Rain.

Chap. xiv. ver. 22.—Are there any among the vanities of the Gentiles that can cause rain? or can the heavens give showers? Art thou not he, O Lord our God? therefore we will wait upon thee: for thou hast made all these things.

A YOUTH in the South Sea Islands, called Joseph Banks, after Sir Joseph Banks, Captain Cook's companion, had been much abroad, and was a shrewd observer of all that came under his notice. One day, when he was disputing against the superstitions of his country, a priest affirmed that, if the maraes, or temples, were forsaken, there would be no rain, and everything would be burnt up. He replied, "In England and America there are no idols, no tabus, yet there is plenty of rain there, and fine crops too. In Tahiti, and Huahine they have broken the tabus, and destroyed the idols, and worship the God of the white men, yet the rain falls there, and the fruits grow as abundantly as ever. And why should not rain fall, and the ground produce food here as well as elsewhere, when these senseless things are done away?" The priest was confounded.

The Book of Books.

Chap. xv. ver. 16.—Thy word was unto me the joy and rejoicing of mine heart.

"I HAVE many books," says Mr. Newton, "that I cannot sit down to read; they are indeed good and sound, but, like halfpence, there goes a great quantity to a little amount. There are silver books, and a very few golden books; but I have one book worth more than all, called the Bible, and that is a book of bank-notes.

God's Eyes.

Chap. xvi. ver. 17.—Mine eyes are upon all their ways.

ONE of the heathen philosophers recommended it to his pupils, as the best means to induce and enable them to behave worthily, to imagine that some very distinguished character was always looking upon them. But what was the eye of a Cato to the eye of God? Who would not approve themselves unto him? The celebrated Linnæus had the following inscription placed over the door of the hall in which he gave his lectures:—"Live guiltless—God observes you."

The Great Saviour.

Chap. xvii. ver. 14.—Lord, save me.

A MINISTER asked the maid at an inn in the Netherlands, if she prayed to God? She replied, "She had scarce time to eat, how should she have time to pray?" He promised to give her a little money, if on his return she could assure him she had meanwhile said three words of prayer, night and morning. Only three words and a reward, caught her promise. He solemnly added, "Lord, save me?" For a fortnight she said the words unmeaningly; but one night she wondered what they meant, and why he bade her repeat them. God put it into her heart to look at the Bible, and see if it would tell her. She liked some verses where she opened so well, that next morning she looked again, and so on. When the good man went back, he asked the landlord for her, as a stranger served him. "Oh, Sir! she got too good for my place, and lives with the minister!" So soon as she saw the minister at the door, she cried, "Is it you, you blessed man? I shall thank God through all eternity that I ever saw you; I want not the money, I have reward enough for saying these words!" She then described how salvation by Jesus Christ was taught her by the Bible, in answer to this prayer.

Hope for the Wicked.

Chap. xviii. ver. 12.—They said, There is no hope; but we will walk after our own devices, and we will every one do the imagination of his evil heart.

A YOUNG woman, when Dr. Gifford visited in prison, and who was to be tried for her life, heard him speak a good while in an awful strain, not only unmoved, but at last she laughed in his face. He then altered his tone, and spoke of the love of Jesus, and the mercy provided for chief sinners, till the tears came in her eyes, and she interrupted him by asking, "Why: do you think there can be mercy for *me*?" He said, "Undoubtedly, if you *can* desire it." She replied, "Ah! if I had thought so, I should not have been here; I have long fixed it in my mind that I was absolutely lost, and without hope, and this persuasion made me obstinate in my wickedness, so that I cared not what I did." She was afterwards tried, and sentenced to transportation, and Dr. Gifford, who saw her several times, had a good hope that she was truly converted before she left England.

Child Murder.

Chap. xix. ver. 1.—They have filled this place with the blood of innocents.

MR. ELLIS informs us, that during the year 1829, Mr. Williams, a missionary to the South Sea Islands, had one day sitting in his room three females, the eldest not more than forty years of age. The subject of the murder of infants was introduced, and he remarked that perhaps some of them had been guilty of the crime. On inquiry these females reluctantly confessed that they had destroyed not fewer than twenty-one infants! One had murdered nine, another seven, and the other five. Nor did it appear that these women had been more guilty than their neighbours.

Speaking in God's Name.

Chap. xx. ver. 9.—Then I said, I will not make mention of him, nor speak any more in his name.

THE late Mr. Clark of Trowbridge, one Sabbath afternoon, said to his wife, "My dear, I can never preach again; I have told my people all I have to say." She said, "But you will disappoint the people, and whom can we engage for to-night?" He still urged that he should be unable to say any thing, when a woman was introduced, who said she had come a long way to beg Mr. Clark to preach from this text, "Then I said, I will not make mention of him, nor speak any more in his name: but his word was in mine heart as a burning fire shut up in my bones, and I was weary with forbearing, and I could not stay." He saw the finger of God in it, and preached from that text in the evening, and was never after at any loss.

The Plague.

Chap. xxi. ver. 6.—I will smite the inhabitants of this city,—and they shall die of a great pestilence.

IN a letter, dated August 30, 1830, the Rev. William Glen gives the following account of the ravages of the cholera morbus in Astrachan:—"In general, business of every kind was at a stand. The bank suspended its operations. In the bazaars not a whisper was to be heard, and scarcely a face to be seen; even the public houses were abandoned, and a general gloom was spread over the countenances of the few solitary individuals that were to be seen walking through the streets. According to the best authenticated accounts, when the disease was at its height, the number of funerals, on one particular day, was five hundred, and on another day four hundred and eighty. More than one thousand were buried about that time in a large pit, for want of graves, which could not be got dug so fast as required, nor at a rate the poor could afford to pay for them. Such a time we have never seen, nor did I suppose that such a time was ever seen in Astrachan."

A Coronation Text

Chap. xxii. ver. 30.—Thus saith the Lord, Write ye this man childless, a man that shall not prosper in his days: for no man of his seed shall prosper, sitting upon the throne of David, and ruling any more in Judah.

BOOK OF JEREMIAH.

THE Rev. Mr. Douglas, an eminently pious minister in Edinburgh, had usually the subjects of his discourses so forcibly impressed on his mind, that he seldom or never had any anxiety in choosing a text. Having been appointed to preach at the coronation of Charles II. at Scoon, the above passage was suggested to him as a text. The good man was troubled what to do. To preach from it would bring down the vengeance of the court—to reject it, would perhaps expose him to Divine chastisement. After much anxious and painful deliberation, he resolved to choose another, as much suited to the occasion as possible. The text he selected was 2 Kings xi. 12.—" And he brought forth the king's son, and put the crown upon him, and gave him the testimony: and they made him king, and anointed him; and they clapped their hands, and said, God save the King." It is remarkable that, during the remainder of his life, he laboured under great difficulty in choosing the subjects of his discourses; the wonted aid from above appearing to be withheld, as a correction for his sin, in resisting convictions of duty, from the fear of man that bringeth a snare.

Unsuitable Pastors.

Chap. xxiii. ver. 32.—I sent them not, nor commanded them; therefore they shall not profit this people at all, saith the Lord.

WHEN two or three gentlemen, in company with the late Rev. Robert Hall of Bristol, were discussing the question—Whether a man of no religion can be a successful minister of the gospel?—surprise was expressed that Mr. Hall remained silent. "Sir," said he in in reply, "I would not deny that a sermon from a bad man may sometimes do good; but the general question does not admit of an argument. Is it at all probable that he who is a willing servant of Satan, will fight *against* him with *all his might?* and, if not, what success can be rationally expected?"

Made Captives for God.

Chap. xxiv. ver. 5.—Them that are carried away captive of Judah, whom I have sent out of this place into the land of the Chaldeans for their good.

A MISSIONARY in India, passing one day through the school-room, observed a little boy engaged in prayer, and overheard him saying, "O Lord Jesus, I thank thee for sending big ship into my country, and wicked men to steal me, and bring me here that I might hear about thee, and love thee; and now, Lord Jesus, I have one great favour to ask thee, please to send wicked men with another big ship, and let them catch my father and my mother, and bring them to this country, that they may hear the missionaries preach, and love thee." The missionary, in a few days after, saw him standing on the sea-shore, looking very intently as the ships came in. "What are you looking at, Tom?" "I am looking to see if Jesus Christ answer prayer." For two years he was to be seen day after day, watching the arrival of every ship. One day, as the missionary was viewing him, he observed him capering about, and exhibiting the liveliest joy. "Well, Tom, what occasions so much joy?" "O, Jesus Christ answer prayer—father and mother come in that ship;" which was actually the case.

The Drunken.

Chap. xxv. ver. 27.—Drink ye, and be drunken, and spue, and fall, and rise no more.

A MAN in North America, who, for several years, had been guilty of occasional excess, was, for a week prior to his death, intoxicated every day, and abused his family unmercifully. The morning of the day on which he died he said to his wife, with a horrible oath, "When I drink another glass of rum, I hope God Almighty will strike me dead!" He immediately went to a public-house—drank rum while there—filled his jug—and, returning, beat his wife, and knocked her to the floor, though her peculiar situation demanded the most kind and affectionate treatment from her husband. A little before two o'clock in the afternoon, he took his jug, and going to another room, said, "I swear I will drink till I die, let it be longer or shorter." His wife expostulated, when he swore he would do so, calling the Saviour to witness. He expired before three o'clock; ill prepared, there is every reason to fear, for his departure.

The Entire Word of God.

Chap. xxvi. ver. 2.—Speak unto all the cities of Judah, which come to worship in the Lord's house, all the words that I command thee to speak unto them; diminish not a word.

THE Rev. J. Brewer's (of Birmingham) manner of expounding the Scriptures was very instructive and useful; and his general style of preaching was that, which, by way of distinction and eminence, has been called *scriptural*, because it embodies so large a portion of the sentiment and language of holy writ. This peculiar character of his preaching Mr Brewer attributed, in a great degree, to a remark of the Rev. Edmund Jones, a minister in Wales, who, after hearing his young friend preach, said to him, when he came down from the pulpit, "Young man, I love to hear the sound of scripture in a sermon." It was a word in season, and he never forgot it. "It did me more good," said Mr Brewer, "than all my studies."

The Sorcerers.

Chap. xxvii. ver. 9.—Hearken not to your sorcerers.

"OF the power of this superstition, (sorcery,)" says Mr Stewart in his Journal, "we had a proof in a native of our own household. A thief was put to flight from our yard one day, while we were at dinner. A lad joined in the chase, and seized the culprit, but lost his hold by the tearing of his kichei, or outer garment. The thief was greatly exasperated, and immediately employed a *sorcerer* to pray the boy to death. Information of this reached the lad in the course of the afternoon; and we soon perceived him to be troubled by the intelligence, though he attempted with us to ridicule the superstition. The next morning he did not make his appearance with the other boys; and upon inquiring from them, they said he was sick. We asked the nature of this sickness; to which it was replied, that "he was sick from the prayer of the sorcery, perhaps." We found him lying in one corner of his house, pale with fear, and trembling like an aspen leaf, and discovered that he had not slept during the night: we were satisfied that the whole arose from terror; and compelled him, notwithstanding his declarations that he was sick, to come from his retreat, diverted his mind, and set him at work, and before noon he was as full of life and spirits as ever, laughed at his fears, and began to defy the power of the—'sorcerer's prayer.'"

The Death Prophecy.

Chap. xxviii. ver. 16.—This year thou shalt die.

AN intimate friend of President Davies of New-Jersey College, told him a few days before the beginning of the year in which he died, that a sermon on the first day of it would be expected from him; mentioning that it was President Burr's custom to do so; and that on the new-year's day preceding his death, he preached from Jer. xxviii. 16. "Thus saith the Lord, This year thou shalt die;" which the people afterwards had regarded as premonitory. When the first of January came, Mr Davies preached from the same text; and being seized with his last illness soon after, said, he had been led to preach, as it were, his own funeral sermon. Mr. Davies often referred to this remarkable circumstance on his death-bed.

Seeking God with all the Heart.

Chap. xxix. ver. 12, 13.—Ye shall go and pray unto me, and I will hearken unto you.—And ye shall seek me, and find me, when ye shall search for me with all your heart.

A PERSON, in addressing some children on the subject of prayer, described its importance and advantages; and explained the difference between *praying* and *saying prayers*. A boy in the first class, whose attention had been arrested by the subject, was powerfully affected by the impressive manner in which this duty was urged upon the children. He reflected, that though he had daily been in the habit of *saying* his prayers, yet he then felt convinced that he had never *prayed* as he ought to have done. He left the school under a deep concern for his soul's welfare, and on reaching home, retired to a private apartment in the house, and sought the Lord in prayer with his whole heart. He did not seek in vain. He obtained mercy, through the blood of Christ. He joined in church-fellowship, became a useful teacher in a school, and has continued to adorn the doctrine of the Saviour by a becoming conversation.

The Increase.

Chap. xxx. ver 19.—I will multiply them, and they shall not be few; I will also glorify them, and they shall not be small.

THE following is from a "Narrative of the State of Religion in the United States of America."

"It is our delightful privilege to report, that sixty-eight Presbyteries have been blessed with the special influences of the Holy Spirit, reviving the churches, and bringing perishing sinners to the saving knowledge of the truth. In these highly-favoured Presbyteries, about seven hundred congregations are reported as having been thus visited in rich mercy. In many of these places, thus refreshed by the showers of divine grace, the displays of the power of the Gospel have been glorious, almost beyond example. Several Presbyteries have had their whole territory pervaded by a heavenly influence, and every congregation has become a harvest-field for the ingathering to souls to the fold of the Good Shepherd. These bodies send us the animating message, that all, or nearly all, their churches have enjoyed a precious season of revival. 'Never,' says the report from West Hanover, 'have we had the privilege of recording so many signal triumphs of Almighty grace. The angel having the Everlasting Gospel in his hand, has passed through our borders, and has brought salvation to almost every house. So powerful and extensive has been the divine influences among us, that one district is known where not one adult could be found unconcerned upon the subject of religion. On some occasions, a whole congregation, without one exception, have been prostrated before God, anxiously inquiring for salvation. Eighteen of our congregations have been revived, and in one of them, three hundred hopeful conversions have taken place."

Bereaved Parents.

Chap. xxxi. ver. 15.—A voice was heard in Ramah, lamentation, and bitter weeping; Rachel weeping for her children, refused to be comforted for her children, because they were not.

ONE day, while the lady of Sir Stamford Raffles was almost overwhelmed with grief for the loss of a favourite child, unable to bear the sight of her other children—unable to bear even the light of day—humbled upon her couch by a feeling of misery, she was addressed by a poor, ignorant, uninstructed native woman, of the lowest class, who had been employed about the nursery, in terms of reproach not to be forgotten. "I am come because you have been here many days shut up in a dark room, and no one dares to come near you. Are you not ashamed to grieve in this manner when you ought to be thanking God for having given you the most beautiful child that ever was seen? Did any one ever see him, or speak of him, without admiring him? And instead of letting this child continue in the world till he should be worn out with trouble and sorrow, has not God taken him to heaven in all his beauty? What would you have more? For shame!—leave off weeping, and let me open a window."

God's Mode of Work.

Chap. xxxii. ver. 19.—Great in counsel, and mighty in work.

A PERSON at dinner with Mr. Newton of London, remarked, that the East India Company had overset the college at Calcutta. "What a pity!" said a gentleman present. "No," said Mr N., "no pity—it must do good. If you had a plan in view, and could hinder opposition, would you not prevent it?"—"Yes sir."—"Well, God can hinder all opposition to his plans: he has permitted that to take place, but he will carry on his own plan. I am learning to see God in all things: I believe not a person knocks at my door but is sent by God."

Our Righteousness.

Chap. xxxiii. ver. 16.—The Lord our Righteousness.

"IF it be shameful to renounce error," says Mr Hervey, "and sacrifice all to truth, I do very willing take this shame to myself, in a copy of verses which I formerly wrote, sacred to the memory of a generous benefactor. I remember the following lines:—

'Our wants relieved by thy indulgent care
Shall give thee courage at the dreadful bar,
And stud the crown thou shalt for ever wear.'

These lines, in whatever hands they are lodged, and whatever else of a like kind may have dropped from my pen, I now publicly disclaim; they are the very reverse of my present belief, in which I hope to persevere as long as I have any being. Far be it from me to suppose that any work of mine should, in order to create my peace, or cherish my confidence, be coupled with Christ's most holy acts. I speak the words of our church, and I speak the sense of the prophet, 'I will trust, and not be afraid;' wherefore? because I am inherently holy? rather *God* is my salvation; God manifest in the flesh has finished my transgression, and made an end of my sin; and in this most magnificent work will I rejoice.—Thy Maker is thy Husband: the consequence of which is, all thy debts and deficiencies are upon him, all his consummate righteousness is upon thee."

Let the Slave go Free.

Chap. xxxiv. ver. 9.—That every man should let his man-servant, and every man his maid-servant, being an Hebrew or an Hebrewess, go free.

AFTER Dr. Hopkins of North America had become impressed with the sinfulness of slavery, he did much, in his intercourse with his brethren, to awaken their attention to the subject, and to convince them of their obligations to discountenance that enormity. Visiting at the house of Dr. Bellamy of Connecticut, who was at that time the owner of a slave, he, with his wonted candour, pressed the subject upon the attention of his friend. Dr. B. endeavoured to defend the practice by the usual arguments; but Dr. H. having successfully refuted them, called upon him immediately to free his slave. In answer to this demand, it was urged, that the slave was a most faithful and judicious servant; that in his management of the doctor's farm he could be trusted with everything; and that he was so happy in his servitude, that he would, in the opinion of his master, refuse his freedom, were it offered to him. "Will you consent to his liberation," said Dr. Hopkins, "if he really desires it?"—"Yes," replied Dr. B., "I will." The slave was then at work in the field. "Call him," said Dr. H., "and let us try." The slave came to receive, as he supposed, the commands of his master. "Have you a good master?" said Dr. Hopkins, addressing the slave. "O yes, massa; he very good."—"Are you happy in your present condition?"—"O yes, massa; me very happy."—"Would you be more happy if you were free?"—"O yes, massa; me would be much more happy."—"You have your desire," exclaimed Dr. Bellamy; "from this moment you are free."

Wine Drinking.

Chap. xxxv. ver. 6.—We will drink no wine; for Jonadab the son of Rechab, our father, commanded us, saying, Ye shall drink no wine, neither ye, nor your sons for ever.

AMONG a few individuals who lately met at a Christmas supper in a public-house, there happened to be a tradesman who belonged to the Temperance Society. His unprincipled companions thought it too good an opportunity to be lost of working the fall of the poor man, and of injuring the general cause of temperance. They accordingly made use of every artifice in order to induce him to drink the poisonous cup, though without success, when the landlady, who had been acquainted with the proceeding, immediately stepped between them, and declared that, as he had joined the Temperance Society, *no one should give him one drop of whisky in her house,* but that if he chose he might have ale or porter. The poor man being thus supported took courage; but, wisely considering that it was unsafe for him to take even ale or porter in such company, went home after supper, without drinking anything, to the grievous mortification and disappointment of his drunken companions.

Animosity to the Bible.

Chap. xxxvi. ver. 23.—The king cut it with the pen-knife, and cast it into the fire that was on the hearth, until all the roll was consumed.

A FEW years ago, a party of men, muffled up in greatcoats, entered the house of an unoffending Protestant in Edgeworthstown;

and after having placed a guard on a female who was the only inmate of the house at the time, they proceeded to search the rooms till they found a large Bible, which they carried out, and tore into a thousand fragments in an adjoining ditch. A man, who seemed the principal of the party, stood at the door, and gave orders to the others not to meddle with anything but the thing which they came for. The violence of their animosity was exhibited by trampling the leaves of the Bible in the mire.

Severe Imprisonment.

Chap. xxxvii. ver. 20—Let my supplication, I pray thee, be accepted before thee; that thou cause me not to return to the house of Jonathan the scribe.

SIR JOHN CHARDIN, when mentioning the power that jailors, in Eastern countries, have over the prisoners committed to their charge, relates the story of an eminent Armenian merchant. He was "treated with the greatest caresses upon the jailor's receiving a considerable present from him at first, and fleecing him after from time to time; then upon the party's presenting something considerable, first to the judge, and afterwards to the jailor, who sued the Armenian, the prisoner first felt his privileges retrenched, was then closely confined, and was then treated with such inhumanity as not to be permitted to drink above once in twenty-four hours, and this in the hottest time of the summer, nor anybody suffered to come near him but the servants of the prison, and at length thrown into a dungeon, where he was, in a quarter of an hour, brought to the point to which all this severe usage was intended to force him."

A Prisoner of the Lord.

Chap. xxxviii. ver. 6.—They took Jeremiah, and cast him into the dungeon.

ONE of the witnesses of the truth, when imprisoned for conscience sake in Queen Mary's persecution of the Church, is said to have thus written to a friend :—" A prisoner for Christ! What is this for a poor worm? Such honour have not all his saints. Both the degrees which I took in the University have not set me so high as the honour of becoming a prisoner of the Lord."

Deliverance.

Chap. xxxix. ver. 17.—I will deliver thee in that day, saith the Lord; and thou shalt not be given into the hand of the men of whom thou art afraid.

AUGUSTINE, going on one occasion to preach at a distant town, took with him a guide to direct him in the way. The man, by some unaccountable means, mistook the usual road, and fell into a bye-path. It afterwards proved, that by this means his life had been saved, as some of the Donatists, who were his enemies, had way-laid him, with the design of killing him.

Murder.

Chap. xl. ver. 14.—Dost thou certainly know that Baalis, the king of the Ammonites, hath sent Ishmael—to slay thee? But Gedaliah—believed them not.

THE Regent Murray, who was assassinated by Hamilton of Bothwellhaugh, in 1570, had got information, we are told, the same day on which the murder was committed, respecting the assassin, and the place where he was concealed. He accordingly resolved to proceed to Edinburgh on the road which skirts the outside of the town of Linlithgow; but perceiving the gate through which he intended to pass blockaded by a crowd, he turned the other way, through the principal street, where the assassin, with a musket, took his fatal aim from a window. The *Good Regent* died in the evening of the same day, while the murderer, having a horse in readiness, effected his escape.

Treasure Pits.

Chap. xli. ver. 8.—Ten men were found among them that said unto Ishmael, Slay us not; for we have treasures in the field, of wheat, and of barley, and of oil, and of honey.

MR SHAW informs us, that in Barbary, when the grain is winnowed, they lodge it in *mattamores*, or subterraneous repositories; two or three hundred of which are sometimes together, the smallest holding four hundred bushels. These are very common in other parts of the East, and are in particular mentioned by Dr Russell, as being in great numbers near Aleppo, about the villages. A method, similar to this, is used in the Holy Land. Le Bruyn speaks of deep pits at Rama, which he was told were designed for corn; and Rauwolf mentions three very large vaults at Joppa, which were used for the purpose of laying up grain when he visited that place. The treasures of wheat, &c., might be laid up by these ten men in the same kind of repositories.

Dissembling in Heart.

Chap. xlii. ver. 20.—Ye dissembled in your hearts, when ye sent me unto the Lord your God, saying, Pray for us unto the Lord our God; and according unto all that the Lord our God shall say, so declare unto us, and we will do it.

A WOMAN once came to the Rev. Mr Kilpin of Exeter, with a long preface on the duty and privilege of having the opinion of a minister on the important subject of marriage. She told her tale, and sought advice. Mr Kilpin guessed how matters stood, and unexpectedly inquired if the day for her marriage was not fixed for Tuesday? "O! no, Sir," she hastily replied, "not until Thursday." This gave him an opportunity of pointing out the sin of persons treating the great and blessed God in somewhat the same manner, seeking direction on a subject, clearly stated in his word, with a determination to act as their own feelings and desires dictated, let the voice of God, in his word or providence, be what it might.

Eastern Customs.

Chap. xliii. ver. 10.—Nebuchadnezzar shall spread his royal pavilion over them.

"WHILE we were employed on the theatre of Miletus," says Dr Chandler in his travels, "the Aga of Suki, son-in-law to Elez-Oglu, (a Turkish officer of high rank), crossed the plain towards us, attended by a considerable train of domestics and officers, their vests and turbans of various and lively colours, mounted on long-tailed horses, with showy trappings, and glittering furniture. He returned, after hewking, to Miletus; and we went to visit him, with a present of coffe and sugar; but were told that two favourite birds had flown away, and that he was vexed and tired. A couch was prepared for him beneath a shed, made against a cottage, and covered with green boughs to keep off the sun. He entered, as we were standing by, and fell down on it to sleep, without taking any notice of us."

Worshipping Idols.

Chap. xliv. ver. 18.—Since we left off to burn incense to the queen of heaven, and to pour out drink-offerings unto her, we have wanted all things, and have been consumed by the sword and by the famine.

A HINDOO who had renounced idolatry, was soon after suddenly afflicted, upon which many of his heathen acquaintance came to see him, and said, "This sickness, without doubt, is sent to punish you because you have forsaken Swamy, (the idol), and have destroyed your pagoda; we therefore advise you to renounce Christianity, and again to worship Swamy, and you will soon recover." He said to them, "The great God, whom I now worship, made all things; therefore He alone is able to restore me to health. I do not fear the devil's anger, for without divine permission he cannot accomplish anything; and if my present sickness should be the means of my death, I will die trusting in Christ." After which he remonstrated with them on the folly and sin of worshipping idols, and they departed. He recovered, and is giving evidence of being a sincere follower of Christ.

Badly Spent Years.

Chap. xlv. ver. 5.—Seekest thou great things for thyself? seek them not.

SIR HENRY WOTTON, in the reign of Queen Elizabeth, who had great honours conferred on him, on account of his near relation to the Queen's great favourite, Robert Earl of Essex, was very intimate with the Duke of Tuscany, and with James, then King of Scotland, (and afterwards of England,) and had been sent on several embassies to Holland, Germany, and Venice: after all, he desired to retire with this motto, "That he had learned at length, that the soul grew wiser by retirement;" and consequently, that a man was more happy in a private situation, than it was possible for him to be with those worldly honours which were accompanied with so many troubles. In short, the utmost of his aim in this life, for the future, was to be Provost of Eaton, that there he might enjoy his beloved study and devotion. He was afterwards heard to say, that the day on which he put on his surplice, was the happiest day of his whole life; it being the utmost happiness a man can attain here, to be at leisure, to be and to do good. This great man never reflected on his former years, but he would weep, and say, "How much time have I to repent of! and how little to do it in!"

Mount Tabor.

Chap. xlvi. ver. 18.—Tabor is among the mountains.

"THE view from Mount Tabor," says Dr. Russell, "is extolled by every traveller. Maundrell remarks, "it is impossible for man's eyes to behold a higher gratification of this nature. On the northwest you discern in the distance the noble expanse of the Mediterranean, while all around you see the spacious and beautiful Plains of Esdraelon and Galilee. Turning a little southward, you have in view the high mountains of Gilboa, so fatal to Saul and his sons. Due east, you discover the Sea of Tiberias, distant about one day's journey. A few points to the north appears the Mount of Beatitudes, the place where Christ delivered his sermon to his disciples and the multitude. Not far from this little hill is the city of Saphet, or Szaffad, standing upon elevated and very conspicuous ground. Still farther, in the same direction, is seen a lofty peak covered with snow, a part of the chain of Anti-Lebanus. To the south-west is Carmel, and in the south the hills of Samaria."

Self Mutilation.

Chap. xlvii. ver. 5.—How long wilt thou cut thyself?

"WE often read'" says Harmer, "of people cutting themselves, in Holy Writ, when in great anguish; but we are not commonly told what part they wounded. The modern Arabs, it seems, gash their arms, which with them are often bare. It appears from a passage of Jeremiah, the ancients wounded themselves in the same part. Chap. xlviii. 37, 'Every head shall be bald, and every beard clipped: upon all the hands shall be cuttings, and upon the loins sackcloth.'"

Moab Broken.

Chap. xlviii. ver. 38.—I have broken Moab like a vessel wherein is no pleasure, saith the Lord.

THE Moabites had, in succession, the monarchs of Israel, Babylon, Persia, Greece, Syria, and Egypt, and the Romans, all as their enemies, who brought them to destruction. They now no longer exist; their country is a heap of wild ruins, showing enough of their ancient grandeur to remind us what they once were; and the rude tribes of Bedouin Arabs now dwell in it, living in tents.

The Widow and the Fatherless.

Chap. xlix. ver. 11.—Leave thy fatherless children, I will preserve them alive; and let thy widows trust in me.

"A FRIEND of mine," says Mr. Newton, "in the west of England (a faithful laborious minister, but who, I believe, never was master of five pounds at one time) was dying. His friends advised him to make his will; he replied, 'I have nothing to leave but my wife and children, and I leave them to the care of my gracious God.' Soon after this he died happily. But there appeared no prospect of support for his family at this time. The Lord, however, stirred up a man who had always despised his preaching, to feel for the deceased minister's poor destitute family; and he so exerted himself, that he was the means of £1600 being raised by subscriptions for them; and the clergy of Exeter, who had never countenanced his preachings, gave her a house and garden during her life, so that she lived in far greater plenty than in her husband's life-time."

Punishing the Heathen.

Chap. l. ver. 38.—A drought is upon her waters; and they shall be dried up: for it is the land of graven images, and they are mad upon their idols.

CYRUS having subdued the lesser Asia, as likewise Syria and Arabia, entered Assyria, and bent his march towards Babylon. The siege of this important place was no easy enterprise. The walls were of a prodigious height, the number of men to defend them very great, and the city stored with all sorts of provisions for twenty years. However, these difficulties did not discourage Cyrus from prosecuting his design; who, after spending two entire years before the place, became master of it by stratagem. Upon a festival night, which the Babylonians were accustomed to spend in drinking and debauchery, he ordered the bank of the canal, above the city, leading to the great lake, that had been lately dug by Nitocris, to be broken down; and having thus diverted the course of the river, by turning the whole current into the lake, he caused his troops to march in by the bed of the river, who now penetrated into the heart of the city without opposition, surprised the guards of the palace, and cut them to pieces. The taking of Babylon put an end to the Babylonian empire, and fulfilled the predictions which the prophets Isaiah, Jeremiah and Daniel, had uttered against that proud metropolis.

Graven Images.

Chap. li. ver. 17.—Every founder is confounded by the graven image: for his molten image is falsehood, and there is no breath in them.

"IN the monastery at Isenach," says Luther, "stands an image which I have seen. When a wealthy person came thither to pray to it, (it was Mary with her child,) the child turned away his face from the sinner to the mother; but if the sinner gave liberally to that monastery, then the child turned to him again; and if he promised to give more, then the child showed itself very friendly and loving, and stretched out its arms over him in the form of a cross. But this picture and image was made hollow within, and prepared with locks, lines, and screws; and behind it stood a knave to move them,—and so were the people mocked and deceived, who took it to be a miracle wrought by Divine Providence!"

Vine-dressers and Husbandmen.

Chap. lii. ver. 16.—Nebuzar-adan, the captain of the guard, left certain of the poor of the land for vine-dressers, and for husbandmen.

THE Rev. John Frederic Oberlin was distinguished by his charity and benevolence, and though scarcely a mendicant was ever seen in the valley of the Ban de la Roche, where he resided, sometimes a pauper from the neighbouring communes, attracted by the well-known disposition of the pastor and his people, wandered thither to implore that assistance which, if deserving, he never failed to receive. "Why do you not work?" was Oberlin's usual interrogation. "Because no one will employ me," was the general reply. "Well, then, I will employ you. There—carry these planks—break those stones—fill that bucket with water, and I will repay you for your trouble." Such was his usual mode of proceeding; and idle beggars were taught to come there no more.

BOOK OF LAMENTATIONS.

The Sabbath Day.

Chap. i. ver. 7.—The adversaries did mock at her Sabbaths.

THE late Mr Meikle, surgeon in Carnwath, being on some business at Edinburgh, which detained him to the end of the week, and not finding himself so comfortably lodged as he could have desired, he rose early on Sabbath morning, and went out to the Meadows, that he might get an opportunity for devotional exercises. As he was sitting in the arbour, a young gentleman happened to come in, and, by his singing and conversation, discovered a contempt for the Sabbath. Mr Meikle said to him, "My good Sir, I am just thinking on the fourth commandment, can you help me out with it?"—"Indeed, Sir," said the gentleman, "I cannot."—"Oh," said Mr. M., "I have it. 'Remember the Sabbath-day to keep it holy.'" The young gentleman felt the reproof, and retired, leaving Mr Meikle to proceed with his devotions.

Unjust Enmity.

Chap. ii. ver. 16.—All thine enemies have opened their mouth against thee.

ONE morning as a minister, in one of the north-easterly cantons of France, was employed in his study, he heard a great noise in the village in which he resided. Rushing out, he perceived a foreigner, whom almost the whole population were loading with threatening and abusive language. "A Jew! a Jew!" resounded on all sides, as the minister forced his way through the crowd; and it was with difficulty that he could obtain silence. As soon, however, as he could make himself heard, he rebuked them with great warmth for having proved themselves unworthy the name of Christians, by treating the unfortunate stranger in so cruel a manner. He added, that if this poor man wanted the *name* of a Christian, they wanted the *spirit* of Christians.

Deserved Punishment.

Chap. iii. ver. 39.—Wherefore doth a living man complain, a man for the punishment of his sins.

THE Duke of Condé, when in poverty and retirement, was one day observed and pitied by a lord of Italy, who, out of tenderness, wished him to take better care of himself. The good Duke answered, "Sir, be not troubled; and think not that I am ill provided of conveniences; for I send a messenger before me, who makes ready my lodgings, and takes care that I be royally entertained." The noble lord asked him who was his messenger? He replied, "The knowledge of myself; and the thoughts of what I deserve for my sins, which is eternal torments; and when, with this knowledge, I arrive at my lodging, how unprovided soever I find it, methinks it is better than I deserve; and as the sense of sin, which merits hell, sweetens present difficulties, so do the hopes of the heavenly kingdom."

Animal Affection.

Chap. iv. ver. 3.—Even the sea-monsters draw out the breast, they give suck to their young ones.

THE natural affection of animals appears in the following instance. A whale and her young one had got into an arm of the sea, where the tide nearly left them. The people on the shore beheld their situation, and came down upon them in boats, attacking them with such weapons as could be collected. The animals were soon severely wounded, and the sea coloured with their blood. After several attempts to escape, the old one forced her way over the shallow into deep water. But though in safety herself, she could not bear the danger that threatened her young one; she therefore rushed once more to the place where it was confined, and appeared resolved, if she could not protect, to share its danger. As the tide was then running in, both of the creatures made their escape, though not without receiving a great number of wounds in every part.

Social Tyranny.

Chap. v. ver. 8.—Servants have ruled over us; there is none that doth deliver us out of their hand.

"IN visiting one of the gardens, for which Rosetta, in Egypt, is famous," says Jowett, in his Christian Researches, "we had a singular specimen of the effect of oppression. Seeing fine fruit on every side, but finding the oranges to be of the sour kind, we asked the gardener for some that were sweet. He at first denied that he had any. Our guide told us to show him money. At the sight of this, he produced some delicious oranges. As we peeled them, and ate, he gathered up the peel, and buried it in the earth, in order that soldiers coming into his garden might not see the trace of sweet oranges, and compel him to give them some."

BOOK OF EZEKIEL.

Four Aspects.

Chap. i. ver. 10.—They four had the face of a man, and the face of a lion on the right side; and they four had the face of an ox on the left side; they four also had the face of an eagle.

THE Rev. William Wilson of Perth, and some of his friends, were, on one occasion, enjoying themselves with some innocent pleasantry, by proposing severally to what they might compare the Four Brethren, with whom the Secession in Scotland originated. Different comparisons were suggested. When it came to Mr Wilson's turn, he did not see anything they could be better compared to than the four living creatures in Ezekiel's vision. "Our brother, Mr Erskine," said he, "has the face of a man. Our friend Mr Moncrieff, has the face of a lion. Our neighbour Mr Fisher, has the face of an eagle. And as for myself, I think you will all own that I may claim to be the ox; for, as you know, the laborious part of the business falls to my share."

Faithful Preaching.

Chap. ii. ver. 7.—Thou shalt speak my words unto them, whether they will hear, or whether they will forbear.

THE late Dr. Ritchie, Professor of Divinity in the University of Edinburgh, was one day preaching in Tarbolton church, where he was at that time minister, against profane swearing in common conversation, while one of his principal heritors who was addicted to that sin was present. This gentleman thought that the sermon was designedly addressed to him, and that the eyes of the whole congregation were fixed upon him. Though he felt indignant, he kept his place till the service was concluded, and then waited on the preacher, and asked him to dine with him, as he was quite alone. The invitation being accepted, the gentleman immediately after dinner thus addressed the minister—"Sir, you have insulted me to-day in the church. I have been three times in church lately, and on every one of them you have been holding me up to the derision of the audience; so I tell you, Sir, I shall never more enter the church of Tarbolton, unless you give me your solemn promise that you will abstain from such topics in future, as I am resolved I shall no more furnish you with the theme of your discourse." Mr. Ritchie heard this speech to a conclusion with calmness, and then looking him steadfastly in the face, thus replied, "Very well, Sir, if you took to yourself what I said to-day against swearing, does not your conscience bear witness to its truth? You say you will not enter the church till I cease to reprove your sins; if such is your determination, it is impossible that you can enter it again; for, which of the commandments have you not broken?" On observing his firmness, and feeling that he was wrong in attempting to make the minister of the parish compromise his duty, the gentleman held out his hand to Mr. Ritchie; a mutual explanation took place; and while the minister would abate none of his faithfulness, the heritor endeavoured to overcome his evil habits.

A Dumb Preacher.

Chap. iii. ver. 26.—I will make thy tongue cleave to the roof of thy mouth, that thou shalt be dumb, and shalt not be to them a reprover.

THE Rev. William Tennant, formerly a very eminent minister of the gospel in New England, once took much pains to prepare a sermon to convince a celebrated infidel. But, in attempting to deliver this laboured discourse, Mr T. was so confused that he was obliged to stop and close the service by prayer. This unexpected failure in one who had so often astonished the unbeliever with the force of his eloquence, led the infidel to reflect that Mr T. had been at other times aided by a divine power. This reflection proved the means of his conversion. Thus God accomplished by silence, what his servant meant to effect by persuasive preaching. Mr Tennant used afterwards to say, "His dumb sermon was the most profitable sermon that he had ever delivered."

Forbearance.

Chap. iv. ver. 6.—Thou shalt bear the iniquity of the house of Judah forty days: I have appointed thee each day for a year.

USHER, afterwards Archbishop of Armagh, was very zealous against the Roman Catholics, and averse to tolerating them. He once preached before the officers of the Irish government, from the preceding text. In the course of his sermon, he made an application of the passage which was remarkable. "From this year (1601)," said he, "I reckon forty years; and then those whom you now embrace shall be your ruin, and you shall bear their iniquity." The apparent accomplishment of this prediction in the Irish rebellion of 1641, was a singular occurrence; and, in the opinion of many, perhaps in his own, was regarded as an indication of his prophetic spirit.

Hair in the East.

Chap. v. ver. 1.—Take thee a barber's razor, and cause it to pass upon thine head, and upon thy beard.

THE Mahometans have a very great respect for their beards, and think it criminal to shave. "Conversing one day with a Turk," says Dr. Clarke, "who was playing with his beard, I asked him, 'Why do you not cut off your beard as we Europeans do?' To which he replied, with great emotion, 'Cut off my beard!—Why should I!—God forbid!'"

Repentance.

Chap. vi. ver. 9.—They shall loathe themselves for the evils they have committed.

THE Rev Ralph Erskine, when rebuking a person before the congregtion, for some scandulous offence, said,—"Think upon the case you are in, and meditate on the misery you have exposed yourself unto ; for God will deal with you either in mercy or in wrath. If he deal with you in mercy, then you will surely find more bitterness in sin than ever you found pleasure in it ; and if he deal with you in wrath, you will find sin, like a mountain of lead, weighing you down to the bottom of hell for ever. The Lord make you wise to salvation, that you may flee from the wrath to come."

Riches of no Avail

Chap. vii. ver. 19.—Their silver and their gold shall not be able to deliver them in the day of the wrath of the Lord.

MR. JEREMIAH BURROUGHS, a pious minister, mentions the case of a rich man, who, when he lay on his sick-bed, called for his bags of money ; and having laid a bag of gold to his heart, after a little he bade them take it away, saying, "It will not do ! it will not do !"

Mourning.

Chap. viii. ver. 14.—He brought me to the door of the Lord's house which was toward the north ; and, behold, there sat women weeping for Tammuz.

THE ancient Greeks, we are informed, used to place their dead near the doors of their houses, and to attend them with mourning. The same custom still continues among the modern Greeks, and might, perhaps, be observed by the ancient Jews. Dr. Richard Chandler, when travelling in Greece, observed, at Megara, a woman sitting, with the door of her cottage open, lamenting her dead husband aloud ; and when at Zante, he saw a woman in a house with the door open, bewailing her little son, whose body lay beside her dressed, the hair powdered, the face painted, and bedecked with leaf-gold.

The Spared.

Chap. ix. ver. 6.—Slay utterly old and young, both maids, and little children, and women ; but come not near any man upon whom is the mark.

BEZA, a little before his death, declared to his christian friends, that the Lord had fulfilled to him all the promises contained in the ninety-first psalm, which he heard expounded, when a young man, in the church. As he had been enabled to close with the second verse, in taking the Lord for his God, and got a sure claim that he would be his "refuge and fortress," so he had found remarkably, in the after changes of his life, that the Lord had "delivered him from the snare of the fowler," for he had been in frequent hazard by the lying in wait of many to ensnare him ; and from the "noisome pestilence," for he was sometimes in great hazard from it, in those places where he was called to reside. Amidst the civil wars in France he had most signal deliverances from many imminent dangers, when he was called to be present sometimes with the Protestant princes upon the field, where "thousands did fall about him." On his death-bed, he found that psalm so observably verefied, on which he was caused to hope, that he went through all the promises in it, declaring the comfortable accomplishment of them, how he had found the "Lord giving his angels charge over him, often answering him when he called on him; how he had been with him in trouble, had delivered him, and had satisfied him with long life." "And now," says he, "I have no more to wait for, but the fulfilling of these last words of the psalm—'I will show him my salvation,'—which, with confidence, I wait for."

Religious Ignorance.

Chap. x. ver. 18.—The glory of the Lord departed from off the threshold of the house, and stood over the cherubim.

IT appears from the Rev. H. Lindsay's interesting letter to the Bible Society in 1816, in which he gives an account of his visit to the Seven Churches of Asia, that even in those places, where the light of the gospel first shone, the inhabitants were not only destitute of the Bible, but they had also no distinct idea of the books it contained. They mentioned them indiscriminately, with various idle legends and lives of saints. Leaving Smyrna, the first place Mr. Lindsay visited was Ephesus. "I found there," says he, "but three Christians; two brothers, who keep a shop, and a gardener. They are all three Greeks, and their ignorance is lamentable indeed. In that place which was blessed so long with an apostle's labours, and those of his zealous assistants, are Christians, who have not so much as heard of that apostle, or seem only to recognise the name of Paul as one in the calendar of their saints."

A New Heart.

Chap. xi. ver. 19.—I will take the stony heart out of their flesh, and will give them an heart of flesh.

THE holiest and best men have been usually the most ready to acknowledge the depravity of their hearts, and the greatness of their obligations to the free and sovereign grace of God, in preserving or delivering them from the consequences of that depravity.—During the ministry of the Rev. Ralph Erskine at Dunfermline, a man was executed for robbery, whom he repeatedly visited in prison, and whom he attended on the scaffold. Mr. Erskine addressed both the spectators and the criminal; and, after concluding his speech, he laid his hands on his breast, uttering these words—"But for restraining grace, I had been brought, by this corrupt heart, to the same condition with this unhappy man."

Willing and Unwilling Hearers.

Chap. xii. ver. 2.—They have ears to hear, and hear not.

AN inn-keeper, addicted to intemperance, on hearing of the particularly pleasing mode of singing at a church some miles distant, went to gratify his curiosity, but with a resolution not to hear a word of the sermon. Having with difficulty found admission into a narrow open pew, as soon as the hymn before sermon was sung, which he heard with great attention, he secured both his ears against the sermon with his fore-fingers.—He had not been in this position many minutes, before the prayer finished, and the sermon commenced with an awful appeal to the consciences of the hearers, of the necessity of attending to the things which were made for their everlasting peace; and the minister addressing them solemnly, "He that hath ears to hear, let him hear." Just the moment before these words were pronounced, a fly had fastened on the face of the inn-keeper, and, stinging him sharply, he drew one of his fingers from his ears, and struck off the painful visitant. At that very moment, the words, "He that hath ears to hear, let him hear," pronounced with great solemnity, entered the ear that was opened as a clap of thunder: it struck him with irresistible force: he kept his hand from returning to his ear, and feeling an impression he had never known before, he presently withdrew the other finger, and hearkened with deep attention to the discourse which followed. A salutary change was produced on him. He abandoned his former wicked practices, became truly serious, and for many years went all weathers six miles to the church where he first received the knowledge of divine things. After about eighteen years' faithful and close walk with God, he died rejoicing in the hope of that glory which he now enjoys.

Blind Leaders.

Chap. xiii. ver. 3.—Woe unto the foolish prophets, that follow their own spirit, and have seen nothing.

IN a letter to a friend, Mr. Hervey says, "Warburton has published two volumes of sermons, in which, it seems, he has decried *experimental* religion, disregarded the peculiarities of the gospel, and treated the operations of the Spirit as mere enthusiasm. If this be the effect of his great learning, then, good Lord, deliver us all, say I, from such attainment! If you either have or can borrow them, just let me peep on them. Don't buy them to gratify me; I can relish nothing but what is evangelical."

The Iniquitous Punished.

Chap. xiv. ver. 10.—They shall bear the punishment of their iniquity.

"I HAVE read of King Canute," says an excellent minister, "that he promised to make him the highest man in England who should kill King Edmund his rival; which, when one had performed and expected his reward, he commanded him to be hung on the highest tower in London. So Satan promises great things to people in pursuit of their lusts, but he puts them off with great mischief. The promised crown turns to a halter; the promised comfort, to a torment; the promised honour, into shame; the promised consolation, into desolation; and the promised heaven turns into hell."

Woe to Jerusalem.

Chap. xv. ver. 7.—I will set my face against the inhabitants of Jerusalem; they shall go out from one fire, and another fire shall devour them.

"THERE was," says Josephus, "one Jesus, son of Ananias, a countryman of mean birth, four years before the war against the Jews, at a time when all was in deep peace and tranquillity, who, coming up to the feast of tabernacles, according to the custom, began on a sudden to cry out, and say, 'A voice from the east, a voice from the west, a voice from the four winds, a voice against Jerusalem and the temple, a voice against bridegrooms and brides, a voice against all the people.' Thus he went about all the narrow lanes, crying night and day: and being apprehended and scourged, he still continued the same language under the blows without any other word. And they, upon this, supposing (as it was) that it was some divine motion, brought him to the Roman prefect: and, by his appointment, being wounded by whips, and the flesh torn to the bones, he neither entreated nor shed a tear; but to every blow, in a most lamentable, mournful note, cried out, 'Woe, woe, to Jerusalem." This he continued to do till the time of the siege, seven years together ; and, at last, to his extraordinary note of woe to the city, the people, the temple, adding, 'Woe also to me ;' a stone from the battlements fell down upon him, and killed him."

Like Mother like Daughter.

Chap. xvi. ver. 44.—As is the mother, so is her daughter.

A MINISTER in the country, who frequently visited a widow lady with one daughter, always heard sad complaints from her mother, that her daughter was fond of public amusements One day when this was repeated, the daughter said, "Mother, who took me first to these places ?" Conscience did its office : the mother was silent, and no more was said on the subject.

The Eagle.

Chap. xvii. ver. 3.—A great eagle with great wings—came unto Lebanon, and took the highest branch of the cedar

"IT is not to be expected," Harmer observes, "that the visionary representations made to the prophets should always coincide with natural history ; but it seems this does, (refering to the preceding passage,) 'We employed the rest of the day,' says La Roque, in speaking of the spot where the cedars of Lebanon grow, 'in attentively surveying the beauties of this place, and of its neighbourhood, in measuring some of the cedars, and in cutting off many of their branches, with their cones, which we sent to Beciarrai, with a number of large eagles' feathers, which were found in the same place."

Better Unborn.

Chap. xviii. ver. 10.—If he beget a son that is a robber, a shedder of blood.

A BOY in London, of thirteen years of age, having been left at home one day with a servant, while his parents were gone out, took an opportunity to rob a drawer of a considerable quantity of silver. His father, next day, detected the theft, and reproved him for such shameful conduct, when the wretched boy obtaining possession of a loaded pistol belonging to his father, put a period to his life with it ; in consequence of which, his body was ordered to be buried in the public street. He was of a very morose disposition, and disobedient to his parents.

Finally Overcome.

Chap. xix. ver. 8, 9.—The nations set against him on every side from the provinces, and spread their net over him : he was taken in their pit.—And they put him in ward in chains.

BONAPARTE, after a career of conquest and blood, was completely subdued by the combined Powers of Russia, Prussia, Austria, and Britain. After the decisive battle of Waterloo, he retreated with precipitation to Paris ; but being followed by the allies, he quitted that capital, and went to Rochefort, where vessels were prepared to carry him and his attendants to America, The British government, however, informed of his plan, blockaded this part of the French coast so effectually, that he found himself compelled to surrender to Captain Maitland of the Bellerophon, the commander of the blockading squadron. In this ship he was brought to the coast of England, but not suffered to land ; and about the middle of August 1815, he sailed with part of his suite, in the Northumberland, to the Island of St Helena, where he was kept a prisoner at large during the remainder of his life. He died 5th May, 1821.

Disregarding the Sabbath.

Chap. xx. ver. 21.—They polluted my Sabbaths: then I said, I would pour out my fury upon them.

SOME time ago, W. Pender, a lad who had formerly attended a Sabbath school, engaged to go with some companions a-fishing on a Lord's day. Though it rained very hard, and he was desired not to go, yet, bent on pursuing his own course, he went notwithstanding. They came to the river, where they agreed to stop, and they began their unhallowed sport, and continued for some time, not thinking of any danger, when W. Pender wishing to obtain a better place, tried to jump from the spot where he stood to another; but, in doing so, his foot slipped, he struck his head against a barge, and fell into the river; and, after being sought for some time, was found, and taken out a lifeless corpse. Let Sabbath-breakers take warning by this young man's unhappy end. The way of transgressors is hard.

Using Divination.

Chap. xxi. ver. 21.—The king of Babylon stood at the parting of the way, at the head of the two ways, to use divination: he made his arrows bright.

DELLA VELLA relates the following method of divination by arrows. "He saw at Aleppo a Mahometan, who caused two persons to sit upon the ground, one opposite to the other, and gave them four arrows into their hands, which both of them held with their points downward, and, as it were, in two right lines, united one to the other. Then a question being put to him about any business, he fell to murmur his enchantments, and thereby caused the said four arrows, of their own accord, to unite their points together in the midst, (though he that held them stirred not his hand,) and according to the future event of the matter, those of the right side were placed over those of the left, or on the contrary." This practice Della Vella refers to diabolical influence.

Despising Holy Things.

Chap. xxii. ver. 8.—Thou hast despised mine holy things, and hast profaned my Sabbaths.

THE following fact, communicated by a respectable merchant of New York, is well worthy of notice:—"I have particularly observed, says the gentleman, "that those merchants in New York, who have kept their counting-rooms open on the Sabbath-day, during my residence there, (twenty-five years,) have failed without exception."

An Admonition.

Chap. xxiii. ver. 38.—They have defiled my sanctuary in the same day, and have profaned my Sabbaths.

IN the church-yard of Devizes, is a monument with the following inscription :—

BOOK OF EZEKIEL. 273

"In Memory
Of the unfortunate end of
Robert Merrit, and Susannah, his wife; Elizabeth Tiley
her sister, Martha Carter, and Joseph Derham,
Who were all drowned in the flower of their youth,
In a pond near the town called Drews,
On Sunday the 30th June;
And are together underneath entombed."

On another part of the stone is added—

"Remember the Sabbath-day to keep it holy.
This Monument, as an awful monitor to young people,
To remember their Creator in the days of their youth,
Was erected by subscription."

Bereavement.

Chap. xxiv. ver. 18.—So I spake unto the people in the morning: and at even my wife died.

MR MATTHEW HENRY'S first wife was seized with the small-pox, when in child-bed, and died. Mr Tong, the writer of his life, though living at a distance of eighteen miles, immediately visited the sorrowing family. The first words Mr Henry spoke to him on this occasion, with many tears, were, "I know nothing could support me under such a loss as this, but the good hope I have that she is gone to heaven, and that in a little time I shall follow her thither."

A God Forsaken Land.

Chap. xxv. ver. 7.—I will stretch out mine hand upon thee, and will deliver thee for a spoil to the heathen; and I will cut thee off from the people, and I will cause thee to perish out of the countries.

CHATEAUBRIAND, the French traveller, speaking of the range of mountains that extend from north to south, east of the Jordan, together with the contiguous country, says, "Nothing is to be seen but black perpendicular rocks, which throw their lengthened shadow over the waters of the Dead Sea. The smallest bird of heaven would not find among the rocks a blade of grass for its sustenance; every thing there announces the country of a reprobate people, and seems to breathe the horror and incest whence sprung Ammon and Moab."

Prophecy Concerning Tyre.

Chap. xxvi. ver. 14.—I will make thee like the top of a rock: thou shalt be a place to spread nets upon.

"THE famous Heutius," says Bishop Newton in his Dissertations, "knew one Hadrianus Parvillerius, a Jesuit, a very candid man, and a master of Arabic, who resided ten years in Syria; and he remembers to have heard him sometimes say, that when he approached the ruins of Tyre, and beheld the rocks stretched forth to the sea, and the great stones scattered up and down on the shore, made clean and smooth by the sun, and waves, and winds, and useful only for the drying of fishermen's nets, many of which happened at that time to be spread thereon, it brought to his memory this prophecy of Ezekiel concerning Tyre—'I will make thee like the top of a rock: thou shalt be a place to spread nets upon; thou shalt be built no more; for I the Lord have spoken it, saith the Lord God.'"

The City of Tyre.

Chap. xxvii. ver. 32.—*They shall lament over thee, saying, What city is like Tyrus, like the destroyed in the midst of the sea?*

MR MAUNDRELL, in his "Journey from Aleppo to Jerusalem," describing Tyre, says, "This city, standing in the sea upon a peninsula, promises, at a distance, something very magnificent. But when you come to it, you find no similitude of that glory for which it was so renowned in ancient times, and which the prophet Ezekiel describes. On the north side it has an old Turkish ungarrisoned castle; besides which, you see nothing here but a mere Babel of broken walls, pillars, vaults, &c., there being not so much as one entire house left: its present inhabitants are only a few poor wretches, harbouring themselves in the vaults, and subsisting chiefly upon fishing, who seem to be preserved in this place by Divine Providence, as a visible argument how God has fulfilled his word concerning Tyre, viz., that 'it should be as the top of a rock, a place for fishers to dry their nets on.'"

Pride of Wealth.

Chap. xxviii. ver. 5.—*By thy great wisdom, and by thy traffic, hast thou increased thy riches, and thine heart is lifted up because of thy riches.*

IN the strait between Johor and Rhio, there is a small white rock, called the "White Stone," very little elevated above the water, and so exactly in the centre of the passage, that many vessels, unacquainted with it, have been wrecked upon it. A Portuguese merchant passing this strait, in a vessel of his own, richly laden with gold, and other valuable commodities, asked the pilot when this rock would be passed; but each moment appearing to him long until he was secure from the danger, he repeated his question so often, that the pilot impatiently told him the rock was passed. The merchant, transported with joy, impiously exclaimed, that "God could not now make him poor." But in a little while the vessel struck on the White Stone, and all his wealth was engulphed in the abyss: life alone remained, to make him feel his misery and his punishment.

Effect of Despotic Power.

Chap. xxix. ver. 3.—*Pharaoh hath said, My river is mine own, and I have made it for myself.*

WHEN the force of the current had carried away the temporary bridge which Xerxes had caused to be thrown over the Hellespont, on his grand expedition into Greece, he was so enraged, that he not only ordered the heads of the workmen to be struck off, but, like a madman, inflicted lashes upon the sea, to punish it for its insolence; he, moreover, affected to hold it in future under his control, by throwing fetters into it! "A striking proof," adds the historian, "how much the possession of despotic power tends not only to corrupt the heart, but even to weaken and blind the understanding."

Abandoning Idol Worship.

Chap. xxx. ver. 13.—*I will also destroy the idols, and I will cause their images to cease.*

ONE day, while Mr Wilson was teaching the people of Raiatea, a South Sea island, an old man stood up, and exclaimed, "My forefathers worshipped *Oro*, the god of war, and so have I; nor shall any thing you can say persuade me to forsake this way. And," continued he, addressing the missionary, "what do you want more than you have already? Have you not won over such a chief, and such a chief?—aye, and you have Pomare himself!—what want you more?"—"All—all the people of Raiatea, and you yourself, I want!" replied Mr Wilson. "No, no," cried the old man; "me!—you shall never have me! I will do as my fathers have done:—I will worship Oro: you shall never have me, I assure you." Yet, within six months from that time, this staunch, inflexible, inveterate adherent of the bloody superstition of Oro (the Moloch of the Pacific) abandoned his idol, and became a worshipper of the true God.

No Rank in the Grave.

Chap. xxxi. ver. 14.—They are all delivered unto death, to the nether parts of the earth, in the midst of the children of men, with them that go down to the pit.

A SULTAN, amusing himself with walking, observed a dervise sitting with a human skull in his lap, and appearing to be in a very profound reverie. His attitude and manner surprised the Sultan, who demanded the cause of his being so deeply engaged in reflection. "Sire," said the dervise, "this skull was presented to me this morning; and I have from that moment been endeavouring, in vain, to discover whether it is the skull of a powerful monarch, like your Majesty, or of a poor dervise like myself."—A humbling consideration truly!

"Earth's highest station ends in—*Here he lies:*
And dust to dust concludes her noblest song."

Living and Dead.

Chap. xxxii. ver. 26.—Though their terror was caused in the land of the living, yet have they borne their shame with them that go down to the pit: he is put in the midst of them that be slain.

PHILIP, King of Macedon, as he was wrestling at the Olympic games, fell down in the sand; and, when he rose again, observing the print of his body in the sand, cried out, "O how little a parcel of earth will hold *us*, when we are dead, who are ambitiously seeking after the whole world whilst we are living!"

The Burden of Sin.

Chap. xxxiii. ver. 10.—If our transgressions and our sins be upon us, and we pine away in them, how should we then live?

A MINISTER of the gospel, when preaching from the preceding text, said, "I knew a poor widow who had gone into a little debt that was a burden upon her, which she could not remove, just as sin is a debt or burden upon the conscience, which no man is able to cast off. Well, what could the widow do? Her language to herself was, 'How *can I live* with this burden? My little furniture—my all will be sold!—I must go to the workhouse, where I must mix with bad people, who know not my Saviour, and who take his name in vain!' A benevolent individual hearing of her distress, sent to the creditor, desiring him to bring a receipt in full, and he should have his money. He took the recept, and gave it to the widow. 'O,' said she, 'now *I shall live! I shall live!*'"—This little story the minister applied, in the most simple manner, to the atonement of Christ, and his payment of the debt of his people.

Unfaithful Pastors.

Chap. xxxiv. ver. 3.—Ye eat the fat, and clothe you with the wool, ye kill them that are fed : but do not feed the flock.

AS one of the Princes of Orange was passing through a village one Sabbath-day, he asked the people, "Who is the man in black playing at tennis ?" He was answered, "The man who has the care of our souls."—"Good people," said the Prince, "is this the man who has the care of your souls ; You had best then look about you, and take a little care of them yourselves."

A Perpetual Hatred.

Chap. xxxv. ver. 5.—Thou hast had a perpetual hatred, and hast shed the blood of the children of Israel by the force of the sword.

AMONG the Circassians, the spirit of resentment is so strong, that all the relatives of the murderer are considered as guilty. This customary infatuation to avenge the blood of relatives, generates most of the fueds, and occasions great bloodshed among all the tribes of Caucasus ; for unless pardon be purchased, or obtained by intermarriage between the two families, the principle of revenge is propagated to all succeeding generations. The hatred which the mountainous nations evince against the Russians, arises, in a great measure, from the same source. If the thirst of vengeance is quenched by a price paid to the family of the deceased, this tribute is called *Thlil-Uasa* or *the price of blood;* but neither princes nor *Usdens* accept of such a compensation, as it is an established law among them to demand *blood for blood*.

A New Heart.

Chap. xxxvi. ver. 26.—A new heart also will I give you, and a new spirit will I put within you : and I will take away the stony heart out of your flesh, and will give you an heart of flesh.

THE late Mr Reader of Taunton, having called one day, in the course of his pastoral visits, at the house of a friend, affectionately noticed a child in the room, a little girl about six years of age.—Among other things he asked her if she knew that she had a bad heart, and opening the Bible, pointed her to the passage where the Lord promises to give a new heart. He entreated her to plead this promise in prayer, and she would find the Almighty faithful to his engagement. About seventeen years after, a lady came to him, to propose herself for communion with the church, and how inexpressible was his delight, when he found that she was the very person with whom, when a child, he had so freely conversed on subjects of religion, and that the conversation was blessed for her conversion to God. Taking her Bible, she had retired, as he advised, pleaded the promise, wept, and prayed; and the Lord, in answer to her fervent petitions, gave her what she so earnestly desired—*a new heart*.

The Divine Spirit.

Chap. xxxvii. ver. 5.—Thus saith the Lord God unto these bones, Behold, I will cause breath to enter into you, and ye shall live.

"I REMEMBER," says Rowland Hill, "once conversing with a celebrated sculptor, who had been hewing out a block of marble to represent one of our great patriots—Lord Chatham. 'There,' said he ; 'is not that a fine form ?'—'Now, Sir,' said I, 'can you put life into it ? else, with all its beauty, it is still but a block of marble.'

Christ, by his Spirit, puts life into a beauteous image, and enables the man he forms to live to his praise and glory."

Evil Thoughts.

Chap. xxxviii. ver. 10.—Things shall come into thy mind, and thou shalt think an evil thought.

NICHOLSON, the murderer of Mr and Mrs Bonar at Chiselhurst, in Kent, who paid the forfeit of his life to the violated laws of his country, declared solemnly in writing, after sentence of death was passed upon him, that he had no previous malice towards the parties, nor intention to murder them, five minutes before he committed the horrid deed ; but that suddenly, as he awoke, the thought suggested itself to his mind, and which he can only account for by confessing, " that he had long lived in utter forgetfulness of God, and was in the habit of giving way to the worst passions of the human heart."

God and the Heathen.

Chap. xxxix. ver. 21.—I will set my glory among the heathen.

MR STEWART, in describing a worshipping assembly at Hido, one of the Sandwich Islands, says, "At an early hour of the morning, even before we had taken our breakfast on board ship, a single islander here or there, or a group of three or four, wrapped in their large mantles of various hues, might be seen wending their way among the groves fringing their bay on the east, or descending from the hills and ravines on the north, towards the chapel ; and by degrees their numbers increased, till in a short time, every path along the beach, and over the uplands, presented an almost uninterrupted procession of both sexes, and of every age, all pressing to the house of God. So few canoes were round the ship yesterday, and the landing-place had been so little thronged, as our boats passed to and fro, that one might have thought the district but thinly inhabited ; but now such multitudes were seen gathering from various directions, that the exclamation, 'what crowds of people ! what crowds of people !' was heard from the quarter-deck to the forecastle.—What a change—what a happy change ! when at this very place, only four years ago, the known wishes and example of chiefs of high authority, the daily persuasion of teachers, added to motives of curiosity and novelty, could scarce induce a hundred of the inhabitants to give an irregular, careless, and impatient attendance on the services of the sanctuary : but now,

> "Like a mountain torrent pouring to the main,
> From every glen a living stream came forth ;
> From every hill in crowds they hasten down,
> To worship Him who deigns in humblest fane,
> On wildest shore to meet the upright in heart."

Impressive Preaching.

Chap. xl. ver. 4.—Declare all that thou seest to the house of Israel.

THE late Rev. David Brown of Calcutta was remarkable for a deeply serious and impressive manner in preaching, which had perhaps a greater force than his words : of this, a sensible hearer once observed, " Whosoever may not believe as Mr. Brown preaches, he makes it impossible to suspect he does not believe so himself ; for which reason alone we cannot but be attentive hearers, when we see him evidently so much in earnest."

The Lord's Table,

Chap. xli. ver. 22.—This is the table that is before the Lord.

MR. OLIVER HEYWOOD had been settled at Coley in England, for seven years, during which time the Lord's Supper was not administered, nor, indeed, had been so for nine years previous to his settlement. He was deeply affected with the omission; and having long revolved the subject in his mind, he was now determined to re-establish the divine institution in his chapel. He foresaw that difficulties would arise, as he could not conscientiously admit all persous indiscriminately to the table of the Lord. In a prudent and cautious manner, he gradually introduced the subject to the notice of his people, by preaching a course of sermons on the nature, obligations, and advantages of the ordinance, and the qualifications of candidates. After having prepared the way, he at length announced his intention, and proposed that application should be made to him personally by all who desired to participate in this feast of love. Considerable numbers applied, and the conversations he held with them were mutually beneficial and gratifying. Their names were entered as candidates. After having prepared the way, he at length announced, that if any objection should be taken against individuals, he might be informed of it previous to the administration. Some of his hearers and warmest admirers, whose lives did no honour to their professions, took offence at the proceeding, and declared that they would never come to the table and participate in the ordinance. Their courage, however, failed them, after hearing the "preparation sermon." The ordinance was at length administered; and great was the joy experienced both by Mr Heywood and the commnnicants on this occasion. It was a season of "refreshing from the presence of the Lord," and a day long to be remembered.

The Holy Place.

Chap. xlii. ver. 13.—The place is holy.

A SCOFFING infidel, of considerable talents, being once in company with a person of truly religious character, put the following question to him :—"I understand, Sir, that you expect to go to heaven when you die : can you tell me what sort of a place heaven is?" "Yes, Sir," replied the Christian, "heaven is a prepared place for a prepared people, and if your soul is not prepared for it, with all your boasted wisdom, you will never enter there."

Instructive Writing.

Chap. xliii. ver. 11.—Write it in their sight, that they may keep the whole form thereof, and all the ordinances thereof, and do them.

THE church at Turvey, in which Mr Legh Richmond officiated, had a most appropriate selection of texts of Scripture inscribed on its walls, chosen by him with great care, and exhibiting a complete system of divinity. "I wish," said Mr. Richmond, "when I can no longer preach to my flock, that the walls should remind them of what they have heard from me. The eye, though wandering in thoughtless vacancy, may catch something to affect the heart."

The Hebrews.

Chap. xliv. ver. 12.—They caused the house of Israel to fall into iniquity.

BOOK OF EZEKIEL.

"STEPPING," says one, "into a Hackney stage in London one Saturday evening, I perceived a decent-looking young woman had already taken her seat. In the course of a little conversation, it appeared that she was a Jewess, who had that day been at the synagogue, and was returning to Hackney, where she resided. Being, at that time, a Hebrew student myself, I was pleased with the opportunity of conversing with this young person, on the subject of the Hebrew language, which she seemed to understand. The pleasure of the conversation, however, was interrupted by the circumstance of her occasionally taking God's name in vain. This led me to observe to her, that I was much surprised that she should thus take the Lord's name in vain, in English, since I understood the Jews professed such a peculiar veneration for the Hebrew name *Jehovah*, that they used another word in its place in reading their own Scriptures. The answer which she returned was, 'The Christians do so.'"

Eastern Money.

Chap. xlv. ver. 12.—*The shekel shall be twenty gerahs: twenty shekels, five and twenty shekels, fifteen shekels, shall be your maneh.*

IN a MS., to which Mr Harmer often refers, it is stated, that it is the custom of the East, in their accounts and their reckonings of a sum of money, to specify the different parts of which it is composed. Talking after this manner, I owe twenty-five—of which the half is twelve and one-half, the quarter six and one-fourth, &c. This appears very strange to us; but if it was the custom of those countries, it is no wonder that Ezekiel reckoned after this manner.

Morning and Evening Sacrifice.

Chap. xlvi. ver. 12.—*They shall prepare the lamb, and the meat-offering, and the oil, every morning, for a continual burnt-offering.*

THE morning and evening sacrifice under the law, has often been referred to as emblematical of the morning and evening sacrifices of prayer and praise presented by Christians under the gospel, through faith in the Redeemer; and it is matter of regret that these should, in many instances, be altogether neglected, and in others, but occasionally attended to. In the following case, a reproof for an omission of family prayer comes from an unexpected quarter:—
"I knew a man," says an author, "who once received one of the most severe reproofs he ever met with from his own child, an infant of three years old. Family prayer had been, by some means, neglected one morning, and the child was, as it were, out of his element. At length he came to his father as he sat, and just as the family were going to dinner, the little reprover, leaning on his father's knee, said, with a sigh, 'Pa, you were used to go to prayer with us, but you did not to-day.'—'No, my dear,' said the parent, 'I did not.'—'But, pa, you ought; why did you not?' In short, the father had not a word to reply, and the child's rebuke was as appropriate and effectual as if it had been administered by the most able minister in the land; and, it may be added, had as permanent an influence."

Fish in the Mediterranean.

Chap. xlvii. ver. 10.—*Their fish shall be according to their kinds, as the fish of the great sea, exceeding many.*

DOUBDAN, speaking of his going by sea from Sidon to Joppa, in his way to Jerusalem, says, that on entering into that port, they found it so abounding in fish, "that a great fish pursuing one somewhat less, both of them sprung at the same time about three feet out of the water ; the first dropped into the middle of the bark, and the other fell so near that they had well nigh taken it with their hands ; this happened very luckily, as it afforded our sailors a treat."

God's Presence.

Chap. xlviii. ver. 35.—The Lord is there.

IN some part of the United States of America the attendance at a prayer meeting had so declined, that some persons advised that it should be given up, which was accordingly done. On the following Tuesday, a poor infirm old woman, a constant attendant, was seen, as usual, hobbling along to the chapel. On her return, some one met her and said, "Why, you forgot that the prayer meeting was given up; there was not any one there, was there?" "O yes," said the woman, "there was God the Father, God the Son, and God the Holy Ghost, and a glorious time we had, and they promised to meet me again next Tuesday night." From that time the place was crowded, and nothing more was heard about giving it up.

BOOK OF DANIEL.

Personal Defilement.

Chap. i. ver. 8.—Daniel purposed in his heart that he would not defile himself with the portion of the king's meat, nor with the wine which he drank.

MR. PHILIP mentions that some Dutch merchants opened a storehouse for selling ardent spirits, on the borders of one of the missionary settlements in South Africa, which would have counteracted all the beneficial effects of the gospel on the poor untutored natives, had not the missionaries fallen on a happy expedient for defeating its baneful effects. When they heard of one of their converts entering into the storehouse to purchase ardent spirits, they caused his name on the following Sunday to be read before the congregation, that the minister and the whole church might unite in prayer on behalf of a brother exposed to great and dangerous temptation. This had so salutary an effect, that henceforth not a convert would enter the spirit shop. The storehouse was speedily removed, and caused no farther annoyance.

Warning by Dreams.

Chap. ii. ver. 1.—Nebuchadnezzar dreamed dreams, wherewith his spirit was troubled, and his sleep brake from him.

IN February 1786, Professor Meyer of Halle was sent for by one of his pupils, a medical student who lay dangerously ill. The patient told him that he should certainly die, having had a warning dream to that effect. "I wrote it down," he added, "the morning after it happened, and laid it in a drawer, of which this is the key ; when I am gone, read it over." On the 4th of March, the student died. Professor Meyer opened the drawer of the writing-desk, in which he found this narration:—"I thought I was walking in the churchyard of Halle, admiring the number of excellent epitaphs which are cut on the gravestones there. Passing from one to another, I was struck by a plain tomb-stone, of which I went to read the inscription. With surprise I found upon it my fore-names and surname, and that I died on the 4th of March. With progressive anxiety I tried to read the date of the year; but I thought there was moss over the fourth cipher of 178—. I picked up a stone to scrape the figures clean, and just as I began to discover a 6, with fearful palpitation I awoke.

Conscientious Action.

Chap. iii. ver. 18.—Be it known unto thee, O king, that we will not serve thy gods, nor worship the golden image which thou hast set up.

MR SAMUEL WESLEY, the father of the celebrated Mr John Wesley, being strongly importuned by the friend of *James the Second* to support the measures of the court in favour of Popery, with promises of preferment, absolutely refused even to read the king's declaration; and though surrounded with courtiers, soldiers, and informers, he preached a bold and pointed discourse against it from these words:—"If it be so, our God whom we serve is able to deliver us out of thy hand, O king. But if not, be it known unto thee, O king, that we will not serve thy gods, nor worship the golden image which thou hast set up"

Counsel to Royalty.

Chap. iv. ver. 27.—O king, let my counsel be acceptable unto thee, and break off thy sins by righteousness, and thine iniquities by shewing mercy to the poor.

DURING the illness of the pious King Edward VI., Dr. Ridley, in a sermon which he preached before him, much commended works of charity, and showed that, as they were enjoined on all men, so especially on those in high stations. The same day after dinner, the king sent for the Doctor into the gallery, made him sit in a chair by him, and would not suffer him to be uncovered. After thanking the Doctor for his sermon, he repeated the chief heads of it, and added,—"I took myself to be chiefly touched by your discourse; for as in the kingdom I am next under God, so must I most nearly approach to him in goodness and mercy. As our miseries stand most in the need of help from him, so are we the greatest debtors. And therefore, as you have given me this general exhortation, direct me, I entreat you, by what particular act I may best discharge my duty."

Undue Power.

Chap. v. ver. 19.—Whom he would he slew, and whom he would he kept alive, and whom he would he set up, and whom he would he put down.

AT the court of France, while Louis XIV. was yet in his youth, some abject courtiers were entertaining the prince in public with the policy of the Turkish government. They observed, that the Sultan had nothing to do but to say the word, whatever it was, whether to take off a great man's head, or strip him of his employment or estate, and that there was a train of servants they called mutes, who executed it without reply. "See," said the prince, "what it is to be a king!" The old Count de Grammont, who heard the corrupters of the youth with indignation, immediately interposed: "But, Sire! of these same sultans I have known three strangled by their own mutes within my memory." This silenced the flatterers; and the Duke de Montausier, the French Cato, who was lolling in a chair behind the circle that surrounded the prince, forced his way through the crowd, and publicly thanked the Count de Grammont for his noble and seasonable liberty.

Faithful in Prayer.

Chap. vi. ver. 10.—When Daniel knew that the writing was signed, he went into his house; and his windows being open in his chamber towards Jerusalem, he kneeled upon his knees three times a-day, and prayed, and gave thanks before his God, as he did aforetime.

SOME time ago, a law was passed in the House of Assembly at Kingston, which contained several clauses highly injurious to the missionary cause in Jamaica. No time was lost in carrying its oppressive enactments into effect. A Wesleyan missionary was thrown into prison for the alleged "crime" of preaching till after eight o'clock in the evening. Two persons connected with the congregation at Montego Bay, had their houses levelled with the ground—their feet made fast in the stocks—and were sent in chains to the workhouse, charged with the heinous offence of praying to the God of heaven. One of these, however, proved so incorrigible, that they were obliged to give him up in despair. Having nothing to do besides in the jail, he spent his time—morning, noon, and night—in singing, and in calling upon God; which so annoyed the jailor, that he repeatedly went into his cell and beat him, till at length the jailor brought him again before the court for this sin. The man, however, resolutely declared his purpose to pray. "If you let me go," said he, "me will pray—if you keep me in prison, me will pray—if you flog me, me will pray: pray me must, and pray me will!" The jailor was fairly confounded; and, rather than be annoyed any longer by this "praying fellow," he gave up his fees, and a part of the fine was remitted: and so the man was dismissed, to go and pray elsewhere.

A Dream Verified.

Chap. vii. ver. 1.—In the first year of Belshazzar king of Babylon, Daniel had a dream, and visions of his head upon his bed: then he wrote the dream, and told the sum of the matters.

BEFORE Mr and Mrs Notcult had any idea of removing from their residence in Essex, Mrs N. dreamed one night, that they went to live at Ipswich, and the house in which she imagined they resided was so impressed on her mind, that when she actually went there, some years afterwards, she had a perfect recollection of it. She also dreamed, that as she was going to a closet in the parlour, her nose began to bleed, and that it would be impossible to stop it, until she had lost so much blood as to occasion her death, which event should happen forty years from that day. As her mind was deeply impressed, she wrote down in her pocket-book the day of the month and year in which her dream occurred. Some time after, they went to reside at Ipswich, and Mrs N. was surprised to find the house exactly correspond with the one she had seen in her dream, and also the very same closet, in going to which the fatal accident happened. But parental duties, and the busy concerns of life, engaging her attention, the circumstance was soon forgotten, and the closet frequented for a number of years, without any fear of the accomplishment of her dream. On Christmas day, 1755, as she was reaching a bottle of drops from the closet, to give Mr Notcult, who was confined to a couch in the room, her nose began to bleed. Finding, after some time, all attempts to stop the blood ineffectual, her dream came to her recollection, and she requested one of her attendants to fetch her pocket-book, directing him where to find it. Upon examining it, they found, to their unspeakable surprise, that it was exactly forty years from the time her dream occurred. All methods were tried without effect, and as the medical attendant entered the room, she said to him, "You may try to stop the bleeding, if you please, but you will not be able." After languishing from Thursday till Saturday, she sweetly fell asleep in Jesus.

Near to God.

Chap. viii. ver. 17.—Understand, O son of man; for at the time of the end shall be the vision.

"THANKS to Divine goodness," says Dr. Payson of America, "this has been a good day to me. Was favoured with considerable freedom in the morning, and rejoiced in the Lord through the day. In the evening felt an unusual degree of assistance, both in prayer and study. Since I began to beg God's blessing on my studies, I have done more in one week, than in the whole year before. Surely, it is good to draw near to God at all times."

Answers to Prayer.

Chap. ix. ver. 23.—At the beginning of thy supplications the commandment came forth, and I am come to shew thee; for thou art greatly beloved: therefore understand the matter, and consider the vision.

A GENTLEMAN having been deeply engaged in abstruse speculations as to the distance from one planet to another, and the length of time that would be required to travel such a distance, carried his speculation so far as to inquire,—"Supposing heaven to be a place, what may be supposed its distance, and the time required for locomotion, from one world to the other?" A lady present promptly replied,—"It is not a matter of mere conjecture, but it admits of a satisfactory and scriptural solution. While a godly man prays and makes confession with supplication to his God, there is time enough for the commandment to go forth in heaven, and an angel, swift in flight, to reach earth with an answer of mercy."

A Great Vision.

Chap. x. ver. 8.—I was left alone, and saw this great vision, and there remained no strength in me: for my comeliness was turned in me unto corruption, and I retained no strength.

THE Rev. William Tennant of America had preached one Lord's day morning to his congregation, and in the intermission had walked into the woods for meditation, the weather being warm. He was reflecting on the infinite wisdom of God, as manifested in all his works, and particularly in the wonderful method of salvation through the death and sufferings of his beloved Son. This subject suddenly opened on his mind with such a flood of light, that his views of the glory and the infinite majesty of Jehovah were so inexpressibly great, as entirely to overwhelm him; and he fell almost lifeless to the ground. When he had revived a little, all he could do was to raise a fervent prayer, that God would withdraw himself from him, or that he must perish under a view of his ineffable glory. When able to reflect on his situation, he could not but abhor himself as a weak and despicable worm; and seemed to be overcome with astonishment, that a creature so unworthy and insufficient had ever dared to attempt the instruction of his fellow-men in the nature and attributes of so glorious a Being. Overstaying his usual time, some of his elders went in search of him, and found him prostrate on the ground, unable to rise, and incapable of informing them of the cause. They raised him up, and, after some time, brought him to the church, and supported him to the pulpit, which he ascended on his hands and knees, to the no small astonishment of the congregation. He remained silent a considerable time, earnestly supplicating Almighty God to hide himself from him, that he might be enabled to address his people, who were by this time lost in wonder to know what had produced this uncommon event. His prayers were heard, and he became able to stand up, by holding the desk; and in a most affecting and pathetic address, he gave an account of the views he had of the infinite wisdom of God, and deplored his own incapacity to speak to them concerning a Being so infinitely glorious beyond all his powers of description. He then broke out into so fervent and expressive a prayer, as greatly to surprise the congregation, and draw tears from every eye. A sermon followed, which continued the solemn scene, and made very lasting impressions on the hearers.

Strong through God.

Chap. xi. ver. 32.—The people that do know their God shall be strong, and do exploits.

"I HAVE lately had the honour," said Captain Parry, at a public meeting in 1826, "and I may truly say, the happiness of commanding British seamen under circumstances requiring the utmost activity, implicit and immediate obedience, and the most rigid attention to discipline and good order; and I am sure, that the maintenance of all these was, in a great measure, owing to the blessing of God upon our humble endeavours to improve the religious and moral character of our men. In the schools established on board our ships during the winter, religion was made the primary object, and the result was every way gratifying and satisfactory. It has convinced me, that true religion is so far from being a hindrance to the arduous duties of that station in which it has pleased Providence to cast the seaman's lot, that, on the contrary, it will always incite him to their performance, from the highest and most powerful of motives; and I will venture to predict, that in proportion as this spring of action is more and more introduced among our seamen, they would become such as every Englishman would wish to see them. To this fact, at least, I can, on a small scale, bear the most decided testimony; and the friends of religion will feel a pleasure in having the fact announced, that *the very best seamen* on board the Hecla—such, I mean, as were always called upon in any cases of extraordinary emergency—were, *without exception*, those who had thought the most seriously on religious subjects; and if a still more scrupulous selection were to be made out of that number, the choice would fall, *without hesitation*, on two or three individuals possessing dispositions and sentiments eminently *Christian*."

A Divine Promise.

Chap. xii. ver. 13.—But go thou thy way till the end be: for thou shalt rest, and stand in thy lot at the end of the days.

IN a certain town in Providence, there lived two young men, who were intimate acquaintances. The one was truly pious; and the other, a shopman, paid no regard to the importance of divine things.

The shopman took up a leaf of the Bible, and was about to tear it in pieces, and use it for packing up some small parcels in the shop, when the other said, "Do not tear that, it contains the word of eternal life." The young man, though he did not relish the reproof of his kind and pious friend, folded up the leaf and put it in his pocket. A while after this he said within himself, "Now I will see what kind of life it is of which this leaf speaks." On unfolding the leaf, the first words that caught his eye were the last in the book of Daniel—"But go thou thy way till the end be: for thou shalt rest, and stand in thy lot at the end of the days." He began immediately to enquire what his lot would be at the end of the days, and from this occurrence became truly pious.

BOOK OF HOSEA.

A Changed People.

Chap. i. ver. 10.—In the place where it was said unto them, Ye are not my people, there it shall be said unto them, Ye are the sons of the living God.

THE late Rev. Robert Hall of Bristol, when describing the character of Mr Robinson of Leicester, says—"It was the boast of Augustus, that he found the city of Rome built of brick, and that he left it built of marble. Mr Robinson might say, without arrogance, that he had been the instrument of effecting a far more beneficial and momentous change. He came to this place while it was sunk in vice and irreligion; he left it eminently distinguished by sobriety of manners, and the practice of warm, serious, and enlightened piety. He did not add aqueducts and palaces, nor increase the splendour of its public edifices; but he embellished it with undecaying ornaments. He renovated the minds of its inhabitants, and turned a large portion of them from darkness to light, and from the power of Satan to God. He embellished it with living stones, and replenished it with numerous temples of the Holy Ghost. He enlarged its intercourse with heaven, and trained a great portion of its inhabitants for the enjoyment of celestial bliss."

God's People.

Chap. ii. ver. 23.—I will say to them which were not my people, Thou art my people; and they shall say, Thou art my God.

ON one occasion, when the late Mr. Brown of Haddington was exhorting his students not to rest satisfied with a mere speculative acquaintance with the truths of Scripture, in the systems, or with treasuring them up in their memories, but to be concerned to have them engraven on their hearts by the spirit of God, He took occasion to mention something of his own experience, of which he was usually very sparing. "I recollect," said he, "that when sitting on the brae of Abernethy, hearing Mr Wilson of Perth, I got more insight into that marrow of the gospel, *thy* God and *my* God, than I ever got before or since: alas! that it was so long ago."

Eastern Custom.

Chap. iii. ver. 2.—I bought her to me for fifteen pieces of silver, and for an homer of barley, and an half homer of barley.

"SIR JOHN CHARDIN," says Harmer, "observed in the East, that in their contracts for their temporary wives,—which are known to be frequent there, which contracts are made before the Cadi,—there is always the formality of a measure of corn mentioned, over and above the sum of money that is stipulated. I do not know of any thing that should occasion this formality of late days in the East; it may possibly be very ancient, as it is apparent this sort of wife is: if it be, it will perhaps account for Hosea's purchasing a woman of this sort for fifteen pieces of silver, and a certain quantity of barley."

Ignorance.

Chap. iv. ver. 6.—My people are destroyed for lack of knowledge.

DR FORD, formerly ordinary of Newgate, who had continual opportunities of investigating the fatal cause of depravity, ascribed the commission of crimes to the want of religious, as well as every moral principle. Of this the following is a melancholy proof:—"Going into the desk," says the doctor, "at the chapel in Newgate, the first Sunday after the Session, I saw twelve men in the condemned felon's pew, whose deportment and dress were decent and respectable. When I announced the day of the month, and mentioned the psalm, I was astonished to observe that none of those convicts took up a prayer-book, though several lay before them; neither did any of them seem to know a particle of the church service, or when to stand, sit, or kneel. In conversation with one next day, I inquired how it happened that none of them opened a prayer-book during divine service. Upon this there was rather an appearance of confusion, and a dead silence ensued. I put the question a second time, when one of them hesitatingly stammered out, "Sir, I cannot read; nor I, nor I, nor I," was rapidly uttered by them all."

Seeking God in Affliction.

Chap. v. ver. 15.—In their affliction they will seek me early.

VAVASOR POWEL, an eminent minister, being appointed to preach on a certain day in a meadow in Cardiganshire, a number of idle persons, enemies to religion, agreed to meet at the same time and place, to play at foot-ball, and thereby create a disturbance. Among them was a young man, named Morgan Howell, of respectable family in that neighbourhood, lately returned from school, having finished his education, who, being nimble-footed and dexterous at the game, had obtained possession of the ball, intending to kick it in the face of the preacher. At this instant another person ran towards him and tripped up his heels. By the fall his leg was broken; and after lying on the ground in great agony, he expressed a wish to see the minister, to whom, on his arrival, he confessed his wicked intention, and acknowledged that the just judgment of God had befallen him. The minister having represented to him the evil and danger of sin, preached the power of the Saviour, and at the request of the young man, accompanied him to his father's house. So great was the change produced in him by means of this affliction, that on his recovery he began to preach, and was for many years the most laborious preacher in those parts.

Effervescent Goodness.

Chap. vi. ver. 4.—Your goodness is as a morning cloud, and as the early dew it goeth away.

"THE dew of the night," says Dr. Shaw, " as we have only the heavens for our covering, would frequently wet us to the skin ; but no sooner was the sun risen, and the atmosphere a little heated, than the mists were dispersed, and the copious moisture, which the *dew* communicated to the sands, would be entirely evaporated."

Evil Influences of Wine,

Chap. vii. ver. 5—In the day of our king: the princes have made him sick with bottles of wine : he stretched out his hand with scorners.

CYRUS, when a youth, being at the court of his grandfather Cambyses, undertook, one day, to be a cup-bearer at table. It was the duty of this officer to taste the liquor before it was presented to the king. Cyrus, without performing this ceremony, delivered the cup in a very graceful manner to his grandfather. The king observed the omission, which he imputed to forgetfulness. "No," replied Cyrus, "I was afraid to taste, because I apprehended there was poison in the liquor ; for not long since, at an entertainment which you gave, I observed that the lords of your court, after drinking of it, became noisy, quarrelsome, and frantic. Even you, Sir, seemed to have forgotten that you were a king."

Forgetting God.

Chap. viii. ver. 14—Israel hath forgotten his Maker.

THE Rev. John Brown of Haddington offered the following advice to one of his hearers, whose father was an eminent Christian :— "Well, Horn, mind these words—'Thou art my God, I will prepare thee an habitation ; my father's God, I will exalt thee.' We should reckon him a madman, who would throw away a father's estate ; but he is much more foolish who throws away a father's God."

Dispersion of the Jews.

Chap. ix. ver. 17.—My God will cast them away, because they did not hearken unto him: and they shall be wanderers among the nations.

PAINS had been early taken by some of the Prince of Condé's supposed friends to shake his belief of Christianity ; he always replied, "You give yourselves a great deal of unnecessary trouble ; the dispersion of the Jews will always be an undeniable proof to me of the truth of our holy religion."

Deferring Decision.

Chap. x. ver. 2.—Their heart is divided ; now shall they be found faulty.

NUMBERS of the Greenlanders, who for a time adhered to the Moravian Missionaries, and promised well, drew back, and walked no more with them ; while the greater part of those who were wavering, seduced by the concourse of their heathen countrymen, again joined the multitude. One being asked why he could not stay, answered, "I have bought a great deal of powder and shot, which I must spend first in the south, in shooting rein-deer ;" another, "I must first have my fill of bears' flesh ;" and a third, "I must have a good boat, and then I will believe."

Refusal to Serve God.

Chap. xi. ver. 7.—Though they called them to the Most High, none at all would exalt him.

ON the day appointed for the National Fast in England, some of the parishioners in Timsbury, near Bath, when going to the parish church, met a young man of their acquaintance, but a leader in crime among his companions. They asked him to accompany them to church. "What should I go to church for?" "O!" replied they, "everybody goes to church to-day." "I shan't go to church till I am *carried* there." On the Friday after, he was employed to blow up the root of a tree with gunpowder; and though, after having communicated fire to the fuse, he retired to an unusually great distance, yet when the explosion took place, a shivered splint hit him on the forehead, and in six hours he was a corpse. The effects produced in the parish are said to have been extensively and solemnly made manifest in the conversion of more than a hundred of the most dissolute and abandoned of the inhabitants, who have, by the relinquishment of criminal practices, and a devout attendance on divine ordinances, evinced the sincerity of their repentance.

Answer to Prayer.

Chap. xii. ver. 4.—He had power over the angel, and prevailed: he wept and made supplication unto him.

THE Rev. Ralph Erskine was, on one occasion, requested by an afflicted friend to remember him in prayer. From the urgency of other affairs, the pious request, for a time, escaped his memory; but happening to recollect it during the night, he rose out of bed, and prayed with great fervour in behalf of that individual. Not long after, he had the happiness to receive information of his recovery, and found, that at the very hour in which he had wrestled for him with the God of Jacob, the sufferer had obtained effectual relief.

The Humble shall be Exalted.

Chap. xiii. ver. 1.—When Ephraim spake trembling, he exalted himself in Israel.

THE Rev. Henry Erskine, minister of Falkirk, and son of the Rev. Ralph Erskine, during his last illness, discovered deep abasement, mingled with a lively hope. "The prayer of the publican," said he, "must be my prayer; 'God be merciful to me a sinner.'" When his brother James at one time made this pious remark, "We all need to settle our accounts with God betimes;" Henry replied, "I know no way, dear brother, of settling my accounts, but by receiving a free pardon from my Redeemer."

Hope for the Backsliding.

Chap. xiv. ver. 4.—I will heal their backsliding, I will love them freely; for mine anger is turned away from him.

IT is said of a Mr. Gunn that he lay languishing in distress of mind for five years; during which he took no comfort in meat or drink, nor any pleasure in life; being under a sense of some backsliding, he was distressed as if he had been in the deepest pit of hell. If he ate his food, it was not from any appetite, but with a view to defer his damnation, thinking within himself that he must needs be lost so soon as his breath was out of his body. Yet, after all this, he was set at liberty, received great consolation, and afterwards lived altogether a heavenly life. Let not the tempted believer then despond, nor the returning backslider fear lest he should be rejected.

BOOK OF JOEL.

An Invasion.

Chap. I. ver. 6.—A nation is come up upon my land, strong and without number.

IN the year 1690, a cloud of locusts was seen to enter Russia, in three different places, and from thence to spread themselves over Poland and Lithuania in such astonishing multitudes that the air was darkened, and the earth covered with their numbers. In some places they were seen lying dead, heaped upon each other four feet deep ; in others they covered the surface like a black cloth ; the trees bent beneath their weight, and the damage which the country sustained exceeded computation.

The Invasion Overcome.

Chap. ii. ver. 20.—I will remove far off from you the northern army and will drive him into a land barren and desolate, with his face towards the east sea and his hinder part toward the utmost sea : and his stink shall come up, and his ill savour.

BARON DE TOTT, speaking of the locust, says, "I have often seen the shores of the Pontus Euxinus, towards the Bosphorus of Thrace, covered with their dried remains in such multitudes, that one could not walk along the strand without sinking half leg deep into a bed of these skinny skeletons. Curious to know the true cause of their destruction, I sought the moment of observation, and was a witness of their ruin by a storm, which overtook them so near the shore that their bodies were cast upon the land while yet entire. This produced an infection so great, that it was several days before they could be approached."

Degrading Influence of Drink.

Chap. iii. ver. 3.—They have sold a girl for wine that they might drink.

A FEW years ago, an old woman in London went into a dram shop and called for a glass of gin, which she drank off as soon as it was served to her. She then produced a Bible from under her apron, saying she had no money, but would leave that in pledge and redeem it in half an hour ; she however never returned. A woman in Glasgow, some time since, in order to gratify her immoderate craving for ardent spirits, was said to have offered her *own child for sale as a subject for dissection !*

BOOK OF AMOS.

Cruel and Pitiless.

Chap. i. ver. 11.—He did cast off all pity.

"BONAPARTE," says Sir Robert Wilson, "having carried the town of Jaffa by assault, many of the garrison were put to the sword, but the greater part flying into the Mosques, and imploring mercy from their pursuers, were granted their lives. Three days afterwards, Bonaparte, who had expressed much resentment at the compassion manifested by his troops, and determined to relieve himself from the maintenance and care of 3800 prisoners, ordered them to be marched to a rising ground near Jaffa, where a division of French Infantry formed against them. When the Turks had entered into their fatal alignment, and the mournful preparations were completed, the signal gun fired. Volleys of musquetry and grape instantly played against them, and Bonaparte, who had been regarding the scene through a telescope, when he saw the smoke ascending, could not contain his joy."

Wine Drinking.

Chap. ii. ver. 12.—Ye gave the Nazarites wine to drink.

IN a village within ten miles of Elgin, a transaction occurred which it is impossible to condemn in sufficiently strong language. A man called on a publican in this village, in order to settle an account, and was asked to take a dram; this was declined by the man on account of being a member of the Temperance Society. The publican first began to ridicule and then to tempt him; telling him, that he would give him a *real good one*, and that, besides, a *gien dram* would never be objected to. The simple man at length yielded to the tempter, and having yielded, was the more ready to sink before other even less powerful temptations; he did so, and is no longer a temperate man, or a member of a Temperance Society. It may be observed, that the *mere circumstance* of being a member of the Temperance Society, will not, and cannot be expected to enable a man to resist temptation, otherwise than as a lawful means under God; unless, therefore, we ask for his assistance, our best resolutions will be insufficient to secure our safety. The atrocious conduct of this publican consisted in tempting the man, after he was made aware of his conscientious reasons for total abstinence. If his unhappy victim die the death of the drunkard, who will say, he is guiltless of the loss of that man's soul?

The Lion.

Chap. iii. ver. 8.—The lion hath roared, who will not fear?

A LION having escaped from the menagerie of the great Duke of Tuscany, entered Florence, everywhere spreading terror. Among the fugitives was a woman with a child in her arms, which she let fall. He seized, and seemed ready to devour it, when the mother, transported with the tender affections of nature, ran back, threw herself before the lion, and by her gestures demanded the child. The lion looked at her stedfastly, her cries and tears seemed to affect him, till at last he laid down the child without doing it the least injury.

Prepared to meet God.

Chap. iv. ver. 12.—Prepare to meet thy God, O Israel.

THE late Rev. Mr. Madan was educated for the bar. His conversion arose from the following circumstance:—He was desired one evening, by some of his companions who were with him at a coffee-house, to go and hear Mr. John Wesley, who they were told was to preach in the neighbourhood, and to return and exhibit his *manners and discourse* for their entertainment. He went with that intention, and just as he entered the place, Mr. Wesley named as his text, "Prepare to meet thy God," with a solemnity of accent which struck him, and which inspired a seriousness that increased as the good man proceeded in exhorting his hearers to repentance. Mr. M. returned to the coffee-room, and was asked by his acquaintance, "if he had taken off the old Methodist?" To which he answered, "No, gentlemen, but he has taken me off;" and from that time he left their company altogether, and in future associated with serious people, and became a serious character.

Believe and Live.

Chap. v. ver. 6.—Seek the Lord, and ye shall live.

"I MUST never," says the Rev. George Burder, "forget my birthday, June 5th, 1762. It was on a Sabbath; and after tea, and before family worship, my father was accustomed to catechise me, and examine what I remembered of the sermons of the day. That evening he talked to me very affectionately, and reminded me that I was now ten years of age; that it was high time I began to seek the Lord, and to become truly religious. He particularly insisted upon the necessity of an interest in Christ, and showed me that, as a sinner, I must perish without it, and recommended me to begin that night to pray for it. After family worship, when my father and mother used to retire to their closets for private devotion, I also went into a chamber, the same room in which I was born, and then, I trust, sincerely and earnestly, and as far as I can recollect, for the first time, I poured out my soul to God, beseeching him to give me an interest in Christ, and desiring, above all things, to be found in him. Reflecting on this evening, I have often been ready to conclude, that surely I was born of God at that time, surely I then was brought to believe in Christ, surely there was something more than nature in all this."

Ill-timed Levity.

Chap. vi. ver. 5, 6.—That chant to the sound of the viol, and invent to themselves instruments of music, like David; that drink wine in bowls, and anoint themselves with the chief ointments; but they are not grieved for the affliction of Joseph.

THE tragical scenes which came under Mr Fisk's observation while in Greece, had become so common, that they began to be regarded with indifference by many classes of people. Parties of pleasure and vain amusements were revived and engaged in, as though all were peace. Thousands had fled for their lives, and the streets of Smyrna were crimsoned with Grecian blood. It was estimated that 2000 had been massacred, and heavy exactions of money were demanded from others for the privilege of living. The bodies of the slain were seen frequently floating in the bay. In a word, exactions, imprisonment, or death, met the defenceless Greeks in every direction;—and yet, strange to tell, multitudes, only because they were better protected from Turkish violence, went thoughtlessly to the assembly room and the dance, as though all were peace and security. While the countenance of many gathered blackness through fear, that of others exhibited only the expression of a thoughtless, ill-timed levity.

Powerful Words.

Chap. vii. ver. 10.—Amaziah, the priest of Beth-el, sent to Jeroboam king of Israel, saying, Amos hath conspired against thee in the midst of the house of Israel; the land is not able to bear all his words.

BISHOP LATIMER, in preaching before King Henry the Eighth, spoke his mind very plainly; which some of his enemies thought to make their advantage of, by complaining of him to the king, that they might thus get him out of the way. Soon after his sermon, he and several others being called before the king to speak their minds on certain matters, one of them kneeled before his majesty, and accused Latimer of having preached seditious doctrines. The king turned to Latimer, and said, "What say you to that, Sir?" Latimer kneeled down, and turning first to his accuser, said, "What form of preaching would you appoint me to preach before a king? would you have me to preach nothing concerning a king in a king's sermon? Have you any commission to appoint me what I shall preach?" He asked him several other questions, but he would answer none at all; nor had he anything to say. Then he turned to the king, and said, "I never thought myself worthy, nor ever sued, to be a preacher before your Grace. But I was called to it: and would be willing, if you mislike me, to give place to my betters. But if your Grace allow me for a preacher, I would desire your Grace to discharge my conscience, give me leave to frame my discourse according to mine audience. I had been a very dolt to have preached so at the borders of your realm, as I preach before your Grace." These words were well received by the king as Latimer concluded, because the king presently turned to another subject. Some of his friends came to him with tears in their eyes, and told him, they looked for nothing but that he should have been sent to the Tower the same night.

Seeking the Scriptures.

Chap. viii. ver. 12.—They shall wander from sea to sea, and from the north even to the east; they shall run to and fro to seek the word of the Lord, and shall not find it.

MR. HENDERSON, in his Journal, says, "In the east of Iceland I fell in with a clergyman, who has been seeking in vain to obtain a Bible for the long period of seventeen years! His joy on my arrival was inexpressible. I passed through a parish lately, in which were only *two* Bibles, and another considerably more populous, in which there are *none at all!*"

Sea Serpents.

Chap. ix. ver. 3.—Though they be hid from my sight in the bottom of the sea, thence will I command the serpent, and he shall bite them.

IN the year 1807, a stout young fisherman in the neighbourhood of Culcutta, in the East Indies, was bit on the point of the middle finger of his right hand by a sea snake, which had been entangled in his net, and considering it harmless, he threw it into the sea, and thought nothing of the bite. About an hour afterwards, he complained of a slight pain in the bitten finger, which extended along the inside of the right arm. The pain increased, he felt giddiness, attended with weakness in the loins and legs, which was followed with violent spasms, and early in the morning he died in convulsions.

BOOK OF OBADIAH.

Robbers by Night.

Ver. 5.—If thieves came to thee, if robbers by night, would they not have stolen till they had enough?

AT an assizes held at York, J. Fourniss and G. Wilkinson were tried for a burglary in the house of George Holroyd, a clothier, at Hartshead. These villains having entered the house, came to the bedside of Holroyd, about one in the morning, demanding his money, and repeatedly threatening to kill him if he refused to discover it. It happened that Holroyd had only a single sixpence in the house, as he solemnly assured them; but not believing him, they persevered in the threatening to kill him, with a case-knife, which Fourniss held in his hand. Holroyd then begged they would let him pray before he died. Wilkinson consented, saying, "Let him pray." He did so for a few minutes; after which Wilkinson seemed to relent; for when the other said, "He will not show us where his money is : we must kill him!" Wilkinson said, "No; we will not kill him."—Soon after which both left the house, taking with them some bacon, butter, and eggs. The jury found the prisoners *guilty;* but recommended Wilkinson to mercy, on account of the compassion he discovered.—Such was the good effect of prayer even upon a thief.

BOOK OF JONAH.

Asleep amidst Danger.

Chap. i. ver. 5, 6.—Jonah was gone down into the sides of the ship; and he lay, and was fast asleep. So the shipmaster came to him, and said unto him, What meanest thou, O sleeper? arise, call upon thy God.

TWO or three miles above the falls of Niagara, an Indian canoe was one day observed floating quietly along, with its paddle upon its side. At first it was supposed to be empty ; no one could imagine that a man would expose himself to such well known and imminent danger. But a turn in the current soon gave the travellers a sight of an Indian lying idly asleep at the bottom. They were shocked, and called aloud, but he did not hear; they shouted in an agony of pity and alarm ; but he was deaf to their saving cry. It chanced that the current, which was now hurrying along with increased speed as it neared the fatal precipice, drove the little boat against a point of rock with such violence, that it was whirled round and round several times. He's safe ! He's safe ! cried the spectators, joyfully ; the man is safe; that shock must wake him. But, alas! no. Fatigue, or drunkenness, (to which savages are particularly addicted) had so oppressed his senses, that it seemed more like death than sleep which held him; it was indeed the sleep of death. All hope was gone, and they hurried along the shore in alarm to see the end. It soon came, for the torrent was now rolling so rapidly, that they could scarce keep pace with the object of their interest. At length the roar of the water, which had been hitherto almost buried within the high banks below, by a sudden change of the wind broke upon them with double violence. This dreadful noise, with which the Indian ear was so familiar, did at last arouse him. He was seen to start up and snatch his paddle. But it was too late; the same dunning sound which had roused him from insensibility, told him at the same time, that it was in vain to seek for safety now by rowing; nor, indeed, had he time to try; upright as he stood, he went over the awful precipice, and the boat and its occupant were seen no more.

Encompassed by the Waters.

Chap. ii. ver. 5.—The waters compassed me about, even to the soul: the depth closed me round about.

"I ONCE," says Dr Currie of Liverpool, "heard—for it was night, and I could not see—a traveller drowning, not in the Annan, but in the Firth of Solway, close by the mouth of that river. The influx of the tide had unhorsed him in the night as he was passing the sands from Cumberland. The west wind blew a tempest; and according to the common expression, brought in the water three feet abreast. The traveller got upon a standing net a little way from the shore. There he lashed himself to the post, shouting for half-an-hour for assistance, till the tide rose over his head! In the darkness of the night, and amidst the pauses of the hurricane, his voice, heard at intervals, was exquisitely mournful. No one could go to his assistance—no one knew where he was—the sound seemed to proceed from the spirit of the waters. But morning rose—the tide had ebbed—and the poor traveller was found lashed to the pole of the net, and bleaching to the wind."

Wise Preaching.

Chap. iii. ver. 2.—Preach unto Nineveh the preaching that I bid thee.

A CELEBRATED preacher, now deceased, in a charge which he delivered to a young minister at his ordination, thus addressed him:—"Let me remind you, Sir, that when you come into this place, and address this people, you are not to bring your *little self* with you. I repeat this again, Sir, that it may more deeply impress your memory: I say, that you are never to bring your *little self* with you. No, Sir, when you stand in this sacred place, it is your duty to hold up your GREAT MASTER to your people, in his character, in his offices, in his precepts, in his promises, and in his glory. This picture you are to hold up to the view of your hearers, while you are to stand behind it, and not let so much as your little finger be seen."

Giving way to Passion.

Chap. iv. ver. 9.—I do well to be angry, even unto death.

"I WAS lately taking a journey from home," says one, "and happened one day to be drinking tea with a clergyman, who said that he had just had a very awful death in his parish. I thought it was some drunkard, or swearer, or Sabbath-breaker, who had perhaps been cut off in his sins; and I never for a moment supposed that it could be a little child. But how was I shocked when he told me the story! A very little child, about three years old, had its naughty will crossed by its mother, and flew into a violent passion. She screamed and cried, and stamped with her feet on the ground, and was like a mad creature with rage. And oh! (dreadful to relate) it pleased God to strike her dead in the midst of her passion. Whether she broke a blood-vessel with her rage, or how it was, I do not know; but she died in the midst of her sins, and is gone to the world of spirits."

BOOK OF MICAH.

Wailing in the Streets.

Chap. i. ver. 8.—I will wail and howl;—I will make a wailing like the dragons, and mourning as the owls.

"WHILE I was at Saphetta," (in Galilee,) says Biddulph, the chaplain to the English factory at Aleppo, in the reign of Queen Elizabeth, "many Turks departed from thence towards Mecca in Arabia. And the same morning they went, we saw many women playing with timbrels as they went along the streets, who made a yelling, or shrieking noise, as if they cried. We asked what they meant in so doing? It was answered us, that they mourned for the departure of their husbands, who were gone that morning on pilgrimage to Mecca; and they feared that they should never see them again, because it was a long way and dangerous, and many died there every year. It seemed strange to us that they should mourn with music about the streets; for music is used in other places at times of mirth, and not at times of mourning."

Warning against Strong Drink,

Chap. ii. ver. 11.—I will prophesy unto thee of wine and strong drink.

THE following is Sir Astley Cooper's opinion of dram-drinking, in answer to an application by the secretary of the Temperance Society, for his support and patronage.

"My dear Sir,—No person has greater hostility to dram-drinking than myself, insomuch that I never suffer any ardent spirits in my house, thinking them EVIL SPIRITS. And if the poor could witness the white livers, the dropsies, and the shattered nervous systems which I have seen, as the consequence of drinking, they would be aware that SPIRITS and POISONS were synonymous terms. But still I think the scheme so Utopian, that I cannot annex my name to it; for I could as soon believe that I could, by my own efforts, stop the cataract of Niagara, as prevent the poor of London from destroying themselves by intemperance."

Preaching of Transgression and Sin.

Chap. iii. ver. 8.—Truly I am full of power by the Spirit of the Lord, and of judgment, and of might, to declare unto Jacob his transgression, and to Israel his sin.

THE biographer of Mr Legh Richmond one day submitted to him the following question:—"What is the scriptural and right way to preach to the Jews?"—"I know of no scriptural way," he replied, "of preaching to men, otherwise than as *sinners;* and why the Jews, whose sins are of so aggravated a nature, should be dealt with *in a different way,* I do not see. I would address the Jew as I would address any other man;—that is, *as a sinner;* and till he is convinced of his sin, he will never believe in a Saviour. 'Christ crucified,' is declared to be 'to the Greeks foolishness, and to the Jews a stumblingblock; but to them that believe, the power of God and the wisdom of God.' No man will ever feel the power of God, whether he be Jew or Gentile, till he learns it at the foot of the cross."

Everlasting Peace.

Chap. iv. ver. 3.—They shall beat their swords into ploughshares, and their spears into pruning-hooks; nation shall not lift up a sword against nation, neither shall they learn war any more.

"I HAVE been labouring," says the Rev. Mr Ellis, in a speech at the anniversary of the Naval and Military Bible Society, "among a people who once delighted in war, but since Christianity has prevailed, there war has ceased altogether; and they are astonished how they ever engaged in all those deeds of savage cruelty, which, according to their usual practice, threatened the extermination of their race; but now the Prince of Peace reigns there. I have seen the musket barrel taken from the stock and carried to the anvil, and beaten into a spade or hoe, though not into a ploughshare, for the plough does not yet turn up their fruitful soil; and the warrior who has used it in battle, now employs it in cultivating the land. They have even gone further in illustration of this beautiful description of the prophet, for they have devoted the implements of war to the service of the sanctuary! The last Sabbath I was there, I went into one their chapels, and ministered to a large congregation of about fifteen hundred persons. A rude sort of pulpit was erected, and the stairs led up to it, the railings of which, smooth and polished, were literally composed of the handles of warriors' spears, who had thus transferred their weapons with themselves to a nobler and better purpose—the service of the sanctuary of God!"

No More Witchcraft.

Chap. v. ver. 12.—I will cut off witchcrafts out of thine hand; and thou shalt have no more soothsayers.

ON two estates in the Island of Lequan, in the West Indies, the plan of appointing catechists for the purpose of reading the Scriptures to the negroes at weekly meetings, has been adopted, and the benefit resulting from it on one of them is thus described by a correspondent:—"A manager of these estates informed me, that the negroes do three times the work they formerly did, and are quite cheerful and happy. I was first requested to visit this estate by the proprietor, on account of the prevalence of Obiah or Witchcraft, which rendered the negroes wretched, and had been the death of some, from its miserable influence upon their minds. But the truths of the Bible banished this from the estate; and I will venture to say, that while the Bible remains in their hands, and the love of it in their hearts, no Obiah will be found among them."

In the Presence of God.

Chap. vi. ver. 6.—Wherewith shall I come before the Lord, and bow myself before the high God?

MR WEIR, a minister, having been visited by a young candidate for the ministry, one Sabbath day, invited him to preach. The young gentleman consented, and delivered an ingenious sermon, though his prayer was very orthodox. When the service was over, Mr Weir thanked him for his kindness, praised him for his ingenuity, but told him, that, as they did not agree in sentiment, he could not invite him to preach again; but, he continued, "I have a favour to ask you: When you go home, will you sit down and write a prayer, to agree with the sentiments you have this day been preaching?—will you commit it to memory, go into your closet, and repeat it to God?" The young man promised to do it. Accordingly, when he went home, he wrote the prayer, committed it to memory, went into his closet, and attempted to repeat it; but found through the power of conscience, that he could not.—A few years afterwards he called on Mr Weir, who soon recollected him, and received him very cordially. The young gentleman offered to preach for him, and Mr Weir, with some reluctance consenting, he went into the pulpit, and, to the surprise of Mr Weir, delivered a sound, sensible sermon. The preacher being asked why he had altered his sentiments, he related the circumstances of Mr Weir's request, and added, that, being greatly agitated, as well as surprised, he had carefully examined his sentiments, and reasoned thus with himself:—"Can it be proper for me to *preach* to a congregation what I cannot offer up in *prayer* to God?"

Mine Enemy.

Chap. vii. ver. 10.—Then she that is mine enemy, shall see it, and shame shall cover her which said unto me, Where is the Lord thy God? mine eyes shall behold her: now shall she be trodden down as the mire of the streets.

WHEN Dr. Dodd, who suffered for forgery in 1777, was led to the place of execution, several of the populace seemed to exult at the condemnation of the dignified ecclesiastic; and a woman reproachfully called out to him, "Where is now thy God?" He instantly referred her to the seventh chapter of Micah, 7—10. "Therefore I will look unto the Lord; I will wait for the God of my salvation: my God will hear me. Rejoice not against me, O mine enemy: when I fall, I shall arise; when I sit in darkness, the Lord shall be a light unto me. I will bear the indignation of the Lord, because I have sinned against him, until he plead my cause, and execute judgment for me; he will bring me forth to the light, and I shall behold his righteousness. Then she that is mine enemy shall see it, and shame shall cover her which said unto me, Where is the Lord thy God? mine eyes shall behold her: now shall she be trodden down as the mire of the streets." The wretched woman, proceeding to witness the execution, was thrown down in the pressure of the throng, and literally trodden to death!

BOOK OF NAHUM.

Drink and Death.

Chap. i. ver. 10.—While they are drunken as drunkards, they shall be devoured as stubble fully dry.

THREE Warsaw butchers went to a tippling-house, abandoned themselves to every sort of excess, and drank till they were so intoxicated that they were carried home senseless. A few hours had scarcely elapsed, when the miserable men were seized with all the symptoms of cholera, which advanced with such rapidity, as to prove fatal to the whole three within four hours.

The Lion.

Chap. ii. ver. 11.—Where is the dwelling of the lions, and the feeding of the young lions?

IN the beginning of March, 1810, five horsemen, stationed at a village near Hansi, having heard that a pig had been carried away by a tiger, went to the spot on foot, when they found a lion and lioness feeding upon it. The latter, on a patch of grass being set on fire, went off; but the former advanced slowly, with his main and tail erect; when the men fired with so good an effect, as induced them to go up and destroy him with their swords, which was accomplished after one man had been severely wounded. The animal appeared to be a full grown lion, in most respects like the African one. A lioness, a few days previous, had been sent in from Hissan, having been killed by a party of horsemen. These facts prove, contrary to the general opinion, that lions are to be found in India as well as Africa.

The Battle Field.

Chap. iii. ver. 3.—The horseman lifteth up the bright sword and the glittering spear: and there is a multitude of slain

AS Napoleon Bonaparte once passed over a field of battle in Italy, with some of his generals, he saw a houseless dog lying on the slain body of his master. The creature came towards them, then returned to the dead body, moaned over it pitifully, and seemed to ask their assistance. "Whether it were the feeling of the moment," continued Napoleon, "the scene, the hour, or the circumstance itself, I was never so deeply affected by any thing which I have seen upon a field of battle. That man, I thought, has, perhaps, had a house, friends, comrades, and here lies deserted by every one but his DOG! How mysterious are the impressions to which we are subject. I was in the habit, without emotion, of ordering battles, which must decide the fate of a campaign, and could look with a dry eye on the execution of manœuvres, which must be attended with much loss; and here I was moved—nay, painfully affected—by the cries and the grief of a dog. It is certain, that at that moment, I should have been more accessible to a suppliant enemy, and could better understand the conduct of Achilles, in restoring the body of Hector to the tears of Priam."

BOOK OF HABAKKUK.

Strange Worship.

Chap. i. ver. 16.—They sacrifice unto their net, and burn incense unto their drag.

A BLACKSMITH, who had been employed one day on the Mission premises in India, fetched away his tools next morning for the purpose of worshipping them, it being the day on which the Hindoos pay divine honours to the implements of their various trades : the files and hammers of the smiths, the chisels and saws of the carpenter, the diamond of the glazier, the crucible of the goldsmith, &c &c., all become idols on this anniversary.

The Just.

Chap. ii. ver. 4.—The just shall live by his faith.

TWO men of learning were conversing with each other respecting the method they should take in reference to a certain regulation imposed upom them by the higher powers, and to which they had conscientious scruples. One of them impiously swore, "By my faith I shall live." The other calmly and pleasantly replied, "I hope to live by my faith too, though I do not swear by it." The result was, that the man who resolved by grace to venture his temporal interest for conscience sake, lived in prosperity to see the other begging, and to contribute to his relief.

Rejoicing in God.

Chap. iii. ver. 17, 18.—Although the fig-tree shall not blossom, neither shall fruit be in the vines ; the labour of the olive shall fail, and the fields shall yield no meat ; the flock shall be cut off from the fold, and there shall be no herd in the stalls ; yet I will rejoice in the Lord, I will joy in the God of my salvation.

TWO religious persons lived in one place, who had been intimately acquainted in early life. Providence favoured one of them with a tide of prosperity. The other, fearing for his friend, lest his heart should be overcharged with the cares of this life, and the deceitfulness of riches, one day asked him whether he did not find prosperity a snare to him. He paused, and answered, "I am not conscious that I do, for I enjoy God in all things." Some years after, his affairs took another turn. He lost, if not the whole, yet the far greater part of what he had once gained, and was greatly reduced. His old friend being one day in his company, renewed his question, whether he did not find what had lately befallen him to be too much for him. Again he paused, and answered, "I am not conscious that I do, for now I enjoy all things in God."

BOOK OF ZEPHANIAH.

Neglect of Privilege.

Chap. i. ver. 6.—Those that have not sought the Lord, nor enquired for him.

ONE evening, a lady and her little daughter attended a religious meeting, and while the minister was speaking of the neglect of family duties, of reading the Scriptures, and of family prayer, the little daughter, who listened attentively, and perceived that the preacher was describing a neglect that she had witnessed herself, whispered to her mother this question—" Ma, is Mr Jones talking to you?" This was powerful preaching to the mother; she was immediately brought under deep convictions, which resulted in her hopeful conversion.

Singing of Birds.

Chap. ii. ver. 14.—Their voice shall sing in the windows.

"I FOUND also in this place," says Le Bruyn, in describing the ruins of Persepolis, "besides the birds I have already mentioned, four or five sorts of small birds, who keep constantly in these ruins and the adjoining mountain, and which make the most agreeable warbling in the world. The singing of the largest approaches very near to that of the nightingale. Some of them are almost all black; others have the head and body spotted, of the size of a swallow; others are smaller, and of different colours, yellowish, grey, and quite white, shaped like a chaffinch."

Trusting in God.

Chap. iii. ver. 12.—I will also leave in the midst of thee an afflicted and poor people, and they shall trust in the name of the Lord.

THE Rev. Oliver Heywood's pecuniary circumstances were sometimes very trying, but the special interpositions of Providence were not less remarkable. "While I was musing," says he, "and pondering how to get my rent discharged, and had no way, at this time, but to borrow it, there came a dear friend to me, and brought me five pounds, which did furnish me with an overplus besides my rent. It was a seasonable present, sent to me by a liberal hand; yet I own God chiefly in it, who cares for me, as in this, and several other experiences, is evident. O what a sweet thing is the life of faith! That is a perfumed gift, which thus comes from God as a token of love, after the actings of faith in prayer. How good is God to me! I live nobly, and am so far from wanting, that I have all and abound; and where supplies fail one way, God makes them up in another."

BOOK OF HAGGAI.

Unthankful Withholding.

Chap. i. ver. 9.—Ye looked for much, and lo, it came to little; and when ye brought it home, I did blow upon it. Why? saith the Lord of hosts. Because of mine house that is waste, and ye run every man unto his own house.

SOME years ago, a poor boy came to town in search of a situation as errand boy; he made many unsuccessful applications, and was on the eve of returning to his parents, when a gentleman, being prepossessed by his appearance, took him into his employment, and after a few months, bound him apprentice. He so conducted himself during his apprenticeship, as to gain the love and esteem of every one who knew him; and after he had served his time his master advanced a capital for him to commence business. He retired to his closet with a heart glowing with gratitude to his Maker for his goodness, and then solemnly vowed that he would devote a tenth part of his annual income to the service of God. The first year his donation amounted to ten pounds, which he gave cheerfully, and continued to do so until it amounted to £500; he then thought that was *a great deal of money to give*, and that he need not be *so particular* as to the exact amount. That year he lost a ship and cargo to the value of £15,000 by a storm! This caused him to repent, and he again commenced his contributions, with a resolution never to retract; he was more successful every year, and at length retired. He then devoted a tenth part of his annual income for some years, till he became acquainted with *men of the world*, who by degrees drew him aside from God: he discontinued his donations, made large speculations, *lost every thing*, and became almost as poor as when he came to town as an errand boy!

Blessed in Giving.

Chap. ii. ver. 18, 19.—From the day that the foundation of the Lord's temple was laid, consider it—from this day will I bless you.

"SOME years ago," says one, "I recollect reading a striking sermon by the late Mr. Simpson of Macclesfield; the subject, I think, was Christian liberality; but what most forcibly struck my mind, was a passage quoted from Malachi iii. 10. 'Bring ye all the tithes into the store house,' &c. I cannot describe how my mind was impressed with the manner in which Jehovah here condescended to challenge his people, when he says, 'And prove me now herewith,' &c. Suffice it to say, that the subject made such an impression, I found it my duty to do more for the cause of God than I ever had done. I did so, and on closing that year accounts, I found that I had gained more than in any two years preceding it. Some time afterwards, I thought the Redeemer's cause had an additional claim, as the place in which we worshipped him wanted some repairs. The sum I then gave was £20; and in a very little time afterwards I received £40, which I had long given up as lost."

BOOK OF ZECHARIAH.

Life is Short.

Chap. i. ver. 5.—Your fathers, where are they? and the prophets do they live for ever?

"WE need no reed," say Mr. Matthew Henry, "no pole, no measuring line, wherewith to take the dimensions of our days, nor any skill in arithmetic, wherewith to compute the number of them. No; we have the standard of them at our fingers' end; and there is no multiplication of it; it is but one *hand-breadth* in all."

Conversion of the Nations.

Chap. ii. ver. 11.—Many nations shall be joined to the Lord in that day, and shall be my people.

"IN the year 1813," says Mr. Campbell, "after having visited several nations in the interior of Africa, beyond the colony of the Cape of Good Hope, when returning, I halted at the town of Paarl, within thirty-six miles of Cape Town; here I was requested by friends to relate publicly the state of the nations in the interior of Africa. About one hundred free persons, with some slaves, attended. At the close, several hundred rix-dollars were contributed by the white friends present for the Missionary Society. After the whites had all left the house, a slave woman and her daughter called upon me, and said, 'Sir, will you take anything from a poor slave, to help to send the gospel to *the poor things beyond us?*' On my saying, 'Most certainly I will,' she gave me eightpence, and her daughter fourpence. Having done so, they hastily went out clapping their hands, and ran to some slave men who were waiting to hear the result. On hearing from her that I cheerfully took subscriptions from slaves, they rushed into my room, and every one threw down all that they had, to send the gospel to *the poor things beyond them!*"

Neighbours.

Chap. iii. ver. 10.—Ye shall call every man his neighbour under the vine, and under the fig-tree.

DR. RICHARD CHANDLER, in his Travels in Asia Minor, informs us, "that a Greek at Philadelphia sent them a small earthen vessel full of choice wine; and that some families, who were sitting beneath some trees, by a rill of water, invited them to alight and partake of their refreshments. The taking their repasts thus in public expressed safety and pleasure; and the calling to passengers to partake with them, a spirit of friendliness and generosity."

Religion Elevates.

Chap. iv. ver. 6.—Not by might, nor by power, but by my Spirit, saith the Lord of Hosts.

"I AM by birth," said a converted Hindoo, when addressing a number of his countrymen, "of an insignificant and contemptible caste; so low, that if a Brahim should chance to touch me, he must go and bathe in the Ganges for the purpose of purification; and yet God has been pleased to call me, not merely to the knowledge of the gospel, but to the high office of teaching it to others. My friends do you know the reason of God's conduct? It is this: if God had selected one of your learned Brahmins, and made you the preacher, when you were successful in making converts, by-standers would have said it was the amazing learning of the Brahmin, and his great weight of character, that were the cause; but now, when any one is convinced by my instrumentality, no one thinks of ascribing any of the praise to me; and God, as is his due, has all the glory."

Profane Swearing.

Chap. v. ver. 3.—Every one that sweareth shall be cut off as on that side.

THREE soldiers passing through a wood, a storm of thunder and lightning came on. One of the soldiers to show his contempt of God and his judgments, began to swear, when a large tree, torn up by the fury of the tempest, fell upon him and crushed him to pieces.

Prophecy Regarding Christ.

Chap. vi. ver. 13.—He shall build the temple of the Lord; and he shall bear the glory, and shall sit and rule upon his throne; and he shall be a priest upon his throne; and the counsel of peace shall be between them both.

"IN the afternoon," says Toplady, in his Diary, "called on William Perry of Southertown. Our discourse happened to take a serious turn. Among other subjects, we spoke concerning the divinity of the ever-blessed Son of God. I could scarce help smiling, at the same time that I heartily applauded the honest zeal of my well-meaning parishioner :—'Let any man,' said he, 'but search the Scriptures, and if he does not find that Christ, as a divine person, subsisted, not only previous to his birth of the Virgin Mary, but from everlasting, I will lose my head.' This brought to my mind that just observation of the late excellent Mr. Hervey, who, speaking of Christ's atonement, says, 'Ask any of your serious tenants, what ideas arise in their minds upon a perusal of the fore-mentioned texts? I dare venture that, artless and unimproved as their understandings are, they will not hesitate for an answer. They will neither complain of obscurity, nor ask the assistance of learning, but will immediately discern, in all these passages, a gracious Redeemer suffering in their stead; and by his bitter but expiatory passion, procuring the pardon of their sins. Nay, farther, as they are not accustomed to the finesse of criticism, I apprehend they will be at a loss to conceive how it is possible to understand such passages in any other sense.'"

Hardened Hearts.

Chap. vii. ver. 12.—They made their hearts as an adamant-stone, lest they should hear the law, and the words which the Lord of hosts hath sent in his Spirit by the former prophets.

BISHOP MASSILLON, in the first sermon he ever preached, found the whole audience, upon his getting into the pulpit, in a disposition no way favourable to his intentions. Their nods, whispers, or drowsy behaviour, showed him that there was no great profit to be expected from his sowing in a soil so improper. However, he soon changed the disposition of his audience by his manner of beginning. "If," says he, "a cause, the most important that could be conceived, were to be tried at the bar, before qualified judges; if this cause interested ourselves in particular; if the eyes of the whole kingdom were fixed upon the events; if the most eminent counsel were employed on both sides; and if we had heard from our infancy of this yet undetermined trial,—would you not all sit with due attention, and warm expectation, to the pleadings on each side? Would not all your hopes and fears be hinged on the final decision? And yet, let me tell you, you have this moment a cause, where not one nation, but all the world are spectators; tried not before a fallible tribunal, but the awful throne of heaven, where not your temporal and transitory interests are the subject of debate, but your eternal happiness or misery; where the cause is still undetermined, but, perhaps, the very moment I am speaking may fix the irrevocable decree that shall last for ever; and yet, notwithstanding all this, you can hardly sit with patience to hear the tidings of your own salvation. I plead the cause of heaven, and yet I am scarcely attended to."

Truthfulness.

Chap. viii. ver. 16.—Speak ye every man, the truth to his neighbour.

"SOME time ago," says a teacher, "I called upon the mother of one of my scholars, to inqure the reason of her son's absence from school: she told me that he had lately got a situation, and promised that he should attend more regularly in future. She was acquainted with the parents of another of my scholars, and as we were conversing about her own boy, she said that she hoped he would be as good a boy as his school-fellow was; for, added she, 'his mother had told me that she never knew him *tell a lie in his life.*' I knew the master and mistress with whom this same boy went to live, and they told me, that though he was not quite so active as they could wish, yet they liked him for one thing particularly, which was, *he always told the truth;* even when he had done anything amiss, he never tried to conceal it by telling a falsehood."

Extension of Christ's Kingdom.

Chap. ix. ver. 10.—He shall speak peace unto the heathen; and his dominion shall be from sea even unto sea, and from the river even to the ends of the earth.

THE late Mr John Croumbie of Haddington, some time before his death, calling on one of his customers, his friend said unto him, "I am sure, Mr Croumbie, you need not care for business." He replied, "It is true, Mrs Barr, but if I were to give over business, I would not be so able to assist the various societies that are formed for diffusing the knowledge of the gospel through the world." The same excellent person, in his last illness, after expressing his surprise that some Christians kept back from the support of these excellent institutions, said, with peculiar emphasis, "O how I pity the poor heathen, who have nothing to support their minds in the *prospect of eternity!*" His feelings were evidently excited by his own situation, and a conviction of the misery he would feel, if his mind had not been supported by the gospel in the near prospect of entering into an eternal state.

Fortune-Tellers Converted.

Chap. x. ver. 2.—The diviners have seen a lie.

A REFORMED gipsy, making a visit to a parish in which one of her children was born, near Basingstoke, entered the cottage of an old couple who sold fruit, &c. Tea being proposed, the old woman expressed her surprise that she had not seen her visitor for so long a time, saying she was glad she was come, as she wanted to tell her many things, meaning future events. She mentioned a great deal that another gipsy woman had told her; on which the reformed one exclaimed—"Don't believe her, dame. It is all lies. She knows no more about it than you do. If you trust to what she says, you will be deceived." The old woman was still more surprised, and asked *how she*, who had so often told their fortunes, and had promised them such good luck, could be so much altered? The woman, taking her Testament from her bosom, replied, "I have learned from this blessed book, and from my kind friends, 'that all liars shall have their portion in the lake that burneth with brimstone and fire;' and rather than tell fortunes again, I would starve."

Cut off Suddenly.

Chap. xi. ver. 8.—Three shepherds also I cut off in one month.

A CLERGYMAN was spending an evening—not in his closet, wrestling with God in prayer—not in his study, searching the Scriptures, and meditating on divine truth, with the view of being prepared for public usefulness—nor in pastoral visits to the flock under his care—but at the card-table! He left the room for a few moments, desiring his wife to deal his cards till his return. This she had done, but he did not come back. The cards waited, the conversation was kept up, still he returned not. At length, surprised at his absence, his wife withdrew to seek him. She found him in his chamber a lifeless corpse! It is observable, that within a very few years, this was the third character (clerical, it is presumed,) in the same neighbourhood, who had been suddenly taken from the pleasures of a card-table to the bar of God!

The Spirit of Man.

Chap. xii. ver. 1.—The Lord—which formeth the spirit of man within him.

"AT a catechising of one of the schools," says a missionary in India, "a Brahmin interrupted us by saying that *the spirit of man and the Spirit of God were one.* In order to show him the absurdity of such a declaration, we called upon the boys to refute it, by telling us the difference between the spirit of man and God. They readily gave the following answer :—'The spirit of man is created—God is its Creator: the spirit of man is full of sin—God is a pure Spirit: the spirit of man is subject to grief—God is infinitely blessed, and incapable of suffering: these two spirits, therefore,' replied the boys, '*can never be one.*'"

Being Chastened.

Chap. xiii. ver 9.—I will bring the third part through the fire, and will refine them as silver is refined.

SARAH HOWARD, a poor old widow, who had been bedridden fourteen years, when visited by her minister, thus spoke of her afflictions :—"I can set to my seal that the Lord has chastened me sore, but he hath not given me over unto death. I have been chastened in my person, and am quite helpless, by long and severe illness; I have been chastened in my circumstances ever since I was left a widow: yes, I know what oppressing a widow, what bad debts and hard creditors are: I have been chastened in my family, by a son, whom I was doatingly fond of, running away and going to sea. Besides all these, I have been chastened in mind, 'walking in darkness and having no light:' yet, after all, I trust I can say with David, 'Before I was afflicted I went astray, but now I have kept thy word.' And I hope I can say that I am now returned to the Shepherd and Bishop of souls."

The Triumphant End.

Chap. xiv. ver. 7.—At evening time it shall be light.

MR ROBERT GLOVER, one of the English martyrs, a little before his death, had lost the sense of God's favour, which occasioned great heaviness and grief; but when he came within sight of the stake at which he was to suffer, he experienced such abundant comfort and heavenly joy, that, clapping his hands together, he cried out, "He is come, he is come!" and died triumphantly.

BOOK OF MALACHI.

Unseemly Weariness.

Chap. i. ver. 13.—Ye said also, Behold, what a weariness is it!

ONE Sabbath morning, a minister in Wakefield had not proceeded far in his discourse, when he observed an individual in a pew just before him rise from his seat, and turn round to look at the clock in the front of the gallery, as if the service were a weariness to him. The unseemly act called forth the following rebuke :—" A remarkable change," said the speaker, " has taken place among the people of this country in regard to the public service of religion. Our forefathers put their clocks on the outside of their places of worship, that they might not be too late in their attendance. We have transferred them to the inside of the house of God, lest we should stay too long in the service. A sad and an ominous change!"

The Wife.

Chap. ii. ver. 14.—The Lord hath been witness between thee and the wife of thy youth, against whom thou has dealt treacherously: yet is she thy companion, and the wife of thy covenant.

"I WAS called," says the Rev. Richard Cecil, "to visit a woman whose mind was disordered; and, on my observing that it was a case which required the assistance of a physician rather than that of a clergyman, her husband replied, 'Sir, we sent to you, because it is a religious case; her mind has been injured by constantly reading the Bible.'—I have known many instances, said I, of persons brought to their senses by reading the Bible; but it is possible that too intense an application to that, as well as to any other subject, may have disordered your wife. 'There is every proof of it,' said he; and was proceeding to multiply his proofs, till his brother interrupted him by thus addressing me :—'Sir, I have no longer patience to stand by and see you thus imposed on. The truth of the matter is this : My brother has forsaken his wife, and has been long connected with a loose woman. He had the best of wives in her, and one who was strongly attached to him; but she has seen his heart and property given to another, and, in her solitude and distress, went to the Bible as the only consolations left her. Her health and spirits at last sunk under her troubles, and there she lies distracted, not from reading her Bible, but from the infidelity and cruelty of her husband.'—Does the reader wish to know what reply the husband made to this?—He made no reply at all; but left the room with confusion of face!"

Christ the Purifier.

Chap. iii. ver. 3.—He shall sit as a refined and purifier of silver.

A SHORT time ago there were a few ladies in Dublin who met together to read the Scriptures and converse upon them. When reading the third chapter of Malachi, one of the ladies gave it as it as her opinion that the fuller's soap and the refiner of silver were only the same image, intended to convey the same view of the sanctifying influences of the grace of Christ. " No," said another, " they are not just the same image: there is something remarkable in the expression in the third verse, ' He shall *sit* as a refiner and purifier of silver.'" They all said that possibly it might be so. This lady was to call on a silversmith, and promised to report to them what he said on the subject. She went, without telling him the object of her errand, and begged to know the process of refining silver, which he fully described to her. "But do you sit, Sir," said she, "while you are refining?" "O yes, Madam, I must sit with my eye steadily fixed on the furnace, since if the silver remain too long it is sure to be injured." "And how do you know when it is sufficiently refined, Sir?" "Whenever I see my own image reflected in it, I know the process is completed." She at once saw the beauty and the comfort too of the expression, "he shall *sit* as a refiner and purifier of silver." Christ sees it is needful to put his children into the furnace, but he is seated by the side of it. His eye is steadily intent on the work of purifying, and his wisdom and love are engaged to do all in the best manner for them. Their trials do not come at random; the very hairs of their head are all numbered.

Sun of Righteousness.

Chap. iv. ver. 2.—Unto you that fear my name shall the Sun of Righteousness arise with healing in his wings.

KAIARNACK, the first Greenland convert of the Moravian missionaries, had a peculiar felicity in communicating instruction to the savages, and could illustrate divine truths to them better than they, introducing striking remarks and profitable observations, which could not easily have been done by his teachers, while his exemplary walk gave force to his words. Once when invited to a sun-dance, "I have now," answered he, "another kind of joy, for another Sun, Jesus, has arisen on my heart;" and then explained to them the origin and nature of his joy, in a manner that silenced and amazed them.

INSTRUCTIVE ANECDOTES

ILLUSTRATING THE

NEW TESTAMENT

PREFACE
TO
NEW TESTAMENT.

MANY persons will perhaps be ready to acknowledge that, while almost the whole of a sermon, or other discourse, has been forgotten, some striking incident related in it, besides making a peculiar impression at the moment, has been long afterwards remembered. Transferring this idea to the record of our faith, it has been thought that the attention may, by this means, be secured and directed with some effect to "the things which belong to our peace." In the course of reading New Testament Scripture in a family or school, the parent or teacher is therefore furnished, in the present work, with an anecdote or two under each chapter, by relating which, he may fix and enliven the attention of his children or pupils, and, at the same time, by agreeable associations, impress the passages illustrated more deeply on their youthful recollections. The publication, though chiefly intended for the benefit of the young, may not, however, be uninteresting to more advanced readers.

The Author is sensible that the anecdotes are

not all of equally direct bearing on the passages to which they are applied. This, in any case, could not reasonably be expected, and more particularly, as the compiler has been precluded from the use of upwards of five hundred anecdotes in the enlarged editions of his other works, most of which would have suited this volume, but which it was deemed improper to admit.

It is the prayer of the compiler, that the blessing of God may accompany the perusal of this little work.

INSTRUCTIVE ANECDOTES

OF THE

NEW TESTAMENT.

MATTHEW.

The Birth of Christ.

Chap. i. ver. 21.—She shall bring forth a son, and thou shalt call his name JESUS: for he shall save his people from their sins.

THE late Rev. John Brown of Haddington, in his last illness, having heard the bells ringing, and understanding it to be the King's Birth-day, said, "O, blessed be God, however worthy our Sovereign be, we have a better King's Birth-day to celebrate. Unto us was born, in the city of David, a Saviour, who is Christ the Lord! On account of that event, the Gospel-bells have been sounding for ages past; and they will ring louder and louder still. O a Saviour!—The Son of God, our Saviour! O His kindness, His kindness! A Saviour, a husband to sinners, to me!"

It was well observed by a minister, in a sermon on 1 Tim. i. 15, that "The *compassion* of Christ *inclines* Him to save sinners,—the *power* of Christ *enables* Him to save sinners,—and the *promise* of Christ *binds* Him to save sinners."

God with Us.

Chap. i. ver. 23.—They shall call his name IMMANUEL, which, being interpreted, is God with us.

THE Rev. Henry Martyn, when at Dinapore, in India, writes thus:— "Upon showing the Moonshee the first part of John iii. he instantly caught at those words of our Lord, in which He first describes Himself as having *come down* from heaven, and then calls Himself 'the Son of Man which is *in* heaven.' He said that this was what the philosophers called 'nickal,' or impossible,—even for God to make a thing to be in two different places at the same time. I explained to him, as soon as his heat was a little subsided, that the difficulty was not so much in conceiving how the Son of Man could be, at the same time, in two different places, as in comprehending that union of the two natures in Him, which made this possible. I told him that I could not explain this union; but showed him the design and wisdom of God in effecting our redemption by this method. I was much at a loss for words, but I believe that he collected my meaning, and received some information which he did not possess before."

Heartless Slaughter.

Chap. ii. ver. 16.—Herod was exceeding wroth, and sent forth, and slew all the children that were in Bethlehem, and in all the coasts thereof, from two years old and under.

IN 1641, Sir Phelim O'Neal, and other Papists, commenced a universal massacre of the Protestants in Ireland. "No age," says Hume, "no sex, no condition, was spared. The wife, weeping for her butchered husband, and embracing her *helpless children*, was pierced with *them*, and perished by the same stroke. In vain did flight save from the first assault. Destruction was everywhere let loose, and met the hunted victims at every turn. They were stripped of their very clothes, and turned out naked and defenceless in all the rigours of winter. The feeble age of *children*, the tender sex of women, soon sunk under the multiplied rigours of cold and hunger. Here the husband, bidding a final adieu to his expiring family, envied them that fate which he himself expected so soon to share! There the son, having long supported his aged parent, with reluctance obeyed his last command, and abandoning him in his utmost distress, reserved himself to the hopes of avenging that death which all his efforts could not prevent or delay." Forty thousand persons, according to the lowest computation, perished in these massacres!

Eastern Mourning.

Chap. ii. ver. 18.—In Ramah was there a voice heard, lamentation, and weeping, and great mourning, Rachel weeping for her children, and would not be comforted, because they are not.

WE learn from Le Brune's voyage to Syria, that the women go in companies, on certain days, to the tombs of their relations, in order to weep there; and when they are arrived, they display very deep expressions of grief. "While I was at Ramah," says he, "I saw a very great company of these weeping women, who went out of the town. I followed them, and, after having observed the place they visited, adjacent to their sepulchres, in order to make their usual lamentations, I placed myself on an elevated spot. They first went and seated themselves on the sepulchres, and wept there; where, after having remained about half an hour, some of them rose up, and formed a ring, holding each other by the hand. Quickly two of them quitted the others, and placed themselves in the centre of the circle, where they made so much noise by screaming, and clapping their hands, as, together with their various contortions, might have subjected themselves to the suspicion of madness. After that they returned, and seated themselves to weep again, till they gradually withdrew to their homes. The dresses they wore were such as they generally used, white, or any other colour; but when they rose up to form a circle together, they put on a black veil over the upper parts of their persons."

The Wrath to Come.

Chap. iii. ver. 7.—But when he saw many of the Pharisees and Sadducees come to his baptism, he said unto them, O generation of vipers! who hath warned you to flee from the wrath to come?

AN irreligious young man went to hear Mr Whitefield, who took the above passage for his text: "Mr Whitefield," said the young man, "described the Sadducean character; this did not touch me,—I thought myself as good a Christian as any man in England. From this he went to that of the Pharisees. He described their exterior decency, but observed, that the poison of the viper rankled in their hearts. This rather shook me. At length, in the course of his sermon, he abruptly broke off, paused for a few moments, then burst into a flood of tears; lifted up his hands and eyes, and exclaimed, 'Oh my hearers! the wrath to come! the wrath to come!' These words sunk deep into my heart, like lead in the waters. I wept, and, when the sermon was ended, retired alone. For days and weeks I could think of little else. Those awful words would follow me wherever I went. 'The wrath to come! the wrath to come!'" The result was, that the young man soon after made a public profession of religion, and in a short time became a very eminent preacher.

Repentance.

Chap. iii. ver. 8.—Bring forth, therefore, fruits meet for repentance.

"I PAY more attention," says Mr Booth, "to people's lives than to their deaths. In all the visits I have paid to the sick during the course of a long ministry, I never met with *one*, who was not previously serious, that ever recovered from what he supposed the brink of death, who afterwards performed his vows, and became religious, notwithstanding the very great appearance there was in their favour when they thought they could not recover."

Tempted by Satan.

Chap. iv. ver. 10.—Then saith Jesus unto him, Get thee hence, Satan.

THE Rev. Joseph Alleine, having shortly before his death a conflict with Satan, said, "Away! thou foul fiend, thou enemy of all mankind, thou subtle sophister! Art thou come now to molest me, now I am just going—now I am so weak, and death upon me! Trouble me not, for I am none of thine; I am the Lord's; Christ is mine, and I am His; His by covenant; I have sworn myself to be the Lord's, and His I will be;—therefore begone!" These last words he often repeated, "which," says Mrs Alleine, "I took much notice of, that his covenanting with God was the means he used to expel the devil and all his temptations."

Fishers of Men.

Chap. iv. ver. 19.—I will make you fishers of men.

"IT is now fifteen years," says the Rev. Risdon Darracott, in a letter, "since I was settled in this place (Wellington); and though I found religion at a very low ebb, it pleased God, by my poor ministration, to revive it soon on my first coming, and to continue it, more or less, in a flourishing state to this day. Every year there have been additions, and, in some years, very large, to the Church, of such as I hope will be saved. Upwards of two hundred have been taken into communion, upon a credible profession, since my settlement; many of them the most profligate in the places round us, whose change has been so remarkable, that the world at once bears their testimony to, and expresses their astonishment of it; many of them so very ignorant, as not to know the plainest and most common principles of religion; yea, were not able to read a letter, who are now making the Word of God their daily study and delight; many who never prayed in all their lives, and lived without God in the world, who have attained to such a gift in prayer, as to be engaged, on particular occasions, in public, to the pleasure and edification of all present, and whose houses, which were once dens of thieves, are now become Bethels, in which family worship is constantly and seriously performed. O, my dear sir, rejoice with me, and let us exalt His name together! You would be more astonished, did you know by what a poor, weak, sinful instrument this has been done. I assure you it has often humbled me to the dust when I think of it, and yet I am not humbled enough. O that

I could lie lower before the Lord! And that I were more affected by such grace, the very quintessence of grace."

Forgiveness.

Chap. v. ver. 23, 24.—If thou bring thy gift to the altar, and there rememberest that thy brother hath ought against thee; leave there thy gift before the altar, and go thy way; first be reconciled to thy brother, and then come and offer thy gift.

HIS late Majesty, George IV., wishing to take the sacrament, sent for the Bishop of Winchester to administer it. The messenger having loitered on his way, a considerable time elapsed before the bishop arrived, and some irritation had been manifested by the king. On the arrival of the reverend prelate, his delay was complained of, and its cause explained. His Majesty immediately rang his bell, and commanded the attendance of the messenger. On his entering the room, he rebuked him sharply, and dismissed him from his service. Having done this, he addressed the bishop thus: "Now, my Lord if you please, we will proceed." His Lordship, with great mildness, but at the same time with firmness, refused to administer the sacrament whilst any irritation or anger towards a fellow-creature remained on the mind of His Majesty, who, suddenly recollecting himself, said, "My Lord, you are right;" and then sent for the offending party, whose forgiveness and restoration to favour he pronounced in terms of great kindness and condescension.

Be Perfect.

Chap. v. 48.—Be ye therefore perfect, even as your Father which is in heaven is perfect.

A FOLLOWER of Mr. Wesley once asked the Rev. Mr. Dunn of Portsea, whether he thought a state of sinless perfection attainable in this life? Mr. D. replied, "Let us, my friend, seek after it as eagerly as if it were attainable."

The Supreme Being.

Chap. vi. ver. 9.—Our Father which art in heaven.

"HOW do you call the Supreme Being?" said a Parsee to a Jew. "We call him," said the Jew, "Jehovah, Adona, the Lord, who is, and was, and is to come." "Your appellation," said he, "is grand and sublime, but it is awful too." A Christian then approached, and said, "We call Him FATHER,—this is the word of the heart." They all raised their eyes to heaven, and said, "Our Father!" and then took each other by the hand, and called one another brothers.

The First Quest.

Chap. 6. ver. 33.—Seek ye first the kingdom of God and his righteousness.

WHEN a young man made an open profession of the Gospel, his father, greatly offended, gave him this advice,—"James, you should *first* get yourself established in a good *trade*, and then think of and determine about religion." "Father," said the son, "Christ advises me differently; He says, 'Seek ye *first* the kingdom of God.'"

Trust in Providence.

Chap. vi. ver. 34.—Take therefore no thought for the morrow; for the morrow shall take thought for the things of itself.

MR. LAWRENCE, who was a sufferer for the conscience' sake, if he would have consulted with flesh and blood, as was said of

one of the martyrs, had eleven good arguments against suffering : viz.
a wife and ten children. Being once asked how he meant to maintain
them all, he cheerfully replied, "They must all live on Matt. vi. 34,
'Take therefore no thought for the morrow,'" etc. Contentment and
resignation, in such trying circumstances, are not only blessings to
the possessors, but they fill observers with astonishment. "Hence,"
said Dr. Wisley to a poor minister, "I wonder, Mr. W., how you con-
trive to live so comfortably; methinks, with your numerous family,
you live more plentifully on the providence of God, than I can with all
the benefits of my parish."

The Straitgate.

Chap. vii. ver. 13, 14.—Enter ye in at the strait gate; for wide is
the gate and broad is the way, that leadeth to destruction, and many
there be which go in thereat : Because strait is the gate, and narrow
is the way, which leadeth unto life, and few there be that find it.

THE Duke of Hamilton, from a child, was remarkably serious, and
took delight in reading his Bible. His mother, the Duchess,
told a relation, that when he was playing about the room at nine
years of age, she said to him, "Come, write me a few verses, and I
will give you a crown." He sat down, took pen and paper, and in a
few minutes produced the following lines :—

> "As o'er the sea-beat shore I took my way,
> I met an aged man who bade me stay ;
> 'Be wise,' said he, 'and mark the path you go.
> This leads to heaven, and that to hell below;
> The way to life is difficult and steep,
> The broad and easy leads you to the deep.'"

Life and Conversation.

Chap. vii. ver. 20.—Wherefore by their fruits ye shall know them.

A GENTLEMAN lately deceased, who was eminent in the literary
world, had his mind in early life deeply imbued with infidel
sentiments. He and one of his companions of the same way of thinking, often carried on their conversation in the hearing of a religious,
but illiterate countryman. The gentleman having afterwards become a serious Christian, was concerned for the countryman, lest his
faith in the Christian religion should have been shaken by their remarks. One day he took the liberty to ask him, whether what had
so frequently been advanced in his hearing had not produced this
effect upon him? "By no means," answered the countryman; "it
never made the least impression upon me." "No impression on you!"
said the gentleman; "why you must know that we had read and
thought on these things much more than you had an opportunity of
doing." "O yes," said the other, "but your conversation plainly
showed me that you had never read nor thought much on your Bible;
and besides, I knew also your manner of living; I knew that to
maintain such a course of conduct, you found it *necessary* to renounce
Christianity."

The Lepers.

Chap. viii. ver. 2.—There came a leper, and worshipped him, saying, Lord, if thou wilt, thou canst make me clean.

IN the south of Africa there is a large lazar-house for lepers. It is
an immense space, enclosed by a very high wall, and containing
fields, which the lepers cultivate. There is only one entrance, which

is strictly guarded. Whenever any one is found with the marks of leprosy upon him, he is brought to this gate, and obliged to enter in, never to return. No one who enters in by that awful gate is ever allowed to come out again. Within this abode of misery, there are multitudes of lepers in all stages of the disease. Dr. Halbeck, a missionary of the Church of England, from the top of a neighbouring hill, saw them at work. He noticed two particularly, sowing peas in the field. The one had no hands, the other had no feet—these members being wasted away by disease. The one who wanted the hands was carrying the other who wanted the feet upon his back, and he again carried in his hands the bag of seed, and dropped a pea every now and then, which the other pressed into the ground with his foot; and so they managed the work of one man between the two.—Two Moravian missionaries, impelled by an ardent love for souls, have chosen the lazar-house as their field of labour. They entered it, never to come out again; and it is said that as soon as these die, other Moravians are quite ready to fill their place. "Ah! my dear friends," adds the late Rev. Robert M'Cheyne, "may we not blush and be ashamed before God, that we, redeemed with the same blood, and taught by the same Spirit, should yet be so unlike these men in vehement, heart-consuming love to Jesus and the souls of men."

Future Punishment.

Chap. viii. ver. 29.—Art thou come hither to torment us before the time?

AN aged elder, still living, remarkable for the kindliness of his manner, and the unobtrusive facility with which he can introduce religious topics and pious counsel in ordinary conversation, was one day lately a passenger in one of the Forth and Clyde canal boats, in company with a number of soldiers, who shocked him exceedingly with their profane swearing. Aware that an abrupt reproof, instead of producing the effect intended, might only provoke to an aggravation of the crime, he entered into familiar conversation with them, and, seizing a proper opportunity, inquired if any of them could tell him what that sin was, in the commission of which men exceeded devils in wickedness? As he anticipated, the singularity or the question arrested their attention, and engaged them in an unsuccessful attempt to point out the character of the sin. Having thus excited their curiosity, he quoted the above passage, in which the devils address our Saviour, and remarked, that when men wantonly call upon God to damn their souls, they are far more wicked than the devils, who, knowing by experience how dreadful it is to suffer under the wrath of the Almighty, earnestly entreated our Saviour not to add to their torments. Such was the awe produced on their minds by this remark, that not an oath was uttered during the rest of the passage; and at parting, the sergeant in charge of the company, shook hands with him, and cordially thanked him for his kind admonition and advice.

The Forgiveness of Sins.

Chap. ix. ver. 2.—Son, be of good cheer; thy sins be forgiven thee.

PROFESSOR WODROW relates the following anecdote of Mr. Donald Cargill:—"Mr. Cargill was under very deep convictions of sin before his entry into the ministry, and while a student; and that, with grievous temptations and fiery darts mixed in with it, and his too great reservedness, and not communicating his case to such as might have given him counsel and support under it, drove him to terrible excesses; in short, he came to the very height of despair; and, through indulging melancholy, and hearkening to temptations, he at length came to the resolution of putting an end to his miserable life. He was then living with his father, or some relations, in the parish of Bothwell, and, in the horrible hurry of these fiery darts, he went out once or twice to the river of Clyde, with a dreadful resolution to drown himself. He was still diverted by somebody or other coming by him, which prevented his design at that time. But the temptations continuing, and his horror by yielding to it increasing, he fell upon a method, in the execution of which he thought he should not be prevented. On a summer morning, very early, he went from the house where he dwelt to a more unfrequented place, where there were some old coal pits, and, on coming up to one of them, was fully determined to throw himself in; but, when very near it, a thought struck him, that the coat and vest he had upon him being new, might be of some use to others, though he was unworthy to live, and deserved to be in hell; and so he stepped back and threw them off, and then came up to the very brink of the pit; and when just going to leap in, these words entered his mind, 'Son, be of good cheer; thy sins are forgiven thee.' He said it came with that power and life upon his spirit, which it was impossible for him to express, and he did not know whether it was by an immediate impression on his mind, or a direct voice from heaven (which last he was inclined to think), but it had such an evidence and energy accompanying it, as at once put an end to all his fears and doubts, and which he could no more resist, than he could do the light of a sunbeam darting upon his eye."

Moved with Compassion.

Chap. ix. ver. 36.—When he saw the multitudes, he was moved with compassion on them, because they fainted, and were scattered abroad, as sheep having no shepherd.

"GIVE hundred millions of souls," exclaims a missionary, "are represented as being unenlightened! I cannot, if I would, give up the idea of being a missionary, while I reflect upon this vast number of my fellow-sinners, who are perishing for lack of knowledge. Five hundred millions! intrudes itself upon my mind wherever I go, and however I am employed. When I go to bed, it is the last thing that recurs to my memory; if I awake in the night, it is to meditate on it alone; and in the morning, it is generally the first thing that occupies my thoughts."

Servant and Lord.

Chap. x. ver. 25.—It is enough for the disciple that he be as his master, and the servant as his lord.

WHEN the Mexican emperor, Gatimozan, was put upon the rack by the soldiers of Cortes, one of the nobles, who lay in torture at the same time, complained piteously to his sovereign of the pain he endured. "Do you think," said Gatimozin, "that I lie upon roses?" The nobleman ceased moaning, and expired in silence. "When a Christian," adds the pious Bishop Horne, "thinks his sufferings for sin, in sickness or pain, etc., intolerable, let him remember those of *his* Lord, endured patiently on that bed of sorrow, the *cross*, and he will think so no longer."

Trust and Believe.

Chap. x. 31.—Fear ye not, therefore, ye are of more value than many sparrows.

THE Rev. Mr Nosworthy, who died in 1677, had, from the persecuting spirit of the times, been imprisoned in Winchester, where he met with much cruel usage. After his release, he was several times reduced to great straits. Once, when he and his family had breakfasted, and had nothing left for another meal, his wife, lamenting her condition, exclaimed, "What shall I do with my poor children?" He persuaded her to walk abroad with him, and, seeing a little bird, he said, "Take notice how that little bird sits and chirps, though we cannot tell whether it has been at breakfast; and if it has, it knows not whither to go for a dinner. Therefore be of good cheer, and do not distrust the providence of God; for are we not better than many sparrows?" Before dinner they had plenty of provisions brought them. Thus was the promise fulfilled, "They who trust in the Lord shall not want any good thing."

Resignation.

Chap. xi. ver. 26.—Even so, Father; for so it seemed good in thy sight.

SEVERAL gentlemen visited a school in France, in which was a boy who was both deaf and dumb. One of the gentlemen asked him, who made the world? The boy took his slate and wrote the first verse of the Bible, "In the beginning God created the heaven and the earth." He was then asked, "How do you hope to be saved?" The child wrote, "This is a faithful saying, and worthy of all acceptation, that Christ Jesus came into the world to save sinners." The last question proposed was,—"How is it that God has made *you* deaf and dumb, while all those around you can hear and speak?" The poor boy seemed puzzled for a moment, and a suggestion of unbelief seemed to pass through his mind, but quickly recovering himself, he wrote, "Even so, Father, for so it seemed good in Thy sight."

Christ's Yoke.

Chap. xi. ver. 30.—My yoke is easy, and my burden is light.

"I REMEMBER," says the Rev. Matthew Henry, in writing the account of his father's life, "a passage of his, in a lecture in the year 1674, which much affected many. He was preaching on that text, Matt. xi. 30, 'My yoke is easy;' and after many things insisted upon, to prove the yoke of Christ an easy yoke, he at last appealed to the experiences of all that had drawn in that yoke: 'Call now, if there be any that will answer you, and to which of the saints will you turn? Turn to which you will, and they will all agree that they have found wisdom's ways pleasantness, and Christ's commandments not grievous; and (saith he) I will here witness for one, who, through grace, has in some poor measure been drawing this yoke now above thirty years, and I have found it an easy yoke, and like my choice too well to change.'"

Charity.

Chap. xii. ver. 7.—I will have mercy, and not sacrifice.

ARCHBISHOP TILLOTSON gave the most exemplary proof of his charity, at the revocation of the edict of Nantz, when thousands of Huguenots were driven over to this country, many of whom settled at Canterbury, where their posterity still continue. The king having granted briefs to collect alms for their relief, Dr T. was peculiarly active in promoting their success ; Dr Beveridge, one of the prebendaries of Canterbury, refused to read the briefs as being contrary to the rubrics ; he was silenced by Dr Tillotson, with this energetic reply, " Doctor, Doctor, charity is above rubrics."

Keeping the Sabbath.

Chap. xii. ver. 11.—What man shall there be among you that shall have one sheep, and if it fall into a pit on the Sabbath-day, will he not lay hold on it, and lift it out ?

A NATIVE of one of the South Sea Islands came and told the missionaries, that while he was attending public worship, a pig broke into his garden ; that on his return, he saw him devour the sweet potatoes, sugar-cane, taro and other productions, but that he did not drive it out, because he was convinced it would immediately return, unless he repaired the broken fence, and *that* he supposed was a kind of labour prohibited on the Sabbath. He therefore allowed the pig to remain till he was satisfied, and did not mend the fence till the following morning. He, however, wished to know, and the people in general were interested in the inquiry,—whether, in the event of a similar occurrence at any future period, he should do wrong in driving out the animal, and repairing the fence. He was told that the most secure way would be to keep the fence in good repair ; but that, if pigs should break in on the Sabbath, they ought by all means to be driven out, and the breaches they had made so far repaired, as to secure the inclosure till the following day.

Idle Words.

Chap. xii. ver. 36.—I say unto you, that every idle word that men shall speak, they shall give account thereof in the day 'of judgment.

"THE story is well known," says Mr Scott, " of a person who invited a company of his friends that were accustomed to take the Lord's name in vain, and contrived to have their discourse taken down, and read to them. Now, if they could not bear to hear their words repeated which they had spoken during a few hours, how shall they bear to have all they have uttered, through a long course of years, brought forth as evidence against them at the tribunal of God ?"

Open Air Preaching.

Chap. xiii. 1, 2.—Jesus sat by the sea-side, and great multitudes were gathered together unto him.

GEORGE WISHART, one of the first Scottish martyrs at the time of the Reformation, being desired to preach one Lord's day in the church of Mauchline, went thither with that design ; but the sheriff of Ayr had, in the night time, put a garrison of soldiers into the church to keep him out. Hugh Campbell of Kinzeancleugh, with others in the parish, were exceedingly offended at this impiety, and would have entered the church by force ; but Wishart would not suffer it, saying, " Brethren, it is the word of peace which I preach unto you ; the blood of no man shall be shed for it this day. Jesus Christ is as mighty in the fields as in the church ; and He Himself, while He lived in the flesh, preached oftener in the desert and on the seaside than in the temple of Jerusalem." Upon this the people were appeased, and went with him to the edge of a moor on the south-west of Mauchline, where, having placed himself upon a mound of earth, he preached to a great multitude. He continued speaking for more than three hours, God working wondrously by him, insomuch that Lawrence Ranken, the Laird of Shield, a very profane person, was converted by his discourse. The tears ran from his eyes, to the astonishment of all present; and the whole of his after life witnessed that his profession was without hypocrisy.

The Kingdom of Heaven.

Chap. xiii. ver. 45, 46.—The kingdom of heaven is like unto a merchantman seeking goodly pearls; who, when he had found one pearl of great price, went and sold all that he had and bought it.

A WEALTHY lady of Java, having been married to an English merchant, came to reside in England. Being unacquainted with the language, together with the customs and manners of the country, nearly the whole of her time was spent in playing with her children, of whom she was very fond, and decking herself in her jewels and pearls, of which she had a large and costly collection. She often called for her treasure-box, and amused herself by first looking at a fine necklace, then at a beautiful pair of ear-rings, and held them up to glitter in the sun. There her treasure was, there was her heart also; and she thought there was little happiness beyond the contents of her box, and such like stones. Her Scotch nurse being one day in her room, in broken English she said to her—"Nurse, this poor place— poor place!" "Why, Madam?" asked her nurse. "Me look out of the window," replied the lady, "and see no woman in the street with jewels on—no jewels to be seen. In my country, all covered with diamonds and pearls. We dig into hills in our country, and we get gold and silver, and precious jewels. You dig into your hills, and get nothing but stones." The nurse replied, "O yes, Madam, we have a pearl in our country—a pearl of great price." The Javanese lady caught her words with great eagerness and surprise. "Pearl of great price! Have you, indeed? O that my husband was come home! He buy me this pearl; me part with all my pearls when he come home, to get this pearl of so great price." "O," said the nurse, "this pearl is not to wear. It is not to be had in the way you think. It is a precious pearl, indeed; and they who have it cannot lose it. They who have it are at peace, and have all they wish for." "Indeed," said the astonished lady, "what can this pearl be?" "The pearl," said the nurse, "is the Lord Jesus, who said that He came into the world to save sinners. All who truly receive this saying, and have Christ in their hearts as the hope of glory, have that which makes them rich and happy, whatever else they want; and so precious is Jesus to them, that they count all things but loss for the excellency of the knowledge of Him." It pleased God to bless the nurse's words. She got a believing view of Christ, in whom are hid all the treasures of wisdom and knowledge; and this world's gems ceased to shine and attract, just as the stars lose their brightness before the morning sun. Sometime after, the lady died; and on her death-bed, she desired that her jewels might be sold, and the produce go towards sending the knowledge of the PEARL OF GREAT PRICE to those in far countries who have it not. She felt its value, and she wished that all the world might feel it too.

Salvation.

Chap. xiv. ver. 30.—Lord, save me.

A MINISTER asked the maid at an inn in the Netherlands, if she prayed to God? She replied, "She had scarce time to eat, how should she have time to pray?" He promised to give her a little money, if, on his return, she could assure him she had meanwhile said three words of prayer, night and morning. Only three words and a reward caught her promise. He solemnly added, "Lord, save me!" For a fortnight she said the words unmeaningly; but one night she wondered what they meant, and why he bade her repeat them. God put it into her heart to look at the Bible, and see if it would tell her. She liked some verses where she opened so well, that next morning she looked again, and so on. When the good man went back, he asked the landlord for her, as a stranger served him. "Oh, Sir! she got too good for my place, and lives with the minister!" So soon as she saw the minister at the door, she cried, "It is you, you blessed man? I shall thank God through all eternity that I ever saw you; I want not the money, I have reward enough for saying those words!" She then described how salvation by Jesus Christ was taught her by the Bible, in answer to this prayer.

Obedience.

Chap. xv. ver. 4.—Honour thy father and mother.

A BOY was once tempted by his companions to pluck some ripe cherries from a tree which his father had forbidden him to touch. "You need not be afraid," said they, "for if your father should find out that you have taken them, he is so kind that he will not hurt you." "For that very reason," replied the boy, "1 ought not to touch them; for though my father may not hurt me, my disobedience would hurt my father."

Unscriptural Teaching.

Chap. xv. ver. 9.—In vain they do worship me, teaching for doctrines the commandments of men.

"A SERIOUS man from a neighbouring parish," says Dr Latrobe, "being one evening at my house on secular business, took occasion to inform me, that there was a great revival of religion in his neighbourhood. I expressed much pleasure at the intelligence, but asked him in what manner this happy revival discovered itself—whether the people appeared more humble, more meek and peaceable, more kind and charitable, better united in their social relations, more virtuous in their lives, etc. He could not answer particularly with respect to these things, but said, 'People were much engaged in attending religious meetings; they had private lectures as often as a preacher could be obtained, and they had conferences almost every evening.' I observed to him, that an attendance on the word preached was highly important, and a hopeful sign; but asked him how it was on the Lord's day—whether they attended on the instituted worship of that day better than they used to do (for I knew they had been shamefully negligent of that duty). 'Why, no,' said he, 'we don't go to meeting on the Sabbath.' What! I inquired, do you neglect God's institutions to observe your own? The prophet marks this as a token of *decay* in religion."

Giving Offence in Preaching.

Chap. xv. ver. 12.—Then came his disciples, and said unto him, Knowest thou that the Pharisees were offended, after they heard this saying?

MR DOD having preached against the profanation of the Sabbath, which much prevailed in his parish, and especially among the more wealthy inhabitants, the servant of a nobleman, who was one of them, came to him and said, "Sir, you have offended my lord to-day." Mr Dod replied, "I should not have offended your lord, except he had been conscious to himself that he had first offended my Lord; and if *your* lord will offend *my* Lord, let him be offended."

Various Keys.

Chap. xvi. ver. 19.—I will give unto thee the keys of the kingdom of heaven: and whatsoever thou shalt bind on earth shall be bound in heaven; and whatsoever thou shalt loose on earth shall be loosed in heaven.

ONCE from the pulpit, at an ordination of elders, the late Rev. Mr. M'Cheyne made the following declaration:—"When I first entered upon the work of the ministry among you, I was exceedingly ignorant of the vast importance of church discipline. I thought that my great and almost only work was to pray and preach. I saw your souls to be so precious, and the time so short, that I devoted all my time, and care, and strength, to labour in word and doctrine. When cases of discipline were brought before me and the elders, I regarded them with something like abhorrence. It was a duty I shrank from and I may truly say it nearly drove me from the work of the ministry among you altogether. But it pleased God, who teaches His servants in another way than man teaches, to bless some of the cases of discipline to the manifest and undeniable conversion of the souls of those under our care; and from that hour a new light broke in upon my mind, and I saw that if preaching be an ordinance of Christ, so is church discipline. I now feel very deeply persuaded that both are of God; that two keys are committed to us by Christ—the one the key of doctrine, by means of which we unlock the treasures of the Bible— the other the key of discipline, by which we open or shut the way to the sealing ordinances of the faith. Both are Christ's gift, and neither is to be resigned without sin."

Profit and Loss.

Chap. xvi. ver. 26.—What is a man profited, if he shall gain the whole world and lose his own soul? or what shall a man give in exchange for his soul?

A PERSON lately deceased, and who possessed a speculative acquaintance with divine truth, had, by unremitting industry, and carefully watching every opportunity of increasing his wealth, accumulated the sum of twenty-five thousand pounds. But alas! he became engrossed and entangled with the world, and to its acquisitions he appears to have sacrificed infinitely higher interests. A dangerous sickness, that brought death near to his view, awakened his fears. Conscience reminded him of his neglect of eternal concerns, and filled him with awful forebodings of future misery. A little before he expired he was heard to say, "My possessions amount to twenty-five thousand pounds. One half of this my property I would give, so that I might live one fortnight longer, to repent and seek salvation; and the other half I would give to my dear and only son."

The Change.

Chap. xvii. ver. 21.—Howbeit this kind goeth not out but by prayer and fasting.

THE following instance will serve to show the efficacy of prayer in expelling Satan from his usurped dominion in the soul; and

may, in a way of accomodation, illustrate the passage to which it is applied :—
A minister from England happening some time since to be at Edinburgh, was accosted very civilly by a young man in the street, with an apology for the liberty he was taking. "I think, Sir," said he, "I have heard you at Spafields Chapel." "You probably may, Sir, for I have sometimes ministered there." "Do you remember," said he, "a note put up by an afflicted widow, begging the prayers of the congregation for the conversion of an ungodly son?" "I do very well remember such a circumstance." "Sir," said he, "I am the very person; and, wonderful to tell, the prayer was effectual. Going on a frolic with some other abandoned young men, one Sunday, through the Spafields, and passing by the chapel, I was struck with its appearance; and hearing it was a Methodist chapel, we agreed to mingle with the crowd, and stop for a few minutes, to laugh and mock at the preacher and the people. We had only just entered the chapel, when you, Sir, read the note, requesting the prayers of the congregation for an afflicted widow's son. I heard it with a sensation I cannot express. I was struck to the heart; and though I had no idea that I was the very individual meant, I felt that it expressed the bitterness of a widow's heart, who had a child as wicked as I knew myself to be. My mind was instantly solemnized. I could not laugh; my attention was rivetted on the preacher. I heard his prayer and sermon with an impression very different from that which had carried me into the chapel. From that moment, the truths of the Gospel penetrated my heart; I joined the congregation; cried to God, in Christ, for mercy, and found peace in believing; became my mother's comfort, as I had long been her heavy cross, and through grace have ever since continued in the good ways of the Lord. An opening having lately been made for advantageous settlement in my own country, I came hither with my excellent mother, and for some time past, have endeavoured to dry up the widow's tears, which I had so often caused to flow; and to be the comfort and support of her old age, as I had been the torment and affliction of her former days. We live together in the enjoyment of every mercy, happy and thankful; and every day I acknowledged the kind hand of my Lord, that led me to the Spafields Chapel."

Payment of Taxes.

Chap. xvii. ver. 27.—Notwithstanding, lest we should offend them, go thou to the sea, and cast an hook, and take up the fish that first cometh up; and when thou hast opened his mouth, thou shalt find a piece of money; that take, and give unto them for me and thee.

"FOR your taxes and tributes," says Justin Martyr to the emperor's, "we are, above all other men, everywhere ready to bring them to your collectors and officers, being taught so to do by our great Master, who bade those that asked the question, Whether they might pay tribute unto Cæsar? to give unto Cæsar the things that are Cæsar's, and unto God the things that are God's."

Humbling Oneself.

Chap. xviii. ver. 4.—Whosoever, therefore, shall humble himself as this little child, the same is greatest in the kingdom of heaven.

THE celebrated Dr. Franklin, of America, once received a very useful lesson from the excellent Dr. Cotton Mather, which he thus relates in a letter to his son, Dr. Samuel Mather, dated Passy, 12th

May 1781;—"The last time I saw your father was in 1724. On taking my leave, he showed me a shorter way out of the house, through a narrow passage, which was crossed by a beam over-head. We were still talking as I withdrew, he accompanying me behind, and I turning towards him; when he said hastily, Stoop—stoop! I did not understand him till I felt my head hit against the beam. He was a man who never was missed an occasion of giving instruction: and upon this he said to me, *You are young, and have the world before you,* STOOP *as you go through it, and you will miss many hard thumps.* This advice, thus beat into my head, has frequently been of use to me; and I often think of it when I see pride mortified, and misfortunes brought upon people by carrying their heads too high."

Quiet Expostulation.

Chap. xviii. ver. 15.—If thy brother shall trespass against thee, go and tell him his fault between thee and him alone.

WHEN any member of Mr. Kilpin's church at Exeter came with details of real or supposed injuries, received from a fellow-member, after listening to the reporter, Mr. K. would inquire if they had mentioned these grievances to their offending brother or sister. If the reply was in the negative, and usually it was so, he would then calmly order a messenger to fetch them, remarking, that it would be ungenerous to decide, and unscriptural to act, merely from hearing the statement of one party. This determination always produced alarm, and the request that nothing might be mentioned to the parties implicated. This plan had a peaceful influence, and often produced humility and self-accusation. Assertions and proofs are very different grounds for the exercise of judgment, and are more distinct than angry persons imagine.

Husband and Wife.

Chap. xix. ver. 6.—What, therefore, God hath joined together, let not man put asunder.

THE wife of a pious man told him one day that if he did not give over running after the missionaries, a name often applied to serious ministers of different denominations, she would certainly leave him. Finding that he continued obstinate, she on one occasion sent for him from the harvest field, and informed him that she was about to carry her threat into execution; and that, before she left the house, she wished some articles divided, to prevent future disputes. She first produced a web of linen, which she insisted should be divided. "No, no," said the husband; "you have been, upon the whole, a good wife to me: if you will leave me, though the thought makes my heart sore, you must take the whole with you; you well deserve it all" The same answer was given to a similar proposal respecting some other articles. At last the wife said, "So you wish me to leave you?" "Far from that," said the husband, "I would do anything but sin to make you stay, but if you will go, I wish you to go in comfort." "Then," said she, "you have overcome me by your kindness; I will never leave you."

Deceitfulness of Riches.

Chap. xix. ver. 23.—Then said Jesus unto his disciples, Verily I say unto you, that a rich man shall hardly enter into the kingdom of heaven

"I HAD been known." says one, "to Mr Cecil, as an occasional hearer at St John's, and by soliciting his advice at my commencing master of a family; but some years had passed since I enjoyed the pleasure of speaking to him, when he called at my house on horseback, being then unable to walk, and desired to speak with me. After the usual salutations, he addressed me thus:—'I understand you are very dangerously situated?' He then paused. I replied, that I was not aware of it. He answered, "I thought it was probable you were not; and therefore I called on you: I hear you are getting rich; take care, for it is the road by which the devil leads thousands to destruction!' This was spoken with such solemnity and earnestness, that the impression will ever remain on my memory."

Receiving an Hundredfold.

Chap. xix. ver. 29.—Every one that hath forsaken houses, or brethren, or sisters, or father, or mother, or wife, or children, or lands, for my name's sake, shall receive an hundredfold, and shall inherit everlasting life.

MR JOHN PRICE, a pious old man, lately deceased, was walking one day on the road from his farm to the sanctuary, with the New Testament in his hand, when a friend met him and and said, "Good morning, Mr Price." "Ah! good morning," replied the aged pilgrim, "I am reading my Father's will as I walk along." "Well, and what has He left you?" said the friend. "Why, he has bequeathed me a hundredfold more in this life, and in the world to come life everlasting." This shrewd and beautiful reply produced a happy effect on the mind of his Christian friend, who was in sorrowful circumstances, and he went on his way rejoicing.

The Eleventh Hour.

Chap. xx. ver. 6.—And about the eleventh hour he went out, and found others standing idle, and saith unto them, Why stand ye here all the day idle?

AN old sailor, who was very ragged, and whose white head spoke of the lapse of many years, was leaning against a post in conversation with another sailor. A member of the Bethel Union spoke to them, and particularly invited the old man to attend the prayer-meeting. His companion, after hearing the nature of the invitation, said, "Thomas, go in; Come! come! man, go into the meeting; it won't hurt you." "Puh! puh!" cried the old seaman, "I should not know what to do with myself. I never go to church or prayer-meetings; besides, I am too old. I am upwards of seventy, and I am very wicked, and have always been so; it is too late for me to begin, it is of no use: all is over with me, I must go to the devil." After a moment's pause, the member, looking with pity upon the old veteran, answered, "You are the very man the prayer-meeting is held for." "How so?" (with much surprise). "Because Jesus Christ came into the world to save the chief of sinners. When young, I suppose, you were tempted to think it would be time enough to be religious when you came to be old?" "Ah! that I did," replied the sailor. "Now you are old, you say it is too late. Listen no longer to these suggestions; come with me: no time is to be lost, for Jesus is waiting to save you, poor sinner, or he would have sent you to that place where hope never comes, before this; your sins deserve it." His companion then said, "Thomas, go to the prayer-meeting. You have need, at your time of life, to prepare to die." He went, and attended regularly.

Some time after, he was asked, "Well, my aged friend, do you think you are too much in years to be saved? too old in sin for the blood of Christ to cleanse you?" "No, Sir," said he; "I bless God, I do feel a hope, a blessed hope, which I would not give up for worlds; a hope which encourages me to think that God will be merciful to me and pardon me, old sinner as I am."

Unwise Asking.

Chap. xx. ver. 22.—Ye know not what ye ask.

A FOND father was in great distress for a favourite child, whom he apprehended to be dying in its infancy. Several of his friends endeavoured to assuage his grief, but he refused to be comforted. At length the minister on whom he attended, offered to pray with him, and desired him to compose his mind, and give up his favourite son to the Divine disposal, since there was no probable hope of his recovery. He replied, "I cannot give him up; and it is my importunate request that God would spare this child to me, whatever may be the consequence." He had his desire; the child recovered, and grew up, if possible, more and more his darling; but he lived to be a thorn in his side, and to pierce his heart with many sorrows. For just as he came to maturity, he robbed his excellent master, whom before he had often injured. He was seized by the hand of justice, tried, condemned, and died one of the most hardened wretches that ever went out of life in that ignominous manner. Upon the fatal day of execution, the mourning father was made to remember his former rash petition with grief and tears; and, humbled in the dust, confessed his folly and his sin.

The Sunday School.

Chap. xxi. ver. 16.—Out of the mouths of babes and sucklings thou hast perfected praise.

A SABBATH School having been opened near Hereford, a labouring man, who had a large family, sent his children there for the benefit of instruction; the good effects of which soon appeared. It happened that, very near to this man's house, a place was opened for the worship of God, where service was performed every Sunday evening at seven o'clock; and this man and part of his family were in the habit of attending regularly. One Sabbath evening, the weather being very snowy, the man thought prudent to leave his children at home, and went alone. Some of these young ones, doubtless, were much disappointed in not being permitted to accompany their father, and thought they would have a meeting amongst themselves. The father, on his return home, was surprised at seeing a light up-stairs in his cottage, and thought that the children must be retiring to bed. He opened the door of the cottage, and went softly up-stairs, when, to his astonishment, he heard his youngest daughter, a child not more than six years old, in humble strains pouring forth her prayers to that God, through whose tender mercy it was that she had been taught to "remember the Sabbath-day, to keep it holy." When she had finished her prayer, she called upon one of her little brothers to pray (for they were met together for that purpose), and thus they finished this blessed day; experiencing, it is hoped, the blessedness of that promise, "Where two or three are gathered together in My name there am I in the midst of them."

The Prayer of Faith.

Chap. xxi. ver. 22.—All things whatsoever ye shall ask in prayer, believing, ye shall receive.

IN the life of the Rev. Robert Blair, a Scottish minister of the seventeenth century, the following passage occurs:—"There having been incessant rain for a month in harvest, the corn was growing a finger length in the sheaves, and the whole crop was in hazard of perishing. In this deplorable situation, the people resolved solemnly, by humiliation and fasting, to beseech the Lord to avert the threatened famine. When the day came, it rained heavily from morning to night; so that the Lord seemed to be thrusting out their prayers from Him. But that same night he sent a mighty wind, which did fully dry the corn, and check the growing; and this wind continuing to blow fair for two days, the people ceased, neither night nor day, till the whole corn was got in. During these two days, I and two neighbouring ministers were continuing our supplications and thanksgivings to the Lord for this great mercy."

Clothed in Righteousness.

Chap. xxii. ver. 11.—And when the king came in to see the guests, he saw there a man which had not on a wedding-garment.

A PERSON who had been for some time labouring under mental dejection, having dressed himself one Sabbath morning for church, and finding he had a few minutes to spend previous to leaving the house, took up his Bible with the intention of reading a portion of Scripture. The first passage that caught his eye was the above, "And when the king came in to see the guests," etc. The words strongly impressed his mind, particularly as connected with the design he had of observing the ordinance of the Lord's Supper that day. When leaving his pew to go to the communion-table, they recurred with such discouraging force to his recollection, as to prevent his going forward, and led him to return to his seat. He afterwards considered he was wrong in having yielded so far to groundless apprehensions, and that a comparison of our state and character with the word of God, is the rational and proper way of ascertaining our fitness or unfitness to approach the table of the Lord.

Caesar and God.

Chap. xxii. ver. 21.—Render therefore unto Cæsar the things which are Cæsar's; and unto God the things that are God's..

A BOY about nine years of age, who attended a Sabbath School at Sunderland, requested his mother not to allow his brother to bring home any thing that was smuggled when he went to sea. "Why do you wish that, my child?" said the mother. He answered, "Because my catechism says it is wrong." The mother replied, "But that is only the word of a man." He said, "Mother, it is the word of a man which said, 'Render unto Cæsar the things which are Cæsar's?'" This reply entirely silenced the mother; but his father still attempting to defend the practice of smuggling, the boy said to him, "Father, whether is it worse to rob one or to rob many?" By these questions and answers, the boy silenced both his parents on the subject of smuggling.

Entering the Kingdom.

Chap. xxiii. ver. 13.—Ye shut up the kingdom of heaven against men: for ye neither go in yourselves, neither suffer ye them that are entering to go in.

A CHILD of nine years old, in St. Giles, London, had gone for a long time to a school, in which the children of Roman Catholics are taught by Protestants to read the Bible. The little girl was taken very ill, and when there seemed no hope of her getting better, her parents sent for a Popish priest. When he came, he thus spake to her:—"Child, you are in an awful state; you are just going to die. I beg you, before you depart, to make your dying request to your father and mother, that they will not send your brothers and sisters to the school that you went to." The little girl raised herself up in bed, and said, "My dear father and mother, I make it my dying request, that you WILL send my brothers and sisters to that school; for there I was first taught that I was a sinner, and that I must depend alone upon Jesus Christ for salvation." She then laid her head back, and expired.

Inconsistency.

Chap. xxiii. ver. 24.—Ye strain at a gnat, and swallow a camel.

A NEAPOLITAN shepherd came in great anguish to his priest: "Father, have mercy on a miserable sinner! It is the holy season of Lent; and while I was busy at work, some whey, spurting from the cheese-press, flew into my mouth, and wretched man, I swallowed it. Free my distressed soul from its agonies, by absolving me from my guilt!" "Have you no other sins to confess?" said his spiritual guide. "No; I do not know that I have committed any other." "There are," said the priest, "many robberies and murders from time to time committed on your mountains, and I have reason to believe you are one of the persons concerned in them." "Yes," he replied, "I am but these are never accounted a crime: it is a thing practised by us all, and there needs no confession on that account."

The Second Coming.

Chap. xxiv. ver. 36.—Of that day and hour knoweth no man, no, not the angels of heaven, but my Father only.

AT a village a few miles from London, a woman was endeavouring to vend some printed trash, which she said contained a prophecy, that on the approaching Whitmonday, the world would be at an end. On hearing this, a girl about seven years of age, standing at the door of her father's house, ran in somewhat alarmed, and, telling her mother what the woman had been saying, asked her whether she believed it? A sister of the little girl, between nine and ten years of age, who had been educated in a Sabbath school, happening to be present, could not refrain from speaking: "Ann," said she, "you must not mind what the woman has been saying; she, I am sure, cannot know when the world is to be at an end; for, don't you remember what the word of God says, 'Of that day and hour knoweth no man, no, not the angels of heaven, but My Father only?'"

Unfulfilled Obligations.

Chap. xxiv. ver. 50, 51.—The Lord of that servant shall come in a day when he looketh not for him, and in an hour that he is not aware of, and shall cut him asunder, and appoint him his portion with the hypocrites.

COSROES, King of Persia, in conversation with two philosophers and his vizier, asked, "What situation of man is most to be deplored?" One of the philosophers maintained that it was old age, accompanied with extreme poverty; the other, that it was to have the body oppressed by infirmities, the mind worn out, and the heart broken by a heavy series of misfortunes. "I know a condition more to be pitied," said the vizier, "and it is that of him who has passed through life without doing good, and who, unexpectedly surprised by death, is sent to appear before the tribunal of the sovereign Judge."

Eastern Marriages.

Chap. xxv. ver. 10.—And the door was shut.

MR. WARD has given the following descriptions of a Hindoo wedding which furnishes a striking parallel to the parable of the wedding feast in the Gospel. "At a marriage, the procession of which I saw some years ago, the bridegroom came from a distance, and the bride lived at Serampore, to which place the bridegroom was to come by water. After waiting two or three hours, at length, near midnight, it was announced, as if in the very words of Scripture, Behold the bridegroom cometh, go ye out to meet him. All the persons employed now lighted their lamps, and ran with them in their hands to fill up their stations in all procession; some of them had lost their lights, and were unprepared, but it was then too late to seek them, and the cavalcade moved forward to the house of the bride, at which place the company entered a large and splendidly illuminated area, before the house, covered with an awning, where a great multitude of friends dressed in their best apparel, were seated upon mats. The bridegroom was carried in the arms of a friend, and placed on a superb seat in the midst of the company, where he sat a short time, and then went into the house, the door of which was immediately shut, and guarded by Sepoys. I and others expostulated with the door-keepers, but in vain. Never was I so struck with our Lord's beautiful parable, as at this moment: 'And the door was shut!'"

The Son of Man.

Chap. xxv. ver. 13.—Watch therefore: for ye know neither the day nor the hour wherein the Son of man cometh.

THE following striking fact is taken from the Edinburgh Advertiser, Dec. 7, 1810. "Died at Waterford, Nov. 4, the Rev. B. Dickinson minister of the Baptist congregation in that city, while zealously employed in the discharge of his functions. Mr. Dickinson had taken for his text, 2 Cor. v. 10, 'We must all appear before the judgment-seat of Christ;' and had advanced but a short way in its illustration, when he fell down in the pulpit, and instantly expired!" What an impressive lesson to those who preach, and to those who hear the everlasting Gospel! And how becoming for every minister to adopt the lines of Baxter:

"I preach as if I ne'er should preach again."
And as a dying man to dying men."

Clothing the Naked.

Chap. xxv. ver. 36.—Naked, and ye clothed me.

ON one occasion, as the Rev. Edmund Jones was returning home over the mountains, from places where he had been dispensing the word of life, he accidentally met a poor creature, almost naked, and perishing with cold. Such an object could not fail to work upon the tender sympathies of his heart Having no money, he actually stripped himself of his shirt, and what other clothes he could spare, and gave them to him; and after conversing with him about the state of his soul, and commending the miserable creature to God in prayer, he pursued his journey. As soon as he entered his house, Mrs Jones was alarmed at his extraordinary appearance, and hastily inquired if any thing disastrous had happened to him. The good man soon quieted her fears, by relating the particulars of what had occurred. "You did well, my dear," said she; "you have other clothes to put on; let us be thankful to God that we are not in the poor man's circumstances."

Temptation.

Chap. xxvi. ver. 41.—Watch and pray, that ye enter not into temptation.

A converted and emancipated slave in the vicinity of Philadelphia, accosted a person thus:—"Massa, me hear you are going to study to be a minister." "Yes." "Will you let poor Tom say one thing to you?" "Yes." "Well, you know the good Master says, 'Watch and pray.' Now you may watch all the time, and if you no pray, the devil will get in. You may pray all the time, and if you no watch too, the devil will get in. But if you watch and pray all the time, the devil no get in; for it is just like the sword of God put into the hand of the angel at the entering of the garden—it turns every way. If the devil come before, it turn there; if the devil come behind, it turn there. Yes, massa, it turn every way."

Denying the Lord.

Chap. xxvi. ver. 75.—Peter remembered the word of Jesus, which said unto him, Before the cock crow, thou shalt deny me thrice. And he went out, and wept bitterly.

"BISHOP JEWEL," says Fuller, "being by the violence of Popish inquisitors, assulted on a sudden to *subscribe*, he took a pen in his hand, and said, smiling, 'Have you a mind to see how well I can write?' and thereupon underwrit their opinions." Jewel, however, by his cowardly compliance, made his foes no fewer without, and one the more, a guilty conscience within him. His life being way-laid for, with great difficulty he got over into Germany. Having arrived at Frankfort, by the advice of some friends, he made a solemn and affecting recantation of his subscription, in a full congregation of English Protestants, on a Sabbath morning, after having preached a most tender, penitential sermon. "It was," said he, "my abject and cowardly mind, and faint heart, that made my weak hand commit this wickedness." He bitterly bewailed his fall; and with sighs and tears, supplicated forgiveness of the God whose truth he had denied, and of the Church of Christ, which he had so grievously offended. The congregation were melted into tears, and "all embraced him as a brother in Christ; yea, as an angel of God." "Whoever seriously considers the high parts of Mr. Jewel," adds Fuller, "will conclude, that his *fall* was necessary for his *humiliation*."

The Crown of Thorns.

Chap. xxvii. ver. 29.—And when they had platted a crown of thorns, they put it upon his head.

WHEN John Huss, the Bohemian martyr, was brought out to be burnt, they put on his head a triple crown of paper, with painted devils on it. On seeing it, he said, "My Lord Jesus Christ, for my sake, wore a crown of thorns ; why should not I then, for His sake, wear this light crown, be it ever so ignominious ? Truly I will do it, and that willingly." When it was set upon his head, the bishops said, " Now, we commit thy soul to the devil," " But I," said Huss, lifting up his eyes towards heaven, " do commit my spirit into Thy hands, O Lord Jesus Christ ; to Thee I commend my Spirit, which Thou hast redeemed."

Dying Words.

Chap. xxvii. ver. 46.—Jesus cried with a loud voice, saying, My God, my God, why hast thou forsaken me ?

MR. JOB THROGMORTON, a puritan divine, who was described by his contemporaries as being "as holy and as choice a preacher as any in England," is said to have lived thirty-seven years without any comfortable assurance as to his spiritual condition. When dying, he addressed the venerable Mr. Dod in the following words, "What will you say of him who is going out of the world, and can find no comfort ?" "What will say of him," replied Mr. Dod, "who, when he was going out of the world, found no comfort, but cried, 'My God, My God, why hast Thou forsaken Me ?" This prompt reply administered consolation to the troubled spirit of his dying friend, who departed an hour after, rejoicing in the Lord.

Baptizing in the East.

Chap. xxviii. ver. 19.—Baptizing them in the name of the Father and of the Son, and of the Holy Ghost.

IN the following account, given by the Rev. Pliny Fisk, late American missionary in Palestine, we see a departure from Scripture simplicity in the dispensing of baptism ; "I went," says he, one morning to the Syrian church to witness a baptism. The administrator was the bishop, Abdool Messeeh. The resident bishop, Abdool Ahad, was present, and assisted in the service. When I arrived at the church, I found about a dozen persons present going through with the prayers and ceremonies preparatory to the baptism. One part of the service was explained to me as intended to expel the devil from the child. When ready for the baptism, the font was uncovered, and a small quantity, first of warm, and then of cold water, was poured into it. The child, in a state of perfect nudity, was then taken by the bishop, who held it in one hand, while with the other he anointed the whole body with oil. He then held the child in the font, its feet and legs being in the water, and with his right hand he took up water, and poured it on the child, in the name of the Father, the Son, and the Holy Ghost. After this, he anointed it with oil, and returned it to the parents."

Christ with Us.

Chap. xxviii. ver. 20.—Lo, I am with you always, even unto the end of the world.

MR ROBERT BRUCE, an eminent minister in Scotland, having to preach on a solemn occasion, was late in coming to the congregation. Some of the people beginning to be weary, and others wondering at his stay, the bells having been rung long, and the time far spent, the beadle was desired to go and inquire the reason ; who coming to his house, and finding his chamber-door shut, and hearing a sound, drew near, and listening, overheard Mr Bruce often, and with much seriousness, say, " I protest I will not go, except Thou go with me."

Whereupon the man, supposing that some person was in company with him, withdrew without knocking at the door. On being asked, at his return, the cause of Mr Bruce's delay, he answered he could not tell; but supposed that some person was with him, who was unwilling to come to church, and he was engaged in pressing him to come peremptorily, declaring he would not go without him. Mr Bruce soon after came, accompanied with no man, but he came in the fulness of the blessings of the Gospel of Christ; and his speech and his preaching were with such evidence and demonstration of the Spirit, that it was easy for the hearers to perceive he had been in the mount with God, and that he enjoyed the presence of his Divine Master.

MARK.

Locusts and Honey.

Chap. i. ver. 6.—John did eat locusts and wild honey.

A GOOD old French bishop, in paying his annual visit to his clergy was very much afflicted by the representations they made of their extreme poverty, which, indeed, the appearance of their houses and families corroborated. While he was deploring the state of things which had reduced them to this sad condition, he arrived at the house of a curate, who, living amongst a poor set of parishioners, would, he feared, be in a still more awful plight than the others. Contrary, however, to his expectations, he found appearances very much improved. Every thing about the house wore the aspect of comfort and plenty. The good bishop was amazed. "How is this, my friend?" said he; "you are the first man that I have met with a cheerful face, and a plentiful board. Have you any income independent of your cure?" "Yes, Sir," said the clergyman, "I have; my family would starve on the pittance I receive from the poor people I instruct. Come with me into the garden, and I will show you the *stock* that yields me an excellent interest." On going to the garden, he showed the bishop a large range of bee-hives. "There is the bank from which I draw an annual dividend. It never stops payment."

Morning Prayer.

Chap. i. ver. 35.—And in the morning, rising up a great while before day, he went out, and departed into a solitary place, and there prayed.

COLONEL GARDINER used constantly to rise at four in the morning, and to spend his time till six in the secret exercises of the closet, reading, meditation, and prayer; in which last he acquired such a fervency of spirit, as, "I believe," says his biographer, "few men living ever attained. This certainly very much contributed to strengthen that firm faith in God, and reverent animating sense of His presence, for which he was so eminently remarkable, and which carried him through the trials and services of life with such steadiness, and with such activity; for he indeed endured and acted as if always seeing Him who is invisible. If at any time he was obliged to go out before six in the morning, he rose proportionally sooner; so that, when a journey or a march has required him to be on horseback by four, he would be at his devotions by two."

God and the Starving.

Chap. ii. ver. 25, 26.—Have ye never read what David did, when he had need, and was an hungered, he, and they that were with him? How he went into the house of God, in the days of Abiathar the high-priest, and did eat the shew-bread, which is not lawful to eat but for the priests, and gave also to them that were with him.

WHEN the Romans had ravaged the province of Azazane, and 7000 Persians were brought to Armida, where they suffered extreme want, Acases, the bishop of that city, observed, that as God said, "I love mercy better than sacrifice," He would certainly be better pleased with the relief of His suffering creatures, than with being served with gold and silver in their churches. The clergy were of the same opinion. The consecrated vessels were sold; and, with the proceeds, the 7000 Persians were not only maintained during the war, but sent home at its conclusion with money in their pockets. Varenes, the Persian monarch, was so charmed with this humane action, that he invited the bishop to his capital, where he received him with the utmost reverence, and for his sake conferred many favours on the Christians.

The Ordained.

Chap. iii. ver. 14.—And he ordained twelve, that they should be with him, and that he might send them forth to preach.

THE Rev. John Howe being introduced to one of the bishops, formerly an acquaintance, his lordship expostulated with him respecting his non-conformity. Mr Howe told him he could not have time, without greatly trespassing upon his patience, to go through the several objections he had to make to the terms of conformity. The bishop pressed him to name any one that he reckoned to be of weight. He instanced the point of *re-ordination*. "Pray, Sir," said the bishop to him, "what hurt is there in being twice ordained?" "Hurt! my lord," said Mr Howe, "the thought is shocking; it hurts my understanding; it is an absurdity: for nothing can have two beginnings. I am sure I am a minister of Christ, and am ready to debate that matter with your Lordship, if you please; and I cannot begin again to be a minister." The bishop then dropped the matter, and told Mr H. that if he would come in amongst them he might have considerable preferment, and at length dismissed him in a very friendly manner.

Hearing and Believing.

Chap. iv. ver. 9.—He that hath ears to hear, let him hear.

AN INNKEEPER, addicted to intemperance, on hearing of the particularly pleasing mode of singing at a church some miles distant, went to gratify his curiosity, but with a resolution not to hear a word of the sermon. Having with difficulty found admission into a narrow open pew, as soon as the hymn before sermon was sung, which he heard with great attention, he secured both his ears against the sermon with his fore-fingers. He had not been in this position many minutes, before the prayer finished, and the sermon commenced with an awful appeal to the consciences of the hearers, of the necessity of attending to the things which belonged to their everlasting peace; and the minister, addressing them solemnly, said, "He that hath ears to hear, let him hear." Just the moment before these words were pronounced, a fly had fastened on the face of the innkeeper, and, stinging him sharply, he drew one of his fingers from his ears, and struck off the painful visitant. At that very moment the words, "He that hath ears to hear, let him hear," pronounced with great solemnity, entered the ear that was opened, as a clap of thunder. It struck him with irresistible force: he kept his hand from returning to his ear, and, feeling an impression he had never known before, he presently withdrew the other finger, and hearkened with deep attention to the discourse which followed. A salutary change was produced on him. He abandoned his former wicked practices, became truly serious, and for many years went, during all weathers, six miles to the church where he first received the knowledge of divine things. After about eighteen years faithful and close walk with God, he died rejoicing in the hope of that glory which he now enjoys.

Controlling the Sea.

Chap. iv. ver. 39.—And he arose, and rebuked the wind, and said unto the sea, Peace, be still. And the wind ceased, and there was a great calm.

MR HERVEY, in a sermon which he preached to the sailors at Biddeford, says,—"What we have mentioned of our Lord's saying *Peace* to the raging waves, may instruct you whom I address in the hour of danger; may also teach the wisdom of securing an interest in the Lord Jesus, whose divine word even the winds and sea obey. The hour is coming, dear sailors, when you shall hail with shouts your native land no more. Oh! then, come unto Christ; get an interest in His merits; give yourselves up to His guidance; let His word be your compass; let His grace hold the helm, and steer your course; let His blessing fill your sails; let His blood, His righteousness, His Spirit, be the prize of your calling; let this be the precious merchandise you court—this the pearl of price you seek."

Reformed through Christ.

Chap. v. ver. 15.—They come to Jesus, and see him that was possessed with the devil, and had the legion, sitting, and clothed, and in his right mind.

A YOUNG man, an apprentice in an extensive tin manufactory in the State of Massachusetts, who had been very profligate, but was converted by reading a religious tract, having applied for admission into a church, the minister called on his master to inquire whether any change had been wrought in his conduct, and whether he had any objection to his reception. When the minister had made the customary inquiries, his master, with evident emotion, though he was not a professor of religion, replied in substance as follows: Pointing to an iron chain hanging up in the room, "Do you see that chain?" said he. "That chain was forged for Wenn. I was obliged to chain him to the bench by the week together, to keep him at work. He was the worst boy I had in the whole establishment. No punishment seemed to have any salutary influence upon him. I could not trust him out of my sight; but now, Sir, he is completely changed; he has really become a lamb. He is one of my best apprentices. I would trust him with untold gold. I have no objection to his being received into communion. I wish all my boys were prepared to go with him."

Thankfulness to God.

Chap. v. ver. 19.—Jesus saith unto him, Go home to thy friends, and tell them how great things the Lord hath done for thee, and hath had compassion on thee.

A SAILOR of the name of Campbell, on board a Guineaman on the Congo, a river in Africa, while in a state of intoxication, bathed in that river. When he had swam some distance from the vessel, some persons on board discovered an alligator making towards him. His escape was now considered impossible; two shots were fired at the formidable creature, but without effect. The report of the piece, and the noise on board, made Campbell acquainted with his danger; he saw the creature advancing towards him, and with all the strength and skill he possessed, made for the shore. On approaching within a very short distance of some canes and shrubs that covered the bank, while closely pursued by the alligator, a ferocious tiger sprang towards him, at the instant the jaws of his first enemy were expanded to devour him. At this awful moment Campbell was preserved. The eager tiger, by overleaping him, encountered the grip of the amphibious monster. A conflict ensued between them; the water was coloured with the blood of the tiger, whose efforts to tear the scaly covering of the alligator were unavailing, while the latter had also the advantage of keeping his adversary under water, by which the victory was presently obtained, for the tiger's death was now effected. They both sank to the bottom, and the alligator was no more seen. Campbell was recovered, and instantly conveyed on board. His danger had sobered him, and the moment he leaped on deck, he fell on his knees, and returned thanks to Providence, who had so wonderfully preserved him; and what is more singular, "from that time to the time I am writing," says the narrator, "he has never been seen the least intoxicated, nor has he ever been heard to utter a single oath. If there ever was a reformed being in the universe, Campbell is the man."

Dancing.

Chap. vi. ver. 22.—The daughter of Herodias came in, and danced, and pleased Herod and them that sat with him.

A YOUNG lady, having requested her pious father to permit her to learn to dance, he replied, "No, my child, I cannot consent to comply with a request which may subject me to your censures at some future period." "No, father, I will never censure you for complying with my request." "Nor can I consent," replied the father, "to give you an opportunity. If you learn, I have no doubt but you will excel; and when you leave school, you may then want to go into company to exhibit your skill. If I then object to let you, as I most likely should, you would very naturally reply, 'Why, father, did you first permit me to learn, if I am not permitted to practise?'" This reply convinced her that her father acted wisely, though he opposed her inclination. She has now become a parent, has often mentioned this occurrence as having had a powerful moral influence over her mind, in the days of her juvenile vanity, and has incorporated this maxim into her system of domestic economy—Never to comply with a request which may subject her to any future reflections from her children.

Blessing at Table.

Chap. vi. ver. 41.—Jesus looked up to heaven, and blessed, and break the loaves.

"I CAME from my last voyage before Christmas," says a sailor, "and hastened home. Being late when I arrived, I had not the opportunity of seeing my eldest girl until the following day. At dinner time, when we had sat down, I began to eat what was before me, without ever thinking of my heavenly Father, that provided my daily bread; but, glancing my eye towards this girl, of whom I was doatingly fond, I observed her looking at me with astonishment. After a moment's pause, she asked me, in a solemn and serious manner, 'Father, do you never ask a blessing before eating?' Her mother observed me looking hard at her, and holding my knife and fork motionless; it was not anger—it was a rush of conviction which struck me like lightning. Apprehending some reproof from me, and wishing to pass it by in a trifling way, she said, 'Do you say grace, Nanny?' My eyes were still rivetted upon the child, for I felt conscious I had never instructed her to pray, nor even set an example, by praying with my family when at home. The child, seeing me waiting for her to begin, put her hands together, lifted her hands up to heaven, breathed the sweetest prayer I ever heard. This was too much for me; the knife and fork dropt from my hands, and I gave vent to my feelings in tears." It appears that, through the instrumentality of this child, not more than six years of age, who had attended a Sabbath school, together with her subsequent attendance on the public worship of God, the father has been led to saving views of divine truth.

Honour to Parents.

Chap. vii. ver. 10.—Honour thy father and thy mother; and, whoso curseth father or mother, let him die the death.

THE Roman Catholic clergy manifest the greatest hostility to the schools established in Ireland, in which the Scriptures are read. A gentleman, on expostulating with a young priest on the subject, was told in reply, that he was only obeying the orders of his bishop, whom he was bound to obey, by the most solemn and sacred oaths taken at his ordination, and of which bishop frequently reminded him, nor did he execute his direction with that *severity he ought*: for he was positively directed by his bishop to bring all the children who were sent by their parents to the school in the place before him; and while he denounced all the curses of the Church against their parents by *name*, the children were ordered to *curse their own parents*, by pronouncing audibly at the end of each verse, Amen!!

Evil Thoughts.

Chap. vii. ver. 21.—Out of the heart of men, proceed evil thoughts.

THE late Dr. Lawson of Selkirk, in travelling with a young friend, the conversation turned on the corruption of the human heart. The youth, who had the highest sense of his wisdom and sanctity, said to him, "I do not think you would need to fear much, though your thoughts were laid open." Dr. L. replied, "I could not bear that the course of my thoughts, even for one hour, should be exposed. Most needful is the prayer, 'Cleanse Thou me from secret faults; keep back thy servant also from presumptuous sins.'"

Giving Thanks.

Chap. viii. ver. 6.—Jesus took the seven loaves, and gave thanks.

AT Lebanon, in the state of New York, there dwelt a certain man, about fifty years of age, who had not only lived a very careless life, but was an open opposer of the Gospel-plan of salvation, and of the work of God in the late revival of religion in that part of the country ; he was, however, brought under serious convictions in the following manner :—One day there came into his house a traveller with a burden on his back ; the family being about to sit down to dinner, the stranger was invited to partake with them, which he accordingly did. When the repast was finished, and the members of the family were withdrawing from their seats, the stranger said, "Don't let us forget to give thanks to God." He accordingly gave thanks, and departed. The man of the house felt reproved and confounded. The words of the stranger were fastened on his mind by the power of God. He was led to reflect on his wickedness in being unmindful of God, and in neglecting prayer and thanksgiving ; he was also led to reflect on his manifold sins, which soon appeared to him a burden infinitely greater than that which the traveller bore. He found no relief until he sought it in that very way which he used formerly to despise, through the peace-speaking blood of the Lord Jesus Christ.

Loyalty to Christ.

Chap. viii. ver. 38.—Whosoever therefore shall be ashamed of me, and my words, in this adulterous and sinful generation, of him also shall the Son of Man be ashamed, when he cometh in the glory of his Father, with the holy angels.

DAVID STRAITON, one of the Scottish martyrs, was brought to the knowledge of the truth through the instrumentality of John Erskine of Dun. One day, having retired with the young laird of Laurieston to a quiet and solitary place in the fields, to have the New Testament read to him, it so happened, that in the course of reading, these words of our Saviour occurred, " He that denieth Me before men, in the midst of this wicked generation, him will I deny in the presence of My Father and His angels." On hearing them, he became of a sudden, as one enraptured or inspired. He threw himself on his knees, extended his hands, and, after looking for some time earnestly towards heaven, he burst forth in these words, " O Lord, I have been wicked, and justly mayest Thou withdraw Thy grace from me ; but, Lord, for Thy mercies' sake, let me never deny Thee nor Thy truth, for fear of death and corporal pains." The issue proved that his prayer was not in vain. For at his trial and death, he displayed much firmness and constancy in the defence of the truth, and gave great encouragement to another gentleman, Norman Gourlay, who suffered along with him.

The Evil Spirit.

Chap. ix. ver. 29.—This kind can come forth by nothing, but by prayer and fasting.

RICHARD COOK, a pious man, during Mr. Baxter's residence at Kidderminster, went to live in the next house to him. After some time he was seized with melancholy, which ended in madness. The most skilful help was obtained, but all in vain. While he was in this state, some pious persons wished to meet to fast and pray on behalf of the sufferer ; but Mr. Baxter in this instance, dissuaded them from it, as he apprehended the case to be hopeless, and thought they would expose prayer to contempt in the eyes of worldly persons, when they saw it unsuccessful. When ten or a dozen years of affliction had passed over Richard Cook, some of the pious men referred to would no longer be dissuaded, but fasted and prayed at his house. They continued this practice once a fortnight for several months ; at length the sufferer began to amend, his health and reason returned, and, adds Mr. Baxter, "he is now as well almost as ever he was, and so hath continued for a considerable time."

Be Humble Minded.

Chap. ix. ver. 35.—If any man desire to be first, the same shall be last of all, and servant of all.

ONE day Mr. John Elliot, a little before his death, after a very distinct and useful exposition of the eighty-third Psalm, concluded with an apology to his hearers, begging them "to pardon the poorness and meanness, and brokenness of his meditations ; but," added he, with singular humility, "my dear brother here will by and by mend all."

The Kingdom of Heaven.

Chap. x. ver. 14.—Suffer the little children to come unto me, and forbid them not : for of such is the kingdom of God.

A LITTLE girl between six and seven years of age, when on her death-bed, seeing her elder sister with a Bible in her hand, requested her to read it. The preceding passage having been read, and the book closed, the child said "How kind ! I shall soon go to Jesus ; He will soon take *me* up in His arms, bless me too ; no disciple shall keep me away." Her sister kissed her, and said, "Do you love me ?" "Yes, my dear," she replied, "but, do not be angry, I love Jesus better."

The Rich.

Chap. x. 23.—How hardly shall they that have riches enter into the kingdom of God !

WHEN Garrick showed Dr. Johnson his fine house, gardens, statues, pictures, etc., at Hampton Court, what ideas did they awaken in the mind of that great man ? Instead of a flattering compliment, which was expected, "Ah ! David, David," said the doctor, "these are the things which make a death-bed terrible !"

The Unfruitful.

Chap. xi. ver. 14.—Jesus answered and said unto it, No man eat fruit of thee hereafter for ever.

THE Spirit of God, by means of the Scriptures, convinces of sin, as well as comforts believers by its promises. Cowper, speaking of his distressing convictions, says, "One moment I thought myself shut out from mercy by one chapter, and the next by another. The sword of the Spirit seemed to guard the tree of life from my touch, and to flame against me in every avenue by which I attempted to approach it. I particularly remember, that the parable of the barren fig-tree was to be an inconceivable source of anguish ; and I applied it to myself, with a strong persuasion in my mind, that when our Saviour pronounced a curse upon it, He had me in His eye, and pointed that curse directly at me."

Forgiveness.

Chap. xi. ver. 25.—When ye stand praying, forgive, if ye have ought against any ; that your Father also which is in heaven may forgive you your trespasses.

A WEALTHY planter in Virginia, who had a great number of slaves, found one of them reading the Bible, and reproved him for neglect of his work, saying, there was time enough on Sundays for reading the Bible, and that on other days he ought to be in the tobacco-house. The slave repeated the offence; he ordered him to be whipped. Going near the place of punishment soon after its infliction, curiosity led him to listen to a voice engaged in prayer; and he heard the poor black implore the Almighty to forgive the injustice of his master, to touch his heart with a sense of his sin, and to make him a good Christian. Struck with remorse, he made an immediate change in his life, which had been careless and dissipated, burnt his profane books and cards, liberated all his slaves, and appears now to study how to render his wealth and talents useful to others.

True Speaking.

Chap. xii. ver. 12.—They sought to lay hold on him, but feared the people; for they knew that he had spoken the parable against them.

DURING the Protectorate, a certain knight in the county of Surrey had a law-suit with the minister of his parish; and whilst the dispute was pending, Sir John imagined that the sermons which were delivered at church were preached at him. He therefore complained against the minister to Oliver Cromwell, who inquired of the preacher concerning it; and having found that he merely reproved common sins, he dismissed the complaining knight, saying, "Go home, Sir John, and hereafter live in good friendship with your minister; the word of the Lord is a searching word, and it seems as if it had found you out."

The Mites.

Chap. xii. ver. 42.—There came a certain poor widow, and she threw in two mites, which make a farthing.

THE fire at Ratcliffe, in July 1794, was more destructive, and consumed more houses, than any conflagration since the memorable fire of London in 1666. Out of twelve hundred houses, not more than five hundred and seventy were preserved. The distress of the miserable inhabitants was beyond description, not less than one thousand four hundred persons being thrown on the benevolence of the public; nor was it slow in their support. Government immediately sent one hundred and fifty tents for the wretched sufferers. The city subscribed £1000 for their relief, and Lloyd's £700 The East India Company also gave £210. The collection from the visitants who crowded to see the encampment, amounted to upwards of £800, of which £426 was in copper, including £38 14s. in *farthings*, each a poor man's mite.

The Horrors of Famine.

Chap. xiii. ver. 8.—There shall be famines.

DURING the siege of Jerusalem, the extremity of the famine was such, that a Jewess of noble family, urged by the intolerant cravings of hunger, slew her infant child, and prepared it for a meal. She had actually eaten one-half of it, when the soldiers, allured by the smell of food, threatened her with instant death, if she refused to discover it. Intimidated by this menace, she immediately produced the remains of her son, which struck them with horror. At the recital of this melancholy and affecting occurrence, the whole city stood aghast, congratulating those whom death had hurried away from such heart-rending scenes. Indeed, humanity at once shudders and sickens at the narration; nor can any one of the least sensibility reflect upon the pitiable condition to which the female part of the inhabitants must at this time have been reduced, without experiencing the tenderest emotion of sympathy, or refraining from tears, when he reads our Saviour's pathetic address to the women who bewailed Him as He was led to Calvary, wherein He evidently refers to these very calamities.

Brothers.

Chap. xiii. ver. 12.—The brother shall betray the brother to death.

JOHN DIAZIUS, a native of Spain, having embraced the Protestant faith, came afterwards to Germany, where he visited Malvinda, the Pope's agent there. Having attempted in vain to bring him back to the Church of Rome, Malvinda sent to Rome for his brother Alphonsus Diazius, who, hearing that his brother had become a Protestant, came into Germany with an assassin, resolving either to draw him back to Popery, or to destroy him. Alphonsus finding his brother so stedfast in his belief of the truths of the Gospel, that neither the promises nor threats of the Pope's agent, nor his own pretensions of brotherly love, could prevail on him to return to Popery, feigned to take a most friendly and affectionate farewell and then departed. Having soon returned, he sent in the ruffian who accompanied him, with letters to his brother, himself following behind; and while his brother was reading them, the assassin cleft his head with a hatchet which they purchased on their way from a carpenter; and, taking horse, they both rode of. Alphonsus, though highly applauded by the Papists, became the prey of a guilty conscience. His horror and dread of mind were so insupportable, that, being at Trent during the general council like another Judas, he put an end to his life by hanging himself.

Unrighteous Blame.

Chap. xiv. ver. 4.—Some had indignation within themselves, and said, Why was this waste of the ointment made?

A CHRISTIAN gentleman, when blamed by his commercial partner for doing so much for the cause of God, made this reply,—"Your fox-hounds cost more in one year than my religion ever cost in *two*."

Willing Service.

Chap. xiv. ver. 8.—She hath done what she could.

AT a meeting held, with the view of forming an auxiliary society in aid of the Wesleyan mission, the following anecdote was related by one of the speakers:—A woman of Wakefield, well known to be in very needy circumstances, offered to subscribe a penny a-week to the Missionary fund. "Surely *you*," said one, "are too poor to afford this?" She replied, "I spin so many hanks of yarn for a maintenance; I will spin ONE MORE, and that will be a penny for the Society." "I would rather," said the speaker, "see that hank suspended in the poor woman's cottage—a token of her zeal for the triumph of the Gospel—than military trophies in the halls of heroes, the proud memorials of victories obtained over the physical strength of men!"

The Crown of Thorns.

Chap. xv. ver. 17.—They platted a crown of thorns, and put it about his head.

A YOUNG believer, full of faith and joy, was offered a present of flowers for her hair. She would not take them. She was pressed to accept them; still she refused. Why will you not? "Ah!" she said, "how can I wear roses on my brow, when Christ wore thorns on His?"

Heartless Mockery.

Chap. xv. ver. 20.—And when they had mocked him, they took off the purple from him, and put his own clothes on him, and led him out to crucify him.

AFTER Archbishop Crammer had been condemned, in the beginning of Queen Mary's reign, to suffer death, they proceeded afterwards to degrade him. To make this appear as ridiculous as possible, they put on him an episcopal habit made of canvas and old rags; Bonner, in the meantime, by way of insult and mockery, called him *Mr. Canterbury*, and such like. He bore all with his wonted fortitude and patience; telling them, the degradation gave him no concern, for he had long despised these ornaments. When they had stript him of all his habits, they put upon his jacket an old gown, threadbare and ill-shaped, and a townsman's cap, and so delivered him to the secular power, to be carried back to prison, where he was kept entirely destitute of money, and totally secluded from his friends. Such was the iniquity of the times, that a gentleman who gave him a little money to buy provisions, narrowly escaped being brought to trial for it.

The World and the Gospel.

Chap. xvi. ver. 15.—Go ye into all the world, and preach the Gospel to every creature.

"I HOPE," says Mr Knill of Petersburg, in a letter. "the subject of devoting ourselves and our children to God and to His service, will be more thought of, and more acted upon, than it has been hitherto. I am more and more convinced, that if St Paul had ever preached from, 'Go ye into all the world, and preach the Gospel to every creature,' he would have laid great stress on the word 'go.' On your peril do not substitute another word for 'go.' Preach is a good word. Direct is a good word. Collect is a good word. Give is a good word. They are all important in their places, and cannot be dispensed with. The Lord bless and prosper those who are so engaged, but still lay the stress on the word 'go!' for, how can they hear without a preacher, and how can they preach except they be sent?' Six hundred millions of the human race are perishing and there are perhaps thirty among all the Christians in Britain, who are at this moment preparing to 'go.' Alas! my hand shakes, and my heart trembles. 'Is this thy kindness to thy friend!'"

Spread of the Gospel.

Chap. xvi. ver 20.—They went forth and preached every where, the Lord working with them, and confirming the word with signs following.

ARNOBIUS, a heathen philosopher, who became a Christian, speaking of the power which the Christian faith had over the minds of men, says, "Who would not believe it, when he sees in how short a time it has conquered so great knowledge? Orators, grammarians, rhetoricians, lawyers, physicians, and philosophers, have thrown up those opinions which but a little before they held, and have embraced the doctrines of the Gospel!"

"Though but of yesterday," said Tertullian, "yet have we filled your cities, islands, castles, corporations, councils, your armies themselves, your tribes, companies, the palace, the senate, the courts of justice; only your temples have we left you free."

LUKE.

The Writer of this Gospel.

Chap. i. ver. 3.—It seemeth good to me also, having had perfect understanding of all things from the very first, to write unto thee in order, most excellent Theophilus.

MR. HILL, missionary at Berhampore, on one occasion distributed a number of tracts. He further states, "I had reserved a Gospel of Luke to use on the way, if occasion should require; but a man followed me, and constrained me to give it to him, by pleading my promise on the past night. When he had received it, he took hold of my horse-reins, and said, 'Sir, I will not let you depart, until I have some clue to the meaning of the book, otherwise it will be useless to me when you are gone.—Here, sir, what is this Mungal Somachar?' 'Good news.'—'What is this Luke?' 'Luke is the man's name who wrote this book.'—'Kutrick—what is that?' 'Written; and the whole sentence means, the Gospel written by Luke.'—'Who was Luke?' 'He was a man acquainted with all which the Lord Jesus Christ did and said on earth, with the reason of Christ's coming into the world, and with the manner of his death; and these are the things contained in this book.'—'That will do, sir; now, I shall understand what I read.' I left him, and prayed that the Lord would give him understanding."

The Ways of Peace.

Chap. i. ver. 79.—To guide our feet into the way of peace.

A PIOUS father, the evening before his departure, desired all his children to come into his chamber; and placing them around his dying bed, thus addressed them:—"You all know that I am soon going to be transplanted out of this world into a better. I hope I shall there be permitted to watch over you, and I trust that you are walking the same road, and will soon follow me. You all know *the road*; great pains have been taken to show it to you. Where is it to be found?" The children all instantly replied, "In the Bible." The dying parent proceeded: "Keep hold of that chain; it will never mislead you. When you are in doubt whether this or that be right, ask your Bible; see if your Saviour would have done so."

Good Tidings.

Chap. ii. ver. 10.—The angel said unto them, Fear not; for behold I bring you good tidings of great joy, which shall be to all people.

IN the year 1753, Mr Lindley Murray was placed in a good school in the city of New York. A very strong, and, he thought, beneficial impression was made upon his mind about this period (in his eighth or ninth year), by a piece which was given him to write. The sheet was decorated with a frame-work of "pleasing figures," in the centre of which he was to transcribe the visit and salutation of the angels to the shepherds of Bethlehem. To use his own words, "The beauty of the sheet, the property I was to have in it, and the distinction which I expected from performing the work in a handsome manner, prepared my mind for relishing the solemn narrative, and the interesting language of the angels to the shepherds. The impression was so strong and delightful, that it has often occurred to me through life with great satisfaction ; and, at this hour, it is remembered with pleasure. If parents and others who have the care of young persons, would be studious to seize occasion of presenting the Holy Scriptures to them, under favourable and inviting points of view, a veneration for these sacred volumes, and a pleasure in perusing them, may be excited by agreeable and interesting associations ; and these impressions, thus early made, there is reason to believe, would accompany the mind through the whole of life."

Dying in Peace.

Chap. ii. ver. 29, 30.—Lord, now lettest thou thy servant depart in peace, according to thy word ; for mine eyes have seen thy salvation.

MR. HERVEY, when dying, expressed his gratitude to his physician for his visits, though it had been long out of the power of medicine to cure him. He then paused a little, and with great serenity and sweetness in his countenance, though the pangs of death were upon him, being raised a little in his chair, repeated these words : "*Lord, now lettest Thou Thy servant depart in peace, according to Thy most holy and comfortable word; for mine eyes have seen Thy precious salvation.* Here, doctor, is my cordial ; what are all the cordials given to support the dying, in comparison to that which arises from the promises of salvation by Christ? This, this now supports me." About three o'clock, he said, "The great conflict is over, —now all is done."

After which he scarcely spoke any other word intelligibly, except twice or thrice, *precious salvation!* and then leaning his head against the side of the chair on which he sat, he shut his eyes, and on Christmas-day, the 25th of December 1758, between four and five in the afternoon, fell asleep in Jesus.

Repentance.

Chap. iii. ver. 7, 8.—Then said he to the multitude that came forth to be baptized of him, O generation of vipers, who hath warned you to flee from the wrath to come ? Bring forth, therefore, fruits worthy of repentance.

THE late Dr. A. Thomson, when minister at Sprouston, having seen a member of his congregation coming out of a public-house in a state of intoxication, resolved to seize the first opportunity to rebuke him for his sin, and warn him of his danger. Nor was it long before such an opportunity occurred. In a few days after, the man came to him, requesting baptism for his child. This Dr. T. decidedly refused until he acknowledged his sin, and promised amendment ; informing him, at the same time, that he himself had been an eye-witness of his inebriety. The man immediately commenced an apology, in which he happened to stumble on another occasion than that to which the minister alluded ; which furnished Dr. T. with additional matter of solemn and pointed rebukes. This was too much for the stubborn delinquent, who immediately left the house in a rage. Shortly after, however, his wife called on Dr. T., and earnestly entreated him to receive her husband again into the communion of the church.

"Most certainly," replied Dr. Thomson, "provided he candidly acknowledges his offence against God, and gives me the solemn promise that he will abandon the sin of intemperance." To this the now humbled penitent agreed, and in due time received baptism for his child.

The Spirit of God.

Chap. iv. ver. 18.—The Spirit of the Lord is upon me, because he hath anointed me to preach the Gospel to the poor.

THE biographer of Mr. Elliot, the missionary, says of him,—"He liked no preaching but what had been well studied; and he would very much commend a sermon which he could perceive had required some good thinking and reading in the author of it. I have heard him thus express himself: 'Brother, there was oil required for the service of the sanctuary; but it was to be beaten oil; I praise God that I saw your oil so well beaten to-day; the Lord help us always, by good study, to beat our oil, that there may be no knots in our sermons left undissolved, and that there may be a clear light thereby given to the house of God!' He likewise looked for something in a sermon beside and beyond the mere study of man; he was for having the *Spirit of God* breathing in it, and with it; and he was for speaking those things from those impressions, and with those affections, which might compel the hearer to say, *The Spirit of God was here!* I have heard him complain, 'It is a sad thing, when a sermon shall have this one thing, *the Spirit of God*, wanting in it.'"

Catching Men.

Chap. v. ver. 10.—Jesus saith unto Simon, Fear not; from henceforth thou shalt catch men.

THE late Rev. Henry Venn, in a letter, descriptive of a tour through different parts of England, says—"From Bath through Bristol and Gloucester, we arrived at Trevecca, in Wales. Howell Harris is the father of that settlement, and the founder. After labouring for fifteen years, more violently than any other of the servants of Christ, in this revival, he was so hurt in body as to be confined to his own house for seven years. Upon the beginning of his confinement, first one and then another whom the Lord had converted under His word, to the number of nearly a hundred, came and desired to live with him, saying that they would work and get their bread. By this means, nearly one hundred and twenty men and children, from very distant parts of Wales, came and fixed their tents at Trevecca. We were there three days, and heard their experience, which they spoke in Welsh to Mr. Harris, and he interpreted to us. Of all the people I ever saw, this society seems to be the most advanced in grace. They speak as men and women who feel themselves every moment worthy of eternal punishment, and infinitely base, and yet, at the same time, have such certainty of salvation through the second Man, the Lord from heaven, as is indeed delightful to behold. My heart received a blessing from them and their pastor, which will abide with me."

Spiritual Wonders.

Chap. v. ver. 26.—We have seen strange things to-day

DR. Philip, in a late speech at the anniversary of the London Missionary Society, alludes to a remark made by Mr. Newton.— "When I got to heaven, I shall see three wonders there;—the first wonder will be to see many people there whom I did not expect to see—the second wonder will be to miss many people whom I did expect to see—and the third, the greatest wonder of all, will be to find myself there." "I have also," said Dr. P., "seen three wonders; I have seen men of great wealth, and great talent, who have had many opportunities of forwarding the cause of God, do nothing; I have seen many humble and despised individuals, but whose hearts were right with God, do wonders; but the greatest wonder of all is to find that so humble an individual as I am, should have been at all useful in the work. I take nothing unto myself but shame and humility before God."

Persecuted for Godliness.

Chap. vi. ver. 22.—Blessed are ye when men shall hate you, and when they shall separate you from their company, and shall reproach you, and cast out your name as evil, for the Son of Man's sake.

SIX students were expelled the University of Oxford in 1768, for praying, reading, and expounding the Scriptures in a private house. Mr. Stedding defended their doctrines from the thirty-nine articles of the Established Church, and spoke in the highest terms of the piety and exemplariness of their lives; but his motion was over-ruled, and sentence pronounced against them. Dr. Jebbe, one of the heads of the houses present, observed, that as these six gentlemen were expelled for having too much religion, it would be very proper to inquire into the conduct of some who had too little. What a state must religion have been in at Oxford, that out of so many hundred students, only six should be found guilty of such a pretended crime!

Kindness to Enemies.

Chap. vi. ver. 28.—Pray for them which despitefully use you.

MR. LAMB, a violent persecutor of the Puritans, being on a journey in the country, and having the misfortune to break his leg, was brought to the same inn where Mr. Herring, a pious minister, whom he had in a special manner persecuted, was stopping all night. The good man was called on to conduct the devotion of the family, and prayed so fervently and affectionately for the doctor, as greatly surprised those who were present. Being asked why he manifested so much respect towards a man so unworthy of it, he replied, "The greater enemy he is, the more need he hath of our prayers. We must prove ourselves to be the disciples of Christ, by loving our enemies, and praying for our persecutors."

Visiting the Sick.

Chap. vii. ver. 2, 3.—And a certain centurion's servant, who was dear unto him, was sick, and ready to die. And when he heard of Jesus, he sent unto him the elders of the Jews, beseeching him that he would come and heal his servant.

"I REMEMBER," says Dr. Doddridge in his Life of Colonel Gardiner, "I had once occasion to visit one of his dragoons in his last illness at Harborough, and I found the man upon the borders of eternity; a circumstance which, as he apprehended himself, must add some peculiar weight and credibility to his discourse. And he then told me, in his colonel's absence, that he questioned not but he should have everlasting reason to bless God on Colonel Gardiner's account; for he had been a father to him in all his interests, both temporal and spiritual. He added, that he had visited him almost every day during his illness, with religious advice and instruction, as well as taken care that he should want for nothing that might conduce to the recovery of his health. And he did not speak of this as the result of any particular attachment to him, but as the manner in which he was accustomed to treat those under his command."

The Dead.

Chap. vii. 12.—Now, when he came nigh to the gate of the city, behold, there was a dead man carried out, the only son of his mother, and she was a widow.

IT is recorded of the late Countess of Huntingdon, who afterwards so warmly espoused the cause of God and His truth, in her early youth, when about nine years old, the sight of a corpse about her own age, carried to the grave, induced her to attend the funeral, and then the first impressions of deep seriousness respecting an eternal world laid hold of her conscience. With many tears, she cried earnestly on the spot to God, that whenever He was pleased to call her hence, He would deliver her from all her fears, and give her a happy departure: she often afterwards visited the grave of this young person, and always preserved a lively sense of the affecting scene.

Changed Women.

Chap. viii. ver. 2.—And certain women, which had been healed of evil spirits and infirmities, Mary called Magdalene, out of whom went seven devils.

MR. ROMAINE had been chosen to the rectory of Blackfriars in 1764; but, by the opposition of some who were unfriendly to the Gospel, was kept out of the pulpit till early in the year 1766, when the Lord Chancellor, to the inexpressible joy of thousands, terminated the dispute in his favour. His election is said to have been principally owing to the influence of a publican. Mr. Romaine being informed of this circumstance, we are told, waited upon him to thank him for the zeal he had shown on that occasion. "Indeed, sir," he replied, "I am more indebted to you than you to me, for you have made my wife, who was one of the worst, the best woman in the world."

Faith.

Chap. viii. ver. 24, 25.—And they came to him, and awoke him, saying, Master, Master, we perish! Then he arose, and rebuked the wind and the raging to the water; and they ceased, and there was a calm. And he said unto them, Where is your faith?

SOME years ago, an officer in the army, who was a pious man, was drafted abroad with his regiment. He accordingly embarked with his wife and children. They had not been many days at sea, when a violent storm arose, which threatened the destruction of the ship, and the loss of all their lives. Consternation and terror prevailed among the crew and passengers; his wife also was greatly alarmed. In the midst of all he was perfectly calm and composed: his wife observing this, began to upbraid him with want of affection to her and her children, urging, that if he was not concerned for his own safety, he ought to be for theirs. He made no reply, but immediately left the cabin, to which he returned in a short time with his sword drawn in his hand, and with a stern countenance pointed it to her breast; but she, smiling, did not appear at all disconcerted or afraid. "What!" said he, are you not afraid when a drawn sword is at your breast?" "No," answered she, "not when I know that it is in the hand of one who loves me." "And would you have me," replied he, "to be afraid of this storm and tempest, when I know it to be in the hand of my heavenly Father, who loves me?"

Asleep at the Wrong Time.

Chap. ix. ver. 32.—But Peter and they that were with him were heavy with sleep; and when they were awake they saw his glory, and the two men that stood with him.

THE late Rev. Mr. More, minister of the Gospel, Selkirk, while preaching from these words of Moses, "I beseech thee show me Thy glory," observing many of his hearers fast asleep, made a pause, on which they awoke. He then, in a very solemn manner, addressed them to the following effect:—"Do you think, my friends, had Moses been asleep while the glory of God passed by him, that he would have seen it? The glory of God, in the dispensation of the Gospel, has just been passing by you, and yet you were all asleep!" It need not be added, that during that day, at least, he had a more attentive audience.

Judging Rightly.

Chap. ix. ver. 42.—And John answered and said, Master we saw one casting out devils in thy name; and we forbade him, because he followeth not with us.

"SEEING a tree growing somewhat irregular, in a very neat orchard," says Mr Flavel, "I told the owner, it was a pity that tree should stand there; and that, if it were mine, I would root it up, and thereby reduce the orchard to an exact uniformity. He replied, 'that he rather regarded the fruit than the form; and that this light inconveniency was abundantly preponderated by a more considerable advantage. This tree,' said he, 'which you would root up, hath yielded me more fruit than any of those trees which have nothing else to commend them but their regular situation.' I could not but yield to the reason of this answer; and could wish it had been spoken so loud that all our uniformity men had heard it, who would not stick to root up many hundreds of the best bearers in the Lord's orchard, because they stand not in exact order with other more conformable, but less beneficial, trees, who do destroy the fruits to preserve the form."

Fruitful and Unfruitful Preaching.

Chap. x. ver. 6.—And if the son of peace be there, your peace shall rest upon it; if not, it shall turn to you again.

A PIOUS minister, perceiving that all his labours among the people of his charge were wholly in vain, was so extremely grieved and dejected, that he determined to leave his flock, and to preach his farewell sermon; but he was suddenly struck with the words, Luke x. 6, "And if the son of peace be there, your peace shall rest upon it; if not, it shall turn to you again." He felt as if his Lord and Master had addressed him thus: "Ungrateful servant, art thou not satisfied with My promise, that My despised peace shall return to you again? Go on then to proclaim peace." Which accordingly he did, with renewed vigour and zeal.

Unlearned yet Wise.

Chap. x. ver. 21.—Thou hast hid these things from the wise and prudent, and hast revealed them unto babes. Even so, Father, for so it seemed good in thy sight.

A PIOUS minister gives the following account of a poor deranged woman, who case appears to illustrate the sovereignty of Divine grace.—"She was a pauper, who usually claimed to herself the title of Lady Pitreavie, and was well known in my neighbourhood by that name. Shortly after I came here, one of my hearers, who knew she had been in my meeting-house, said to her, 'Well, my lady, what do you think of our minister?' She replied, with great energy, 'Your minister! why, I think so much of his Master, that I think little of him in comparison.' Passing by her one day, she accosted me, 'Mr Bain, I must have you and Mr Horne to meet with me some day, that I may get my titles to the house of Pitreavie settled." I said to her, 'My lady, the best house which you can now possess, is the house eternal in the heavens.' She made answer, 'True, but the more evidence I have of a title to a house eternal in the heavens, the better right have I to a house on earth.' On another occasion, on my addressing her, 'How are you to-day, my lady?' she answered, 'Whether do you mean as I am in myself, or as I am in Christ?' I told her she might take it either way.—'If,' said she 'you mean how am I in myself, I am a poor sinner: but if you mean how am I as in Christ, I answer, I am complete in Him."

Temptations.

Chap. xi. ver. 4.—And lead us not into temptation, but deliver us from evil.

"HE that is not satisfied," says Bishop Wilson, "that plays are an unlawful diversion, let him, *if he dare*, offer up this prayer to God *before he goes*, 'Lord lead me not into temptation, and bless me in what I am now to be employed.'" There are many other occupations and amusements, in which the same advice is worth attending to.

Encountering Difficulties.

Chap. xi. ver. 52.—Woe unto you, lawyers! for ye have taken away the key of knowledge: ye enter not in yourselves, and them that were entering in ye hindered.

A FEW years ago, a pilot in Quebec, a Roman Catholic, who cared nothing at all about religion, picked up an old Bible which had been cast ashore from the wreck of a ship. He read it through; and it opened his eyes so much, that he could not forbear from disputing with his priest upon certain points of religion. The priest was much surprised to find him so knowing, and inquired how he had received his information; upon which the pilot showed him his Bible. The priest declared it was not a fit book for him to read, and desired he would give it into his charge. This the pilot refused, and the priest threatened to write to the bishop, and have him excommunicated as a heretic. But finding that neither threats nor entreaties had any effect, he requested he would just keep it to himself, and let none of his neighbours know he had such a book. The old pilot declared that he considered the finding of that book the happiest event of his life, in consequence of the comfort which he received from perusing it.

Striving after Riches.

Chap. xii. ver. 20.—But God said unto him, Thou fool, this night thy soul shall be required of thee: then whose shall these things be which thou hast provided?

JOHN CAMERON, Bishop of Glasgow, was so given to covetousness, extortion, violence, and oppression, especially upon his own tenants and vassals, that he would scarcely afford them bread to eat, or clothes to cover their nakedness. But the night before Christmas day, and in the midst of his cruelties, as he lay in bed at his house in Lockwood, he heard a voice summoning him to appear before the tribunal of Christ, and give an account of his actions. Being terrified with this notice, and the pangs of a guilty conscience, he called up his servants, commanding them to bring lights, and stay in the room with him. He himself took a book in his hand, and began to read, but the voice being heard a second time, struck all the servants with horror. The same voice repeating the summons a third time, and with a louder and more dreadful accent, the bishop, after a lamentable and frightful groan, was found dead in his bed with his tongue hanging out of his mouth, a dreadful spectacle to all beholders. This relation is made by the celebrated historian Buchanan, who records it as a remarkable example of God's judgment against the sin of oppression.

Devotion to Duty.

Chap. xii. ver. 43.—Blessed is that servant, whom his Lord, when he cometh, shall find so doing.

MR CARTER, a pious minister, once coming softly behind a religious man of his own acquaintance, who was busily employed in tanning a hide, and giving him a tap on the shoulder, the man started, looked behind, and with a blushing countenance said, "Sir, I am ashamed that you should find me thus." To whom Mr Carter replied, "Let Christ, when he cometh, find me so doing." "What," said the man, "doing thus?" "Yes," said Mr Carter, "faithfully performing the duties of my calling."

Repentance.

Chap. xiii. ver. 3.—Except ye repent, ye shall all likewise perish.

IT is said of a Mr Tain and three of his associates, that to enliven a company, they once undertook to mimic a celebrated preacher. The proposition was highly gratifying to all present, and a wager was agreed upon, to inspire each individual with a desire of excelling in his impious attempt. That their jovial auditors might adjudge the prize to the most adroit performer, it was concluded that each should open the Bible, and hold forth from the first text that should present itself to his eye. Accordingly, three in their turns mounted the table, and entertained their wicked companions at the expense of everything sacred. When they had exhausted their little stock of buffoonery, it devolved on Mr T. to close this very irreverent scene. Much elated, and confident of success, he exclaimed, as he ascended the table, "I shall beat you all!" When the Bible was handed to him, he had not the slightest preconception what text of Scripture he should make the subject of his banter. However, by the guidance of an unerring Providence, it opened at the above passage—"Except ye repent, ye shall all likewise perish." No sooner had he uttered the words, than his mind was affected in a very extraordinary manner. The sharpest pangs of conviction now seized him, and conscience denounced vengeance upon his soul. In a moment he was favoured with a clear view of his subject, and divided his discourse more like a divine, than one who never thought on religious topics, except for the purpose of ridicule. He found no deficiency of matter, no want of utterance;

and he has been frequently heard to declare, "If ever I preached in my life by the assistance of the Spirit of God, it was at that time." The impression which the subject made upon his mind, had such an effect upon his manner, that the most ignorant and profane could not but perceive that what he had spoken was with the greatest sincerity.

Cumberers.

Chap. xiii. ver. 7.—Cut it down; why cumbereth it the ground.

THERE was a man bitterly hostile to religion, who had long been the opposer of his pious wife, who one Sabbath morning took his axe upon his shoulder, and went to his wood-lot to fell trees. As he looked around, he saw one tree dead and dry, with its leafless branches extended into the air, and he said to himself, "That tree I will cut down; it is dead and dry, fit only to burn." And at that moment the thought rushed into his mind, "Am not I a dead tree, fit only to burn?" He tried to banish the thought, but it was an arrow from the quiver of the Almighty. He went to the tree and struck a few blows with his axe. But the thought still rankled in his heart, "Am not I a dead tree, fit only to burn? Will not God say concerning me, 'Cut him down, for he cumbereth the ground?'" Again and again he tried to drive away the unwelcome and harrowing thought. But there it was, a barbed arrow fixed in his heart, and he could not tear it out. He plied his axe with increasing vigour, but every blow seemed but to deepen the conviction of his own spiritual deadness. At last he could endure it no longer. He shouldered his axe, returned to his home, went to his chamber, fell upon his knees before God, and cried for mercy. With a penitent and broken heart, he implored forgiveness through atoning blood, and found that peace which the penitent never seeks in vain. He erected the family altar in his dwelling, united himself with the Church of Christ, is now apparently journeying fast to heaven, a new creature in Jesus Christ.

Helping on Sunday.

Chap. xiv. ver. 5.—Which of you shall have an ass or an ox fall into a pit, and will not straightway pull him out on the Sabbath-day?

A MAN belonging to one of the South Sea Islands, came to the missionaries at a Monday evening meeting, and said his mind was troubled, as he feared he had done wrong. He was asked in what respect; when he answered, that on the preceding day, which was the Sabbath, when returning from public worship, he observed that the tide, having risen higher than usual, had washed out to sea a large pair of double canoes, which he had left on the beach. At first he thought of taking a smaller canoe, fetching back the larger ones, and fixing them in a place of security; but while he was deliberating, it occurred to his recollection that it was the Sabbath, and that the Scriptures prohibited any work. He therefore allowed the canoes to drift towards the reef, until they were broken on the rocks. But, he added, though he did not work on the Sabbath, his mind was troubled on account of the loss he had sustained, and *that* he thought was wrong. He was immediately told that he would have done right, had he fetched the canoes to the shore on the Sabbath. While these scruples, to a person of enlarged information, will appear unnecessary, the conscientious feeling which they manifest ought to be respected.

Humility

Chap. xiv. ver. 11.—Whosoever exalteth himself, shall be abased; and he that humbleth himself, shall be exalted.

IN the evening of the day Sir Eardly Wilmot kissed his Majesty's hands on being appointed chief justice, one of his sons, a youth of seventeen, attended him to his bed-side. "Now," said he, "my son, I will tell you a secret worth your knowing and remembering. The elevation I have met with in life, particularly this last instance of it, has not been owing to any superior merit or abilities, but to my *humility;* to my not having set up myself above others, and to an uniform endeavour to pass through life void of offence towards God and man."

Repentance.

Chap. xv. ver. 7.—Joy shall be in heaven over one sinner that repenteth.

MAHOMED RAHEM, a Persian, having been asked respecting the change that had taken place in his religious sentiments, gave the following account:—"In the year 1223 of the Hegira, there came to this city an Englishman, who taught the religion of Christ with a boldness hitherto unparalleled in Persia, in the midst of scorn and much ill-treatment from our mollahs, as well as the rabble. He was a beardless youth, and evidently enfeebled by disease. He dwelt amongst us for more than a year. I was then a decided enemy to infidels, as the Christians are termed by the followers of Mahomet, and I visited this teacher of the despised sect, with the declared object of treating him with scorn, and exposing his doctrines to contempt. Although I persevered for some time in this behaviour towards him, I found that every interview not only increased my respect for the individual, but diminished my confidence in the faith in which I was educated. His extreme forbearance towards the violence of his opponents, the calm and yet convincing manner in which he exposed the fallacies and sophistries by which he was assailed, for he spoke Persian excellently, gradually inclined me to listen to his arguments, to inquire dispassionately into the subject of them, and finally, to read a tract which he had written in reply to a defence of Islamism, by our chief mollahs. Need I detain you longer? The result of my examination was a conviction that the young disputant was right. Shame, or rather fear, withheld me from avowing this opinion; I even avoided the society of the Christian teacher, though he remained in the city so long. Just before he quitted Shiraz, I could not refrain from paying him a farewell visit. Our conversation—the memory of it will never fade from the tablet of my mind—sealed my conversion.—He gave me a book,—it has ever been my constant companion; the study of it has formed my most delightful occupation,—its contents have often consoled me. Upon this he put into my hands a copy of the New Testament in Persian; on one of the blank leaves was written—

'THERE IS JOY IN HEAVEN OVER ONE SINNER THAT REPENTETH.

HENRY MARTYN.'"

The Prodigal.

Chap. xv. ver. 12, 13.—And he divided unto them his living, And not many days after, the younger son gathered all together, and took his journey into a far country, and there wasted his substance with riotous living.

THE late Admiral Williams, when young, was gay, and so addicted to expensive pleasures, that no remonstrances had the power to reclaim him, being so enamoured with ruinous folly. When his father died, he joined the rest of the family to hear the will read. His name did not occur amongst those of the other children, and he looked upon the omission as a testimony of his father's resentment against him: At the close of it, however, he found himself brought in as residuary legatee, or, who was to receive all that remained of his father's property, after paying the other legacies, in these words:— "All the rest of my estate and effects I leave to my son Peer Williams, knowing that he will spend it all." On hearing this, the young gentleman burst into tears: "My father," said he, "has touched the right string, and his reproach shall not be thrown away." From that time he altered his conduct, and became an ornament to his profession.

Stewardship.

Chap. xvi. ver. 2.—Give an account of thy stewardship; for thou mayest be no longer steward.

A WEALTHY but niggardly gentleman was waited on by the advocates of a charitable institution, for which they solicited his aid, reminding him of the divine declaration (Prov. xix. 17), "He that hath pity on the poor, lendeth unto the Lord; and that what he hath given will he pay him again." To this he replied, "The security, no doubt, is good, and the interest liberal; but I cannot give such long credit." Poor rich man! the day of payment was much nearer than he anticipated. Not a fortnight had elapsed from his refusing to honour this claim of God upon his substance, before he received a summons with which he could not refuse to comply. It was, "This night thy soul shall be required of thee, then whose shall those things be which thou hast withheld?"

The Rich Man in Hell.

Chap. xvi. ver. 22, 23.—The rich man also died; and in hell he lifted up his eyes, being in torments.

A NOBLEMAN who lived in the neighbourhood of the Rev. Mr Dunn, one day asked him to dine with him. Before dinner they walked into the garden, and after viewing the various productions and rarities with which it abounded, his lordship exclaimed, "Well, Mr Dunn, you see I want for nothing; I have all that my heart can wish for." As Mr Dunn made no reply, but appeared thoughtful, his lordship asked him the reason? "Why, my Lord," said the old man, "I have been thinking, that a man may have all these things, and go to hell after all." The words powerfully struck the nobleman, and through the blessing of God terminated in his conversion.

Thankfulness.

Chap. xvii. ver. 15, 16.—And one of them, when he saw that he was healed, turned back, and with a loud voice glorified God, and fell down on his face at his feet, giving him thanks; and he was a Samaritan.

ADMIRAL BENBOW, after many years of hard service, for he had only merit to recommend him, visited Shrewsbury, his native town, and, on his arrival, preceeded to the house of his nativity, which was then occupied by people in no way related to him ; yet he entered the house as if it had been his own, walked up stairs, went into the room where he first drew breath, fell on his knees, and returned thanks to the Great Disposer of events, for His protection and support through his past eventful life.

Unimproved Privileges

Chap. xvii. ver. 22.—The days will come, when ye shall desire to see one of the days of the Son of Man, and ye shall not see it.

" A GAY and thoughtless young man," says Mr. Innes, in his useful work on domestic duties, "who had often opposed a pious father's wishes, by spending the Sabbath in idleness and folly, instead of accompanying his parents to the house of God, was taking a ride one Sabbath morning. After riding for some time at great speed, he suddenly pulled up his horse, when the animal, by stopping more suddenly than he expected, gave him such a sudden jerk, that it injured the spinal marrow ; and when he came to his father's door, he had totally lost the use of the lower extremities of his body. He was lifted from his horse, and laid on that bed which was destined to prove to him the bed of death ; and there he had leisure to reflect on his ways. It was when in this situation I was asked to visit him, and he then discovered the deepest solicitude about the things that belonged to his eternal peace. He eagerly listened to the representation that was given him respecting the evil of sin, its dreadful consequences, and the ground of hope to the guilty. He seemed much impressed with a sense of his need of pardoning mercy, and thankfully to receive it in the way that God had revealed. Many parts of the conversations I had with him now escape my recollection, but some of his expressions I shall not easily forget. On one occasion, when referring to his past life, and finding himself now unable to attend public worship, he exclaimed, 'O ! what would I give now for some of those Sabbaths which I formerly treated with contempt !' He seemed deeply to feel and to deplore his guilt in having so heinously misimproved the precious opportunities of waiting on the public ordinances of religion, which, in the day of health, he had enjoyed."

Prayer.

Chap. xviii. ver. 1—And he spake a parable unto them to this end that men ought always to pray, and not to faint.

MR. Elliot was eminent for prayer ; and whenever any remarkable difficulty lay before him, he took the way of prayer in order to encounter and overcome it ; being of Dr. Preston's mind, "That where he would have any great things to be accomplished, the best policy is to work by an engine which the world sees nothing of." When he heard any important news, he usually said, "Let us turn all this into prayer." And if he came to a house where he was intimately acquainted, he used frequently to say, "Come, let us not have a visit without a prayer. Let us, before we part, pray for the blessing of heaven on our family."

Sacrifice for Christ.

Chap. xviii. ver. 29, 30.—Verily I say unto you, There is no man that hath left house, or parents, or brethren, or wife, or children, for the kingdom of God's sake, who shall not receive manifold more in this present time, and in the world to come life everlasting.

A YOUNG person who had been a Sabbath scholar, went to live in a family in which religion was wholly neglected. On the other side of the street a pious family resided, who strictly observed the Sabbath. The young woman perceived that the servants were allowed to attend public worship twice every Lord's day, while she could not go once to church, as her master generally invited company to dinner on that day. She reminded her mistress of this circumstance, and requested she might go to chapel one part of the Sabbath. This was refused, on the ground that she could not be spared. She then resolved, that if any vacancy occurred in the family opposite, she would offer herself. This happening soon after, she waited upon the lady, who observed, "I am afraid that, as you have high wages where you now live, my place will not suit you, as I give but five pounds a-year, but if you will come for that, I will try you." The young woman consented, and entered into the family. A gentleman visiting in the house, being acquainted with the case, presented her with a Bible, on the blank leaf of which he wrote—Luke xviii. 29, 30. "Verily I say unto you, There is no man who hath left house, or parents, or brethren, or wife, or children, for the kingdom of God's sake, who shall not receive manifold more in this present time, and in the world to come life everlasting."

Temporal Restoration.

Chap. xix. ver. 8.—Behold, Lord, the half of my goods I give to the poor; and if I have taken anything from any man by false accusation, I restore him fourfold.

ONE of the Moorish kings of Spain wished to build a pavillion on a field near his garden, and offered to purchase it of the woman to whom it belonged, but she would not consent to part with the inheritance of her fathers. The field, however, was seized, and the building was erected. The poor woman complained to a cadi, who promised to do all in his power to serve her. One day, while the king was in the field, the cadi came with an empty sack, and asked permission to fill it with the earth on which he was treading. He obtained leave, and when the sack was filled, he requested the king to complete his kindness by assisting him to load his ass with it. The monarch laughed, and tried to lift it, but soon let it fall, complaining of its enormous weight. "It is however," said the cadi, "only a small part of the ground which thou hast wrested from one of thy subjects; how then wilt thou bear the weight of the whole field when thou shalt appear before the Great Judge laden with this iniquity?" The king thanked him for his reproof; and not only restored the field to its owner, but gave her the building which he had erected, and all the wealth which it contained.

Waiting God's Time.

Chap. xix. ver. 13.—Occupy till I come.

WHEN Mr. Whitefield was last in America, Mr. Tennent paid him a visit, as he was passing through New Jersey; and one day dined with other ministers at a gentleman's house. After dinner, Mr W. adverted to the difficulties attending the gospel ministry; lamented that all their zeal availed but little; said that he was weary with the burdens of the day; declared his great consolation that in a short time his work would be done, when he should depart and be with Christ. He then appealed to the ministers if it was not their great comfort that they should go to rest. They generally assented, except Mr. T., who sat next to Mr. W. in silence, and by his countenance discovered but little pleasure in the conversation. On which Mr. W., tapping him on the knee, said, "Well, brother Tennent, you are the oldest man among us; do you not rejoice to think that your time is so near at hand, when you will be called home?" Mr. T. bluntly answered, "I have no wish about it." Mr. W. pressed him again; Mr. T. again answered, "No, sir, it is no pleasure to me at all; and if you knew your duty, it would be none to you. I have nothing to do with death; my business is to live as long as I can—as well as I can—and serve my Master as faithfully as I can, until He shall think proper to call me home." Mr. W. still urged for an explicit answer to his question, in case the time of death were left to his own choice. Mr. T. replied, "I have no choice about it; I am God's servant, and have engaged to do His business as long as he pleases to continue me therein. But now, brother, let me ask you a question. What do you think I would say, if I was to send my man into the field to plough; and if at noon I should go to the field, and find him lounging under a tree, and complaining, 'Master, the sun is very hot and the ploughing hard, I am weary of the work you have appointed me, and am overdone with the heat and burden of the day. Do, master, let me return home, and be discharged from this hard service?' What would I say? Why, that he was a lazy fellow; that it was his business to do the work that I had appointed him, until I should think fit to call him home."

Unfulfilled Obligations.

Chap. xx. ver. 15, 16.—So they cast him out of the vineyard, and killed him. What therefore shall the Lord of the vineyard do unto them? He shall come and destroy these husbandmen, and shall give the vineyard to others.

THE awful calamities that came on the Jews, soon after our Saviour's ascension, are well known, and furnish a dreadful illustration of the above passage. At the Passover, when it was supposed there were upwards of two millions of people in the city of Jerusalem, the Romans surrounded it with their armies, and cast trenches, and raised walls round it, in order that none might escape. Fierce factions raged within, and destroyed one another. Titus, the Roman general, earnestly endeavoured to persuade the Jews to an advantageous surrender; but they scorned every proposal. From extremity of famine, they were compelled to feed on human flesh, and even noble women were known to murder and devour their own children. Numbers were carried off by the pestilence. After a siege of six months, the city was taken; and, provoked by their obstinacy, the Romans made terrible havoc among the inhabitants The temple was burnt to ashes, and its very foundations ploughed up. In Jerusalem alone, 1,100,000 are said to have perished by the sword, famine and pestilence, besides multitudes who were destroyed in various parts of the country.

God and Money

Chap. xx. ver. 24, 25.—Show me a penny. Whose image and superscription hath it? They answered and said, Cæsar's. And he said unto them, Render therefore unto Cæsar the things which be Cæsar's, and unto God the things which be God's.

THE preparing and circulating of counterfeit coin is undoubtedly among the worst species of fraud. In the following instance, the reading of the Scriptures, by the Divine blessing, proved an effectual check to this iniquitous practice.

Some time ago, a man travelling in Ireland, being benighted, opened a cabin door, and requested permission to lodge there, which was granted. The poor man who inhabited the house, was, according to his usual custom, reading a chapter of the Bible to his family. When the stranger was seated, he resumed his reading; and, having prayed, the family retired to rest. In the morning, the same thing again took place, which seemed to excite the attention of the stranger. On rising from their knees, the stranger thanked his kind host for his hospitality, and informed him that he had travelled into that part of the country, in order to attend a fair, for the wicked purpose of passing bad maney; that he had brought with him base coin to the amount of four pounds; that this was the first time he had taken up such a practice, but that what he had heard in the cabin, had made such an impression on his mind, that he had resolved it should be the last. He then took out of his pocket a small bag, containing the counterfeits, and threw it into the fire.

The Widow's Mite.

Chap. xxi. ver. 3, 4.—Of a truth I say unto you, That this poor widow hath cast in more than they all: For all these have of their abundance cast it unto the offerings of God: but she of her penury hath cast in all the living that she had.

THE Rev. Dr. Dickson of Edinburgh, at the Anniversary of the London Missionary Society in 1829, related the following anecdote:—"Once when I was soliciting contributions on behalf of the Scottish Missionary Society, I preached in Paisley. The next day, I was met by an old and meanly dressed woman, who asked me how I did. I replied, I did not know who she was. She answered, 'Sir, I heard you preach yesterday. I was out of work four days, but Providence relieved me. Now, I do not like to be present at a Missionary meeting when I have nothing to give; so I went to some friends, and told what you had said; so one gave me 6d., another 4d., and another a 1d., and several others one halfpenny, making altogether 19½d. I could do nothing less than show my gratitude to God, for the straits from which he has relieved me." I thought more of that nineteen-pence-half-penny than of the tens and fifties of pounds I had previously received; for it is the spirit with which it is given that sanctifies the gift. If, then, God has prospered you more than formerly, I intreat you to act in the spirit of the poor woman of Paisley; and not only to cheer the hearts of the Christian directors of this Institution, but to enable them to cheer the hearts of the millions of human beings, who, but for you, may never hear of the way to eternal life."

The Unexpected Day.

Chap. xxi. ver. 34.—Take heed to yourselves, lest at any time your hearts be overcharged with surfeiting, and drunkenness, and cares of this life, and so that day come upon your unawares.

IN that part of the country of the Grisons which adjoins to the state of Venice, formerly stood the ancient town of Pleuers, built on a rising ground near the foot of a mountain. The situation was considered healthy; the gardens were delightful, and hither the neighbouring gentry used to come on Sabbath, and spend the day in all manner of riot and debauchery. Their voluptuousness was great, and the enormity of their crimes was aggravated by their abuse of the blessings of Divine Providence. A lady told Bishop Burnet that she had heard her mother often repeat some passages of a Protestant's minister's sermons, who preached in a little church in the neighbourhood of this place. He intimated in his discourse, that nothing but a timely repentance, and the forsaking of their evil ways, would screen them from Divine justice, which would soon be executed upon them in a most signal manner. This was good advice; but, alas! it was slighted, and the people continued to go on in the same manner as before.

On the 25th of August 1618, an inhabitant came, and told them to be gone, for he saw the mountian cleaving, and that it would soon fall upon them; but he was only laughed at. He had a daughter, whom he persuaded to leave all, and go with him: but when she had got out of town, she recollected that she had not locked the door of a room in which she had left several things of value. She accordingly went back; but in the meantime the mountain fell, and she was buried in the ruins, together with every person there present, not one escaping. The fall of the mountain choking up the river that ran near the bottom, first spread the alarm over the neighbouring country. "I could hear no particular character," says Bishop Burnet, "of the man who escaped, so I must leave the secret reason of so singular preservation to the great discovery at the last day, when those steps of Divine Providence, which we cannot now account for, will be disclosed."

The Cup.

Chap. xxii. ver. 20.—Likewise also the cup after supper, saying, This cup is the New Testament in my blood, which is shed for you.

"IN the twelfth year of my age," says Mr. Robert Blair, in giving an account of his life, "the supper of the Lord having been celebrated in Irvine, I was admirably taken with the sermon; and, my spirit having been likewise greatly ravished with the first exhortation at the table, I earnestly desired to communicate; but having got breakfast, I durst not, for it was then a generally received opinion, that the sacrament behoved to be received fasting; and, being also greatly moved with the second exhortation, I secretly lamented that my bodily breakfast should bereave me of a soul banquet; but observing these words 'after supper,' in the third exhortation, I thus reasoned with myself: Did Christ and His disciples celebrate this sacrament after supper, and can it be a fault in me to celebrate the same after breakfast? Surely it can be none; and so I sat down at the next table, and communicated. This was the Lord's work to His poor child, to make me his covenanted and sealed servant."

Lacking Nothing.

Chap. xxii. ver. 35.—When I sent you without purse, and scrip, and shoes, lacked ye anything; And they said, Nothing.

MR. Mason was an acting magistrate for the county of Surrey; an excellent man, and the author of many evangelical works. In reference to the preceding passage, he says, "These were precious words to me. With tears of thankfulness I record the goodness of my Lord to the chief of sinners. Upwards of twenty years ago, when it pleased God to call me by His grace, and make me happy in His love, my name was cast out as evil—friends became foes—their hands were against me—they withdrew their favours from me, and derided me. Under narrow circumstances, tender feelings for a large family, carnal reasonings of my corrupt nature, and strong temptations from the enemy, I was sore distressed. But the Lord was gracious: and often did He bring this text to my mind, *Lackest thou anything?* I was constrained with gratitude to reply, *Nothing, Lord.* Christ is a most precious Master to serve! I have proved it." Thus too shall all His servants have to say. Let us, then, under the darkest dispensation of His providence, trust in Him and not be afraid.

They Know Not.

Chap. xxiii. ver. 34.—Father, forgive them; for they know not what they do.

A WEALTHY merchant, in America, lately gave the following account;—as he was standing at his door, a venerable greyheaded man approached him and asked an alms. He answered him with severity, and demanded why he lived so useless a life The beggar answered, that "age disabled him for labour, and he had committed himself to the providence of God, and the kindness of good people." The rich man was at this time an infidel. He ordered the old man to depart, at the same time casting some reflections on the providence of God. The venerable beggar descended the steps, kneeling at the bottom offered up the following prayer:—"O my gracious God, I thank Thee that my bread and water are sure; but I pray Thee, in Thy intercession above, to remember this man; he hath reflected on Thy providence. Father! forgive him, he knows not what he saith." Thus the present scene ended. The words, "Father! forgive him, he knows not what he saith," constantly rung in the ears of the rich man. He was much disconcerted during the following night. The next day, being called on business to a neighbouring town, he overtook the old man on the road. As he afterwards confessed, the sight almost petrified him with guilt and fear. He dismounted, when a interesting conversation ensued. At the close of it the old man remarked:—"Yesterday, I was hungry, and called at the door of a rich man. He was angry, and told me he did not believe in the providence of God, and bid me depart; but at the next house I had a plentiful meal. And this, mark ye! was at the house of a *poor woman*." The wealthy man confessed that at this moment he was pierced with a sense of guilt. He then gave some money to the poor man, of whom he never could hear afterwards; yet the sound of these words being impressed on his mind by the last interview —"He knows not what he saith,"—never left him, till he was brought to Christian repentance.

The Sabbath Day.

Chap. xxiii. ver. 56.—They rested the Sabbath day, according to the commandment.

SOUTHEY, in his life of Wesley, tells us, that John Nelson, a Methodist preacher, being once desired by his master's foreman to work on the Lord's day, on the ground that the king's business required despatch, and that it was common to work on the Sabbath for his Majesty when anything was wanted in a particular haste, Nelson boldly declared, "That he would not work upon the Sabbath for any man in the kingdom, except it were to quench fire, or something that required immediate help." "Religion," says the foreman, "has made you a rebel against the king." "No, sir," replied he, "it has made me a better subject than ever I was. The greatest enemies the kings has, are Sabbath-breakers, swearers, drunkards, and whoremongers; for these bring down God's judgments upon the king and country." He was told he should lose his employment if he would not obey his orders; his answer was, "he would rather want bread than wilfully offend God. The foreman swore he would be as mad as Whitefield if he went on. "What hast thou done," said he, "that thou needest make so much ado about salvation? I always took thee to be as honest a man as I have in the work, and would have trusted thee with £500." "So you might," answered Nelson, "and not have lost a penny by me." "I have a worse opinion of thee now," said the foreman. "Master," rejoined he, "I have the odds of you, for I have a worse opinion of myself than you can have." The issue, however, was that the work was not pursued on the Sabbath; and Nelson rose in the good opinion of his employer, for having shown a sense of his duty as a Christian.

The Scriptures and Christ.

Chap. xxiv. ver. 27.—And beginning at Moses and all the prophets, he expounded unto them in all the Scriptures the things concerning himself.

MR COTTON paid a visit to Dr Young, author of "Night Thoughts," about a fortnight before his last illness. The subject of conversation was "Newton on the Prophecies," when Dr Young closed the conversation thus:—"My friend, there are three considerations upon which my faith in Christ it built, as upon a rock: The fall of man, the redemption of man, and the resurrection of man. These three cardinal articles of our religion are such as human ingenuity could never have invented; therefore they must be divine. The other argument was this: If the prophecies have been fulfilled, of which there is abundant demonstration, the Scriptures must be the word of God; and, if the Scripture is the word of God, Christianity must be true."

Understanding the Scriptures.

Chap. xxiv. ver. 45.—Then opened he their understanding, that they might understand the Scriptures.

"I SEE," said the Rev. John Cowper, brother of the poet, "the rock upon which I once split, and see the rock of my salvation. I have peace in myself; and if I live, I hope it will be that I may be made a messenger of peace to others. I have learned that in a moment, which I could not have learned by reading many books for many years. I have often studied these points, and studied them with great attention, but was blinded by prejudice; and, unless He who alone is worthy to unloose the seals, had opened the book, I had been blinded still. Now they appear so plain, that though I am convinced no comment could ever have made me understand them, I wonder I did not see them before. Yet, great as my doubts and difficulties were, they have only served to pave the way, and being solved, they make it plainer.—The subjects crowd upon me faster than I can give them utterance.—How plain do many texts appear, to which, after consulting all the commentaries, I could hardly affix a meaning; and now I have their true meaning without any comment at all."

JOHN.

The Word.

Chap. i. ver. 14.—The Word was made flesh, and dwelt among us.

THE late Mr William Greenfield was once in company, at the house of a friend, with a gentleman of deistical principles, a stranger to him, who put to him the following among many other questions: "Can you give me the reason why Jesus Christ is called the Word? What is meant by the Word? It is a curious term." Mr Greenfield, unconscious of the motive of the sceptical principles of the inquirer, replied with the mild simplicity and decision by which his character was marked, "I suppose, as words are the medium of communication between us, the term is used in the sacred Scriptures to demonstrate that HE is the only medium between God and man; I know no other reason." The deist's mouth was shut.

The Lamb of God.

Chap. i. ver. 29.—Behold the Lamb of God, which taketh away the sin of the world!

A LITTLE boy reading to his mother about the lion, in a book of natural history, said, "Mamma, the lion is a noble animal, but I love the lamb better; and I will tell you why I love it better; because Jesus Christ is called the Lamb of God, which taketh away the sin of the world."

Water-pots of the East.

Chap. ii. ver. 6—And there were set there six water-pots of stone, after the manner of the purifying of the Jews, containing two or three firkins a-piece.

"THE ruins of a church," says Dr Clarke in his Travels, "are shown in this place (Cana of Galilee,) which is said to have been erected over the spot where the marriage-feast of Cana was celebrated. It is worthy of notice, that walking among these ruins, we saw large mossy *stone* water-pots, answering to the description given of the ancient vessels of the country; not preserved, or exhibited as relics, but lying about disregarded by the present inhabitants, as antiquities with whose original use they were unacquainted. From their appearance, and the number of them, it is quite evident that a practice of keeping water in large *stone* pots, each holding from eighteen to twenty-seven gallons, was once common in the country."

Universality of the Atonement

Chap. iii. ver. 16.—For God so loved the world, that he gave his only-begotten Son, that whosoever believeth in him should not perish, but have everlasting life.

MR NOTT, missionary in the South Sea Islands, was on one occasion reading a portion of the Gospel of John to a number of natives. When he had finished the sixteenth verse of the third chapter, a native, who had listened with avidity and joy to the words, interrupted him, and said, "What words were those you read? What sounds were those I heard? Let me hear those words again." Mr Nott again read the verse, "God so loved," etc., when the native rose from his seat, and said, "Is that true? Can that be true? God loved the world, when the world not love Him. God so loved the world, as to give His Son to die, that man might not die. Can that be true?" Mr Nott again read the verse, "God so loved the world," etc.; told him it was true, and that it was the message God had sent to them; and that whosoever believed in Him would not perish, but be happy after death. The overwhelming feelings of the wondering native were too powerful for expression or restraint. He burst into tears, and as these chased each other down his countenance, he retired to meditate in private on the amazing love of God, which had that day touched his soul; and there is every reason to believe he was afterwards raised to share the peace and happiness resulting from the love of God shed abroad in his heart.

Evil Doing.

Chap. iii. ver. 20.—Every one that doeth evil hateth the light, neither cometh to the light, lest his deeds should be reproved.

A GENTLEMAN once visiting an acquaintance of his, whose conduct was as irregular as his principles were erroneous, was astonished to see a large Bible in the hall chained fast to the floor. He ventured to inquire the reason.—"Sir," replied his infidel friend, "I am obliged to chain down that book to prevent its flying in my face." Such persons hate the Bible as Ahab did Micaiah, because it never speaks good concerning them, but evil.

The Water of Life.

Chap. iv. ver. 14, 15.—Whosoever drinketh of the water that I shall give him shall never thirst. The woman saith unto him, Sir, give me this water, that I thirst not, neither come hither to draw.

"WHEN in the market-place," say the Rev. Jonas King, missionary in Greece, "I saw several women who had water to sell: good water here is scarce, and brought from the monastery, which is a considerable distance from the city. As I passed by them, one of them asked me to drink. I told her that I had plenty of good water at my house; still, however, she asked me again if I would not drink. I replied, 'There is one who can give us water, of which if we drink we shall never thirst. He that drinks of this water will thirst again: but the other is the water of eternal life; and he who drinks of it will thirst no more.' This reply, which I supposed would be understood, seemed to excite some wonder and curiosity; and several young men who were near, came around me to hear what I had said to the woman. One of the young men said, 'Sir, where is that water? We wish for it. Where is he who has it?' I said, 'Come with me to my house, and I will show you. It is Jesus Christ.' Still they did not seem to understand; and some said 'He must be a physician; he will give us something which will prevent us from thirsting.' As many began to collect, I thought it best to go away, and returned to my lodgings. Several young men, however, followed me, and expressed a desire to know where that water, of which I had spoken, could be found: so I took the New Testament, and read to them a part of the fourth chapter of St. John's Gospel, from the fifth to fifteenth verse; and gave them the book to carry with them to the market-place to read the whole chapter, and explain what I had said to those who were desirous of knowing. 'Ah!' said one of them, after I had read the portion above mentioned, 'I perceive that he is speaking in a figure:' and went on explaining to the others what he supposed I intended to say."

Spiritual Food.

Chap. iv. ver. 31, 32.—His disciples prayed him, saying, Master, eat. But he said unto them, I have meat to eat that ye know not of.

ON a sacramental occasion in 1741, Mr Colin Brown, an eminently pious man, and who had formerly been Provost of Perth, from the deep interest he felt in the solemn introductory services of the day, which the Rev. Mr Wilson had been conducting, continued in the church beyond the ordinary time, without retiring for refreshment. When entreated by his friends to retire, he excused himself by saying—"Here I have been getting much of that meat to eat, which the world knoweth not of."

Everlasting Life.

Chap. v. ver. 24, 25.—Verily, verily, I say unto you, He that heareth my word, and believeth on him that sent me, hath everlasting life, and shall not come into condemnation; but is passed from death unto life. Verily, verily, I say unto you, The hour is coming, and now is, when the dead shall hear the voice of the Son of God; and they that hear shall live.

THE following examination took place on the fifth chapter of John's Gospel, in one of the schools of the Hibernian Society. "I asked the meaning," says the visitor, "of the 24th verse. 'He that heareth My word, and believeth on Him that sent Me, hath everlasting life, and shall not come into condemnation, but is passed from death unto life.' A boy about thirteen years of age answered, 'Jesus said, he that heareth My words, and believeth on God the Father, who sent Me into this world, hath everlasting life.' I asked what was everlasting life. He answered, 'Heaven and glory for ever.' I asked what was the meaning of not coming into condemnation; and he said, 'Not to be condemned with the wicked to everlasting punishment, but to pass from death unto life, by believing in Jesus Christ.' I again asked what was the voice of the Son of God, mentioned in the 25th verse. He answered, 'The Scripture is the voice, and the dead in sins, that will hear the Scriptures, which speak of Jesus, shall live for ever.' I also asked who was the Son of Man mentioned in the 27th verse. He replied, 'Jesus was the Son of Man.' I said, How can Jesus be the Son of God and the Son of Man? He answered, 'Because He came from heaven He was the Son of God, and because He was born of the Jews He was the Son of Man.'"

Searching the Scriptures.

Chap. v. ver. 39.—Search the Scriptures; for in them ye think ye have eternal life: and they are they which testify of me.

A SERMON having been preached for the Bible Society a number of years ago in England, the next day the poor people of the place brought their little contributions to the clergyman's house. A little girl, four or five years old, accompanied her elder sister; and after listening with eager attention to all that passed, at last cried out, "I will go for my money too, that I will." The clergyman, thinking that so young a child could not understand the meaning of what had been said, asked her what she wanted to do with her money? "To give it to you," she replied, "that you may buy Bibles for the poor negroes." "But what good will the Bible do them, my dear?" "Oh it will tell them all about Jesus Christ; and how to get to heaven.—So be sure to buy Bibles with my money, and send them to the poor black men," she added, with great earnestness, and tears in her eyes.

Waste Not.

Chap. vi. ver. 12.—Gather up the fragments that remain, that nothing be lost.

WHEN the late M. Jackues Laffitte came to Paris, in 1778, the extent of his ambition was to find a situation in a bankinghouse; and to attain this object he called on M. Perregaux, the rich Swiss banker, to whom he had a letter of recommendation. Being introduced into the presence of the banker, he modestly stated the object of his visit. "It is impossible for me to admit you into my establishment, at least for the present," replied the banker: "all my offices have their full complement. If I require any one at a future time, I will see what can be done. but in the meantime I advise you to seek elsewhere, for I do not expect to have a vacancy for some time. With a disappointed heart the young aspirant for employment left the office; and while with a downcast look he traversed the courtyard, he stopped to pick up a pin which lay in his path, and which he carefully stuck in the lappel of his coat. Little did he think that this trivial action was to have so important an influence on his future destiny. From the window of his cabinet, M. Perregaux had observed the action of the young man. The Swiss banker was one of those keen observers of human actions, who estimated the value of circumstances apparently trifling in themselves, and which would pass unnoticed by the majority of mankind. He was delighted with the conduct of the young stranger. In this simple action he saw the revelation of a character; it was a guarantee of a love of order and economy, a pledge of all the qualities which should be possessed by a good financier. A young man who would pick up a pin could not fail to make a good clerk, merit the confidence of his employer, and attain a high degree of prosperity. In the evening of the same day, M. Laffitte received the following note from M. Perregaux:—"A place is made for you in my office, which you may take possession of to-morrow morning." The anticipations of the banker were not deceived. The young Laffitte possessed every desirable quality, and even more than was at first expected. From simple clerk he soon rose to be cashier—then partner—then head of the first banking-house in Paris; and, afterwards in rapid succession, a deputy and president of the Council of Ministers, the highest point to which a citizen can aspire.

The Bread of Life.

Chap. vi. ver. 32.—My Father giveth you the true bread from heaven.

WHEN the Rev. Ebenezer Erskine's doctrine was impugned, and his discourses complained of before the ecclesiastical courts, he was enabled to vindicate himself with great dignity and courage; and expressions sometimes fell from his lips, which, for a time, overawed and confounded his enemies. On one occasion, at a meeting of the Synod of Fife, according to the account of a respectable witness, when some members were denying the Father's gift of our Lord Jesus to sinners of mankind, he rose and said, "Moderator, our Lord Jesus says of Himself, 'My Father giveth you the true bread from heaven.' This He uttered to a promiscuous multitude; and let me see the man who dares to affirm that He said wrong?" This short speech, aided by the solemnity and energy with which it was delivered, made an uncommon impression on the Synod, and on all that were present.

Coming to Christ.

Chap. vi. ver. 37.—Him that cometh to me I will in no wise cast out.

A CLERGYMAN was called to visit a poor dying woman, who was quite ignorant of the truth. After conversing with her on the depravity of human nature, and the way of salvation by Jesus Christ, that it was all of grace, and that there was no limitation as to person or state; the woman listened to every word with great attention; the tears began to trickle down her cheeks; and at last she said, "I know nothing of the Man of whom you have been speaking;" immediately adding, "I was never brought up in the way of religion; never taught to know a letter of a book, nor attend any place of worship." The clergyman visiting her next day, began to discourse upon the suitableness, the ability, and willingness of Jesus to save perishing sinners. "And do you think, sir," said she, "He will save such a vile wretch as I am?" He observed, the promise ran thus, "Him that cometh unto Me I will in no wise cast out." Here she found a basis to rest on. Her knowledge of divine things rapidly increased; and her fervent devotions seemed now to be the perpetual breathings of her soul. She continued in this state about six weeks, soliciting the company of all Christian friends to converse and pray with her, giving evident marks of being a subject of that grace to which she had so long been a stranger.

Needless Exposure of Life.

Chap. vii. ver. 1.—Jesus walked in Galilee; for he would not walk in Jewry, because the Jews sought to kill him.

IN Tourney, about 1544, a very noted professor of the Protestant religion, being earnestly sought after, had concealed himself so closely, that his persecutors were unable to discover where he was hid. Contrary, however, to the advice and entreaty of his wife and friends, he gave himself up, desirous of the glory of martyrdom; but being adjudged to be burnt, he recanted and abjured the faith, in order to be beheaded. The Papists improved this, in order to decoy his fellow-sufferers, to the like recantation; but they replied, "He had tempted God by rushing upon danger without a call, but they had to the utmost of their power shunned it, and hoped that since He had called them to suffer, He would support them under it." And it so happened, they went to the fire in solemn pomp, and were consumed loudly singing the praise of God even in the flames, till their strength was exhausted. We are not to court sufferings; it is enough if we cheerfully endure them when, in the providence of God, we are called to it. Our Lord Himself says to His disciples, "When they persecute you in one city, flee ye into another."

The Power of the Gospel.

Chap. vii. ver. 45, 46.—The Pharisees said unto them, Why have ye not brought him? The officers answered, Never man spake like this man.

MR POWELL, a minister of the Gospel, being informed that an officer was come to apprehend him for preaching the Gospel, quietly resigned himself into his hands, requesting only that he might be permitted to join with his wife and children in prayer before he was dragged to prison. With this request the officer complied; and the family being together, the officer was so struck with the ardent and tender prayers of this suffering servant of God for his family, for the Church, and for his persecutors in particular, that he declared he would die rather than have a hand in apprehending such a man.

Dying in Sin.

Chap. viii. ver. 24.—If ye believe not that I am he, ye shall die in your sins.

VOLTAIRE spent his whole life in malignant but vain attempts to ridicule and overturn Christianity. He was the idol of a large portion of the French nation; but just when they were decreeing new honours for him, and loading him with fresh applause, then the hour of his ignominy and shame was fully come. In a moment the approach of death dissipated his delusive dreams, and filled his guilty soul with inexpressible horror. As if moved by magic, conscience started from her long slumbers, and unfolded before him the broad extended roll of all his crimes. Ah! whither could he fly for relief? Fury and despair succeeded each other by turns, and he had more the appearance of a demon than a man. To his physician he said, "Doctor, I will give you half of what I am worth. if you will give me six month's life." The doctor answered, "Sir, you cannot live six weeks." Voltaire replied, "Then shall I go to hell, and you shall go with me;" and soon after expired.

The Devil.

Chap. viii. ver. 44.—Ye are of your father the devil.

OF Mr Haynes the coloured preacher, it is said, that some time after the publication of his sermon on the text, "Ye shall not surely die," two reckless young men having agreed together to try his wit, one of them said, "Father Haynes, have you heard the good news?" "No," said Mr Haynes, "what is it?" "It is great news indeed," said the other, "and, if true, your business is done." "What is it," again inquired Mr Haynes. "Why," said the first, "the devil is dead." In a moment the old gentleman replied, lifting up both hands, and placing them on the heads of the young men, and in a tone of solemn concern, " Oh, poor fatherless children! what will become of you?"

The Useful Life.

Chap. ix. ver. 4.—I must work the works of him that sent me while it is day: the night cometh, when no man can work.

AN eminent divine, suffering under chronic disease, consulted three physicians, who declared, on being questioned by the sick man, that his disease would be followed by death in a longer or shorter time, according to the manner in which he lived: but they unanimously advised him to give up his office, because, in his situation, mental agitation would be fatal to him. "If I give myself to repose," inquired the divine, "how long, gentlemen, will you guarantee my life?" "Six years," answered the doctors. "And if I continue in office?" "Three years at most." "Your servant, gentlemen," he replied: "I should prefer living two or three years in doing some good, to living six in idleness."

Who's Disciple.

Chap. ix. ver. 28.—Thou art his disciple; but we are Moses' disciples.

ONE day, as Mr. Whitefield walked along, a sailor, apparently a little intoxicated, but it would seem wishing to appear more so, frequently stumbled in Mr. Whitefield's way, notwithstanding, took no notice of him ; at length he so much interrupted the way as to prevent Mr. Whitefield getting forward. On which he took him by the shoulder, and thrust him to one side. What do you mean?" said the sailor : "don't you know I am one of your disciples?" "I am afraid of that," replied the good man ; "had you been one of my Master's, I should have had better hopes of you."

The Right Entrance.

Chap. x. ver. 1.—He that entereth not by the door into the sheep-fold, but climbeth up some other way, the same is a thief and a robber.

THE celebrated Mr. Alexander Henderson, who lived in the seventeenth century, was presented by Archbishop Gladstanes to the parish of Leuchars in Fife. His settlement was so unpopular, that on the day of ordination, the church-doors were shut and secured by the people, so that the ministers who attended, together with the precentor, were obliged to go in by the window. Shortly after, having heard of a communion in the neighbourhood, at which the excellent Mr. Bruce was to be an assistant, he went thither secretly ; and, fearful of attracting notice, placed him in a dark corner of the church, where he might not be readily seen or known. Mr. Bruce having come into the pulpit, paused for a little, as was his usual manner, a circumstance which excited Mr. Henderson's surprise ; but it astonished him much more when he heard him read as his text these very striking words, *He that entereth not in by the door, but climbeth up some other way, the same is a* THIEF *and a* ROBBER ; which words, by the blessing of God, and the effectual working of the Holy Spirit, took such hold on him at that very instant, and left such an impression on his heart afterwards, that they proved the very first means of his conversion unto Christ. Ever after he retained a great affection for Mr Bruce, and used to make mention of him with marks of the highest respect.

Shepherding in the East.

Chap. x. ver. 3.—The sheep hear his voice ; and he calleth his own sheep by name, and leadeth them out.

"I HAVE met with an illustration of a passage of Scripture," says Mr. Hartly, missionary in Greece, " which interests me. Having had my attention directed last night to the words, John x. 3, 'The sheep, hear His voice, and He calleth His own sheep by name,' etc., I asked my man if it was usual in Greece to give names to the sheep ; he informed me that it was, and that the sheep obeyed the shepherd, when he called them by their names. This morning I had an opportunity of verifying the truth of this remark. Passing a flock of sheep, I asked the shepherd the same question which I had put to my servant, and he gave me the same answer. I then bade him call one of his sheep ; he did so, and it instantly left its pasturage and its companions, and ran up to the hand of the shepherd with signs of pleasure, and with a prompt obedience which I had never before observed in any other animal. It is also true of the sheep in this country, that a stranger they will not follow, but will flee from him ; for they know not the voice of strangers. The shepherd told me that many of his sheep are still WILD ; that they had not yet learned their names ; but that by teaching they would all learn them. The others which knew their names, he also called TAME. How natural an application to the state of the human race, does this description of the sheep admit of! The Good Shepherd laid down His life for His sheep; but many of them are still wild; they know not His voice. Others have learned to obey His call, and to follow Him; and we rejoice to think, that even to those not yet in His fold, the words are applicable,—'Them also I must bring; and they shall hear My voice; and there shall be one fold and one Shepherd.'"

The New Life

Chap. xi. ver. 25.—Jesus said unto her, I am the resurrection and the life: he hath believeth in me, though he were dead, yet shall he live.

WHEN a naval officer was inspecting one of the schools in the island of Barbadoes, containing two hundred negro boys and girls, a sign was made by one of the children (by holding up his hand), intimating that he wished to speak to the master. On going up to the child, who was past eight years of age, the master inquired what was the matter. "Massa," he replied, with a look of horror and indignation, which the officer said he should never forget, and pointing to a little boy of the same age who sat beside him, "Massa, this boy says he does not believe in the resurrection." "This is very bad," said the master; "but do you, my little fellow (addressing the young informer), believe in the resurrection yourself?" "Yes, Massa, I do." "But can you prove it from the Bible?" "Yes, Massa; Jesus says, *I am the resurrection and the life: he that believeth in Me, though he were dead, yet shall he live;* and, in another place, *'Because I live, ye shall live also.'*" The master added, "Can you prove it from the Old Testament also?" "Yes; for Job says, 'I know that my Redeemer liveth, and that He shall stand at the latter day upon the earth; and though, after my skin, worms destroy this body, yet in my flesh shall I see God!' And David says in one of his psalms, 'I shall be satisfied, when I awake, with Thy likeness.'" "But are you sure these passages are in the Bible? Here is a Bible, point them out to us." The little boy instantly turned up all the passages, and read them aloud.

Wrongful Arrestment.

Chap. xi. ver. 57.—Now both the chief priests, and the Pharisees had given a commandment, that if any man knew where he were, he should show it, that they might take him.

MR. GILBERT RULE was minister of Alnwick in Northumberland during the time of the persecution. When he was forced to leave his charge at Alnwick, he went to Berwick, where he practised surgery for the support of his family. His enemies continued their persecutions. They engaged some of the baser sort to waylay him. That he might be brought into this snare, a messenger was despatched at midnight to request him to visit a person in the country whom he should represent as very ill. The good man expressed so much sympathy for the sick person, and showed such readiness to run to his relief, though at midnight, that the messenger's heart relented (for he was privy to the plot), and was so filled with remorse, that he discovered the whole affair to Mr. Rule, which happily prevented his meeting a premature death.

The Present.

Chap. xii. ver. 35.—Yet a little while is the light with you: **walk** while ye have the light, lest darkness come upon you.

FROM the notion which some entertained of *St Columba* being able to foretell future events, a man asked him one day how long he had to live. "If your curiosity on that head could be satisfied," said the saint, "it could be of no use to you. But it is only God, who appoints the days of man, that knows when they are to terminate. Our business is to do our duty, not to pry into our destiny. God in mercy hath concealed from man the knowledge of his end. If he knew it was near, he would be disqualified for the duties of life ; and if he knew it were distant, he would delay his preparation. You should therefore be satisfied with knowing that it is certain ; and the safest way is to believe that it may be also near, and to make no delay in getting ready, lest it overtake you unprepared."

Vanity.

Chap. xii. ver. 43.—They loved the praise of men.

"I ONCE knew," says Mr. Abbot, "a little boy of unusually bright and animated countenance. Every one who entered the house noticed the child, and spoke of his beauty. One day a gentleman called upon business, and being engaged in conversation, did not pay that attention to the child to which he was accustomed, and which he now began to expect as his due. The vain little fellow made many efforts to attract notice, but not succeeding, he at last placed himself full in front of the gentleman, and asked, 'Why don't you see how beautiful I be ?'"

Knowing and Obeying.

Chap. xiii. ver. 17.—If ye know these things, happy are ye if ye do them.

MR. ELLIS having been engaged in conversation on religious subjects with the governor of Owhyhee, such as the resurrection of the body, etc., was asked by him, how he knew these things. "I asked for his Bible," says Mr. E., "and translated the passages which inculcate the doctrine of the resurrection, etc., and told him it was from that book we obtained all our knowledge of these things, and that it was the contents of that book which we had come to teach the people of Owhyhee. He then asked if all the people were in our native countries were acquainted with the Bible. I answered, that from the abundant means of instruction there, the greater portion of the people had either read the book, or had, in some other way, become acquainted with its principal contents. He then said, How is it that such numbers of them swear, get intoxicated, and do many things prohibited in this book ? He was told, that there was a vast difference between *knowing* the word of God, and *obeying* it : and that it was most likely those persons knew their conduct was displeasing to God, yet persisted in it, because most agreeable to their corrupt inclinations."

Truth of Prophecy.

Chap. xiii. ver. 19.—Now I tell you before it come, that, when it is come to pass, ye may believe that I am he.

BISHOP NEWTON, in the dedication of his work on the Prophecies, says, "What first suggested the design, were some conversations formerly with a great general (Marshal Wade), who had for many years the chief command in the army, and was a man of good understanding, and of some reading, but unhappily had no great regard for revealed religion or the clergy. When the prophecies were urged as a proof of revelation, he constantly derided the notion, asserted that there was no such thing, and that the prophecies, which were pretended, were written after the events. It was immediately replied, that though such a thing might with less scruple and more confidence be affirmed of some prophecies fulfilled long ago, yet it could never be proved of any: the contrary might be proved almost to a demonstration; but it could not be so much as affirmed of several prophecies without manifest absurdity; for there were several prophecies in Scripture which were not fulfilled till these later ages, are fulfilling even now, and consequently could not be framed after the events, but undeniably were written and published many ages before. He was startled at this, and said he must acknowledge that if this point could be proved to satisfaction, there would be no argument against such a plain matter of fact; it would certainly convince him, and he believed would be the readiest way to convince every reasonable man, of the truth of revelation."

The Holy Spirit's Guidance.

Chap. xiv. ver. 26.—The Holy Ghost—shall teach you all things, and bring all things to your remembrance.

MR. NEWTON, telling in company, one day, how much his memory was decayed, "There," said he, "last Wednesday, after dinner, I asked Mrs. Cane what I had been about that forenoon, for I could not recollect. Why, said she, you have been preaching at St. Mary's. Yet it is wonderful, when I am in the pulpit, I can recollect any passage of Scripture I want to introduce into my sermon from Genesis to Revelation."

Going to the Father.

Chap. xiv. ver. 28.—If ye loved me, ye would rejoice, because I said, I go unto the Father; for my Father is greater than I.

A LOVELY young lady, in her near approach to dissolution, observing her father overcome with grief, thus pertinently remonstrated with him: "Why, sir, so much grief? Had an offer of marriage been made me by one who in himself was all you could wish, and whose situation in life was far superior to mine, but whose residence must be in a remote part of the kingdom, perhaps the consideration of advantage and promotion to me would have reconciled you to my removal, though it would have been little other than a separation for life. But I am now about to be promoted incomparably beyond anything that could have occurred in this world. Then why this reluctance? Our next meeting will be in circumstances of high improvement, joyful and perpetual."

Divine Correction.

Chap. xv. ver. 2.—Every branch that beareth fruit, he purgeth it, that it may bring forth more fruit.

"I HAVE heard Mr. Cecil mention, with much feeling," says his biographer, "many deep and secret conflicts of mind, with which he was exercised, while at college; added to which, he had to meet many insults, which profligate men offer to piety. Under these impressions he was one day walking in the physic gardens, where he observed a very fine pomegranate tree cut almost through the stems near the root. On asking the gardener the reason of this, 'Sir,' said he, 'this tree used to shoot so strong, that it bore nothing but leaves, I was therefore obliged to cut it in this manner; and, when it was almost cut through, then it began to bear plenty of fruit.' The gardener's explanation of this act conveyed a striking illustration to Mr. Cecil's mind, and he went back to his room comforted and instructed by this image."

Dislike to the Good.

Chap. xv. ver. 19.—Because ye are not of the world, but I have chosen you out of the world, therefore the world hateth you.

"IT HAPPENED once," says Dr. Cotton Mather, "to be present in the room where a dying man could not leave the world until he lamented to a minister (whom he had sent for on his account), the unjust calumnies and injuries which he had often cast upon him. The minister asked the poor penitent what was the occasion of this abusive conduct; whether he had been imposed upon by any false report. The man made this answer, 'No, sir, it was merely this; I thought you were a good man, and that you did much good in the world, and therefore I hated you. Is it possible, is it possible,' he added, 'for such a wretch to find pardon?'"

Devilish Infatuation.

Chap. xvi. ver. 3.—The time cometh, that whosoever killeth you will think he doeth God service.

ONE of the most horrid circumstances attending the massacre of the Protestants under Charles IX. of France was, that when the news of this event reached Rome, Pope Gregory XIII. instituted the most solemn rejoicing, giving thanks to Almighty God for this glorious victory over the heretics!!

Tribulation.

Chap. xvi. ver. 33—In the world ye shall have tribulation.

SOME time ago, as a gentleman was passing over one of the extensive downs in the west of England, about mid-day, where a large flock of sheep was feeding, and observing the shepherd sitting by the road side, preparing to eat his dinner, he stopped his horse, and entered into conversation with him to this effect :—" Well, shepherd, you look cheerful and contented, and I dare say have very few cares to vex you. I, who am a man of pretty large property, cannot but look at such men as you with a kind of envy." "Why, sir," replied the shepherd, "'tis true I have not troubles like yours; and I could do well enough, was it not for that black ewe that you see yonder amongst my flock. I have often begged my master to kill or sell her; but he won't, though she is the plague of my life; for no sooner do I sit down to look at my book, or take up my wallet to get my dinner, but away she sets off over the down, and the rest follow her; so that I have many a weary step after them: There you see she's off, and they are all after her!"—"Ah, friend," said the gentleman to the shepherd before he started, "I see every man has a black ewe in his flock to plague him as well as I!"—The reader can make the application.

Gospel Truth.

Chap. xvii. ver. 17.—Sanctify them through thy truth; thy word is truth.

"TO preach *practical* sermons, as they are called," says Bishop Horne, "*i.e.* sermons upon virtues and vices, without inculcating those great scripture truths of redemption, grace, etc., which alone can incite and enable us to forsake sin and follow after righteousness, what is it but to put together the wheels, and set the hands of a watch, forgetting the *spring*, which is to make them all go?"

The Son's Glory.

Chap. xvii. ver. 24.—Father, I will that they also whom thou hast given me be with me where I am; that they may behold my glory, which thou hast given me.

THE late Rev. Alexander Fisher of Dumfermline, an excellent young minister, in the afternoon of the day on which he died, inquired what the hour was, and on being informed, said, "What would you think if I were in heaven to-night?" It was answered, "Then you will be with your Saviour, and see Him face to face." His pale emaciated countenance seemed to beam with delight, and his faltering lips uttered, "Glory, glory, glory!"

The Truth.

Chap. xviii. ver. 38.—Pilate saith unto him, What is truth?

FATHER FULGENTIO, the friend and biographer of the celebrated Paul Sarpi, both of them secret friends to the progress of religious reformation, was once preaching upon Pilate's question, "What is truth?" He told the audience, that he had at last, after many searches, found it out; and, holding forth a New Testament, said, "Here it is, my friends," but added sorrowfully, as he returned it to his pocket, "*It is a sealed book!*" It has been since the glory of the Reformation to break the seal which priestcraft had imposed upon it, and to lay its blessed treasures open to the universal participation of mankind.

Christ or Barabbas.

Chap. xviii. ver. 40.—Then cried they all again, saying, Not this man, but Barabbas.

TREMELLIUS was a Jew, from whose heart the veil had been taken away, and who had been led by the Holy Spirit to acknowledge Jesus as the Messiah and the Son of God.—The Jews who had condemned our Saviour, had said, "Not this man, but Barabbas;" Tremellius, when near his end, glorying in Christ alone, and renouncing whatever came in competition with Him, used very different words, "Not Barabbas, but Jesus."

The Verdict.

Chap. xix. ver. 6.—When the chief priests therefore and officers saw him, they cried out, saying, Crucify him, crucify him.

IT is said of Dr. Robertson, the celebrated historian, that preaching once in the forenoon, he affirmed, in the words of the ancient heathen, "That if perfect virtue were to descend to the earth clothed in a human form, all the world would fall prostrate and worship her." In the afternoon, Dr. Erskine, his colleague, remarked, on the contrary, "That perfect virtue, in the human nature of the Saviour of mankind, had indeed appeared on the earth; but, instead of being universally worshipped, the general cry of his countrymen was, 'Crucify Him, crucify Him!'"

Mother and Son.

Chap. xix ver. 26, 27.—He saith unto his mother, Woman, behold thy son! Then saith he to the disciple, Behold thy mother! And from that hour that disciple took her unto his own home.

A PIOUS young man, who was desirous of devoting himself to the work of the ministry among the heathen, and had been recommended with that view to the committee of the London Missionary Society, on undergoing the usual examination, stated that he had one difficulty; he had an aged mother entirely dependent upon an elder brother and himself for maintenance; and in case of that brother's death, he should wish to be at liberty to return to this country, if his mother were still living, to contribute to her support. Scarcely had he made this ingenuous statement, when a harsh voice exclaimed, "If you love your mother more than the Lord Jesus Christ, you will not do for *us*." Abashed and confounded, the young man was silent. Some murmurs escaped the committee; and he was directed to retire while his proposal was taken into consideration. On his being again sent for, the venerable chairman, Dr. Waugh, in tones of unaffected kindness, and with a patriarchal benignity of mien, acquainted him that the committee did not feel themselves authorised to accept of his services on a condition involving uncertainty as to the term: but immediately added,—"We think none the worse of you, my good lad, for your dutiful regard for your aged parent. You are but acting in conformity to the example of Him whose Gospel you wished to proclaim among the heathen, who, as He hung upon the cross in dying agonies, beholding His mother and the beloved disciple standing by, said to the one, 'Woman, behold thy son!' and to John, 'Behold thy mother!' My good lad, we think none the worse of you."

Going to the Father.

Chap. xx. ver. 17.—I ascend unto my Father, and your Father; and to my God, and your God.

THE Rev. Joseph Alleine being asked by a friend, how he could be contented to be so long under such weakness as he then suffered, he answered, "What! is God my Father; Jesus Christ my Saviour; and the Spirit my sweet friend, my comforter, and sanctifier; and heaven my inheritance; and shall I not be content without limbs and health? Through grace, I am fully satisfied with my Father's pleasure." To another who proposed a similar question, he said, "I have chosen God, and He is become mine, and I know with whom I have trusted myself: which is enough. He is an unreasonable wretch that cannot be content with God, though he has nothing else. My interest in God is all my joy."

The Scriptures.

Chap. xx. ver. 31.—These are written, that ye might believe that Jesus is the Christ, the Son of God; and that believing, ye might have life through his name.

A MAN who had been very much connected with infidels was taken dangerously ill; and, feeling that he could not recover, became alarmed for the safety of his soul. He found that his infidel principles gave him no comfort. He began, for the first time, to examine into the Christian religion. He embraced it, and found it to be the power of God to salvation, enabling him to triumph over the fear of death. In the mean time his infidel friends hearing of his sickness, and that he was not expected to recover, showed a degree of feeling and integrity, which, it is hoped, may prove the first happy step to their own conversion. They were not aware that their dying friend had become a Christian. They called to see him; and actually told him

Spiritual Food.

Chap. xxi. ver. 16.—Feed my sheep.

MR NEWTON once paid a visit to a minister who affected great accuracy in his discourses, and who, on that Sabbath day, had occupied nearly an hour in insisting on several laboured and nice distinctions made in his subject. As he had a high estimation of Mr Newton's judgment, he inquired of him, as they walked home, whether he thought the distinctions just now insisted on were full and judicious? Mr N. said he thought them not *full*, as a very important one had been omitted. "What can that be?" said the minister, "for I have taken more than ordinary care to enumerate them fully." "I think not," replied Mr N.; "for when many of your congregation had travelled several miles for a meal, I think you should not have forgotten the important distinction between MEAT and BONES."

Mr Christopher Richardson, minister of Kirk Heaton, in Yorkshire, was much followed: a neighbouring minister, whose flock used to go to hear him, complaining once to him that he drew away his flock, Mr Richardson answered, "Feed them better, and they will not stray."

Death Approaching.

Chap. xxi. ver. 19.—This spake he, signifying by what death he should glorify God.

THE Rev. Dr. Simpson was for many years tutor in the college at Hoxton, and while he stood very low in his own esteem, he ranked high in that of others. After a long life spent in the service of Christ, he approached his end with holy joy. He spoke with disapprobation of a phrase often used by some good people, "venturing on Christ." "When I consider," said he, "the infinite dignity and allsufficiency of Christ, I am ashamed to talk of venturing on Him. Oh! had I ten thousand souls, I would, at this moment, cast them all into His hands with the utmost confidence." A few hours before his dissolution, he addressed himself to the last enemy in a strain like that of the apostle, when he exclaimed, "O death! where is thy sting?" Displaying his characteristic fervour, as though he saw the tyrant approaching, he said, "What art thou? I am not afraid of thee. Thou art a vanquished enemy through the blood of the cross."

ACTS.

The Reward of Iniquity.

Chap. i. ver. 18.—This man purchased a field with the reward of iniquity; and falling headlong, he burst asunder in the midst, and all his bowels gushed out.

THE Duke of Buckingham, having by an unfortunate accident lost the army which he had raised against the usurper Richard II., was forced to flee for his life without page or attendant. At last he took refuge in the house of Humphrey Bannister of Shrewsbury, who being one of his servants, and having been formerly raised by him from a low condition, would, he trusted, be ready to afford him every possible protection. Bannister, however, upon the king's proclamation, promising £1000 reward to him that should apprehend the duke, betrayed his master to John Merton, high sheriff at Shropshire, who sent him under a strong guard to Salisbury, where the king then was, by whom he was condemned to be beheaded. But divine vengeance pursued the traitor and his family; for, on demanding the £1000, that was the price of the master's blood, King Richard refused to pay it, saying, "He that would be false to so good a master, ought not to be encouraged." He was afterwards hanged for manslaughter; his eldest son soon fell into a state of derangement, and died in a hogsty; his second became deformed and lame; his third son was drowned in a small pool of water, and the rest of his family perished miserably.

Ordained a Witness.

Chap. i. ver. 22.—One must be ordained to be a witness with us of his resurrection.

THE Rev. Samuel Lavington, of Bideford, at the ordination of the Rev. Mr. Seward, introduced his discourse by using the following language :—" What a multitude is here assembled to see an ordination ! Many of you were perhaps never present at such a solemnity before ; and I should be very sorry if, when the assembly breaks up, you should go away with a visible disappointment, and say, 'Is that all?' Why, 'what came ye out to see?' Did you expect to see a number of apostles met together, to lay their hands upon the head of a young minister, and to communicate to him some miraculous powers? Alas! we have not them ourselves. If we had, you should not take all this trouble for nothing. If we had, you should have something by which to remember an ordination as long as you live. If the Holy Ghost were at our command, most gladly would we lay our hands upon you all; and this assembly should be like that mentioned in the Acts of the Apostles: 'While Peter yet spake these words, the Holy Ghost fell on all them which heard the word.' But what we cannot command we may humbly and earnestly supplicate. Shall I then beg the favour of you, to join with me in this short ejaculation to the God of all grace?—O God the Lord, to whom belong the issues from death, pour out thy Spirit upon all this assembly; and command on every one of us a blessing out of Zion, even life for evermore. Amen." The congregation, abstracted for the moment from all other objects, forgot the order of worship, rose from their seats, joined in the collect, and then resumed their places with the greatest solemnity.

Foreign Mission Work.

Chap ii. ver. 4.—They began to speak with other tongues as the Spirit gave them utterance.

THE Rev. Pliny Fisk, in a letter to the Society of Inquiry respecting Missions at Andover, soon after his arrival at Smyrna, writes— "I beg leave to submit to you one remark, which seems to me important, respecting the qualifications of a missionary. It is this; *more knowledge of languages should be acquired.* I say, more *knowledge* of languages, rather than a knowledge of *more* languages. To have such an acquaintance with Latin, Greek, and Hebrew, as will enable you not only to read them with familiarity, but to *speak* and *write* them, would be of very great utility in this country, and I presume, in any part of Asia, probably in any part of the world. And let me add, that it would be well if the wife of a missionary were to know Italian, French, and Latin."

Visions and Dreams.

Chap. ii. ver. 17.—Your young men shall see visions, and your old men shall dream dreams.

ALTHOUGH little or no attention is to be paid to dreams in general, it cannot be denied that these are sometimes remarkable, and followed by striking effects. The following is an instance of this kind, in the case of a lame boy who had been very wicked and undutiful:—Adjoining the room where he lay was a passage. He dreamed that this was on fire, and thought it was hell. He imagined that he saw many devils flying about in the flames, and that they were coming to take him away. Awaking in great terror, he attempted to alarm his mother; and put out his hand to her, but in vain. Though he said nothing of his dream for several months, a great alteration had been remarked in his temper. He was very desirous that his mother should read the Scriptures to him, and some hymn-books. He delighted in reading, as he could, the Scripture texts on the reward tickets, which his brothers and sisters obtained at a Sabbath school. So great was the pleasure he derived from the word of God, that he would say in an evening, "I could keep awake all night to hear my mother read the Bible."—His mother sitting by his bedside, he said to her, "Mother, though I am in so much pain, I am happy." She replied, "What makes you happy, my dear?" "Because," said he, "I am not afraid to die." "My dear, do you know that death has a sting?" "Yes," he replied, "but Christ has taken it away."—A little before his departure, he was heard saying, "He will never, never forsake me." Soon after, he looked up, and exclaimed, "Jesus and His angels! Hallelujah! Hallelujah! Praise ye the Lord!"

Better than Gold.

Chap. iii. ver. 6.—Then Peter said, silver and gold have I none; but such as I have give I thee, In the name of Jesus Christ of Nazareth, rise up and walk.

THOMAS AQUINAS, surnamed the Angelical Doctor, who was highly esteemed by Pope Innocent IV., going one day into the Pope's chamber, where they were reckoning large sums of money, the Pope, addressing himself to Aquinas, said, "You see the Church is no longer in an age in which she can say, 'Silver and gold have I none.'" "It is true, holy father," replied the Angelical Doctor, "nor can she now say to the lame man, Rise and walk."

Killing the Prince of Life.

Chap. iii. ver. 15.—And killed the Prince of life, whom God hath raised from the dead; whereof ye are witnesses.

A JEW, in a letter to one of the same nation, writes:—"One day I overheard your worthy gardener, William, tell another Christian servant that the sermon had been that morning on these words, 'Ye have killed the Prince of Life.' Fears what would become of me if that were true, so agitated me the whole night, that, after a short and suddenly interrupted sleep, I rose early to walk in your garden. There I soon met William, who, with honest and undissembled goodness, asked me, 'What vexes you? Often, when you imagined you was not seen, I have observed you in the garden sighing, wringing your hands, and lifting up your eyes to heaven. Are you unhappy?' 'I am as wretched as possible!' 'How, sir? you are a man of fortune, and being unmarried, have no kind of family distress!' 'Yes, but I am a Jew!' 'Well, you are not at all the worse on that account. Thousands of your nation live merrily!' 'But if it be true what your minister preached yesterday!'—William leaping back some paces, asked, full of surprise, 'How know you what my minister preached?' 'I heard you tell it yesterday to John.' 'Well, but with the same breath, Peter told his countrymen, *Now, brethren, I wot that through ignorance ye did it.*' 'Be it so, William; but I, who see strong proofs of your religion around me, and even in my own wandering and depressed nation, am less excusable.' 'Yet the Prince of Life prayed for His murderers, and commanded that to them, first, remission of sins should be preached. You are of the nation beloved for the fathers' sake.' He would have said more; when seeing you, he broke off, and whispered in my ear, 'My Jesus loves even His murderers.' Soon after, as I was stepping into a schute, I stumbled, and probably should have been drowned, had not the minister of the village, whom I had the day before, against my conscience, joined you in ridiculing, caught hold of me with his hand. 'Honest man,' said I. 'what virtue is this, to rescue from death one of a nation which killed your Prince of Life!' He kindly replied, 'My master loves even his murderers.' I can not express what I felt when I heard these words repeated, and what anxiety has filled my mind ever since."

Salvation.

Chap. iv. ver. 12.—Neither is there salvation in any other.

"I HAVE not time to add more," says Cowper the poet, in a letter, "except just to add, that if I am ever enabled to look forward to death with comfort, which I thank God is sometimes the case with me, I do not take my view of it from the top of my own works and deservings, though God is witness that the labour of my life is to keep a conscience void of offence towards Him. Death is always formidable to me, but when I see him disarmed of his sting, by having sheathed it in the body of Jesus Christ."

Hearkening unto God.

Chap. iv. ver. 19, 20.—Whether be it right in the sight of God to hearken unto you more than unto God, judge ye. For we cannot but speak the things which we have seen and heard.

WHEN the Assembly met at Edinburgh, 1582, Andrew Melville inveighed against the absolute authority which was making its way into the church, whereby he said they intended to pull down the crown from Christ's head, and wrest the sceptre out of His hand; and when several articles of the same tenor with this speech were presented by the commission of the Assembly to the King and Council, craving redress, the Earl of Arran cried out, "Is there any here that dare subscribe these articles?" Upon which Melville went forward and said, "We dare, and will render our lives in the cause;" and then took up the pen and subscribed.

Divine Punishment.

Chap. v. ver. 10.—Then she fell down straightway at his feet, and yielded up the ghost.

SOME years ago, a poor woman in the workhouse at Milburn Port, being charged with having stolen some trivial article, which was amissing, wished God might strike her dumb, blind, and dead if she knew anything of it. About six o'clock she ate her supper as well as usual: soon after her speech faltered, her eyes closed, and before seven she was a breathless corpse without any apparent cause.

Loyalty to God.

Chap. v. ver. 29.—Peter and the other apostles answered and said, We ought to obey God rather than men.

PHILIP, Bishop of Heraclea, in the beginning of the 4th century, was dragged by the feet through the streets, severely scourged, and then brought again to the governor, who charged him with obstinate rashness, in continuing disobedient to the imperial decrees; but he boldly replied, "My present behaviour is not the effect of rashness, but proceeds from my love and fear of God, who made the world, and who will judge the living and the dead, whose commands I dare not transgress. I have hitherto done my duty to the emperors, and am always ready to comply with their just orders, according to the doctrine of our Lord Christ, who bids us give both to Cæsar and to God their due; and I am obliged to prefer heaven to earth, and to obey God rather than man." The governor, on hearing this speech, immediately passed sentence on him to be burnt, which was executed accordingly, and the martyr expired, singing praises to God in the midst of the flames.

At the period of the Bartholomew massacre, when the King of France sent his orders to the commanders in the different provinces to massacre the Huguenots, one of them returned him this answer: "In my district your majesty has many brave soldiers, but no butchers." It is pleasing to add, that the humane and virtuous governor never felt any effects of the royal resentment.

Devotion to Duty.

Chap. vi. ver. 4.—We will give ourselves continually to prayer, and to the ministry of the word.

"NOTHING seems important to me," says Mr Cecil, "but so far as it is connected with religion. The end—the *cui bono?*—enters into my view of everything. Even the highest acts of the intellect become criminal trifling, when they occupy much of the time of a moral creature, and especially of a minister. If the mind cannot feel and treat mathematics and music, and all such things, as trifles, it has been seduced and enslaved. Brainerd, and Grimshaw, and Fletcher, were men. Most of us are dwarfs."

Religious Disputations.

Chap. vi. ver. 9.—There arose certain of the synagogue which is called the synagogue of the Libertines, and Cyrenians, and Alexandrians, and them of Cilicia and of Asia, disputing with Stephen.

MR GRIMSHAW was once in company with a nobleman, who unhappily employed his talents in the service of infidelity. He had some time before been engaged in a long dispute with two eminent divines, in which, as usual in such cases, the victory was claimed by both sides. Meeting afterwards with Mr G., he wished to draw him likewise into a dispute, but he declined it nearly in these words: "My lord, if you needed information, I would gladly do my utmost to assist you; but the fault is not in your *head*, but in your *heart*.

which can only be reached by a divine power; I shall pray for you, but I cannot dispute with you." His lordship, far from being offended, treated him with particular respect, and declared afterwards, that he was more pleased and more struck by the freedom, firmness, and simplicity of his answer, than by anything he heard on the side of his opponents.

Wrong-Doing Punished.

Chap. vii. ver. 24.—And seeing one of them suffer wrong, he defended him, and avenged him that was oppressed, and smote the Egyptian.

THE Emperor Kaung-hi, one of the most celebrated of the Chinese monarchs, in one of his visits to the provinces, having retired a little way from his attendants, perceived an old man weeping bitterly. "What do you weep for?" said the emperor. "My lord," replied the old man, who did not know the person of his sovereign, "I had only one son in whom all my hopes were centred, and who might have become the support of my family; a Tartar mandarin has torn him from me. I am now deprived of every assistance, and know not where to seek relief; for how can a feeble old man like me obtain justice against a powerful man?" "Your son will be restored," said the emperor, without making himself known. "Conduct me to the house of the mandarin who has been guilty of this act of violence." The old man obeyed, and after having travelled two hours they arrived at the mandarin's house, who little expected such a visit. The emperor immediately condemned him to lose his head; and this sentence was executed upon the spot. The emperor, then turning towards the old man, with a grave tone addressed him: "I appoint you to the office of the criminal whom I have now put to death; be careful to discharge the duties of it with more moderation than your predecessor, lest yourself become an example to others."

True Prayer.

Chap. vii. ver. 60.—He kneeled down, and cried with a loud voice, Lord, lay not this sin to their charge.

JOHN WREN, a pious young man, was employed in a large manufactory, the overseer of which took every opportunity of exposing him to the ridicule of his companions on account of his religion, and because he refused to join in their drinking parties and Sabbath frolics. As they lived in the same house, the overseer one day heard him at prayer, and resolved to listen; when, to his great surprise, he found himself the subject of the young man's supplications, who was spreading his case of infidelity and hardness of heart before God, and supplicating earnestly for him, that God would give him repentance unto salvation, and create in him a new heart, and put a right spirit within him. The man was deeply penetrated with what he heard. He had never entertained an idea of the power or nature of true prayer: he wondered at the eloquence and fervour with which his own unhappy case had been pleaded before God. I never, said he to himself, thus prayed to God for myself. The impression dwelt upon his mind. The next day he took John aside; "I wish," said he, "John, you would preach to me a little." John, who only thought his grave face was meant to turn the subject into ridicule, said, "Mr. Melville, you know I am no preacher, I don't pretend to it." "Nay," said Mr. M., "I don't know how you can preach to-day; but I heard you yesterday make such a description of my state, as convinces me you can do it very well; and I shall be much obliged to you to repeat it." "Oh," says John, "it is true I was at prayer, and did, indeed, heartily pray for you." "Very well," said he, "pray, do it again; for I never heard anything in my life which so deeply affected me." John did not wait for much entreaty; they knelt down together, and cried to the God of all grace, and found acceptance. From that day they were bosom friends; went to the same place of worship, and frequently bowed their knees together, and joined in praise and thanksgiving. Their conversation adorned their profession; and the mocker became a confessor of the grace which he had so often abused and turned into ridicule.

The Church Persecuted.

Chap. viii. ver. 1.—There was a great persecution against the church which was at Jerusalem; and they were all scattered abroad throughout the region of Judea and Samaria, except the apostles.

DURING the reign of the bigoted and persecuting Mary of England, many of the Protestants sought refuge in Germany, where, by the good providence of God, they were comfortably provided for till the death of the Queen. "It is no less pleasant to consider," says Fuller, "than admirable to conceive, how the exiles subsisted so long, and so far from their native country, in so comfortable a condition; especially, seeing Gardiner, Bishop of Winchester, solemnly vowed, so to stop the sending of all supplies to them, that, *for very hunger, they should eat their own nails, and then feed on their fingers' ends.* But threatened folks live long; and, before these banished men were brought to that short bill of fare, the bishop was eaten up of *worms* himself."

Gold.

Chap. viii. ver. 20.—Peter said unto him, Thy money perish with thee, because thou hast thought that the gift of God may be purchased with money.

POPE JULIUS II. began the building of the magnificent church at Rome, but left it unfinished. His successor, Leo X., was desirous to complete this superb edifice, but being involved in debt, and finding the apostolic treasury exhausted, he had recourse to the selling of indulgences, a gainful traffic, for the procuring of a sufficient sum of money. Accordingly, in 1517, he published general indulgences throughout all Europe to such as would contribute to the building of St Peter's. The sum of *ten shillings* was sufficient to purchase the pardon of sins, and the ransom of a soul from purgatory!

Conversion to God.

Chap. ix. ver. 8.—Saul arose from the earth; and when his eyes were opened, he saw no man; but they led him by the hand, and brought him into Damascus.

MR. ELLIS, when speaking of the conversion of an old blind priest of the fisherman's temple at Parea, says:—"When the majority of the inhabitants embraced Christianity, he declared he would not abandon the idols, nor unite in the worship of the God of the Christians; and in order to show his determination, on the Sabbath day, when the people went to the chapel, he went to work in, I think, a part of the ground belonging to the temple: while thus engaged in mending a fence, a bough struck his eyes, and not only inflicted great pain, but deprived him of his sight, and, like Elymas, he was obliged to be led home. This circumstance deeply affected his mind; he became a firm believer in the true God, maintained an upright and resigned frame of mind, and when baptized, adopted the name of Paul, from the similarity in the means employed in humbling and converting him, and those used to bring the apostle to a sense of the power and mercy of the Saviour."

Waiting to Kill.

Chap. ix. ver. 23, 24.—The Jews took counsel to kill him. But their laying await was known of Saul : and they watched the gates day and night to kill him.

MR. BRADBURY possessed an ardent zeal in the cause of civil and religious liberty, and had many admirers. This exposed him to the hatred of the popish faction, whose designs in respect of the Jacobitish succession he had often exposed. They once employed a person to take away his life. To make himself fully acquainted with Mr. Bradbury's person, the man frequently attended at places of worship where he preached, placed himself in front of the gallery, with his countenance stedfastly fixed on the preacher. It was scarcely possible, in such circumstances, wholly to avoid listening to what was said. Mr. Bradbury's forcible way of presenting divine truth awakened the man's attention ; the truth entered his understanding, and became the means of changing his heart. He came to the preacher with trembling and confusion, told his affecting tale, gave evidence of his conversion, became a member of Mr. Bradbury's church, and was, to his death, an ornament to the Gospel which he possessed.

Praying Soldiers.

Chap. x. ver. 7.—A devout soldier of them that waited on him continually.

DURING the late unhappy commotions in Ireland, a private soldier in the army of Lord Cornwallis was daily observed to be absent from his quarters, and from the company of his fellow-soldiers. He began to be suspected of withdrawing himself for the purpose of holding intercourse with the rebels ; and, on this suspicion, probably increased by the malice of his wicked comrades, he was tried by a court-martial, and condemned to die. The marquis, hearing of this, wished to examine the minutes of the trial ; and, not being satisfied, sent for the man to converse with him. Upon being interrogated, the prisoner solemnly disavowed every treasonable practice or intention, declared his sincere attachment to his sovereign, and his readiness to live and die in his service ; he affirmed, that the real cause of his frequent absence was, that he might obtain a place of retirement for the purpose of private prayer, for which his lordship knew he had no opportunity among his profane comrades, who had become his enemies merely on account of his profession of religion. He said he had made this defence on his trial, but the officers thought it so improbable that they paid no attention to it. The marquis, in order to satisfy himself as to the truth of his defence, observed, that if so, he must have acquired considerable aptness in this exercise. The poor man replied, that, as to ability, he had nothing to boast of. The marquis then insisted on his kneeling down, and praying aloud before him ; which he did, and poured forth his soul before God, with such copiousness, fluency, and ardour, that the marquis took him by the hand, and said, he was satisfied that no man could pray in that manner who did not live in the habit of intercourse with his God. He not only revoked

Judging the Quick and Dead.

Chap. x. ver. 42.—He was ordained of God to be the Judge of quick and dead.

ADALBERT, who lived in the 10th century, was appointed Archbishop of Prague. This preferment seemed to give him so little satisfaction, that he was never seen to smile afterwards; and, on being asked the reason, he replied, "It is an easy thing to wear a mitre and a cross, but an awful thing to give an account of a bishopric before the Judge of quick and dead."

Methodical Instruction.

Chap. xi. ver. 4.—Peter rehearsed the matter from the beginning; and expounded it by order unto them.

"I DON'T know," said a gentleman to the late Rev. Andrew Fuller, "how it is that I can remember your sermons better than those of any other minister, but such is the fact." "I cannot tell," replied Mr. Fuller, "unless it be owing to simplicity of arrangement; I pay particular attention to this part of composition, always placing things together that are related to each other, and that naturally follow each other in succession. For instance," added he, "suppose I were to say to my servant, 'Betty, you must go and buy some butter, and starch, and cream, and soap, and tea, and blue, and sugar, and cakes,' Betty would be very apt to say, 'Master! I shall never be able to remember all these.' But suppose I were to say, 'Betty, you know that your mistress is going to have some friends to tea to-morrow, and that you are going to wash the day following; and that for the tea party, you will want tea, and sugar, and cream, and cakes, and butter; and for the washing you will want soap, and starch, and blue;' Betty would instantly reply, 'Yes, master, I can now remember them all very well.'"

Repentance.

Chap. xi. ver. 18.—Then hath God also to the Gentiles granted repentance unto life.

IN one of the counties in England which is famous for its mines, lived a collier, who had spent a great portion of his life in a careless and ungodly manner. Not accustomed to attend the preaching of the Gospel, he was grossly ignorant of divine things. From his habits of vice, and aversion to the worship of God, his case appeared very hopeless. God was pleased, however, to accomplish his conversion to Himself in a way exceedingly simple, yet truly marvellous. Though regardless of concern for his own spiritual welfare, he was induced to permit the attendance of his children at a Sabbath school. It pleased God to visit one of the daughters of this wicked father with a mortal sickness; but before her death, she was rendered instrumental in exciting the attention of her parent to the concerns of his soul. "Father," inquired the dying child, "can you spell repentance?" This he became desirous of knowing, and ultimately was taught its sacred meaning. He also discovered that he needed repentance, that he was a guilty sinner, deserving God's everlasting wrath. Repentance unto life was granted him, and he was enabled by grace to bring forth the fruits of righteousness in his conversation

Answer to Prayer.

Chap. xii. ver. 5.—*Peter therefore was kept in prison; but prayer was made without ceasing of the church unto God for him.*

MR. ELLIOT, who laboured as a missionary among the American Indians, was eminent in prayer; and several instances are recorded of remarkable answers having been given to his petitions; the following is striking:—

Mr. Foster, a godly gentleman of Charleston, was, with his son, taken by the Turks; and the barbarous prince, in whose dominions he was become a slave, was resolved that, in his lifetime, no captive should be released; so that Mr. Foster's friends, when they heard the sad news, concluded that all hope was lost. Upon this, Mr. Elliot, in some of his next prayers before a great congregation, addressed the throne of grace in the following very plain language:—" Heavenly Father, work for the redemption of Thy poor servant Foster. And if the prince who detains him will not, as they say, dismiss him as long as himself lives, Lord, we pray Thee, kill that cruel prince: kill him, and glorify Thyself upon him." In answer to this singular prayer, Mr. Foster quickly returned from captivity, and brought an account, that the prince who had detained him had come to an untimely death; by which means he had been set at liberty. "Thus we knew," says Dr. Cotton Mather, "that a prophet had been among us."

Deliverance from Death.

Chap. xii. ver. 11.—*When Peter was come to himself, he said, Now I know of a surety, that the Lord hath sent his angel and hath delivered me out of the hand of Herod, and from all the expectation of the people of the Jews.*

ONE Mr. Barber, a Protestant, was, in the reign of Queen Mary, condemned to the flames. The morning of execution arrived. The intended martyr walked to Smithfield, and was bound to the stake. The faggots were piled around him, and the executioner only waited for the word of command to apply the torch. Just at this crisis, tidings came of the queen's death; which obliged the officers to stop their proceedings until the pleasure of the new queen (Elizabeth) should be known. In memory of so providential a deliverance, by which the good man was as *a brand plucked out of the fire*, he was no sooner released from his imprisonment and troubles, than he got a picture of Queen Elizabeth made, decorated round with significant ornaments, and ordered in his will that the picture should be transmitted as a memorial to future times in the eldest branch of his family.

Perverting the Church.

Chap. xiii. ver. 10.—*Paul said, O full of all subtilty and all mischief, thou child of the devil, thou enemy of all righteousness, wilt thou not cease to pervert the right ways of the Lord?*

WHEN Polycarp was at Rome, he employed his time in confirming the faithful, and convincing gainsayers, whereby he reclaimed many who had been infected with the pernicious heresies of Marcian and Valentius; and so very fervent was his affection for the truth, that whenever he heard of any of the mischievous opinions of his time mentioned, he used to stop his ears, and cry out, "Good God, to what times hast Thou reserved me, that I should hear such things!" And one day meeting Marcian, who called to him, saying, "Polycarp own us," he replied, "I own thee to be the first born of Satan."

Despisers of Religion.

Chap. xiii. 40, 41.—Beware, therefore, lest that come upon you which is spoken of in the prophets ; Behold, ye despisers, and wonder, and perish.

ONE Mr. Soper, while residing at Alfriston, in England, having been called to the knowledge of the truth, separated himself from his former gay associates. Some of these giddy youths meeting him one day when going to the chapel, thus addressed him : "Well, Soper, you seem to be very zealous for religion ; we shall soon hear that you are a preacher. Come, can't you preach us a sermon?" Soper very gravely replied, "No ; I will name a text, and will leave you to preach the sermon." Then, with great emphasis, he recited the above passage ; "Beware, therefore, lest that come upon you which is spoken of in the prophets : Behold, ye despisers, and wonder, and perish ; for I work a work in your days, a work which ye shall in nowise believe, though a man declare it unto you." The words fell with such weight on their minds that not one of them could make a reply, nor did they ever ridicule him any more.

Stirring up Evil.

Chap. xiv. ver. 2.—The unbelieving Jews stirred up the Gentiles, and made their hearts evil affected against the brethren.

ABOUT the beginning of 1825, Mr. King, the American missionary, spent about six months in Tyre in Syria, and made some efforts to establish a school there for the instruction of Tyrian females. He was very near succeeding, when one of the principal priests rose up and said, "It is by no means expedient to teach women to read the word of God. It is better for them to remain in ignorance, than to know how to read and write. They are quite bad enough with what little they know ; teach them to read and write, and there would be no living with them." These arguments were sufficient to convince all the Greek and Catholic population of the impropriety of female education.

Only Men.

Chap. xiv. ver. 15.—We also are men with like passions with you.

WHEN the French ambassador visited the illustrious Bacon in his last illness, and found him in bed with the curtains drawn, he addressed this fulsome compliment to him : "You are like the angels, of whom we hear and read much, but have not the pleasure of seeing them."—The reply was the sentiment of a philosopher, and language not unworthy of a Christian,—"If the complaisance of others compares me to an angel, my infirmities tell me I am a man."

Disputations in the Church.

Chap. xv. ver. 2.—Paul and Barnabas had no small dissension and disputation with them.

A GENTLEMAN who was in company with the late Mr. John Newton of London, lamented the violent disputes that often take place among Christians respecting the non-essentials of Christianity, and particularly church government. "Many," he said, "seem to give their chief attention to such topics, and take more pleasure in talking on these disputable points, than on spiritual religion, the love of Christ, and the privileges of His people." "Sir," said the venerable old man, "did you ever see a whale ship? I am told that when the fish is struck with the harpoon, and feels the smart of the wound, it sometimes makes for the boat, and would probably dash it to pieces. To prevent this, they throw a cask overboard; and when it is staved to pieces, they throw over another. Now, sir," added Mr. Newton, "church government is the tub which Satan has thrown over to the people of whom you speak."

Saved by Grace.

Chap. xv. ver. 11.—We believe that, through the grace of the Lord Jesus Christ, we shall be saved even as they.

THE late Rev. Andrew Fuller, one day during his last illness, complained of great depression and sinking, saying that he must die. A friend replied, "I do not know of any person, sir, who is in a more enviable situation than yourself; a good man on the verge of a blessed immortality." He humbly acquiesced, and hoped it was so; and then lifting up his hands, exclaimed, "If I am saved, it must be by great sovereign grace,—by great sovereign grace."

Listening Willingly.

Chap. xvi. ver. 14.—A certain woman named Lydia, whose heart the Lord had opened, that she attended unto the things which were spoken of Paul.

THE late Rev. John Pattison of Edinburgh, having occasion to preach on a Sabbath day in Dundee, had, previously to his leaving home, laid aside, and ordered to be packed up with some other necessary articles, a certain note-book, which contained a sermon, on which the good man had bestowed considerable pains, and which he hoped might not be unacceptable to a congregation of Christians, who then enjoyed the stated labours of the late excellent Mr. M'Ewen. On his arrival in Dundee, however, which was not till the Saturday evening, and on examining the contents of his saddle-bags, he found the note-book wanting, nor had any other been substituted in its place. He was, therefore, late as it was, obliged to make choice of a new subject, and to cast his thoughts together upon it, in the best manner he could; and after all his pains, and all his prayers, was not a little apprehensive that such defective preparation would not only affect the respectability of his appearance in the pulpit, but in some measure mar the success of his work. "Not by might," however, "nor by power, but by my Spirit, saith the Lord." It happened in adorable providence, on the afternoon of that Sabbath, that a poor fish woman, notorious for clamour and profanity, stumbled into the meeting, and felt the sermon, particularly in the application, come home with such life and peculiar energy to her soul, as instantly to produce the most happy effect on the dispositions of her heart, and tenor of her conduct. On Monday she attended with her fish-basket at market as usual,— but, O how changed! Instead of her former noise and profanity, she was quiet and calm as a lamb—instead of asking from her customers double or triple the value of her fish, she spoke to them with discretion and told the lowest price at once. Surprised at this new behaviour of the woman, some who were present, judging she might be indisposed, began to inquire for her health; one of them in particular said to her, "Dear Margaret, what is the matter with you? you are not at all as you used to be." "No," replied Margaret, "and I hope never shall." It pleased God to lead me yesterday to Mr. M'Ewen's meeting-house, where I heard words I will never forget, and found something come over me. the like of which I never knew before."—The woman lived to give the most satisfactory evidence of the soundness of her conversion, by a walk and conversation becoming the Gospel.

Do Thyself no Harm.

Chap. xvi. ver. 28.—Do thyself no harm; for we are all here.

AN ingenious young man, having come to London in the hope of getting some employment, was unsuccessful in his attempt, and being reduced to extreme poverty, came to the awful resolution of throwing himself into the Thames. On passing near the Royal Exchange to effect his desperate purpose, he saw the carriage of the late excellent Mr Hanway, under the arms of which was the motto, "Never despair." The singular occurrence of this sentence had, under Providence, such an effect on the young man, that he immediately desisted from his horrid design, gained soon afterwards a considerable establishment, and died in good circumstances in the common course of mortality.

Reasoning from Scripture.

Chap. xvii. ver. 2.—Paul reasoned with them out of the Scriptures.

THE late Mrs Graham of New York regarded with particular esteem the works of Dr Owen, the Rev. William Romaine, and the Rev. John Newton, and read them with pleasure and profit. One day she remarked to Mr Banner, her son-in-law, that she preferred the ancient writers on theology to the modern, because they dealt more in italics. "Dear mother," he replied, "what religion can there be in *italics?*" "You know," she said, "that old writers expected credit for the doctrines they taught, by proving them from the word of God to be correct; they inserted the Scripture passages in italics, and their works have been sometimes one half in italics. Modern writers on theology, on the contrary, give us a long train of reasoning to persuade us to their opinion, but very little in *italics*."

Mockers.

Chap. xvii. ver. 18.—Certain philosophers of the Epicureans, and of the Stoics, encountered him. And some said, What will this babbler say? other some, He seemeth to be a setter forth of strange gods; because he preached unto them Jesus, and the resurrection.

"THIS has been one of the worst nights," says Mr Bampton, one of the missionaries in India, "I ever endured. Mockery! mockery! cruel mockery! almost unbearable. I talked for a while, and was heard by some, on the blessings to be enjoyed by faith in Jesus Christ; when a man came with a hell-hardened countenance, and that peculiar constant laugh which I can hardly bear. The burden of his cry was 'Juggernaut is the foundation! Juggernaut is completely god! victory to Juggernaut!' He clapped his hands—he shouted—he laughed, and induced the rest, or a great part of them, to do the same. On the ground of reason, I fear no one; and rage I commonly bear very well; but these everlasting laughing buffoons are nearly too much for me. It is my one great care, that amidst a reviling, laughing, shouting crowd, I do not seem abashed."

Earning a Living.

Chap. xviii. ver. 3.—And because he was of the same craft, he abode with them and wrought; for by their occupation they were tentmakers.

A VIOLENT Welsh squire having taken offence at a poor curate who employed his leisure hours in mending clocks and watches, applied to the Bishop of St Asaph, with a formal complaint against him, for impiously carrying on a trade, contrary to the statute. His lordship having heard the complaint, told the squire he might depend upon the strictest justice being done in the case. Accordingly the mechanic divine was sent for a few days after, when the bishop asked him, "How he dared to disgrace his diocese by becoming a mender of clocks and watches." The other, with all humility, answered, "To satisfy the wants of a wife and ten children." "That won't do with me," rejoined the prelate, "I will inflict such a punishment upon you as shall make you leave off your pitiful trade, I promise you;" and immediately, calling in his secretary, ordered him to make out a presentation for the astonished curate to a living of at least one hundred and fifty pounds per annum.

Expounding the Way to God.

Chap. xviii. ver. 26.—He began to speak boldly in the synagogue; whom, when Aquila and Priscilla had heard, they took him unto them, and expounded unto him the way of God more perfectly.

IT is said of the Rev. Ebenezer Erskine, that, for some time after his ordination, his views of divine truth, in common with those of a large proportion of godly ministers of the Church of Scotland in that age, were not quite clear and correct, but consisted of a confused mixture of legal and evangelical doctrine. It pleased God, however, to give him more accurate and satisfactory conceptions of the truth, and to bless for that purpose the interviews he had with his brother Ralph, and others. Nay, according to his own ingenious acknowledgments to his children and friends, he was more deeply indebted to no one, as an instrument of helping him to understand "the way of God more perfectly," than to his amiable partner, Alison Turpie, a young lady of engaging dispositions and eminent piety, whom he married soon after his settlement in Portmoak. A confidential conversation, which he overheard betwixt her and his brother Ralph, on the subject of their religious experience, is thought to have contributed greatly towards the happy change that took place in Ebenezer's views and impressions with relation to the Gospel. Whilst they were freely opening their minds to each other, in a bower in his garden, immediately beneath the window of his study, which then happened to be open, he listened with much eagerness to their interesting communications. Their views and feelings appeared so different from his own, that he was immediately struck with the idea that they possessed valuable attainments to which he was a stranger; and the impression seemed to have remained, till, with regard to vital and evangelical Christianity, he became not merely almost, but altogether, as they were.

Profane Books.

Chap. xix. ver. 19.—Many of them also which used curious arts, brought their books together, and burned them before all men.

THE Earl of Rochester, of whom it has been said, that he was "a great wit, a great scholar, a great poet, a great sinner, and a great penitent," left a strict charge to the person in whose custody his papers were, to burn all his profane and lewd writings, as being only fit to promote vice and immorality, by which he had so highly offended

God, and shamed and blasphemed that holy religion into which he had been baptized. Dr Watts refers to him in the following lines:—

"Stephen of noble blood and mind,
(For ever shine his name!)
As death approached, his soul refined,
And gave his looser sonnets to the flame.
'Burn, burn,' he cried, with sacred rage;
'Hell is the due of every page,
Hell be the fate.' But, O, indulgent heaven!
So vile the muse, and yet the man forgiven!"

Do Nothing Rashly.

Chap. xix. ver. 36.—Ye ought to be quiet, and to do nothing rashly.

"I HAVE heard one say," observes Dr Mather, "that there was a gentleman mentioned in the 19th chapter of the Acts, to whom he was more indebted than to any man in the world. This was he whom our translation calls the town-clerk of Ephesus, whose counsel it was *to do nothing rashly.* Upon any proposal of consequence, it was a usual speech with him—'We will first advise with the town-clerk of Ephesus.' One, in a fond compliance with a friend, forgetting the town-clerk, may do that in haste, which he may repent at leisure —may do what may cost him several hundreds of pounds, besides trouble, which he would not have undergone for thousands."

Sleeping at Service.

Chap. xx. ver. 9.—As Paul was long preaching, Eutychus sank down with sleep.

ONE Lord's day afternoon, the late Mr Fuller of Kettering perceiving some of his hearers to be drowsy, as soon as he had read his text, he struck the Bible three times against the side of the pulpit, calling out, "What! asleep already! I am often afraid I should *preach* you asleep: but the fault cannot be mine to-day, for I have not yet begun!"

Repentance and Faith.

Chap. xx. ver. 21.—Testifying both to the Jews, and also to the Greeks, repentance toward God, and faith toward our Lord Jesus Christ.

IN the year 1680, the Rev. Philip Henry preached on the doctrine of faith and repentance, from several texts of Scripture. He used to say, that he had been told concerning the famous Mr Dod, that some called him in scorn, *faith* and *repentance,* because he insisted so much upon these two in all his preaching. "But," says he, "if this be to be vile, I will be yet more vile, for faith and repentance are all in all in Christianity." Concerning repentance, he has sometimes said, "If I were to die in the pulpit, I would desire to die preaching repentance; or if I die out of the pulpit, I would desire to be practising repentance." And he had often this saying concerning repentance, "He that repents every day for the sins of every day, when he comes to die, will have the sins but of one day to repent of."

Incurring Danger for Christ's Sake.

Chap. xxi. ver. 13.—Then Paul answered, What mean ye to weep and to break mine heart? for I am ready not to be bound only, but also to die at Jerusalem for the name of the Lord Jesus

WHEN Luther was summoned to attend the diet at Worms, his friends, notwithstanding the safe conduct granted to him by the Emperor Charles V., apprehending danger to his person, would have dissuaded him from going thither. Luther replied, "I am determined to enter the city in the name of the Lord Jesus Christ, though as many devils should oppose me as there are tiles upon all the houses at Worms." He was accompanied from Wittemberg by some divines, and one hundred horse; but he took only eight horsemen into Worms. When he stept out of the carriage, he said, in presence of a great number of persons, "God shall be on my side."

Submission to God.

Chap. xxi. ver. 14.—The will of the Lord be done.

"WHEN I was in the United States of America," says a Christian writer, "I heard of the conversion of a complete man of the world: which, as far as means were concerned, owed its existence to the following circumstances :—God laid his hand on a lovely, and I think an only daughter; and the affliction terminated in death. When the terrible moment arrived in which the object of his affections must die, he stood at the head of her bed, almost frantic with grief; and, having no consolatson above what nature and education supplied, as is frequently the case, his grief terminated in rage; he was almost ready to curse the God who, as he thought, could be so cruel as to deprive him of so dear a child. His wife, an amiable and sensible woman, at the same time stood at the foot of the bed. Her eyes were suffused with tears, her hands lifted up to heaven; and, while every feature spoke the feelings of her soul, she exclaimed, 'The will of the Lord be done! The will of the Lord be done! The will of the Lord be done!' These exclamations very naturally called the attention of her frantic husband from his dying daughter to herself; and, as he afterwards confessed, he was on the point of wreaking his vengeance on what he then considered an unfeeling wife, and an unnatural, hard-hearted mother. After a while, however, the storm of passion gave place to reflection. He was a man of eminence at the bar, a colonel at the army; he prided himself on being a philosopher; and was therefore led to examine how his courage and philosophy had supported him on the day of trial. Here he saw reason to reflect on his conduct with shame; the more so, as he contrasted it with the conduct of his amiable and pious partner. 'How is this?' he could not but exclaim; "I am a man and a soldier. I boast of my courage and pride myself in my philosophy, in which I am versed, as being equal to the support of man in every emergency. But in the hour of trial I acted an unworthy part. My wife, a delicate female, and, notwithstanding my suspicions to the contrary, one of the most affectionate of mothers, was alone the magnanimous sufferer on this trying occasion. What, under circumstances so directly opposite, could lead to such contrary results?' 'She is a Christian," said a still small voice; "and I am not; surely the secret is here!" This train of thought led to the most pleasing consequences. He concluded that there must be a reality in that religion which he had hitherto despised; and, if so, that it is the one thing needful. He conferred not with flesh and blood; but immediately began to seek the consolations of true religion, and, ere long, found

'What nothing earthly gives, or can destroy;
The soul's calm sunshine, and the heartfelt joy.'"

The Vision.

Chap. xxii. ver. 6, 7.—As I made my journey, and was come nigh unto Damascus about noon, suddenly there shone from heaven a great light round about me. And I fell unto the ground, and heard a voice saying unto me, Saul, Saul, why persecutest thou me?

COLONEL GARDINER, on the memorable day of his conversion, had spent the preceding part of the evening in gay company; and having a criminal assignation with a married woman at twelve o'clock (the company having broken up at eleven), he took up a book entitled, "The Christian Soldier, or heaven taken by storm," which his pious mother or aunt had slipt into his portmanteau, expecting to find something that might afford him a little diversion. While reading it, he thought he saw an unusual blaze of light fall on the book, which he at first imagined might happen by some accident in the candle. But, lifting up his eyes, he apprehended, to his extreme amazement, that there was before him, as it were, suspended in the air, a visible representation of the Lord Jesus Christ upon the cross, surrounded on all sides with a glory; and was impressed as if a voice, or something equivalent to a voice, had come to him to this effect, "Oh, sinner! did I suffer this for thee, and are these thy returns?" But whether this were an audible voice, or only a strong impression on his mind, equally striking, he did not seem very confident, "though," says his biographer, "to the best of my remembrance, he rather judged it to be the former. Struck with so amazing a phenomenon as this, there hardly remained any life in him, so that he sunk down in the arm-chair in which he sat, and continued, he knew not exactly how long, insensible (which was one circumstance that made me several times to take the liberty to suggest that he might possibly be all the while asleep); but however that were, he quickly after opened his eyes, and saw nothing more than usual."

Eastern Custom.

Chap. xxii. ver. 23,—They cried out, and cast off their clothes, and threw dust into the air.

A GREAT similarity appears between the conduct of the Jews, when the chief captain of the Roman garrison at Jerusalem presented himself in the temple, and the behaviour of the Persian peasants, when they go to court to complain of the governors under whom they live, upon their oppressions becoming intolerable. Sir John Chardin tells us respecting them, that they carry their complaints against their governors by companies, consisting of several hundreds, and sometimes of a thousand; they repair to that gate of the palace near to which their prince is most likely to be, where they begin to make the most horrid cries, tearing their garments, and throwing dust into the air, at the same time demanding justice. The king, upon hearing these cries, sends to know the occasion of them. The people deliver their complaint in writing, upon which he lets them know that he will commit the cognizance of the affair to some one, by whom justice is usually done them.

Unjust Judging.

Chap. xxiii. ver. 3.—Then said Paul unto him, God shall smite thee thou whited wall; for sittest thou to judge me after the law, and commandest me to be smitten contrary to the law?

MR. JOSEPH SHERWOOD, one of the nonconformist ministers of England, having preached on that text, "I will avenge the quarrel of my covenant," was carried to a petty session of justices, where one Mr. Robinson sat as chairman, who greatly reviled Mr. Sherwood, and called him a rebel, etc., which he bore patiently, only making this reply, "That as he was a minister of the Gospel, and at the church where there were so great an assembly, he could not but have compassion on the multitude, and give them a word of exhortation." Mr. Robinson said, "But did ever man preach from such a rebellious text?" "Sir," replied Mr. Sherwood, "I know man is a rebel against his Creator, but I never knew that the Creator could be a rebel against His creature." On which Robinson cried out, "Write his mittimus for Launceston jail." And then, turning to Mr. Sherwood, said, "I say, sir, it was a rebellious text." Mr. Sherwood looked him full in the face, and addressed him in these words: "Sir, if you die the common death of all men, God never spake by me." He was then sent to prison, where he found favour with the keepers, and had liberty to walk about the castle and town. Robinson returned home; and a few days after, walking in the fields, a bull that had been very tame, came up to a gate where he stood, and his servant-maid before him, who had been milking, when the creature turned her aside with his horns, ran directly upon Robinson, and tore out his bowels! He was carried home in this miserable state, and soon afterwards died.

Ready to Kill.

Chap. xxiii. ver. 15.—We, or ever he come near, are ready to kill him.

MR THOROWGOOD, a minister of the 17th century, having reproved the sin of swearing, one of his hearers, sensible of his guilt, and thinking he was the person particularly intended, resolved to kill him; and in order to do it, he hid himself behind a hedge, which he knew Mr Thorowgood would ride by when he went to preach his weekly lecture. When Mr T. came to the place, he prepared to shoot him, but his piece failed, and only flashed in the pan. The next week he lay in the same place with the same design. When Mr T. came up, the wretched man attempted to fire again, but the piece would not go off. Upon this, his conscience accusing him for such wickedness, he went after him, and, falling down on his knees, with tears in his eyes related the whole to him, and begged his pardon. This providence was the means of his conversion, and he became, from that time, a serious Christian.

A Pure Conscience.

Chap. xxiv. ver. 16.—And herein do I exercise myself, to have always a conscience void of offence toward God and toward men.

TWO monks having come one day to William Rufus, king of England, to buy an Abbot's place, who outreached each other in the sums they offered, the king said to a third monk, who stood by, "What wilt thou give for the place?" "Not a penny," answered the monk, "for it is against my conscience." "Then," replied the king, "thou of the three best deservest it," and instantly gave it to him.

Bribery.

Chap. xxiv. ver. 26.—He hoped also that money should have been given him of Paul, that he might loose him: wherefore he sent for him oftener, and communed with him.

A CASE was tried before a young Cadi at Smyrna, the merits of which were as follow :—A poor man claimed a house which a rich man usurped. The former held his deeds and documents to prove his right ; but the latter had provided a number of witnesses to invalidate his title. In order to support their evidence effectually, he presented the Cadi with a bag containing 500 ducats. When the day arrived for hearing the cause, the poor man told his story, and produced his writings, but could not support his case by witnesses ; the other rested the whole case on his witnesses, and on his adversary's defect in law, who would produce none ; he urged the Cadi, therefore, to give sentence in his favour. After the most pressing solicitations, the judge calmly drew out from under his sofa the bag of ducats, which the rich man had given him as a bribe, saying to him very gravely, "You have been much mistaken in the suit, for if the poor man could produce no witnesses in confirmation of his right, I myself can produce at least five hundred." He then threw away the bag with reproach and indignation, and decreed the house to the poor plaintiff. Such was the noble decision of a Turkish judge, whose disinterested conduct was the reverse of the unjust, time-serving Felix.

False Accusations.

Chap. xxv. ver. 7.—And when he was come, the Jews which came down from Jerusalem stood round about, and laid many and grievous complaints against Paul, which they could not prove.

WHEN the first missionaries from America reached the Sandwich Islands, in the spring of 1820, an effort was made by some of the foreigners to have their landing and establishment at the islands forbidden by the government. With this view, their motives were misrepresented by them to the king and chiefs. It was asserted, that while the ostensible object of the mission was good, the secret and ultimate design was the subjugation of the islands, and the enslavement of the people, and, by way of corroboration, the treatment of the Mexicans and aborigines of South America and the West Indies by the Spaniards, and the possession of Hindostan by the British, were gravely related. It was in consequence of this misrepresentation, that a delay of eight days occurred before the missionaries could secure permission to disembark. In answer to these allegations, the more intelligent of the chiefs remarked, "The missionaries speak well ; they say they have come from America only to do us good : if they intend to seize our islands, why are they so few in number ? where are their guns ? and why have they brought their wives ?" To this it was replied, "It is true their number is small ; a few only have come now, the more fully to deceive. But soon many more will arrive and your islands will be lost." The chiefs again answered, "They say they will do us good ; they are few in number ; we will try them for one year, and if we find they deceive us, it will then be time enough to send them away." Permission to land was accordingly granted. Mr. Young, it is said, was the only foreigner who advocated their reception.

Zeal in Godliness.

Chap. xxvi. ver. 24.—Festus said with a loud voice, Paul, thou art beside thyself : much learning doth make thee mad.

AS soon as the late Mr. Berridge, vicar of Everton, began to preach in a different strain from the neighbouring clergy, it was observed, they found themselves hurt at the emptiness of their own churches, and the fulness of his. The squire of the parish, too, was much offended; he did not like to see so many strangers, and be so incommoded, and endeavoured to turn Mr. Berridge out of his living, by a complaint to his Bishop. Mr. Berridge being sent for by his lordship, he was accosted in the following manner:—"Well, Berridge, they tell me you go about preaching out of your parish; did I institue you to any other than Everton?" "No, my lord." "Well, but you go and preach where you have no right so to do." "It is true, my lord; I remember seeing five or six clergymen out of their own parishes playing at bowls." "Pho," said his lordship, "if you don't desist, you will very likely be sent to Huntingdon jail." "As to that, my lord, I have no greater likings to a jail than other people; but I had rather go there with a good conscience, than be at liberty with a bad one." Here his lordship, looking hard at Berridge, gravely assured him, "he was beside himself, and that in a few months' time he would be either better or worse." "Then," said he, "my lord, you may make yourself easy in this business; for if I am better, you must suppose I shall desist of my own accord; and if worse, you need not send me to Huntingdon jail, and I shall be provided with an accommodation in bedlam."

Saved from the Storm.

Chap. xxvii. ver. 20.—And when neither sun nor stars in many days appeared, and no small tempest lay on us, all hope that we should be saved was then taken away.

IN the year 1709, a packet boat, returning from Holland to England, was so damaged by a tempest, that she sprung a leak, and was in the utmost extremity of danger. When all the mariners and passengers were in the last distress, and the pumps had been worked to carry off the water, but all to little purpose, by a good providence the hole filled, and was stopped seemingly of itself. This struck them all with wonder and astonishment. No sooner did they get safe into port, than they examined the ship to ascertain the cause, and found a fish sticking in the very hole, which had been driven into it by the force of the tempest. But for this wonderful Providence, they must all have perished.

Trust in God.

Chap. xxvii. ver. 25.—Wherefore, sirs, be of good cheer; for I believe God, that it shall be even as it was told me.

SOME years ago, a minister was preaching in Plymouth, when a written paper was given him to this effect:—"The thanksgivings of this congregation are desired to Almighty God, by the chaplain, passengers, and crew of the——, West Indiaman, for their merciful escape from shipwreck during the late awful tempest."—The next day the minister went on board the vessel, with some friends from the shore; and, talking with the passengers, a lady, thus expressed herself:—"Oh, sir, what a blessing must true religion be! Never did I see it more than in my poor negress, Ellen, during the dreadful storm. When, sir, we were tossed to the heavens, and sunk again to the depths, and expecting every wave would break over the vessel and entomb us all, my mind was in a horrible state—I was afraid to die—I could not think to appear before God, but in dread dismay. Ellen would come to me and say, with all possible composure, 'Never mind, missa; look to Jesus Christ—He gave—He rule de sea—He prepare to die.' And when, sir, we neared the shore, and were at a loss to know on what part of the coast we were, fearing every minute to be dashed to atoms on the rocks, my mind still in a distracted state—I feared to die—I knew nothing of religion,—poor Ellen, with the same composure as before, came to me and said, 'Don't be fear, missa, look to Jesus Christ, He de rock; no shipwreck on dat rock; He save to de utmost; don't be fear, missa, look to Jesus Christ.' I determined, sir, I hope in Divine strength, that if ever we reached the shore in safety, I would seek to possess that religion which so supported the heart of a poor negress in the midst of such dreadful danger and alarms."

Imprisoned for the Gospel's Sake.

Chap. xxviii. ver. 20.—For the hope of Israel I am bound with this chain.

GUY DE BREZ, a French minister, was prisoner in the castle of Tournay. A lady who visited him said, "She wondered how he could eat, or drink, or sleep in quiet." "Madam," said he, "my chains do not terrify me, or break my sleep; on the contrary, I glory and take delight therein, esteeming them at an higher rate than chains and rings of gold, or jewels of any price whatever. The rattling of my chains is like the effect of an instrument of music in my ears: not that such an effect comes merely from my chains, because it is I am bound therewith for maintaining the truth of the Gospel."

ROMANS.

Practical Knowledge of God.

Chap. i. ver. 21.—Because that, when they knew God, they glorified him not as God.

A GENTLEMAN, who seemed strongly impressed with the opinion that in order to exalt revelation, it is necessary to maintain that there is no such thing at all as natural religion, visiting a celebrated public seminary in Edinburgh, on occasion of some mention of the ancient philosophers in a passage which the pupils were then reading, asked a blind boy the following questions:—"What did their philosophy do for them?" The boy returned no answer. "Did it, resumed the examiner, "lead them to any knowledge of religion?" "They had no RIGHT knowledge of God." "But could they be said," rejoined the visitor in a marked tone of disapprobation, "to have any knowledge of God at all?" After a moment's thought, the child answered, "Yes." "That," observed the gentleman to the superintendents, "is by no means a right answer." Upon which the pupil was asked whether he had any reason for making this answer, to which he replied, "Yes," "What is it?" "The Apostle Paul, in the first of the Romans, says, that when THEY KNEW GOD," laying an emphasis on these words, "they glorified Him not as God."

Without Christian Teaching.

Chap. i. ver. 31.—Without natural affection, implacable, unmerciful.

MR. ELLIS, in his Missionary Tour, relates the following shocking instance of infanticide. A man and his wife, tenants of Mr.

Young, who has for many years held, under the king, the small district of Kukuwaw, situated on the centre of Waiakea Bay, resided not far from Maaro's house. They had one child, a fine little boy. A quarrel arose between them on one occasion respecting this child. The wife refusing to accede to the wishes of the husband, he, in revenge, caught up the child by the head and the feet, broke its back across his knee, and then threw it down in expiring agonies before her. Struck with the atrocity of the act, Mr. Young seized the man, led him before the king Tamehameha, who was then at Waiakea, and requested that he might be punished. The king inquired, "To whom did the child he has murdered belong?" Mr. Young answered, that it was his own son. "Then," said the king, "neither you nor I have any right to interfere; I cannot say anything to him."

Not Christians in Heart.

Chap. ii. ver. 23, 24.—Thou that makest thy boast of the law, through breaking the law dishonourest thou God? For the name of God is blasphemed among the Gentiles through you.

MR. BRAINERD informs us, that when among the American Indians, at one place, where there was a great number, he halted, and offered to instruct them in the truths of Christianity. "Why," said one of them, "should you desire the Indians to become Christians, seeing the Christians are so much worse than the Indians? The Christians lie, steal, and drink, worse than the Indians. They first taught the Indians to be drunk. They steal to that degree, that their rulers are obliged to hang them for it; and that is not enough to deter others from the practice. But none of the Indians were ever hanged for stealing; and yet they do not steal half so much. We will not consent, therefore, to become Christians, lest we should be as bad as they. We will live as our fathers lived, and go where our fathers are when we die." Notwithstanding Mr. B. did all he could to explain to them that these were not Christians in heart, and that he did not want them to become such as these, he could not prevail, but left them, mortified at the thought, that the wickedness of some called Christians should engender such prejudices.

Christ's Atonement.

Chap. iii. ver. 25.—Whom God hath set forth to be a propitiation through faith in His blood, to declare his righteousness for the remission of sins that are past, through the forbearance of God.

COWPER, the poet, speaking of his religious experience, says, "But the happy period which was now to shake off my fetters, and afford me a clear opening of the free mercy of God in Christ Jesus, was now arrived. I flung myself into a chair near the window, and seeing a Bible there, ventured once more to apply to it for comfort and instruction. The first verse I saw was the 25th of the third of Romans: 'Whom God hath set forth to be a propitiation through faith in His blood, to declare His righteousness for the remission of sins that are past, through the forbearance of God.' Immediately I received strength to believe, and the full beams of the Sun of Righteousness shone upon me. I saw the sufficiency of the atonement He had made, my pardon sealed in His blood, and all the fulness and completeness of His justification. In a moment I believed, and received the Gospel. Whatever my friend Madan had said to me so long before, revived in all its clearness, with demonstration of the Spirit, and with power."

Justification by Faith.

Chap. iii. ver. 26.—That he might be just, and the justifier of him which believeth in Jesus.

IN a conversation which the Rev. Mr Innes had with an infidel on his sick bed, he told him that, when he was taken ill, he thought he would rely on the general mercy of God; that as he never had done anything very bad, he hoped all would be well. "But as my weakness increased," he added, "I began to think, is not God a just Being as well as merciful? Now, what reason have I to think He will treat me with mercy, and not with justice; and if I am treated with justice," said he, with much emotion, "where am I?" "I showed him," says Mr Innes, "that this was the very difficulty the Gospel was sent to remove, as it showed how mercy could be exercised in perfect consistency with the strictest demands of justice, while it was bestowed by the atonement made by Jesus Christ. After explaining this doctrine, and pressing it on his attention and acceptance, one of the last things he said to me, before leaving him, was, 'Well, I believe it must come to this. I confess I here see a solid footing to rest on, which, on my former principles, I could never find.'"

Belief in Christ.

Chap. iv. ver. 5.—To him that worketh not, but believeth on him that justifieth the ungodly, his faith is counted for righteousness.

MR SAMUEL WALKER of Truro was for some time a preacher before he experienced the power of godliness on his own heart. He was brought to right views in the following manner:—About a year after he came to Truro, being in company with some friends, the subject of whose conversation turned upon the nature of justifying and saving faith, he, as he freely owned afterwards, became sensible that he was totally unacquainted with that faith which had been the topic of discourse; and also convinced that he was destitute of something, which was of the greatest importance to his own, as well as the salvation of the people committed to his charge. He said nothing at that time of the concern he was brought under, but was ever ready, afterwards as opportunity offered, to enter upon the subject. He now began to discover that he had hitherto been ignorant of the Gospel salvation, inattentive to the spiritual state of his own, and the souls of others, and governed in all his conduct, not by the only Christian motives of love to God and man, but purely by such as were sensual and selfish; he found he was a slave to the desire of man's esteem; and in short, as he himself expressed it, had been all *wrong* both within and without. Having, by prayer, and study of the Scriptures, under the divine blessing, obtained just views of divine truth, and experienced the power of religion on his own mind, he became a distinguished and successful preacher of the Gospel, whose praise is in all the churches.

Peace with God.

Chap. v. ver. 1.—Therefore, being justified by faith, we have peace with God through our Lord Jesus Christ.

A MINISTER of the Gospel was once preaching in a public hospital. There was an aged woman present, who for several weeks had been aroused to attend to the concerns of her soul; and was now in a state of wretchedness approaching to despair. When she heard the word of God from the lips of his servant, she trembled like a criminal in the hands of the executioner. She was an object of pity to all who knew her. Formerly she had entertained hope of acceptance with God; but she had departed from her comforter, and now she was the prey of a guilty conscience. A short time after this, the same minister was preaching in the same place; but during the first prayer, his text, and the whole arrangement of his discourse, went completely from him, he could not recollect a single sentence of either; but Romans v. 1 took possession of his whole soul: "Therefore, being justified by faith, we have peace with God through our Lord Jesus Christ." He considered this a sufficient intimation of his duty, and descanted freely on justification by faith, and a sinner's peace with God, through the atonement of Christ. It was the hour of mercy to this poor distracted woman. A ray of divine consolation now penetrated her soul; and she said to the minister, when taking his leave, "I am a poor vile sinner, but I think, being justified by faith, I begin again to have peace with God through our Lord Jesus Christ. I think Christ has now got the highest place in my heart; and, oh! I pray God, He would always keep him there.

Love to Sinners.

Chap. v. ver. 8.—God commendeth his love towards us, in that, while we were yet sinners, Christ died for us.

"DURING a sea voyage, a few years since," says Dr. Parker, of the United States, in his interesting book, "Invitation to True Happiness," "I was conversing with the mate of the vessel on this topic, when he concurred in the view presented, and observed that it called to mind one of the most thrilling scenes he had ever beheld. With this he related the following story:—'I was at sea, on the broad Atlantic, as we now are. It was just such a bright moonlight night as this, and the sea was quite as rough. The captain had turned in, and I was upon watch, when suddenly there was a cry of a man overboard. To go out in a boat was exceedingly dangerous. I could hardly make up my mind to command the hands to expose themselves. I volunteered to go myself if two more would accompany me. Two generous fellows came forward, and in a moment the boat was lowered, and we were tossed upon a most frightful sea. As we rose upon a mountain wave we discovered the man upon a distant billow. We heard his cry, and responded "coming." As we descended into the trough of the sea, we lost sight of the man, and heard nothing but the roar of the ocean. As we rose on the next wave, we again saw him, and distinctly heard his call. We gave him another word of encouragement, and pulled with all our strength. At the top of each successive wave we saw and heard him, and our hearts were filled with encouragement. As often, in the trough of the sea, we almost abandoned the hope of success. The time seemed long, and the struggle was such as men never made but for life. We reached him just as he was ready to sink from exhaustion. When we had drawn him into the boat, he was helpless and speechless. Our minds were now turned towards the ship. She had rounded to. But, exhausted as we were, the distance between us and the vessel was frightful. One false movement would have filled our boat, and consigned us all to a watery grave. Yet we reached the vessel, and were drawn safely upon the deck. We were all exhausted, but the rescued man could neither speak nor walk; yet he had a full sense of his condition. He clasped our feet and began to kiss them. We disengaged ourselves from his embrace. He then crawled after us, and as we stepped back to avoid him he followed us, looking up at one moment with smiles and tears, and then patting our wet foot-prints with his hand, he kissed them with an eager fondness. I never witnessed such a scene in my life. I suppose if he had been our greatest enemy he would have been perfectly subdued by our kindness. The man was a passenger. During the whole remaining part of the voyage he showed the deepest gratitude, and when we reached the port he loaded us with presents.'"

What gratitude do we owe to Him who loved us, and gave Himself for us, to deliver us from the "fiery burning lake?"

"O for this love, let rocks and hills,
Their lasting silence break;
And all harmonious human tongues
The Saviour's praises speak."

Changed from Sin.

Chap. vi. ver. 6.—Knowing this, and that our old man is crucified with him, that the body of sin might be destroyed, that henceforth we should not serve sin.

"FIVE persons," says Mr Brooks, "were studying what were the best means to mortify sin; one said, to meditate on death; the second, to meditate on judgment; the third, to meditate on the joys of heaven; the fourth, to meditate on the torments of hell; the fifth, to meditate on the blood and sufferings of Jesus Christ; and certainly the last is the choicest and strongest motive of all. If ever we would cast off our despairing thoughts, we must dwell and muse much upon, and apply this precious blood to our own souls; so shall sorrow and mourning flee away."

Changed.

Chap. vi. ver. 17.—Ye were the servants of sin; but ye have obeyed from the heart that form of doctrine which was delivered you.

A PERSON who had expressed doubts, whether the negroes had received any real advantage by hearing the Gospel, was asked whether he did not think one named Jack was the better for the preaching! He replied, "Why I must confess that he was a drunkard a liar, and a thief, but, certainly, he is now a sober boy, and I can trust him with anything; and since he has talked about religion, I have tried to make him drunk but failed in the attempt."

The Law and the Gospel.

Chap. vii. ver. 9.—I was alive without the law once; but when the commandment came, sin revived, and I died.

THE following remarks of one of the Christian negroes may be considered as illustrative of the above passage:—"Yesterday morning," said he, "when you preach, you show me that the law be our schoolmaster to bring us to Christ. You talk about the ten commandments. You begin at the first, and me say to myself, 'Me guilty!' the second, 'Me guilty!' the third, 'Me guilty!' the fourth, 'Me guilty!' the fifth, 'Me guilty!' Then you say the sixth, I suppose plenty live here, who say,—'Me no guilty of that!' Me say again in my heart, 'Ah! me no guilty!' 'Did you never hate any person? Did you never wish that such a person, such a man or such a woman, was dead?' Massa, you talk plenty about that; and what I feel that time I can't tell you. I talk in my heart, and say, Me the same person. My heart began to beat—me want to cry—my heart heave so much, me don't know what to do. Massa, me think me kill ten people before breakfast. I never think I so bad. Afterward you talk about the Lord Jesus Christ, how He take all our sins. I think I stand the same like a person that have a big stone upon his head, and can't walk—want to fall down. O, Massa! I have trouble too much—I no sleep all night, and wept much.—I hope the Lord Jesus Christ will take my sins from me! Suppose He no save me, I shall go to hell for ever."

The Flesh and the Spirit.

Chap. vii. ver. 22, 23.—For I delight in the law of God after the inward man : but I see another law in my members warring against the law of my mind, and bringing me into captivity to the law of sin which is in my members.

THE Rev. William Johnston, missionary in Africa, gives the following account :—" One woman was much distressed, and wept, and said that she had two hearts, which troubled her so much, that she did not know what to do. One was the new heart, that told her all things that she had ever been doing. The same heart told her she must go to Jesus Christ, and tell Him all her sins, as she had heard at church ; but her old heart told her 'Never mind, God no save black man, but white man. How know He died for black man ?' Her new heart said, 'Go, cry to Him, and ask.' Old heart tell me, do my work first, fetch water, make fire, wash, and then go pray. When work done, then me forget to pray. I don't know what I do. I read to her the seventh chapter of the Romans, and showed that the Apostle Paul felt the same things, and spoke of two principles in man. When I came to the verse, *O wretched man that I am ! who shall deliver me from the body of this death ?* she said, 'Ah, Massa, that me—me not know what to do.' I added the words of St. Paul—*I thank God, through Jesus Christ;* and explained to her the love of Christ, how He died for sinners like her. She burst into tears ; and has continued ever since, so far as I know, to follow her Saviour."

Present Sufferings.

Chap. viii. ver. 18.—I reckon that the sufferings of this present time are not worthy to be compared with the glory which shall be revealed in us.

"I WAS called upon," says the Rev. Mr. Trefit, an American minister, "some years ago, to visit an individual in the state of New York, from Ireland, who had resided for many years in that city. Part of his face had been eaten away by a most loathsome cancer. Fixing my eyes on this man in his sufferings and in his agony, I said, 'Supposing that Almighty God were to give you your choice : whether would you prefer your cancer, your pain, and your sufferings, with a certainty of death before you, but of immortality hereafter ; or would you prefer health, prosperity, long life in the world, and run the risk of losing your immortal soul !' 'Ah, sir !' said the man in the midst of his agony, 'give me the cancer, the pain, the Bible, the hope of heaven ; and others may take the world, long life, and prosperity !'"

The Spirit Strengtheneth.

Chap. viii. ver. 26.—Likewise the Spirit also helpeth our infirmities ; for we know not what we should pray for as we ought.

MR. CAYTON, a pious gentleman lately deceased, was on a visit to an intimate friend, whose sister, a pious lady, was lying on her death-bed. Religion, together with the means of promoting its growth in the heart, formed the subject of conversation. Mr. C. having taken occasion to recommend the duty of family worship, his friend remarked, that he was sensible of the importance of the duty : but having hitherto been a stranger to the practice of it, he felt a difficulty in commencing it; that, however, if Mr. C. would assist him in getting over that difficulty by giving the duty a beginning, he would afterwards endeavour to continue the practice of it. To such a mind as Mr. C.'s this proposal was embarrassing. If he complied with it, he knew he had no resource but to undertake the duty without the customary help of a prayer-book ; and from this his modesty revolted. If he declined it, he had reason to apprehend that his declining it might operate unfavourably on his friend's establishment and growth in grace. The possibility of such a result he could not suffer to be hazarded. In the option of difficulties, the benevolent desire of usefulness prevailed. The family was convened at the hour of prayer, and the guest presided in their family worship. At first he was somewhat agitated, and his voice began to falter. But his mind soon recovered its tone, and the solemn duty was performed with ease and with propriety. The success which attended this first attempt encouraged him to lay his formulary aside ; and experience soon taught him, that when the spirit of devotion in truth prevails, there is rarely any difficulty in giving expression to the feelings which it excites.

Ultimate Good.

Chap. viii. ver. 28.—All things work together for good to them that love God.

WHEN the Rev. Bernard Gilpin was on his way to London, to be tried before the Popish party, he broke his leg by a fall, which put a stop for some time to his journey. The person in whose custody he was, took occasion from this circumstance to retort upon him an observation he used frequently to make, "That nothing happens to us but what is intended for our good." He answered meekly, "He made no question but it was." And, indeed, so it proved ; for before he was able to travel, Queen Mary died. Being thus providentially rescued, he returned to Houghton through crowds of people expressing the utmost joy, and blessing God for his deliverance.

God's Justice.

Chap. ix. ver. 14.—What shall we say then? Is there unrighteousness with God? God forbid.

A PIOUS gentleman was once called to visit an unhappy old man, who lay at the point of death. For several years he had been an avowed infidel. He had been accustomed to scoff at Scripture ; but he principally exercised his profane wit in ridiculing the justice of God, and the future punishment of the wicked. He died convinced, but not converted. His death was truly awful. With his last quivering breath he exclaimed. "Now I know there is a hell, for I feel it !" and expired It is a fearful thing to fall into the hands of the living God.

Vessels of Wrath.

Chap. ix. ver. 22, 23.—What if God, willing to show his wrath, and to make his power known, endured with much long-suffering the vessels of wrath fitted to destruction ; and that he might make known the riches of his glory on the vessels of mercy, which he had afore prepared unto glory?

A CERTAIN minister, having changed his views of some parts of divine truth, was waited upon by an old acquaintance, who wished to reclaim him to his former creed. Finding he could not succeed in his object, he became warm, and told his friend in plain terms that God had given him "up to strong delusion," and that he was "a vessel of wrath fitted to destruction." "I think, brother," replied the one who was charged with the departure from the faith, with great calmness, "I think, brother, that you have mistaken the sense of the passage you last referred to. Vessels are denominated according to their contents. A chemist, in conducting a stranger through his laboratory, would say, 'This is a vessel of turpentine, that of vitriol,' etc., always giving to the vessel the name of the article it contains. Now, when I see a man full of the holy and lovely spirit of Christ, devoted to His service, and imitating His example, I say that man is a vessel of mercy, whom God hath afore prepared unto glory; but when I see a man full of everything but the spirit of the Bible—opposed to the moral government of God—seeking his own things rather than those which are Christ's—and filled with malice, wrath, and *all uncharitableness*, I am compelled to consider him 'a vessel of wrath, fitted to destruction.'"

Confessing Christ.

Chap. x. ver. 10.—With the heart man believeth unto righteousness; and with the mouth confession is made unto salvation.

THERE was one Victorinus, famous in Rome for teaching rhetoric to the senators: this man in his old age was converted to Christianity, and came to Simplicianus, who was an eminent man, whispering softly in his ears these words: "I am a Christian;" but this holy man answered, "I will not believe it, nor count thee so, till I see thee among the Christians in the church." At which he laughed, saying, "Do then those walls make a Christian? Cannot I be such except I openly profess it, and let the world know the same?" A while after, being more confirmed in the faith, and considering that, if he should thus continue ashamed of Christ, Christ would be ashamed of him in the last day, he changed his language, and came to Simplicianus, saying, "Let us go to the church; I will now in earnest be a Christian." And there, though a private confession of his faith might have been sufficient, yet he chose to make it open, saying, "That he had openly professed rhetoric, which was not a matter of salvation, and should he be afraid to own the word of God in the congregation of the faithful!"

The Scriptures.

Chap. x. ver. 17.—Faith cometh by hearing, and hearing by the word of God.

A VERY poor woman in Edinburgh, who was so nearly blind as not to be able to peruse the Bible, could get no one to read it to her. She was greatly distressed to live day after day without the comfort and direction of this blessed book. She thought of many plans, and made many inquiries, but all in vain. At last she made a bargain with another woman to read to her a chapter every night; and for this service she paid her a penny a-week out of her scanty pittance.

Because of Unbelief.

Chap. xi. ver. 19, 20.—Thou wilt say, then, The branches were broken off, that I might be graffed in. Well, because of unbelief they were broken off, and thou standest by faith. Be not high-minded but fear.

"HAD I," says D'Israeli, "to sketch the situation of the Jews in the 9th century, and to exhibit at the same time the character of that age of bigotry, could I do it more effectually than by the following anecdote, which a learned friend discovered in some manuscript records:—'A Jew at Rouen, in Normandy, sells a house to a Christian inhabitant of that city. After some time of residence, a storm happens, lightning falls on the house, and does considerable damage. The Christian, unenlightened and villainous, cites the trembling descendant of Israel into court for damages. His eloquent advocate hurls an admirable philippic against this detestable nation of heretics, and concludes by proving, that it was owing to this house having been the interdicted property of an Israelite, that a thunderbolt fell upon the roof. The judges, as it may be supposed, were not long in terminating this suit. They decreed that God had damaged this house as a mark of His vengeance against the property of a Jew, and that therefore it was just the repairs should be at his cost!'"

The Great Centre.

Chap. xi. ver. 36.—For of him, and through him, and to him, are all things.

"I HAVE read of an author," says Mr Ashburner, "who, whilst he was writing a book he was about to publish, would every now and then look back to the title, to see if his work corresponded thereto, and if it answered the expectation raised thereby. Now the use I would make hereof, and would recommend to you is, for thee, O sinner, to look back every now and then, and consider for what thou wast created; and for thee, O saint, to look back every now and then, and consider for what thou wast redeemed."

Industry and Fervency.

Chap. xii. ver. 11.—Not slothful in business; fervent in spirit, serving the Lord.

MR CRUDEN, during the last year of his life, lived in terms of the strictest intimacy with the Rev. David Wilson, minister of the Presbyterian congregation, Bow Lane, London. The two friends were in the habit of paying frequent visits to Mr Gordon, a pious nurseryman in the neighbourhood of the metropolis. One evening, Mr Gordon informed Mr Wilson, that a young Scottish gardener in his employment, who usually attended divine service at Bow Lane, sometimes absented himself from public worship without a sufficient cause, and was besides rather indolent, desiring the minister to admonish him. The young man was according called into the parlour, and Mr Wilson concluded a solemn address with these words: "Remember the Sabbath-day, to keep it holy." "Have you done, sir?" said Mr Cruden. "Yes," replied Mr Wilson. "Then," rejoined Mr Cruden, "you have forgotten one-half of the commandment: Six days shalt thou labour, and do all thy work, etc.; for if a man does not labour six days of the week, he is not likely to rest properly on the seventh."

Thine Enemy.

Chap. xii. ver. 20.—If thine enemy hunger, feed him; if he thirst, give him drink.

A SLAVE in one of the West India Islands, who had been brought from Africa, became a Christian, and behaved so well that his master raised him to a situation of great trust on his estate. He once employed him to select twenty slaves in the market, with the view of making a purchase. While looking at some who were offered, he perceived an old broken-down slave, and immediately told his master that he wished very much that he might be one of the number to be bought. The master was much surprised, and at first refused; but the slave begged so hard that his wish might be granted, that the master allowed the purchase to be made. The slaves were soon taken to the plantation, and the master, with some degree of wonder, observed his servant pay the greatest attention to the old African. He took him to his house, laid him on his own bed, and fed him at his own table. When it was cold, he carried him into the sunshine, and when it was hot, he placed him under the shade of the cocoa-trees. The master supposed that the old man must be some relation to his favourite, and asked him if he were his father. "Sir, massa," said the poor fellow, "he no my fader." "Is he then an elder brother?" "No, massa." "Perhaps your uncle, or some other relation?" "No, massa, he no be of my kindred at all, not even my friend." "Why, then," asked the master, "do you treat him so kindly?" "He my enemy, massa," replied the slave; "he sold me to the slave dealer; my Bible tell me, when my enemy hunger, feed him; when he thirst, give him drink."

Taking Human Life.

Chap. xiii. ver. 9.—Thou shalt not kill.

THE Rev. Ebenezer Erskine, after travelling at one time, toward the end of the week, from Portmoak to the banks of the Forth, on his way to Edinburgh, was, with several others, prevented by a storm from crossing that firth. Thus obliged to remain in Fife during the Sabbath, he was employed to preach, it is believed, in Kinghorn. Conformably to his usual practice, he prayed earnestly in the morning for the Divine countenance and aid in the work of the day; but suddenly missing his note-book, he knew not what to do. His thoughts, however, were directed to the command, "Thou shalt not kill;" and having studied the subject with as much care as the time would permit, he delivered a short sermon on it in the forenoon. Having returned to his lodging, he gave strict injunctions to the servant that no one should be allowed to see him during the interval of worship. A stranger, however, who was also one of the persons detained by the state of the weather, expressed an earnest desire to see the minister; and having with difficulty obtained admittance, appeared much agitated, and asked him, with great eagerness, whether he knew him, or had ever seen or heard of him. On receiving assurance that he was totally unacquainted with his face, character, and history, the gentleman proceeded to state that his sermon on the sixth commandment had reached his conscience; that he was a *murderer;* that being the second son of a Highland laird, he had some time before, from base and selfish motives, cruelly suffocated his elder brother, who slept in the same bed with him; and that now he had no peace of mind, and wished to surrender himself to justice, to suffer the punishment due to his horrid and unnatural crime. Mr Erskine asked him if any other person knew anything of his guilt. His answer was, that so far as he was aware, not a single individual had the least suspicion of it; on which the good man exhorted him to be deeply affected with a sense of his atrocious sin, to make an immediate application to the blood of sprinkling, and to bring forth fruits meet for repentance; but at the same time, since, in providence, his crime had hitherto remained a secret, not to disclose it, or give himself up to public justice. The unhappy gentleman embraced this well intended counsel in all its parts, became truly pious, and maintained a friendly cerrespondence with Mr Erskine in future life.

Salvation Nearer.

Chap. xiii. ver. 11.—Now is our salvation nearer than when we believed.

MR VENN in one of his excursions to preach for the Countess of Huntingdon, while riding on the road, fell into company with a person who had the appearance of a clergyman. After riding together for some time, conversing on different subjects, the stranger, looking in his face said, "Sir, I think you are on the wrong side of fifty." "On the wrong side of fifty!" answered Mr Venn, "No, sir, I am on the right side of fifty." "Surely," the clergyman replied, "you must be turned of fifty?" "Yes, sir," added Mr Venn, "but I am on the right side of fifty, for I am nearer my crown of glory."

Living to God.

Chap. xiv. ver. 8.—Whether we live, we live unto the Lord; and whether we die, we die unto the Lord.

THE following lines, which Dr Doddridge wrote on the motto of his family arms, have been much admired, as expressing, in a lively and pointed manner, the genuine spirit of a faithful servant of God. Dr Johnson, when speaking of this epigram, praised it as one of the finest in the English language. "Whilst we live, let us live," was the motto of the family arms, on which the Doctor wrote—

> "Live whilst you live," the Epicure would say,
> And seize the pleasures of the present day;
> "Live whilst you live," the sacred preacher cries,
> And give to God each moment as it flies;
> Lord, in my views, let both united be;
> I live in pleasure whilst I live to Thee.

Our Accountability.

Chap. xiv. ver. 12.—Every one of us shall give an account of himself to God.

THE late Rev. Herbert Mends of Plymouth, speaking of his early religious impressions, says, "If any particular circumstance might be considered as making a more deep, lasting, and serious impression than others, it was a dream which I had when at school at Ottery. I felt the apprehension of the approach of the last great judgment-day. I well remember all the attending circumstances; and observed that they were perfectly corresponding to the description of that awful event recorded in the Gospel of Matthew. After I had perceived vast multitudes of the human race appearing before the throne of Christ, some being approved, and others rejected, I at length beheld my beloved father and mother, and several of the family, summoned to appear. Great agitation was awakened in my breast; but I heard them distinctly examined, and as distinctly heard the Judge say, ' Well done,' etc. At this period, my whole soul was filled with horror indescribable, being conscious that I was not prepared to pass my final scrutiny. At length my name was announced, and I felt all the agonies of a mind fully expecting to be banished from the presence of God, and the glory of His power. The Judge then, with a stern countenance, and in language which struck me with mingled shame and hope, said, 'Well, what sayest thou?' I fell at His feet, and implored mercy, and uttered these words : 'Lord, spare me yet a little longer, and when thou shalt call for me again, I hope to be ready.' With a smile which tranquillized my spirits, the Lord replied, 'Go, then, and improve the time given thee.' The extreme agitation of my mind awoke me. But so deep was the impression, that I have never forgotten it; indeed, I soon after arose, and committed the whole to paper, with many other attendant circumstances, not proper to be here recorded."

Preaching the Gospel.

Chap. xv. ver. 20, 21.—Yea, so I have strived to preach the gospel, not where Christ was named, lest I should build upon another man's foundation: But as it is written, To whom he was not spoken of, they shall see: and they that have not heard shall understand.

"THE last time I was with Mr Grimshaw," says Mr Newton, "as we were standing together upon a hill near Haworth, and surveying the romantic prospect around us, he expressed himself to the following purport, and I believe I nearly retain his very words, for they made a deep impression upon me while he spoke—'When I first came into this country, if I had gone half a day's journey on horseback towards the east, west, north, and south, I could not have met with or hear of one truly serious person;—but now, through the blessing of God upon the poor services of the most unworthy of His ministers, besides a considerable number whom I have seen or known to have departed this life, like Simeon, rejoicing in the Lord's salvation ; and besides five dissenting churches or congregations, of which the ministers, and nearly every one of the members, were first awakened under my ministry; I have still at my sacrament, if the weather is favourable, from three to five hundred communicants, of the greater part of whom, so far as man, who cannot see the heart, and who can therefore only determine by appearances, profession, and conduct, may judge, I can give almost as particular an account as I can of myself. I know the state of their progress in religion. By my frequent visits and converse with them, I am acquainted with their several temptations, trials, and exercises, both personal and domestic, both spiritual and temporal, almost as intimately as if I had lived in their families.'"

The Church at Home.

Chap. xvi. ver. 5.—Greet the church that is in their house.

A FAMILY in which the worship of God is observed, morning and evening, may, in a subordinate sense, be called "A church in the house." The following is an instance of the advantages of family worship.—An old servant of a respectable family, having been constrained to give herself to the public profession of the Gospel, by commemorating with a Christian church the dying love of Christ, said that she was first excited to give religion a serious attention by the habitual observance of family worship. Here her mind was prepared to receive those impressions which laid the foundation of permanent religious character, and "a good hope through grace."

Knowledge through the Scriptures.

Chap. xvi. ver. 26.—But now is made manifest, and by the scriptures of the prophets, according to the commandment of the everlasting God, made known to all nations for the obedience of faith.

IN Iceland, a custom prevails among the people, of spending their long evenings in a manner which must powerfully tend to promote their religious improvement. The whole family assembles at dusk around the lamp, every one except the reader having some kind of work to perform. The reader is frequently interrupted, either by the head, or some of the most intelligent members of the family, who make remarks on various parts of the story, and propose questions, with a view to exercise the ingenuity of the children and servants. In this kind of exercise, the Bible is preferred to every other book. Before separating, a prayer is offered up, and the evening closed with singing a psalm.

FIRST CORINTHIANS

Speaking Advisedly.

Chap. i. ver. 17.—Not with wisdom of words, lest the cross of Christ should be made of none effect.

THE Rev. J. Thorowgood, a dissenting minister in England, though a learned critic himself, did not approve of introducing any parade of criticism into the pulpit. In a letter to an intimate friend, written in the first year of his ministry, he mentions an instance of his indiscretion one time in preaching:—"I bite my lips," says he, "with vexation at my folly last Lord's day. I was preaching upon a very alarming subject. My people were all silence and attention, when, in the midst of an important theme, I meanly stopped to divert them with a trifling criticism. O, how did I blush at my folly!—This I mention, my dear friend, for your caution."

Christ.

Chap. i. ver. 24.—Christ the power of God, and the wisdom of God.

TWO of Dr. Priestly's followers, eminent men, once called on an old gentleman of the Society of Friends, to ask what was *his* opinion of the person of Christ. After a little consideration, he replied:—"The apostle says, We preach Christ crucified, unto the Jews a stumbling-block, because they expected a *temporal* Messiah; to the Greeks foolishness, because He was crucified as a malefactor: but unto them which are called, both Jews and Greeks, Christ the power of God, and the wisdom of God. Now, if you can separate the power of God from God, and the wisdom of God from God, I will come over to your opinions."—They were both struck dumb, and did not attempt to utter a single word in reply.

Preaching Wisely and Well.

Chap. ii. ver. 4.—My speech and my preaching was not with enticing words of man's wisdom, but in demonstration of the Spirit and of power.

IT is related of Dr. Manton, that having to preach before the Lord Mayor and Aldermen of London, he chose a subject in which he had an opportunity of displaying his learning and judgment. He was heard with admiration and applause by the intelligent part of his audience; but as he was returning from dinner with the Lord Mayor, a poor man following him, pulled him by the sleeve of his gown, and asked him if he was the gentleman that preached before the Lord Mayor. He replied he was. "Sir," said he, "I came with hopes of getting some good to my soul, but I was greatly disappointed, for I could not understand a great deal of what you said; you were quite above my comprehension. "Friend," said the doctor, "if I have not given you a sermon, you have given me one: By the grace of God, I will not play the fool in such a manner again."

Spiritual Preaching.

Chap. ii. ver. 13.—Which things also we speak, not in the words which man's wisdom teacheth, but which the Holy Ghost teacheth.

SOME time after the conversion of Mr John Cotton, it came to his turn to preach at St Mary's, when a high expectation from his known abilities was raised through the University, that they should have a sermon set off with all the learning and eloquence of the place. Mr Cotton had now many difficulties in his own mind concerning the course he was to pursue. On the one hand, he considered that if he should preach with a scriptural and Christian plainness, he should not only wound his own fame, but also tempt carnal men to renew an old cavil, that religion made scholars turn dunces; whereby the honour of God might suffer not a little. On the other hand, he considered that it was his duty to preach with such plainness as became the oracles of the living God. He therefore resolved to preach a plain sermon; such a one as he might in his own conscience think would be most pleasing to the Lord Jesus Christ; and accordingly he did so. But when he had finished, the wits of the University discovered their resentment, by their not humming, as according to their absurd custom they had formerly done; and the vice-chancellor, too, showed much dissatisfaction. He had, however, many encouragements from some doctors, who, having a better sense of religion, prayed him to persevere in that good way of preaching he had now taken. But the greatest consolation was, that by the sermon he became a spiritual father to Dr. Preston, one of the most eminent men of his time.

Preaching to Unlearned.

Chap. iii. ver. 2.—I have fed you with milk, and not with meat; for hitherto ye were not able to bear it, neither yet now are ye able.

AT a meeting held at Wittemberg by the leading parties of the Reformation, with a view to promote the harmony of the whole, it was agreed that Albert Bucer and Luther should be the preachers. At the close of the services, Luther requested Bucer to be his guest, to which Bucer readily acceded. In the course of the evening Luther found an opportunity to make his remarks on the sermon delivered by his sage friend. He spoke highly in its praises, but added, "*Bucer, I can preach better than you.*" Such an observation sounded oddly to the ear of his friend, who, however, took it in good part, and readily replied, *Every person of course will agree, that Luther should bear the palm.*" Luther immediately changed his tone of voice, and with indescribable seriousness addressed his friend to this effect: "Do not mistake me, my dear brother, as though I spoke merely in the praise of myself. I am fully aware of my weakness, and am conscious of my inability to deliver a sermon so learned and judicious as the one I have heard from your lips this afternoon. But my method is, when I enter the pulpit, to look at the people that sit in the aisles; because they are principally Vandals.—(By this term he meant the ignorant common people, and alluded to the circumstance of those parts having been formerly overrun by hordes of savage Vandals.) I keep my eye on the Vandals, and endeavour to preach what they can comprehend. But you shot over their heads; your sermon was adapted for learned hearers, but my Vandals could not understand you. I compare them to a crying babe, who is sooner satisfied with the breast of its mother, than with the richest confectionaries; so my people are more nourished by the simple word of the Gospel, than by the deepest erudition, though accompanied with all the embellishments of eloquence."

All Things.

Chap. iii. ver. 21, 22.—All things are yours; whether Paul, or Apollos, or Cephas, or the world, or life, or death, or things present, or things to come; all are yours.

DR. STONEHOUSE, who attended Mr. Hervey during his last illness, seeing the great difficulty and pain with which he spoke, and finding by his pulse that the pangs of death were then coming on, desired that he would spare himself:—"No," said he, "Doctor, no: You tell me I have but a few minutes to live; O! let me spend them in adoring our great Redeemer. Though my flesh and my heart fail me, yet God is the strength of my heart, and my portion for ever." He then expatiated in the most striking manner on these words of Paul, "All things are yours; life and death; things present, and things to come; all are yours; and ye are Christ's, and Christ is God's.' "Here," says he, "is the treasure of a Christian, and a noble treasure it is. Death is reckoned in this inventory: how thankful am I for it, as it is the passage through which I get to the Lord and giver of eternal life; and as it frees me from all the misery you see me now endure, and which I am willing to endure as long as God thinks fit; for I know He will by and by, in His good time, dismiss me from the body. These light afflictions are but for a moment, and then comes an eternal weight of glory. O welcome, welcome, death! thou mayest well be reckoned among the treasures of the Christians. To live is Christ, but to die is gain."

Serving God.

Chap. iv. ver. 4.—For I know nothing by myself; yet am I not hereby justified; but he that judgeth me is the Lord.

THE celebrated Mr. Shepherd, when on his death-bed, said to some young ministers who had come to see him, "Your work is great, and calls for great seriousness." With respect to himself, he told these three things: First, That the studying of his sermons very frequently cost him tears. Secondly, Before he preached any sermon to others, he got good by it himself. And, thirdly, That he always went to the pulpit, as if he were immediately after to render an account to his Master.

Defamed in God's Service.

Chap. iv. ver. 13.—Being defamed, we entreat; we are made as the filth of the world, and are the offscouring of all things unto this day.

"ONE Sabbath afternoon," says Mr. Lacey, a missionary in the East Indies, "the people were extremely violent, shouting, 'A lie; a lie!' at every word spoken. Some called aloud, to drown my voice; others made impudent gestures, and excited a loud obscene laugh; and, in short, all means of diverting the attention of the hearers were resorted to. Some few, I observed, were more backward in the crowd, more serious, and seemed to feel the force of truth; these encouraged me to proceed. Upon others, persecution seemed to make a favourable impression; these came and complained of the folly and ignorance of the mob; and soon had their mouths stopped by hearing, 'Ah? are you of the caste, to blaspheme the mara poboo? It is blaspheming to hear the idiot's words, come away!' The epithets, fool, thief, liar, etc., were liberally bestowed this evening. Brother Bampton came up, followed by a mob, shouting him away. We both retired together, amidst the shouts and hisses of the multitude, and a shower of dust and broken pots."

Keeping the Feast.

Chap. v. ver. 8.—Let us keep the feast, not with old leaven, neither with the leaven of malice and wickedness; but with the unleavened bread of sincerity and truth.

GENERAL BURN, in recording his experience, says, "One Lord's day, when I was to receive the sacrament, before I approached that sacred ordinance, my conscience so keenly accused me on account of this beloved idol (playing at cards) that I hardly knew what to do with myself. I tried to pacify it by a renewal of all my resolutions, with many additions and amendments. I parleyed and reasoned the matter over for hours, trying, if possible, to come to some terms of accommodation, but still the obstinate monitor within cried out, 'There's an Achan in the camp; approach the table of the Lord if you dare!' Scared at the threat, and yet unwilling to part with my darling lust, I became like one possessed. Restless and uneasy, I flew out of the house, to vent my misery with more freedom in the fields, under the wide canopy of heaven. Here I was led to meditate on the happiness of the righteous, and the misery of the wicked in a future state. The importance of eternity falling with a ponderous weight upon my soul, raised such vehement indignation against *the accursed thing* within, that, crying to God for help, I kneeled down under a hedge, and taking heaven and earth to witness, wrote on a piece of paper with my pencil a solemn vow, that I would never play at cards, on my pretence whatsoever, so long as I lived. No sooner had I put my name to that solemn vow, than I felt myself another creature. Sorrow took wing and flew away, and a delightful peace succeeded. The intolerable burden being removed from my mind, I approached the sacred table of the Lord with an unusual degree of pleasure and delight. This was not my only idol. I had many others to contend with. But while I was endeavouring to heal my wounded soul in one place, ere I was aware sin broke out in another."

Irreligious Company.

Chap. v. ver. 9, 10.—I wrote unto you in an epistle not to company with fornicators: yet not altogether with the fornicators of this world, or with the covetous, or extortioners, or with idolators; for then must ye needs go out of the world.

MR ROBERT BLAIR, in a memoir of his life, written by himself, says, "That year (1616) having, upon an evening, been engaged in company with some irreligious persons, when I returned to my chamber, and went to my ordinary devotion, the Lord did show so much displeasure and wrath, that I was driven from prayer, and heavily threatened to be deserted of God. For this I had a restless night, and resolved to spend the next day in extraordinary humiliation, fasting, and prayer; and, toward the evening of that day, I found access to God, with sweet peace, through Jesus Christ, and learned to beware of such company; but then I did run into another extreme of rudeness and incivility toward such as were profane and irreligious, so hard a thing is it for short-sighted sinners to hold the right and the straight way."

Christians going to Law.

Chap. vi. ver. 7.—There is utterly a fault among you, because ye go to law one with another: why do ye not rather take wrong? why do ye not rather suffer yourselves to be defrauded?

MR PHILIP HENRY relates a remarkable story concerning a good old friend of his, who when young, being an orphan, was greatly wronged by his uncle. His portion, which was £200, was put into the hands of that uncle; who, when he grew up, shuffled with him, and would give him but £40, instead of his £200, and he had no way of recovering his right but by law. But, before he would engage in that, he was willing to advise with his minister, who was the famous Dr Twiss of Newberry. The counsel he gave him, all things considered, was, for peace sake, and for the preventing of sin, and snares, and troubles, to take the £40 rather than contend; "and, Thomas," said the doctor, "if thou dost so, assure thyself that God will make it up to thee and thine some other way, and they that defraud will be the losers by it at last." He did so, and it pleased God so to bless that little which he began the world with, that when he died in a good old age, he left his son possessed of some hundreds a year, whilst he that had wronged him fell into poverty.

Drunkards.

Chap. vi. ver. 10.—Drunkards shall not inherit the kingdom of God.

A PARENT once said to a Sabbath school teacher, "O, sir! I am very glad that you have got a school for boys on Sunday nights. I had such a reprimand and sermon from my little lad the other night, as I never had before in my life. After he came home last Sunday night, he sat down very thoughtful, and at last began to cry, and said, 'O father; if you go and get drunk, you will go to hell; and if I were to go to heaven, and see you on the left hand, O how I should cry, and wish you to come to me!'"

Husband and Wife.

Chap. vii. ver. 16.—What knowest thou, O wife, whether thou shalt save thy husband?

A LADY in Germany, who had been a sincere follower of Christ, but whose husband was still unrenewed, was very much afflicted on his account, and told a clergyman that she had done all in her power in persuading and beseeching him to turn from his evil practices, to no effect. "Madam," said he, "Talk more to God about your husband, and less to your husband about God." A few weeks after, the lady called upon him, full of joy that her prayers to God had been heard, and that a change was wrought upon her husband.

Wise Possession.

Chap. vii. ver. 30.—It remaineth, that both they that have wives be as though they had none;—and they that buy as though they possessed not.

"BEING with my friend in a garden," says Mr Flavel, "we gathered each of us a rose. He handled his tenderly; smelt it but seldom, and sparingly. I always kept mine to my nose, or squeezed it in my hand, whereby, in a very short time, it lost both its colour and sweetness; but *his* still remained as sweet and fragrant as if it had been growing upon its own root. These roses, said I, are the true emblems of the best and sweetest creature enjoyments in the world,—which, being moderately and cautiously used and enjoyed, may for a long time yield sweetness to the possessor of them; but if once the affections seize too greedily upon them, and squeeze them too hard, they quickly wither in our hands, and we lose the comfort of them; and that, either through the soul surfeiting upon them, or the Lord's righteous and just removal of them, because of the excess of our affections to them."

Love to God.

Chap. viii. ver. 3.—If any man love God, the same is known of him.

AN aged Christian, in great distress of mind, was once complaining to a friend of his miserable condition; and, among other things, said, "That which troubles me most is, that God will be dishonoured by my fall." His friend hastily caught at this, and used it for the purpose of comforting him:—"Art thou careful of the honour of God? And dost thou think that God hath no care for thee, and of thy salvation? A soul forsaken of God, cares not what becomes of the honour of God; therefore be of good cheer; if God's heart were not towards thee, thine would not be towards God, or towards the remembrance of His name."

Self-Denial.

Chap. viii. ver. 13.—If meat make my brother to offend, I will eat no flesh while the world standeth, lest I make my brother to offend.

"A CHIEF of Hauhine once asked me," says Mr Ellis, missionary to the South Sea Islands, "whether it would be right, supposing he was walking in his garden on that day (the Sabbath), and saw ripe plantains hanging from the trees that grew by the side of the path, to gather and eat them; I answered that I thought it would not be wrong. 'I felt inclined to do so,' said he, 'last Sabbath, when walking in my garden; but on reflecting that I had other fruit ready plucked and prepared, I hesitated, not because I believed it would be in itself sinful, but lest my attendants should notice it, and do so too, and it should be a general practice with the people to go to their gardens and gather fruit on the Sabbath, which would be very unfavourable to the proper observance of that sacred day.'"

The Incorruptible Crown.

Chap. ix. ver. 25.—They do it to obtain a corruptible crown, but we an incorruptible.

THE Rev. H. Davies, sometimes called "The Welsh Apostle," was walking early one Sabbath morning to a place where he was to preach. He was overtaken by a clergyman on horseback, who complained that he could not get above half-a-guinea for a discourse.

"O, sir," said Mr Davies, "I preach for a crown!" "Do you?" replied the stranger, "then you are a disgrace to the cloth." To this rude observation he returned this meek answer, "Perhaps I shall be held in still greater disgrace in your estimation, when I inform you that I am now going nine miles to preach, and have but sevenpence in my pocket to bear my expenses out and in; but I look forward to that *crown of glory* which my Lord and Saviour will freely bestow upon me, when He makes His appearance before an assembled world."

All as One.

Chap. x. ver. 17.—For we being many are one bread and one body: for we are all partakers of that one bread.

"I WAS once permitted to unite," says the Rev. R. M'Cheyne, "in celebrating the Lord's Supper in an upper room in Jerusalem. There were fourteen present, the most of whom, I had good reason to believe, knew and loved the Lord Jesus Christ. Several were godly Episcopalians, two were converted Jews, and one a Christian from Nazareth, converted under the American missionaries. The bread and wine were dispensed in the Episcopal manner, and most were kneeling as they received them. We felt it to be sweet fellowship with Christ, and with the brethren; and as we left the upper room, and looked out upon the Mount of Olives, we remembered with calm joy the prayer from our Lord, that ascended from one of its shady ravines after the first Lord's Supper:—'Neither pray I for these alone, but for them also which shall believe in me through their word, and they all may be ONE.'"

Seeking Another's Good.

Chap. x. ver. 24.—Let no man seek his own, but every man another's wealth.

MR HOWE, when chaplain to Cromwell, was applied to for protection by men of all parties, in those eventful times; and it is said of him that he never refused his assistance to any person of worth, whatever might be his religious tenets. "Mr Howe," said the Protector to his chaplain, "you have asked favours for everybody besides yourself, pray, when does *your* turn come?" "*My* turn, my Lord Protector," said Mr Howe, "is always come when I can serve *another*."

The Bread and the Body.

Chap. xi. ver. 24.—Take, eat; this is my body which is broken for you.

A ROMAN Catholic gentleman in England being engaged to marry a Protestant lady, it was mutually agreed that there should be no contests on the subject of religion. For some years after their union this agreement was scrupulously observed; but, in the course of time, the priest, who had paid them frequent visits, expecting to find no difficulty in making a convert of the lady, began to talk about the peculiarities of his religion. He particularly insisted upon the doctrine of transubstantiation, and grew troublesome by his importunity. To avoid being further teased by him, she one day seemed to be overcome by his arguments, and agreed to attend at mass with her husband the following Sabbath, provided she might be allowed to prepare the wafer herself. The priest, not suspecting anything, and glad on any terms to secure such a good convert, gave his consent. The lady, accordingly, appeared at the chapel with her husband; and, after the consecration of the wafers which she had brought with her, she solemnly demanded of the priest whether it was really converted into the body of Christ? to which question he without hesitation replied, *That there was a conversion made of the whole substance of the bread into the body of Christ, and there remained no more of its form or substance.* "If that be really the case," said she, "you may eat the wafer without any danger; but as for *myself*, I should be afraid to touch it as it is mixed with arsenic." The priest was overwhelmed by a discovery so unexpected, and was too wise to hazard his life upon a doctrine for which he had, however, contended with all the earnestness of perfect assurance. The lady's husband was so struck by this practical confutation of a doctrine which he had before implicitly believed, that he never afterwards appeared at the mass.

The Spiritual Weak.

Chap. xi. ver. 30.—For this cause many are weak and sickly among you, and many sleep.

WHEN Mr Joseph Woodward, one of the Nonconformist ministers in England, was settled in Dursley, he vigorously set about the reformation of many disorders in discipline and manners that existed among the people. In particular, he declared his resolution to admit none to the Lord's Supper but those who, besides a visible probity of conversion, had a competent knowledge of divine things. A certain person said, "He would not submit to examination; and if Mr Woodward would not give him the sacrament, he would take it!" In pursuance of his impious resolution, this man was coming to church on the sacrament-day, but he had scarcely set one foot over the threshold before he fell down dead.

Heathen Worship.

Chap. xii. ver. 2.—Ye know that we were Gentiles, carried away unto these dumb idols, even as ye were led.

BRITISH Christians ought to recollect, that their ancestors were once blind idolaters, serving them that by nature are no gods. Dr Plaifere, in a sermon preached before the University of Cambridge, in 1573, remarks, "that before the preaching of the Gospel of Christ, no church here existed, but the temple of an idol; no priesthood but that of paganism; no God but the sun, the moon, or some hideous image. To the cruel rites of the Druidical worship, succeeded the abominations of the Roman idolatry. In Scotland stood the temple of Mars; in Cornwall, the temple of Mercury; in Bangor, the temple of Minerva; at Maiden, the temple of Victoria; in Bath, the temple of Apollo; at Leicester, the temple of Janus; at York, where St Peter's now stands, the temple of Bellona; in London, on the site of St Paul's Cathedral, the temple of Diana; and at Westminster, where the Abbey rears its venerable pile, a temple of Apollo." Through the mercy of God, our country is now blessed with thousands of Christian churches, and multitudes of Gospel ministers. The land is full of Bibles; and British Christians, sensible of their privileges, are engaged in diffusing the light of divine truth among the benighted nations.

All Members of Use.

Chap. xii. ver. 15.—If the foot shall say, Because I am not the hand, I am not of the body; is it therefore not of the body?

THE Rev. Ambrose Morton was generally esteemed a good scholar, and remarkably humble, sanctified, and holy, but was inclined to melancholy, to his own discouragement. In his younger days, when he was assistant to another minister, some good people, in his hearing, speaking of their conversion, and ascribing it under God to that minister's preaching, he seemed cast down as if he was of no use. A sensible countryman, who was present, and who had a particular value for his ministry, made this observation for his encouragement: "An ordinary workman may hew down timber, but it must be an accomplished artist that shall frame it for the building." Mr M. therefore rose up, and cheerfully replied, "If I am of any use I am satisfied." Indeed, his preaching was always solid and judicious, and highly esteemed by all but himself; and was especially useful to experienced Christians.

Unselfish.

Chap. xiii. ver. 5.—Seeketh not her own.

MR HAMMOND frequently remitted his rights when he thought the party unable to pay. Once he had made a bargain with one of his parishioners to have so much for the tithe of a large meadow; and, according to his agreement, received part of the money at the beginning of the year. It happened, however, that the produces was afterwards spoiled, and carried away by a flood. When the tenant came to make the last payment, the doctor not only refused it, but returned the former sum, saying to the poor man, "God forbid that I should take the tenth, where you have not the nine parts."

Knowing Fully.

Chap. xiii. ver. 12.—Now we see through a glass darkly; but then face to face: now I know in part; but then shall I know even as also I am known.

AN old Hottentot having been taken ill, was visited by Mr Reid, a missionary. He said, "This is the message of death! I shall now go and see the other country, where I have never been, but which I long to see! I am weary of everything here! I commit too much sin here, I wish to be free from it; I cannot understand things well here, and you cannot understand me. The Lord has spoken much to me, though I cannot explain it."

Simple Phraseology.

Chap. xiv. ver. 9.—So likewise ye, except ye utter by the tongue words easy to be understood, how shall it be known what is spoken? for ye shall speak into the air.

A GENTLEWOMAN went one day to hear Dr Gordon preach, and, as usual, carried a pocket Bible with her, that she might turn to any of the passages the preacher might happen to refer to. But she found that she had no use for her Bible there; and, on coming away, said to a friend, "I should have left my Bible at home to-day, and have brought my dictionary. The doctor does not deal in Scripture, but in such learned words and phrases as require the help of an interpreter to render them intelligible."

Hearing without Response.

Chap. xiv. ver. 21.—In the law it is written, With men of other tongues and other lips will I speak unto this people; and yet for all that will they not hear me, saith the Lord.

A MUSICAL amateur of eminence, who had often observed Mr. Cadogan's inattention to his performances, said to him one day, "Come, I am determined to make you feel the force of music,—pay particular attention to this piece." It accordingly was played. "Well, what do you say now?" "Why, just what I said before." "What! can you hear this and not be charmed? Well, I am quite surprised at your insensibility. *Where are your ears?*" "Bear with me, my lord," replied Mr. Cadogan, "since I too have had my surprise: I have often from the pulpit set before you the most striking and affecting truths; I have sounded notes that have raised the dead! I have said, Surely he will feel now; but you never seemed charmed with my music, though infinitely more interesting than yours. I too have been ready to say with astonishment, *Where are his ears?*"

Bad Companionship.

Chap. xv. ver. 33.—Evil communications corrupt good manners.

A POOR boy who had been educated in the Stockport Sabbath-school, conducted himself so well and made so great proficiency in learning, that he was appointed teacher of one of the junior classes. About this time his father died, and his mother being reduced to indigent circumstances, she was obliged to engage him in one of the cotton factories, where he met with boys of his own age, who were matured in vice, and hardened in crime. Through the force of their evil example, he lost by degrees all his serious impressions; and having thrown off the fear of God, became addicted to intemperance, and the commission of petty thefts. His dissolute conduct soon brought him into the army. The regiment was sent to Spain, where his habit of excessive drinking was confirmed; and, not satisfied with the advantages he reaped as the fruits of many a splendid victory, he plundered the innocent and peaceful inhabitants. On the close of the war in the Peninsula, he returned home with his regiment; and soon after landing on the coast of Hampshire, he, with others of his companions, whose principles he had vitiated, broke into several houses; till at length he was detected, arraigned at the tribunal of justice, and condemned to an ignominious death, at the age of twenty-one. "Sin, when it is finished, bringeth forth death."

The Resurrection.

Chap. xv. ver. 35.—But some man will say, How are the dead raised up? and with what body do they come?

"A NUMBER of the attendants on the queen's sister," says Mr Ellis in his Polynesian Researches, "soon after the reception of Christianity, came to the meeting, and stated that one of their friends had died a few days before, and that they had buried the corpse according to their ancient manner, not laying it straight in a coffin, as Christians were accustomed to do, but placing it in a sitting posture, with the face between the knees, the hands under the thighs, and the whole body bound round with cords. Since the interment (they added), they had been thinking about the resurrection, and wished to know how the body would then appear, whether, if left in that manner, it would rise deformed, and whether they had not better disinter the corpse, and deposit it in a straight or horizontal position. A suitable reply was of course returned. They were directed to let it remain undisturbed—that probably long before the resurrection it would be so completely dissolved, and mingled with the surrounding earth, that no trace would be left of the form in which it had been deposited."

The Weekly Offering.

Chap. xvi. ver. 2.—Upon the first day of the week, let every one of you lay by him in store, as God hath prospered him.

AT a public meeting, one of the orators addressed the assembly as follows :—"My dear brethren, it has been the usual custom for an audience to testify their approbation of the speaker by clapping their hands ; but I beg to recommend to your adoption a new method of clapping, less tumultuous, and much more pleasing.—When you leave this place, clap your hands into your pockets, and clap your money into the plate held to receive it, and the Lord give it His blessing." This address had the desired effect.

Love and Christ.

Chap. xvi. ver. 22.—If any man love not the Lord Jesus Christ, let him be Anathema Maran-atha.

MR FLAVEL, on one occasion, preached from the above passage. The discourse was unusually solemn, particularly the explanation of the words *anathema maran-atha*—" cursed with a curse, cursed of God with a bitter and grievous curse." At the conclusion of the service, when Mr Flavel rose to pronounce the benediction, he paused, and said, "How shall I bless this whole assembly, when every person in it, who loveth not the Lord Jesus Christ, is anathema maran-atha ?" The solemnity of this address affected the audience ; and one gentleman, a person of rank, was so overcome by his feelings, that he fell senseless to the floor. In the congregation was a lad, named Luke Short, then about fifteen years old, and a native of Dartmouth. Soon after he went to America, where he passed the rest of his life, first at Marblehead, and afterwards at Middleborough, Massachusetts. Mr Short's life was lengthened much beyond the usual time. When *an hundred years old*, he had sufficient strength to work on his farm, and his mental faculties were very little impaired. Hitherto he had lived in carelessness and sin ; he was now "a sinner an hundred years old," and apparently ready to "die accursed." But one day as he sat in the field, he busied himself in reflecting on his past life. Recurring to the events of his youth, his memory fixed upon Mr Flavel's discourse, above alluded to, a considerable part of which he was able to recollect. The affectionate earnestness of the preacher's manner, the important truths he delivered, and the effects produced on the congregation, were brought fresh to his mind. The blessing of God accompanied his meditation : he felt that he had not "loved the Lord Jesus Christ ;" he feared the dreadful "anathema ;" conviction was followed by repentance ; and at length this aged sinner obtained peace through the blood of the atonement, and was "found in the way of righteousness." He joined the congregational church in Middleborough, and to the day of his death, which took place in his 116th *year*, gave pleasing evidences of piety.

SECOND CORINTHIANS.

Suffering and Consolation.

Chap. i. ver. 5.—As the sufferings of Christ abound in us, so our consolation also aboundeth by Christ.

WHEN Mr James Bainham, who suffered under Henry VIII. of England, was in the midst of the flames, which had half consumed his arms and legs, he said aloud,—"O ye Papists, ye look for miracles, and here now you may see a miracle ; for in this fire I feel no more pain than if I were in a bed of down, but it is to me a bed of roses."

God's Promises.

Chap. i. ver. 20.—All the promises of God in him are Yea, and in him Amen, unto the glory of God by us.

THE faith of Dr Watts in the promises of God was lively and unshaken. "I believe them enough," said he, "to venture an eternity on them." To a religious friend, at another time, he thus expressed himself : "I remember an aged minister used to say, that the most learned and knowing Christians, when they come to die, have only the same plain promises for their support as the common and unlearned ; and so," continued he, "I find it. It is the plain promises of the Gospel that are my support : and I bless God they *are* plain promises, which do not require much labour and pains to understand them ; for I can do nothing now but look into my Bible for some promise to support me, and live upon that."

Love to Christ.

Chap. ii. ver. 8.—Wherefore I beseech you, that ye would confirm your love toward him.

SOME friends were conversing about a person, who, in spite of many remonstrances, and many opportunities of knowing the path of duty, seemed perfectly steeled against every proper impression, and determined to go on in his evil courses. One of the company, who, before he knew the Gospel, had gone to great excess in wickedness, himself, remarked that he saw no necessity for his friends troubling themselves any further with such a character ; adding, "If he has an opportunity of knowing the truth, and will not attend to it, let him take the consequences." A lady sitting by, who knew this person's history, gently reminded him,—"Ah ! Mr Sayn, what might have been your state to-day, if others had argued thus in regard to you ?" He had himself been indebted to the affectionate and persevering assiduities of a Christian friend, as the means, under the blessing of God, of leading his attention to the revelation of divine mercy.

Increase of Responsibility.

Chap. ii. ver. 16.—To the one we are the savour of death unto death.

WHEN the Rev. Mr Fletcher of Madeley was once preaching on Noah as a type of Christ, and while in the midst of a most animated description of the terrible day of the Lord, he suddenly paused. Every feature of his expressive countenance was marked with painful feeling ; and, striking his forehead with the palm of his hand, he exclaimed, "Wretched man that I am ! Beloved brethren, it often cuts me to the soul, as it does at this moment, to reflect, that while I have been endeavouring, by the force of truth, by the beauty of holiness, and even by the terrors of the Lord, to bring you to walk in the peaceable paths of righteousness, I am, with respect to many of you who reject the Gospel, only tying millstones round your neck, to sink you deeper in perdition?" The whole church was electrified, and it was some time before he could resume his discourse.

Humility.

Chap. iii. ver. 5.—Not that we are sufficient of ourselves to think anything as ourselves, but our sufficiency is of God.

THE Rev. Thomas Hooker, some time after his settlement, at Hartford, having to preach among his old friends at Newton on a Lord's day in the afternoon, his great fame had collected together a vast concourse of people. When he came to preach, he found himself so entirely at a loss what to say, that, after a few shattered attempts to proceed, he was obliged to stop and say, that what he had prepared was altogether taken from him. He therefore requested the congregation to sing a psalm while he retired. Upon his return, he preached a most admirable sermon with the greatest readiness and propriety. After the public service was closed, some of his friends speaking to him of the Lord's withholding His assistance, he meekly replied, "We daily confess that we have nothing and can be nothing without Christ; and what if Christ will make this manifest before our congregations? Must we not be humbly contented?"

The Old Testament and Christ.

Chap. iii. ver. 14.—Their minds were blinded: for until this day remaineth the same vail untaken away in the reading of the Old Testament; which vail is done away in Christ.

A LEARNED rabbi of the Jews, at Aleppo, being dangerously ill, called his friends together, and desired them seriously to consider the various former captivities endured by their nation, as a punishment for the hardness of their hearts, and their present captivity, which was continued sixteen hundred years, "the occasion of which," said he, "is doubtless our unbelief. We have long looked for the Messiah, and the Christians have believed in one Jesus, of our nation, who was of the seed of Abraham and David, and born in Bethlehem, and, for aught we know, may be the true Messiah; and we may have suffered this long captivity because we have rejected Him. Therefore, my advice is, as my last words, that if the Messiah, which we expect, do not come at or about the year 1650, reckoning from the birth of their Christ, then you may know and believe that this Jesus is the Christ, and you shall have no other."

The Physical and the Spiritual.

Chap. iv. ver. 7.—We have this treasure in earthen vessels, that the excellency of the power may be of God, and not of us.

SOMETIMES God is pleased to enrich, with a more than ordinary measure of grace and knowledge of Gospel truth, persons of feeble constitutions. Dr Doddridge, at his birth, showed so small symptoms of life, that he was laid aside as dead. But one of the attendants, thinking she perceived some motion of breath, took that necessary care of him upon which, in those tender circumstances, the feeble flame of life depended, which was so nearly expiring, as soon as it was kindled. He had from his infancy an infirm constitution, and a thin consumptive habit, which made himself and his friends apprehensive that his life would be very short; and he frequently, especially on the returns of his birth-day, expressed his wonder and thankfulness that he was so long preserved.

Eternity.

Chap. iv. ver. 18.—The things which are not seen are eternal.

A CERTAIN lady, having spent the afternoon and evening at cards, and in gay company, when she came home, found her servant-maid reading a pious book. "Poor melancholy soul," said she, "what pleasure canst thou find in poring so long over a book like that?"— When the lady went to bed, she could not fall asleep, but lay sighing and weeping so much, that her servant overhearing her, came and asked her, once and again, what was the matter with her. At length she burst out into a flood of tears, and said, "Oh! it was one word I saw in your book that troubles me; there I saw that word ETERNITY." The consequences of this impression was, that she laid aside her cards, forsook her gay company, and set herself seriously to prepare for another world.

Heaven.

Chap. v. ver. 2.—In this we groan, earnestly desiring to be clothed upon with our house which is from heaven.

MR DOD, in the sixty-third year of his age, had a fever with very threatening symptoms; but things turning happily at the crisis, and the physician having thereupon said to him, "Now I have hopes of your recovery;" Mr Dod answered, "You think to comfort me by this; but you make my heart sad. It is as if you should tell a man, who, after being sorely weather-beaten at sea, had just arrived at the haven where his soul longed to be, that he must return to the ocean, to be tossed again with winds and waves."

In Christ.

Chap. v. ver. 17.—If any man be in Christ, he is a new creature: old things are passed away; behold all things are become new.

THE Rev. Legh Richmond, on his return from Scotland some years ago, passed through Stockport, at the time when radical opinions first agitated the country. In consequence of his lameness, he was never able to walk far without resting. He was leaning on his stick, and looking about him, when a poor fellow ran up to him and offered his hand, inquiring with considerable earnestness, "Pray, sir, are you a radical?" "Yes, my friend," replied Mr Richmond, "I am a radical, a thorough radical." "Then," said the man," give me your hand." "Stop, sir, stop; I must explain myself: we all need a radical reformation, our hearts are full of disorders; the root and principle within is altogether corrupt. Let you and me mend matters there, and then all will be well, and we shall cease to complain of the times and the government." "Right, sir," replied the radical, "you are right, sir;" and bowing respectfully, he retired.

The Ministry.

Chap. vi. ver. 3. Giving no offence in any thing, that the ministry be not blamed.

DOCTOR BROCKMAND, Bishop of Zealand, was once present at a wedding, which was attended by a large promiscuous company of all ranks. At table, the conversation turned upon the conduct of a certain disorderly clergyman; some of the company reprobated, and others pitied him. But a lady of rank, no doubt one of those who take the lead where busy scandal feasts her votaries, gave a new turn to the subject, and with a scornful mien, added, "What a pretty set of creatures our clergy are!" It grieved Brockmand to hear the whole clergy thus vilified, yet he did not think proper to offer a serious reply. But shortly after, he related an anecdote of a noble lady, notorious for ill conduct, concluding with these words,—"It does not follow, however, that all our noble ladies should resemble her."

Marriage.

Chap. vi. ver. 14.—Be ye not unequally yoked with unbelievers.

ELIZA EMBERT, a young Parisian lady, resolutely discarded a gentleman, to whom she was to have been married, because he ridiculed religion. Having given him a gentle reproof, he replied, "That a man of the world could not be so old-fashioned as to regard God and religion." Eliza started!—but on recovering herself, said, "From this moment, sir, when I discover that you do not regard religion, I cease to be yours. He who does not love and honour God, can never love his wife constantly and sincerely."

God Comforteth.

Chap. vii. ver. 6.—God, that comforteth those that are cast down.

DURING the ministry of the late Mr Willison of Dundee, a serious woman who had been hearing him preach from Psalm lv. 22, "Cast thy burden upon the Lord, and He will sustain thee," came to his house in the evening, with a broken and oppressed mind, in order to make known to him her perplexed case. The poor woman, as she passed through the house to his room, heard a little girl repeating the text, which came with such power to her heart, as effectually dispelled her fears, and set her at liberty. When she was introduced to Mr W., she told him that she was come to make known her distress: but the Lord, by means of his grandchild repeating the text, as she came through the house, had graciously dispelled her fears, and removed her burden, and now she only desired to give thanks for her spiritual recovery.

The Conscience.

Chap. vii. ver. 11.—For behold this self-same thing, that ye sorrowed after a godly sort, what carefulness it wrought in you; yea, what revenge.

IN the bloody reign of Queen Mary of England, Archbishop Cranmer became obnoxious to her persecuting spirit. She was determined to bring him to the stake; but previously employed emissaries to persuade him, by means of flattery and false promises, to renounce his faith. The good man was overcome, and subscribed the errors of the Church of Rome. His conscience smote him; he returned to his former persuasion; and, when brought to the stake, he stretched forth the hand that had made the unhappy signature, and held it in the flames till it was entirely consumed, frequently exclaiming, "That unworthy hand;" after which he patiently suffered martyrdom, and ascended to receive its reward.

The Will and the Power.

Chap. viii. ver. 11.—Perform the doing of it; that as there was a readiness to will, so there may be a performance also out of that which ye have.

KARAMSIN, the Russian traveller, having witnessed Lavater's diligence in study, visiting the sick, and relieving the poor, greatly surprised at his fortitude and activity, said to him, "Whence have you so much strength of mind and power of endurance?" "My friend," replied he, "man rarely wants the power to work, when he possesses *the will;* the more I labour in the discharge of my duties, so much the more ability and inclination to labour do I constantly find within myself."

Want and Abundance.

Chap. viii. ver. 14.—At this time your abundance may be a supply for their want, that their abundance may be a supply for your want.

THE Rev. Edward Jones was particularly noted for his charitable disposition. A friend once made him a present of a sum of money that he might purchase malt to make beer for the use of his family. Returning home from the house of his friend, he happened to pass through a village where there were several poor families, some of whom were sick, and others in very needy circumstances. Hearing of their distresses, he went into their houses, in order to address some serious advice to them. But his heart was so much affected with the miseries he beheld, that he distributed among them what his friend had given him to supply his own wants. When he reached home, he told his wife what he had done. She cheerfully applauded his generosity, and at the same time acquainted him, that, in his absence, God had inclined the heart of a neighbouring farmer to send the very quantity of malt that his friend's money would have purchased.

Giving Cheerfully.

Chap. ix. ver. 7.—Every man, according as he purposeth in his heart, so let him give, not grudgingly, nor of necessity; for God loveth a cheerful giver.

MRS GRAHAM of New York made it a rule to appropriate a tenth part of her earnings to be expended for pious and charitable purposes; she had taken a lease of two lots of ground in Greenwich Street, from the corporation of Trinity Church, with the view of building a house on them for her own accommodation: the building, however, she never commenced, and by a sale which her son-in-law, Mr Bethune, made of the lease in 1795 for her, she got an advance of one thousand pounds. So large a profit was new to her. "Quick, quick," said she, "let me appropriate the tenth before my heart grows hard." What fidelity in duty; What distrust of herself! Fifty pounds of this money she sent to Mr Mason, in aid of the funds he was collecting for the establishment of a theological seminary.

Giving to the Poor.

Chap. ix. ver. 9.—He hath dispersed abroad : he hath given to the poor: his righteousness remaineth for ever.

THE late John Thornton, Esq. of Clapham, was distinguished by his great liberality: he disposed of large sums in various charitable designs, with unremitting constancy, during a long course of years. His charities were much larger than is common with wealthy persons of good reputation for beneficence, insomuch that he was almost regarded as a prodigy. He was the patron of all pious, exemplary, and laborious ministers of the Gospel; frequently educating young men whom he found to be religiously disposed, and

purchasing many livings, which he gave to ministers, in order that
the Gospel might be preached in those places where he supposed the
people were perishing for lack of knowledge. He also dispersed a
number of Bibles, in different languages, in distant countries, perhaps
in all the four quarters of the globe, and with them vast quantities
of religious books, calculated to alarm the conscience, and affect the
heart with the importance of eternal things. He also patronised
every undertaking which was suited to supply the wants, to relieve
the distresses, or to increase the comforts of the human species, in
whatever climate, or of whatever description, provided they properly
fell within his sphere of action.

Spiritual Weapons.

Chap. x. ver. 4.—The weapons of our warfare are not carnal, but
mighty through God to the pulling down of strongholds.

THE preaching of the late Rev. J. Scott having been made effectual
to the production of a great change in a young lady, the daughter
of a country gentleman, so that she could no longer join the family
in their usual dissipations, and appeared to them as melancholy, or
approaching to it,—her father, who was a very gay man, looking upon
Mr Scott as the sole cause of what he deemed his daughter's misfortune, became exceedingly enraged at him ; so much so, that he actually
lay in wait, in order to shoot him. Mr S. being providentially
apprised of it, was enabled to escape the danger. The diabolical
design of the gentleman being thus defeated, he sent Mr S. a challenge.
Mr S. might have availed himself of the law, and prosecuted him, but
he took another method. He waited upon him at his house, was introduced to him in his parlour, and, with his characteristic boldness
and intrepidity, thus addressed him :—"Sir, I hear you have designed
to shoot me,—by which you would have been guilty of murder : failing in this, you sent me a challenge : and what a coward you must be,
sir, to wish to engage with a blind man (alluding to his being short-
sighted). As you have given me a challenge, it is now my right to
choose the time, the place, and the weapon ; I, therefore, appoint the
present moment, sir, the place where we now are, and the sword for
the weapon, to which I have been most accustomed." The gentleman
was evidently greatly terrified : when Mr Scott, having attained his
end, produced a pocket Bible, and exclaimed, "This is my sword, sir,
the only weapon I wish to engage with." "Never," said Mr S. to a
friend to whom he related this anecdote, "never was a poor careless
sinner so delighted with the sight of a Bible before." Mr Scott
reasoned with the gentleman on the impropriety of his conduct in
treating him as he had done, for no other reason than because he had
preached the everlasting Gospel. The result was, the gentleman
took him by the hand, begged his pardon, expressed his sorrow for
his conduct, and became afterwards very friendly to him.

Appearances.

Chap. x. ver. 10.—His letters (they say) are weighty and powerful ;
but his bodily presence is weak, and his speech contemptible.

MR HERBERT PALMER, an eminent divine in the 17th century,
sometimes preached in the French congregation at Canterbury,
at the request of their Eldership, being master of that language, to
the great edification of his hearers. A French gentlewoman, when
the saw him the first time coming into the pulpit, being startled at
the smallness of his personal appearance, and the weakness of his

look, cried out in the hearing of those that sat by her, "Alas! what should this child say to us?" But having heard him pray and preach with so much spiritual strength and vigour, she lifted up her hands to heaven with admiration and joy, blessing God for what she heard.

Perils at Sea.

Chap. xi. ver. 26.—In perils in the sea.

NATHANIEL, an assistant to the Moravian missionaries in Greenland, when engaged in the seal-fishery, being in company with another brother, who was yet inexperienced in the management of a kayak (a Greenland boat), he met a Neitsersoak, the largest kind of seal, which he killed. He then discovered his companion upon a flake of ice, endeavouring to kill another of the same species, and in danger; he, therefore, left his dead seal, kept buoyant by the bladder, and hastened to help his brother. They succeeded in killing the seal; but suddenly a strong north wind arose, and carried off both the kayaks to sea; nor could they discover any kayaks in the neighbourhood. They cried aloud for help, but in vain. Meanwhile the wind rose in strength, and carried both the kayaks, and also the piece of ice, swiftly along with the waves. Having lost sight of the kayaks, they now saw themselves without the least hope of deliverance. Nathaniel continued praying to his Saviour, and thought with great grief of the situation of his poor family, but felt a small degree of hope arising in his breast. Unexpectedly, he saw his dead seal floating towards him, and was exceedingly surprised at its approaching against the wind, till it came so near the flake of ice that they could secure it. But how shall a dead seal become the means of their deliverance? and what was now to be done? All at once Nathaniel resolved, at a venture, to seat himself upon the dead floating seal; and, by the help of his paddle, which he had happily kept in his hand when he joined his brother on the ice, to go in quest of the kayaks. Though the sea and waves continually overflowed him, yet he kept his seat, made after the kayaks, and succeeded in overtaking his own, into which he crept, and went in quest of that of his companion, which he likewise found. He also kept possession of the seal; and now hastened in search of the flake of ice on which his companion was most anxiously looking out for him; having reached it, he brought him his kayak, and enabled him to secure the other seal, when both returned home in safety. When relating his dangerous adventure, he ascribed his preservation, not to his own contrivance, but to the mercy of God alone.

Escape from Danger.

Chap. xi. ver. 32, 33.—The Governor, under Aretas the king, kept the city of the Damascenes with a garrison, desirous to apprehend me; and through a window, in a basket, was I let down by the wall, and escaped his hands.

ARCHBISHOP BANCROFT having received information that Mr Robert Parker, a Puritan divine, was concealed in a certain citizen's house in London, immediately sent a person to watch the house, while others were prepared with a warrant to search for him. The person having fixed himself at the door, boasted that he had him now secure. Mr Parker, at this juncture, resolved to dress himself in the habit of a citizen, and venture out, whereby he might possibly escape; but if he remained in the house, he would be sure to be taken. Accordingly, in his strang garb he went forth; and

God so ordered it that, just at the moment of his going out, the watchman at the door spied his intended bride passing on the other side of the street; and, while he was just stepping over to speak to her, the good man escaped. When the officers came with the warrant to search the house, to their great mortification he could not be found. After this signal providential deliverance, he retired to the house of a friend in the neighbourhood of London, where a treacherous servant in the family gave information to the bishop's officers, who came and actually searched the house where he was; but, by the special providence of God, he was again most remarkably preserved; for the only room in the house which they neglected to search, was that in which he was concealed, from whence he heard them swearing and quarrelling one with another; one protesting that they had not searched that room, and another as confidently asserting the contrary, and refusing to suffer it to be searched again. Had he been taken, he must have been cast into prison, where, without doubt, says the narrator, he **must have died.**

Spiritual Visions.

Chap xii. ver. 3, 4.—I knew such a man (whether in the body, or out of the body, I cannot tell: God knoweth), how that he was caught up into paradise, and heard unspeakable words, which it is not lawful for a man to utter.

MR. JOHN HOLLAND, the day before he died, called for the Bible, saying, "Come, O come! death approaches, let us gather some flowers to comfort this hour." And turning with his own hand to the 8th chapter of Romans, he gave the book to Mr. Leigh, and bade him read: at the end of every verse, he paused, and then gave the sense, to his own comfort, but more to the joy and wonder of his friends. Having continued his meditations on the 8th of the Romans, thus read to him, for two hours or more, on a sudden he said, "O stay your reading. What brightness is this I see? Have you lighted up any candles?" Mr Leigh answered, "No, it is the sunshine;" for it was about five o'clock in a clear summer evening. "Sunshine!" said he, "nay, it is my Saviour's shine. Now, farewell world; welcome heaven. The day-star from on high hath visited my heart. O speak it when I am gone, and preach it at my funeral; God dealeth familiarly with man. I feel His mercy; I see His majesty; whether in the body or out of the body, I cannot tell, God knoweth; but I see things that are unutterable." Thus ravished in spirit, he roamed towards heaven with a cheerful look, and soft sweet voice; but what he said could not be understood.

The Grace of God.

Chap. xii. ver. 9.—My grace is sufficient for thee; for my strength is made perfect in weakness.

A MINISTER of the Gospel was one evening preaching in Bristol, from these words, "My grace is sufficient for thee," when he took occasion to relate the circumstance of a pious young woman's labouring under a strong temptation to put a period to her life by drowning herself, from which she was delivered in a manner strikingly providential. She had gone to the river in order to comply with the enemy's suggestion; but as she was adjusting her clothes to prevent her from floating, she felt something in her pocket, which proved to be her Bible. She thought she would take it out, and look in it for the last time. She did so, and the above-mentioned text caught her eye. Through the Divine blessing attending them, the words struck her with peculiar force, when the snare was instantly broken, the temptation vanished, and she returned home blessing and praising Him who had given her the victory. It is stated that the relation of this circumstance was blessed to the conversion of a man and his wife who were present, who had lived in an almost continual state of enmity, and whose habitation exhibited a terrifying scene of discord and confusion. In one of those unhappy intervals of sullen silence, which both parties were accustomed to maintain after their quarrels, the wife came to the dreadful determination of drowning herself. She accordingly left her house for that purpose, and approached the river, but owing to its being too light, she apprehended she should be detected before she could accomplish her design. She therefore deferred the fatal act till it should have grown dark, and, in the interim, wandered about, not knowing whither to go. At length she observed a place of worship open, and thought she would go in to pass the time. Mr W. was preaching, and she listened to him with attention, especially when he related the matter above mentioned. Instead of drowning herself, she returned home after the sermon, with a countenance which, however expressive before of a malevolent disposition, now indicated that a spirit of gentleness had taken possession of her breast. Struck with her appearance, her husband asked her where she had been. On telling him, he immediately said, "And did you see me there?" She replied, "No." He rejoined, "But I was; and blessed be God, I found His grace sufficient for *me* also."

Peace.

Chap. xiii. ver. 11.—Be of one mind, live in peace; and the God of love and peace shall be with you.

MR JOHNSTON of West Africa, in one of his late journals, relates the following very pleasing and instructive incident:—"In visiting a sick communicant, his wife, who was formerly in our school, was present. I asked several questions, viz. if they prayed together, read a part of the Scriptures (the woman can read), constantly attended public worship, and lived in peace with their neighbours. All these questions were answered in the affirmative. I then asked if they lived in peace together. The man answered, 'Sometimes I say a word my wife no like, or my wife talk or do what I no like; but when we want to quarrel, then we shake hands together, shut the door, and go to prayer, and so we get peace again.' This method of keeping peace quite delighted me."

A Divine Blessing.

Chap. xiii. ver. 14.—The grace of the Lord Jesus Christ, and the love of God, and the communion of the Holy Ghost, be with you all. Amen.

MR VENN was on a visit at the house of a very intimate friend, where a lady of great piety was ill of a dangerous and exquisitely painful disorder. The physician who attended her one day observed to Mr Venn, that he was quite at a loss to explain how she was enabled to bear such a severity of suffering, as he well knew attended her complaint, with so much tranquillity, and so little symptom of murmuring and restlessness. "Can you account for it, sir?" added he. "Sir," said Mr Venn, "that lady happily possesses what you and

I ought to pray for,—the grace of our Lord Jesus Christ, the love of God, and the fellowship of the Holy Ghost."

GALATIANS.

Faithful to God.

Chap. i. ver. 10.—Do I seek to please men? for if I yet pleased men, I should not be the servant of Christ.

THE Rev. Joseph Alleine was very faithful and impartial in administering reproof. Once when employed in a work of this kind, he said to a Christian friend, "I am now going about that which is likely to make a very dear and obliging friend become an enemy. But, however, it cannot be omitted; it is better to lose man's favour than God's." But, so far from becoming his enemy for his conscientious faithfulness to him, he rather loved him the more ever after, as long as he lived.

Changed in Spirit.

Chap. i. ver. 23.—He which persecuted us in times past, now preacheth the faith which once he destroyed.

THE Rev. J. Perkins, one of the American missionaries, has recorded the following remarkable anecdote in his Journal. A physician who had been personally acquainted with the infidel Paine, had embraced his sentiments, and was very profane and dissipated. After more than a year striving against the convictions of the Spirit of God, which were so powerful, and his stubbornness so great, like a bullock unaccustomed to the yoke, as to bring him to a bed of long confinement, and the most awful depression of mind, he became a humble, zealous, and exemplary Christian. And as soon as his health was recovered, he qualified himself by preparatory studies, to go forth to the world and preach that Jesus, whom he for many years considered as an impostor, whose name he had habitually blasphemed, and whose religion he had counted foolishness, and a base imposition on the world.

The Poor.

Chap. ii. ver. 10.—Only they would that we should remember the poor; the same which I also was forward to do.

AMONG the graces for which Mr Fox, the celebrated Martyrologist, was eminent, may be noticed his extensive liberality to the poor. He was so bountiful to them while he lived, that he had no ready money to leave to them at his death. A friend once inquiring of him, "Whether he recollected a certain poor man whom he used to relieve?" he replied, "Yes, I remember him well; and I willingly forget lords and ladies to remember such as he."

Faith and Works.

Chap. ii. ver. 16.—We have believed in Jesus Christ, that we might be justified by the faith of Christ, and not by the works of the law; for by the works of the law shall no flesh be justified.

THE views of the Rev. Martin Boos, a late Catholic clergyman in Austria, though afterwards decidedly evangelical, were at the commencement of his ministry erroneous. About the year 1788, he went to visit a woman distinguished for her humility and piety, who was dangerously ill. In endeavouring to prepare her for death, he said to her, "I doubt not but you will die calm and happy." "Wherefore?" asked the sick woman. "Because your life has all been made up of a series of good works." The sick woman sighed: "If I die," said she, "confiding in the good works which you call to my recollection, I know for certain that I shall be condemned; but what renders me calm at this solemn hour is, that I trust solely in Jesus Christ my Saviour." "These few words," said Boos, "from the mouth of a dying woman who was reputed a saint, opened my eyes for the first time. I learned what that was—'*Christ for us.*'—Like Abraham, I saw His day: from that time, I announced to others the Saviour of sinners, whom I had myself found, and there are many of them who rejoice in Him along with me."

Receiving the Spirit.

Chap. iii. ver. 2.—Received ye the Spirit by the works of the law, or by the hearing of faith?

"I PREACHED up santification very earnestly for six years in a former parish," says the Rev. Mr Bennet in a letter, "and never brought one soul to Christ. I did the same at this parish, for two years, without having any success at all; but as soon as ever I preached Jesus Christ, and faith in His blood, then believers were added to the church occasionally; then people flocked from all parts to hear the glorious sound of the Gospel, some coming six, others eight, and others ten miles, and that constantly. The reason why my ministry was not blessed, when I preached up salvation partly by faith, and partly by works, is, because the doctrine is not of God; and He will prosper no ministers, but such as preach salvation in His own appointed way, viz. by faith in Jesus Christ."

The Law.

Chap. iii. ver. 13.—Christ hath redeemed us from the curse of the law, being made a curse for us.

IN a conversation the Rev. Mr Innes had with an infidel on his sick-bed, the latter told Mr Innes that when he was taken ill, he thought he would rely on the general mercy of God; that as he never had done anything very bad, he hoped all would be well. "But as my weakness increased," he added, "I began to think, is not God a just Being, as well as merciful. Now, what reason have I to think He will treat me with mercy, and not with justice; and if I am treated with justice," he said, with much emotion, "where am I?" "I showed him," says Mr Innes, "that this was the very difficulty the Gospel met and removed, as it showed how mercy could be exercised in perfect consistency with the strictest demands of justice, while it was bestowed through the atonement made by Jesus Christ. After explaining this doctrine, and pressing it on his attention and acceptance, one of the last things he said to me before leaving him was, "Well, I believe it must come to this. I confess I here see a solid footing to rest on, which, on my former principles, I could never find!"

Sacred Seasons.

Chap. iv. ver. 10.—Ye observe days, and months, and times, and years.

SOON after the coronation of Henry II. of France, a tailor was apprehended for working on a saint's day; and, being asked why he gave such offence to religion, his reply was, "I am a poor man, and have nothing but my labour to depend upon ; necessity requires that I should be industrious, and my conscience tells me there is no day but the Sabbath which I ought to keep sacred from labour." Having thus expressed himself, he was committed to prison, and being brought to trial, was by his iniquitous judges condemned to be burnt.

In Doubt.

Chap. iv. ver. 20.—I desire to be present with you now, and to change my voice ; for I stand in doubt of you.

MR Whitefield, in a sermon he preached at Haworth, having spoken severely of those professors of the Gospel, who by their loose and evil conduct caused the ways of truth to be evil spoken of, intimated his hope, that it was not necessary to enlarge much upon that topic to the congregation before him, who had so long enjoyed the benefit of an able and faithful preacher, and he was willing to believe that their profiting appeared to all men. This roused Mr Grimshaw's spirit, and notwithstanding his great regard for the preacher, he stood up and interrupted him, saying with a loud voice, "Oh, sir, for God's sake do not speak so, I pray you do not flatter ; I fear the greatest part of them are going to hell with their eyes open."

Temptations.

Chap. v. ver. 17.—The flesh lusteth against the Spirit, and the Spirit against the flesh ; and these are contrary the one to the other, so that ye cannnot do the things that ye would.

AN Indian visiting his white neighbours, asked for a little tobacco to smoke, and one of them having some loose in his pocket, gave him a handful. The day following, the Indian came back, inquiring for the donor, saying he had found a quarter of a dollar among the tobacco. Being told, that as it was given him, he might as well keep it ; he answered, pointing to his breast, "I got a good man and a bad man here, and the good man say, it is not mine, I must return it to the owner ; the bad man say, why, he gave it you, and it is your own now ; the good man say, that not right, the tobacco is yours, not the money ; the bad man say, never mind, you got it, go buy some dram ; the good man say, no, no, you must not do so ; so I don't know what to do ; and I think to go to sleep ; but the good man and the bad man kept talking all night and trouble me ; and now I bring the money back, I feel good."

Evil Dissipation.

Chap. v. ver. 21.—Drunkenness, revellings, and such like—they which do such things shall not inherit the kingdom of God.

IN a journal written by Mr William Seward, a gentleman who accompanied Mr Whitefield in his travels, is found the following notice :—"Heard of a drinking club that had a negro boy attending them, who used to mimic people for their diversion. The gentlemen bade him mimic Mr Whitefield, which he was very unwilling to do, but they insisted upon it. He stood up and said, 'I speak the truth in Christ, I lie not ; unless you repent, you will be damned ?' This unexpected speech broke up the club, which has not met since."

Individual Responsibility.

Chap. vi. ver. 5.—Every man shall bear his own burden.

BISHOP BURNET, in his charges to the clergy of his diocese, used to be extremely vehement in his declamations against pluralities. In his first visitation to Salisbury, he urged the authority of St Bernard ; who being consulted by one of his followers, whether he might accept of two benefices, replied, "And how will you be able to serve them both ?" "I intend," answered the priest, "to officiate in one of them by a deputy." "Will your deputy suffer eternal punishment for you too ?" asked the saint. "Believe me, you may serve your cure by proxy, but you must suffer the penalty in person." This anecdote made such an impression on Mr Kelsey, a pious and wealthy clergyman then present, that he immediately resigned the rectory of Bernerton, in Berkshire, worth two hundred a-year, which he then held with one of great value."

Doing Good.

Chap. vi. ver. 10.—As we have therefore opportunity, let us do good unto all men, especially unto them who are of the household of faith.

THE celebrated Dr Franklin informs us, that all the good he ever did to his country or mankind, he owed to a small book which he accidentally met with, entitled, "Essays to do Good," in several sermons from Gal. vi. 10. These sermons were written by Dr Cotton Mather, a very able and pious minister of the Gospel in Boston. "This little book," says he, "he studied with care and attention— laid up the sentiments in his memory, and resolved from that time, which was in his early youth, that he would make *doing good* the great purpose and business of his life."

EPHESIANS.

The Forgiveness of Sin.

Chap. i. ver. 7.—In whom we have redemption through His blood the forgiveness of sins, according to the riches of His grace.

WHEN the eminent prelate, Bishop Butler, lay on his death-bed, he called for his chaplain, and said, "Though I have endeavoured to avoid sin and please God to the utmost of my power, yet, from the consciousness of perpetual infirmities, I am still afraid to die." "My lord," said the chaplain, "you have forgotten that Jesus Christ is a Saviour." "True," was the answer, "but how shall I know that he was a Saviour for me ?" "My lord, it is written, ' Him that cometh to me I will in no wise cast out.' " "True," said the bishop, "and though I have read that Scripture a thousand times over, I never felt its virtue till this moment, and now I die happy."

A Vision of the Future.

Chap. i. ver. 18.—The eyes of your understanding being enlightened ;

that ye may know what is the hope of his calling, and what the riches of the glory of his inheritance in the saints.

MR FLAVEL, at one time on a journey, set himself to improve his time by meditation ; when his mind grew intent, till at length he had such ravishing tastes of heavenly joy, and such full assurance of his interest therein, that he utterly lost the sight and sense of this world and all its concerns, so that he knew not where he was. At last, perceiving himself faint from a great loss of blood from his nose, he alighted from his horse, and sat down at a spring, where he washed and refreshed himself, earnestly desiring, if it were the will of God, that he might there leave the world. His spirits reviving, he finished his journey in the same delightful frame. He passed that night without any sleep, the joy of the Lord still overflowing him, so that he seemed an inhabitant of the other world. After this, a heavenly serenity and sweet peace long continued with him ; and for many years he called that day "one of the days of heaven!" and professed he understood more of the life of heaven by it, than by all the discourses he had heard, or the books he ever read.

Spiritual Quickening.

Chap. ii. ver. 1.—You hath he quickened, who were dead in trespasses and sins.

IN 1812, the Rev. Robert Hall, who then resided at Leicester, paid one of his periodical visits to Bristol, and preached a most solemn and impressive sermon on the text, "Dead in trespasses and sins," of which the concluding appeals were remarkably sublime and awful. The moment he had delivered the last sentence, Dr Ryland, then the pastor of the church, hastened part of the way up the pulpit stairs ; and, while the tears trickled down his venerable face, exclaimed with a vehemence which astonished both the preacher and the congregation—"Let all that are alive in Jerusalem, pray for the dead that they may live."

Saved by Grace.

Chap. ii. ver. 8.—By grace are ye saved.

MR McLAREN and Mr Gustart were both ministers of the Tolbooth Church, Edinburgh. When Mr M'Laren was dying, Mr G. paid him a visit, and put the question to him, "What are you doing, brother!" His answer was, "I'll tell you what I am doing, brother ; I am gathering together all my prayers, all my sermons, all my good deeds, all my ill deeds ; and I am going to throw them all overboard, and swim to glory on the plank of Free Grace."

Unsearchable Riches.

Chap. iii. ver. 8.—That I should preach among the Gentiles the unsearchable riches of Christ.

MR CONYERS was for some years a preacher before he had an experimental knowledge of the truths of the Gospel. One day, studying his Greek Testament, as his custom was, he came, in the course of his reading to Ephesians iii. 8. "Unto me, who am less than the least of all saints, is this grace given, that I should preach among the Gentiles the unsearchable riches of Christ." "Riches of Christ!" said he to himself, "unsearchable riches! What have I preached of these? What do I know of these?" Such was the beginning of new views, new sentiments, new declarations, with this truly conscientious pastor, who had the honesty to inform his people on the very next Sabbath, that he feared he had been a blind leader of the blind, but that he was now determined to begin afresh : he trusted the Lord would lead him aright, and as he should be led, so he would lead them. The broad seal of the Spirit convincing, converting, sanctifying multitudes through his ministry, put it beyond a doubt who had been the author of this revolution in his opinions and feelings, and that the "vision was of the Lord."

The Love of Christ.

Chap. iii. ver. 19.—And to know the love of Christ, which passeth knowledge.

ON one occasion, the Rev. Rowland Hill was endeavouring to convey to his hearers, by a variety of striking illustrations, some idea of his conceptions of the Divine love ; but suddenly casting his eyes towards heaven, he exclaimed, "But I am unable to reach the lofty theme !—yet I do not think that the smallest fish that swims in the boundless ocean ever complains of the immeasurable vastness of the deep. So it is with me ; I can plunge, with my puny capacity, into a subject, the immensity of which I shall never be able fully to comprehend !"

Righteous Anger.

Chap. iv. ver. 26.—Be ye angry, and sin not ; let not the sun go down upon your wrath.

A PIOUS little boy, one day seeing his little sister in a passion, thus spoke to her : "Mary, look at the sun, it will soon go down ; it will soon be out of sight ; it is going, it is gone down. Mary, let not the sun go down upon your wrath."

Helpful Work.

Chap. iv. ver. 28.—Let him labour, working with his hands the thing which is good, that he may have to give to him that needeth.

A MAN in America, who depended for support entirely on his own exertions, subscribed five dollars annually in support of the Bombay schools. His friends inquired, "why he gave so much, and how he could afford it ?" He replied, "I have for sometime been wishing to do something for Christ's cause, but I cannot preach, neither can I pray in public, to any one's edification, nor can I talk to people, but I have hands, and I can work."

Value of Time.

Chap. v. ver. 16.—Redeeming the time.

AN American clergyman, in the early part of his ministry, being in London, called on the late Rev. Matthew Wilks. He received him with courtesy, and entered into conversation, which was kept up briskly, till the most important religious intelligence in possession of each had been imparted. Suddenly there was a pause,—it was broken by Mr Wilks. "Have you anything more to communicate ?" "No, nothing of special interest." "Any further inquiries to make ?" "None." "Then you must leave me ; I have my Master's business to attend to ;—good morning." "Here," says the minister, "I received a lesson on the impropriety of intrusion, and on the most manly method of preventing it."

Temperance.

Chap. v. ver. 18.—Be not drunk with wine, wherein is excess.

A STRIKING exemplification of the relation which temperance bears to the pauperism of the country, is shown in the experience of the State of Massachusetts during a recent year. According to an estimate of Mr Williams, the Temperance agent, the pauper tax of Massachusetts amounted a few years ago to 200,000 dollars, eight-tenths of which was ascertained to be the result of ardent spirits. Two years before this tax was reduced to 136,000 dollars, and the last year it amounted to only 41,000 dollars. This great reduction is to be accounted for by the cheering fact, that within these few years there have been 30,000 drunkards reformed. Thus has the Temperance movement, besides bringing life, health, and hope to the lost, and comfort and happiness to thousands of homes, put thousands of dollars into the pockets of the tax-payers of that single State. Who can be an enemy to so useful and excellent a work? Mr Williams also states that in the town of Worcester, within three years, the number of inmates in the poor-house has been reduced from 469 to 11, by the operation of the same cause; a reformation so strikingly and obviously beneficial, that the town voted, at its annual meeting, to contribute 500 dollars a year to the treasury of the Washingtonian Society. Money could not be better laid out.

Masters and Servants.

Chap. vi. ver. 9.—Ye masters, do the same things unto them, forbearing threatening: knowing that your Master also is in heaven; neither is their respect of persons with him.

A CELEBRATED tutor in Paris was in the habit of relating to his pupils, as they stood in a half circle before him, anecdotes of illustrious men, and obtaining their opinions respecting them, rewarding those who answered well with tickets of merit. On one of these occasions, he mentioned to them an anecdote of Marshal Turenne. "On a fine summer's day," said he, "while the Marshal was leaning out of his window, the skirts of his coat hanging off from the lower part of his body, his valet entered the room, and approaching his master with a soft step, gave him a violent blow with his hand. The pain occasioned by it brought the Marshal instantly round, when he beheld his valet on his knees imploring his forgiveness, saying that he thought it had been George his fellow-servant." The question was then put to each of the scholars, "What would you have done to the servant had you been in the Marshal's situation?" A haughty French boy, who stood first, said,—"Done! I would have run him through with my sword." This reply filled the whole school with surprise, and the master sentenced the boy to the forfeiture of his tickets. After putting the question to the other children, and receiving different answers, he came at length to a little English girl, about eight years of age. "Well, my dear, and what would you have done on this occasion, supposing you had been Marshal Turenne?" She replied, with all the sedateness of her nation, "I should have said, suppose it *had been* George, why strike so hard?" The simplicity and sweetness of this reply drew smiles of approbation from the whole school, and the master awarded the prize and all the forfeitures to this little girl.

The Holy Spirit.

Chap. vi. ver. 17.—The sword of the Spirit, which is the word of God.

ADMIRAL COUNT VERHUEL attended the anniversary of the British and Foreign Bible Society in London in 1822, as the representative of the French Bible Society, and occupied a seat next to Admiral Lord Gambier. He was asked some time after, by a reverend gentleman, what were his feelings on that occasion. He replied, "I remember the time when Lord Gambier and myself could not have stood so near each other, without each holding a sword in his hand. At this time we did not feel the want of our swords: we suffered them to remain in the scabbard; we had no sword but the sword of the Spirit, and the sword of the Spirit is the word of God." "Would it not," the minister added, "be a matter of regret to you to be again engaged in a war with Great Britian?" "I should always," he added, "regret to be at war with a country that is so nobly engaged in sending the Gospel of peace throughout the world."

PHILIPPIANS.

If Christ be Preached.

Chap. i. ver. 18.—Christ is preached; and I therein do rejoice, yea, and will rejoice.

A WORTHY minister, who used to preach a week-day lecture in the city of London, heard a person expressing his regret that it was so ill attended. "Oh, that is of little consequence," replied the minister, "as the Gospel is preached by several others in the same neighbourhood; and in such a situation, for any one to be very desirous that people should come and hear the Gospel from *him*, instead of others, seems as unreasonable, as it would be for one of the salesmen in a large shop to wish all the customers to come to his particular part of the counter. If the customers come at all, and the goods go off, in so far as he feels an interest in the prosperity of the shop, he will rejoice."

Dying in Faith.

Chap. i. ver. 21.—For me—to die is gain.

"I AM no longer disposed," says a Jew in writing to another, "to laugh at religion, or to plead that Christianity has no comforts in death. I witnessed the last moments of my worthy gardener, and wish I may die his death: and, if there is happiness in another life, this disciple of Jesus is assuredly happy. When the physician told him he was in extreme danger, 'How,' said he, 'can that be, when God is my Father, Jesus my Redeemer, heaven my country, and death the messenger of peace! The greatest risk I run is to die, but to die is to enter into complete and endless bliss.' His last words were, 'I die, but what needs that trouble me? My Jesus is the true God, and eternal life.'"

Leaving this World.

Chap. i. ver. 23.—Having a desire to depart, and to be with Christ, which is far better.

ARCHBISHOP LEIGHTON was conversing one day, in his wonted strain of holy animation, of the blessedness of being fixed as a pillar in the heavenly Jerusalem to go no more out, when he was interrupted by a near relation exclaiming, "Ah! but you have assurance." "No, truly," he replied; "only a good hope, and a *great desire* to see what they are doing on the other side, for of this world I am heartily weary."

Unselfishness.

Chap. ii. ver. 4.—Look not every man on his own things, but every man on the things of others.

OF the benevolent temper of the Rev. Mr Gilpin, the following instance is related. One day, returning home, he saw in a field several people crowding together; and judging something more than ordinary had happened, he rode up, and found that one of the horses in a team had suddenly dropped down, which they were endeavouring to raise, but in vain, for the horse was dead. The owner of it seeming to be much dejected with the misfortune, and declaring how grievous a loss it would be to him, Mr Gilpin bade him not be disheartened:—"I'll let you have," said he, "honest man, that horse of mine," pointing to his servant's. "Ah! master," replied the countryman, "my pocket will not reach such a beast as that." "Come, come," said Mr Gilpin, "take him, take him, and when I demand the money, then thou shalt pay me."

The Gloucestershire Chronicle relates an accident that occurred in a coal-pit near Bitton, when six lives were lost. At the moment of the time when the iron handle of the cage, in which the unfortunate men were, snapped asunder, a man and a boy, who were hanging on the rope above, made a sudden spring, and most providentially laid hold of a chain which is always hanging at the side of the pit as a guide. As soon as possible after the accident was known at the top of the pit, and it was ascertained that some one was clinging to the side, a man was sent down with a rope and noose to render assistance. He came first, in his descent, to a boy named Daniel Harding; and on his reaching him, the noble-minded lad instantly cried out, "Don't mind me, I can still hold on a little; but Joseph Brown, who is a little lower down, is nearly exhausted, save him first." The person went on, and found Joseph Brown, as described by his companion, and after bringing him safely up, again descended, and succeeded in restoring the gallant boy to light and life. When we state that the time which elapsed from the moment of the accident till the boy was brought up was from fifteen to twenty minutes, his fortitude and heroism will be duly appreciated.

Spiritual Striving.

Chap. ii. ver. 12, 13.—Work out your own salvation with fear and trembling: for it is God which worketh in you both to will and to do of his good pleasure.

IT is but too common with some professors, under a pretence of magnifying the grace of God, to excuse their want of zeal, and negligence in the duties of religion, by pleading that they can do nothing without the sensible influence of grace upon their minds.—" I once heard," adds Mr Buck, " a zealous minister (now with God) talking in his sleep, which was a very customary thing with him, and lamenting this disposition in some professors, which he thus reproved: 'I am a poor creature, says one; and I can do nothing, says another. No, and I am afraid you *do not want to do much.* I know you have no strength of your own, but how is it you do not cry to the strong for strength?'"

Righteousness through Faith.

Chap. iii. ver. 9.—Not having mine own righteousness, which is of the law, but that which is through the faith of Christ, and righteousness which is of God by faith.

AN Indian and a white man, being at worship together, were both brought under conviction by the same sermon. The Indian was shortly after led to rejoice in pardoning mercy. The white man, for a long time, was under distress of mind, and at times almost ready to despair, but at length he was also brought to a comfortable experience of forgiving love. Some time after, meeting his *red* brother, he thus addressed him :—" How is it that I should be so long under conviction, when you found comfort so soon?" "O brother," replied the Indian, " me tell you : there come along a rich prince, he propose to give you a *new coat*; you look at your coat, and say, I don't know ; my coat pretty good ; I believe it will do a little longer. He then offer me new coat : I look on my *old blanket;* I say, this good for nothing ; I fling it right away, and accept the new coat. Just so, brother, you try to keep your own righteousness for some time : you loath to give it up ; but I, poor Indian, had none ; therefore I glad at once to receive the righteousness of the Lord Jesus Christ."

Apprehended of Christ.

Chap. iii. ver. 12.—I follow after, if that I may apprehend that for which also I am apprehended of Christ Jesus.

MR JOHN WELSH, grandson of Mr. Welsh of Ayr, being pursued with unrelenting rigour, was one time quite at a loss where to go ; but depending on Scottish hospitality, and especially on the providence of God, he in an evening called at the house of a gentleman of known hostility to field preachers, and particularly to himself. He was kindly received. In the course of conversation, Welsh was mentioned, and the difficulty of getting hold of him. " I know," says the stranger, " where he is to preach to-morrow, and will give you him by the hand." At this the gentleman was very glad, and engaged the company of his guest with great cordiality. They set off next morning, and when they arrived at the congregation, they made way for the minister, and also for his host. He desired the gentleman to sit down on the chair, where he stood and preached. During the sermon, the gentleman seemed much affected. At the close, Mr. Welsh gave him his hand, which he cheerfully received and observed, " You said you were sent to apprehend rebels, and I, a rebellious sinner, have been apprehended this day."

Christian Behaviour.

Chap. iv. ver. 5.—Let your moderation be known unto all men. The Lord is at hand.

A PIOUS officer of the army, travelling through the Mahratta country, was asked by Judge Davidson, a religious gentleman, to accompany him to a public dinner, at which the commanding officer of the district, with all his staff, and various other public characters, were expected to meet. " I expressed a wish to be excused," says the officer, " as I had then no relish for such entertainments, and did not think that much either of pleasure or benefit was to be derived from them." His reply was—" While I feel it my duty to attend on such an occasion, I certainly have as little pleasure in it as you have. But there is one way in which I find I can be present at such meetings, and yet receive no injury from them. I endeavour to conceive to myself the Lord Jesus seated on the opposite side of the table, and to think what He would wish me to do and to say, when placed in such a situation, and as long as I can keep this thought alive on my mind, I find I am free from danger."

Contentment.

Chap. iv. ver. 11.—I have learned, in whatsoever state I am, therewith to be content.

TO a clergyman who once visited Mr Newton when confined by weakness, he said, "The Lord has a sovereign right to do what He pleases with His own. I trust we are His, in the best sense, by purchase, by conquest, and by our own willing consent. As sinners, we have *no right*, and if believing sinners, we have *no reason*, to complain; for all our concerns are in the hand of our best Friend, who has promised that all things shall work together for His glory, and our final benefit. My trial is great;" but I am supported, and have many causes for daily praise.

COLOSSIANS.

The Faithful Pastor.

Chap. i. ver. 7.—Epaphras, a faithful minister of Christ.

MR THOMAS SHEPHERD was an excellent preacher, and took great pains in his preparations for the pulpit. He used to say, "God will curse that man's labour who goes idly up and down all the week, and then goes into his study on a Saturday afternoon. God knows that we have not too much time to pray in, and weep in, and get our hearts into a fit frame for the duties of the Sabbath."

Responsibility for Others.

Chap. i. ver. 28.—Warning every man, and teaching every man in all wisdom; that we may present every man perfect in Christ Jesus.

DURING a recent voyage, sailing in a heavy sea, near a reef of rocks, a minister on board the vessel remarked, in a conversation between the man at the helm and the sailors, an inquiry whether they should be able to clear the rocks without making another tack; when the captain gave orders that they should put off to avoid all risk. The minister observed, "I am rejoiced that we have so careful a commander." The captain replied, "It is necessary I should be very careful, because I have souls on board. I think of my responsibility, and should anything happen through carelessness, these souls are very valuable!"—The minister, turning to some of his congregation, who were upon deck with him, observed, "The captain has preached me a powerful sermon; I hope I shall never forget, when I am addressing my fellow-creatures on the concerns of eternity, that I have *souls on board*."

Christ's Triumph.

Chap. ii. ver. 15.—Having spoiled principalities and powers, he made a show of them openly, triumphing over them in it.

MR VENN, in his last illness, exhibited at times, in the midst of extreme feebleness of body, signs of great joy and gladness. Some of his friends, who visited him in his declining state, endeavoured to encourage his mind, by bringing to his recollection his useful labours in the Lord's vineyard. While one of them was enlarging in the same strain, the dying saint, raised from a state of oppressive languor, and deeply sensible of his own insufficiency, with great animation exclaimed, "Miserable comforters are ye all,—I have had many to visit me, who have endeavoured to comfort me, by telling me what I *have done*. '*He* hath spoiled principalities and powers,—He hath made a show of them openly, triumphing over them in His cross.' *This*, sir, is the source of all my consolation, and not anything I have done."

Affected Humility.

Chap. ii. ver. 23.—Which things have indeed a show of wisdom in will-worship and humility.

CARDINAL VASARI, was a strange compound of affected humility and real pride. While he performed the lowly office of washing the feet of thirteen beggars every morning, his supercilious, obstinate, and tribulent spirit, assumed a proud, overbearing, spiritual authority over his sovereign, whom he was in the habit of treating with all the insolence of a licensed censor.

The Affections.

Chap. iii. ver. 2.—Set your affections on things above, and not on things on the earth.

"I COULD mention the name of a late very opulent and very valuable person," says a writer in the *Gospel Magazine*, "who, though naturally avaricious in the extreme, was liberal and beneficent to a proverb. He was aware of his constitutional sin, and God gave him *victory* over it, by enabling him to *run away* from it. Lest the dormant love of money should awake and stir in his heart, he would not, for many years before his death, trust himself with the *sight* of his revenues. He kept, indeed, his accounts as clearly and exactly as any man in the world, but he dared not receive, because he dared not look at that gold, which he feared would prove a snare to his affections. His stewards received all, and retained all in their own hands, till they received orders how to dispose of it."

Obedience of Children.

Chap. iii. ver. 20.—Children, obey your parents in all things; for this is well pleasing unto the Lord.

WHEN the late Rev. Richard Cecil was but a little boy, his father had occasion to go to the India House, and took his son with him. While he was transacting business, the little fellow was dismissed, and told to wait for his father at one of the doors. His father, on finishing his business, went out at another door, and entirely forgot his son. In the evening, his mother missing the child, inquired where he was; on which his father suddenly recollected that he had directed him to wait at a certain door, said, "You may depend upon it, he is still waiting where I appointed him." He immediately returned to the India House, and found his dear boy on the very spot he had ordered him to remain. He knew that his father expected him to wait, and therefore he would not disappoint him.

Obedience of Servants.

Chap. iii. ver. 22.—Servants, obey in all things your masters.

TWO servants of a certain Raja, in the East Indies, once paid a dreadful penalty for the sin of disobedience. One of them had been strictly ordered to keep away from a cave in a wood, near the residence of the Raja, and to prevent any other person from going there also. This servant, instead of resolving at once to obey the command he had received, began to consider the probable reason of his having been forbidden to enter the cave, and persuaded himself that his master had a great treasure hid there. He at length resolved to get possession of it. Knowing that he could not roll away the stone from the mouth of the cave himself, he communicated his design to a fellow-servant, who willingly engaged in the plot, on being promised a part of the booty. When the night came, and the silvery moon was pursuing her course through the heavens, they stole quietly into the wood, and approached the cave, thinking only of the manner in which they should dispose of their treasure. But, alas! what sudden calamities come upon evil-doers. No sooner had they, with great labour, rolled away the stone, than a tremendous tiger, with eyes glaring like fury, sprang upon them, and tore them to pieces.

Justice to Servants.

Chap. iv. ver. 1.—Masters, give unto your servants that which is just and equal, knowing that ye also have a Master in heaven.

A POOR black boy, the property of a slave-holder in Africa, having heard of the preaching of the missionaries, felt a strong desire to go and hear about Jesus Christ. For this purpose he crept secretly away one evening, but being obliged to pass under the window of the house, his master observed him, and called out, "Where are you going?" The poor fellow came back trembling, and said, "Me go to hear the missionaries, massa." "To hear the missionaries, indeed; if ever you go there, you shall have nine and thirty lashes, and be put in irons." With a disconsolate look, the poor black replied, "Me tell Massa, me tell the great Massa." "Tell the great Massa," replied the master, "what do you mean?" "Me tell the great Massa, the Lord in Heaven, that my massa was angry with me, because I wanted to go and hear His word." The master was struck with astonishment, his colour changed, and, unable to conceal his feelings, he hastily turned away, saying, "Go along, and hear the missionaries." Being thus permitted, the poor boy gladly complied. In the meantime, the mind of the master became restless and uneasy. He had not been accustomed to think that he had a Master in heaven, who knew and observed all his actions; and he at length determined to follow his slave, and see if there could be any peace obtained for his troubled spirit; and creeping unobserved, he slunk into a secret corner, and listened eagerly to the words of the missionary. That day Mr Kircherer addressed the natives from those words—"Lovest thou Me?" "Is there no poor sinner," said he, "who can answer this question? not one poor slave who dares to confess Him?" Here the poor slave boy, unable to restrain any longer, sprang up, and holding up both his hands, while the tears streamed down his cheeks, cried out with eagerness, "Yes, massa, me love the Lord Jesus Christ; me do love Him, me love Him with all my heart." The master was still more astonished, and he went home convinced of the blessings the Gospel brings, and became a decided Christian.

Time Precious.

Chap. iv. ver. 5.—Redeeming the time.

MR JOSEPH ALLEINE, when in health, rose constantly at or before four o'clock, and on Sabbath sooner, if he awoke. He was much troubled if he heard any smiths, or shoemakers, or other tradesmen at work, before he was in his duties with God, often saying to his wife, "O how this noise shames me! Does not my Master deserve more than theirs?" He used often to say, "Give me a Christian that counts his time more precious than gold."

FIRST THESSALONIANS.

Effective Preaching.

Chap. i. ver. 5.—Our gospel came not unto you in word only, but also in power, and in the Holy Ghost, and in much assurance.

ABOUT forty or fifty years ago, a clergyman, who was a widower, married the widow of a deceased clergyman of another denomination. She was a woman highly esteemed for her correct views of Divine truth, and for sincere and consistent piety. She had not accompanied her new companion in this public and social worship a long time before she became pensive and dejected. This awakened the solicitude of her husband. He insisted on knowing the cause. At length, with trembling hesitancy, she observed, "Sir, your preaching would starve all the Christians in the world." "Starve all the Christians in the world!" said the astonished preacher; "why, do I not speak the truth?" "Yes," replied the lady, "and so you would were you to stand in the desk all day, and say my name is Mary. But, sir, there is something beside the letter in the truth of the Gospel." The result was, a very important change in the ministerial efforts of the clergyman; after which his wife sat and heard him preach with great delight.

Waiting for the Son.

Chap. i. ver. 10.—And to wait for his Son from heaven.

LITTLE more than half-an-hour before Dr Watts expired, he was visited by his dear friend Mr Whitefield. The latter asked him how he found himself; the doctor answered, "Here I am, one of Christ's waiting servants." Soon after some medicine was brought in, and Mr Whitefield assisted in raising him up in the bed, that he might with more convenience take the draught. On the doctor's apologising for the trouble he gave Mr Whitefield, the latter replied with his usual amiable politeness, "Surely, my dear brother, I am not too good to wait on a waiting-servant of Christ's." Soon after, Mr Whitefield took his leave, and often afterwards regretted that he had not prolonged his visit, which he would certainly have done, could he have foreseen his friend was but within half-an-hour's distance of the kingdom of glory.

Praise of Men.

Chap. ii. ver. 6.—Nor of men sought we glory.

UPON a certain high churchman's refusing to style Dr Owen *Reverend*, he wrote to him thus: "For the title of *Reverend*, I do give him notice, that I have very little valued it ever since I have considered the saying of Luther, 'Religion never was endangered except among the *most Reverends;*' so that he may, as to me, forbear it for the future, and call me as the Quakers do, and that will suffice. And for that of *Doctor*, it was conferred on me in my *absence*, and against my *consent*, as they have expressed it under their public seal: nor doth anything but *gratitude* and *respect* unto them that make me once own it; and, freed from that obligation, I should never use it more; nor did I use it until some were offended with me, and blamed me for my neglect."

Winning Souls.

Chap. ii. ver. 19, 20.—For what is our hope, or joy, or crown of rejoicing? Are not even ye in the presence of our Lord Jesus Christ at his coming? For ye are our glory and joy.

ARCHBISHOP WILLIAMS once said to a friend of his, "I have passed through many places of honour and trust both in Church and State, more than any of my order in England these seventy years back; yet were I but assured that by my preaching I had but converted one soul to God, I should take therein more spiritual joy and comfort, than in all the honours and offices which have been bestowed upon me."

Pray without Ceasing.

Chap. iii. ver. 10.—Night and day praying exceedingly.

MR HERVEY'S man-servant slept in the room immediately above that of his master. One night, long after the whole family had retired to rest, he awoke, hearing the groans of Mr Hervey in the room beneath, who seemed to be in great distress. He went down stairs, and opened the door of his master's room; but instead of finding him in bed, as he expected, he saw him prostrate on the floor, engaged in earnest and importunate prayer to his God. Disturbed by this unseasonable appearance, Mr Hervey, with his usual mildness, said, "John, you should not have entered the room unless I had rung the bell." Communion with God in prayer will turn night into day.

Those who know not God.

Chap. iv. ver. 5.—The Gentiles which know not God.

"IT is stated in the history of England," says Dr Philip, in an address delivered at one of the London Anniversaries, "that when the first missionary who arrived in Kent presented himself before the king, to solicit permission to preach the Gospel in his dominions, after long deliberation, when a negative was about to be put upon his application, an aged counsellor, with his head silvered over with grey hairs, rose, and by the following speech obtained the permission which was requested: 'Here we are,' said the orator, 'like birds of passage, we know not whence we come, or whither we are going; if this man can tell us, for God's sake let him speak.' I say, if there are six hundred millions of our fellow-creatures, who, like birds of passage, know not whence they came, nor whither they are going, for God's sake let us send them the Gospel, which will tell them whence they came, and which is able to make them wise unto salvation."

Sorrow for the Deceased.

Chap. iv. ver. 13.—I would not have you to be ignorant, brethren, concerning them which are asleep; that ye sorrow not, even as others which have no hope.

MR. NEWTON of London one day said to a gentleman who had lately lost a daughter by death, "Sir, if you were going to the East Indies, I suppose you would like to send a remittance before you. This little girl is just like a remittance sent to heaven before you go yourself. I suppose a gentleman on 'Change is never heard expressing himself thus:—'O my dear ship, I am sorry she has got into port so soon! I am sorry she has escaped the storms that are coming!" Neither should we sorrow for children dying."

Last Words.

Chap. iv. ver. 17.—And so shall we ever be with the Lord.

A CHRISTIAN man, being near the close of life, was attended by an apothecary who was also religious. On his friend's departure, he was desirous of hearing his last words, and, for that purpose, laid his ear to his patient's mouth. He heard him say, "Forever with the Lord, forever with the Lord."

Continuous in Prayer.

Chap. v. ver. 17.—Pray without ceasing.

A SAILOR who had been long absent from his native country, returned home, flushed with money. Coming to London, where he had never been before, he resolved to gratify himself with the sight of whatever was remarkable. Among other places, he visited St Paul's. It happened to be at the time of divine service. When carelessly passing, he heard the words, "Pray without ceasing," uttered by the minister, without having any impression made on his mind by them. Having satisfied his curiosity in London, he returned to his marine pursuits, and continued at sea for seven years, without any remarkable occurrence in his history. One fine evening, when the air was soft, the breeze gentle, the heavens serene, and the ocean calm, he was walking the deck, with his feelings soothed by the pleasing aspect of nature, when all on a sudden darted on his mind the words, "Pray without ceasing!" "Pray without ceasing! What words can these be?" he exclaimed: "I think I have heard them before: where could it be?" After a pause—"O, it was at St Paul's in London, the minister read them from the Bible. What! and do the Scriptures say, 'Pray without ceasing?' Oh what a wretch must I be to have lived so long without praying at all!"—God, who at first caused him to hear this passage in his ear, now caused it to spring up, in a way, at a time, and with a power peculiarly His own. The poor fellow now found the lightning of conviction flash on his conscience, the thunders of the law shake his heart, and the great deep of destruction threaten to swallow him up. Now he began, for the first time, to pray; but praying was not all: "Oh," said he, "if I had a Bible, or some good book!" He rummaged his chest, when, in a corner, he espied a Bible which his anxious mother had, twenty years before, placed in his chest, but which till now he had never opened. He snatched it up, put it to his breast, then read, wept, prayed; he believed, and became a new man.

Be Careful in coming to Conclusions.

Chap. v. ver. 21.—Prove all things: hold fast that which is good.

A GENTLEMAN was once asked in company, what led him to embrace the truths of the Gospel, which formerly he was known to have neglected and despised! He said, "My call and conversion to God my Saviour were produced by very singular means :—A person put into my hands Paine's 'Age of Reason.' I read it with attention, and was much struck with the strong and ridiculous representation he made of many passages in the Bible. I confess, to my shame, I had never read the Bible through; but from what I remembered to have heard at church, and accidentally on other occasions, I could not persuade myself that Paine's report was quite exact, or that the Bible was quite so absurd a book as he represented it. I resolved therefore that I would read the Bible regularly through, and compare the passages when I had done so, that I might give the Bible fair play. I accordingly set myself to the task, and as I advanced I was struck with the majesty which spoke, the awfulness of the truths contained in it, and the strong evidence of its Divine origin, which increased with every page, so that I finished my inquiry with the fullest satisfaction of the truth as it is in Jesus, and my heart was penetrated with a sense of obligation I had never felt before. I resolved henceforth to take the sacred word for my guide, and to be a faithful follower of the Son of God."

SECOND THESSALONIANS.

Retribution follows Evil Doers.

Chap. i. ver. 6.—It is a righteous thing with God to recompense tribulation to them that trouble you.

ABOUT the year 1738, when some of the ministers of the Secession were preaching at Braid's Craigs, in the vicinity of Edinburgh, a man had the hardihood to set fire to some furze bushes in the immediate neighbourhood of the spot where a numerous audience was assembled, concluding, from the direction and force of the wind, that the smoke proceeding from the burning bushes would exceedingly annoy the Seceders. It so happened, however, in the good providence of God, that the wind immediately veered about to another quarter, and the assembly suffered no inconvenience. The impious project, in the meantime, attracted the notice of the ministers as well as the people; Mr Ralph Erskine publicly remarked, that the person who had been guilty of that deed would perhaps live to repent it. That same individual, it is credibly related, was afterwards three times driven from his own dwelling by means of fire. First one house he occupied on Clerkington estate was burned down, and then another; on which his master dismissed him, saying, "*That man would burn all the houses on his property.*" He removed, in consequence, to Prestonpans, where a similar calamity befell him, the truth of which was attested by a very old woman in Edinburgh, who affirmed that, when a child, she made a very narrow escape from the flames of that house, being let down from a window in a blanket.

Future Punishment.

Chap. i. ver. 9.—Who shall be punished with everlasting destruction from the presence of the Lord, and from the glory of his power.

MR WAYN, preaching at a village where a large congregation had come out to hear something new, endeavoured to convince his hearers that there is no punishment after death. At the close of his sermon, he informed the people, that if they wished, he would preach there again in four weeks; then Mr Carr, a respectable merchant, rose, and replied, "Sir, if your doctrine is true, we do not need you; and if it is false, we do not want you."

Antichrist.

Chap. ii. ver. 3, 4.—That man of sin, the son of perdition; who opposeth and exalteth himself above all that is called God, or that is worshipped.

ONE day, after prayer, King Charles I. asked Mr Robert Blair, an eminent Scottish minister, if it was warrantable in prayer to determine a controversy. Mr Blair, taking the hint, said he thought he had determined no controversy in that prayer. "Yes," said the king, "you have determined the Pope to be antichrist, which is a controversy among divines." To this Mr Blair replied, "To me this is no controversy, and I am sorry it should be accounted so by your majesty; sure it was none to your father." This silenced the king, for he was a great defender of his father's opinions; and his testimony, Mr Blair knew well, was of more authority with him than the testimony of any divine.

Salvation through Belief.

Chap. ii. ver. 13.—God hath from the beginning chosen you to salvation, through sanctification of the Spirit, and belief of the truth.

THE Rev. Dr Lawson, in a discourse on the Sovereignty of Grace in the conversion of sinners, made the following declaration:— "For my part, I am firmly persuaded that all my hope must rest upon the richness and sovereignty of the mercy of God in Christ Jesus. I am sensible that I can never make myself a fitter subject of mercy than I am at this moment; and that therefore I must follow to the pit those miserable wretches that are groaning under the wrath of God, unless I accept of the atonement provided by Christ's death. A doctrine so necessary to my hope and peace as the sovereignty of divine mercy, I hope never to renounce."

Bad Company.

Chap. iii. ver. 6.—Withdraw yourselves from every brother that walketh disorderly.

SIR PETER LELY made it a rule never to look at a bad picture, having found by experience, that whenever he did so, his pencil took a taint from it. "Apply this," adds Bishop Horne, "to bad books and bad company."

Idleness.

Chap. iii. ver. 10.—This we commanded you, that if any would not work neither should he eat.

PISISTRATUS, the Grecian general, walking through some of his fields, several persons implored his charity. "If you want *beasts* to plough your land," said he, "I will lend you some; if you want *land*

I will give you some ; if you want *seed* to sow your land, I will give you some ; but I will encourage none in *idleness*." By this conduct, in a short time, there was not a beggar in his dominions.

FIRST TIMOTHY.

The Lawless.

Chap. i. ver. 9.—The law is not made for a righteous man, but for the lawless and disobedient—for murderers of fathers, and murderers of mothers.

IN 1815, a person was brought before the Court of Vannes, in France, accused of the murder of his mother. It appeared by the evidence given on the trial, that he had returned home intoxicated, and wet through with the rain ; on his arrival, he took it into his head to get into the oven in order to warm and dry himself, but the oven having been heated not long before, he burnt his hands and knees in the attempt : this rendered him furious, and he returned to the room in which all the family slept, and which was in total darkness ; he there fell into a passion against his son, a lad of 14 years, for not having told him that the oven had been lately heated, and took up a large bar in order to strike him. His father, more than sixty years old, ran and endeavoured to cool the rage of his son ; but this only enraged him the more, and he was about to strike him, when his mother went to the assistance of her husband. She was no sooner come near him, than the prisoner struck her twice on the head with the bar, of which blows she died in a few hours afterwards, praying Heaven for the pardon of her son. During the trial, the prisoner constantly denied these facts ; but the Jury having unanimously found him guilty, he was sentenced, as a parricide, to be conducted to the place of execution in a shirt, with his feet naked, and his head covered with a black veil, to have his right hand struck off, and afterwards to be beheaded.

The Reformed Pastor.

Chap. i. ver. 12, 13.—Putting me into the ministry ; who was before a blasphemer, and a persecutor, and injurious.

SEVERAL years ago, a charity sermon was preached in a dissenting chapel in the west of England ; and when the preacher ascended the pulpit, he thus addressed his hearers :—" My brethren, before I proceed to the duties of this evening, allow me to relate a short anecdote. Many years have elapsed since I was within the walls of this house. Upon that very evening there came three young men, with the intention not only of scoffing at the minister, but with their pockets filled with stones for the purpose of assaulting him. After a few words, one of them said with an oath—'Let us be at him now ; but the second replied, 'No, stop till we hear what he makes of this point.' The minister went on, when the second said, 'We have heard enough, now throw !' But the third interfered, saying, 'He is not so foolish as I expected, let us hear him out.' The preacher concluded without having been interrupted. Now mark me, my brethren—of these three young men, *one* was executed a few months ago at Newgate, for forgery; the *second* lies under sentence of death at this moment in the jail of this city, for murder : the other (continued the minister with great emotion,) the *third*, through the infinite grace of God, is even now about to address you—listen to him."

Becoming Prayer.

Chap. ii. ver. 8.—I will therefore that men pray every where, lifting up holy hands, without wrath and doubting.

MR JOHN KILPIN, father of the late Rev. Samuel Kilpin of Exeter, having, from some cause, displeased a member of the church; at a prayer meeting, his offended brother used most unbecoming expressions respecting him in prayer. On his family's offering their sympathy, and expressing resentment, he said, with a mind unruffled, "I was not the least hurt on my own account; such *talking* never goes any higher than the ceiling; the God of love never admits it as *prayer*."

Women's Adornment.

Chap. ii. ver. 9.—In like manner also, that women adorn themselves in modest apparel—not with broidered hair, or gold, or pearls, or costly array.

A MINISTER of the Gospel occasionally visiting a gay person, was introduced to a room near to that in which she dressed. After waiting some hours, the lady came in and found him in tears. She inquired the reason of his weeping; the minister replied, "Madam, I weep on reflecting that you can spend so many hours before your glass, and in adorning your person, while I spend so few hours before my God, and in adorning my soul." The rebuke struck her conscience,—she lived and died a monument of grace.

Danger of Conceit.

Chap. iii. ver. 6.—Not a novice, lest being lifted up with pride, he fall into the condemnation of the devil.

"THE apprehension of cursed pride (the sin of young ministers), working in my heart," says Dr Cotton Mather, "filled me with an inexpressible bitterness and confusion before the Lord. In my youth, when some others of my age were playing in the streets, I was preaching to large assemblies, and I was honoured with great respect among the people of God. I feared (and thanks be to God that He made me fear), lest Satan was hereby preparing a snare and a pit for such a novice. I therefore resolved, that I would set apart a day to humble myself before God, for the pride of my own heart, and to supplicate His grace to deliver me from that sin, and from the dreadful wrath it would expose me to."

One Wife.

Chap. iii. ver. 12.—The husbands of one wife.

THE Rev. Robert Moffat, speaking of Titus, brother of Africaner, says,—" He was the only individual of influence on the station who had two wives, and fearing the influence of example, I have occasionally made a delicate reference to the subject, and, by degrees, could make more direct remarks on that point, which was one of the barriers to his happiness; but he remained firm, admitting, at the same time, that a man with two wives was not to be envied; adding, 'He is often in an uproar, and when they quarrel, he does not know whose part to take.' He said he often resolved, when there was a great disturbance, he would pay one off. One morning I thought the anticipated day had come. He approached my door, leading an ox, upon which one of his wives was seated. 'What is the matter?" I inquired. Giving me a shake of his hand, and laughing, he replied, 'Just the old thing over again. Mynheer must not laugh too much at me, for I am now in for it.' The two wives had quarrelled at the outpost, and the one in a rage had thrown a dry rotten stick at the other, which had entered the palm of her hand, and left a piece about an inch long, and the thickness of a finger. The hand had swollen to nearly four times its usual size. 'Why,' I asked, 'did you not bring her sooner?' 'She was afraid to see you, and would not come till I assured her that you were a *maak mensche* (a tame man). Having made an incision, and extracted the piece of wood, she was melted into tears with gratitude, while I earnestly exhorted her to a better course of life."

Godliness.

Chap. iv. ver. 8.—Godliness is profitable unto all things; having promise of the life that now is, and of that which is to come.

"BLESSED be God that I was born," said the pious Halyburton when dying. "I have a father and a mother, and ten brethren and sisters in heaven, and I shall be the eleventh. O blessed the day that I was ever born! O that I were where He is! And yet were God to withdraw from me, I should be weak as water. All that I enjoy, though it be miracle on miracle, would not support me without fresh supplies from God. The thing I rejoice in is this, that God is altogether full; and that in the Mediator Christ Jesus is all the fulness of the Godhead, and it will never run out. Study the power of religion. 'Tis the power of religion, and not a name, that will give the comfort I find. There is telling in this providence, and I shall be telling it to eternity. If there be such a glory in His conduct towards me now, what will it be to see the Lamb in the midst of the throne? My peace hath been like a river." Soon after, one of those about him having said, 'You are now putting your seal to that truth, that great is the gain of godliness," he replied, "Yes, indeed." Then said another, "And I hope you are encouraging yourself in the Lord?" On which, not being able to speak, he lifted up his hands and clapped them; and quickly after, went to the land where the weary are at rest.

Fruitful Pastorates.

Chap. iv. ver. 16.—Take heed unto thyself, and unto the doctrine; continue in them: for in doing this thou shalt both save thyself, and them that hear thee.

AT a minister's meeting at Northampton, a question was discussed, to the following purport:—*To what causes in ministers may much of their want of success be imputed?* The answer turned chiefly upon the want of personal religion; particularly the neglect of close dealing with God in *closest prayer*. Jer. x. 21 was referred to: "Their pastors are become *brutish*, and have not *sought* the Lord; therefore they shall not prosper, and their flocks shall be scattered." Another reason assigned was the want of reading and studying the Scriptures more *as Christians*, for the edification of their own souls. "We are too apt to study them," adds Mr. Fuller, "merely to find out something *to say to others*, without living upon the truth ourselves. If we eat not the book, before we deliver its contents to others, we may expect the Holy Spirit will not much accompany us. If we study the Scriptures as *Christians*, and the more familiar we are with them, the more we shall feel their importance; but, if otherwise, our familiarity with the world will be like that of soldiers and doctors with death—it will wear away all sense of its importance from our minds. To enforce this sentiment, Pro. xxii. 17, 18, was referred to—'Apply thine *heart to* knowledge: the words of the wise will be pleasant if thou keep them within thee; they shall withal be fitted in thy lips.' Another reason was, our want of being emptied of *self-sufficiency*. In proportion as we lean upon our own gifts, or parts, or preparations, we slight the Holy Spirit; and no wonder that, being grieved, He should leave us to do our work alone."

Living in Pleasure.

Chap. v. ver. 6.—She that liveth in pleasure, is dead while she liveth.

THE late pious Mrs Judson, referring to her former neglect of religion, says, "The first circumstance which in any measure awakened me from this sleep of death, was the following:—One Sabbath morning, having prepared myself to attend public worship, just as I was leaving my toilet, I accidentally took up Hannah More's Strictures on Female Education, and the words that caught my eye were, '*She that liveth in pleasure, is dead while she liveth.*' They were printed in Italics, with marks of admiration, and they struck me to the heart. I stood for a moment amazed at the incident, and half inclined to think that some invisible agency had directed my eye to these words. At first, I thought I would live a different life, and be more serious and sedate; but at last, I thought that the words were not applicable to me, as I first imagined, and resolved to think no more of them."

Public Rebuke.

Chap. v. ver. 20, 21.—Them that sin, rebuke before all, that others also may fear.—Doing nothing by partiality.

THE late Mr Barton was entertaining himself one day with seeing some of his parishioners catching salmon. At the same time came Colonel Seton with several gentlemen. As the former, who was at that time a justice of the peace, was swearing in a very profane manner, Mr B. thus addressed him: "Sir, you are a justice of the peace, and a gentleman of family and fortune, therefore your example to all should become the state in which kind Providence has placed you." He answered, "Sir, I will not come and swear in your church." This was spoken with great bitterness. Mr B. then left him; but the fishermen afterwards said that the gentleman was very angry, and declared that if the minister had not gone away he would have beaten him. But his future conduct towards Mr B. became the gentleman; for, some time afterwards, Mr B. having some business to transact with the justice, the latter at first sight thanked him for his reproof, but added, that he should not have given it in so public a manner. Mr B. replied, "Sir, my reason for doing so, was because the fishermen who were present are my parishioners; and as swearing is a prevailing vice with them, I am frequently under the necessity of reproving them. Therefore, sir, reflect but a moment and you will see the propriety of what I did, and of the public manner in which I did it. Would not the fishermen have said, that the minister could reprove *them*, but that he was afraid to reprimand the *justice*, had they not witnessed the contrary?" Suffice it to say, that the gentleman was pleased with Mr B.'s remarks, and ever after treated him with the greatest kindness and respect.

Unprofitable Disputations.

Chap. vi. ver. 5.—Perverse disputings of men of corrupt minds, and destitute of the truth.

WHEN Dr Swift was arguing one day, with great coolness, with a gentleman who had become exceedingly warm in the dispute, one of the company asked him how he could keep his temper so well. "The reason is," replied the Dean, "I have truth on my side."

The Dangers of Riches.

Chap. vi. ver. 9.—They that will be rich, fall into temptation and a snare.

MR NEWTON of London, coming out of church, on a Wednesday, a lady stopped him on the steps, and said, "The ticket, of which I held a quarter, is drawn a prize of ten thousand pounds: I know you will congratulate me upon the occasion." "Madam," said he, "as for a friend under temptation, I will endeavour to pray for you."

Giving Freely.

Chap. vi. ver. 18.—That they do good, that they be rich in good works, ready to distribute, willing to communicate.

A RICH old gentleman residing at Manchester, was lately called upon by some members of the Bible Society there, to subscribe his mite; he replied, "he had been thinking about it, but would first wish to become acquainted with their plans," etc., and wished them to call again. Some time after, they did so, and he told them he had made up his mind to subscribe a guinea a-year, and immediately began to count out upon the table a quantity of guineas: when he had got to twenty-one, the gentlemen stopped him, and said, as their time was rather precious, they should feel obliged if he would give his subscription, that they might go. The old gentleman still continuing to count them out upon the table, they interrupted him a second time, when he simply hoped the gentlemen would suffer him to go on, and on he went till he had counted down eighty guineas. "There, gentlemen," cried the old man, "I promised you a subscription of a guinea a-year; I am eighty years old, and there are the eighty guineas."

SECOND TIMOTHY.

Death and Life.

Chap. 1. ver. 10.—Our Saviour Jesus Christ, who hath abolished death, and hath brought life and immortality to light through the gospel.

GENERAL BURN had, during his residence in France, unhappily imbibed infidel sentiments, so far, at one time, as to doubt the immortality of the soul. Though these sentiments and doubts were afterwards removed, not only by a thorough conviction of the truth of Christianity, and after diligent investigation, but by personal experience of the power of religion on his heart, they nevertheless did him lasting injury, and in after life often afforded Satan the means of distressing this holy man. At one period of extreme weakness and suffering, during his last illness, the great enemy of souls was permitted to harass him, by suggesting the thought, that perhaps annihilation would follow death. He mentioned this temptation to one of his children, standing by the bed-side, who replied, "Life and immortality are brought to light by the Gospel." This passage of Scripture immediately dissipated his fears, and proved a shield against the temptations of the devil;—he reclined his head again on the pillow, and for some time after, his beaming countenance indicated the sweetest serenity and joy.

Sound Doctrine.

Chap. i. ver. 13.—Hold fast the form of sound words, which thou hast heard of me, in faith and love which is in Christ Jesus.

THE celebrated Claude, a French minister, said on his death-bed, "I have carefully examined all religions. No one appears to me worthy of the wisdom of God, and capable of leading men to happiness, but the Christian religion. I have diligently studied Popery and Protestantism. The Protestant religion is, I think, the only good religion. It is all founded on the Holy Scriptures, the Word of God. From this, as from a fountain, all religion must be drawn. Scripture is the root, the Protestant religion is the trunk and branches of the tree. It becomes you all to keep steady to it."

Strong through Grace.

Chap. ii. ver. 1.—Be strong in the grace that is in Christ Jesus.

LUTHER relates concerning one Staupicius, a German divine, that he acknowledged that before he came to understand the free and powerful grace of Christ, he resolved, and vowed a hundred times against a particular sin ; yet could never get power over it, nor his heart purified from it, till he came to see that he trusted too much to his own resolutions, and too little to Jesus Christ ; but when his faith had engaged against his sin, he obtained the victory.

The Power of Meekness.

Chap. ii. ver. 25.—In meekness instructing those that oppose themselves ; if God peradventure will give them repentance to the acknowledging of the truth.

DR DWIGHT mentions a man of his acquaintance, of a vehement temper, who had a dispute with a friend, a professor of religion. He met with so much frankness, humility, and kindness in his Christian friend, that, on returning home, he said to himself, "There must be something more in religion than I have hitherto suspected. Were any one to address me in the tone of haughtiness and provocation with which I accosted my friend this evening, it would be impossible for me to preserve the equanimity of which I have been a witness. There is something in this man's disposition which is not in mine. There is something in the religion which he professes, and which I am forced to believe he feels ; something which makes him so superior, so much better, so much more amiable than I can pretend to be. The subject strikes me in a manner to which I have hitherto been a stranger. It is high time to examine it more thoroughly, with more candour, and with greater solicitude than I have done hitherto."

From this incident, a train of thoughts and emotions commenced in the mind of this man, which terminated in his profession of the Christian religion, his relinquishment of the business in which he was engaged, and his consecration of himself to the ministry of the Gospel.

Blasphemers.

Chap. iii. ver. 2.—Men shall be—blasphemers.

SOME time ago, a party of profligate young men were sitting drinking, and, while in a state of intoxication, two of them agreed, for a sum of money, to try their skill in blasphemy;—the prize to be given to him who should be unanimously considered to have poured out the most horrible imprecations and blasphemies. One of them having had greater opportunities of improvement in vice, and being also perfectly familiar with all kinds of sea-slang, was unanimously acknowledged conqueror. Crowned with this hellish honour, he left the place; but not reaching home so soon as was expected, a person was despatch in search of him. The wretched man was found in a field near a ditch, quite dead, and a scythe near him. From the position of the body, it was supposed he had taken up the scythe, intending either to throw it into the ditch for a frolic, or to try his skill at a stroke; but, being in liquor, he had fallen over on the scythe's sharp edge; for he was found lying in a pool of his own blood, with the main artery of his thigh completely cut through. Thus, in a fit of drunkenness, and bearing off the prize as the most accomplished blasphemer, he was hurried into eternity!

Avoid Undesirable Society.

Chap. iii. ver. 5.—From such turn away.

JUDGE BULLER, when in the company of a young gentleman of sixteen, cautioned him against being led astray by the example or persuasion of others, and said, "If I had listened to the advice of some of those who called themselves my friends when I was young, instead of being a judge of the King's Bench, I should have died long ago a prisoner in the King's Bench."

Rebuke Gently.

Chap. iv. ver. 2.—Reprove, rebuke, exhort, with all long-suffering.

THE natural temper of the late Rev. Andrew Fuller of Kettering, though neither churlish nor morose, was not distinguished by gentleness, meekness, or affability. He could rarely be faithful without being severe; and in giving reproof, he was often betrayed into intemperate zeal. Once, at a meeting of ministers, he took occasion to correct an erroneous opinion, delivered by one of his brethren; and he laid on his censure so heavily, that Dr Ryland called out vehemently, in his own peculiar tone of voice, "Brother Fuller! brother Fuller! you can never admonish a mistaken friend, but you must take up a sledge hammer and knock his brains out!"

The Faithful Pastor.

Chap. iv. ver. 5.—Watch thou in all things, endure afflictions, do the work of an evangelist, make full proof of thy ministry.

TO a person who regretted to Dr Johnson that he had not been a clergyman, because he considered the life of a clergyman an easy and comfortable one, the doctor made this memorable reply: "The life of a conscientious clergyman is not easy. I have always considered a clergyman as the father of a larger family than he is able to maintain. No, sir, I do not envy a clergyman's life as an easy life, nor do I envy the clergyman who makes it an easy life."

TITUS.
Disinterestedness.
Chap. i. ver. 7.—Not given to filthy lucre.

IN the reign of James II., Dr Wallis was then Dean of Waterford, in Ireland, and, during the troubles of that unhappy country at that period, suffered greatly in his private fortune, from his strong attachment to the Protestant faith. After peace was restored, and the Protestant religion firmly established by the accession of King William, Wallis was presented at the court of London, as a gentleman who had well merited the royal patronage. The king had before heard the story of his sufferings: and therefore, immediately turning to the Dean, desired him to choose any church preferment then vacant. Wallis, with all the modesty incident to men of real worth, after a due acknowledgment of the royal favour, requested the deanery of Derry. "How," replied the king, in a transport of surprise, "ask the deanery, when you must know the bishopric of that very place is also vacant?" "True, my liege," replied Wallis, "I do know it; but could not in honesty demand so great a benefice, conscious there are many other gentlemen who have suffered more than myself, and deserve better at your Majesty's hands, I therefore presume to repeat my former request." It is needless to add, his request was granted. They parted; the dean highly satisfied with his visit, and the king astonished at the noble instance of disinterestedness of which he had just been a witness.

Pure in Heart.
Chap. i. ver. 15.—Unto the pure, all things are pure.

A LITTLE girl, not six years old, who attended a Sabbath-school, and had just begun to read in the New Testament, was promised a hymn-book, on condition that she would learn to read the fifth and sixth chapters of Matthew's Gospel within the space of a fortnight. She immediately undertook the task, and some time after, when reading to the gentleman who promised the reward, he caused her to stop at the end of the first twelve verses, in order to inquire of her, which of the qualities described in the beatitudes she should desire most to possess. Pausing a little, with a modest smile, she replied, "I would rather be pure in heart." On being asked the reason of her preference, she answered to this effect: "Sir, if I could but obtain a pure heart, I should then possess all the other good qualities spoken of in this chapter."

Sober Minded.
Chap. ii. ver. 6.—Young men likewise exhort to be sober-minded.

THE late Mr Walker, one of the ministers of Edinburgh, was naturally of a sanguine and somewhat choleric temperament; but his manners and general deportment were singularly patient and calm. He used to give the following account of the conquest which he obtained over his constitutional irritability:—"When I was a young man, I had engaged to be at the marriage of a friend, and promised myself much pleasure on the occasion. I dreamed that I was on the way to the scene of festivity, and that I had a bridge to pass over. When I arrived at it, my horse became restive, and would not proceed. I used the whip and spur without success. I dismounted, and lashed him; but all in vain. My passion was excited in a high degree; and the sensations produced by the impetuosity of my temper awoke me. In the instant of awaking, I beheld the bridge fall; while a voice, as I thought struck my ear,—'YOUNG MAN, BE SOBER-MINDED.' The recollection of this circumstance, though a dream, produced a happy effect for the future in my constitutional impatience."

Honesty.

Chap. ii. ver. 10.—Not purloining, but showing all good fidelity.

SELIM, a poor Turk, had been brought up from his youth with care and kindness by his master Mustapha, When the latter lay at the point of death, Selim was tempted by his fellow-servants to join them in stealing a part of Mustapha's treasures. "No," said he, "Selim is no robber! I fear not to offend my master for the evil he can do me now, but for the good he has done me all my life long."

Deserved Rebuke.

Chap. ii. ver. 15,—Rebuke with all authority. Let no man despise thee.

WHEN the late Rev. Mr. King was settled in his congregation of Sorton, they could not furnish him with a manse, or even with lodgings. In these circumstances, a Captain Parr, in the neighbourhood, though a stranger to religion, generously took him into his family, and gave him his board, it is believed, gratuitously. But our young clergyman soon found himself in very unpleasant circumstances, owing to the captain's usual practice of profane swearing. Satisfied of his duty, however, he determined to perform it at all hazards. Accordingly, one day at table, after a very liberal volley of oaths from the captain, he observed calmly, "Captain, you have certainly on the present occasion made use of a number of very improper terms." The captain, who was rather a choleric man, was instantly in a blaze. "Pray, sir, what improper terms have I used?" "Surely, captain, you must know," replied the clergyman with greater coolness, "and having already put me to the pain of hearing them, you cannot be in earnest in imposing upon me the additional pain of repeating them." "You are right, sir," resumed the captain, "you are right. Support your character, and we will respect you. We have a parcel of clergymen around us here, who seem quite uneasy till they get us to understand that we may use any freedoms we please before them, and we despise them." It ought to be known, that the captain never afterwards repeated the offence in his presence, and always treated Mr King with marked respect, and befriended him in all his interests.

Evil Speaking.

Chap. iii. ver. 2.—Speak evil of no man.

THE late Dr Waugh of London had a marked dislike of everything bordering on slander or defamation. The following is an illustration of his character in this point.—One of his people had travelled all the way from Newtown to his father's, where he usually resided, to communicate to him an unfavourable report concerning another member of his congregation. Some friends being with him, this person was requested to stay and dine with him. After dinner, he took occasion, in a jocular manner, to ask each person, in his turn, how far he had ever known a man travel to tell an evil report of his neighbour, when some gave one reply, and some another; he at last came to this individual, but without waiting for his self-condemning reply, or necessarily exposing him, Dr Waugh stated, that he had lately met with a Christian professor, apparently so zealous for the honour of the church, as to walk fourteen miles with no other object than that of making known to his minister the failings of a brother member. He then in a warm and impressive manner enlarged on the praise of that "charity which covers a multitude of sins; which rejoiceth not in iniquity, but rejoiceth in the truth."

Unprofitable Controversies.

Chap. iii. ver. 9.—Avoid foolish questions, and genealogies, and contentions, and strivings about the law; for they are unprofitable and vain.

WHILE Melancthon was at Spires, he paid a visit to Bretten, to see his mother. This good woman asked him, What she must believe, amidst these disputes? She repeated to him the prayers she was used to make, and which contained nothing that was superstitious. "Continue," said he, "to believe and pray as you have done hitherto, and never trouble yourself about controversies."

PHILEMON.

Faithful unto Death.

Ver. 9.—Being such as one as Paul the aged.

IN a letter, the late Rev. Rowland Hill remarks,—"Old as I am, I am just returned from a long missionary ramble; but I feel I am getting old. O that I may work well to the last!" In all his journeys, even when he had reached a period beyond that usually allotted to man, he was disconcerted if he did not find a pulpit ready for him every evening. In one of his letters, fixing his days for preaching on his road to some place, he says, "Ever since my Master has put me into office, I have ever esteemed it my duty to remember His admonition, 'As ye go, preach.'" His general answer to invitations to houses on his route was, "I shall be happy to come to you, if you can find me a place to preach in."

Preaching while a Prisoner.

Ver. 10.—Onesimus, whom I have begotten in my bonds.

THE Rev. Dr. Malan happened, at one time, to be in the adjoining territory of Savoy, where Romish surveillance is perpetually on the alert. He was suspected as chargeable with the offence of distributing tracts obnoxious to the Roman Catholics; he was seized, and, under the custody of two *gens d'armes*, sent to prison. The charge was without evidence or foundation, and he was not detained; but, nothing daunted by his situation, and conceiving the opportunity to be important and favourable, he preached the Gospel to the poor fellows who attended him in the carriage which conveyed them to the prison; and there is good reason for believing that one of these soldiers, employed to incarcerate the ambassador of Christ, was himself brought to the Saviour, and introduced into the glorious liberty of the sons of God.

Changed.

Ver. 11.—Which in time past was to thee unprofitable, but now profitable to thee and to me.

SOME time ago, the Rev. Rowland Hill preached a funeral sermon, occasioned by the death of his man-servant. In the course of his sermon, he delivered the following affecting relation:—"Many persons present," he said, "were acquainted with the deceased, and have had it in their power to observe his character and conduct. They can bear witness, that for a considerable number of years he proved himself a perfectly honest, sober, industrious, and religious man, faithfully performing, as far as lay in his power, the duties of his station in life, and serving God with constancy and zeal. Yet this very man was once a robber on the highway. More than thirty years ago, he stopped me on the public road, and demanded my money. Not at all intimidated, I argued with him; I asked him what could induce him to pursue so iniquitous and dangerous a course of life? 'I have been a coachman,' said he, 'I am out of place, and I cannot get a character. I am unable to get any employment, and am therefore obliged to resort to this means of gaining a subsistence.' I desired him to call on me. He promised he would, and he kept his word. I talked further with him, and offered to take him into my own service. He consented, and ever since that period, he has served me faithfully, and not me only, but has faithfully served his God. Instead of finishing his life in a public and ignominious manner, with a depraved and hardened mind, as he probably would have done, he died in peace, and, we trust, prepared for the society of just men made perfect. Till this day, the extraordinary circumstance I have related has been confined to his breast and mine. I have never mentioned it to my dearest friend."

HEBREWS.

The Great Creator.

Chap. i. ver. 2.—By whom also he made the worlds.

HERSCHEL estimates the star Lyra to be more than fifty-four thousand times larger than the sun, which fills a cubical space equal to 681,471,000,000,000,000 miles; 100,000,000 of such stars lie within range of the telescope, and between every two there is an interval of more than 200,000,000,000 miles of space. Who can think of what lies beyond the telescopic view? In such a thought, is not the mind lost in sublimity and grandeur?

God's Son.

Chap. i. ver. 6.—When he bringeth in the first-begotten into the world, he saith, And let all the angels of God worship him.

IT was during the reign of Theodosius the Great, in the 4th century, that the Arians, through the lenity of the emperor, made their most vigorous attempts to undermine the doctrine of the divinity of Jesus Christ. The event, however, of his making his son Arcadius partner with himself on his throne, was happily overruled to his seeing the God-dishonouring character of their creed. Among the bishops who came to congratulate him on the occasion, was the famous and esteemed Ampilochus, who, it is said, had suffered much under the Arian persecution. He approached the emperor, and making a very handsome and dutiful address, was going to take his leave. "What," said Theodosius, "do you take no notice of my son? Do you not know that I have made him a partner with me in the empire?" Upon this the good old bishop went to young Arcadius, then about sixteen years of age, and putting his hand upon his head, said, "The Lord bless thee, my son!" and immediately drew back. Even this did not satisfy the emperor. "What," said he, "is this all the respect you pay to a prince, that I have made of equal dignity with myself?" Upon this, the bishop arose, and looking the emperor in the face, with a tone of voice solemnly indignant, said, "Sire, do you so highly resent my apparent neglect of your son, because I do not give him equal honour with yourself? What must the eternal God think of you, who have allowed his co-equal and co-eternal Son to be degraded in His proper divinity in every part of your empire?" This was as a two-edged sword in the heart of the emperor. He felt the reproof to be just and confounding, and no longer would seem to give the least indulgence to that creed, which did not secure divine glory to the "Prince of Peace."

Acceptance of the Atonement.

Chap. ii. ver. 3.—How shall we escape if we neglect so great salvation?

MR BLACKADDER has recorded some instances of the powerful influence of the preaching of Mr Welsh, a contemporary minister. "At one time, after having removed all impediments that might hinder sinners from embracing the salvation offered in the Gospel, he said at the conclusion, 'I must enter my protestation in my Master's name against any here who will not close with the offer, and give their consent.' A woman in the company cried out, 'Hold your hand, sir; do it not, for I give my consent.'"

A minister of the Gospel thus began his address from the pulpit, to his hearers:—"My brethren, I have a very solemn question to propose to you this day. It is a question of the greatest importance; and it is of such a nature that neither you nor I can answer it. No man, not all the men on earth, nay, Satan, with all his knowledge, cannot answer it. No saint in heaven, nor can the highest archangel; nay, the great God Himself cannot answer it. The question is this, 'How shall we escape if we neglect so great salvation?'"

The Fear of Death.

Chap. ii. ver. 15.—And deliver them who, through fear of death, were all their lifetime subject to bondage.

A PERSON who died some years ago, lived in the house of a pious friend, to whom he often communicated his distressing apprehensions. He was not so much disturbed with doubts respecting his interest in Christ, as terrified with the thoughts of dying: and said he thought he should need three or four persons to hold him, if he apprehended death was at hand. His friend proposed scriptual antidotes to this unreasonable dread; and encouraged him to expect that, as his day, so should his strength be. After long illness, the time of his departure approached; and he often expressed a wish that his friend could always be with him. Finding himself dying, he repeatedly sent for his friend to pray with him. He felt uneasy, and said, "Satan whispers that I have been a deceiver, and shall die a hypocrite." He asked his friend to pray again with him, after which he cried, "The Lord is come! Praise God, praise God!" He then lifted up both his hands, which, from weakness, he could scarcely raise before, and several times repeated, "Victory, victory, victory, through the blood of the Lamb!" and expired with the unfinished word on his lips.

The Maker of All.

Chap. iii. ver. 4.—Every house is builded by some man, but he that built all things is God.

"SEE here," says Mr Robinson, "I hold a Bible in my hand, and you see the cover, the leaves, the letters, the words, but you do not see the writers or the printer, the letter-founder, the ink-maker, the paper-maker, or the binder. You never did see them, you never will see them; and yet there is not one of you who will think of disputing or denying the being of these men. I go further, I affirm that you see the very souls of these men, in seeing this book, and you feel yourselves obliged to allow that, by the contrivance, design, memory, fancy, reason, and so on. In the same manner, if you see a picture, you judge there was a painter; if you see a house, you judge there was a builder of it; and if you see a room contrived for this purpose, and another for that, a door to enter, and a window to admit light, a chimney to hold fire, you conclude that the builder was a person of skill and forecast, who formed the house with a view to the accommodation of its inhabitants. In this manner, examine the world, and pity the man who, when he sees the sign of a wheat-sheaf, hath sense enough to know that there is a joiner, and somewhere a painter; but who, when he sees the wheat-sheaf itself, is so stupid, as not to say to himself, this had a wise and good Creator."

The Present Time.

Chap. iii. ver. 15.—To-day, if ye will hear his voice, harden not your hearts.

A GENTLEMAN wishing to convey, together with a gentle reproof, a useful lesson to his gardener, who had neglected to prop a valuable fruit-tree, until it was damaged by a high wind, observed, "You see, gardener, the danger of putting off, from day to day, the doing of any necessary work; yet, in this way, foolish men defer their repentance from one day to another, until, in some unexpected moment, the wind of death comes and blows them into eternity."

Sure Work.

Chap. iv. ver. 1.—Let us therefore fear, lest, a promise being left us of entering into his rest, any of you should seem to come short of it.

MR PHILIP HENRY said to some of his neighbours who came to see him on his death-bed, "O make sure work for your souls, my friends, by getting an interest in Christ while you are in health. If I had that work to do now, what would become of me? I bless

God, I am satisfied. See to it, all of you, that your work be not undone when your time is done, lest you be undone for ever."

Believing on Christ.

Chap. iv. ver. 3.—We which have believed do enter into rest.

MR STEWART, in his journal of a residence in the Sandwich Islands, speaking of a converted sailor, says. "Rae is one of the happiest of creatures. All he says is worth twice its real value, from the manner in which it is communicated. He last night related to me a conversation he had with Carr, a few days since. Carr came to him with a spirit greatly troubled, and wished to know in what manner he had obtained the light and liberty he appeared to enjoy; adding, I believe the Bible to be true, and every word of it to be from God. I know that I can be saved only by the redemption of Jesus Christ. I feel my misery as a sinner. *I believe every thing, but how am I to believe so as to be saved?* I want faith, and how am I to get it? Rae told him it was just so with himself once. I did not know what faith was, or how to obtain it; but I know now what it is, and believe I possess it. But I do not know that I can tell you what it is, or how to get it. I can tell you what it is not. It is not *knocking off swearing, and drinking, and such like;* and it is not *reading the Bible, nor praying, nor being good.* It is none of these; for, even if they would answer for the time to come, there is the *old score* still, and how are you to get clear of that? It is not anything you have done, or can do; it is only believing, and trusting to what *Christ has done.* It is forsaking your sins, and looking for their pardon, and the salvation of your soul, because He died and shed His blood for sin; and it is nothing else. A doctor of divinity might have given poor Carr a more technical and polished answer, but not one more simple or probably satisfactory."

Sympathy with the Ignorant.

Chap. v. ver. 2.—Who can have compassion on the ignorant, and on them that are out of the way.

"I RECEIVED a most useful hint," says Cecil, "from Dr Bacon, then father of the University, when I was at college. I used frequently to visit him at his living, near Oxford; he would frequently say to me, 'What are you doing? What are your studies?' 'I am reading so and so.' 'You are quite wrong. When I was young, I could turn any piece of Hebrew into Greek verse with ease. But when I came into this parish, and had to teach ignorant people, I was wholly at a loss; I had no furniture. They thought me a great man, but that was their ignorance; for I knew as little as they did of what it was most important for them to know. Study chiefly what you can turn to good account in your future life."

Explicit Teaching.

Chap. v. ver. 12.—Ye have need that one teach you again which be the principles of the oracles of God, and are become such as have need of milk, and not of strong meat.

MR GRIMSHAW once apologized for the length of his discourse, to this effect:—" If I were in some situations, I might not think it needful to speak so much; but many of my hearers, who are wicked and careless, are likewise very ignorant, and very slow of apprehension. If they do not understand me, I cannot hope to do them good; and when I think of the uncertainty of life, and perhaps it may be the last opportunity afforded, and that it is possible I may never see them again, till I meet them in the great day, I know not how to be explicit enough; I endeavour to set the subject in a variety of lights; I express the same thoughts in different words, and can scarcely tell how to leave off, lest I should have omitted something, for the want of which my preaching and their hearing might prove in vain; and thus, though I fear I weary others, I am still unable to satisfy myself."

Putting Christ to Shame.

Chap. vi. ver. 6.—They crucify to themselves the Son of God afresh, and put him to an open shame.

BRIDAINE, a celebrated French preacher, discoursing on the passion of Christ, expressed himself thus:—"A man, accused of a crime of which he was innocent, was condemned to death by the iniquity of his judges. He was led to punishment, but no gibbet was prepared, nor was there any executioner to perform the sentence. The people, moved with compassion, hoped that this sufferer would escape death. But one man raised his voice, and said, 'I am going to prepare a gibbet, and I will be the executioner.' You groan with indignation! Well, my brethren, in each of you I behold this cruel man. There are no Jews here to-day, to crucify Jesus Christ; but you dare to rise up and say, 'I will crucify Him.'" These words, pronounced by the preacher, though very young, with all the dignity of an apostle, and with the most powerful emotion, produced such effect, that nothing was heard but the sobs of the auditory.

Our Hope.

Chap. vi. ver. 19.—Which hope we have as an anchor of the soul, both sure and stedfast, and which entereth into that within the vail.

MR W. COWPER, sometime minister of Stirling, and afterwards Bishop of Galloway, thus spoke of his dissolution to his weeping friends: "Death is somewhat dreary, and the streams of that Jordan between us and our Canaan run furiously, but they stand still when the ark comes. Let your anchor be cast within the vail, and fastened to the rock Jesus. Let the end of the threefold cord be buckled to the heart; so shall ye go through."

Made Perfect.

Chap. vii. ver. 19.—The law made nothing perfect, but the bringing in of a better hope did; by the which we draw nigh unto God.

A LADY who was in the habit of close attendance on the Princess Amelia, during her last illness, described some of the latter intercourses which took place between the princess and her royal father, George III., and which seldom failed to turn on the momentous topic of the future world, as being singularly affecting. "My dear child," said his majesty to her, on one of these occasions, "you have ever been a good child to your parents; we have nothing wherewith to reproach you; but I need not tell you, that it is not of yourself alone that you can be saved, and that your acceptance with God must depend on your faith and trust in the merits of the Redeemer." "I know it," replied the princess, mildly, but emphatically, "and I could wish for no better trust."

Saving to the Uttermost.

Chap. vii. ver. 25.—He is able also to save them to the uttermost that come unto God by him, seeing he ever liveth to make intercession for them.

"I WAS one morning called from my study," said a minister at a naval station, to a person who wished to see me. "When I entered the room, his appearance reminded me of Covey, being a sailor with a wooden leg, who, with tears in his eyes, said, 'Here's another Covey come to see you sir.' I replied, 'I am glad to see you, Covey; sit down.' He then informed me that he was a Swede, had been some years in the British service, had lost his limb in the action of the 1st of June, under Lord Howe, and was now cook of one of his majesty's ships in ordinary; it was with reluctance he came into this port, from some report he had heard unfavourable to the place. He had been for some years married to an Englishwoman, who, when on shore, having seen for sale a tract, with the picture of a sailor in the act of having his legs cut off, was induced to purchase it, supposing that it might contain something that would please her husband. It was the tract of COVEY THE SAILOR, which he read with uncommon interest, as he had known him, and had heard of him as having been a brave seaman. He had, previously to this, felt at times considerable compunction for his sins, and fear of future misery, but knew nothing of the Saviour through whom his sins were to be pardoned. He observed, 'When I read the tract, I there saw my own character. Though I thought I could fight as well as Covey, I was afraid I could not die so well. When I came to that part that none need to despair, since poor blaspheming Covey had found mercy, I wept, and took courage. After having read it over many times, I resolved I would hear the minister that Covey heard. I did so; and here I heard of that Saviour who is able and willing to save my soul to the uttermost, and who I humbly hope and believe has saved me.'"

The Better Covenant.

Chap. viii. ver. 6.—He is the mediator of a better covenant, which was established upon better promises.

MR LYFORD, a puritan divine, a few days before his dissolution, being desired by his friends to give them some account of his hope and comforts, he replied, "I will let you know how it is with me, and on what ground I stand. Here is the grave, the wrath of God, and devouring flames, the great punishment of sin, on the one hand; and here am I, a poor sinful creature on the other; but this is my comfort, the covenant of grace, established upon so many sure promises, hath satisfied all. The act of oblivion passed in heaven is, 'I will forgive their iniquities, and their sins will I remember no more, saith the Lord.' This is the blessed privilege of all within the covenant, of whom I am one. For I find the Spirit, which is promised, bestowed upon me, in the blessed effects of it upon my soul, as the pledge of God's eternal love. By this I know my interest in Christ, who is the foundation of the covenant; and therefore, my sins being laid on Him, shall never be charged on me."

All shall know Him.

Chap. viii. ver. 11.—All shall know me, from the least to the greatest.

THE Diary of Mrs Savage abounds with expressions of concern for her children. At one time she writes,—"I read in course, in my closet, Isaiah liv. with the exposition. I was much affected with the 13th verse, 'And all thy children shall be taught of the Lord.' Though it is spoken of the church's children, I would apply it to my own children, in particular, and desire to act faith on it. I am caring and endeavouring that they may be taught and instructed in the good way. This is the inward desire of my soul. Now, saith God, they shall be taught of *Me*, and *all* thy children shall,—a sweet promise, it much satisfies me ; Lord, set in with poor parents, who desire nothing in the world so much as to see their children walk in the narrow way that leads to life."

The Eternal Inheritance.

Chap. ix. ver. 15.—He is the mediator of the New Testament, that by means of death, for the redemption of transgressions, they which are called might receive the promise of eternal inheritance.

MR JOHN AVERY, a pious minister, having been driven from his native country by the persecution of Archbishop Laud, fled to New England. Upon his arrival, he settled for a short time at Newbury ; but, receiving an invitation to Marble Head, he determined upon a removal to that place. Having embarked in a small vessel, together with Mr Anthony Thacker, another worthy minister, there arose a most tremendous storm, by which the vessel struck against a rock, and was dashed to pieces. The whole company, consisting of twenty-three persons, got upon the rock, but were successively washed off and drowned, except Mr Thacker and his wife. Mr Thacker and Mr Avery held each other by the hand a long time, resolving to die together, till, by a tremendous wave, the latter was washed away, and drowned. The moment before this happened, he lifted up his eyes to heaven, saying, "We know not what the pleasure of God may be. I fear we have been too unmindful of former deliverances. Lord, I cannot challenge a promise of the preservation of my life ; but Thou hast promised to deliver us from sin and condemnation, and to bring us safe to heaven, through the all-sufficient satisfaction of Jesus Christ. He had no sooner uttered these words, than he was swept into the mighty deep, and no more seen. Mr Thacker and his wife were also washed off the rock ; but, after being tossed in the waves for some time, the former was cast on shore, where he found his wife a sharer in the deliverance.

Death and Judgment.

Chap. ix. ver. 27, 28.—It is appointed unto men once to die, but after this the judgment : so Christ was once offered to bear the sins of many.

DEATH and judgment can be contemplated with comfort only in connection with a believing view of the atonement of Christ :

"Death's terror is the mountain faith removes."

The late Rev. Archibald Hall of London, when in Scotland, being on a visit to a dying Christian at Borrowstounness, after much serious conversation, he took hold of Mr Hall's hand, and said, "Now, sir, I can with as much pleasure take hold of death by its cold hand. You may justly wonder at this ; for I see and believe myself to be most unworthy ; but, at the same time, I see Christ to be my great propitiation, and faith in His blood gives me ease. I see myself all vile and polluted, but I view Jesus as the fountain opened, and faith in Him supports me under a sense of my vileness."

Sinning Wilfully.

Chap. x. ver. 26, 27.—For if we sin wilfully, after that we have received the knowledge of the truth, there remaineth no more sacrifice for sins; but a certain fearful looking for of judgment and fiery indignation, which shall devour the adversaries.

"I WAS lately," observed Mr Gunn, "called to attend the death-bed of a young man at Hoxton. On my entering the room, I found him in the greatest horror of mind. Thinking perhaps it arose from that deep remorse sometimes attendant on the death-bed of a sinner, I began to point him to Jesus, the sinner's only friend, and to the glorious promises of the Gospel; when, with an agonizing look of despair, he replied, 'Ah! sir, but I've rejected the Gospel. Some years since, I unhappily read Paine's Age of Reason,—it suited my corrupt taste—I imbibed its principles: after this, wherever I went, I did all that lay in my power to hold up the Scriptures to contempt; by this means I led others into the fatal snare, and made proselytes to infidelity. Thus I rejected God, and now He rejects me.' I offered to pray by him, but he replied, 'O no,—it is all in vain to pray for me.' Then, with a dismal groan, he cried out, 'Paine's Age of Reason has ruined my soul!' and instantly expired."

Confidence in Christ.

Chap. x. ver. 35.—Cast not away therefore your confidence, which hath great recompense of reward.

AN eminent minister was much troubled with doubts and fears concerning his *own* salvation, and many of his hearers who laboured under similar distress coming daily to him for direction increased the burden. One day, after much wrestling with God in prayer for deliverance, it was impressed on his mind to go to such a place, and he would find a person that would be of spiritual use to him. Accordingly, on passing through his own church-yard, he met a very aged man, to whom the minister observed, "It is a good day." The old man answered, "I never saw a bad day in my life-time." At hearing this, the minister, fetching a deep sigh, asked him, "How it was that he, who appeared to be so old a man, had never seen a bad day?" To which the other replied, "My mind is so sunk into the will of God, that, knowing His unerring wisdom and goodness, whatever is *His* will is *my* will." "And what," said the minister, "if God was to cast you into hell, would you be resigned to His will in that particular?" To which it was answered, "God hath given me two long arms—the arm of *faith* and the arm of *hope*, and was the Lord even to cast me into hell, I would not let go my hold of Him." This simple word was so blessed to the afflicted minister, that from thenceforward he could *rejoice* in the Lord as his God.

Drawing Back.

Chap. x. ver. 38.—If any man draw back, my soul shall have no pleasure in him.

"I KNEW a man," says Bunyan, "that was once, as I thought, hopefully awakened about his condition. Yea, I knew *two* that were so awakened. But, in course of time, they began to draw back, and to incline again to their lusts. Wherefore God gave them up to the company of three or four men, that in less than three years brought them round to the gallows, where they were hanged like dogs, because they refused to live like honest men."

Dying in Faith.

Chap. xi. ver. 13.—These all died in faith.

A CLERGYMAN having occasion to wait on the late Princess Charlotte, was thus addressed by her:—"Sir, I understand you are a clergyman." "Yes, Madam." "Of the Church of England?" "Yes." "Permit me to ask your opinion, sir, what is it that can make a death-bed easy?" The clergyman was startled at so serious a question from a young and blooming female of so high rank, and modestly expressed his surprise that she should consult him, when she had access to many much more capable of answering the inquiry. She replied, that she had proposed it to many, and wished to collect various opinions on this important subject. The clergyman then felt it his duty to be explicit, and affectionately recommended to her the study of the Scriptures, which, as he stated, uniformly represent faith in the Lord Jesus Christ as the only means to make a death-bed easy. "Ah!" said she, bursting into tears, "that is what my grandfather often told me; but then he used to add, that besides reading the Bible, I must pray for the Holy Spirit to understand its meaning."

Blessing in Faith.

Chap. xi. ver. 21.—By faith Jacob, when he was dying, blessed both the sons of Joseph.

A FEW days previous to his death, the late Rev. Dr Belfrage of Falkirk, hearing his infant son's voice in an adjoining room, desired that he should be brought to him. When the child was lifted into the bed, the dying father placed his hands upon his head, and said in the language of Jacob, "The God before whom my fathers did walk, the God who fed me all my life long to this day, the Angel who redeemed me from all evil, *bless the lad*." When the boy was removed, he added, "Remember and tell John Henry of this; tell him of these prayers, and how earnest I was that he might become early acquainted with his father's God."

Author and Finisher of Faith.

Chap. xii. ver. 2.—Looking unto Jesus, the author and finisher of our faith.

MR EDWARD RIDDELL, an aged Christian in Hull, remarked a few days before his death, to one present: "Some may suppose, that a person at my time of life, and after so long making a profession of religion, has nothing to do but to die and go to heaven; but I find that I have as much need to go to God, through Christ, as a sinner, at the last hour as at the beginning. The blood of Christ, the death of Christ, His victory and fulness, are my only ground of faith, hope, and confidence; there is the same need of Him to be the Finisher of my faith as there was to be the Author of it."

Earthly and Heavenly Fathers.

Chap. xii. ver. 9.—We have had fathers of our flesh which corrected us, and we gave them reverance: shall we not much rather be in subjection to the Father of spirits, and live?

THE son of a minister, lately deceased, had by some means excited the displeasure of his father. His father thought it right to be *reserved* for an hour or two, and when asked a question about the business of the day, he was very short in his answer to his son. The time was nearly arrived when the youth was to repeat his lessons. He came into his father's study, and said, "Papa, I cannot learn my lesson unless you are reconciled; I am sorry I have offended you, I hope you will forgive me, I think I shall never offend you again."

His father replied, "All I wish is to make you sensible of your fault; when you acknowledge it, you know all is easily reconciled with me." "Then, papa," said he, "give the token of reconciliation, and seal it with a kiss." The hand was given, and the seal most heartily exchanged on each side. "Now," exclaimed the dear boy, "I will learn Latin and Greek with anybody;" and fled to his little study. "Stop, stop," cried his father, "have you not a heavenly Father? If what you have done be evil, *He* is displeased, and you must apply to *Him* for forgiveness." With tears starting in his eyes, he said, "Papa, *I went to Him first;* I knew except He was reconciled, I could do nothing;" and with tears, he said, "I hope He has forgiven me, and now I am happy." His father never had occasion to look at him with a shade of disapprobation from that time till his death.

Fitness for Heaven.

Chap. xii. ver. 14.—Follow—holiness, without which no man shall see the Lord.

A PIOUS military officer, desirous to ascertain what were the real feelings and views of a dying soldier, whom he had been instrumental in bringing to the saving knowledge of the truth, respecting the heavenly rest into which "I felt assured," says the officer, "he was about to enter, I said, some time after his awakening to a sense of his ruined state, 'William, I am going to ask you a strange question; suppose you could carry your sins with you to heaven, would that satisfy you?' The poor dying lad replied, with a most affecting smile, 'Why, sir, what sort of a heaven would that be to me? I would be just like a *pig in a parlour.*' I need not add," continues the officer, "that he was panting after a heaven of holiness, and was convinced that if he died in sin, he would be quite out of his element in the heaven of purity."

Contentment.

Chap. xiii. ver. 5.—Be content with such things as ye have.

"WE have heard," said a gentleman to Thomas Mann, a pious waterman on the Thames, "that teaching the poor to read has a tendency to make them discontented with the station in which Providence has placed them. Do you think so?" "No, sir, quite the contrary. All that I have read in the Bible teaches me to be content with the dispensations of Providence, to be industrious and careful. A Christian cannot be an idle or an ungrateful man."

The Earnest Pastor.

Chap. xiii. ver. 17.—They watch for your souls, as they that must give an account.

"I VISIT and examine every district of my large congregation," says Dr Henry Belfrage, in a letter, "every year. My father did so; and though the increasing population of the country has enlarged the congregation considerably, I follow his example. Though urged by my friends to lessen my labour, I still go on; and my vigorous health fits me for a toil that would be oppressive to others. Old Mr Shirra of Kirkcaldy, of whom you must have heard, used sometimes to say to his brethren, when urging them to hard service, 'You will not look the worse at the day of judgment.'"

JAMES.

Yielding to Temptation.

Chap. i. ver. 14, 15.—Every man is tempted, when he is drawn away by his own lust, and enticed. Then, when the lust hath conceived, it bringeth forth sin; and sin, when it is finished, bringeth forth death.

MANY years since, two men were executed at Carlisle for burglary. A minister then living in that city was moved by compassion for the men, and applied to the judge for a respite; he was informed, that on account of the cruelty attending the robbery, capital punishment must be inflicted. His lordship recommended their humane intercessor to use the only means which could now be available to the culprits, in preparing them by Christian instruction for the awful change which awaited them. In the course of his benevolent visits to this gloomy abode, he questioned the prisoners how they had been led from the path of honesty to commit such crimes. In answer to these inquires, one of the unhappy men declared that his first step to ruin was, *taking a half-penny out of his mother's pocket while she was asleep.* From this sin he was led, by small but fatal degrees, to the crimes for which he was so soon to suffer a shameful death.

What is Pure Religion?

Chap. i. ver. 27.—Pure religion, and undefiled, before God and the Father, is this: to visit the fatherless and widows in their affliction, and to keep himself unspotted from the world.

A LITTLE girl, who used to read the Bible to a poor sick woman, who could not read herself, was asked by a gentleman in the Sabbath school at which she attended, why she visited this woman? "Because, sir," said she, "I find it said in the Bible, 'Pure religion and undefiled, before God and the Father, is this, to visit the fatherless and widows in their affliction.'"

The Rich.

Chap. ii. ver. 6.—Do not rich men oppress you?

A RICH man, who was oppressive and unjust, was once overheard speaking thus to himself: "I would willingly give one-half of my wealth to be beloved and respected by my neighbours; but that is impossible; for I have wronged them too much either to love them, or to be beloved by them." This man, in the midst of his riches was poor.

Do not Kill.

Chap. ii, ver. 11.—If thou kill, thou art become a transgressor of the law.

WHEN Dr Donne took possession of his first living, he took a walk into the churchyard, where the sexton was digging a grave, and throwing up a skull. The doctor took it up, and found a rusty headless nail sticking in the temple, which he drew out secretly, and wrapt in the corner of his handkerchief. He then demanded of the grave-digger whether he knew whose skull that was. He said it was a man's who kept a brandy shop, an honest drunken fellow, who one night having taken two quarts, was found dead in his bed next morning. "Had he a wife?" "Yes." "What character does she bear?" "A very good one; only the neighbours reflect on her, because she married the day after her husband was buried." This was enough for the doctor, who, under the pretence of visiting his parishioners, called on her; he asked her several questions, and among others, what sickness her husband had died of. She gave him the same account he had received; upon this he suddenly opened the handkerchief, and cried in an authoritative voice, "Woman, do you know this nail?" She was struck with horror at the unexpected demand, instantly owned the fact, was tried, and executed.

Real Benevolence.

Chap. ii. ver. 15, 16.—If a brother or sister be naked, or destitute of daily food, and one of you say unto them, Depart in peace, be ye warmed and filled, etc.

"NEAR Fua, on my way to Cairo," says Mr Lieder, missionary in Egypt, "when we sailed near the shore, eight or ten naked boys ran along after us, begging alms; and before I could throw them some bread, my Reis (captain of the vessel) repeatedly called to them, 'May God give you; may God help you;' a most common custom in Egypt, when a man will give nothing. I never was so much struck with this custom as now, when it brought to my recollection the practices which St James so strikingly censures.

Ships of the Sea.

Chap. iii. ver. 4.—Behold also the ships.

THE Rev. John Williams, when dining on one occasion with a party of naval gentlemen, a captain present turned to him, and said, "Well, Mr Williams, I and several of my naval friends have read your book (Narrative of Missionary Enterprises); and if you will allow me to be candid, I may tell you, that we can receive it all except that story about the building of a ship; but this really exceeds our belief." "I am very glad, sir," said Mr W., "that you have expressed your doubt now, because there is the Captain who was at Raiatea shortly after 'The Messenger of Peace' arrived there, and to whom therefore I shall refer you for information respecting her." The officer to whom this appeal was made, then described the vessel, and gave such details respecting her as entirely removed the incredulity of the inquirer, and deeply interested the whole company.

The Boastful Spirit.

Chap. iii. ver. 5.—The tongue is a little member, and boasteth great things.

MR CARTER, an eminent minister, being invited to dine, together with several other ministers, at the house of a respectable magistrate at Ipswich, a very vain person who sat at table boasted that he would dispute with any gentleman present, upon any question that should be proposed, either in divinity or philosophy. A profound silence ensued, till Mr Carter addressed him in these words:— "I will go no further than my plate to puzzle you. Here is a *sole;* now tell me the reason why this fish, which hath always lived in *salt* water, should come out *fresh?*" As the bold challenger did not so much as attempt any answer, the scorn and laughter of the company were presently turned on him.

Nearness to God.

Chap. iv. ver. 8.—Draw nigh to God, and he will draw nigh to you.

"I WOULD not," says Mrs Berry in her Diary, "be hired out of my closet for a thousand worlds. I never enjoy such hours of

JAMES

pleasure, and such free and entire communion with God, as I have here; and I wonder that any can live prayerless, and deprive themselves of the greatest privilege allowed to them."

Evil Speaking.

Chap. iv. ver. 11.—Speak not evil one of another, brethren.

DR WAUGH being in company with a number of ministers, the bad conduct of a brother in the ministry became the subject of conversation, and every gentleman in the room joined warmly in condemning him. Dr Waugh sat for a long time silent. At last he walked up to his companions and said, "My dear friends, surely we are not acting in accordance with our profession. The person you speak of is one of ourselves, and we ought not to blow the coal. But do you know that he is as bad a man as he is represented? and if he is, will railing against him do any good? It is cowardly to speak ill of a man behind his back; and I doubt if any of us would have sufficient courage, if our poor friend were to appear among us, to sit down and kindly tell him of his faults. If there be one here who feels himself quite pure, and free from error, let him throw the first stone; but if not, let us be silent, and I confess that I feel that I must not say one word." He resumed his seat, and the company looked at each other, struck silent by this rebuke from one so good and mild.

Profane Swearing.

Chap. v. ver. 12.—Above all things, my brethren, swear not, neither by heaven, neither by the earth, neither by any other oath.

THE late excellent Mr Jack of Glasgow was remarkable for the cheerfulness as well as the fervour of his piety. When he administered a reproof, it was frequently accompanied with a kind of pleasantry, which fixed the attention, and disarmed the resentment of the person whom he addressed. Being once in company when a gentleman occasionally embellished his discourse with the names of devil, deuce, etc., and at last also took the name of God in vain— "Stop, sir," said the old man; "I said nothing while you used only freedoms with the name of your own master, but I insist you shall use no freedoms with the name of mine."

Faith Healing.

Chap. v. ver. 15.—The prayer of faith shall save the sick.

A CLERGYMAN, some time since, concluding a sermon to youth, took occasion to press upon parents the duty of parental faith, and illustrated its power in the following manner:—"About two-and-twenty years ago, a little circle were met around the apparently dying couch of a male infant; the man of God who led their devotions, seemed to forget the sickness of the child in his prayer for his future usefulness. He prayed for the child who had been consecrated to God at its birth, as a man, a Christian, and a minister of the word. The parents laid hold of the horns of the altar, and prayed with him. The child recovered, grew towards manhood, ran far in the ways of folly and sin. One after another of that little circle ascended to heaven; but two of them at least, and one of them the mother, lived to hear him proclaim the everlasting Gospel. It is," said the preacher, "no fiction; that child, that prodigal youth, that preacher, *is he who now addresses you.*"

FIRST PETER.

Love to Christ.

Chap. i. ver. 8.—Whom having not seen, ye love.

JOHN LAMBERT suffered in the year 1538. No man was used at the stake with more cruelty than this holy martyr. They burnt him with a slow fire by inches; for if it kindled higher and stronger than they chose, they removed it away. When his legs were burnt off, and his thighs were mere stumps in the fire, they pitched his poor body upon pikes, and lacerated his broiling flesh with their halberts. But God was with him in the midst of the flame, and supported him in all the anguish of nature. Just before he expired, he lifted up such hands as he had all flaming with fire, and cried out to the people with his dying voice, "None but Christ! None but Christ!" He was at last beat down into the fire, and expired.

Perseverance in the Faith.

Chap. i. ver. 13.—Be sober, and hope to the end for the grace that is to be brought unto you at the revelation of Jesus Christ.

"WE read," says Townson, "that, in certain climates of the world, the gales that spring from the land carry a refreshing smell out to sea, and assure the watchful pilot that he is approaching to a desirable and fruitful coast, when as yet he cannot discern it with his eyes. And, to take up once more the comparison of life to a voyage, in like manner it fares with those who have steadily and religiously pursued the course which heaven pointed out to them. We shall sometimes find, by their conversation towards the end of their days, that they are filled with peace, and hope, and joy, which, like those refreshing gales and reviving odours to the seaman, are breathed forth from Paradise upon their souls, and give them to understand with certainty that God is bringing them unto their desired haven."

> The merchant, who towards spicy regions sails,
> Smells their perfume far off in adverse gales;
> With blasts which thus against the faithful blow,
> Fresh odorous breathings of God's goodness flow.

A Consistent Life.

Chap. ii. ver. 12.—Having your conversation honest among the Gentiles; that, whereas they speak against you as evil-doers, they may by your good works, which they shall behold, glorify God in the day of visitation.

AN under gardener, with whom his Majesty George III. was accustomed familiarly to converse, was missed one day by the king, who inquired of the head gardener where he was. "Please, your Majesty," said the gardener, "he is very troublesome with his religion, and is always talking about it." "Is he dishonest?" said the king, "does he neglect his work?" "No, your Majesty, he is very honest, I have nothing to say against him for that." "Then send for him again," said the monarch, "why should he be turned off? Call me *defender of the faith!* DEFENDER OF THE FAITH? and turn away a man for his religion?" The king had learned from this good man, that the place of worship where he attended was supported by voluntary contribu-

Servants' Conduct.

Chap. ii. ver. 18.—Servants, be subject to your masters with all fear; not only to the good and gentle, but also to the froward.

MR COLLINS, an infidel writer, used occasionally to visit Lord Barrington, who, in conversation, once asked him, "how it was, that though he seemed to have very little religion himself, he yet took so much care that his servants should attend regularly at church." His reply was that he did it to prevent their robbing or murdering him." Surely religion is a good thing, its enemies themselves being judges. Let Christian servants study, by a faithful discharge of the duties of their religion, to adorn the doctrine of God our Saviour in all things.

Wives' Behaviour.

Chap. iii. ver. 1.—Likewise, ye wives, be in subjection to your own husbands; that if any obey not the word, they also may without the word be won by the conversation of the wives.

A WOMAN who had derived spiritual benefit from the discourses of Mr Robinson of Leicester, was often threatened by her wicked husband for going to St Mary's church, in which Mr R. officiated. His feelings were at length wrought up to such a pitch that he declared with an awful oath, that if ever she went to St Mary's again, he would cut off her legs. Having sought direction in prayer, she was strengthened to go to the place where oft she had been made joyful in the Lord. On her return from church, she found her husband waiting her arrival, and as soon as she had shut the door, he said in an angry tone, "Where have you been?" She replied, "At St Mary's." He instantly struck her a violent blow on the face, and she fell to the ground; but rising from the floor, she turned the other side of her face, and in a mild and affectionate manner said, "My dear, if you serve this side the same I hope I shall bear it with patience." Struck with this meek answer, for she had been a very passionate woman, he said, "Where did you learn that?" She replied, in a gentle manner, "At St Mary's church, my dear." "Well," said he, "if that is what you learn at St Mary's, you may go as often as you like, I will never hinder you again." This good woman enjoyed her privileges undisturbed, and also had the pleasure, a short time afterwards, of having her husband to accompany her.

The Wise Woman.

Chap. iii. ver. 3.—Whose adorning let it not be that outward adorning of plaiting the hair, and of wearing of gold, or of putting on of apparel.

"IT is a lamentable fact," says the author of the 'Wife and Mother,' "that at the present day there are hundreds of bankrupts or tradesmen on the very verge of bankruptcy, or persons of limited income in embarrassed circumstances, whose difficulties have originated in the fondness of their wives for dress and display, and some of these wives, women professing godliness! Not very long since, a professional man, with an income, perhaps, of from two to three hundred a year, on which to support himself, a wife, and one child, was arrested for debt. The stir thus occasioned brought to light his general circumstances, when it appeared, that he owed about twelve hundred pounds, more than half that sum being due to mercers, milliners, and jewellers, for his wife's finery."

The Gentle Life.

Chap. iii. ver. 10.—He that will love life, and see good days, let him refrain his tongue from evil, and his lips that they speak no guile.

WHEN Henry III. of France inquired of those about him, what it was that the Duke of Guise did to charm and allure every one's heart; the reply was, "Sire, the Duke of Guise does good to all the world without exception, either directly by himself, or indirectly by his recommendation. He is civil, courteous, liberal, has always some good to say of everybody, but never speaks ill of any; and this is the reason he reigns in men's hearts as absolutely as your Majesty does in your kingdom."

The Disipated.

Chap. iv. ver. 5.—They think it strange, that ye run not with them to the same excess of riot.

A GENTLEMAN, on entering a stage coach, rubbing his head, with a yawn, said, "My head aches dreadfully, I was very drunk last night." A person affecting surprise, replied, "Drunk! sir. What! do you get drunk?" "Yes," said he, "and so does every one at times, I believe. I have no doubt but you do." "No, sir," he replied, "I do not." "What! never?" "No, never; and amongst other reasons I have for it, one is, I never find, being sober, that I have too much sense, and I am loath to lose what little I have."

Suffering as a Christian.

Chap. iv. ver. 16.—If any man suffer as a Christian, let him not be ashamed; but let him glorify God on this behalf.

AS Mr Jeremiah Whittaker was riding with one of his intimate friends past Tyburn (which he had not seen, or not observed before), he asked what that was; and being answered that it was Tyburn, where so many malefactors had been executed, he stopped his horse, and with much feeling expressed himself thus: "Oh! what a shame is it that so many thousands should die for the satisfaction of their lusts, and so few be found willing to lay down their lives for Christ? Why should not we, in a good cause, and upon a good call, be ready to die for Jesus Christ? It would be an everlasting honour; and it is a thousand times better to die for Christ,—to be hanged, or to be burnt for Christ,—than to die in our beds!"

Humility.

Chap. v. ver. 5.—Be clothed with humility; for God resisteth the proud, and giveth grace to the humble.

AUGUSTINE being asked, which is the first step to heaven? he replied, "Humility." And what is the second step? said the inquirer; to which the man of God answered, "Humility." And which is the third step to heaven? He again replied, "Humility." It is one of those modest and retired graces, which best suits a state of dependance and obligation.

Trust in God.

Chap. v. ver. 7.—Casting all your care upon him, for he careth for you.

MR THOMAS PERKINS, a sufferer for conscience' sake, was often in great straits. At one time, a niece of his, whom he had brought up, going, after her marriage, to visit him, in the course of free conversation with her, he said to her, "Child, how much do you think I have to keep my family? But poor threepence." At which she appearing affected, he, with a great deal of cheerfulness, cried out, "Fear not, God will provide;" and in a little time, a gentleman's servant knocked at the door, who brought him a haunch of venison as a present, together with some wheat and malt. Upon which he took his niece by the hand, saying, "Do you see, child, here is venison, which is the noblest flesh, and the finest of the wheat for bread, and good malt for drink. Did not I tell you God would provide for us?" Thus they who trust in Providence shall not be forsaken.

SECOND PETER.

Entering the Kingdom.

Chap. i. ver. 11.—For so an entrance shall be ministered unto you abundantly into the everlasting kingdom of our Lord and Saviour Jesus Christ.

WHEN the Rev. Andrew Fuller was visiting Mr Sutcliff, a pious minister, on his death-bed, he said, on taking leave, "I wish you, my dear brother, an abundant entrance into the everlasting kingdom of our Lord Jesus Christ!". At this Mr S. hesitated, not as doubting his entrance into the kingdom, but as questioning whether the term *abundant* were applicable to him. "That," said he, "is more than I expect. I think I understand the connection and import of those words,—' Add to your faith virtue—give diligence to make your calling and election sure—for so an entrance shall be ministered unto you *abundantly*.' I think the idea is that of a ship coming into harbour, with a fair gale, and a full tide. If I may but reach the heavenly shore, though it be on a board or broken piece of a ship, I shall be satisfied."

Eye Witnesses of Christ.

Chap. i. ver. 16.—We have not followed cunningly devised fables, when we made known unto you the power and coming of our Lord Jesus Christ, but were eye-witnesses of his majesty.

ATHENAGORAS, a famous Athenian philosopher in the second century, not only doubted the truth of the Christian religion, but was determined to write against it. However, upon an intimate inquiry into the facts on which it was supported, in the course of his collecting materials for his intended publication, he was convinced by the blaze of its evidence, and turned his designed invective into an elaborate apology, which is still in existence.

Ignorance and Evil Speaking.

Chap. ii. ver 12.—These speak evil of the things that they understand not

A SHORT time since, an aged clergyman was travelling in a stage coach, and finding himself in the company of two or three young men, who were rather inclined to amuse him and one another by frivolous conversation, he endeavoured to compose himself to sleep. He was shorlty afterwards aroused by one of his companions, who wished for his decision on the point on which they were disputing. One of them had said, "that he would rather believe the Koran than the Bible;" and it was submitted to the clergyman to say, to which of these books he thought the greater credit due. He complained of having been awakened from his sleep to settle their disputes, but, however, said, he was happy to be able to receive some information respecting the Koran, and accordingly inquired of the person who said he would rather believe the Koran than the Bible, what sort of book it was, whether it was divided into chapters and verses, like our Bible, etc. The young man could not inform him; and the minister, suspecting that he ignorant of the book, inquired a little further, and found that he had never seen the Koran, and had never read the Bible. "Now," said he, "gentlemen, is it fair, that I should be awaked from my sleep, to decide a question thus raised by a man who knows nothing of either of the books of which he speaks? Surely it is not too much to ask men to *read* what they condemn; and if you will take my advice, you will immediately apply yourselves to the prayerful study of the Word of God, which is able to make you wise unto salvation. You will then not have occasion to inqiure whether the Koran or any other work is equally entitled to your belief, but you will *know* and be *assured*, that it is indeed the word and truth of God."

Knowing the Truth, but not Doing It.

Chap. ii. ver. 21.—It had been better for them not to have known the way of righteousness, than, after they have known it, to turn from the holy commandment delivered unto them.

A SOCIETY of infidels were in the practice of meeting together on Sabbath mornings, to ridicule religion, and to encourage each other in all manner of wickedness. At length they proceeded so far, as to meet, by previous agreement, to burn their Bibles! They had lately initiated a young man into their awful mysteries, who had been brought up under great religious advantages, and seemed to promise well; but on that occasion, he proceeded the length of his companions, threw his Bible into the fire, and promised with them, never to go into a place of religious worship again. He was soon afterwards taken ill. He was visited by a serious man, who found him in the agonies of a distressed mind. He spoke to him of his past ways. The poor creature said, "It all did well enough while in health, and while I could keep off the thoughts of death;" but when the Redeemer was mentioned to him, he hastily exclaimed, "What's the use of talking to me about mercy?" When urged to look to Christ, he said, "I tell you it's of no use now; 'tis too late, 'tis too late. Once I could pray, but now I can't." He frequently repeated, "I cannot pray; I will not pray." He shortly afterwards expired, uttering the most dreadful imprecations against some of his companions in iniquity who came to see him, and now and then saying, "My Bible! Oh, my Bible!"

Scoffers.

Chap. iii. ver. 3.—Knowing this first, that there shall come in the last days scoffers.

ON one occasion, when a parliamentary friend called upon the late Mr Wilberforce, he was found reading his Bible. He began to rally him for taking up his time with that old musty book, remarking that we saw the course of nature going on as usual, and that there was no reason to expect that those future events the Bible spoke of would ever take place. Mr W. replied, "It is sufficiently singular, that what you have been saying, is just the accomplishment of what I have been reading." Then turning to II PET. III. 3, 4, he thus read, "Knowing this first, that there shall come in the last days scoffers, walking after their own lusts, and saying, where is the promise of His coming? for since the fathers fell asleep, all things continue as they were from the beginning of the creation." The coincidence powerfully struck at the time the gentleman to whom the remark was made, "though I never heard," adds Mr Innes, "that any permanent effect was produced."

High Ideals.

Chap. iii. ver. 11.—Seeing, then, that all these things shall be dissolved, what manner of persons ought ye to be in all holy conversation and godliness?

MR ROGERS, a puritan divine, was styled the Enoch of his day. Bishop Kennet said of him, that England hardly ever brought forth a man who walked more closely with God. He was always remarkable for gravity and seriousness in company. Being once addressed by a gentleman of rank,—"Mr Rogers, I like you and your company well enough, but you are too *precise!*" "Oh, sir, replied Mr R. "I serve a *precise* God!"

FIRST JOHN.

Exalted Companionship.

Chap. i. ver. 3.—Truly our fellowship is with the Father, and with his Son Jesus Christ.

THE Rev. James Owen, a pious minister in Shrewsbury, being asked, when on his death-bed, whether he would have some of his friends sent for to keep him company, replied, "My fellowship is with the Father, and with His Son Jesus Christ; and he that is not satisfied with that company, doth not deserve it."

Cleansed from Sin.

Chap. i. ver. 7.—The blood of Jesus Christ his Son cleanseth us from all sin.

MR WILLIAMS, having visited an old blind warrior in Raiatea, who had been converted to Christianity, intimated, that he thought his sickness would terminate in death, and wished the old man to tell him what he thought of himself in the sight of God, and what was the foundation of his hope. "Oh," he replied, "I have been in great trouble this morning, but I am happy now. I saw an immense mountain with precipitous sides, up which I endeavoured to climb, but when I had attained a considerable height, I lost my hold, and fell to the bottom. Exhausted with perplexity and fatigue, I went to a distance, and sat down to weep, and while weeping, I saw a drop of blood fall upon that mountain, and in a moment it was dissolved." Wishing to have his own ideas of what had been presented to his imagination, Mr W. said, "This was certainly a strange sight; what construction do you put upon it!" After expressing his surprise that Mr W. should be at a loss for the interpretation, he exclaimed, "That mountain was my sins, and the drop which fell upon it, was one drop of the precious blood of Jesus, by which the mountain of my guilt must be melted away." He died soon after, exclaiming, "O death, where is thy sting?"

Real Followers.

Chap. ii. ver. 6.—He that saith he abideth in him, ought himself also so to walk, even as he walked.

SCIPIO AFRICANUS had a son, who had nothing of the father but the name,—a coward.—a dissolute, sorry rake,—the son of one of the greatest generals in the world! This son wore a ring upon his finger, wherein was his father's picture. His life and character were so opposite to those of his father, and so unworthy, that, by an act of the senate, he was commanded to forbear wearing that ring. They judged it unfit that he should have the honour to wear the picture of his father, who would not himself bear the resemblance of his father's excellency. The divine command is, "Let every one that nameth the name of Christ depart from iniquity."

The Divinity of Christ.

Chap. ii. ver. 23.—Whosoever denieth the Son, the same hath not the Father: but he that acknowledgeth the Son, hath the Father also.

DR MILLER, Professor of Theology in Princeton College, North America, in a note prefixed to an ordination sermon, relates part of a conversation that he had with Dr Priestly, two or three years before his death. "The conversation," says he, "was a free and amicable one, on some fundamental doctrines of religion. In reply to a direct avowal on the part of the author (Dr Miller), that he was a Trinitarian, Dr Priestly said, 'I do not wonder that you entertain and express a strongly favourable opinion of us Unitarians. The truth is, there neither can nor ought to be any compromise between us. If *you* are right, *we are not Christians at all*; and if *we* are right, *you are gross idolaters!*'"

The Love of God.

Chap iii. ver. 1.—Behold what manner of love the Father hath bestowed upon us, that we should be called the sons of God!

WHEN the Danish missionaries in India appointed some of their Indian converts to translate a catechism, in which it was mentioned as the privilege of Christians to become the sons of God, one of the translators, startled at so bold a saying as he thought it, said, "It is too much; let me rather render it, they shall be permitted to kiss His feet."

Real Love.

Chap. iii. ver. 18.—My little children, let us not love in word, neither in tongue, but in deed, and in truth.

A RESPECTABLE merchant of London, having been embarrassed in his circumstances, and his misfortunes having been one day the subject of conversation in the Royal Exchange, several persons expressed great sorrow; when a foreigner who was present, said, "I feel five hundred pounds for him, what do *you feel?*"

God first Loved us.

Chap. iv. ver. 10.—Herein is love, not that we loved God, but that he loved us, and sent his Son to be the propitiation for our sins.

THE following lines, composed by a lunatic, were found written on the wall of his cell after his death:—

"Could we with ink the ocean fill,
And were the skies of parchment made,
Were every stalk on earth a quill,
And every man a scribe by trade;
To write the love of God above
Would drain the ocean dry;
Nor could the scroll contain the whole,
Tho' stretch'd from sky to sky."

Consistent Love.

Chap. iv. ver. 21.—This commandment have we from him, That he who loveth God, love his brother also.

"I WAS conversing with a Brahmin one day," says the Rev. H Townly, "respecting the relative morals of Hindoos and Christians, when he said, 'Our religion is superior to yours. See what excellent fruits our religion produces; see what saints we have amongst us Hindoos. Such a man was actuated by the principles of Hindooism; he left wife, and children, and family, and extensive property; he left everything, and spent his life in a wood. Can you produce such a saint as that?' I replied, 'That we should call him a very great sinner.' 'Upon what principle?' said he. I answered, 'God has given us two commandments, Thou shalt love the Lord thy God with all thy heart, and with all thy soul, and with all thy mind, and with all thy strength, and thy neighbour as thyself; and your Hindoo saint, who went to live in a wood, as long as he lived there, was violating the second great commandment; for, forsaking his neighbours, and kindred, and friends, he could not render them any assistance; he had no longer the opportunity of administering food to the hungry, and relieving the miserable; and can a man who is living a life of continued disobedience to one of God's commandments be deemed a saint?'"

The Trinity.

Chap. v. ver. 7.—There are three that bear record in heaven, the Father, the Word, and the Holy Ghost; and these three are one.

A LADY who piqued herself on her skill in ridiculing the sentiments of the Trinitarians, meeting a poor but eminently pious man, with whom she had formerly been unusually affable, thus accosted him, "Friend Orrock, you worship three gods, do you not?" Certainly not, Madam," was the reply. "Nay," retorted the lady, with a sneer, "but you profess to have three, Father, Son, and Spirit; so I suppose you pray a little to the Father, a little to the Son, and a little to the Holy Ghost." The good man, shocked with such profane flippancy, replied, "I wish, Madam, to pray always as did the Apostle Paul,—"The grace of our Lord Jesus Christ, and the love of God, and the fellowship of the Holy Ghost, be with *us all*, Amen." This solemn

The Condition of Fulfilled Prayer.

Chap. v. ver. 14.—This is the confidence that we have in him, that, if we ask anything according to his will, he heareth us.

LORD BOLINGBROKE once asked Lady Huntingdon how she reconciled prayer to God for particular blessings, with absolute resignation to the Divine will. "Very easy," answered her ladyship; "just as if I were to offer a petition to a monarch, of whose kindness and wisdom I have the highest opinion. In such a case, my language would be, I wish you to bestow on me such a favour: but your majesty knows better than I how far it would be agreeable to you, or right in itself, to grant my desire. I therefore content myself with humbly presenting my petition, and leave the event of it entirely to you."

SECOND JOHN.

Thankfulness Regarding Children.

Ver. 4.—I rejoiced greatly that I found thy children walking in truth.

LADY STORMONT, mother of the late Lord Chief Justice Mansfield, on being complimented by another lady, that "she had the three finest sons in Scotland to be proud of," made answer, "No, Madam, I have much to be thankful for, but nothing to be proud of."

A Full Reward.

Ver. 8.—But that we receive a full reward.

A MILITARY gentleman, a stated hearer of the late Rev. John Martin of Forres, who had been long in a weakly state, and whom Mr M. frequently visited in his affliction, remarked to his visitor one day, "Why, Mr Martin, if I had power over the pension list, I would actually have you put upon half-pay for your long and faithful services." Mr M. replied, "Ah! my friend, your master may put you off in your old age with *half-pay*, but my Master will not serve me so meanly. He will give me *full pay*. Through grace I expect a *full* reward!"

THIRD JOHN.

Walking in Truth.

Ver. 4.—I have no greater joy than to hear that my children walk in truth.

DR WITHERSPOON, President of New Jersey College in America, educated five hundred and twenty-three young men, one hundred and fifteen of whom were afterwards ministers of the Gospel. He had the satisfaction to see many of his former pupils filling the first offices of trust under the government; and on returning one day from the General Assembly of the Presbyterian Church, then sitting in Philadelphia, he remarked to a particular friend, "I cannot, my dear sir, express the satisfaction I feel, when I observe that a majority of our General Assembly were once my own pupils."

Christian Help in Journeying.

Ver. 6.—If thou bring them forward on their journey after a godly sort, thou shalt do well.

IN 1819, two missionaries, one of them with his wife and child, landed on the island of St Helena. Soon after one of them had reached the inn, the excellent chaplain, the Rev. Mr Vernon, called, and, with peculiar kindness, offered to do everything for them to make their visit pleasant and beneficial. Several officers also visited them, who were men evidently devoted to God. They spent four days on this island, and found it particularly refreshing to their enfeebled bodies, and wearied minds. On their departure, Mr Solomon, the inn-keeper, said to them, "Gentlemen, you have nothing to pay." Their expenses, which were not less than twenty guineas, had been defrayed by the chaplain and officers, who had done this to show their esteem for Christian missionaries, though of different denominations from themselves. Well might the missionary who related the fact add, "Though it is nearly eleven years ago, I feel my heart heave with gratitude at the recollection of it. Oh! how refreshing it is to see true Christian principles rising above all little selfish party feeling, and reiterating the apostolic benediction, 'Grace be with all them that love our Lord Jesus Christ in sincerity.'"

JUDE.

Deniers of the Lord.

Ver. 4.—Ungodly men turning the grace of our God into lasciviousness, and denying the only Lord God, and our Lord Jesus Christ.

A CLERGYMAN was preaching in a town of America, which was much infected with the heresy, that all men, whatever may be their character, shall ultimately be saved. A preacher of this doctrine, who was present, with a view to "withstand the truth," became greatly enraged in the progress of his discourse. It was no sooner closed, than he began to challenge the preacher to a defence of his doctrines. As it was rather late, the clergyman who had been preaching declined a formal debate, but proposed that each should ask the other three questions, to which a direct answer should be returned. This being agreed to, the challenger began. He put his questions, which were promptly answered. It then came to the clergyman's turn. His first question was, "Do you pray in your family?" Thunderstruck and dismayed, the preacher of smooth things knew not what to say. At length he asked, "Why; what has that to do with the truth of my doctrine?" "Much," was the reply: "By their fruits ye shall know them." At last he frankly confessed that he did not. Then for the second question; "When you get somewhat displeased, do you not sometimes make use of profane language?" This was carrying the war into the innermost temple of his infidel abominations. There was no door of escape. Answer he must. It was of no use to deny it. He confessed he was profane. "I will go no further," said the pious clergyman, "I am satisfied;" and, turning to the congregation, added, "I presume you are also. You dare not trust your welfare to a prayerless and profane guide." Every one saw and felt the force of this practical argument. A dozen lectures on the subject would not have done half so much good.

Ignorance and Evil Speaking.

Ver. 10.—These speak evil of those things which they know not.

WHEN the celebrated Dr Edmund Halley was talking infidelity before Sir Isaac Newton, he addressed him in these words:— "I am always glad to hear you when you talk about astronomy, or other parts of the mathematics, because that is a subject you have studied, and well understand; but you should not talk of Christianity, for you have not studied it. I have; and am certain that *you* know nothing of the matter."

REVELATION.

Profitable Reading.

Chap. i. ver. 3. Blessed is he that readeth, and they that hear the words of prophecy, and keep those things which are written therein.

LADY JANE GRAY was once asked by one of her friends, in a tone of surprise, how she could consent to forego the pleasures of the chase, which her parents were enjoying, and prefer sitting at home reading her Bible. She smilingly answered, "All amusements of that description are but a shadow of the pleasure which I enjoy in reading this book."

Kings and Priests.

Chap. i. ver. 6.—And hath made us kings and priests unto God and his Father.

AN old African negro, who had long served the Lord, when on his death-bed, was visited by his friends, who came around him, lamenting that he was going to die, saying, "Poor Pompey, poor Pompey is dying." The old saint, animated with the prospect before him, said to them, with much earnestness, "Don't call me poor Pompey, I KING Pompey;" referring to the preceding passage, in which the saints are spoken of as being made kings and priests unto God.

The Lord's Day.

Chap. i. ver. 10.—I was in the Spirit on the Lord's Day.

TO a person who inquired whether or not it would be sinful to spend time in registering meteorological observations on Sabbaths, the late Rev. Mr M'Cheyne gave the following reply:— "Dear Friend,—You ask me a hard question. Had you asked me *what I would do in the case*, I could easily tell you. I love the Lord's day too well to be marking down the height of the thermometer and barometer every hour. I have other work to do, higher and better, and more like that of angels above. The more entirely I can give my Sabbaths to God, and half forget that I am not before the throne of the Lamb, with my harp of gold, the happier am I, and I feel it my duty to be as happy as I can be, and as God intended me to be. The joy of the Lord is my strength. But whether another Christian can spend the day in His service, and mark down degrees of heat and atmospherical pressure, without letting down the warmth of his affections, or losing the atmosphere of heaven, I cannot tell. My conscience is not the rule of another man. One thing we may learn from these men of science, namely, to be as careful in marking the changes and progress of our own spirit, as they are in marking the changes of the weather. An hour should never pass without our looking up to God for forgiveness and peace. This is the noblest science, to know how to live in hourly communion with God in Christ. May you and I know more of this, and thank God that we are not among the wise and prudent from whom these things are hid!—The grace of the Lord of the Sabbath be with you."

Ephesus.

Chap. ii. ver. 5.—I will come unto thee quickly, and will remove thy candlestick out of his place, except thou repent.

A LATE missionary traveller, in speaking of Ephesus, says, "The candlestick is out of its place. How doth the city sit solitary that was full of people! The site of this once famous city is now covered with grass or grain. The church of St John stands deserted and in ruins, having been occupied as a mosque, after the country fell into the hands of the Mohammedans. In this church are some immensely large pillars of granite, said to have been taken from the temple of Diana ; having served successively as a Pagan, a Christian, and a Mohammedan place of worship. No human being now lives in Ephesus, a few miserable Turkish huts are alone seen in this desolate spot. The streets are obscured and overgrown ; and a noisy flight of crows seemed to insult its silence. The call of the partridge is heard in the area of the theatre and the stadium. The pomp of its heathen worship is no longer remembered ; and Christianity, which was planted and nursed by the apostle, no longer lingers in this once favoured Church."

Poor yet Rich.

Chap. ii. ver. 9.—I know thy works, and tribulation, and poverty: but thou art rich.

THE following lines were occasioned by the circumstance of a person's going lately into the house of a poor pious man, with a large family, and saying to him, "My friend, you seem to be very poor;" to which the man replied, "How can you call me poor, when, through the grace of Christ, all things are mine?"

> How canst thou call me poor ? All things are mine.
> Whate'er I ask, my God replies, "'Tis thine,
> The world, life, death, things present, things to come."
> Such is my store in Christ ; a countless sum !
> The world may think me poor, as I think them :
> Their treasures I, my riches they, contemn.
> They have their good things now, for mine I wait :
> How worthless theirs at best ; the least of mine how great !

Keeping the Faith.

Chap. iii. ver. 8.—Thou hast kept my word and hast not denied my name.

IN the beginning of the reign of Queen Mary of England, a pursuivant was sent to bring Bishop Latimer to London, of which he had notice six hours before he arrived. But instead of fleeing, he prepared for his journey to London; and, when the pursuivant was come, he said to him, "My friend, you are welcome. I go as willingly to London, to give an account of my faith, as ever I went to any place in the world. And I doubt not, but as the Lord made me worthy formerly to preach the word before two excellent princes, he will now enable me to bear witness to the truth before the third, either to her eternal comfort or discomfort." As he rode on this occasion through Smithfield, he said, "That Smithfield had groaned for him a long time."

Love and Chastening.

Chap. iii. ver. 19.—As many as I love, I rebuke and chasten.

MR NEWTON had a very happy talent of administering reproof. Hearing that a person, in whose welfare he was greatly interested, had met with peculiar success in business, and was deeply immersed in worldly engagements, the first time he called on him, which was usually once a month, he took him by the hand, and drawing him on one side, into the counting-house, told him his apprehensions of his spiritual welfare. His friend, without making any reply, called down his partner in life, who came with her eyes suffused in tears, and unable to speak. Inquiring the cause, he was told that she had just been sent for to one of her children, that was out at nurse, and supposed to be in dying circumstances. Clasping her hands immediately in his, Mr N. cried, "God be thanked, he has not forsaken you! I do not wish your babe to suffer, but I am happy to find He gives you this token of His favour."

Brave as a Lion.

Chap. iv. ver. 7.—And the first beast was like a lion.

AS the four beasts, or living creatures, are understood by many good commentators to be symbolical of the ministers of the Gospel, the lion here may be considered as the emblem of their courage and boldness. Of this the following anecdote will furnish an example:

Bishop Latimer having one day preached before King Henry VIII. a sermon which displeased his majesty, he was ordered to preach again on the next Sabbath, and to make an apology for the offence he had given. After reading his text, the bishop thus began his sermon: —"Hugh Latimer, dost thou know before whom thou art this day to speak? To the high and mighty monarch, the king's most excellent majesty, who can take away thy life if thou offendest; therefore, take heed that thou speakest not a word that may displease; but then consider well, Hugh, dost thou not know from whence thou comest; upon whose message thou art sent? Even by the great and mighty God! who is all-present! and who beholdeth all thy ways! and who is able to cast thy soul into hell! Therefore, take care that thou deliverest thy message faithfully." He then proceeded with the same sermon he had preached the preceding Sabbath, but with considerably more energy. The sermon ended, the court were full of expectation to know what would be the fate of this honest and plain-dealing bishop. After dinner, the king called for Latimer, and, with a stern countenance, asked him how he dared to be so bold as to preach in such a manner. He, falling on his knees, replied, his duty to his God and his prince had enforced him thereto, and that he had merely discharged his duty and his conscience in what he had spoken. Upon which the king, rising from his seat, and taking the good man by the hand, embraced him, saying, "Blessed be God I have so honest a servant!"

The Creator of All Things.

Chap. iv. ver. 11.—Thou art worthy, O Lord, to receive glory, and honour, and power: for thou hast created all things, and for thy pleasure they are and were created.

MR BURNET, who was intimately acquainted with the Honourable Robert Boyle, and wrote his life, says, "It appeared to those who conversed with him on his inquiries into nature, and this main design was to arise in himself and others, vaster thoughts of the greatness and glory, of the wisdom and goodness of God. This was so deep in his thoughts, that he concludes the article of his will, which alludes to that illustrious body the Royal Society, in these words, 'Wishing them a happy success in their laudable attempts to discover the true nature of the works of God; and praying that they, and all other searchers into physical truths, may cordially refer their attainments to the Great Author of nature, and to the comfort of mankind.'"

The Great Atoner.

Chap. v. ver. 6.—In the midst of the throne and of the four beasts and in the midst of the elders, stood a Lamb as it had been slain.

THOMAS, Earl of Kinnoul, a short time before his death, in a long and serious conversation with the late Rev. Dr Kemp of Edinburgh, thus expressed himself:—"I have always considered the atonement to be characteristical of the Gospel, as a system of religion. Strip it of that doctrine, and you reduce it to a scheme of morality, excellent indeed, and such as the world never saw; but to man, in the present state of his faculties, absolutely impracticable. The atonement of Christ, and the truths immediately connected with that fundamental principle, provide a remedy for all the wants and weaknesses of our nature. They who strive to remove those precious doctrines from the word of God, do an irreparable injury to the grand and beautiful system of religion which it contains, as well as to the comforts and hopes of man. For my own part, I am now an old man, and have experienced the infirmities of advanced years. Of late, in the course of dangerous illness, I have been repeatedly brought to the gates of death. My time in this world cannot now be long; but with truth I can declare that, in the midst of all my past afflictions, my heart was supported and comforted by a firm reliance upon the merits and atonement of my Saviour; and now, in the prospect of entering upon an eternal world, this is the only foundation of my confidence and hope." In these sentiments, he steadily persevered, till, on the 27th of December 1787, he expired without a struggle or a groan.

Redeemed to God.

Chap. v. ver. 9.—Thou wast slain, and has redeemed us to God by thy blood, out of every kindred, and tongue, and people, and nation.

AN Indian describing his conversion, says, "After some time, Brother Rauch came into my hut, and sat down by me. He spoke to me nearly as follows:—'I come to you in the name of the Lord of heaven and earth; He sends to let you know that He will make you happy, and deliver you from the misery you lie in at present. To this end He became a man, gave His life a ransom for man, and shed His blood for him.' When he had finished his discourse, he lay down upon a board, fatigued by the journey, and fell into a sound sleep. I then thought, what kind of man is this? Here he lies and sleeps; I might kill him, and throw him into the wood, and who would regard it? But this gives him no concern. However, I could not forget his words. They constantly recurred to my mind. Even when I was asleep, I dreamed of the blood which Christ shed for us. I found this to be something different from what I had ever heard, and I interpreted Christian Henry's words to the other Indians. Thus, through the grace of God, an awakening took place amongst us. I say, therefore, brethren, preach Christ our Saviour, and His sufferings and death, if you would have your words to gain entrance amongst the heathen."

Killing one Another.

Chap. vi. ver. 4.—Power was given to him that sat thereon to take peace from the earth, and that they should kill one another; and there was given unto him a great sword.

IN a German publication, the loss of men, during the war, from 1802 to 1813—in St Domingo, Calabria, Russia, Poland, France, Spain, Portugal, Germany, etc., including the maritime war, contagious diseases, famine, etc., is stated to amount to the dreadful sum of *Five Millions Eight Hundred Thousand !*

Earthquakes.

Chap. vi. ver. 12.—There was a great earthquake.

"THE 26th of March," (1812), says the St Thomas' Gazette, "has been a day of woe and horror to the province of Venezuela. At four in the afternoon, the city of Caraccas stood in all its splendour. A few minutes later, 4500 houses, 19 churches and convents, together with all the other public buildings, etc., were crushed to atoms by a sudden shock of an earthquake, which did not last a minute, and buried thousands of the devoted inhabitants in ruins and desolation. That day happened to be Maunday Thursday, and at the hour when every place of worship was crowded, to commemorate the commencement of our Saviour's passion, by public procession, which was to proceed through the streets a few minutes afterwards. The number of hapless sufferers was thus augmented to an incredible amount, as every church was levelled with the ground, before any person could be aware of danger. The number of sufferers taken out of one of the churches, two days after this disaster, amounted alone to upwards of 300 corpses. An idea of the extent of the number of dead is differently stated, from 4000 to 8000. The next town and sea-port thereto, viz., La Guayra, has in proportion suffered still more, as well as its immediate coast. Huge masses of the mountains detached themselves from the summits, and hurled down into the valleys. Deep clefts and separations of the immense bed of rocks, still threaten future disaster to the hapless survivors, who are now occupied in burying and burning the dead, and in relieving the numerous wounded and cripples perishing for want of surgical aid, shelter, and other comforts."

The Servants of God.

Chap. vii. ver. 3.—Hurt not the earth, neither the sea, nor the trees, till we have sealed the servants of our God in their foreheads.

THE *sealing* here mentioned is considered by commentators as signifying God's marking His people out for safety, both from temporal and spiritual evils. The following anecdote may illustrate the watchful care of Providence over a distinguished servant of God, in circumstances of danger.

Mr Hervey, on one occasion, when returning from London, met with a singular deliverance, which he gratefully records. "I set out for Northampton," says he, "in the new machine, called *The Berlin*, which holds four passengers, is drawn by a pair of horses, and driven in the manner of a post-chaise. On this side Newport, we came up with a stage-coach, and made an attempt to pass it. This the coachman perceiving, mended his pace, which provoked the driver of the Berlin to do the same, till they both lashed their horses into a full career, and were more like running a race than conveying passengers. We very narrowly escaped falling foul on each other's wheels. I called out to the fellows, but to no purpose. It is possible, amidst the rattle and hurry, they did not hear; it is certain they did not regard. Within the space of a minute or two, what I apprehended happened. My vehicle was overturned, and thrown with great violence on the ground; the coachman was tossed off his box, and lay bleeding on the road. There was only one person in the coach, and none but myself in the Berlin; yet neither of us (so singular was the goodness, so tender the care of Divine Providence!) sustained any considerable hurt. I received only a slight bruise, and had the skin razed from my leg, when I might too reasonably have feared the misfortune of broken bones, dislocated limbs, or a fractured skull. Have I not abundant reason to adopt the Psalmist's acknowledgment,—'Thou hast delivered my life from death, mine eyes from tears, and my feet from falling?' Have I not abundant reason to make his grateful inquiry, 'What shall I render to the Lord for all His benefits towards me?' And ought I not to add his holy resolution, 'I will walk before the Lord, in the land of the living?' So long as this life exists, which has been so wonderfully preserved, it shall be devoted to the honour of my great Deliverer."

Out of Great Tribulation.

Chap. vii. ver. 14.—These are they which came out of great tribulation, and have washed their robes, and made them white in the blood of the Lamb.

WILLIAM TOVART, a marty of Antwerp, in a pious letter, thus expressed, as he very safely and scripturally might, his belief of the happiness of martyrs:—"The eternal Son of God will confess their names before His heavenly Father, and His holy angels. They shall be clad with white robes, and shine as the sun in the kingdom of heaven, filled with gladness in the presence of the Lamb. They shall eat of the fruit of the tree of life, which is in the midst of the paradise of God."

An Acceptable Offering.

Chap. viii. ver. 3.—There was given unto him much incense, that he should offer it with the prayers of all saints.

A NUMBER of ministers were assembled for the discussion of difficult questions; and, among others, it was asked, how the command to "pray without ceasing" could be complied with. Various suppositions were started, and at length one of the number was appointed to write an essay upon it to read at the next monthly meeting; which being overheard by a female servant, she exclaimed, "What! a whole month wanted to tell the meaning of that text! It is one of the easiest and best texts in the Bible." "Well, well," said an old minister, "Mary, what can you say about it? Let us know how you understand it; can you pray all the time?" "Oh yes, sir." "What! when you have so many things to do?" "Why, sir, the more I have to do, the more I can pray." "Indeed; well, Mary, do let us know how it is; for most people think otherwise?" "Well, sir," said the girl, "when I first open my eyes in the morning, I pray, Lord, open the eyes of my understanding; and while I am dressing, I pray that I may be clothed with the robe of righteousness; and when I have washed me, I ask for the washing of regeneration; and as I begin work, I pray that I may have strength equal to my day; when I begin to kindle up the fire, I pray that God's work may revive in my soul; and as I sweep out the house, I pray that my heart may be cleansed from all its impurities; and, while preparing and partaking of breakfast, I desire to be fed with the hidden manna, and the sincere milk of the word; and as I am busy with the little children, I look up to God as my Father, and pray for the spirit of adoption that I may be His child, and so on all day; everything I do furnishes me with a thought for prayer." "Enough, enough," cried the old divine, "these things are revealed to babes, and often hid from the wise and prudent. Go on, Mary," said he, "pray without ceasing; and as for us, my brethren, let us bless the Lord for this exposition, and remember that He has said, 'The meek will He guide in judgment.' The essay, as a matter of course, was not considered necessary after this little event occurred.

In God's Hands.

Chap. viii. ver. 5.—There were thunderings and lightnings.

A PROFANE persecutor discovered great terror during a storm of thunder and lightning which overtook him on a journey. His pious wife, who was with him, inquired the reason of his terror. He replied by asking, "Are not you afraid?" She answered, "No, it is the voice of my heavenly Father; and should a child be afraid of its father?" "Surely (thought the man) these Puritans have a divine principle in them which the world seeth not, otherwise they could not have such serenity in their souls, when the rest of the world are filled with dread." Upon this, going to Mr Bolton of Broughton, near Kettering, he lamented the opposition which he had made to his ministry, and became a godly man ever after.

Locusts.

Chap. ix. ver. 3.—There came out of the smoke locusts upon the earth.

THE natural locusts are well known to be a dreadful scourge to the countries they visit. From 1778 to 1780, the empire of Morocco was terribly devastated by them, every green thing was eaten up, not even the bitter bark of the orange and pomegranate escaping. A most dreadful famine ensued. The poor were seen to wander over the country, deriving a miserable subsistence from the roots of plants ; and women and children followed the camels, from whose dung they picked the undigested grains of barley, which they devoured with avidity ; in consequence of this, vast numbers perished, and the roads and streets exhibited the unburied carcasses of the dead. On this sad occasion, fathers sold their children, and husbands their wives.

Heathen Gods.

Chap. ix. ver. 20.—Idols of gold, and silver, and brass, and stone, and of wood ; which neither can see, nor hear, nor walk.

WHEN Mr Money resided, some years since, in the Mahratta country, as his daughter, not then three years old, was walking out with a native servant, they came near an old Hindoo temple, when the man stepped aside, and "made his salaam," as they call it, to a stone idol at the door. The child, in her simple language, said, "Saamy (that was his name), what for you do that ?" "Oh missy," said he, "that my god." "Your god, Saamy ! why your god no see— no hear—no walk—your god stone. My God see everything—my God made you, made me, made everything." Mr M. and his family resided there for some time ; Saamy continued to worship at the temple, and missy to reprove him ; but, when they were about to leave India, the poor heathen said, "What will poor Saamy do when missy go to England ? Saamy no father, no mother ?" The child replied, "Oh Saamy, if you love my God, He will be your father and mother too." He promised to do so. "Then," said she, you must learn my prayers." He agreed ; and she taught him the Lord's Prayer, Creed, and her morning and evening hymns. Some time after this, he desired to learn English, that he might read the Bible ; and he became at length a serious and consistent Christian,

The End of Time.

Chap. x. ver. 6.—And sware by him that liveth for ever and ever, that there should be time no longer.

A YOUNG man, in giving an account of his conversion, says, "One Sabbath, after attending Divine service, and after the rest of the day spent in awful transgression, I returned home in the evening and joined the family, to whom my sister was reading a tract aloud. Contrary to my usual practice, I remained to hear it, and, with my sin fresh in remembrance, I listened with deep concern to its awful truths. It was entitled 'THE END OF TIME.' The passages which particularly struck me were these :—'The end of time !' Then shall the sinner's heart give up its last hope. None are completely miserable before death ; indeed, the vilest men are often the most merry ; but it will not be always so,—their joy will be turned into heaviness. Imagine the Judge upon the throne, calling you to answer these inquiries at His bar, 'How have you spent the many Sabbaths I have afforded ! Did you improve your time well ? Time shall end ! How valuable then while it lasts, particularly to the unprepared ! Every hour you have is a merciful respite. Go forth and meet your offended Sovereign ! Seek him while He may be found ; call on Him while He is near. Go in the name of Jesus, plead His righteousness—His blood—His death—His intercessions, and say, God be merciful to me a sinner!" The young man read the tract, and prayed over it. The Lord was pleased to open the eyes of his understanding, and to begin a good work in him. He is now a candidate for the ministry, and a consistently pious character.

The Dead.

Chap. xi. ver 9.—They shall see their dead bodies three days and a half, and shall not suffer their dead bodies to be put in graves.

ADMIRAL COLIGNY was among the earliest victims of Popish treachery and cruelty, in the bloody massacre at Paris in 1572. One Beheme, a German, was the first that entered his chamber; who said, "Are you the Admiral?" "I am," said he, "but you, young man, should have regard to my hoary head and old age." Beheme struck him with his sword. Several other assassins rushed into the room, and the venerable Coligny fell covered with wounds. The Duke of Guise ordered his body to be thrown out at the window, that the people might be assured it was he. His head was cut off, and sent to the king and queen mother, who got it embalmed, and gave it as a present to the Pope. His body was dragged about the streets for three days together. Such was the end of this brave man, who was the first nobleman in France that professed himself a Protestant, and a defender of the Protestant cause.

Evil Accusers.

Chap. xii. ver. 10.—The accuser of our brethren is cast down, which accused them before our God day and night.

MR DOD, a little before his death, experienced some severe conflicts with Satan; but he was enabled, through grace, to obtain the victory. One morning, about two o'clock, he said to the person who sat up with him, "That he had, from the beginning of the night, been wrestling with Satan; who had accused him as having neither preached nor prayed, nor performed any duty as he should have done, either for manner or end. But," continued he, "I have answered him from the examples of the prodigal and the publican."

The Devil.

Chap. xii. ver. 12.—The devil is come down unto you, having great wrath, because he knoweth that he hath but a short time.

"I ASKED the Rev. Legh Richmond," says one, "how we were to reconcile the increase of religion with the acknowledged growth of crime, as evinced in our courts of justice? He answered, 'Both are true. Bad men are becoming worse, and good men better. The first are ripening for judgment, the latter for glory. The increase of wickedness is, in this respect, a proof of the increase of religion. The devil is wroth, knowing that his time is short.'"

Blasphemy.

Chap. xiii. ver. 6.—He opened his mouth in blasphemy against God.

POPE JULIUS, sitting at dinner one day, and pointing to a peacock which he had not touched, "Keep," said he, "this cold peacock for me against supper, and let me sup in the garden; for I shall have guests." When supper came, the peacock was not brought to the table, on which the Pope, after his wonted manner, fell into an extreme rage. One of his cardinals, sitting by, desired him not to be so moved with a matter of such small weight. "What!" said the Pope, "If God was so angry for an apple, that He cast our first parents out of Paradise for the same, why may not I, being His Vicar, be angry for a peacock, since a peacock is a greater matter than an apple?"

Deceiving the People.

Chap. xiii. ver. 14.—And deceiveth them that dwell on the earth, by the means of those miracles which he had power to do in the sight of the beast.

IN an official and authorized Roman Catholic publication, printed in 1801, we are told that no less than twenty-six pictures of the Virgin Mary opened and shut their eyes at Rome, in the years 1796 and 1797, which was supposed to be an indication of her peculiar grace and favour to the Roman people, on account of their opposition to the French at that period. Among the subscribers to this work are the four Popish archbishops, and eleven Popish bishops of Ireland! It also states, that, on the same occasion, the face of a statue of the Virgin at Torrice changed colour, and perspiration appeared upon it! Surely the senseless block manifested more sensibility than the unblushing relaters of such tales; but the Protestant reader can hardly avoid similar sensations upon hearing such fabrications. It may remind us of the words of the apostle, "They received not the love of the truth, that they might be saved; and for this cause God shall send them strong delusion, that they should believe a lie."

Dying in the Lord.

Chap. xiv. ver. 13.—Blessed are the dead which die in the Lord.

OF Mr Stephen Marshall, an eminent divine of the 17th century, Mr Giles Firman, who knew him in life, and attended him in death, says, "That he left behind him few preachers like himself; that he was a Christian in practice as well as profession; that he lived by faith, and died by faith, and was an example to the believers, in word, in conversation, in charity, in faith, and in purity. And when he, together with some others, conversed with him about his death, he replied, 'I cannot say, as one did, I have not so lived that I should now be afraid to die; but this I may say, I have so *learned Christ*, that I am not afraid to die.'"

Triumphing over the World.

Chap. xv. ver. 2.—I saw them that had gotten the victory over the beast, and over his image, and over his mark, and over the number of his name.

LUTHER, having rejected with disdain the great offers by which Alexander, the Papal legate, attempted to gain him over to the court of Rome; "He is a ferocious brute (exclaimed the legate, equally confounded and disappointed), whom nothing can soften, and who regards riches and honour as mere dirt; otherwise the Pope would long ago have loaded him with favours."

Being Watchful.

Chap. xvi. ver. 15.—Behold I come as a thief. Blessed is he that watcheth.

THE Honourable Robert Boyle was, from early youth, singularly attentive to derive moral and religious improvement from every object in nature, and every occurrence in life. In the year 1648, he made a short excursion to the Hague. Sailing home, between Rotterdam and Gravesend, he saw, through a perspective glass, a vessel imagined to be a pirate, and to give chase to the ship in which he was embarked. The occasion suggested to him the following judicious reflection:—"This glass does, indeed, cause the distrusted vessel to approach; but it causes her to approach only to our eyes, not to our ship. If she be not making up to us, this harmless instrument will prove no loadstone to draw her towards us; and if she be, it will put us in better readiness to receive her. Such an instrument, in relation to death, is the meditation of it, by mortals so much and so causelessly abhorred. For though most men studiously shun all thoughts of death, as if, like a nice acquaintance, he would forbear to visit where he knows he is never thought of; or, as if he would exempt ourselves from being mortal, by forgetting that we are so; yet meditation on this subject brings the awful reality nearer to our view, without at all lessening the real distance betwixt us and death. If our last enemy be not approaching us, this innocent meditation will no more quicken his pace than direct his steps; and if he be, it will, without hastening his arrival, prepare us for his reception."

Hailstones.

Chap. xvi. ver. 21.—And there fell upon men a great hail out of heaven, every stone about the weight of a talent.

NATURAL historians record various instances of surprising showers of hail, in which the hailstones were of extraordinary magnitude. An author, speaking of the war of Louis XII. in Italy, in 1510, relates, that there was for some time a horrible darkness, thicker than that of night; after which the clouds broke into thunder and lightning, and there fell a shower of hailstones, or rather, as he calls them, pebble stones, which destroyed all the fish, birds, and beasts in the country. It was attended by a strong smell of sulphur; and the stones were of a bluish colour, some of them weighing 100 pounds.

Religious Abominations.

Chap. xvii. ver. 5.—Babylon the Great, the mother of harlots, and abominations of the earth.

A JEW went from Paris to Rome, in order to acquire a just idea of the Christian religion, as at the fountain-head. There he beheld simony, intrigue, and abominations of all sorts; and, after gratifying his curiosity in every particular, he returned to France, where he gave a detail of his observations to a friend, by whom he had been long solicited to abjure Judaism. From such a recital the Christian expected nothing but an obstinate perseverance in the old worship; and was struck with amazement when the Jew acquainted him with his resolution of requesting baptism, upon the following grounds of conviction:—"That he had seen at Rome everybody, from the Pope down to the beggar, using all their endeavours to subvert the Christian faith; which, nevertheless, daily took deeper and firmer root, and must therefore be of Divine institution."

The Martyrs.

Chap. xvii. ver. 6.—I saw the woman drunken with the blood of the saints, and with the blood of the martyrs of Jesus; and when I saw her, I wondered with great admiration.

ACCORDING to the calculation of some, about two hundred thousand suffered death in seven years, under Pope Julian; no less than a hundred thousand were massacred by the French in the space of three months; the Waldenses who perished, amounted to one million; within thirty years, the Jesuits destroyed nine hundred thousand; under the Duke of Alva, thirty-six thousand were executed by the common hangman; a hundred and fifty thousand perished in the Inquisition; and a hundred and fifty thousand by the Irish massacre; besides the vast multitude of whom the world could never be particularly informed, who were proscribed, banished, burned, starved, buried alive, smothered, suffocated, drowned, assassinated, chained to the gallies for life, or immured within the horrid walls of the Bastile, or others of their church or state prisons. According to some, the whole number of persons massacred since the rise of Papacy, amounts to fifty millions!

Romish Corruptions.

Chap. xviii. ver. 4.—Come out of her, my people, that ye be not partakers of her sins, and that ye receive not of her plagues.

LUTHER often mentioned to his familiar acquaintance, the advantage which he derived from a visit to Rome in 1501, and used to say that he would not exchange that journey for 1000 florins; so much did it contribute to open his eyes to the corruptions of the Romish court, and to weaken his prejudices.

Slavery.

Chap. xviii. ver. 12, 13.—The merchandise of slaves.

A LATE traveller at the Cape of Good Hope says in a letter to a friend, "Having learned that there was to be a sale of cattle, farm stock, etc., by auction, we stopt our waggon for the purpose of procuring fresh oxen. Among the stock of the farm was a female slave and her three children. The farmer examined them as if they had been so many head of cattle. They were sold separately, and to different purchasers. The tears, the anxiety, the anguish of the mother, while she met the gaze of the multitude, eyed the different countenances of the bidders, or cast a heart-rending look upon the children; and the simplicity and touching sorrow of the poor young ones, while they clung to their distracted parent, wiping their eyes, and half-concealing their faces, contrasted with the marked indifference and laughing countenances of the spectators, furnished a striking commentary on the miseries of slavery, and its debasing effects upon the hearts of its supporters. While the woman was in this distressed situation, she was asked, 'Can you feed sheep?' Her reply was so indistinct, that it escaped me; but it was probably in the negative, for her purchaser rejoined, in a loud and harsh voice, 'Then I will teach you with the sjamboc,'—a whip made of the rhinoceros's hide. The mother and her three children were literally torn from each other."

The Scriptures.

Chap. xix. ver. 9.—These are the true sayings of God.

"WELL, HODGE," said a smart-looking Londoner to a plain cottager, who was on his way home from church, "so you are trudging home, after taking the benefit of the fine balmy breezes in the country this morning." "Sir," said the man, "I have not been strolling about this sacred morning, wasting my time in idleness and neglect of religion; but I have been at the house of God, to worship Him, and to hear His preached word." "Ah, what then, you are one of these simpletons that in these country places are weak enough to believe the Bible? Believe me, my man, that book is nothing but a pack of nonsense; and none but weak and ignorant people now think it true." "Well, Mr Stranger, but do you know, weak and ignorant as we country people are, *we* like to have *two strings to our bow.*" "Two strings to your bow! What do you mean by that?" "Why, sir, I mean, that to believe the Bible, and to act up to it, is like having two strings to one's bow; for, if it is *not* true; I shall be the better man for living according to it, and so it will be for my good in this life—that is one string; and if it *should* be true, it will be better for me in the next life—that is another string; and a pretty strong one it is. But, sir, if you disbelieve the Bible, and on that account do not live as it requires, you have not one string to your bow. And *O! if its tremendous threats prove* TRUE. *O think! what then, sir, will become of* YOU!" This plain appeal silenced the coxcomb, and made him feel, it is hoped, that he was not quite so wise as he supposed.

Satan.

Chap. xx. ver. 7, 8.—And when the thousand years are expired, Satan shall be loosed out of his prison, and shall go out to deceive the nations.

AN islander in the South Seas once proposed the following query to the missionaries:—"You say God is a holy and a powerful Being; that Satan is the cause of a vast increase of moral evil or wickedness in the world, by exciting or disposing men to sin. If Satan be only a dependent creature, and the cause of so much evil, which is displeasing to God, why does God not kill Satan at once, and thereby prevent all the evil of which he is the author?" In answer he was told, "that the facts of Satan's dependence on, or subjection to the Almighty, and his yet being permitted to tempt men to evil, were undeniable from the declarations of Scripture, and the experience of every one accustomed to observe the operations of his own mind. Such an one, it was observed, would often find himself exposed to an influence that could be attributed only to satanic agency; but that, why he was permitted to exert this influence on man, was not made known in the Bible."

The Sea.

Chap. xx. ver. 13.—The sea gave up the dead which were in it.

MR GREENLEAF, editor of the Sailor's Magazine, has kept a register of marine disasters which have come to his knowledge within the year 1836, and the result is appalling. The whole number, counting only those which resulted in a total loss of the vessel, was no less than four hundred and ninety: viz., ships and barques, 94; brigs, 135; schooners, 234; sloops, 12; steam-boats, 15; total, 490. Most of the vessels included in this melancholy list were American. Forty-three of them were lost toward the close of 1836; but the intelligence of their fate was not received here until 1837. Thirty-eight were lost in the month of January, fifty-four in February, twenty-four in March, thirty in April, nineteen in May, fifteen in June, forty-two in July, fifty in August, thirty-two in September, forty-three in October, forty-three in November, and six in December. The precise time when the remaining vessels were lost could not be satisfactorily ascertained. In the above named vessels, 1295 lives are reported as being lost.

What multitudes will be found, at the great rising day, to have been entombed in the mighty deep! What a display of infinite wisdom and almighty power will then be given in raising the bodies of these multitudes, many of which were devoured by voracious fishes! Surely the numerous perils of the sea call on sailors to be men of piety and prayer, and call on all who derive benefit from their labours and hazards (and who, in this sea-girt isle, in one form or another, does not?) at least to remember them in their prayers. Certainly they ought to occupy a place, more frequently than they do, in the public prayers of the church.

Seeking and Finding.

Chap. xxi. ver. 6.—I will give unto him that is athirst of the fountain of the water of life freely.

AN Indian woman, from Mevissing, came to one of the missionaries and told him that as soon as she had a good heart she would turn to the Lord Jesus. "Ah!" replied he, "you want to walk on your head. How can you get a good heart, unless you first come to Jesus for the sanctifying grace of His Holy Spirit?"

Heaven.

Chap. xxi. ver. 27.—And there shall in no wise enter into it anything that defileth.

SOME of the last expressions of [the Rev. Henry Martyn were:— "O when shall time give place to eternity! When shall appear the new heaven and earth, wherein dwelleth righteousness! *There*, there shall in no wise enter in anything that defileth; none of that wickedness which has made men worse than wild beasts, none of those corruptions that add still more to the miseries of mortality, shall be seen or heard of any more!" After breathing forth these heavenly aspirations, he entered into the joy of his Lord.

The Divine Face.

Chap. xxii. ver. 4.—They shall see his face.

AN old Welsh minister, while one day pursuing his studies, his wife being in the room, was suddenly interrupted by her asking him a question, which has not always been so satisfactorily answered. "John Evans, do you think we shall be known to each other in heaven?" "To be sure we shall," he replied; "do you think we shall be greater fools there than we are here?" After a momentary pause, he again proceeded, "But, Margaret, I may be a thousand years by your side in heaven without having seen you; for the first thing which will attract my notice when I arrive there, will be my dear Saviour; and I cannot tell when I shall be for a moment induced to look at any other object."

The Lord's Coming.

Chap. xxii. ver. 7.—Behold I come quickly: blessed is he that keepeth the sayings of the prophecy of this book.

THE 18th of May, 1780, was remarkably dark in Connecticut. Candles were lighted in many houses; the birds were silent, and disappeared; and domestic fowls retired to roost. The people were impressed by the idea that the day of judgment was at hand. This opinion was entertained by the legislature, at that time sitting at Hartford. The house of representatives adjourned; the council proposed to follow the example. Colonel Davenport objected.—"The day of judgment is either approaching, or it is not. If it is not, there is no cause for adjourning; if it is, I choose to be found doing my duty; I wish, therefore, that candles may be brought."

THE END.

www.ingramcontent.com/pod-product-compliance
Lightning Source LLC
Chambersburg PA
CBHW021825220426
43663CB00005B/130